# 1000 GUITAR LICKS

## THE ULTIMATE LICK LIBRARY FOR EVERY GUITARIST

FEATURED GUITAR INSTRUCTORS:

**Greg Harrison**
**John Heussenstamm**
**Chad Johnson**
**Don Linke**
**Johnny Moeller**
**Colin O'Brien**
**Peter Roller**
**Matthew Schroeder**
**Paul Silbergleit**
**Troy Stetina**
**Bill Stone**
**Josh Tovar**
**Ben Woolman**

To access video, visit:
**www.halleonard.com/mylibrary**

Enter Code
4007-5038-6768-0163

ISBN 979-8-3501-5846-5

Visit Hal Leonard Online at
**www.halleonard.com**

World headquarters, contact:
**Hal Leonard**
7777 West Bluemound Road
Milwaukee, WI 53213
Email: info@halleonard.com

In Europe, contact:
**Hal Leonard Europe Limited**
Dettingen Way
Bury St Edmunds, Suffolk, IP33 3YB
Email: info@halleonardeurope.com

In Australia, contact:
**Hal Leonard Australia Pty. Ltd.**
4 Lentara Court
Cheltenham, Victoria, 3192 Australia
Email: info@halleonard.com.au

# CONTENTS

# OVERVIEW

### THE BOOK

Welcome to *1000 Guitar Licks*, the most comprehensive lick collection ever assembled in one volume. Inside, you'll discover a vast library of guitar licks, lead lines, and riffs from blues, rock, acoustic, country, jazz, and many other sub-styles. Each lick is carefully notated in tab and paired with a matching video lesson. All of this is organized into a single reference you can use every day to build your skills, expand your vocabulary, and stay inspired.

### DIFFICULTY & VARIETY

The licks cover a wide range of skill levels, from straightforward phrases accessible to newer players to advanced lines that will stretch even experienced guitarists. Within each style, you'll find both classic vocabulary and modern approaches—from expressive blues bends to fiery rock shred, intricate acoustic fingerpicking, twangy country riffs, and fluid jazz lines. Whether you're looking to improve your soloing, add new colors to your improvisation, or simply find fresh ideas to practice, there is a wealth of material to explore.

### THE INSTRUCTORS

You'll be learning from a roster of exceptional guitarists and educators, each bringing authentic style expertise and clear teaching to the examples. Their performances and explanations make this collection a rich and reliable resource for players at any stage of their musical journey.

### THE VIDEOS

Every lick in this book comes with a video lesson. In each video you'll see:

- On-screen tablature synced with the performance
- The lick played at regular and slow speeds
- A concise explanation from the instructor, highlighting the key techniques and concepts

To access the videos for streaming or downloading, simply go to **www.halleonard.com/mylibrary** and enter the access code printed on page 1 of this book.

# BLUES LICKS

## Instructor: John Heussenstamm

### 1: Penta-Tasty

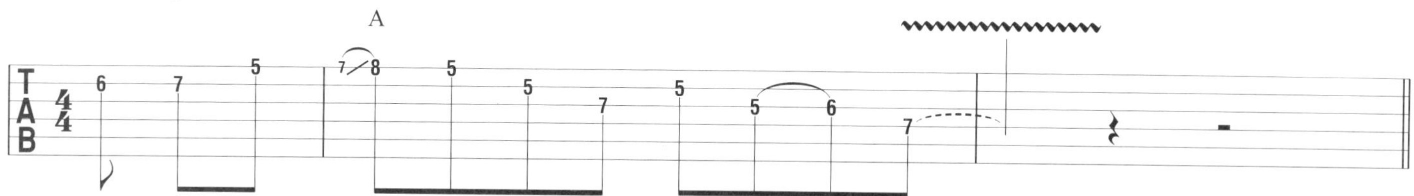


### 2: Blues Resolute

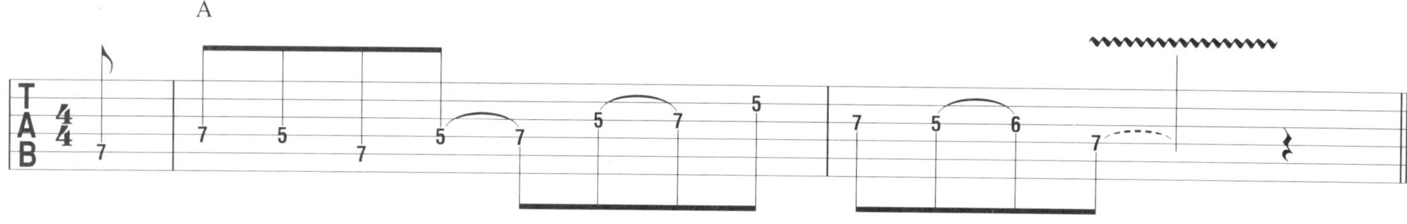


### 3: Added Ingredients

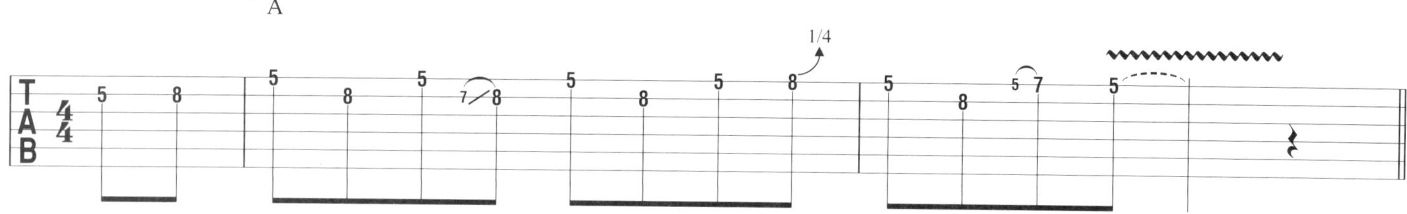


### 4: Cascading Bends

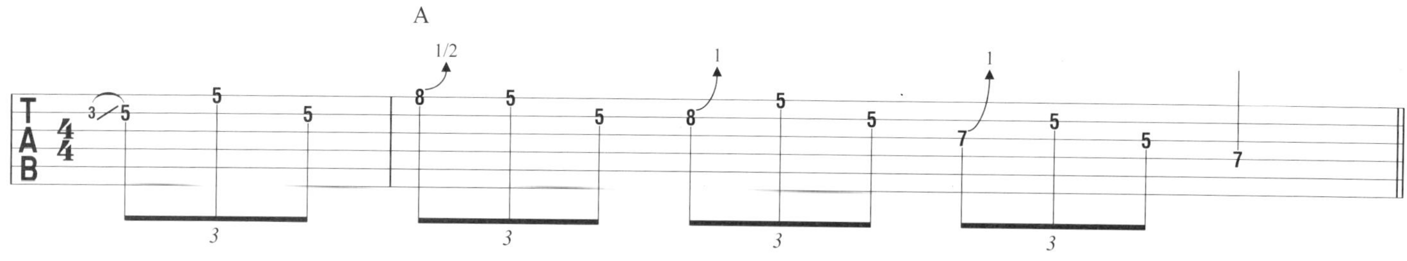


### 5: Blues Peddler

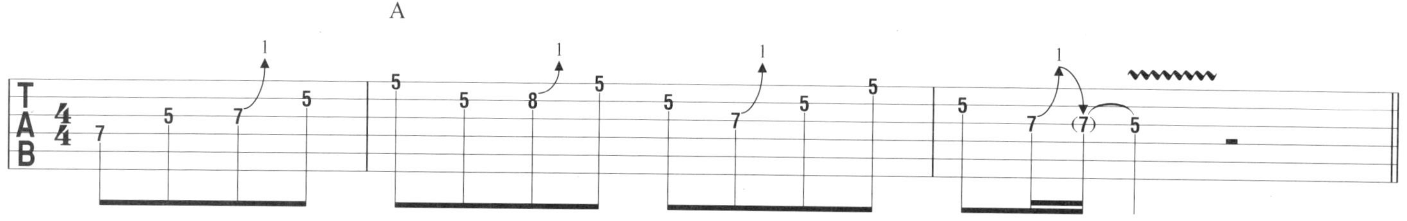

### 6: Climb the Box

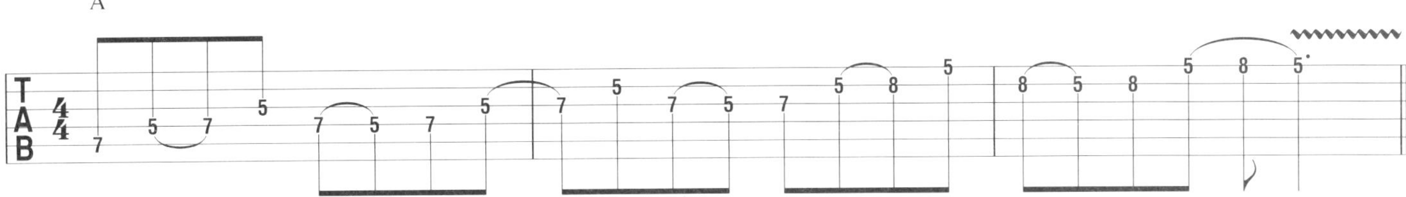


### 7: Position Shifter

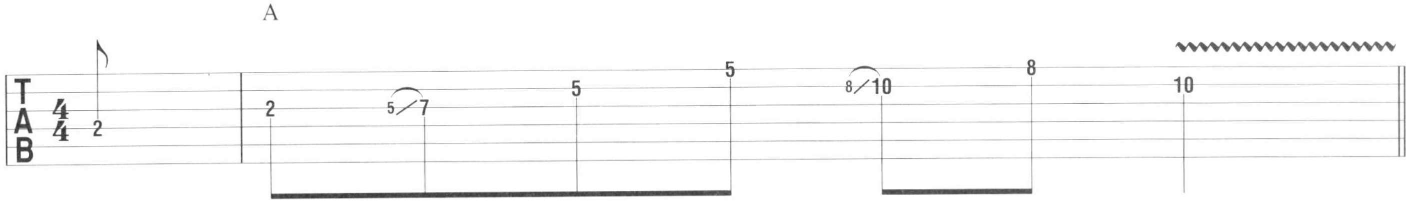


### 8: Melodic Blues

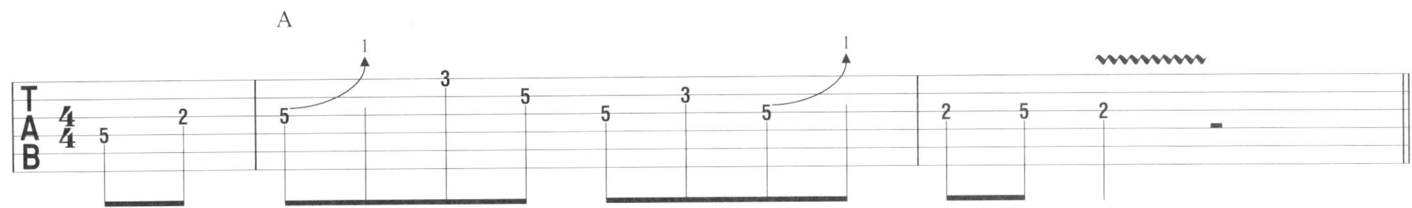


### 9: Jack in the Box

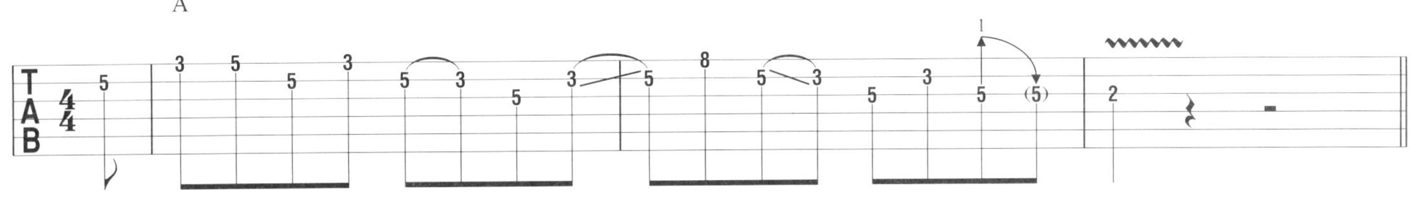


### 10: Blues Scale Blues

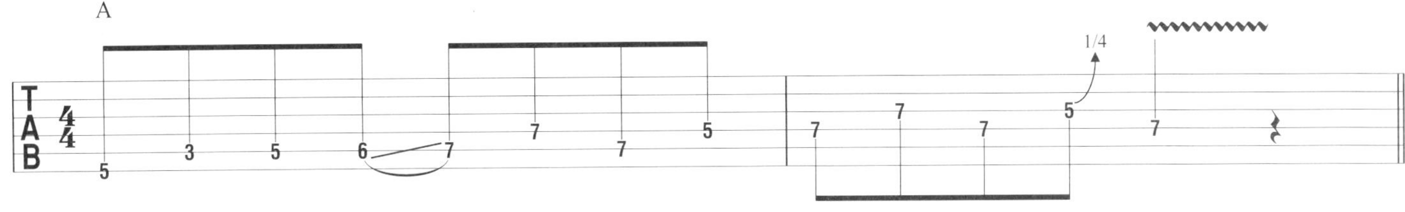


### 11: Fast Sequence

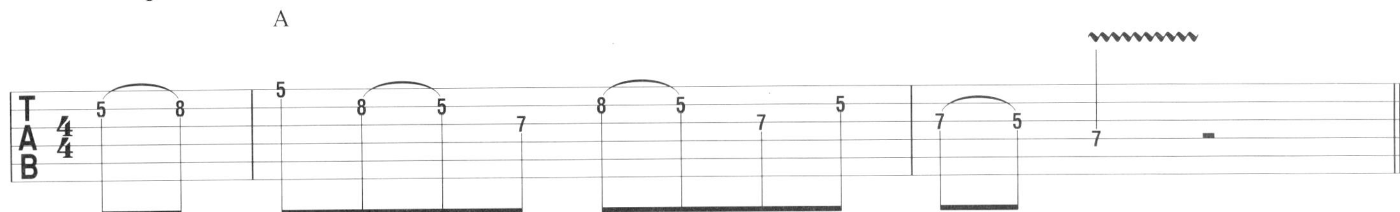

## 12: Milking It

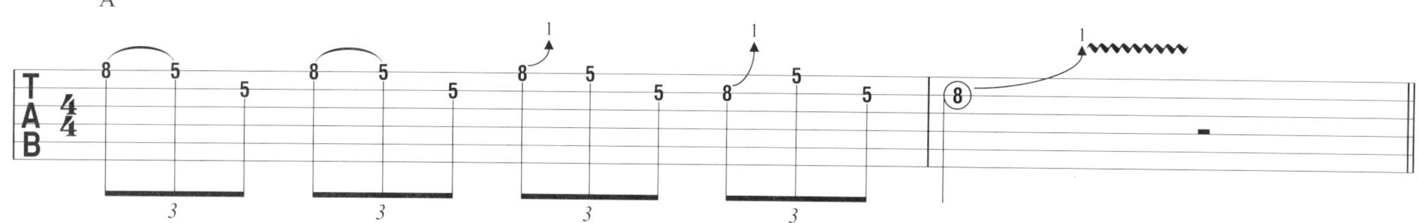


## 13: Major Tasty

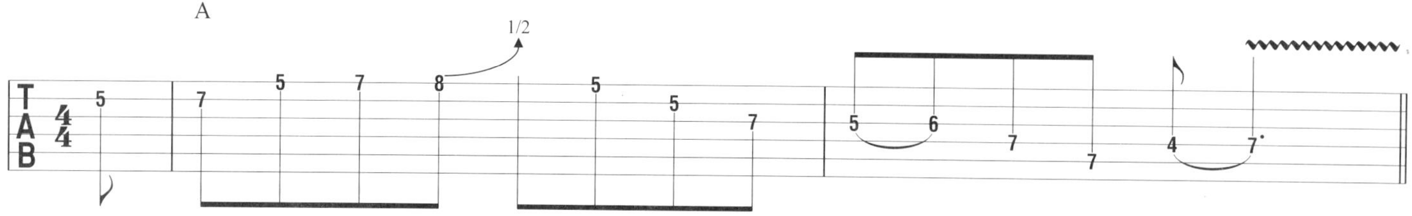


## 14: B.B.'s House

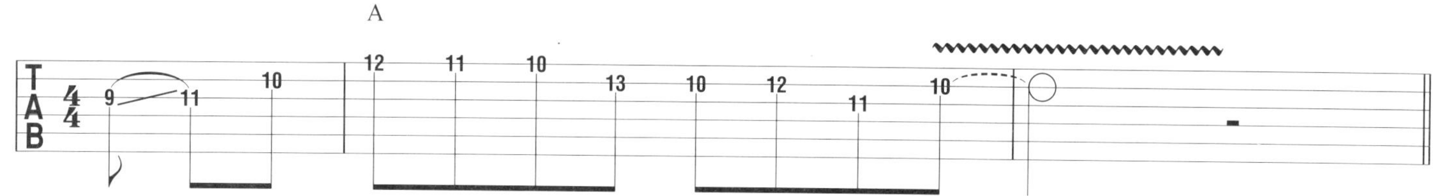


## 15: Kickstart My Harp

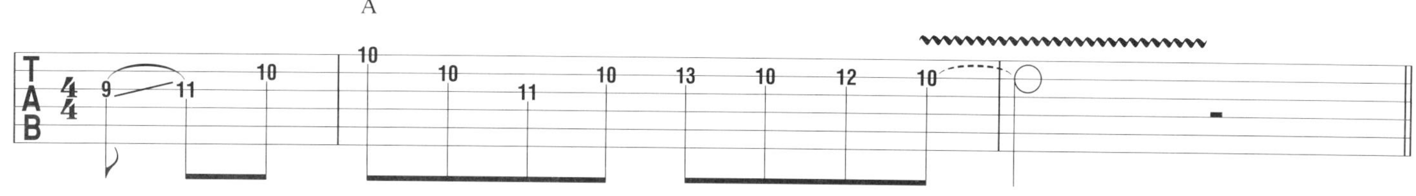


## 16: Trillin'

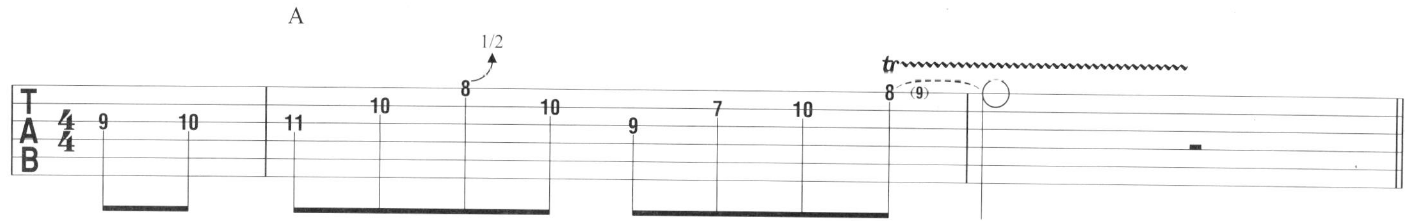


## 17: Penta-Surprise

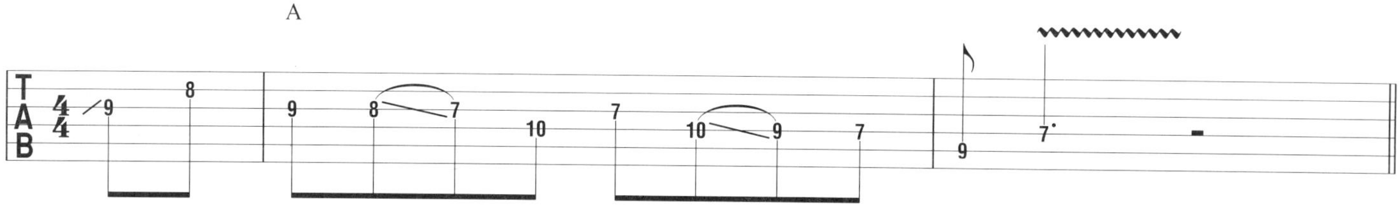

## 18: Sky Blues

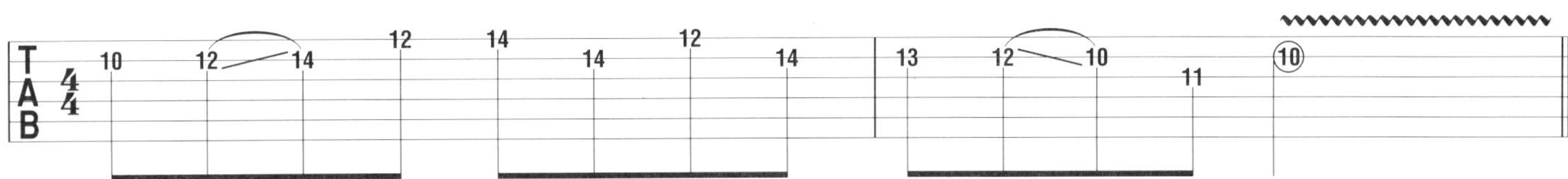


## 19: Double Slider

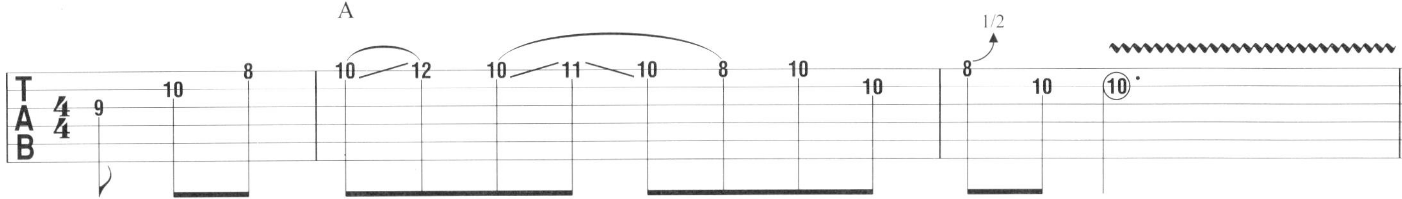


## 20: Drone Tone

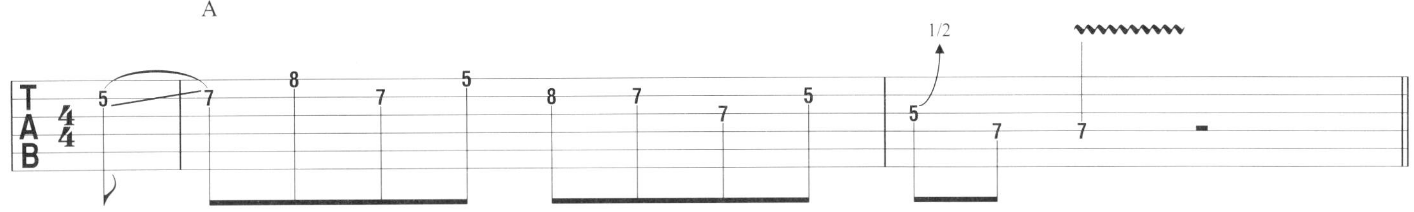


## 21: Triplet Bouncer

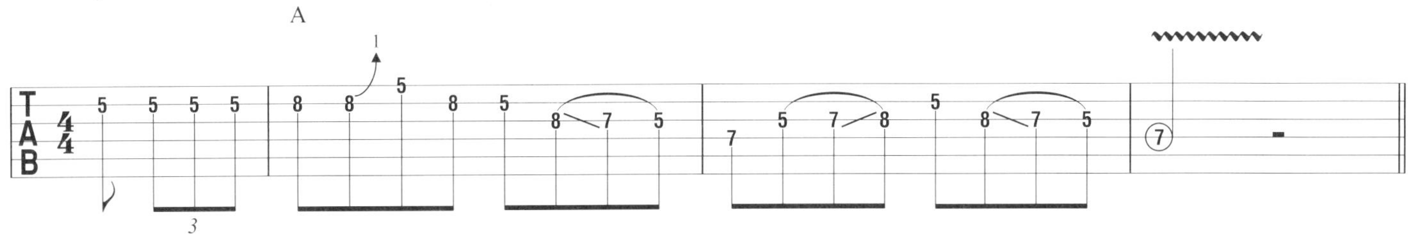


## 22: Bend Sequence

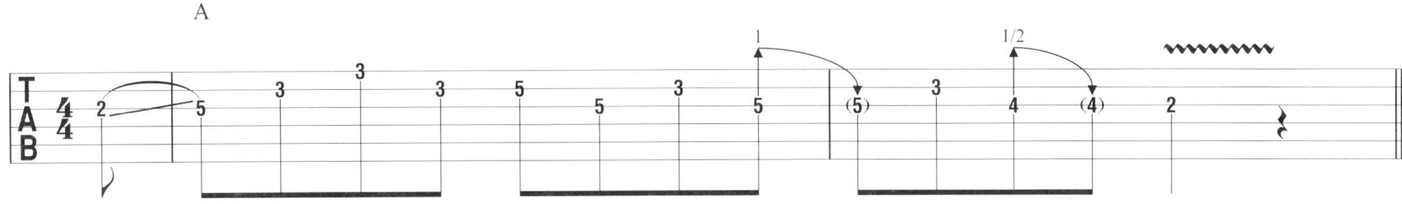


## 23: 6 and 9 Time

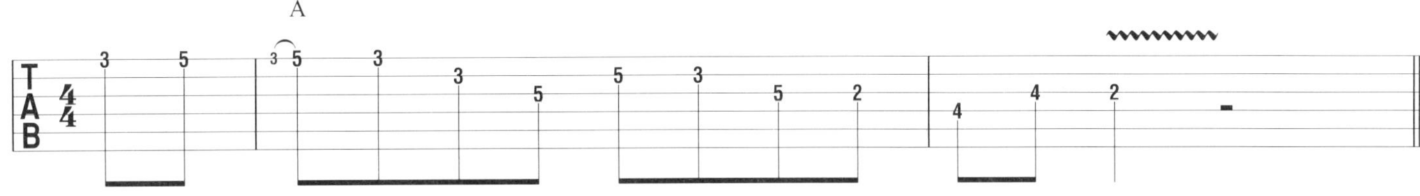

### 24: Open-String Romp

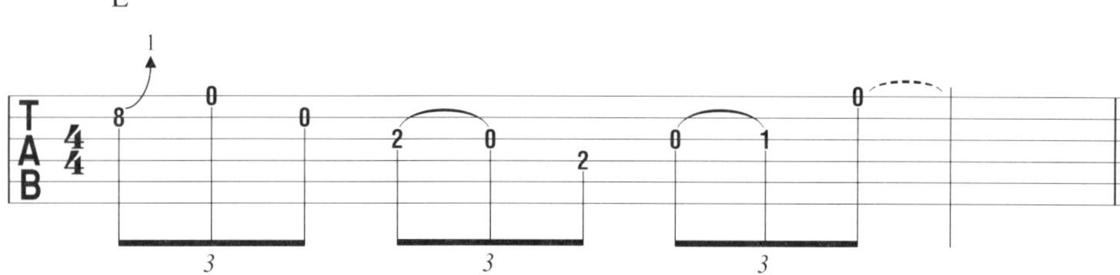


### 25: Countrified

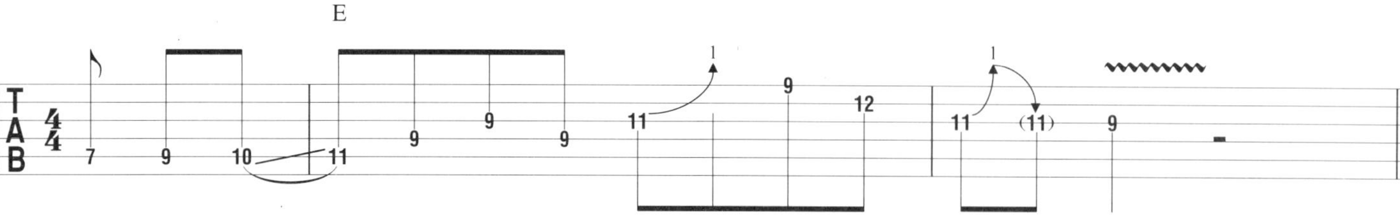


### 26: Pedal Steel Blues

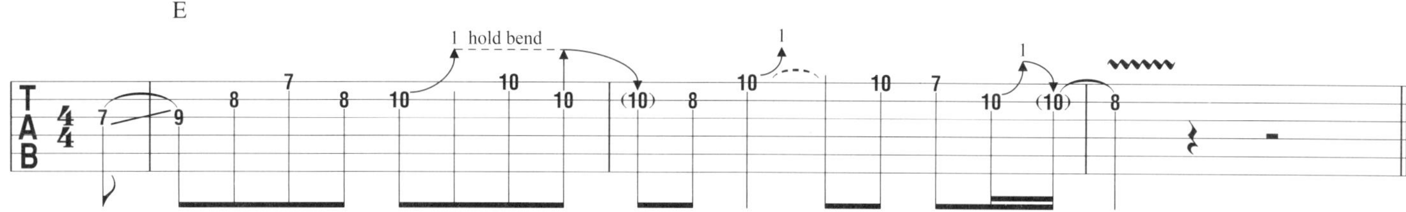


### 27: Target Practice

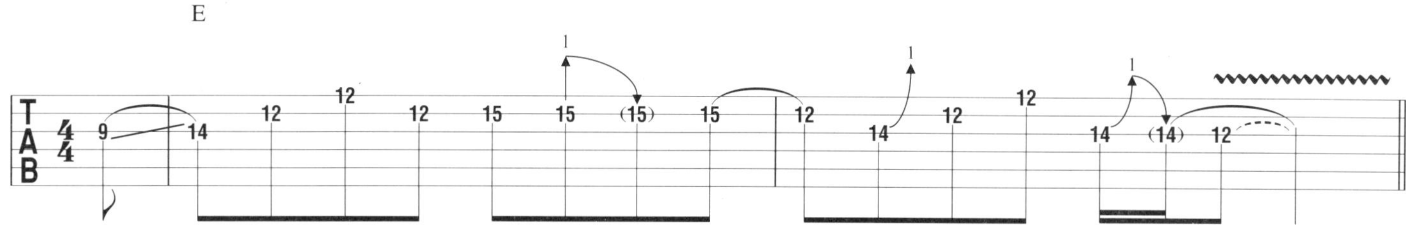


### 28: Hammer-Puller

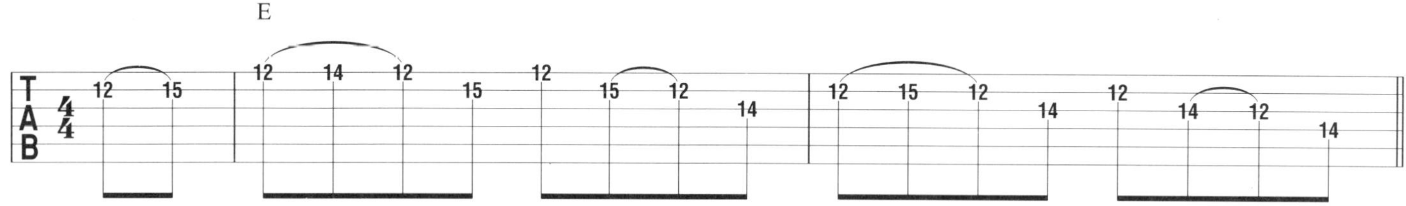


### 29: Parallel Pattern

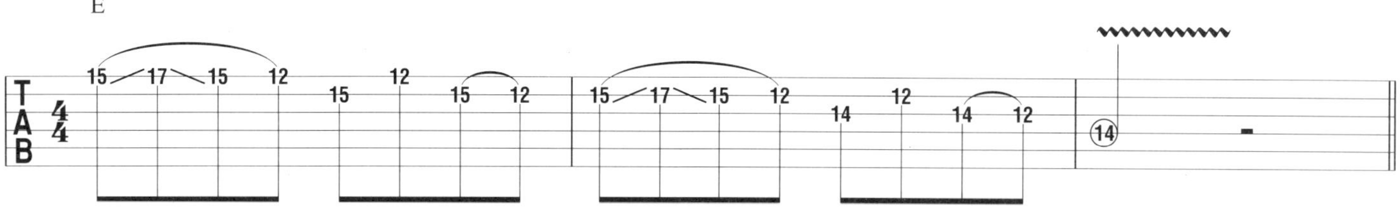

## 30: Triadic Blues

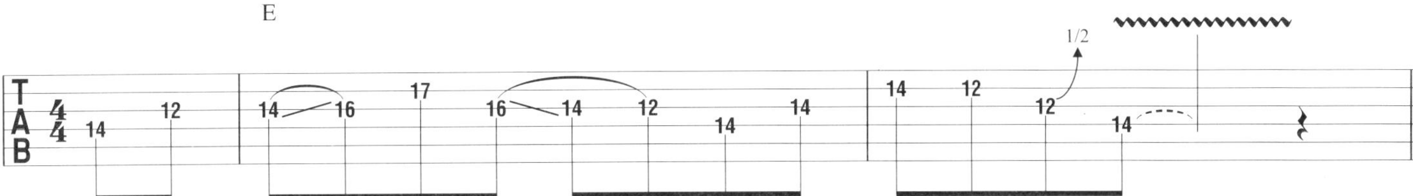


## 31: Dorian Blue

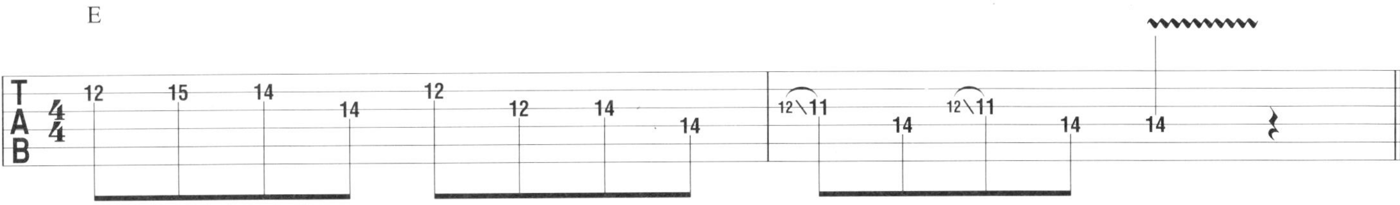


## 32: Melodious Minor

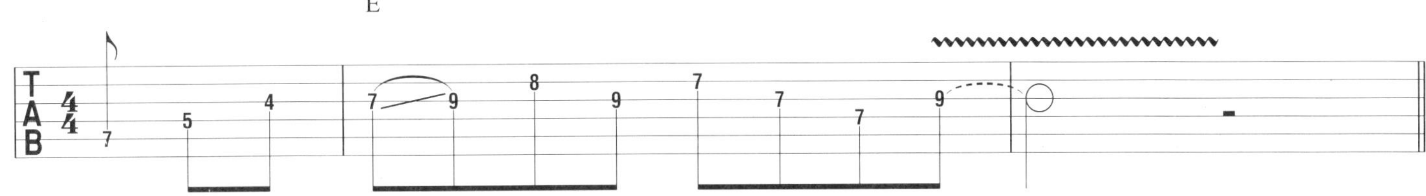


## 33: Barre Time

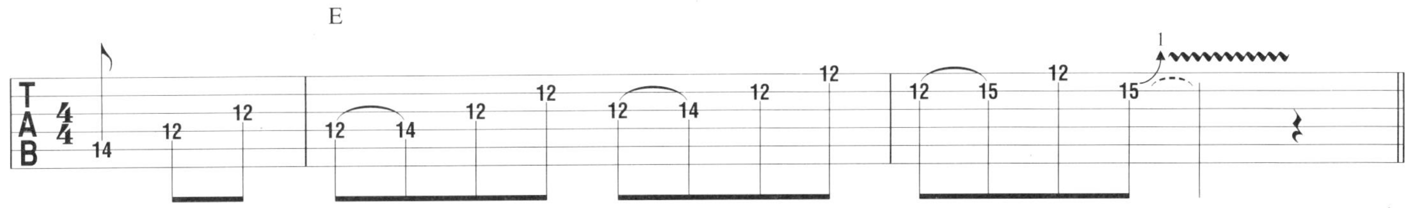


## 34: Triplet Classic

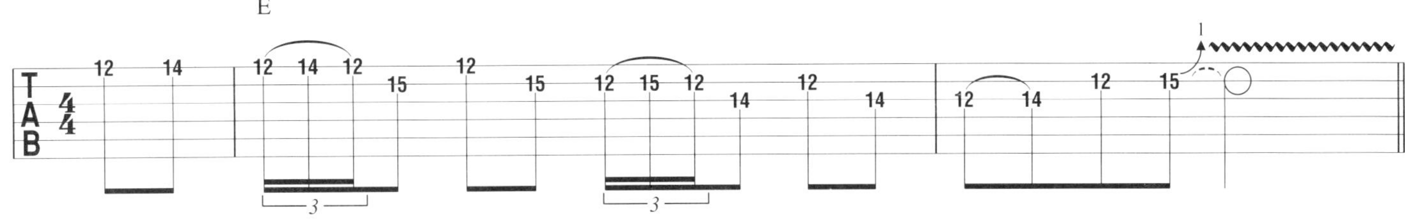


## 35: Soul Stinger

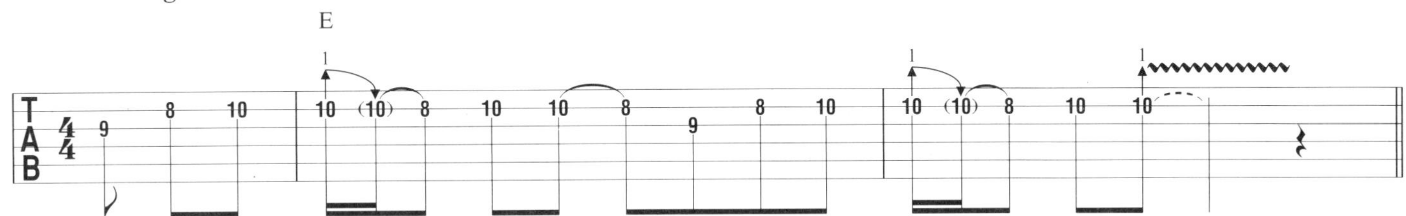

**36: Rolling Blues**

E

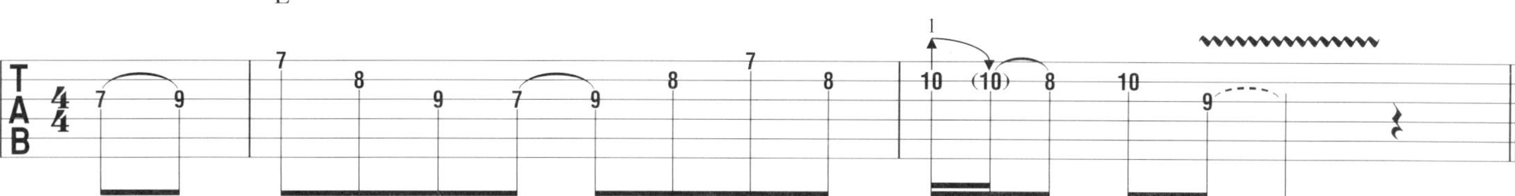

**37: Slip and Slide**

E

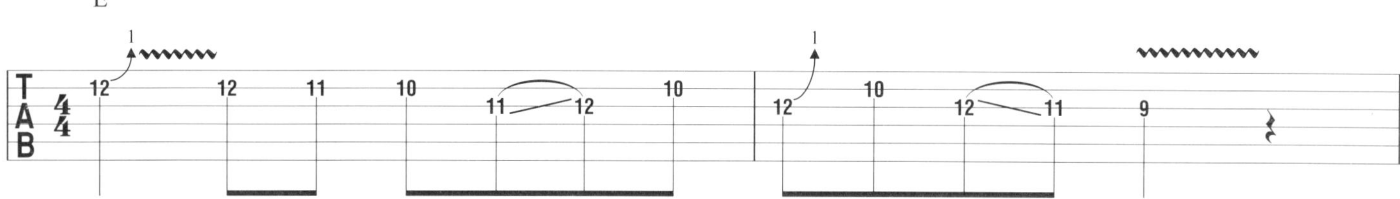

**38: SRV Me**

E

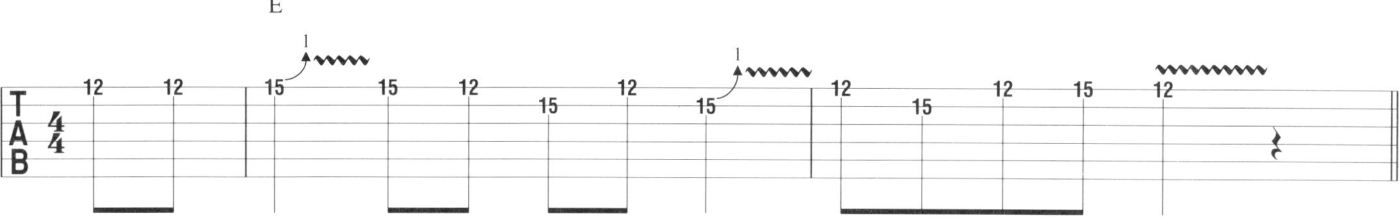

**39: Get Plucky**

D

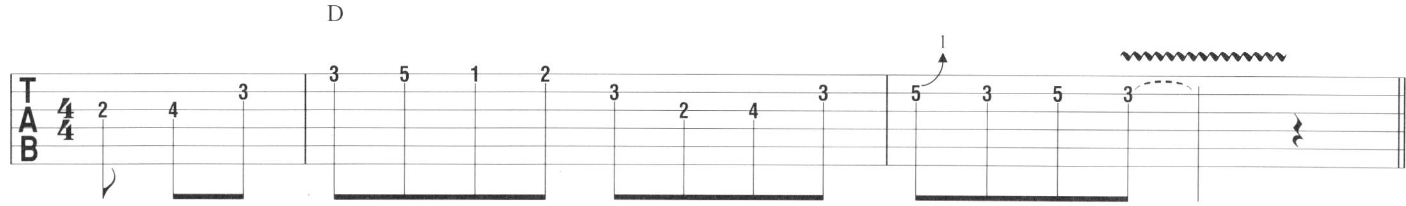

**40: Dorian-Like**

D

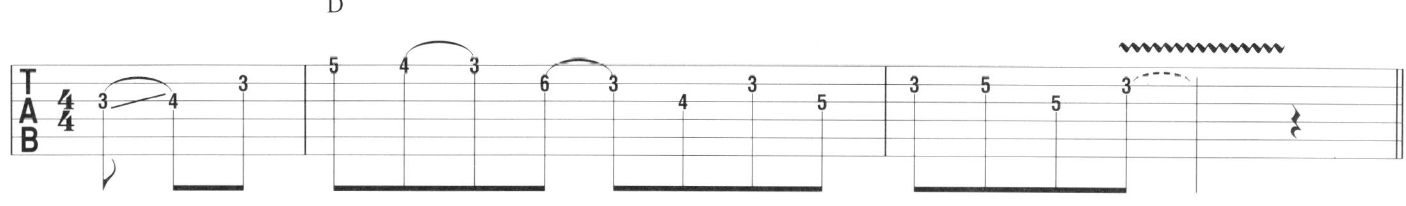

**41: Chromatic Blues**

D

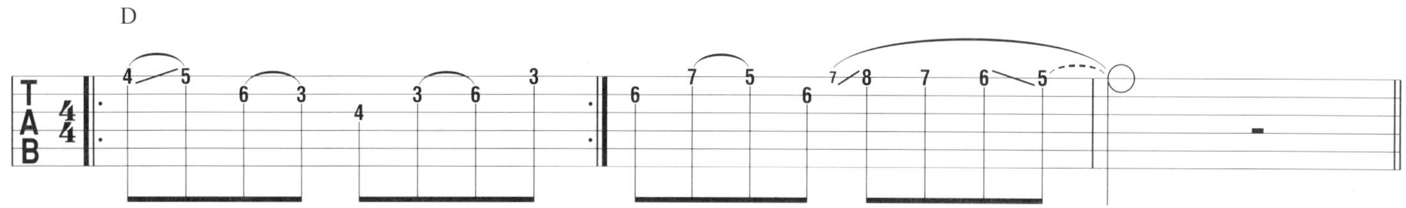

### 42: Final Approach

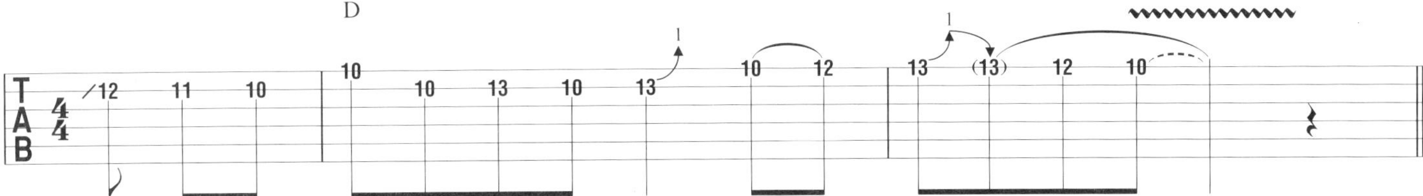

### 43: Throaty & Cool

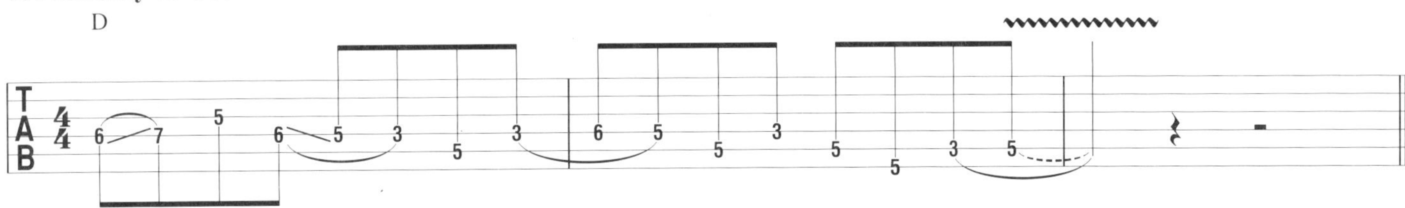

### 44: Penta-Cycle

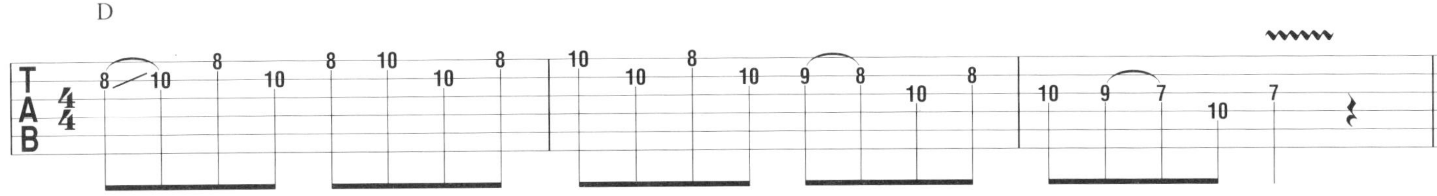

### 45: Diatonic Surprise

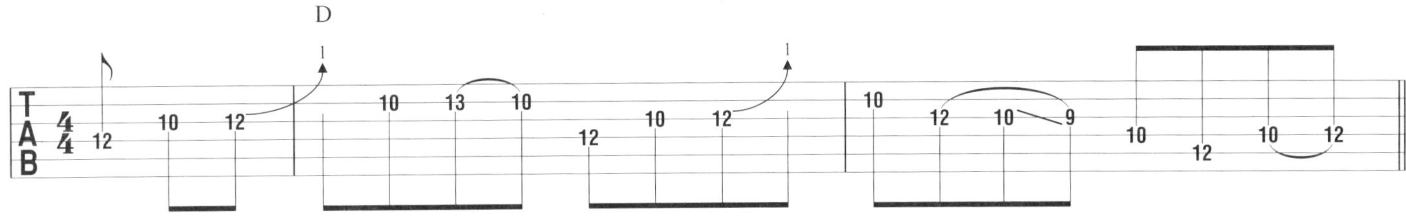

### 46: Waterfalling

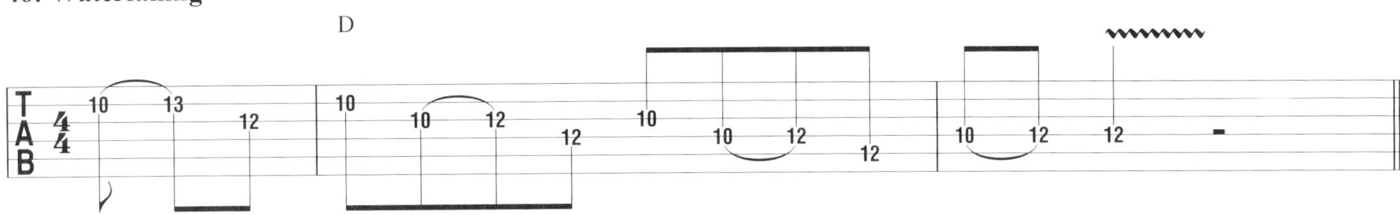

### 47: Sequential Descent

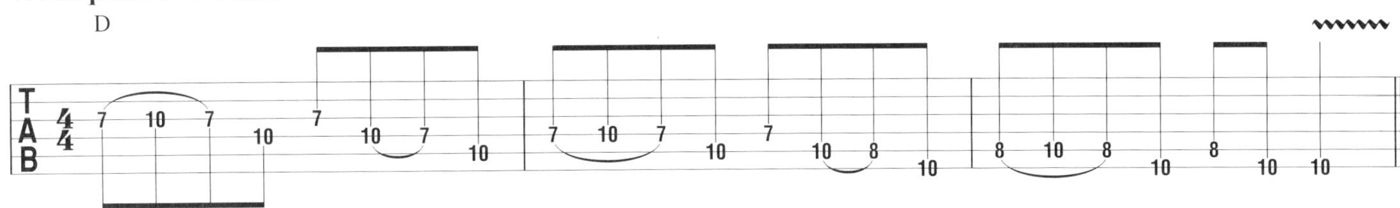

### 48: Blues Rocker

D

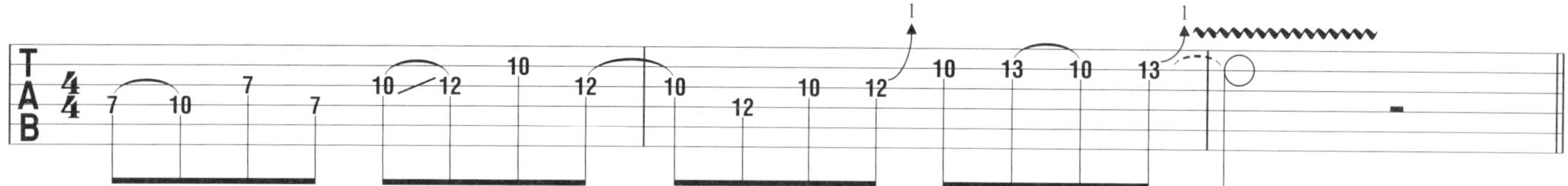

### 49: Cyclic Blues

D

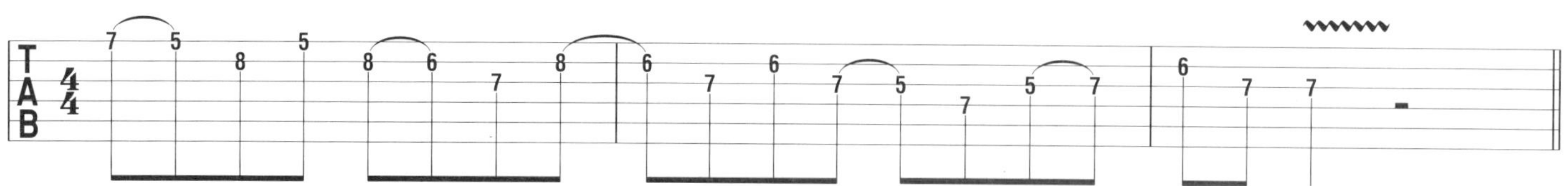

### 50: Up-the-Necker

D

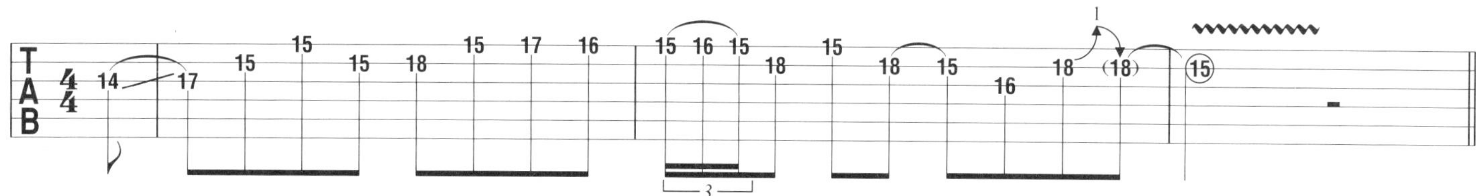

### 51: Bend to the Moon

D

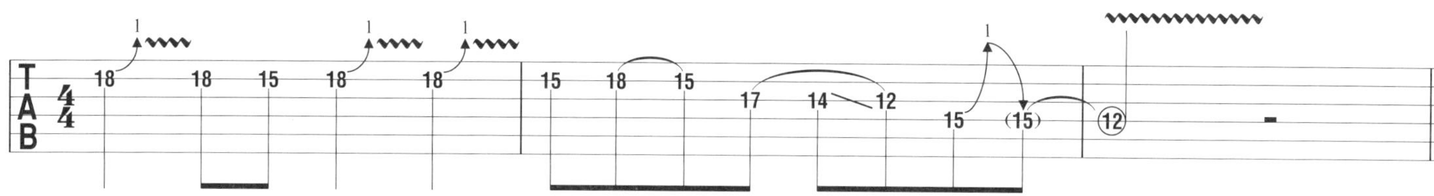

### 52: Southern Rocker

G

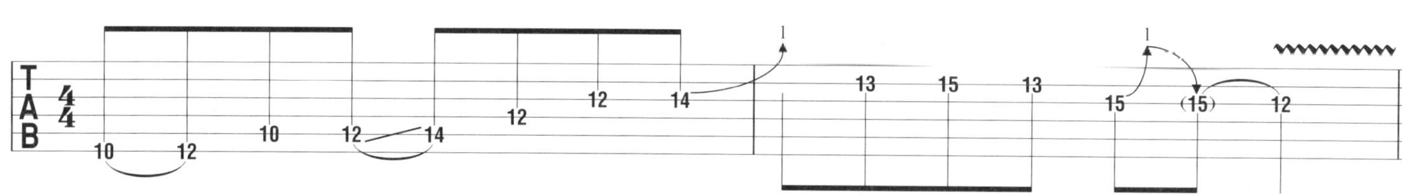

### 53: Choke It

G

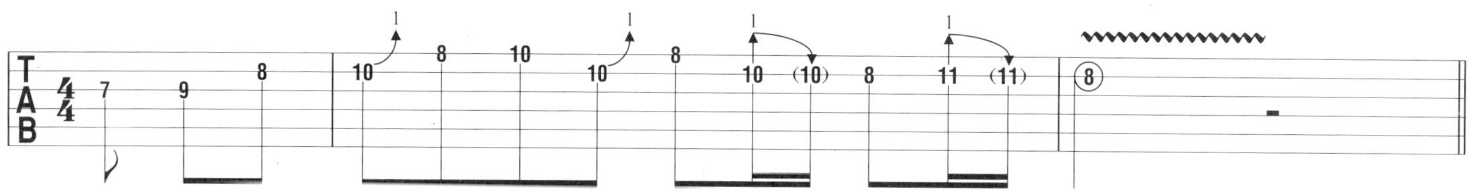

### 54: Fit for a King

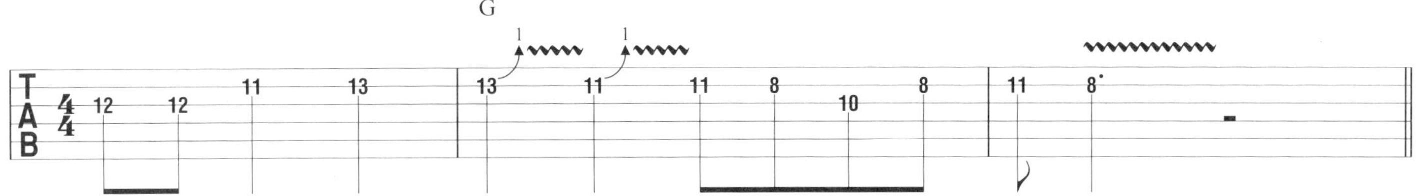


### 55: Chromatic Ascent

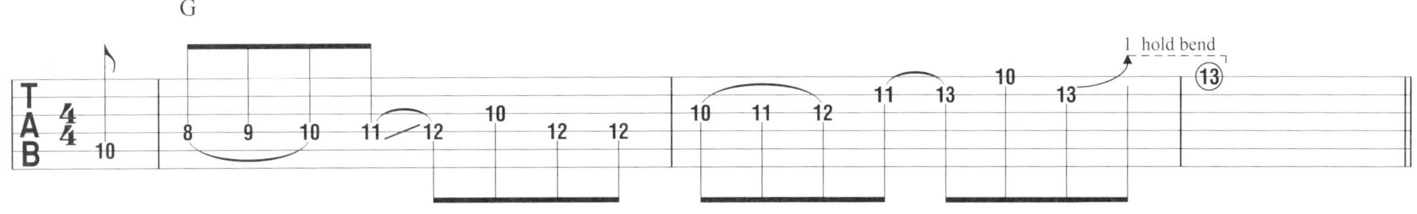


### 56: Melodic Melancholic

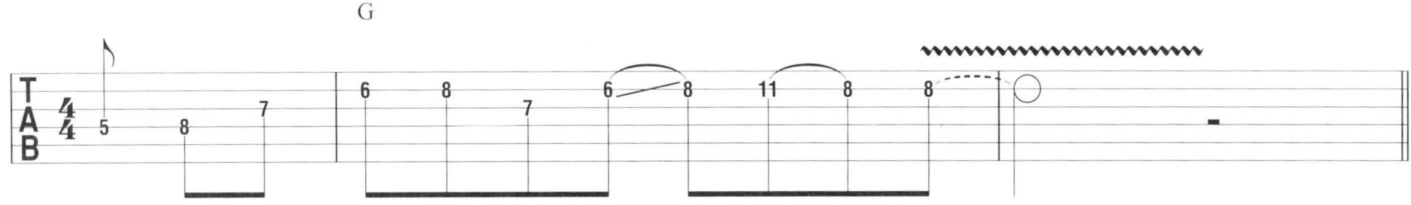


### 57: Feel the Pain

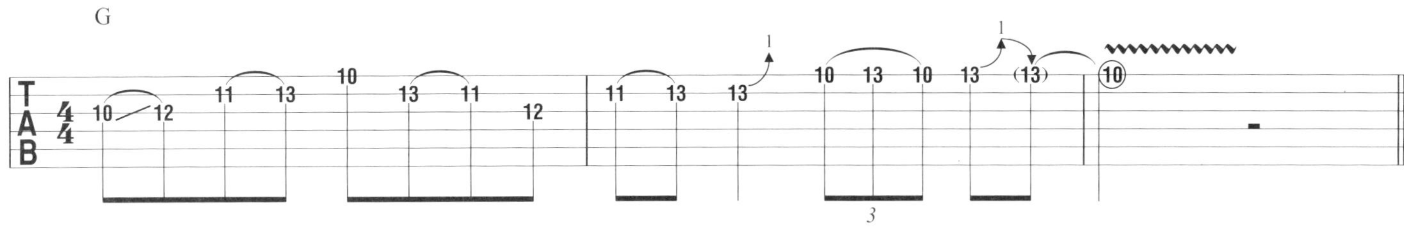


### 58: Mix It Up

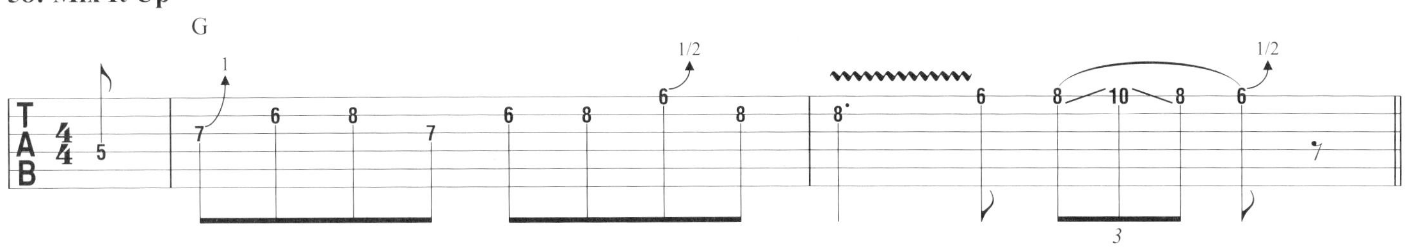


### 59: String Skipper

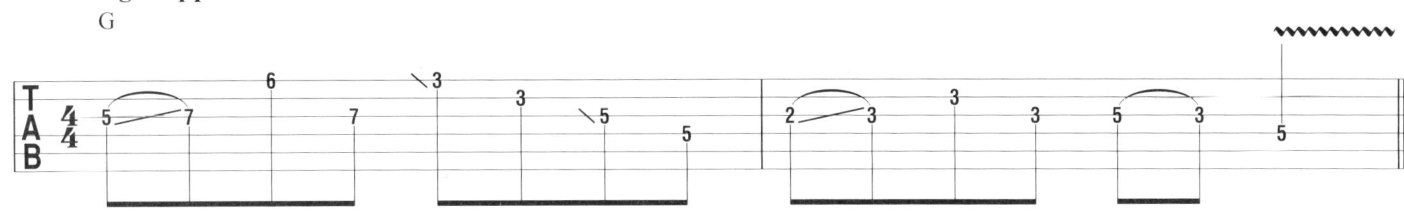

### 60: Fret Jumper

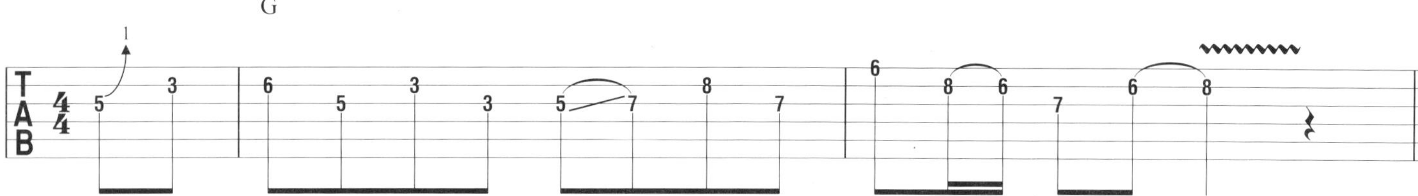

### 61: Angularity

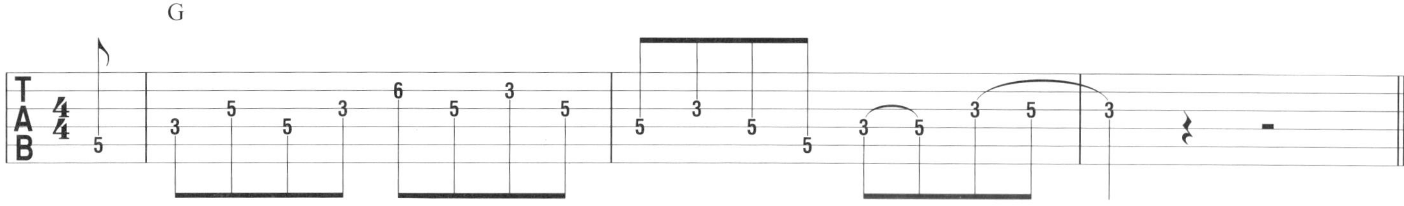

### 62: Über Blues

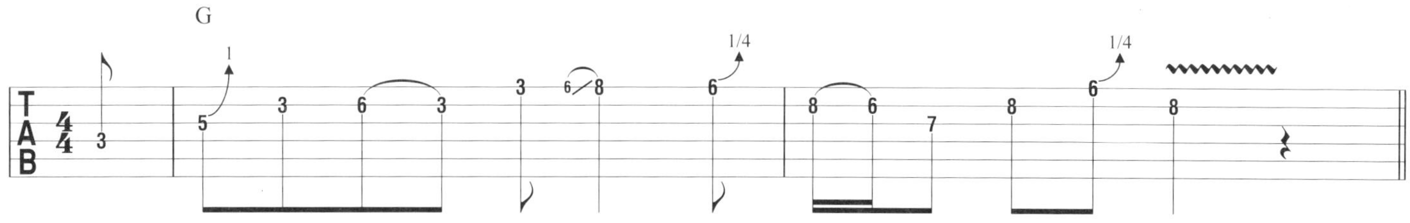

### 63: Minor/Major Mix

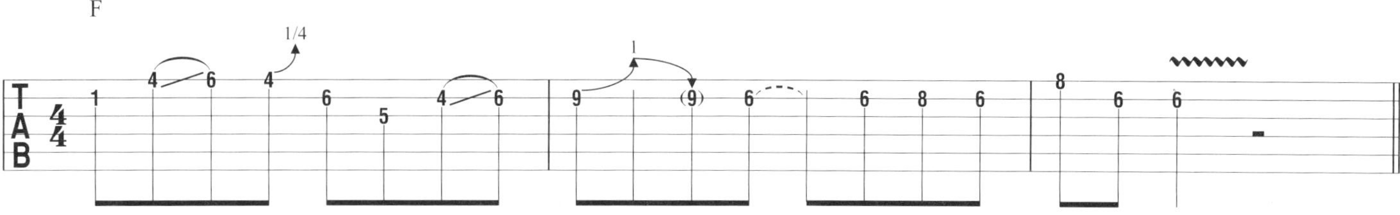

### 64: Claptonian Repeater

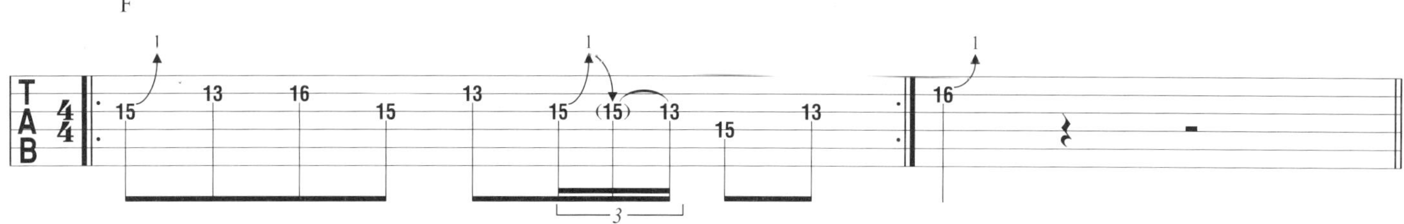

### 65: Chordal Country

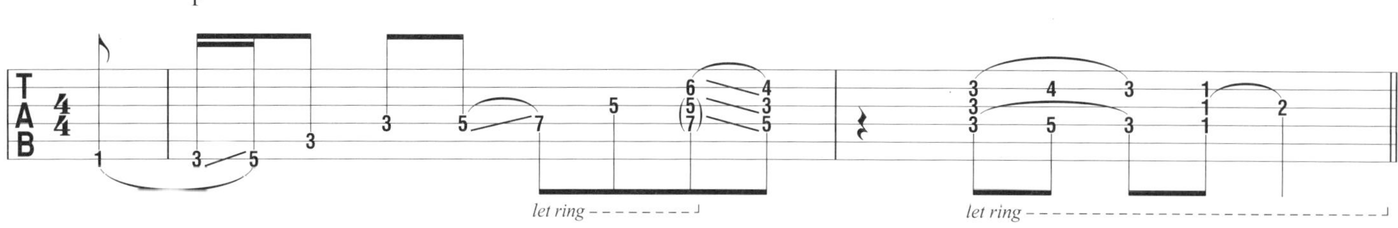

### 66: Scalar Combo

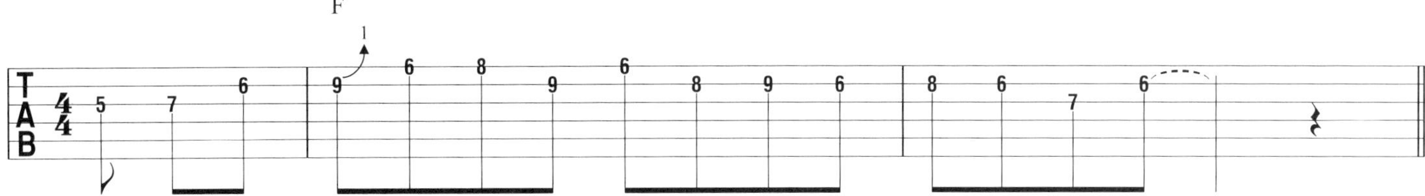


### 67: Gliss Bliss

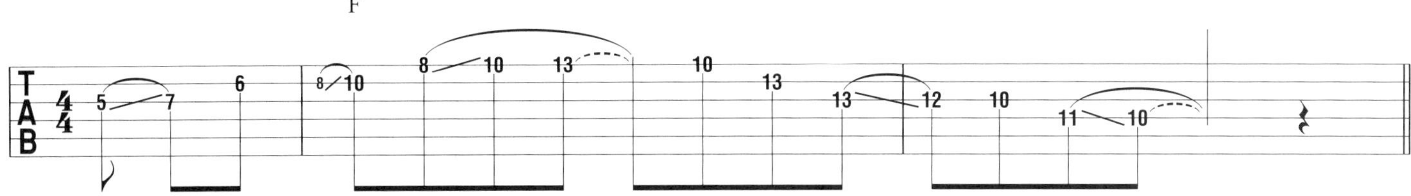


### 68: Arpeggio Delight

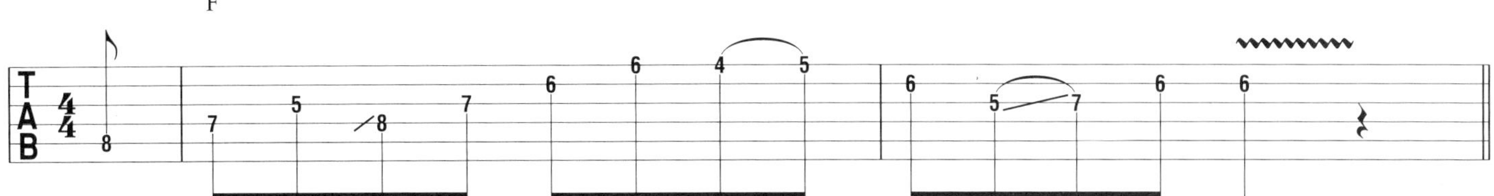


### 69: Pull It Off

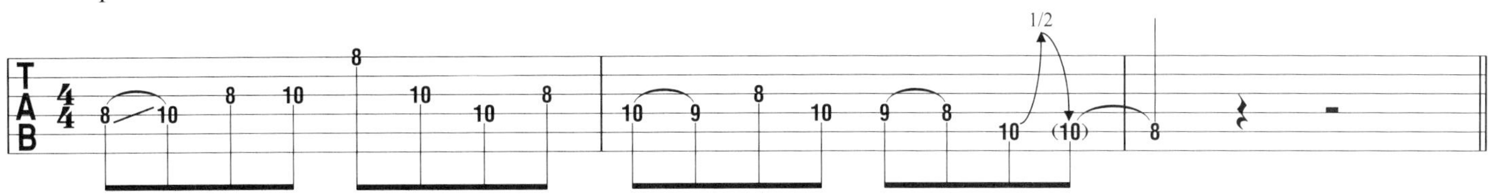


### 70: Non-Linear Line

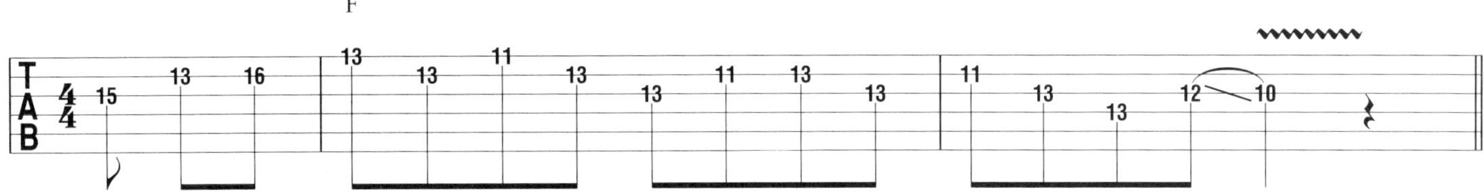


## Instructor: Johnny Moeller

### 71: V-IV-I Intro

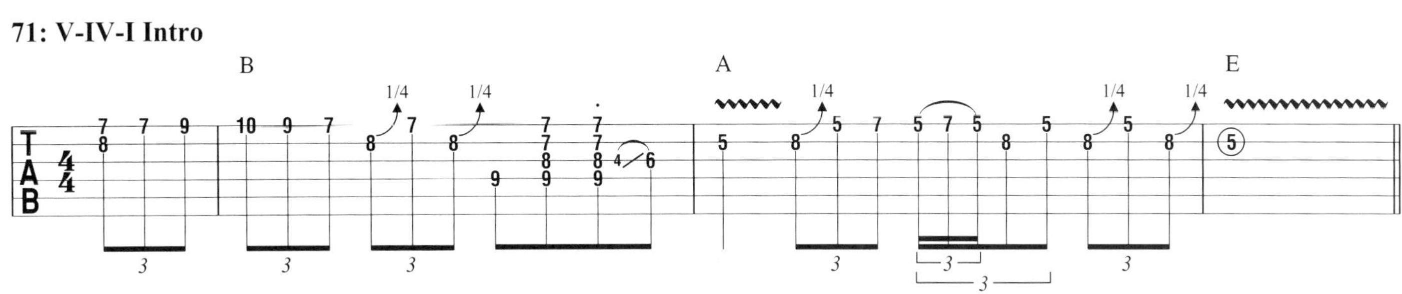

## 72: V-IV-I-V Intro

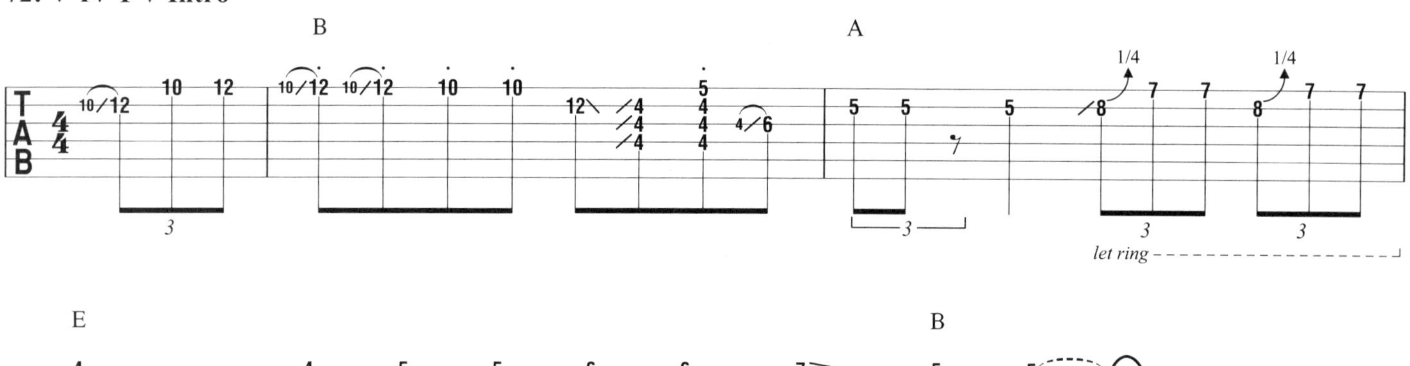


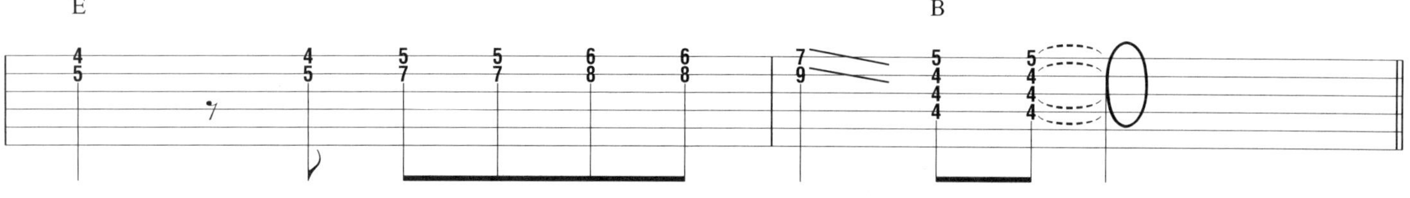


## 73: Solo Starter

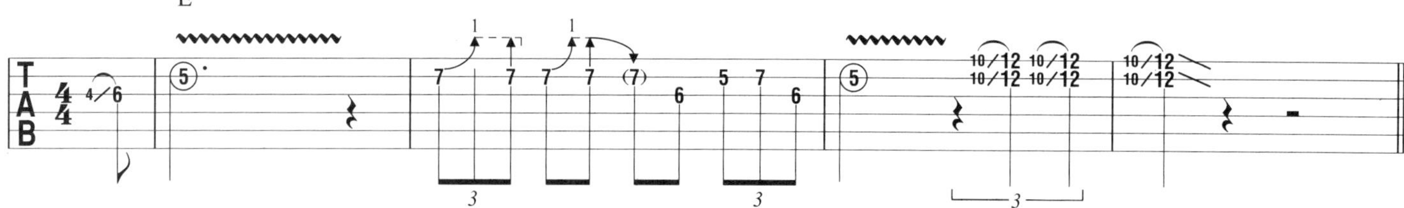


## 74: Kick It Chromatic

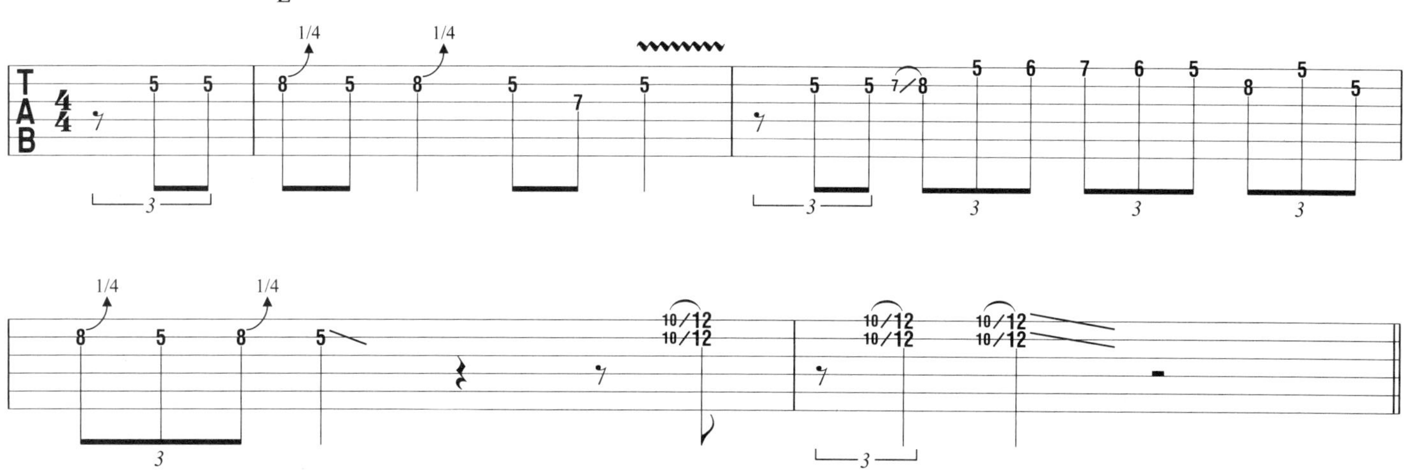

## 75: Grind It

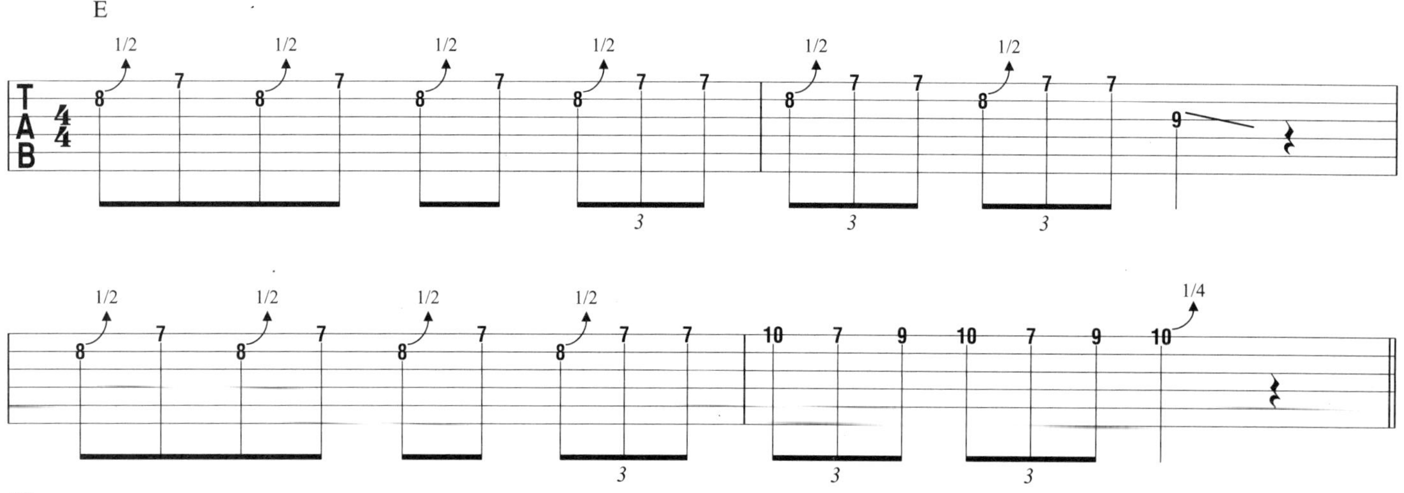

**76: Funky Freddie**

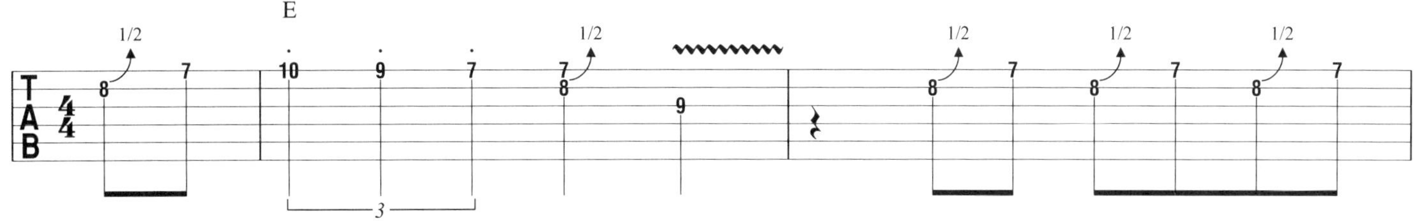


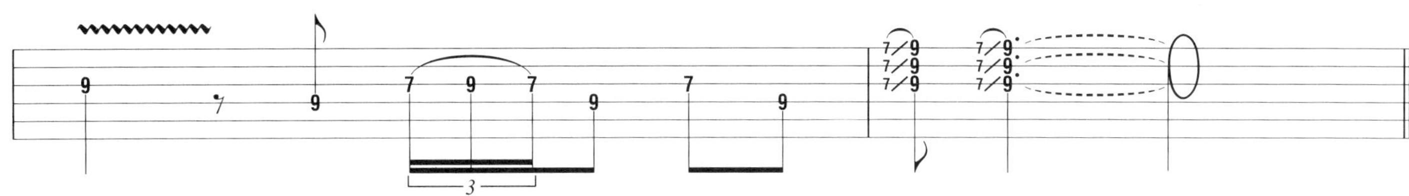

**77: Texas Turnaround**

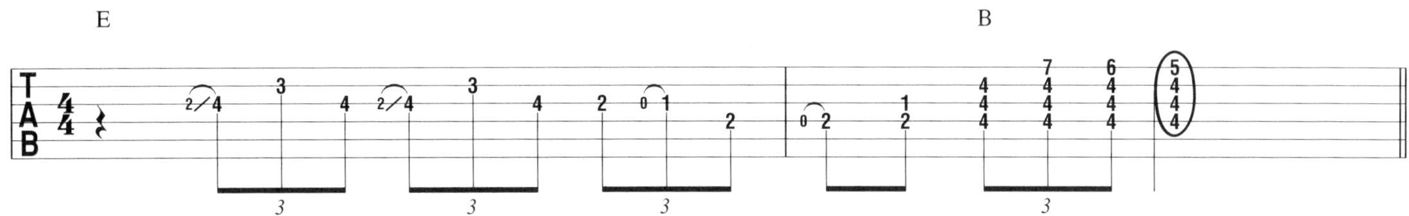


**78: Turn It Around**

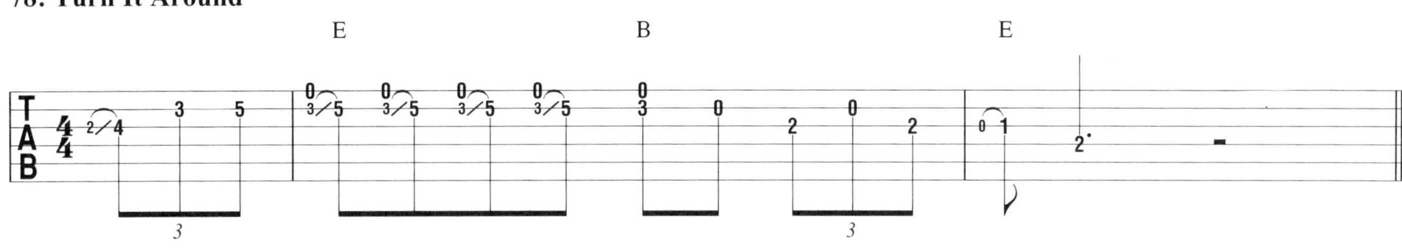

**79: Stop Around**

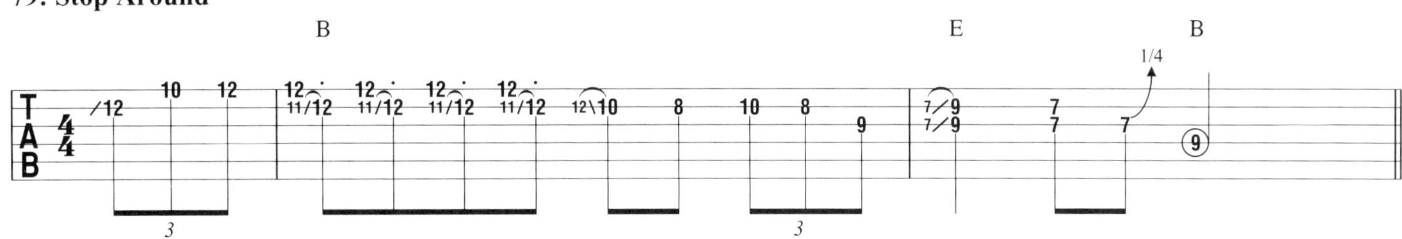


**80: Round and Round**

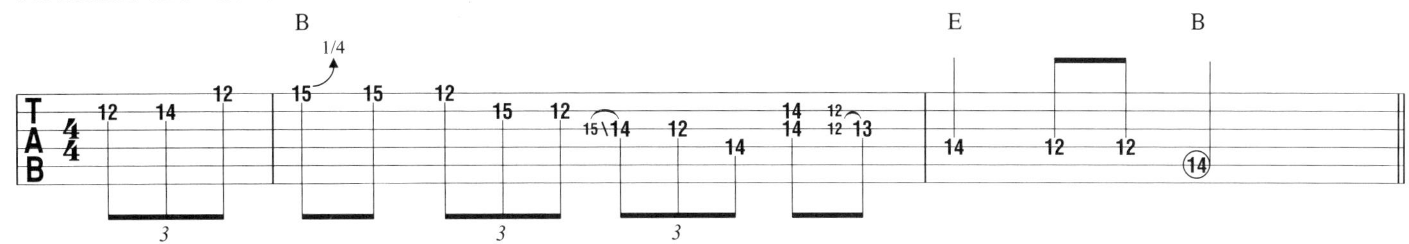

## 81: Rock and Roller

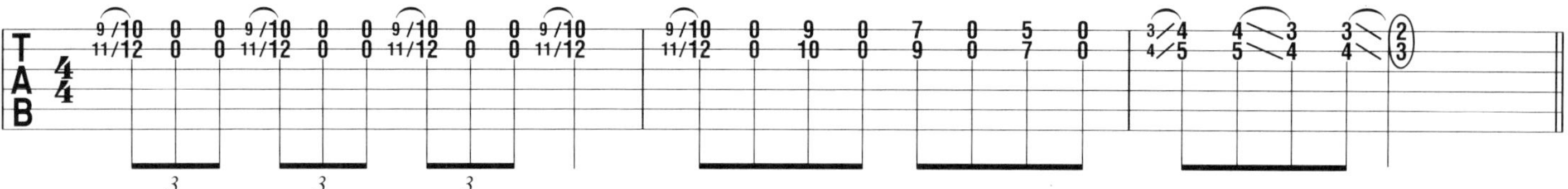


## 82: Hooker Time

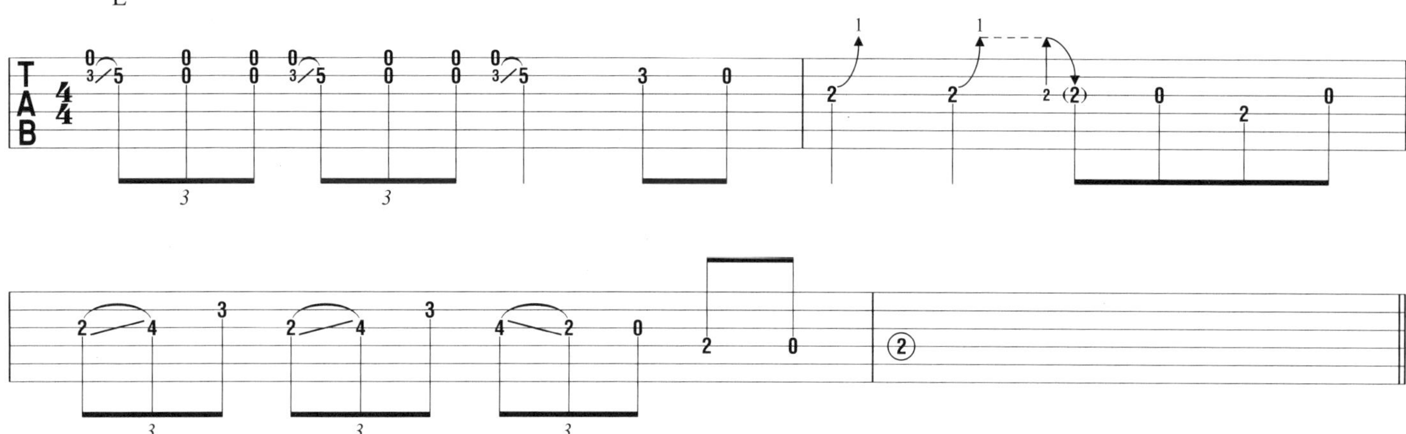


## 83: Droning Blues

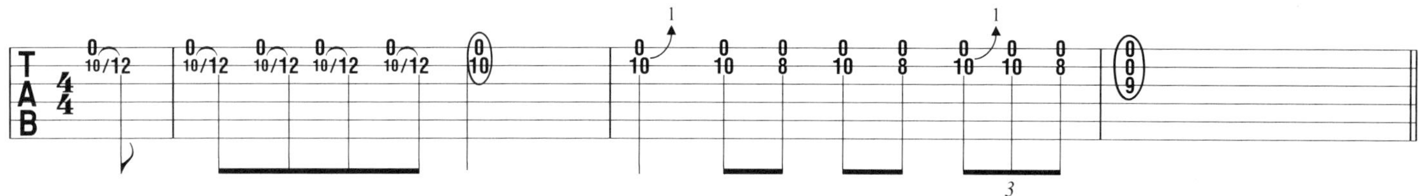


## 84: Twisted Blues

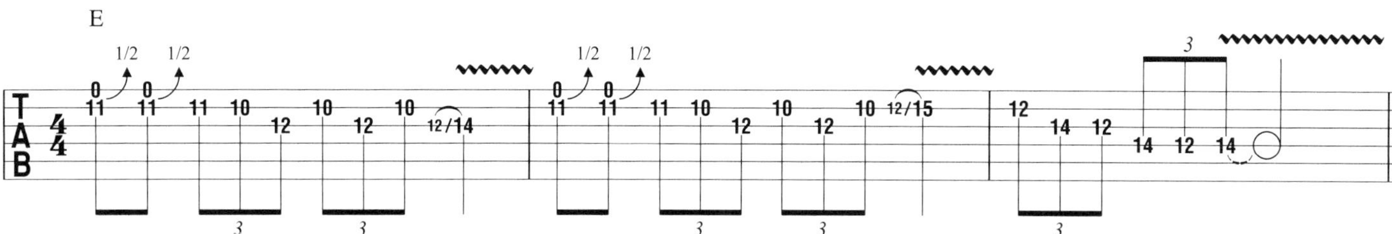


## 85: Fat & Dirty

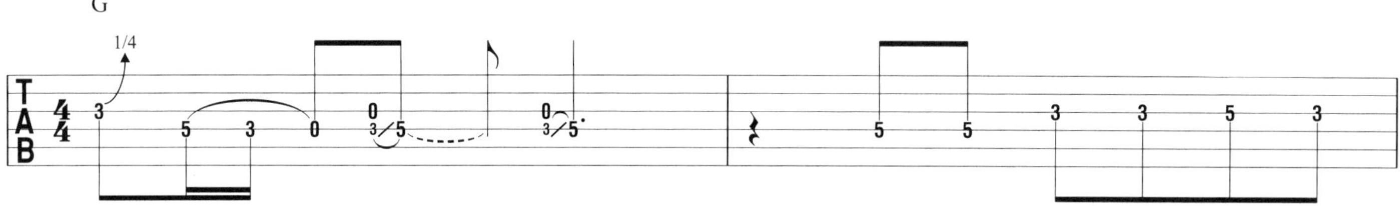


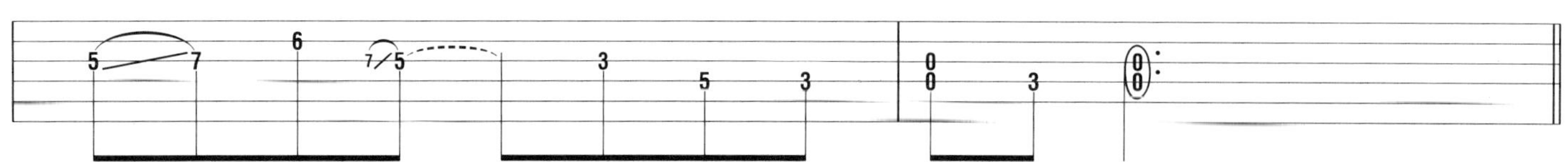

**86: Trippy Blues**

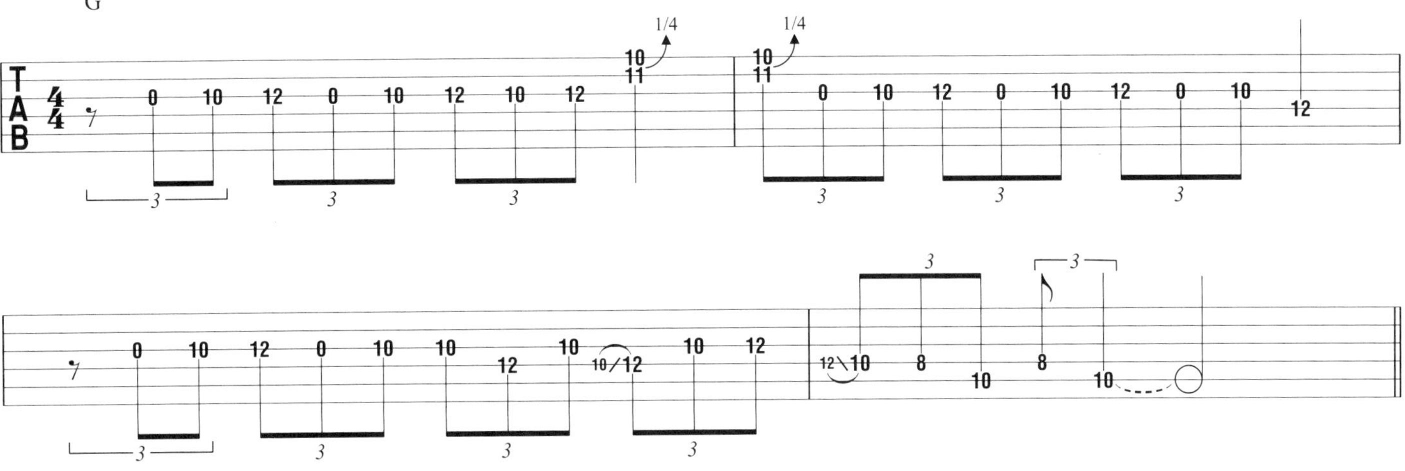


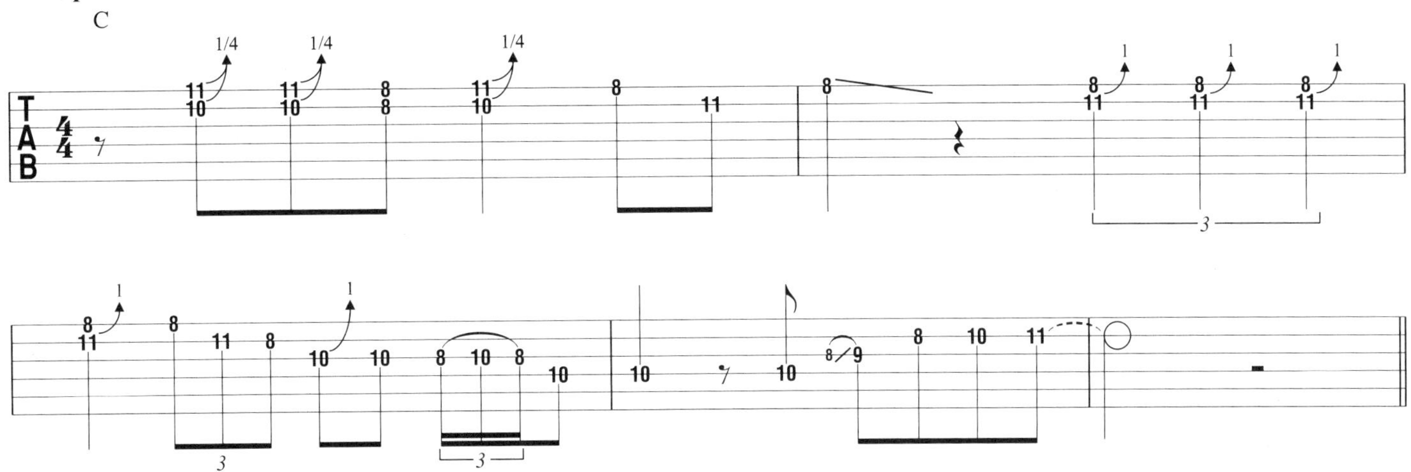

**87: Uptown Shuffle**

**88: Triple-Stoppin'**

C

**89: IV-Chord Shuffle**

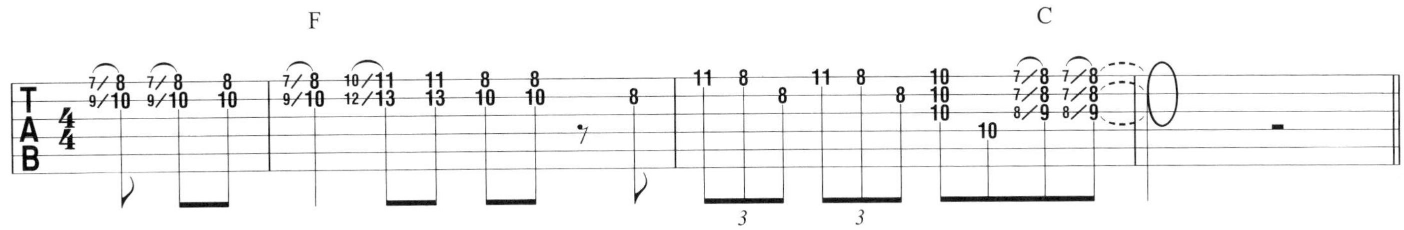

## 90: IV-Chord Walkup

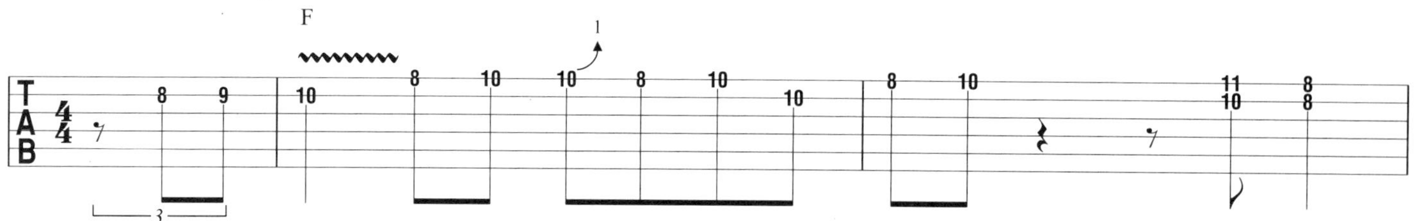


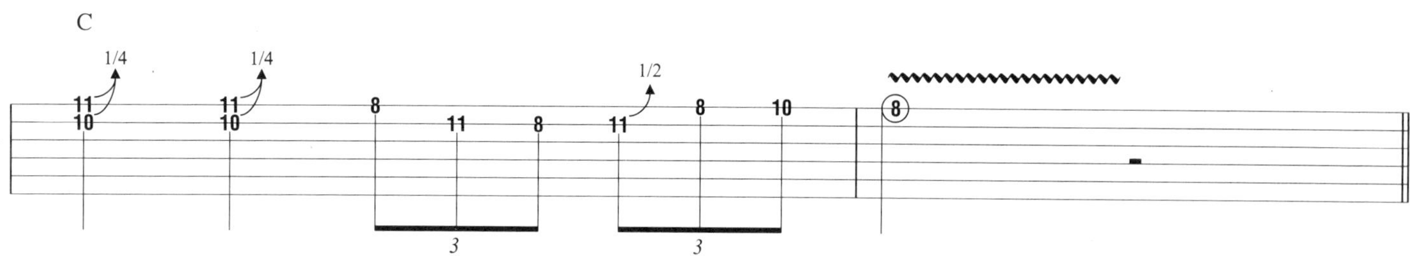


## 91: Double Bender

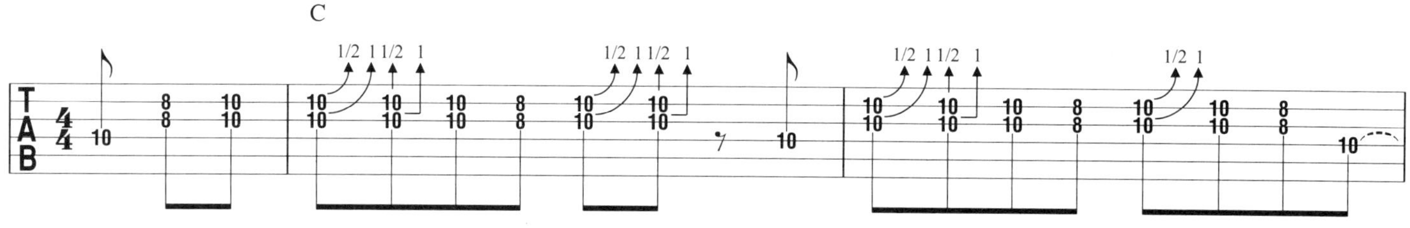


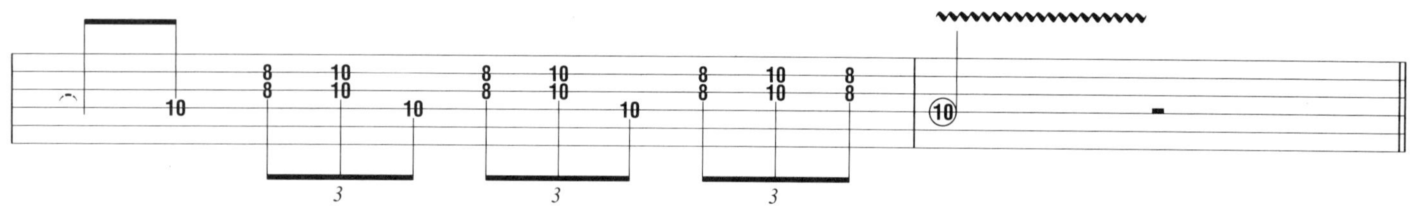

## 92: Triple Bender

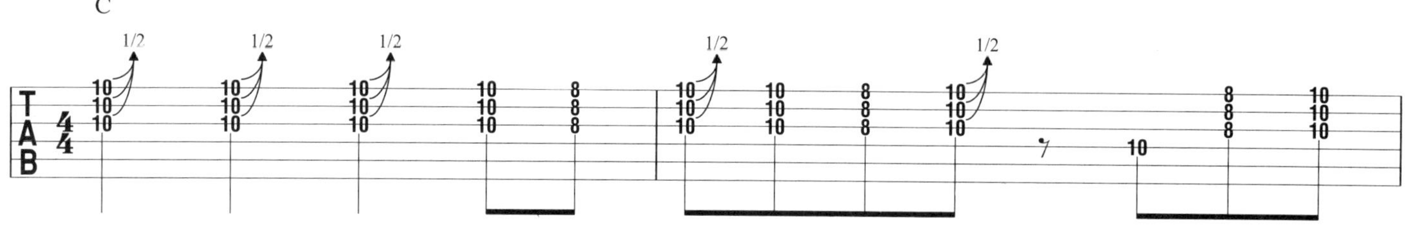


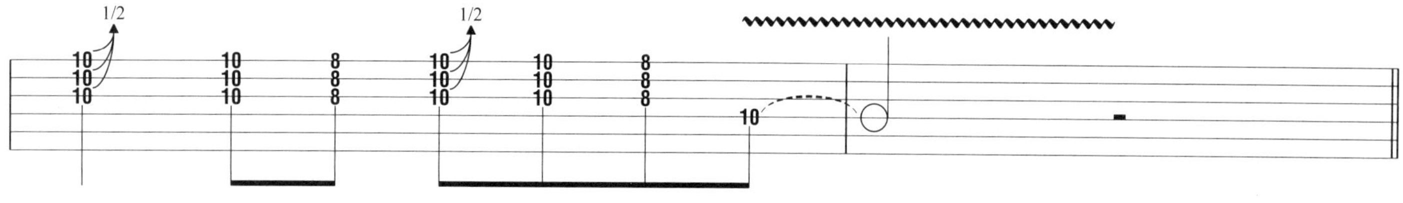

## 93: Rakin' the Blues

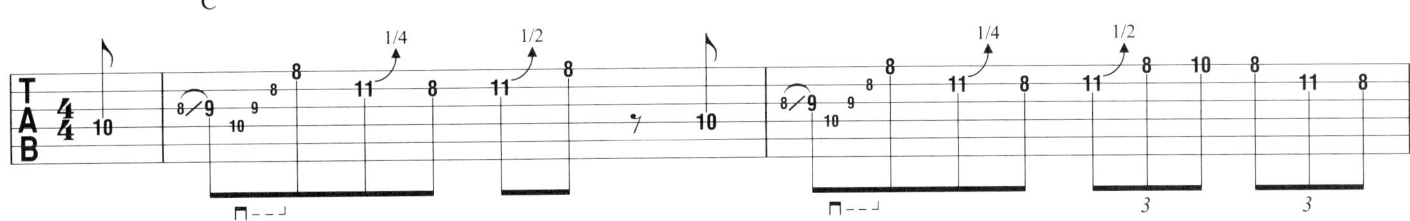


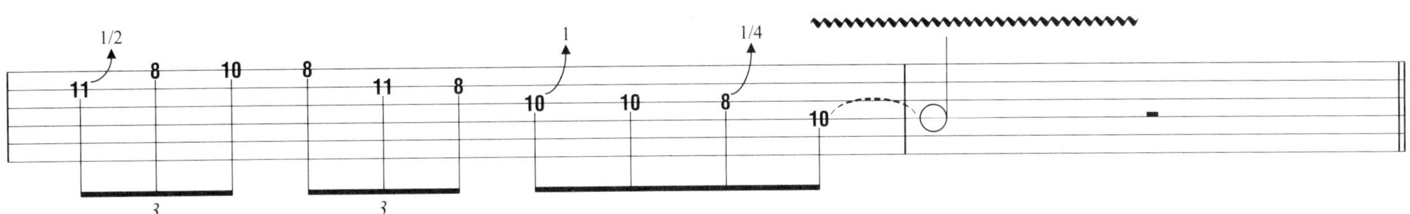

## 94: Rake Me

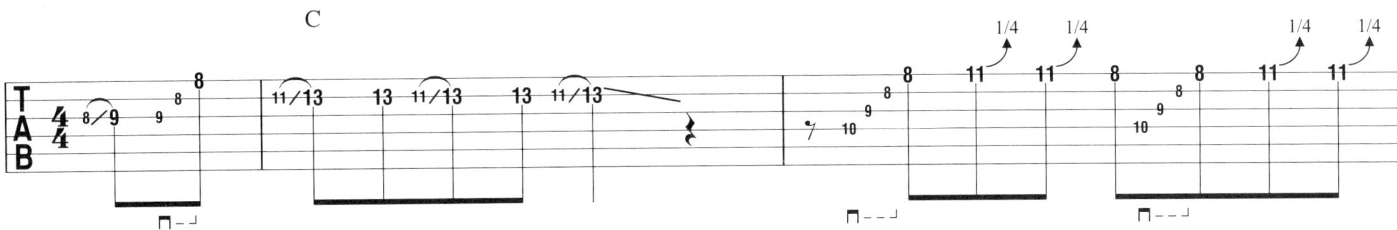


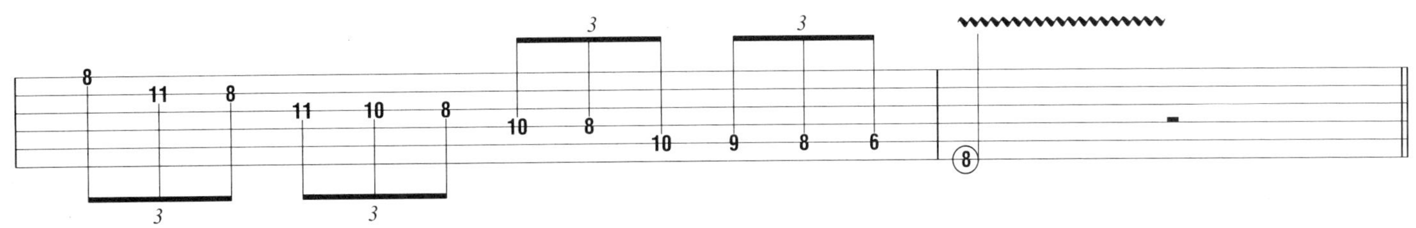

## 95: King's Chords

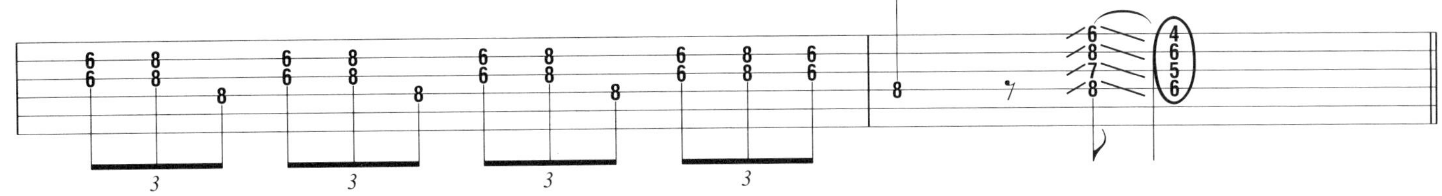

### 96: Buddy's Bends

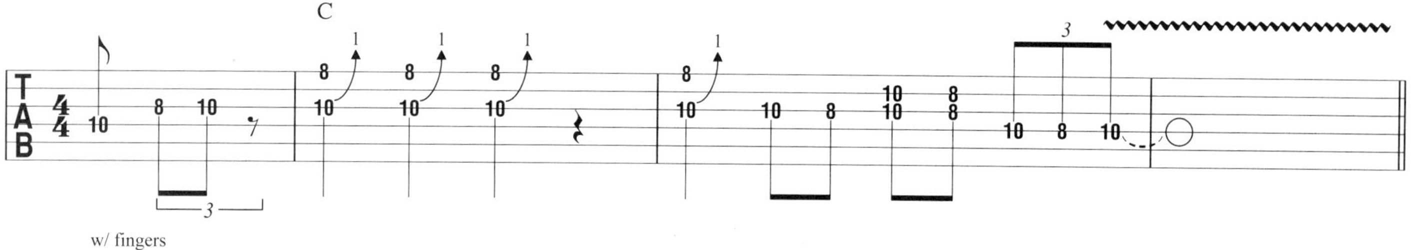


### 97: Sliding Stops

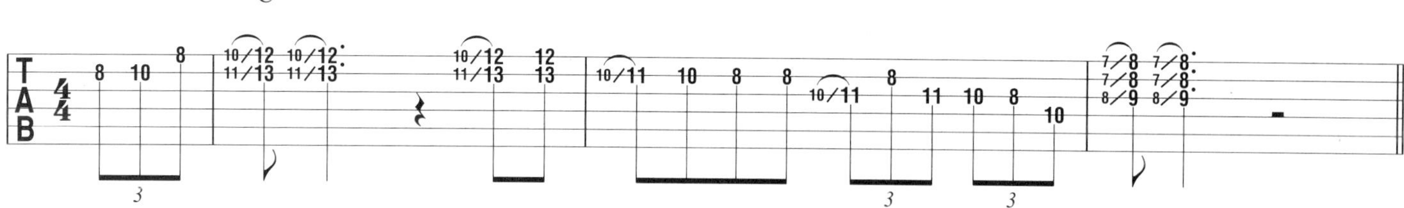


### 98: Swingin' Classic

### 99: Slow Blueser

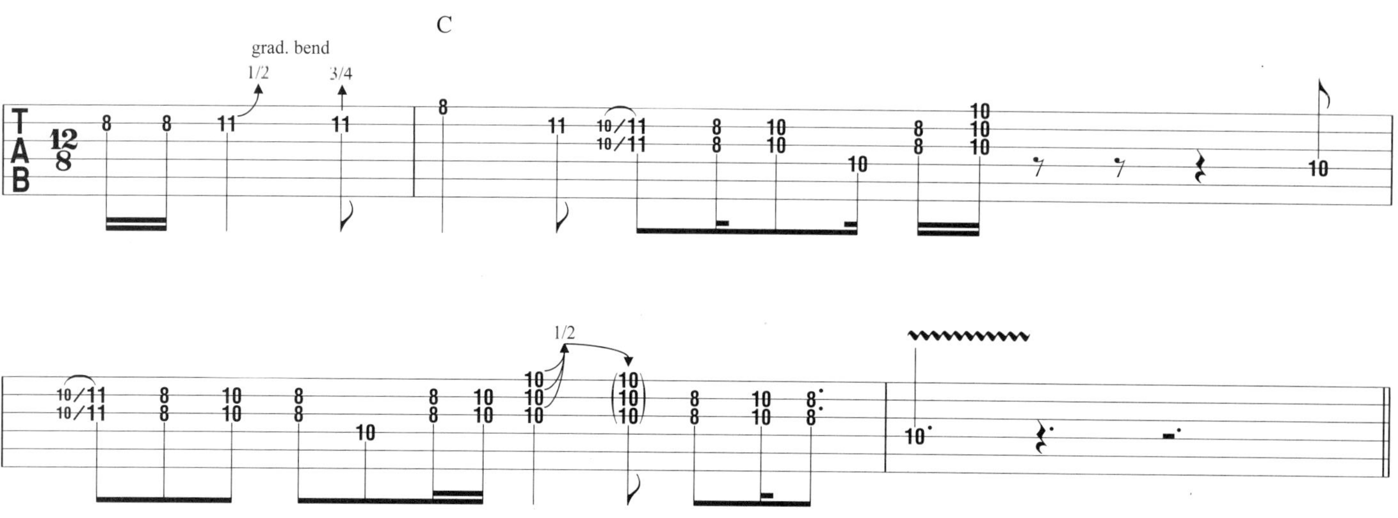

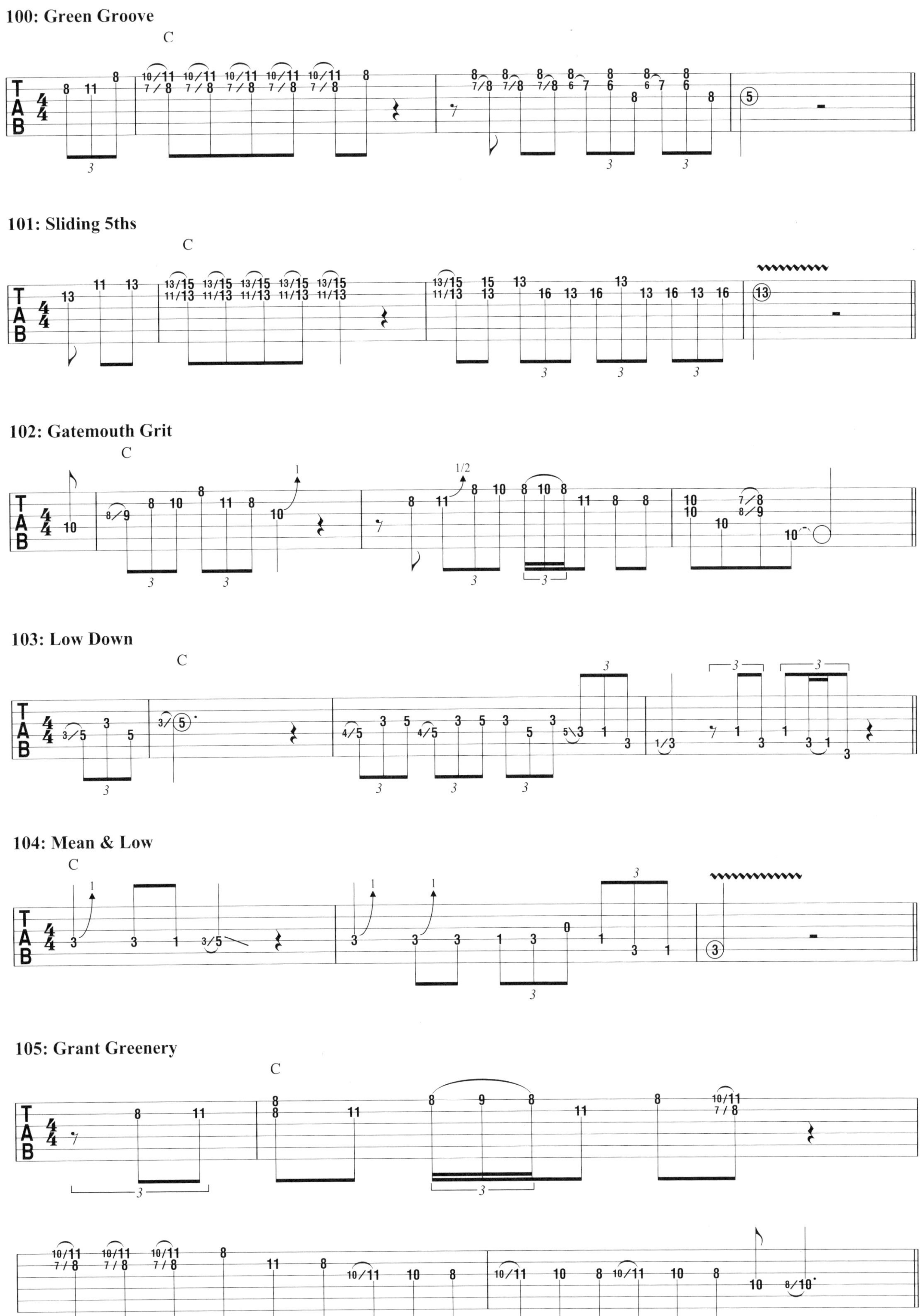
100: Green Groove
C
101: Sliding 5ths
C
102: Gatemouth Grit
C
103: Low Down
C
104: Mean & Low
C
105: Grant Greenery
C

## 106: Chromatic Soul

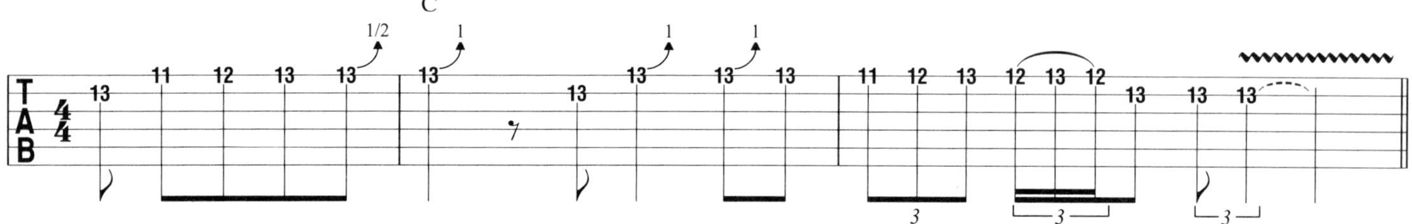

## 107: Chord Bender

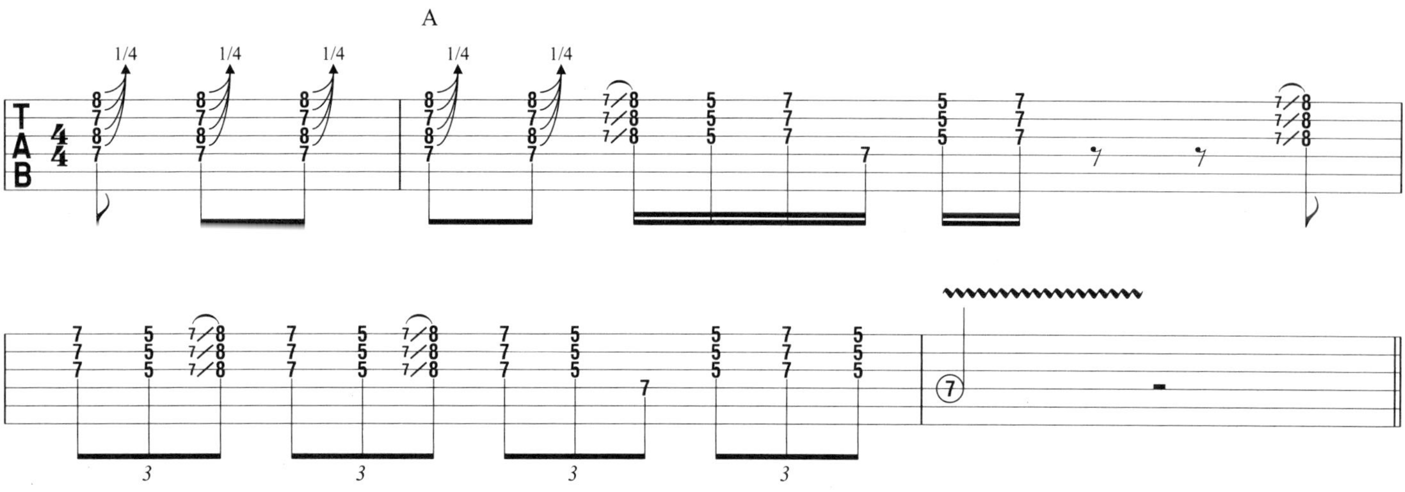

## 108: Funky Blues

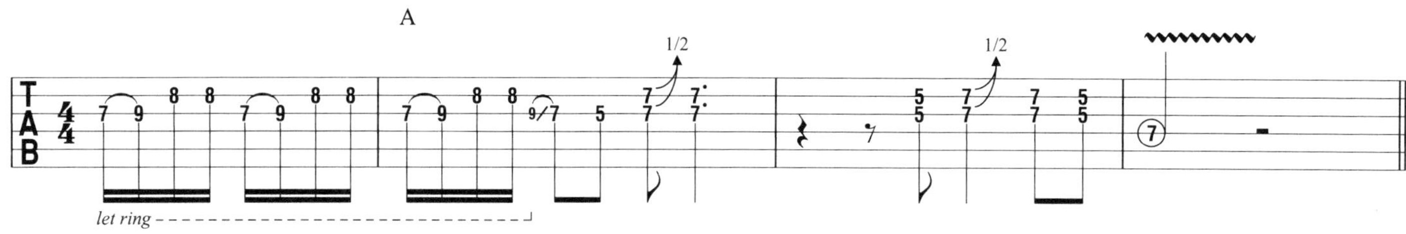

## 109: Double-Stoppin'

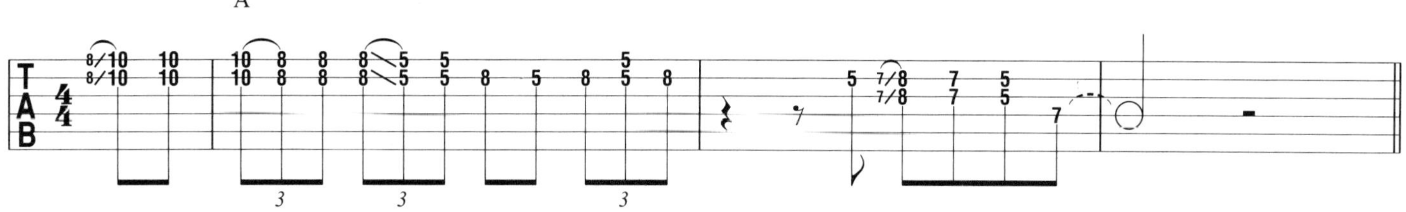

## 110: Funky Diddley

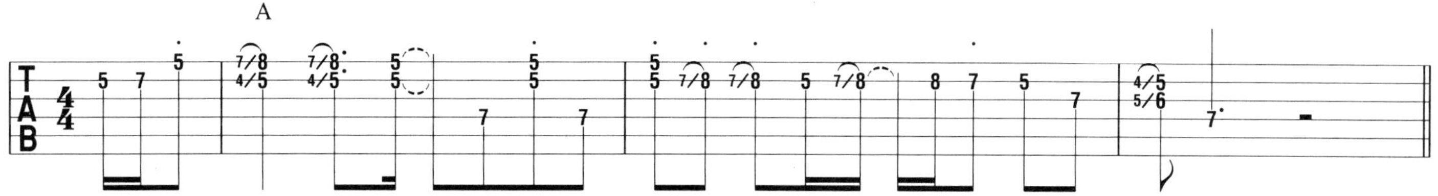

### 111: Freight Train

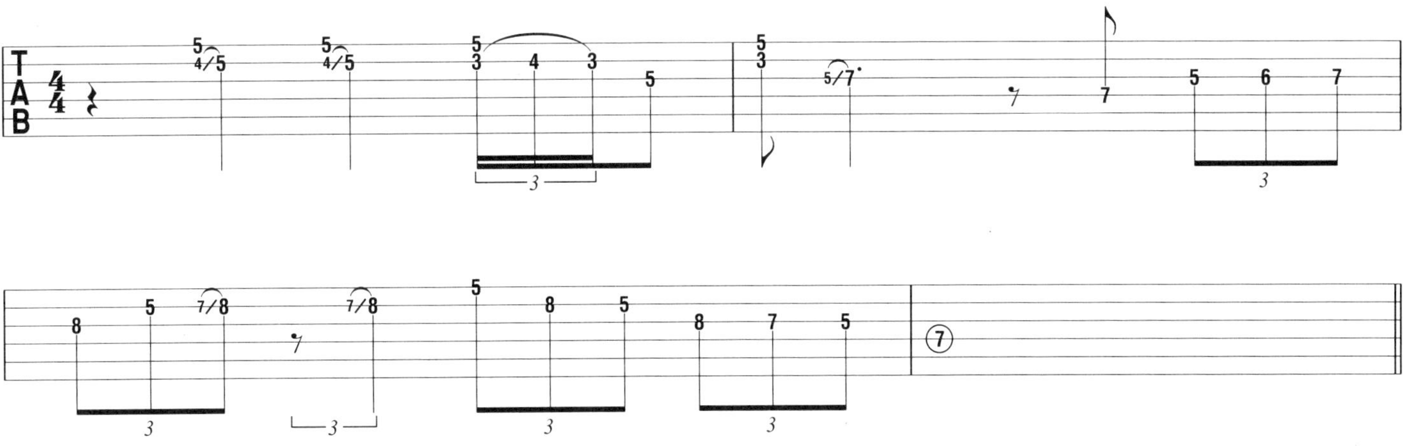


### 112: That's Funky

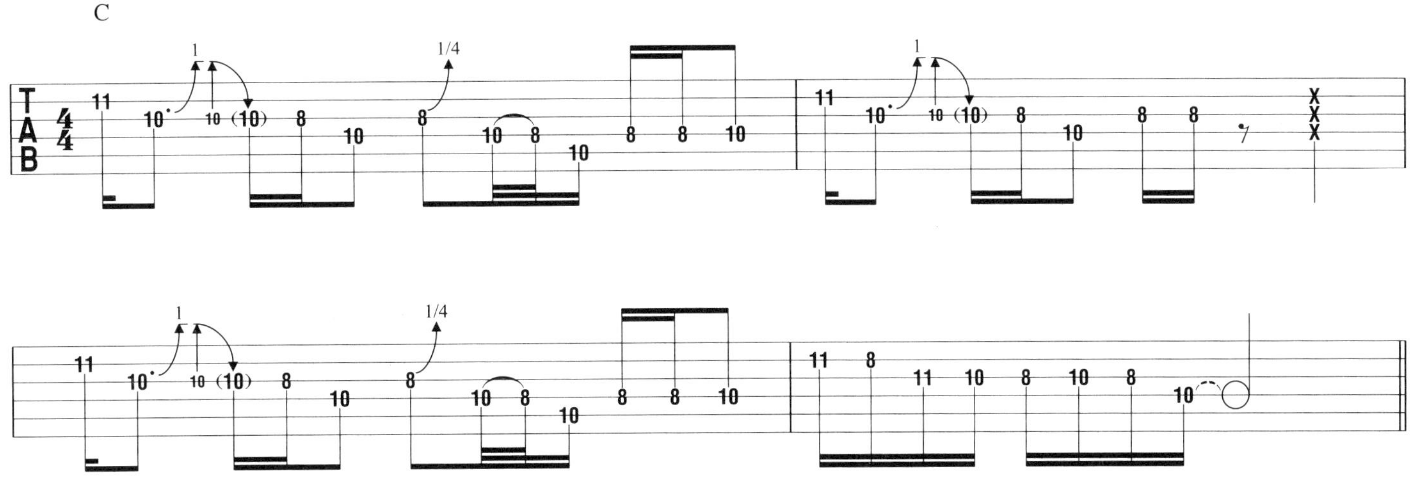


### 113: Fragment Funk

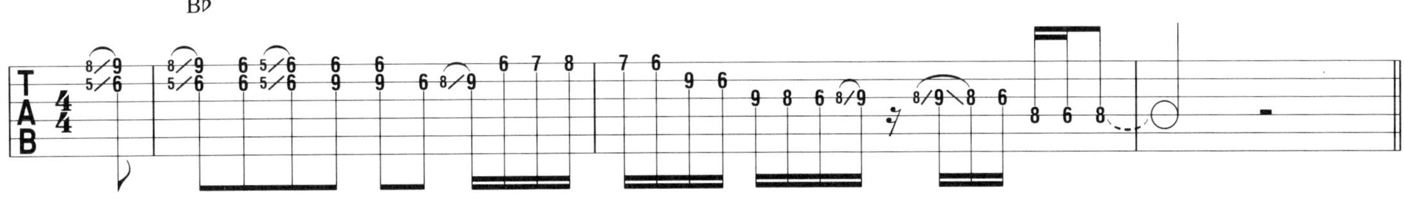


### 114: Hammer Time

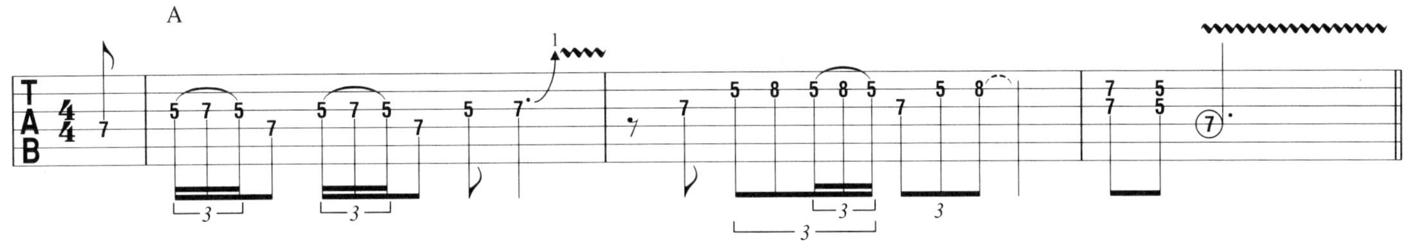

## 115: Tripletized

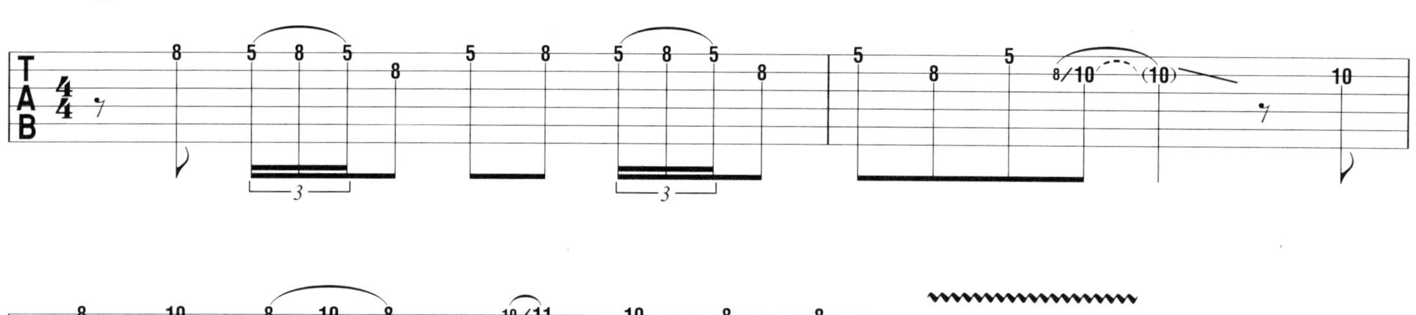


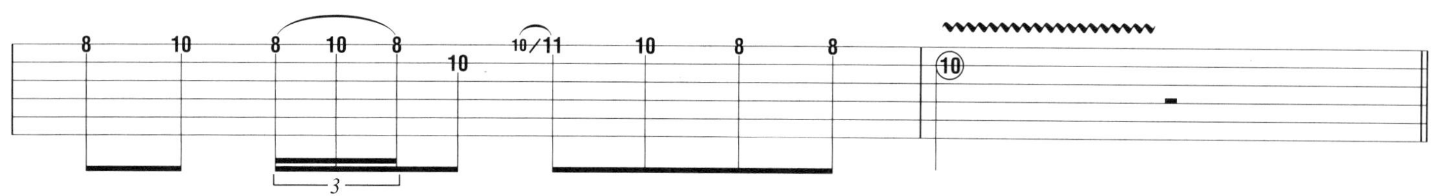

## 116: From the V

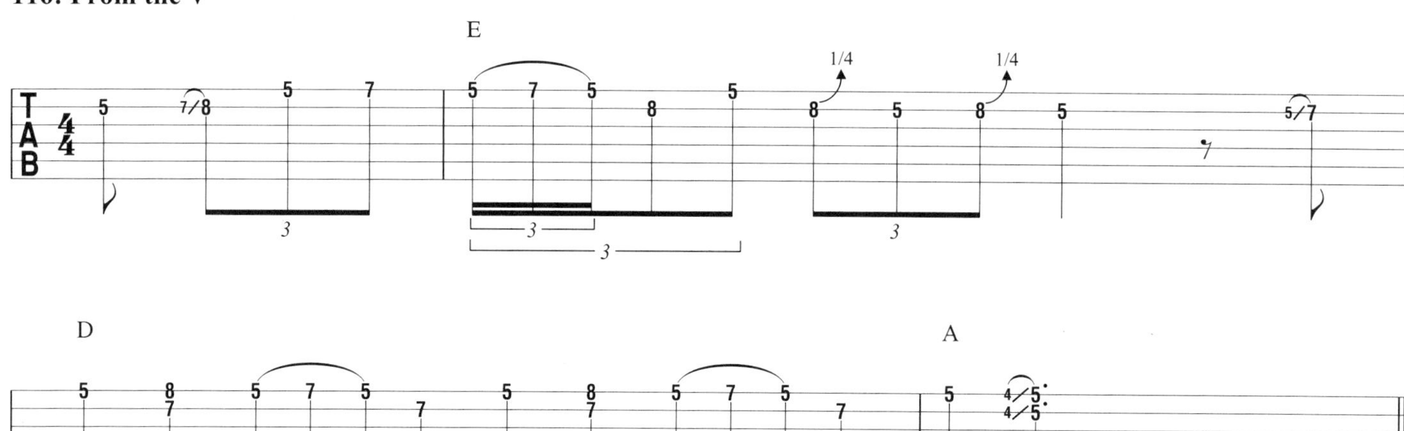


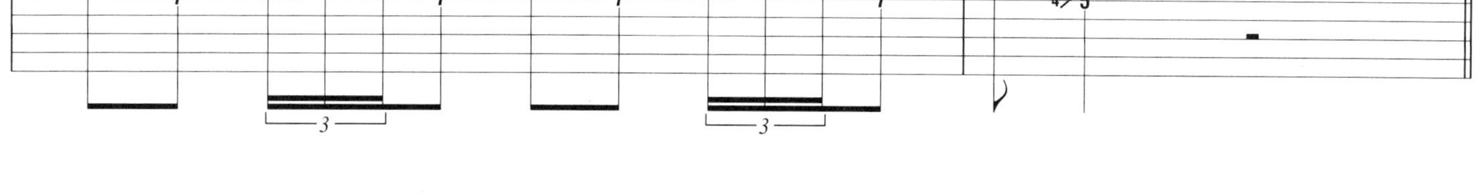


## 117: V-Chord Gallop

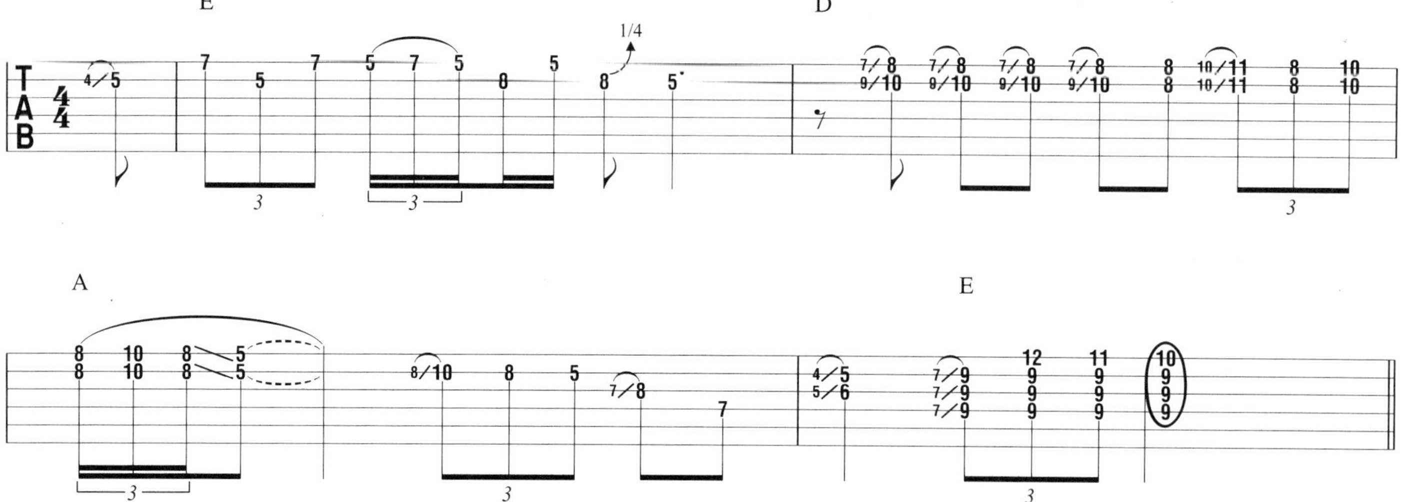

## 118: Funky Strum

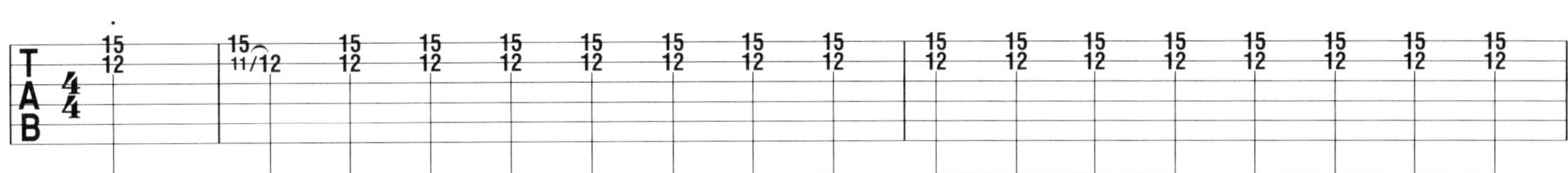


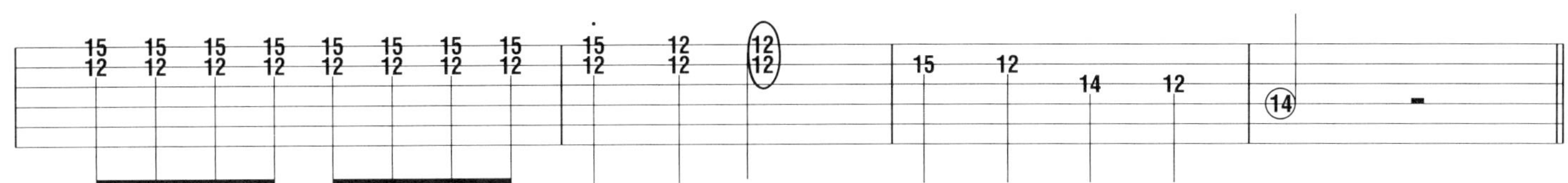

## 119: Uptempo Funk

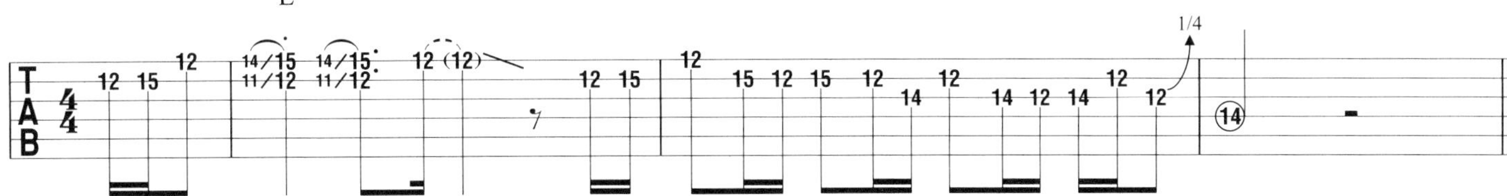


## 120: Playing with Fire

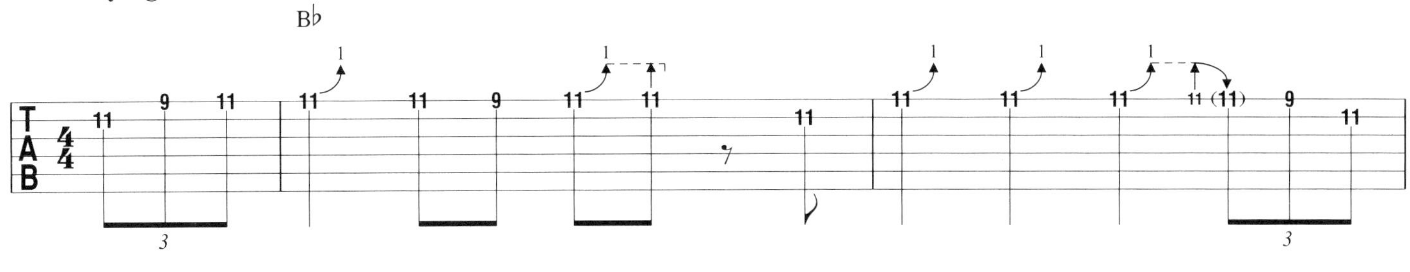


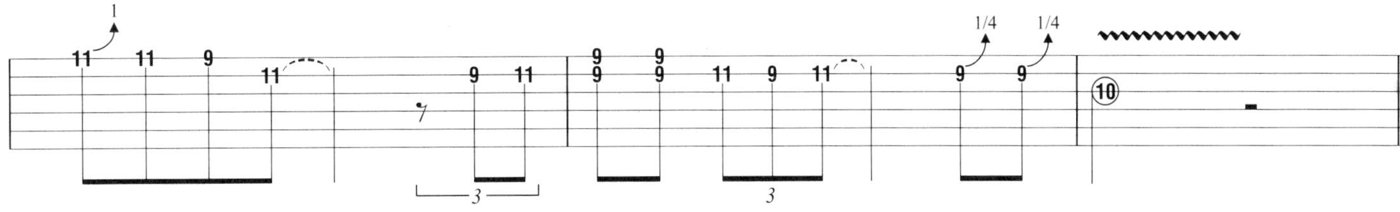

## 121: Blues with Tude

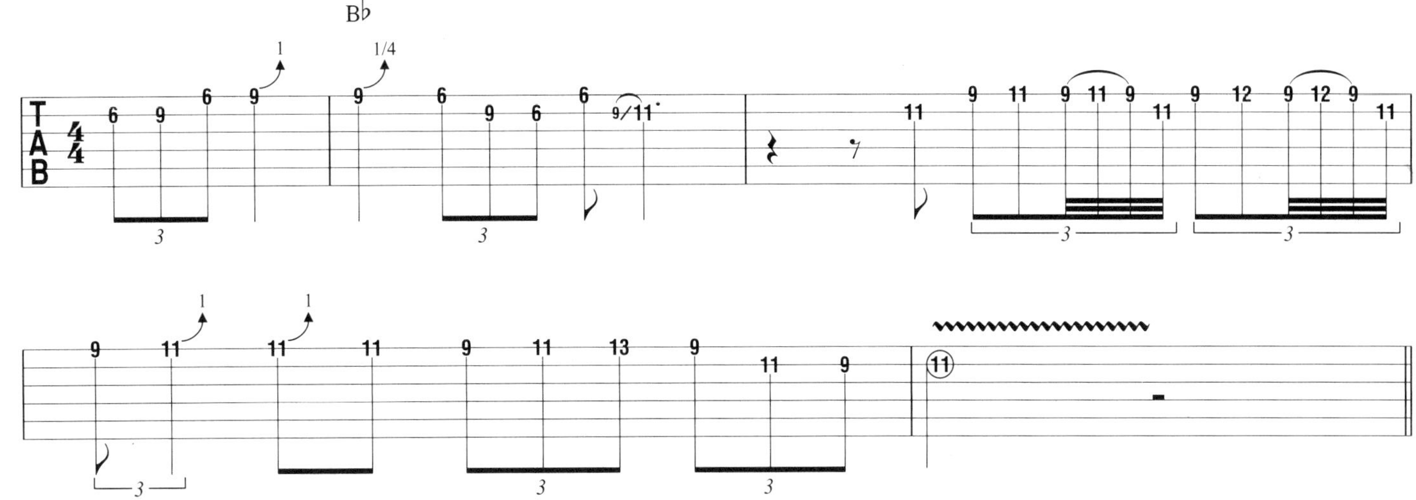

## 122: Fire Blues

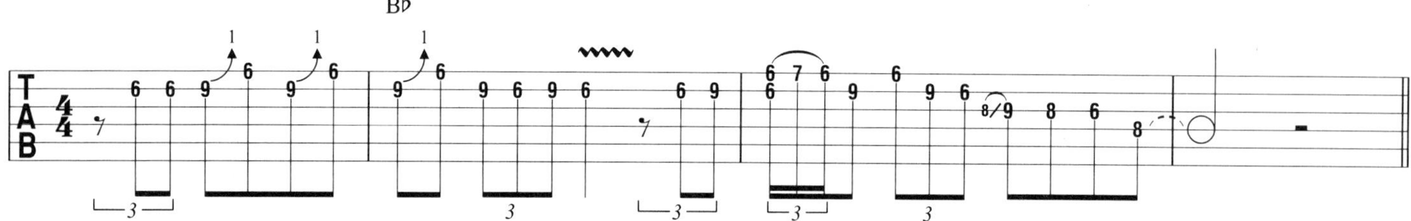


## 123: Thrill Isn't Gone

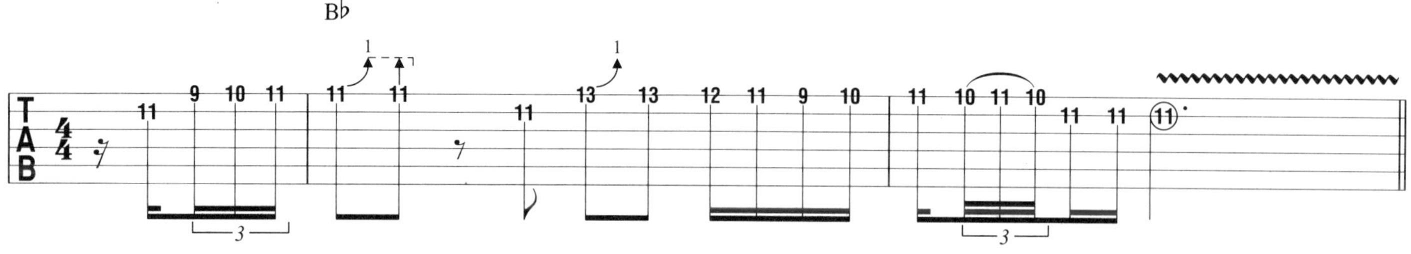


## 124: Tremolo Picker

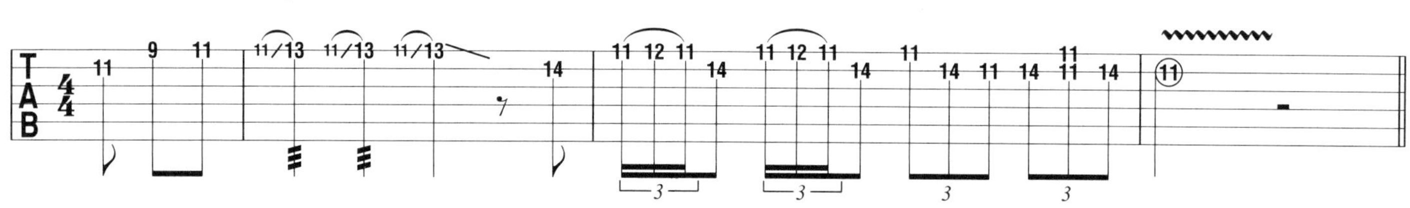


## 125: Call-and-Response

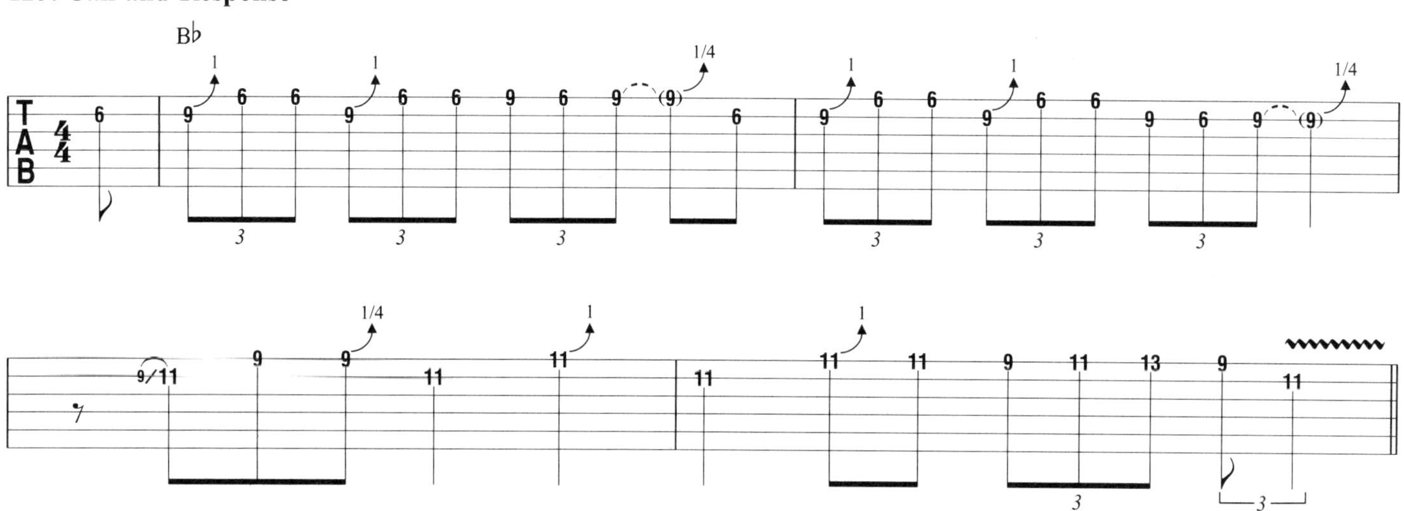


## 126: Classic Turnaround

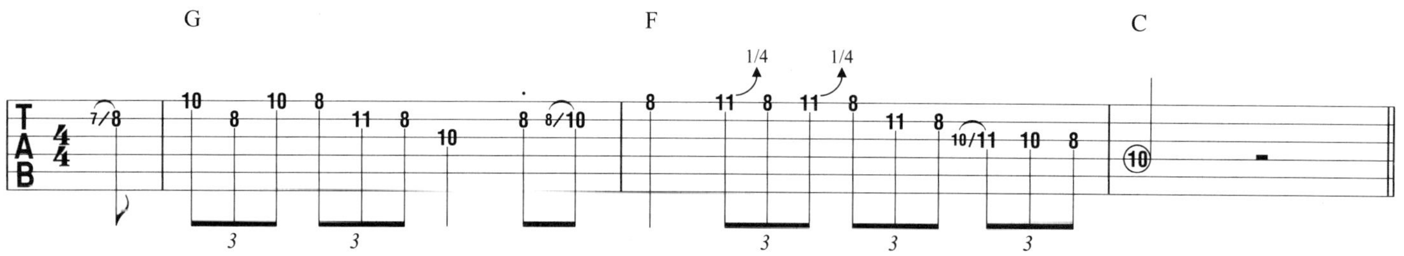

## 127: V-IV-I Turnaround

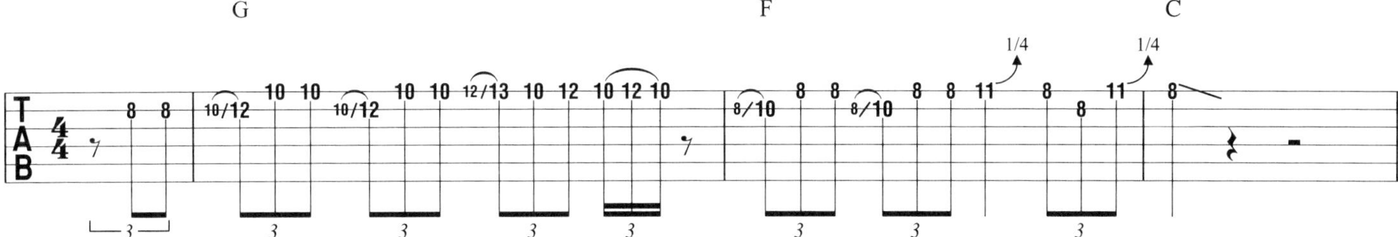

## 128: Take Me Home

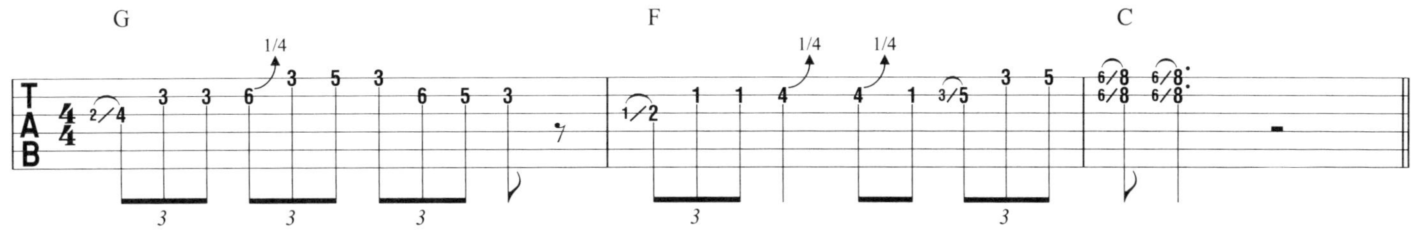

## 129: Back Around

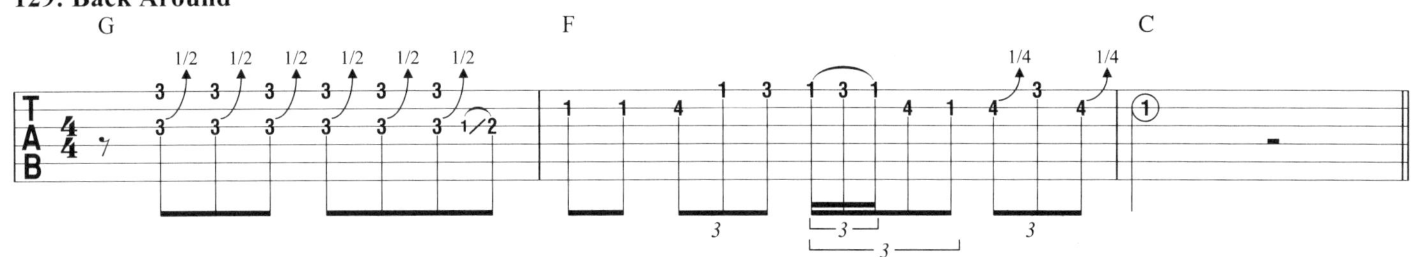


## 130: V-IV-I Me

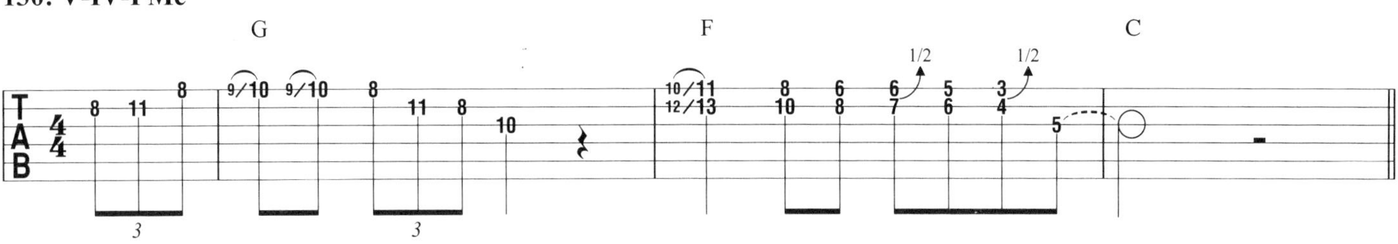


## 131: Simple Turnaround

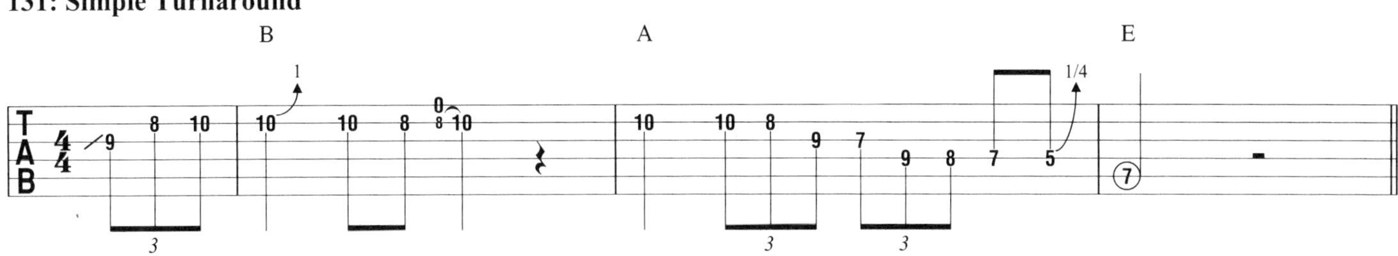


## 132: Shufflin'

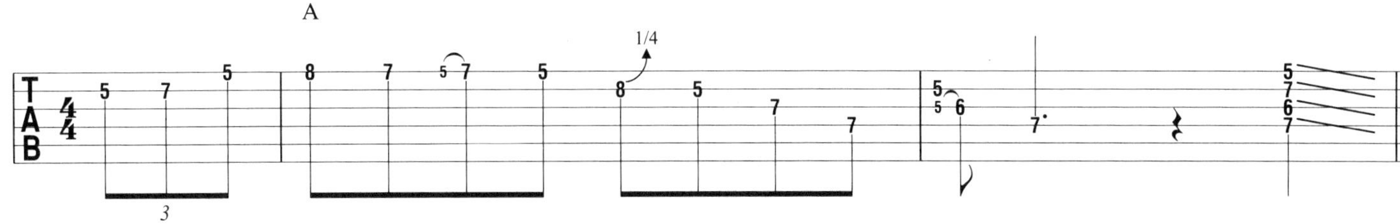

## 133: Sweet Potatoes

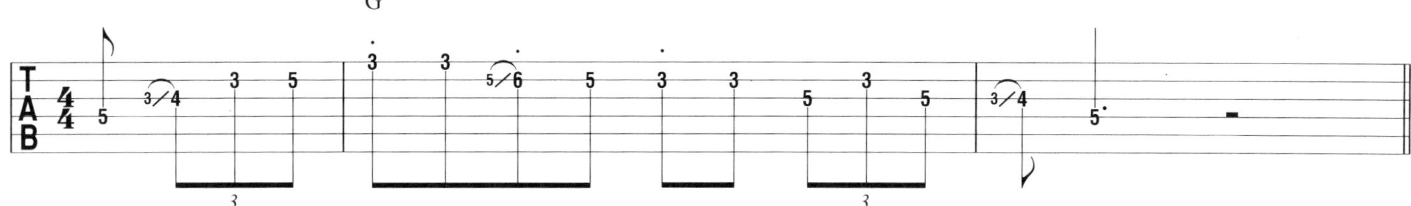


## 134: Upstroker

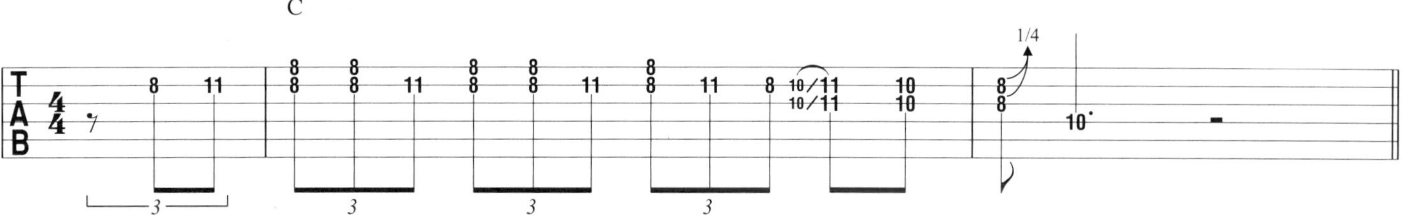


## 135: Blues King

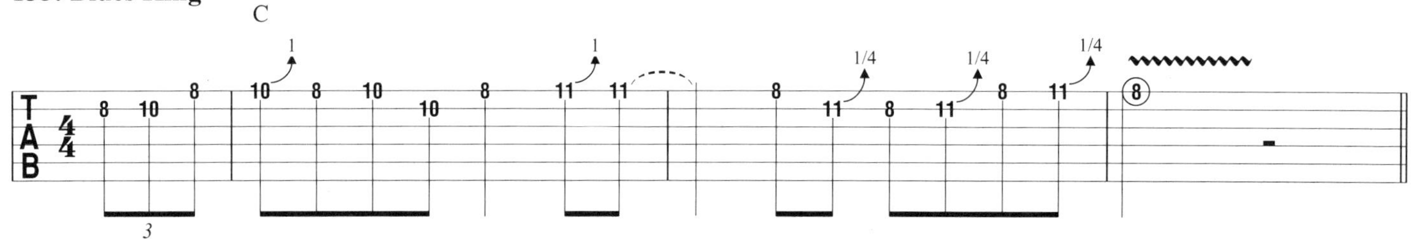


## 136: One More Time

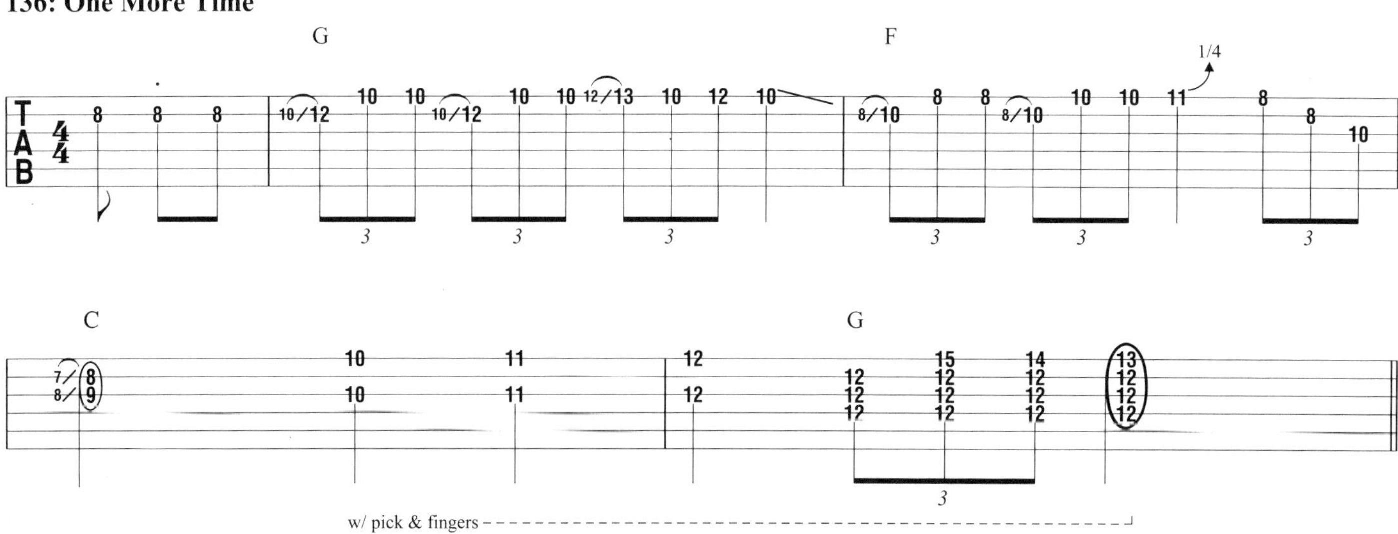

## 137: Bend-O-Rama

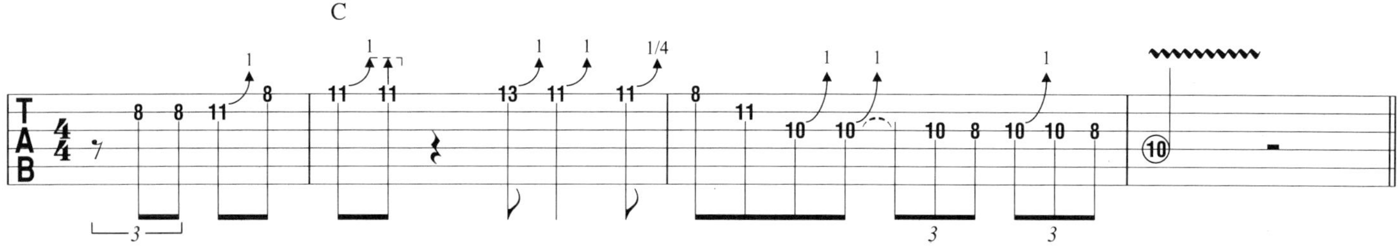

## 138: Vibro-Bender

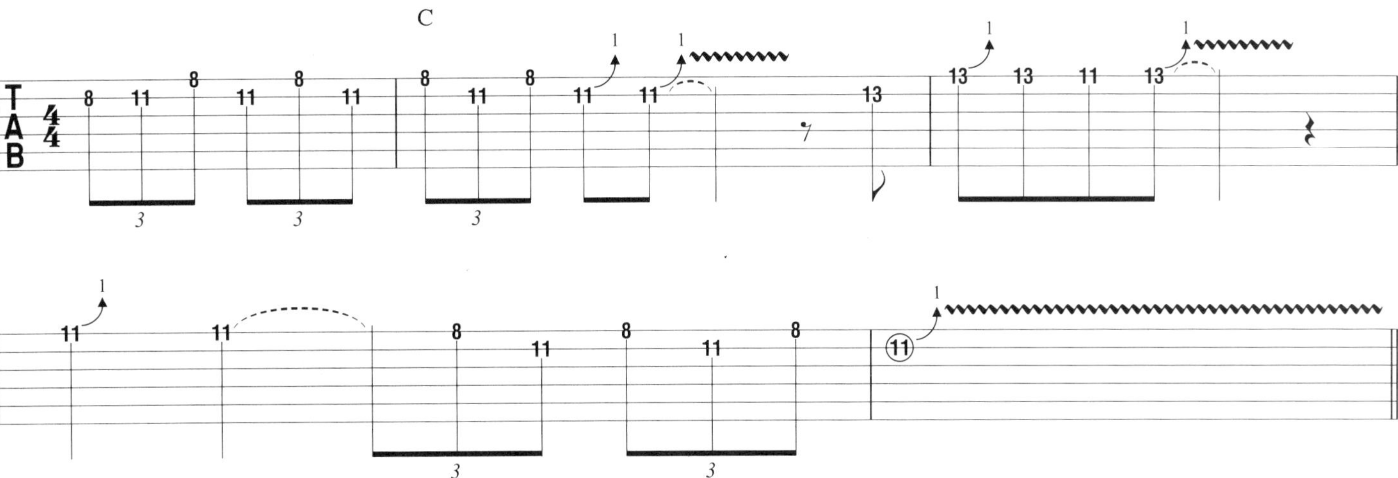


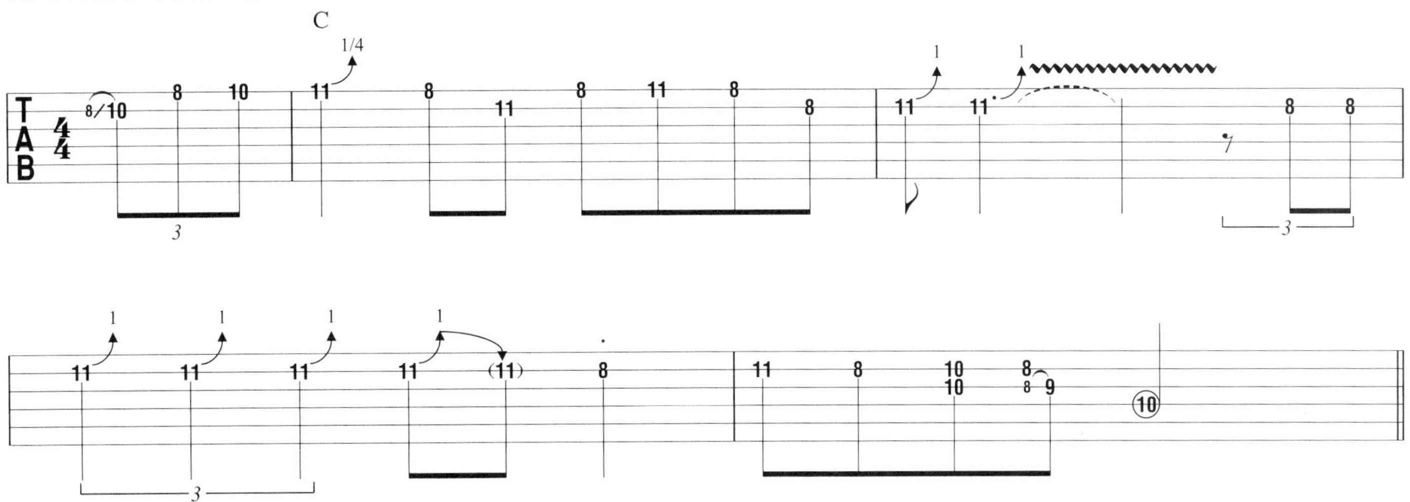


## 139: Otis in the House

## 140: Box of Bends

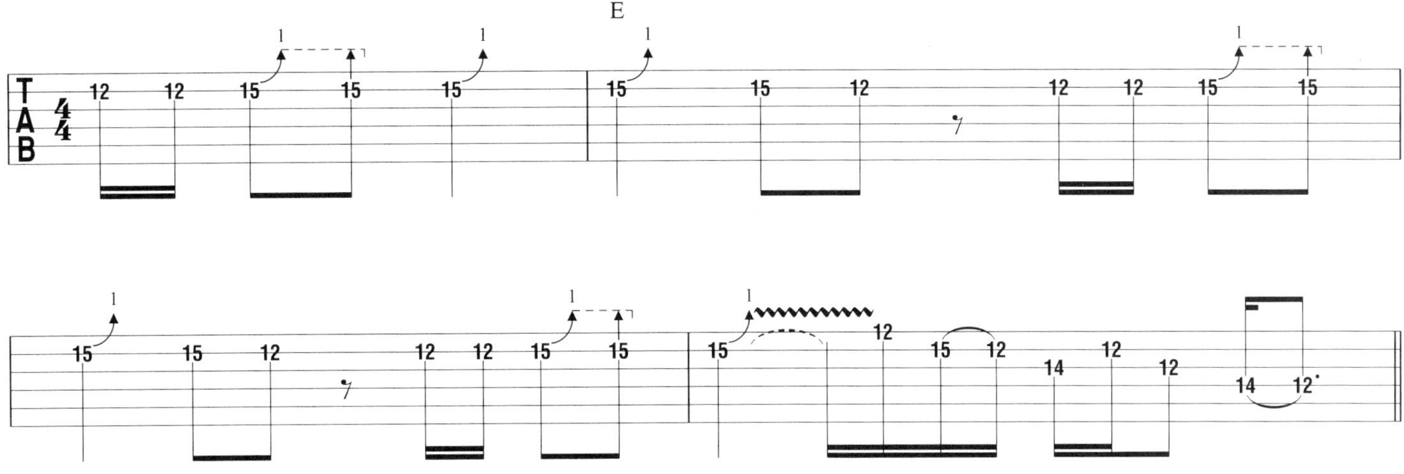


## 141: At Blues End

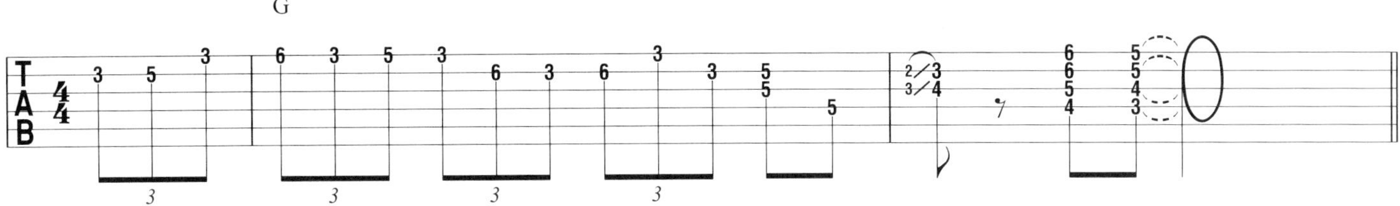

**142: Chordal Ending**

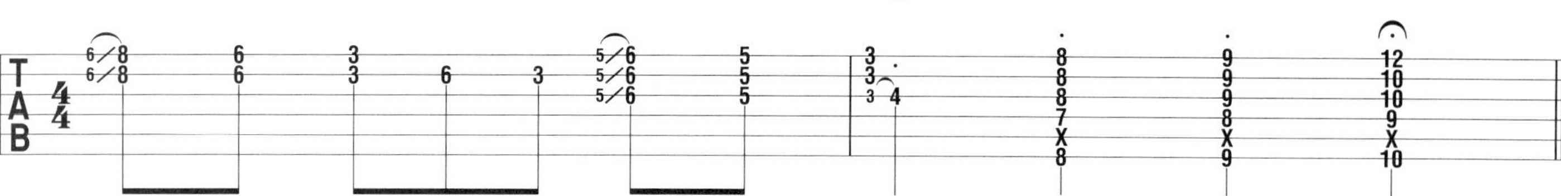

**143: Sophisticated Exit**

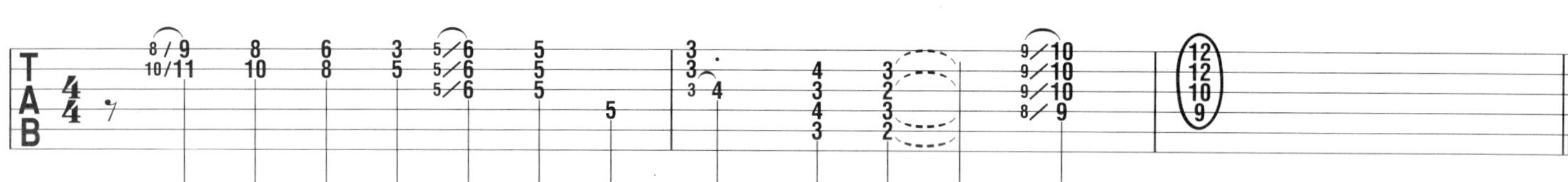

**144: Run It Down**

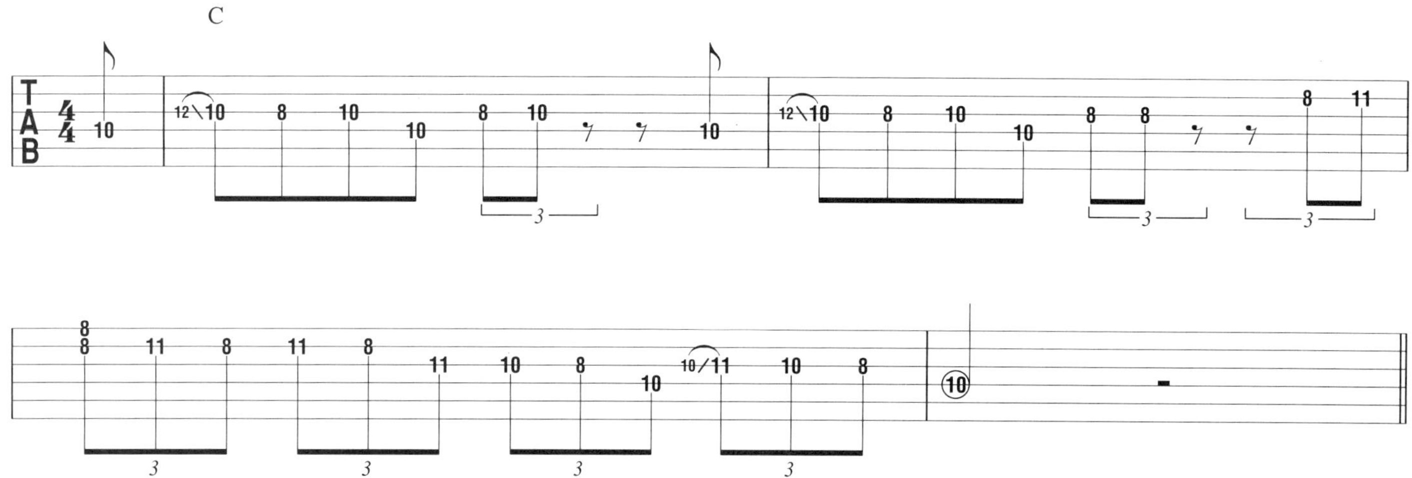

**145: Staccato Funk**

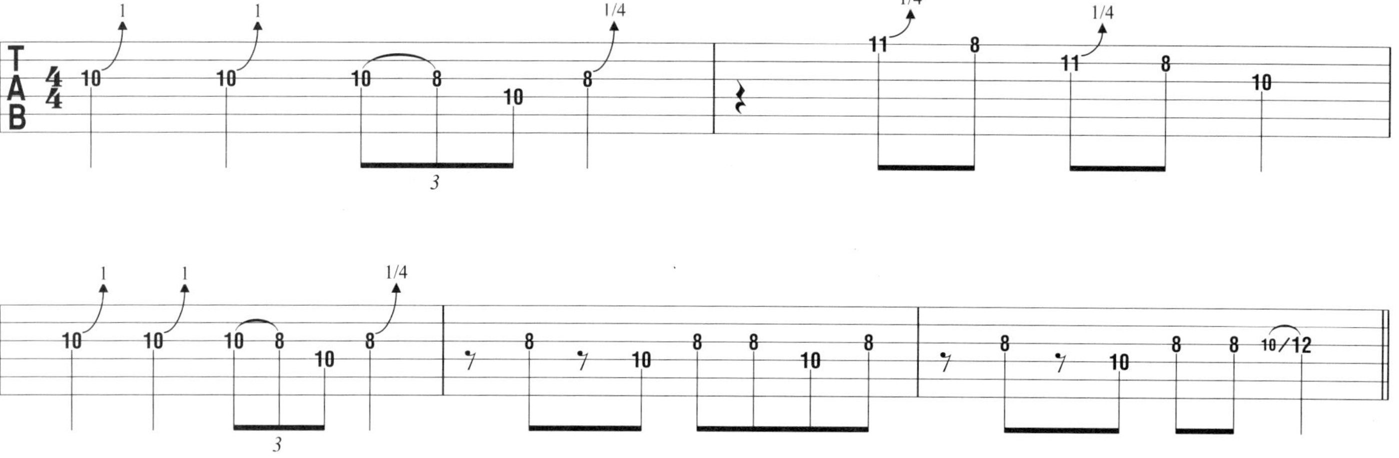

## 146: Rhythm & Lead

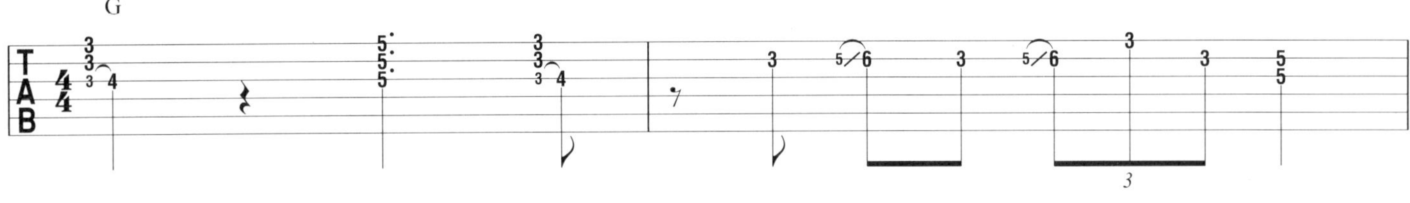


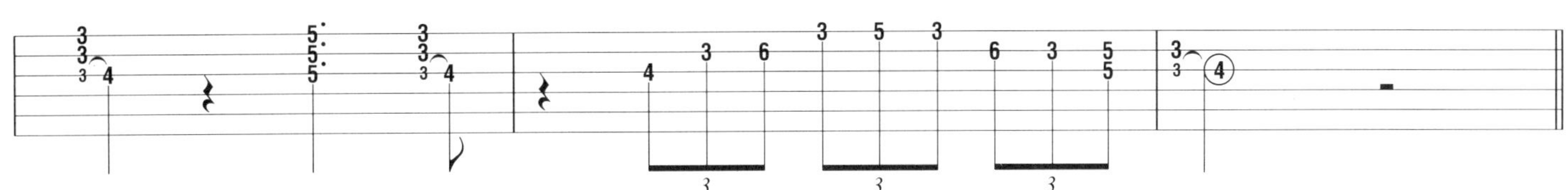

## 147: Back Porchin’

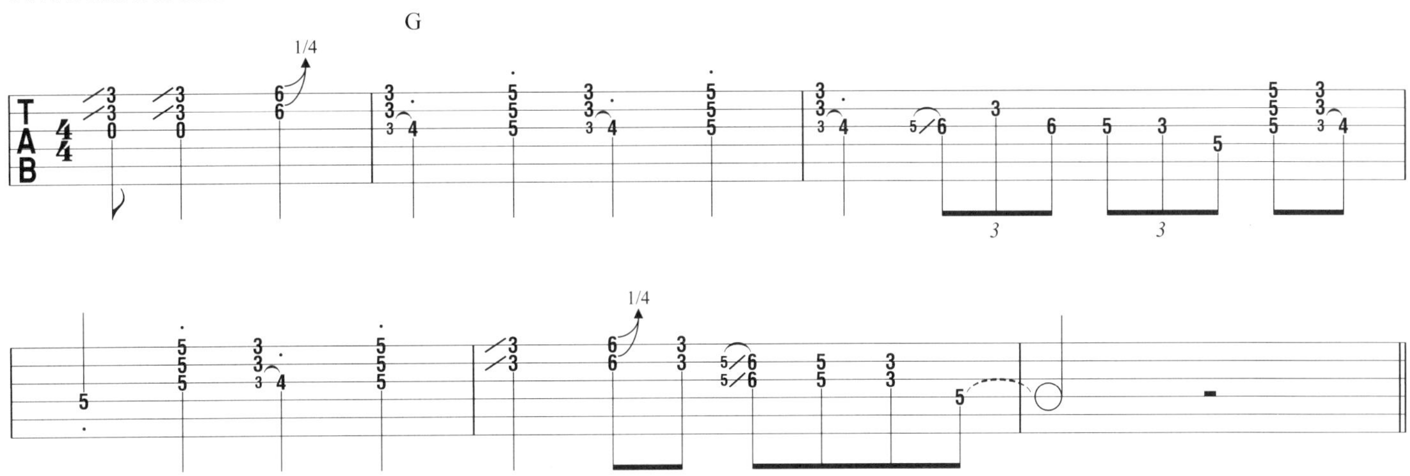


## 148: Groovy Indeed

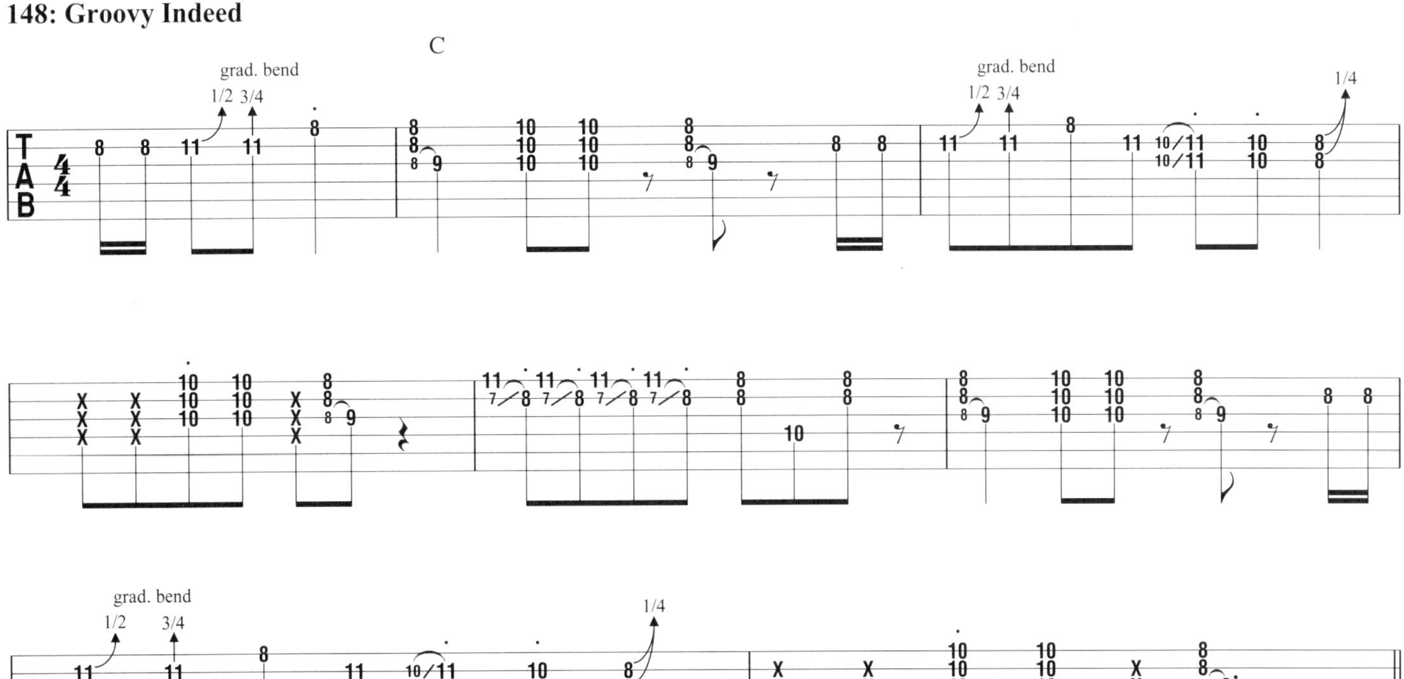

### 149: Old Schooled

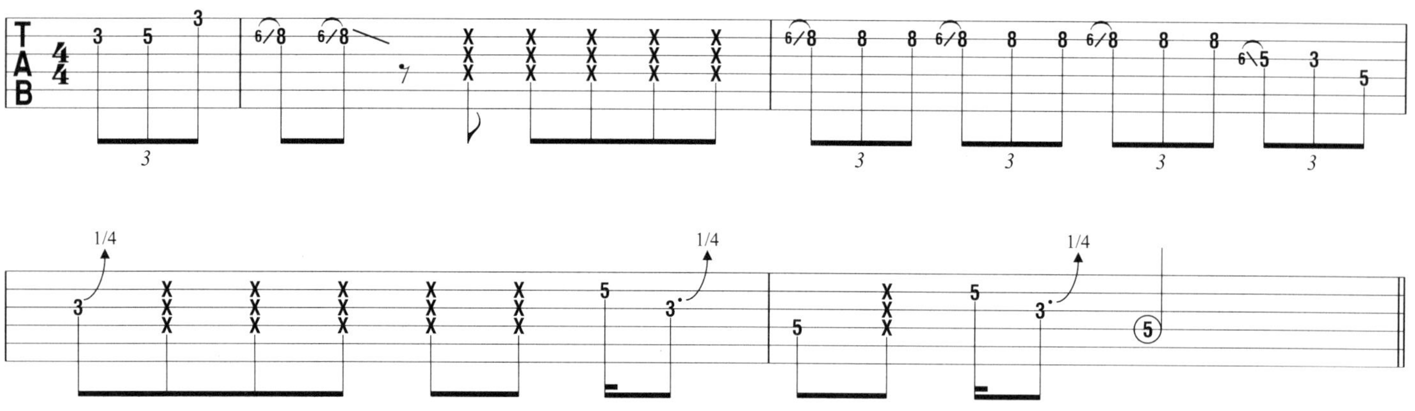


### 150: Workin' It

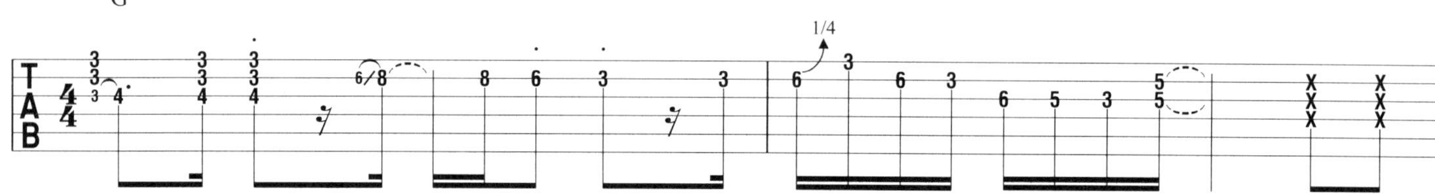


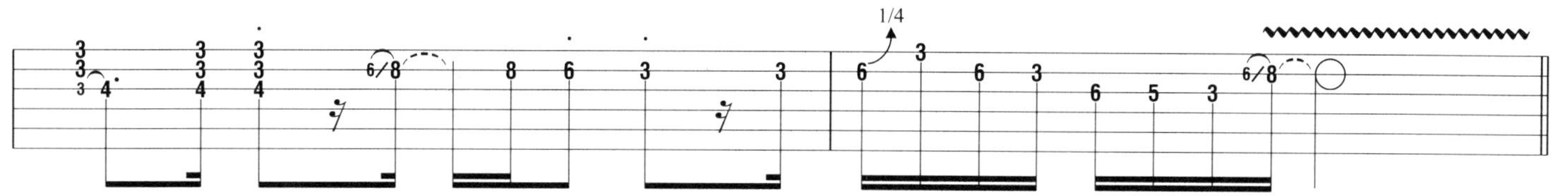

## Instructor: Peter Roller

### 151: Classic Freddie

Swing feel

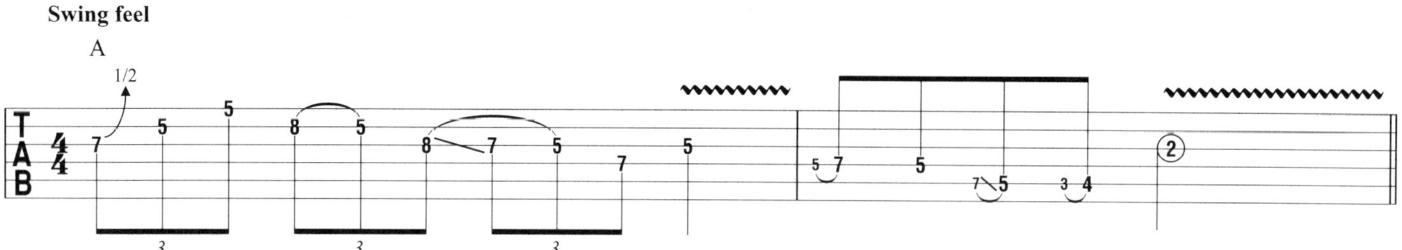


### 152: Turnaround Time

Swing feel

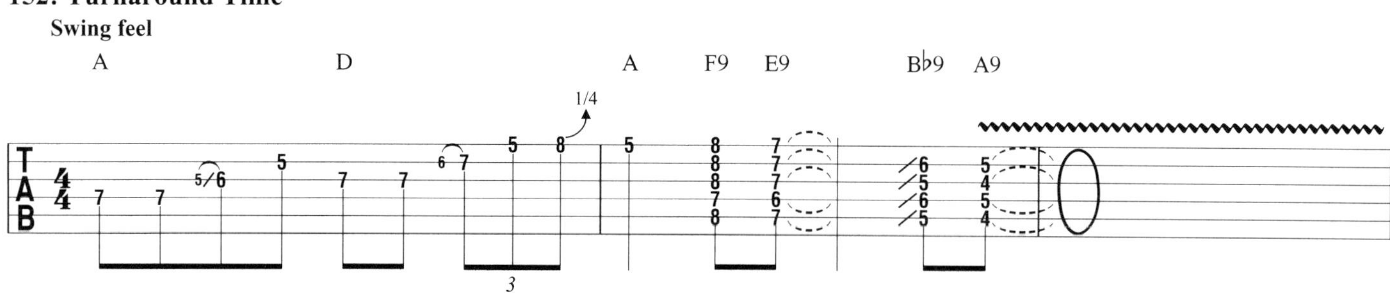

## 153: Early B.B.

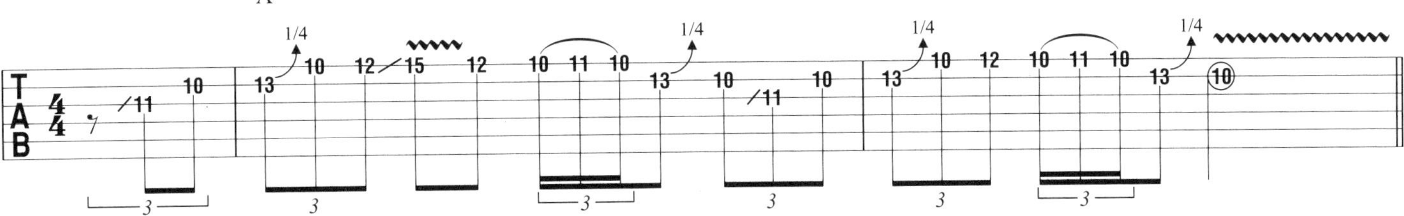


## 154: Bebop Blues

Swing feel

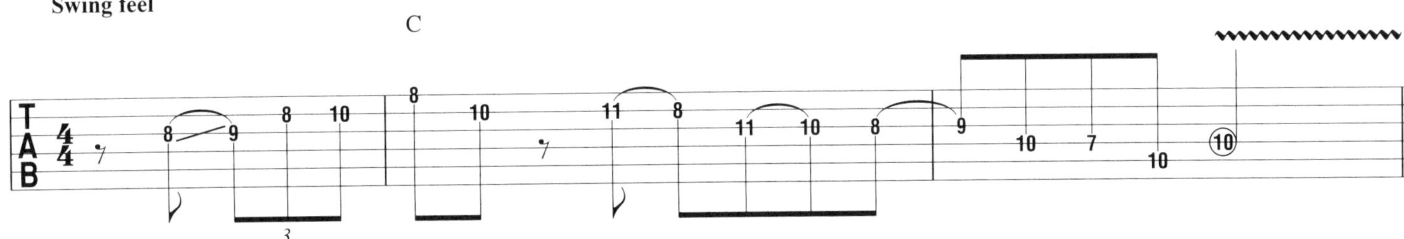


## 155: Vibrato Blues

Swing feel

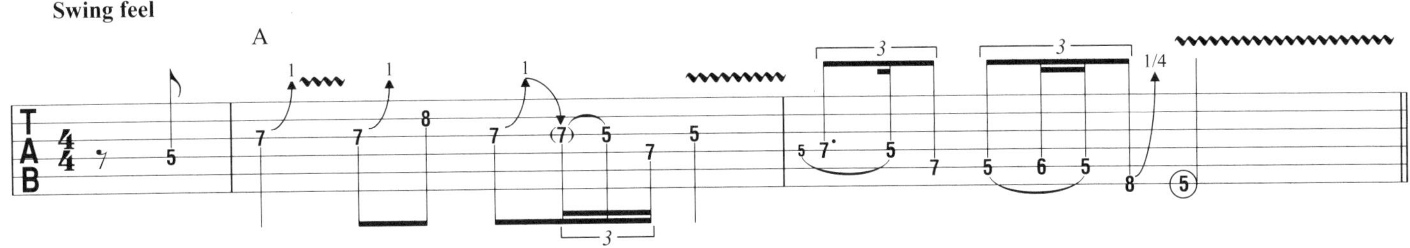


## 156: Blues Country

Swing feel

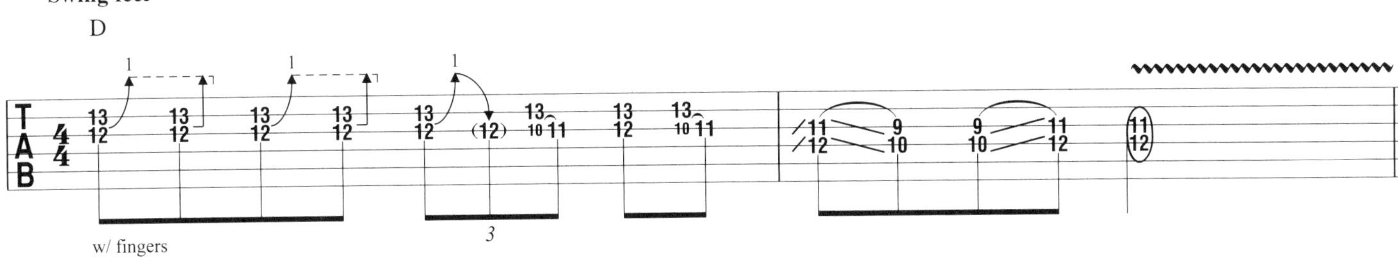


## 157: Triple-Stops

Swing feel

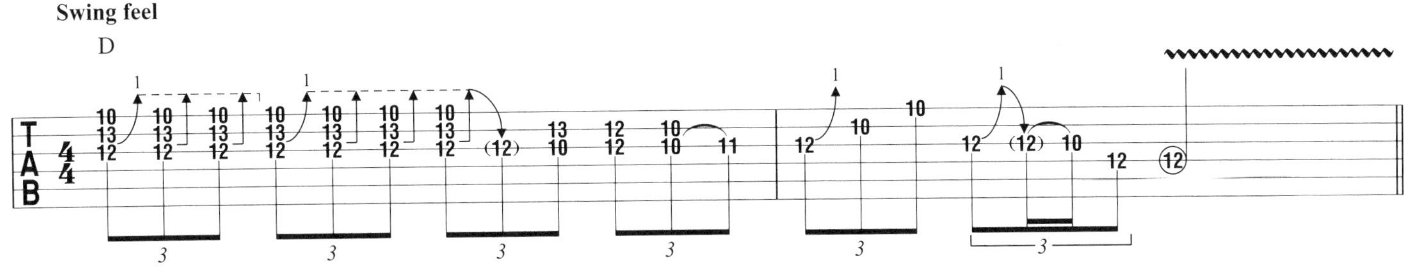

## 158: Steely Bop

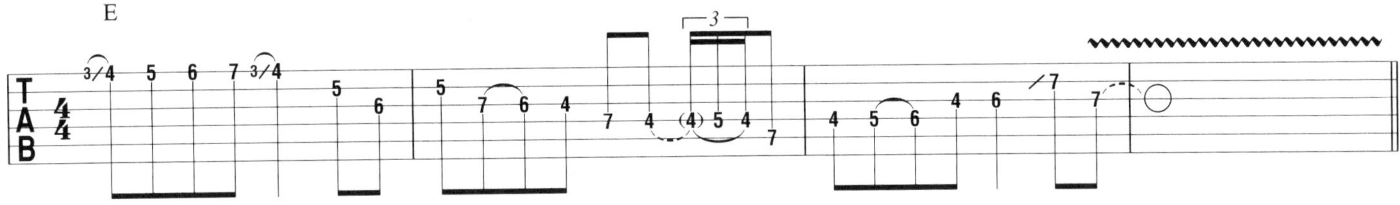

## 159: Berry Blues

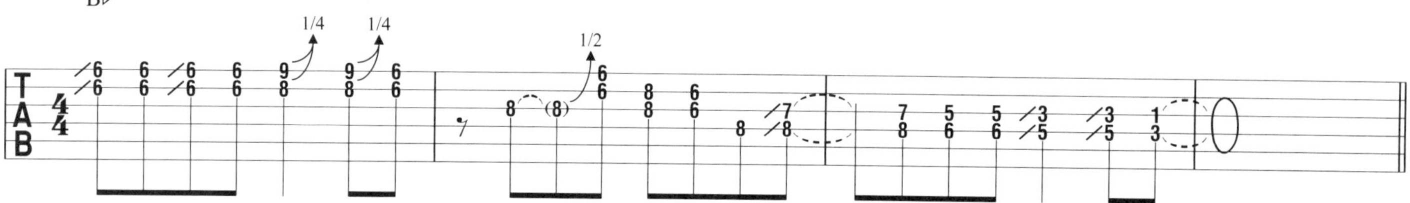


## 160: Slow & Muddy

**Swing feel**

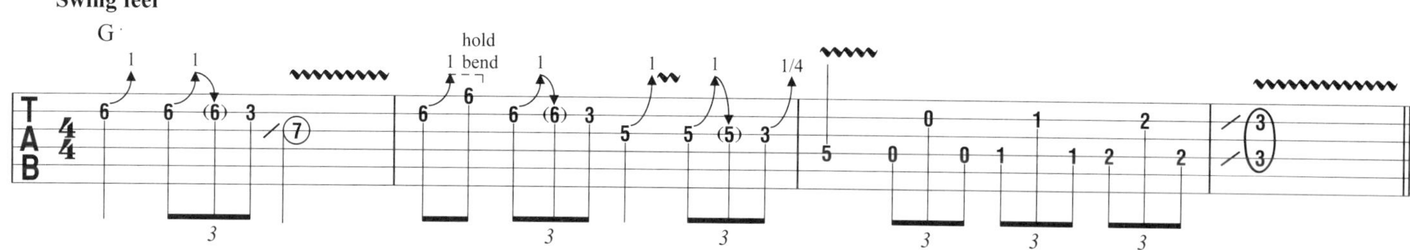


## 161: Elmore to Allman

**D-A-D-F♯-A-D**

**Swing feel**

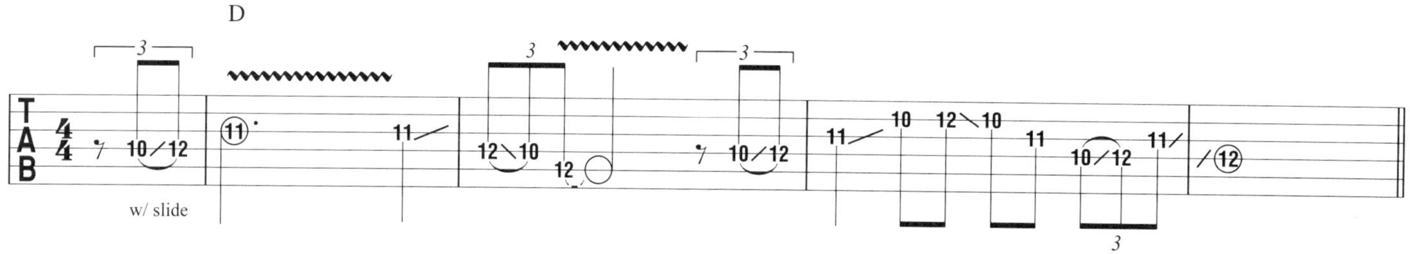


## 162: Southern Slide

**D-A-D-F♯-A-D**

**Swing feel**

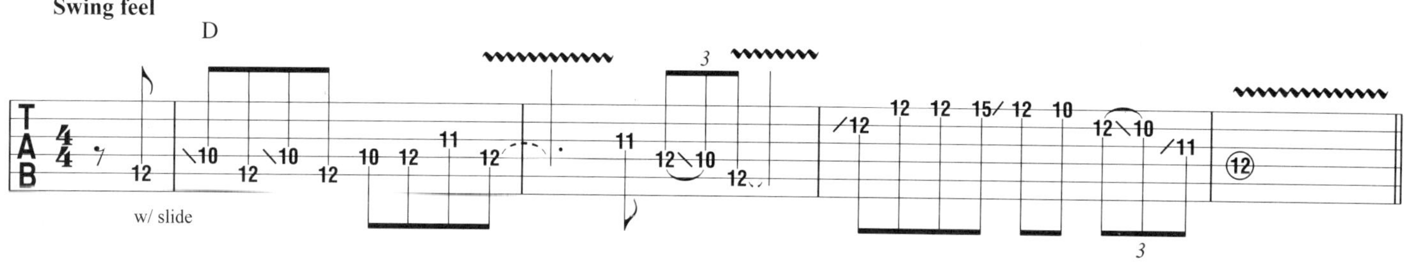


## 163: Winter Time

**D-A-D-F♯-A-D**

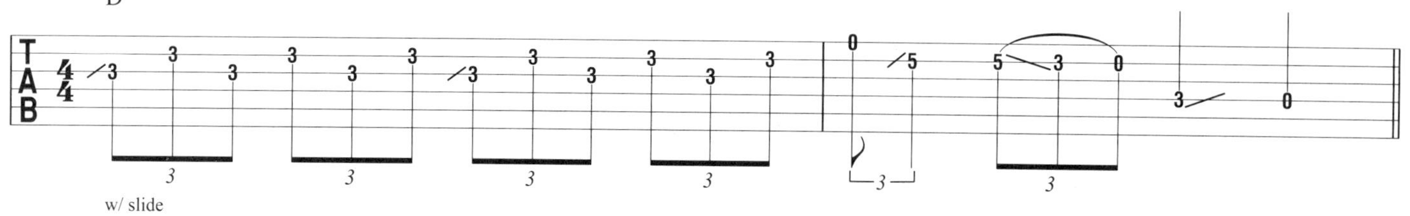

## 164: Melodic Slide

D-A-D-F♯-A-D

Swing feel

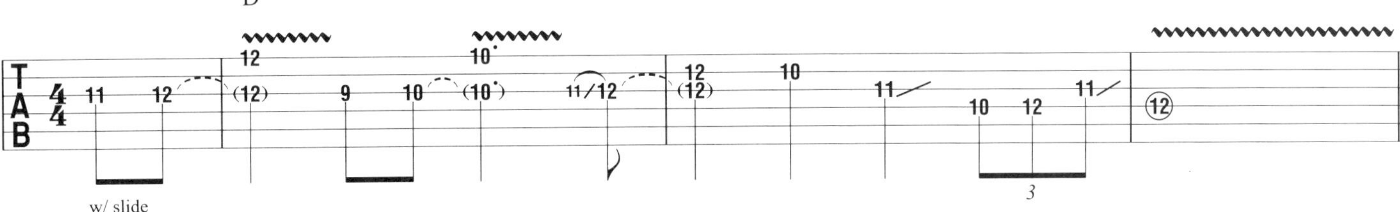


## 165: Speedy Slide

D-A-D-F♯-A-D

Swing feel

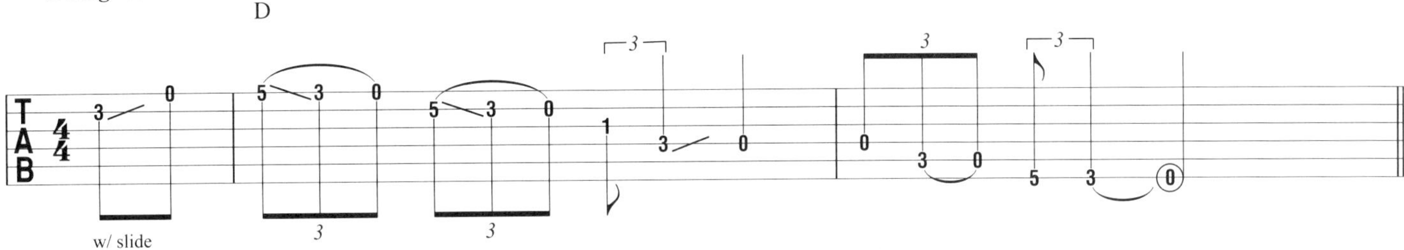


## 166: Horn Line Slide

D-A-D-F♯-A-D

Swing feel

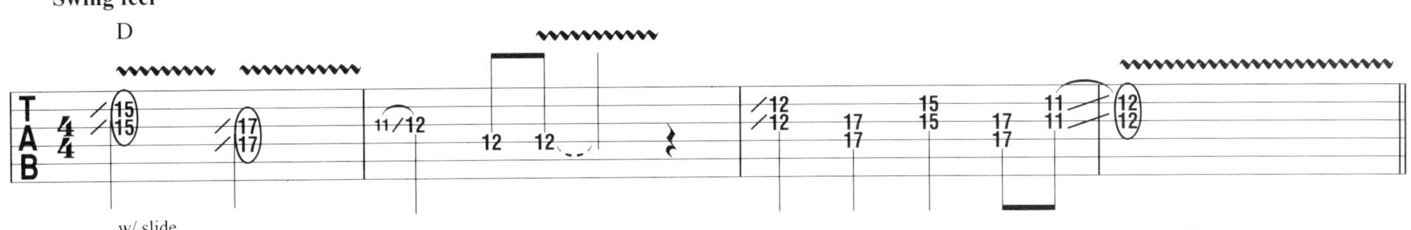


## 167: Octave Slider

D-A-D-F♯-A-D

Swing feel

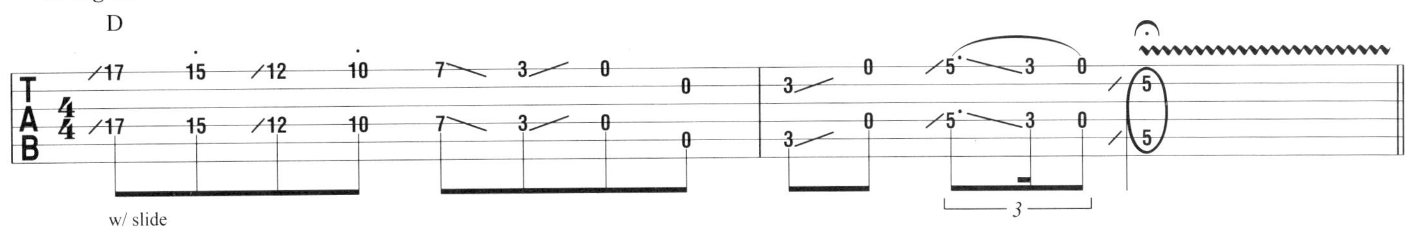


## 168: Classic Slide

Swing feel

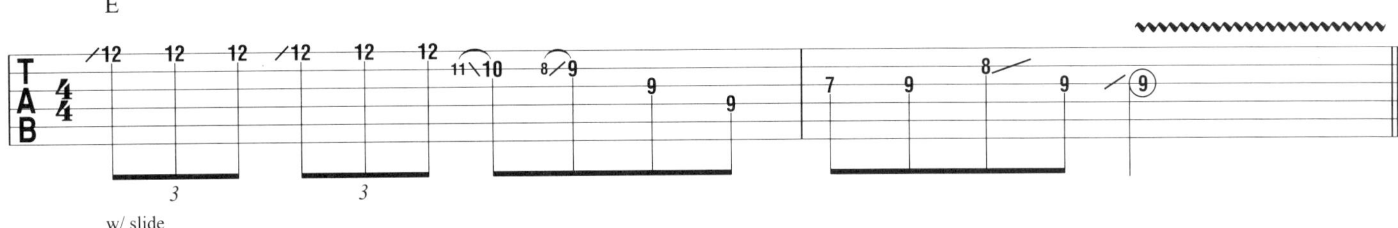

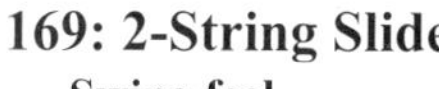

### 169: 2-String Slide

Swing feel

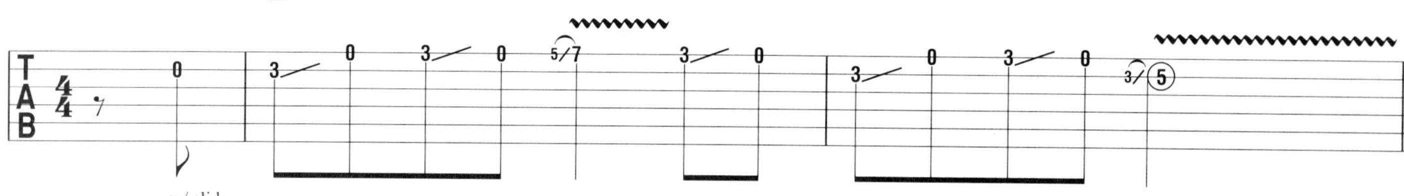


### 170: Slow Waters

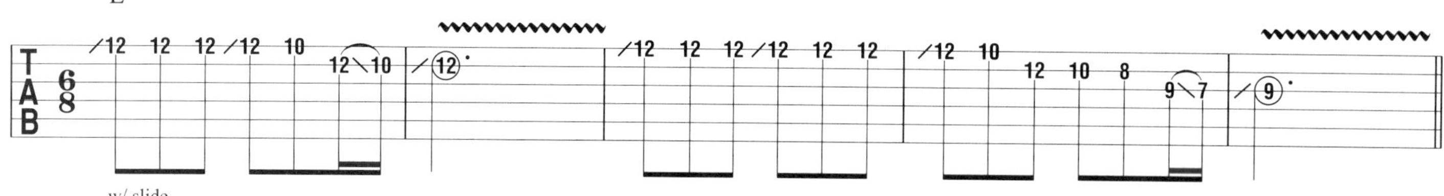


## Instructor: Bill Stone

### 171: Finger Rolls

Swing feel

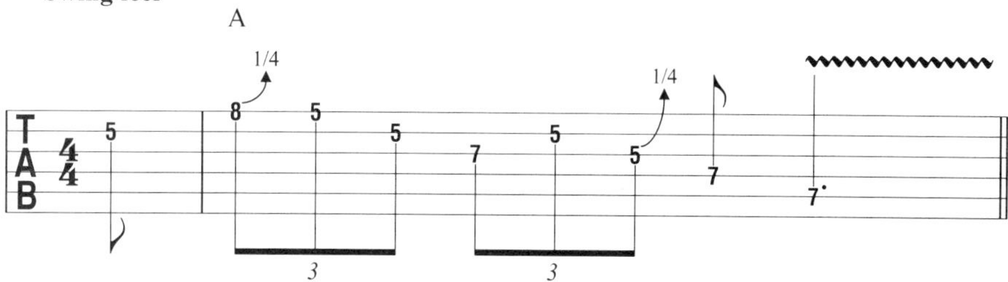


### 172: Upbeat Blues

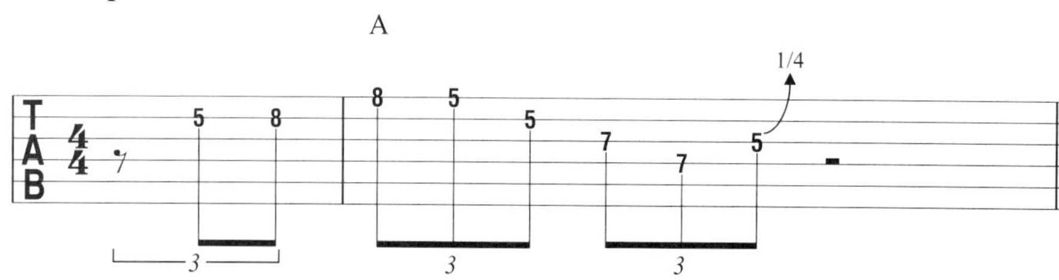


### 173: Upsweep

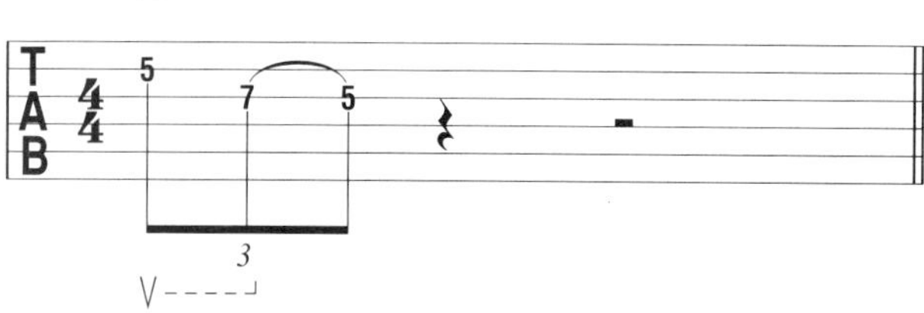


### 174: Downsweep

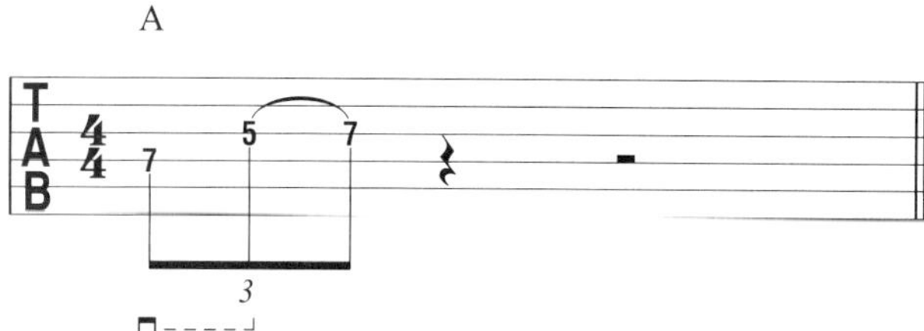

### 175: 4 Notes, 2 Strokes

### 176: Short but Sweep

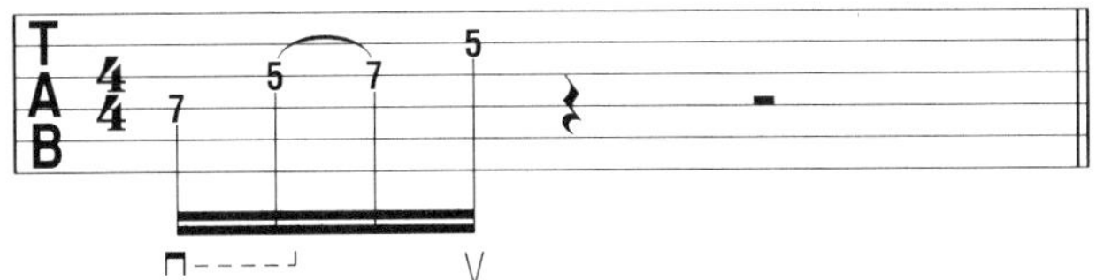


### 177: Smooth Flurry

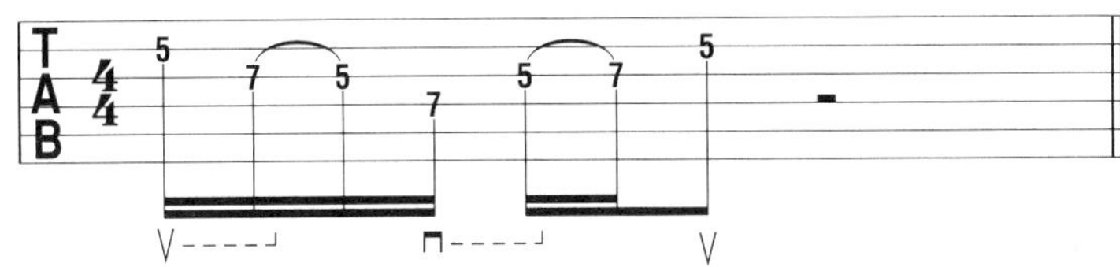


### 178: Up/Down Sweeper

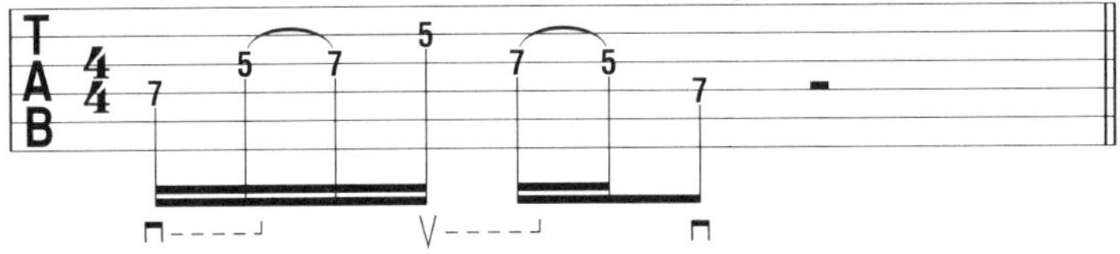


### 179: Step Progression

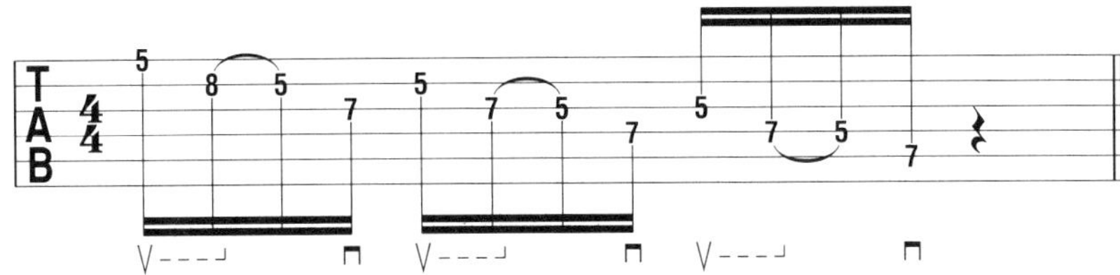


### 180: Alternate Picking

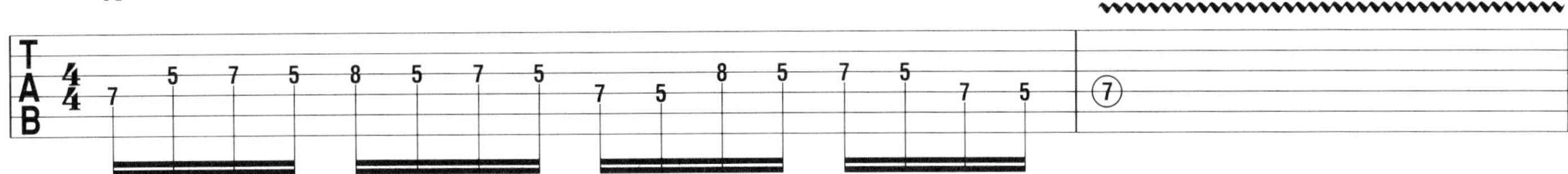

### 181: 16th-Note Blues

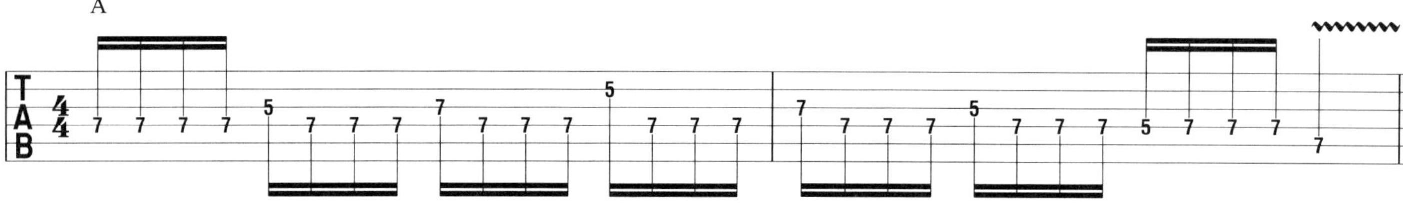


### 182: Pedaling Around

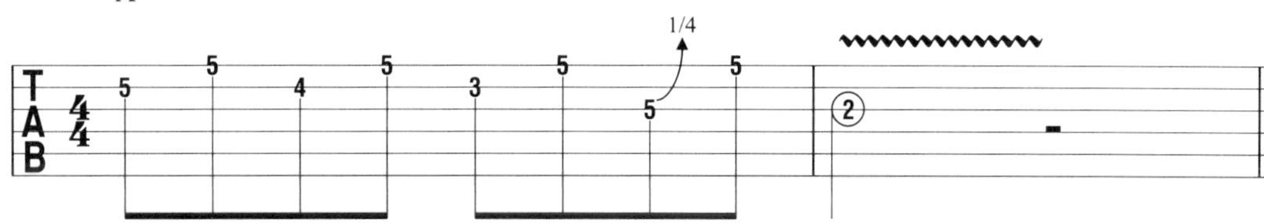


### 183: Pedal Point Blues

Swing feel

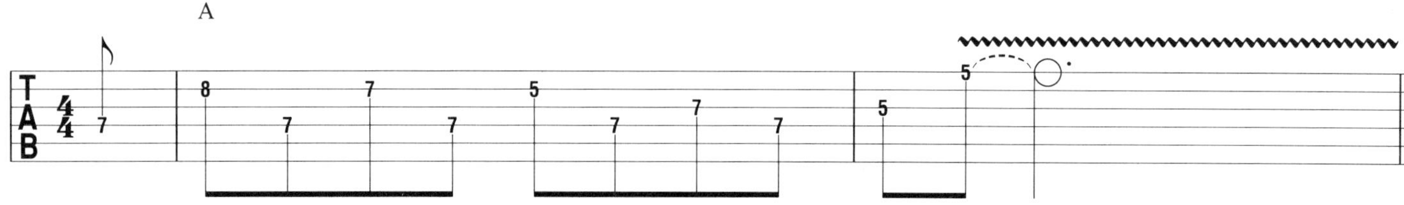


### 184: Syncopated Pedal

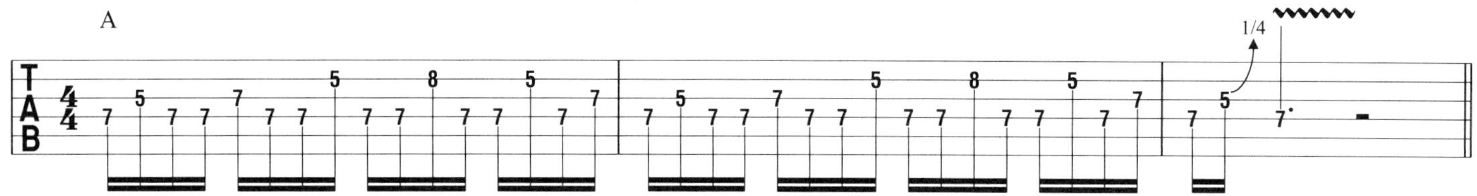


### 185: Expanded Pedal

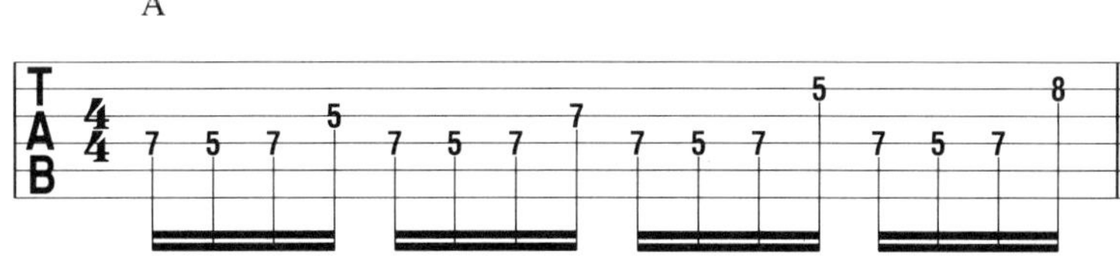


### 186: Melodic Skips

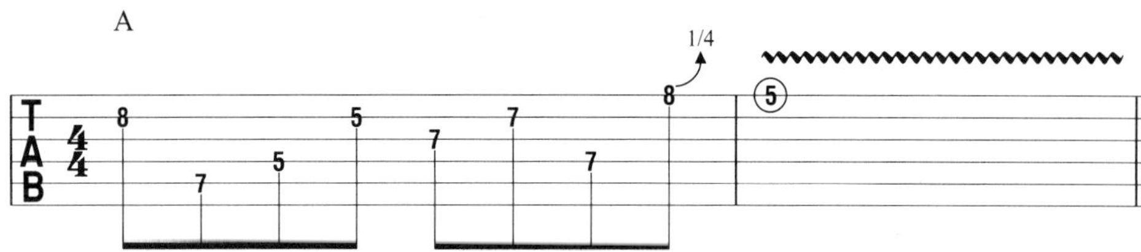

## 187: Melodic Content

Swing feel

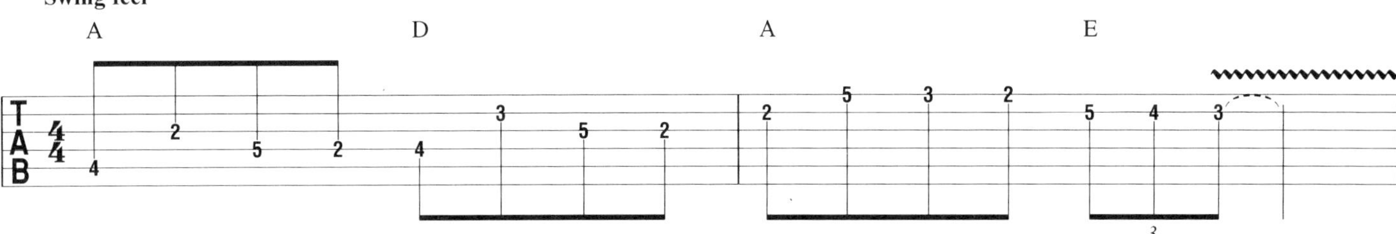

## 188: Melodic Turnaround

Swing feel

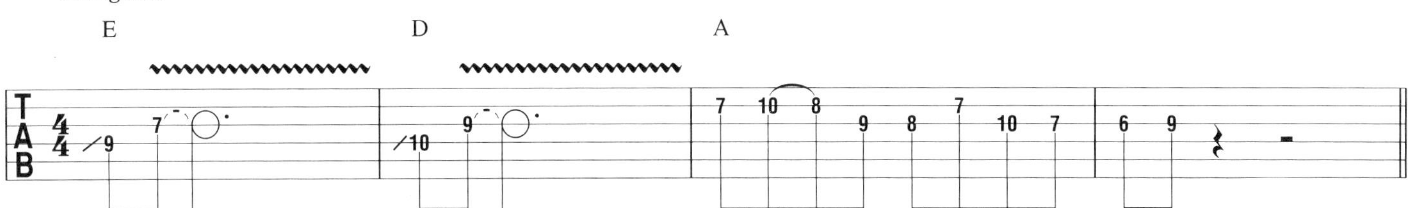

## 189: V-IV-I Melody

Swing feel

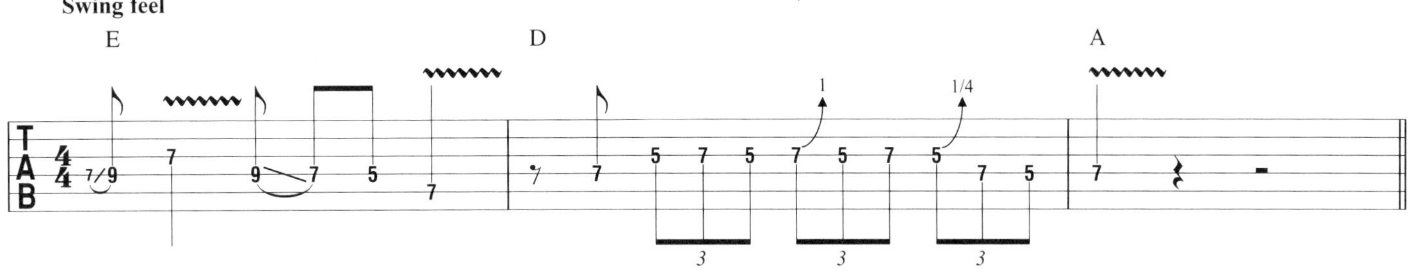

## 190: I-V Chromatic

Swing feel

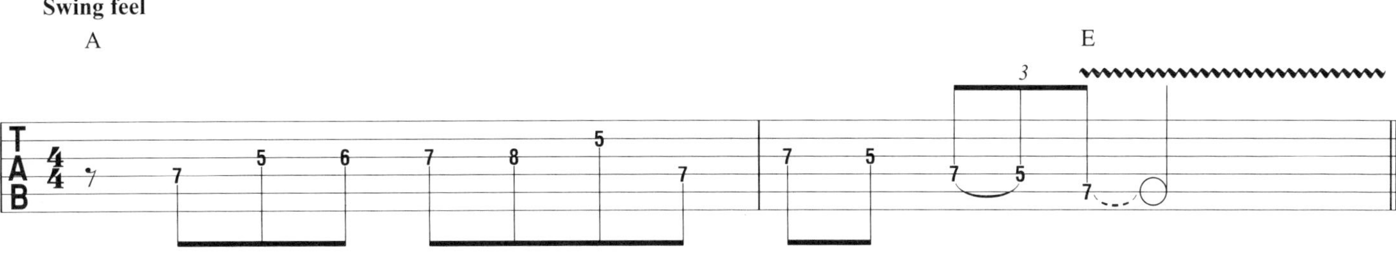

## 191: Polyrhythm Blues

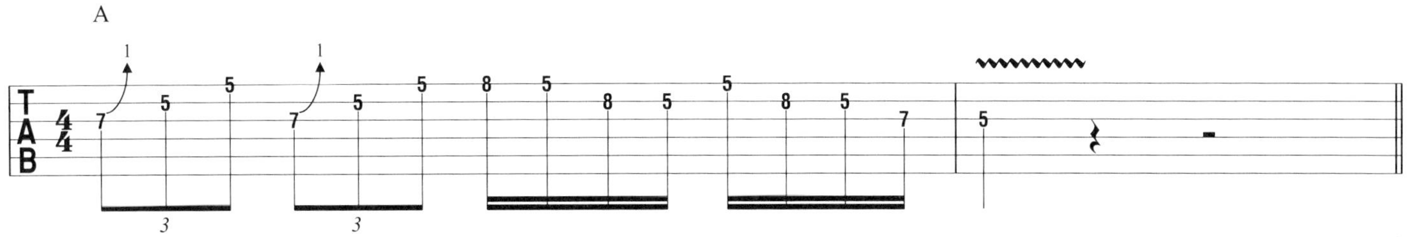

## 192: Picking 4ths

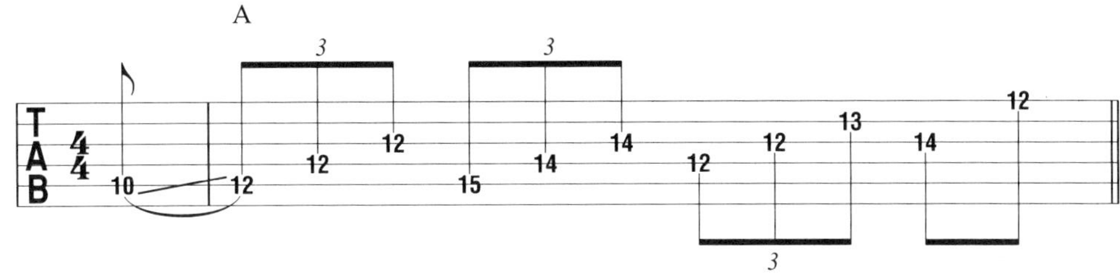

## 193: Blues Fingerings

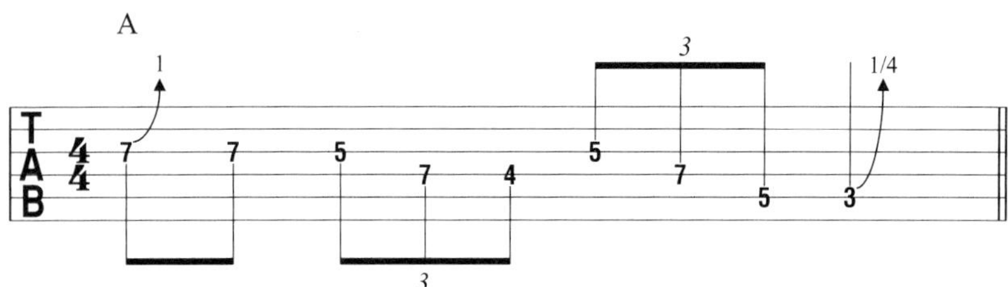


## 194: Jazz It Up

Swing feel

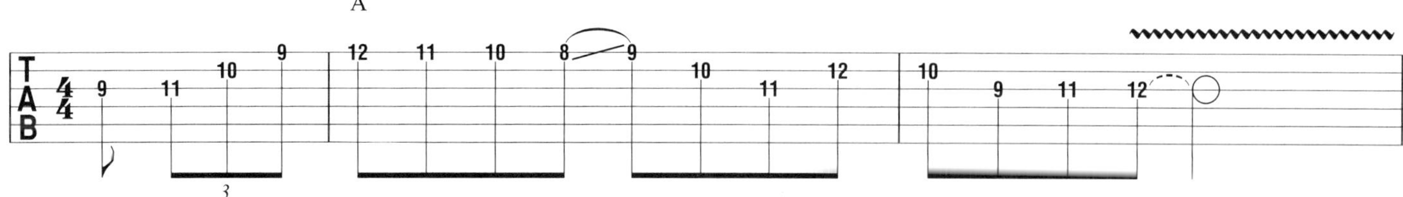


## 195: Bluesy 6ths

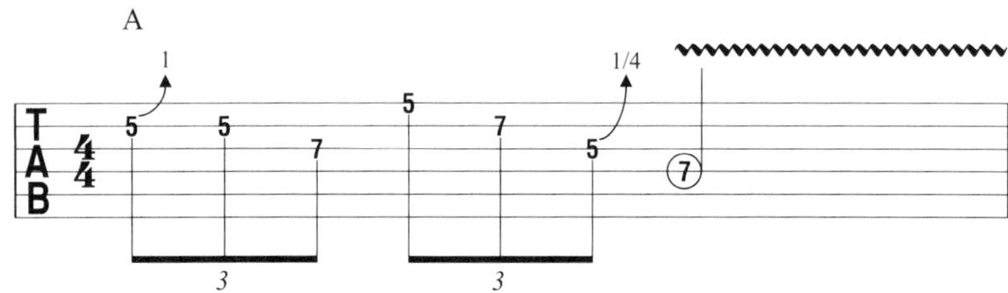


## 196: Muscle Bends

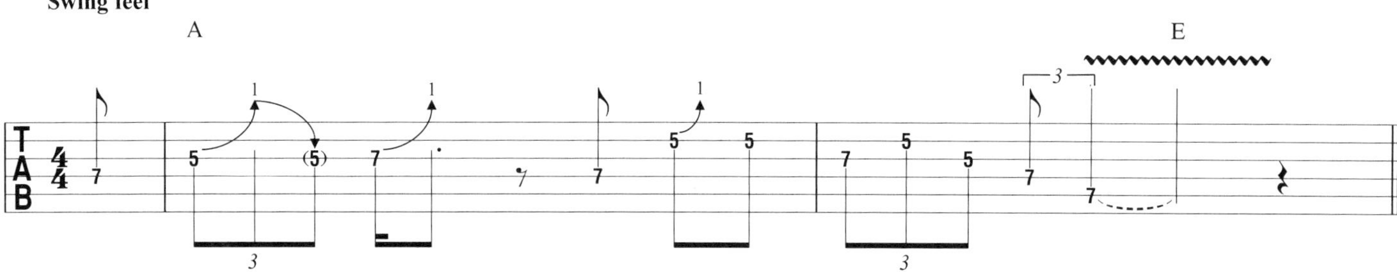


## 197: Vibrato Bends

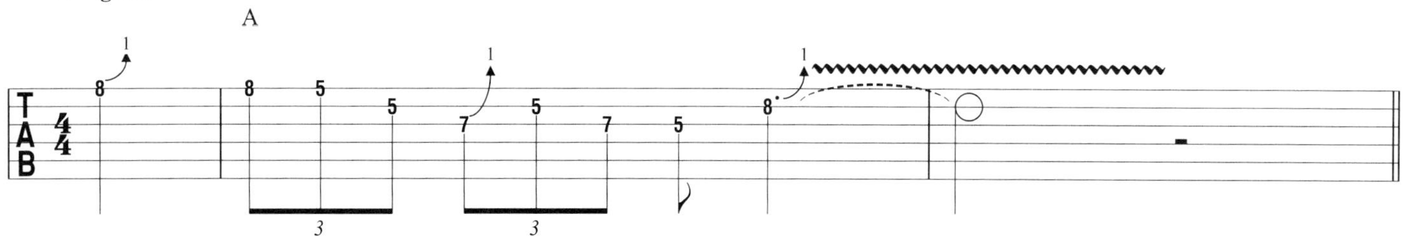


## 198: Crazy Bends

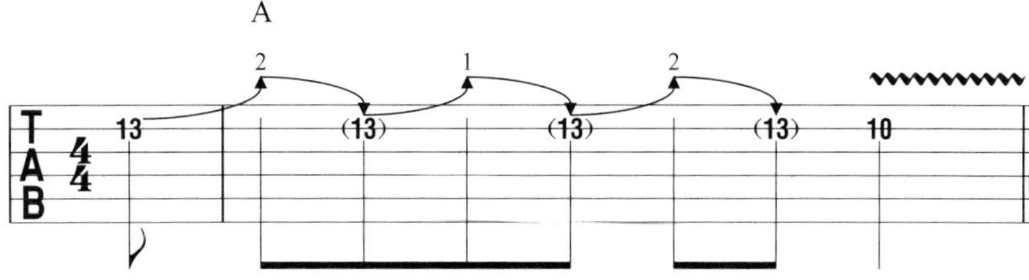

## 199: Using Positions

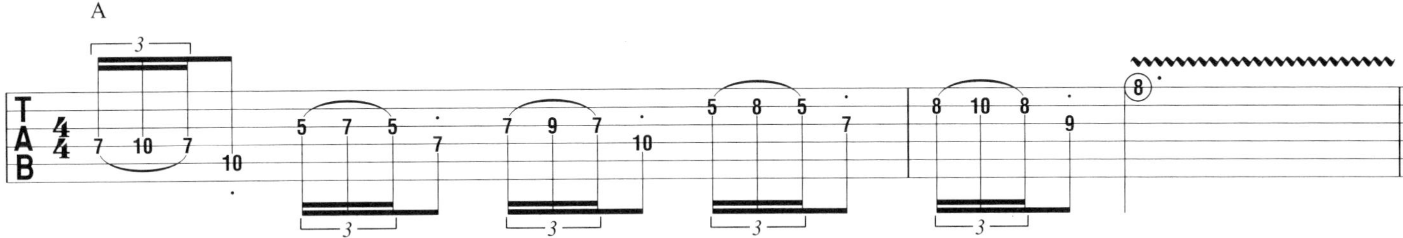


## 200: Fret Jumpin'

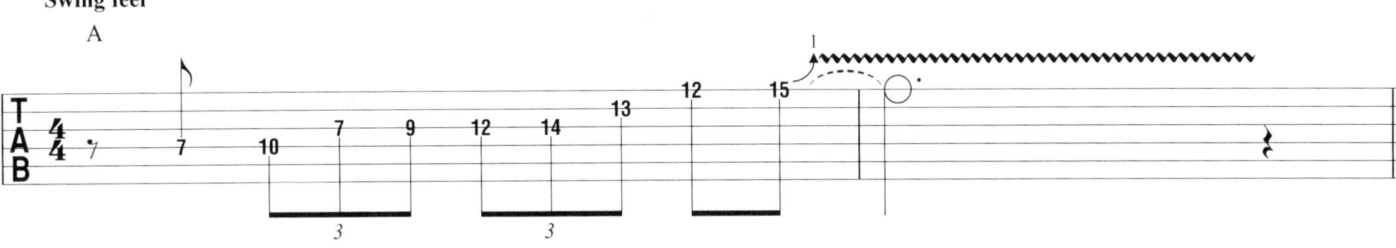

# ROCK LICKS

## Instructor: Troy Stetina

### 201: Penta-Blues

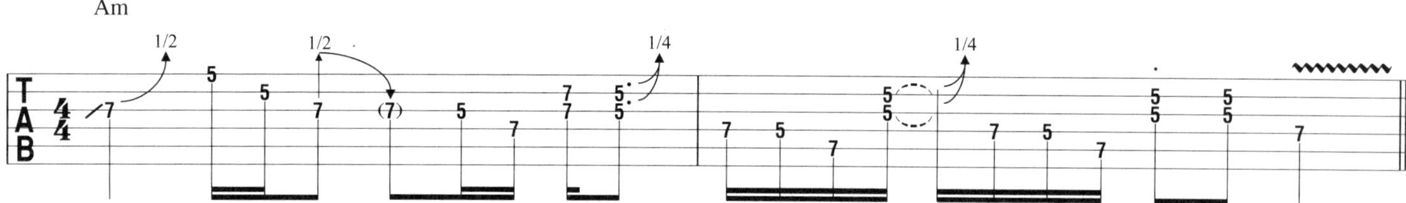


### 202: Hard Blues

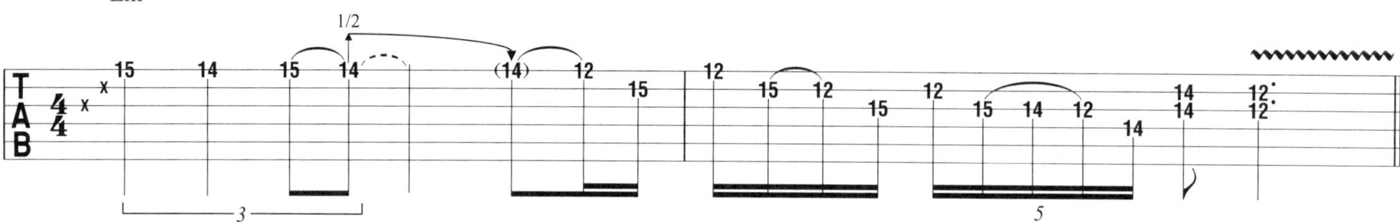


### 203: Classic Rocker

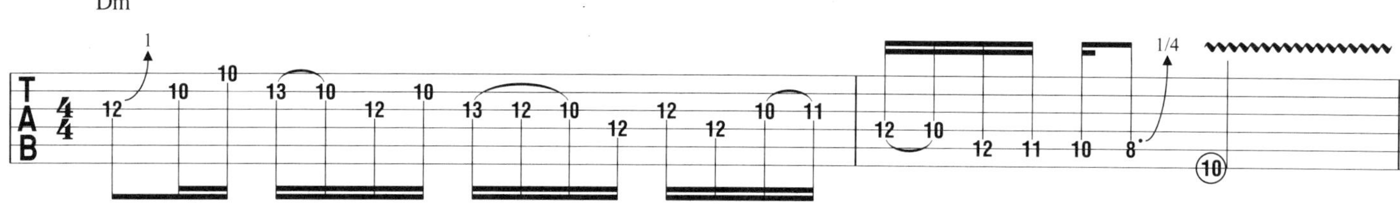


### 204: Rock Repeater

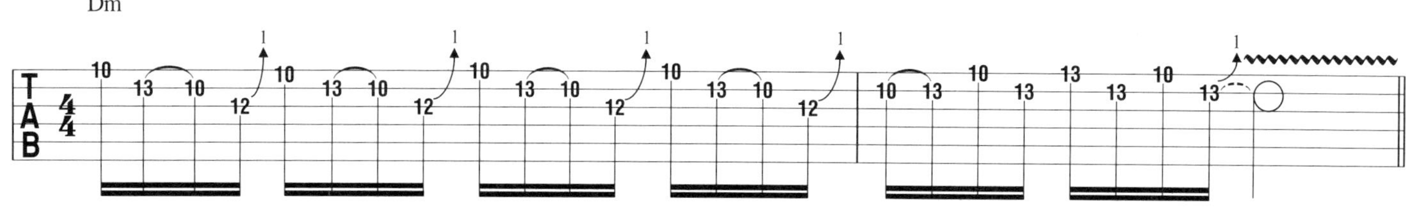


### 205: Sexy Tuplets

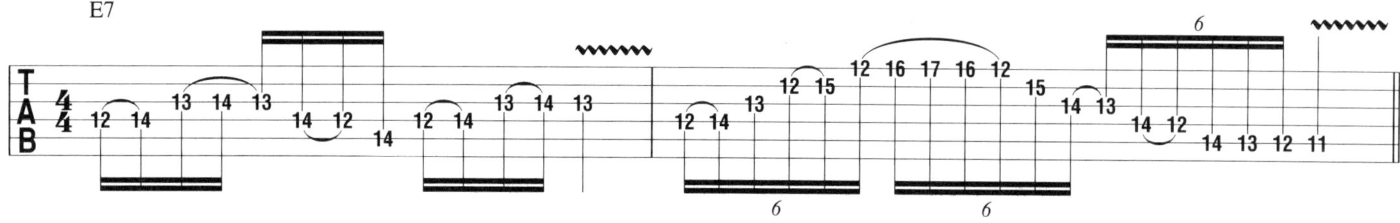


### 206: Country Rocker

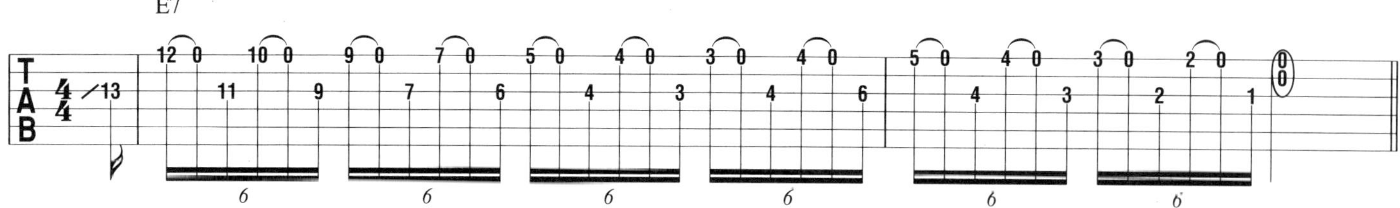

## 207: Rock Hybrid

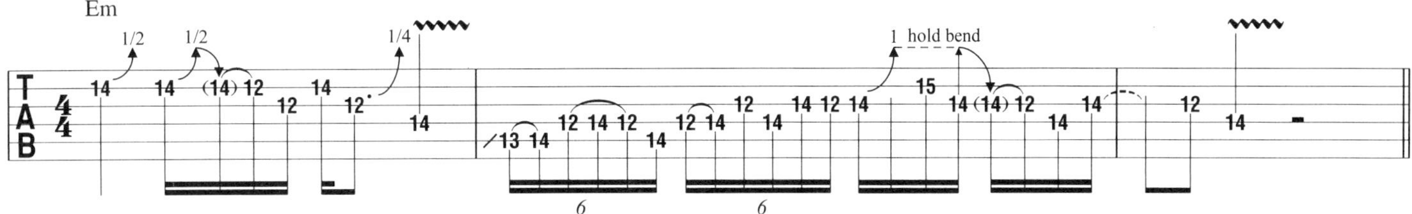


## 208: P.M. Riff

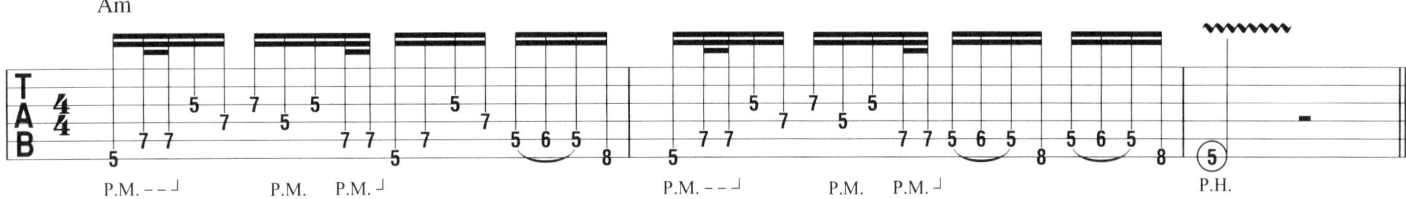


## 209: Penta-Flurry

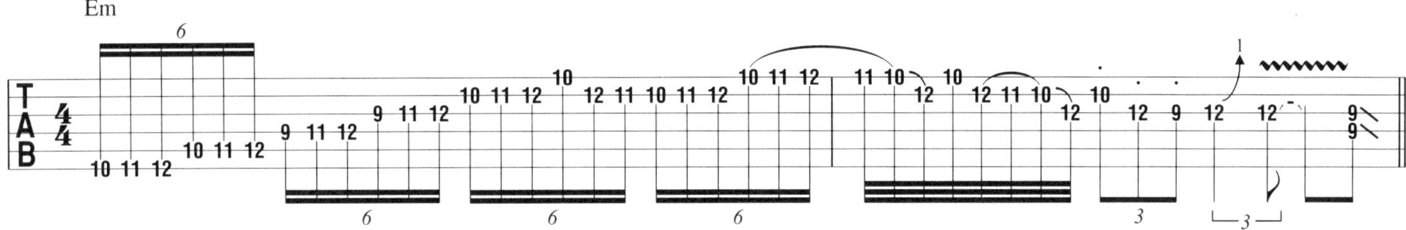


## 210: SRV Rock

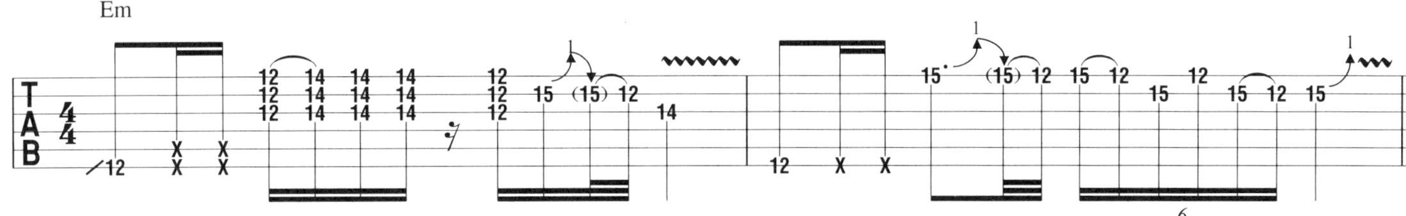


## 211: Octave Pattern

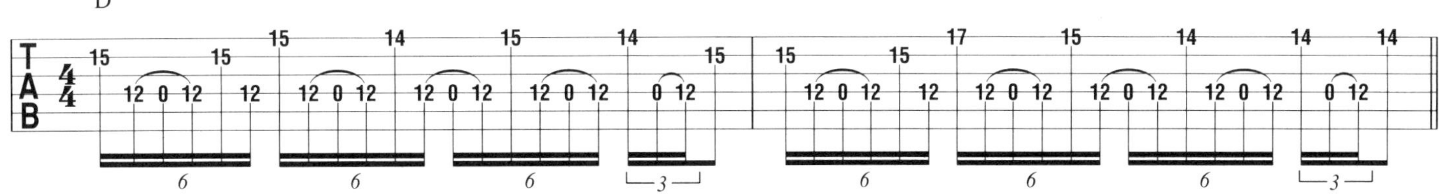


## 212: Jack the Ripper

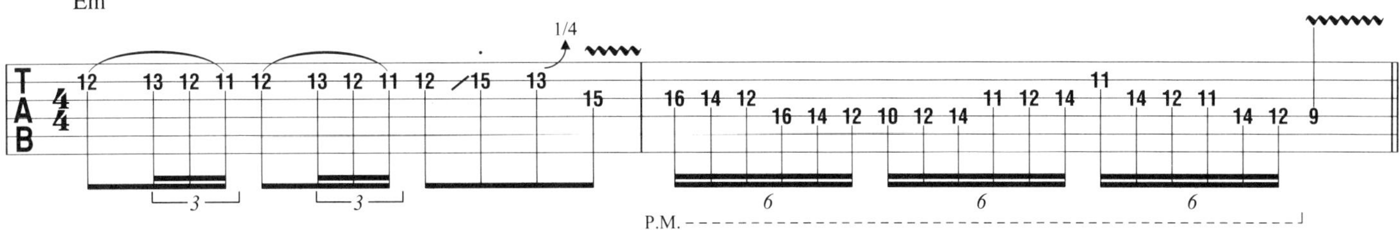


## 213: Minor Run

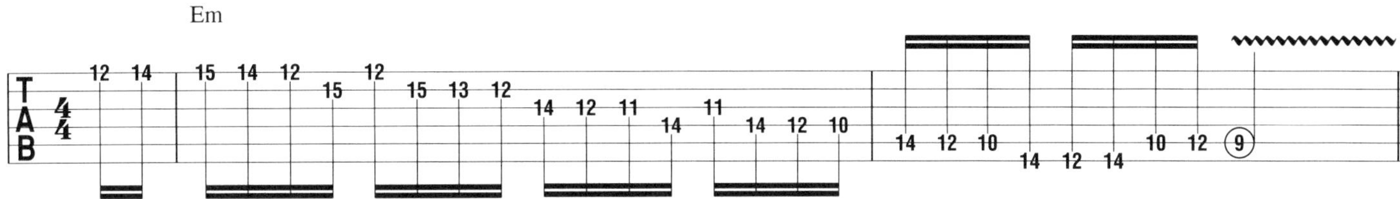

## 214: Arpin' Legato

B7♭9

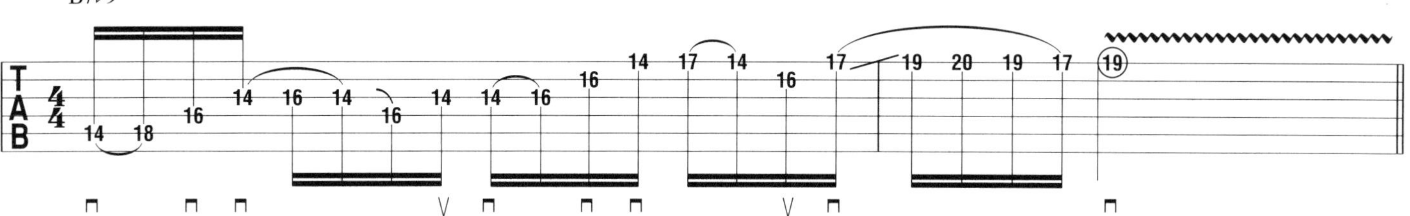

## 215: String Skipping

Am

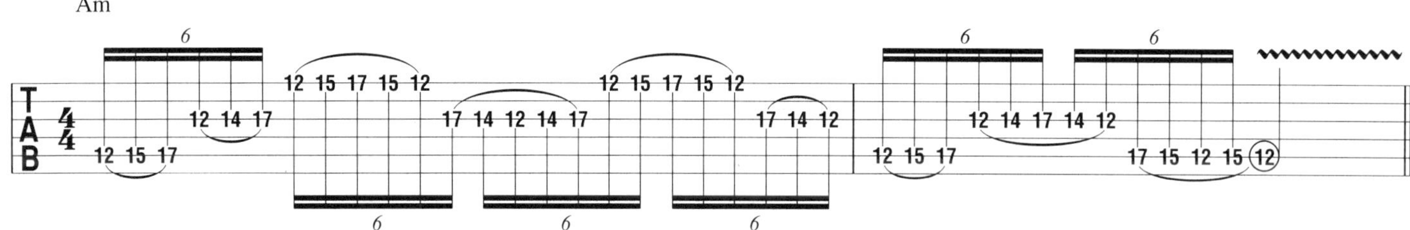

## 216: Blues Contour

Em

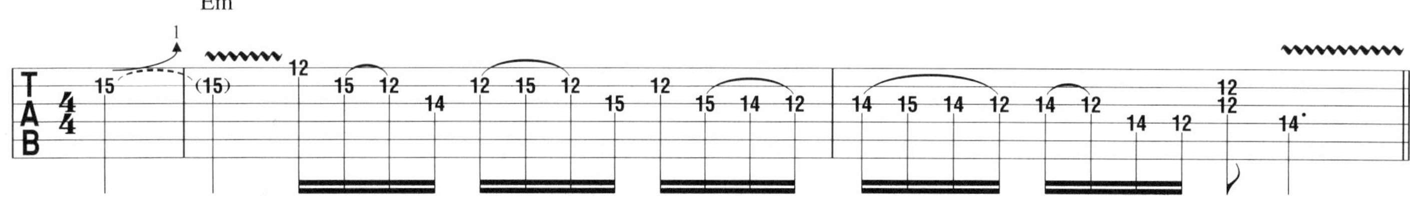

## 217: Tumbling Hemiola

Am

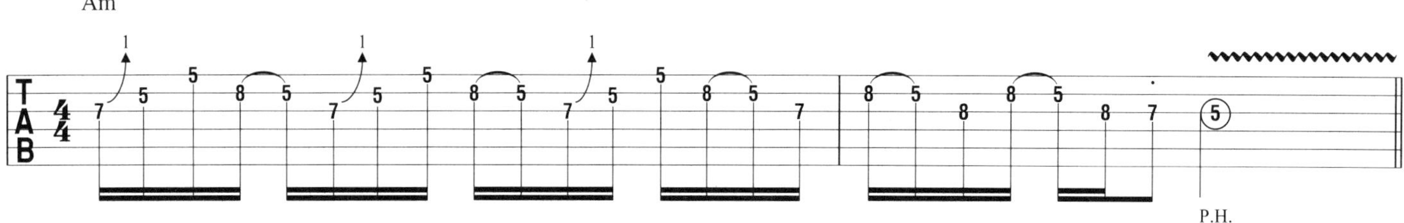


## 218: Liquid Blues

Dm

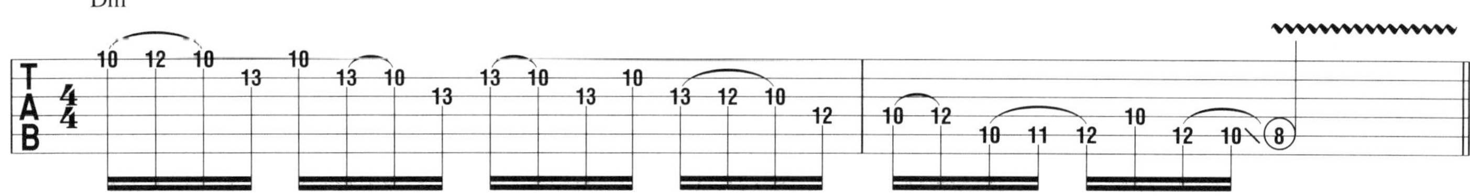

## 219: Wicked Blues

Em

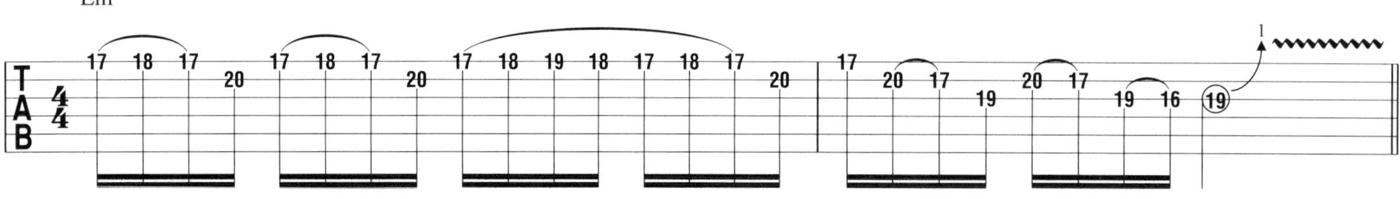

### 220: MAB Style

Em

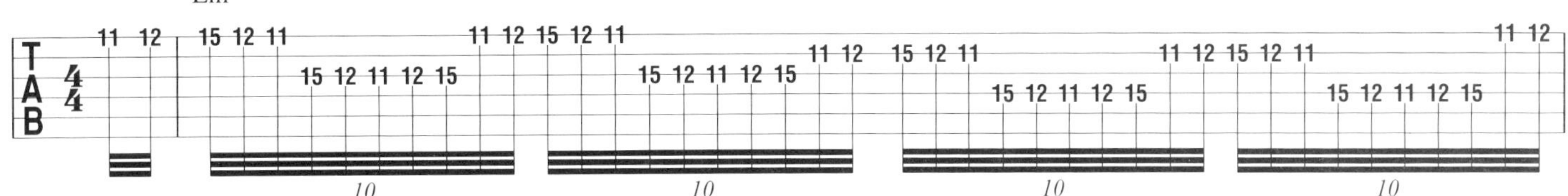

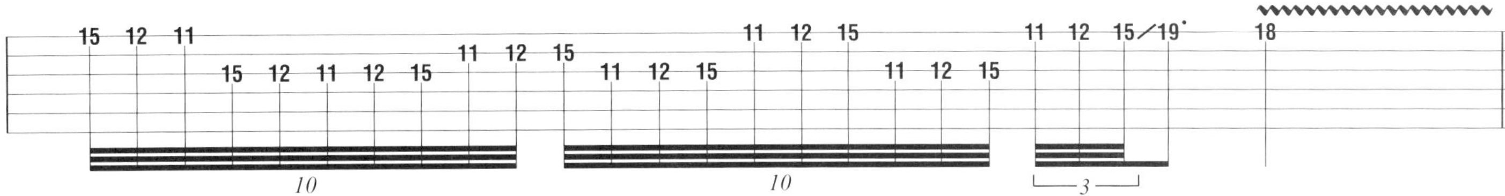

### 221: Pinch It

Am

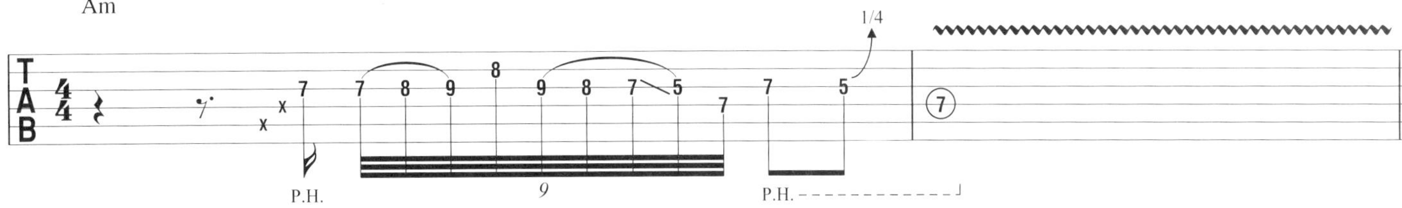


### 222: Chromatica

Am

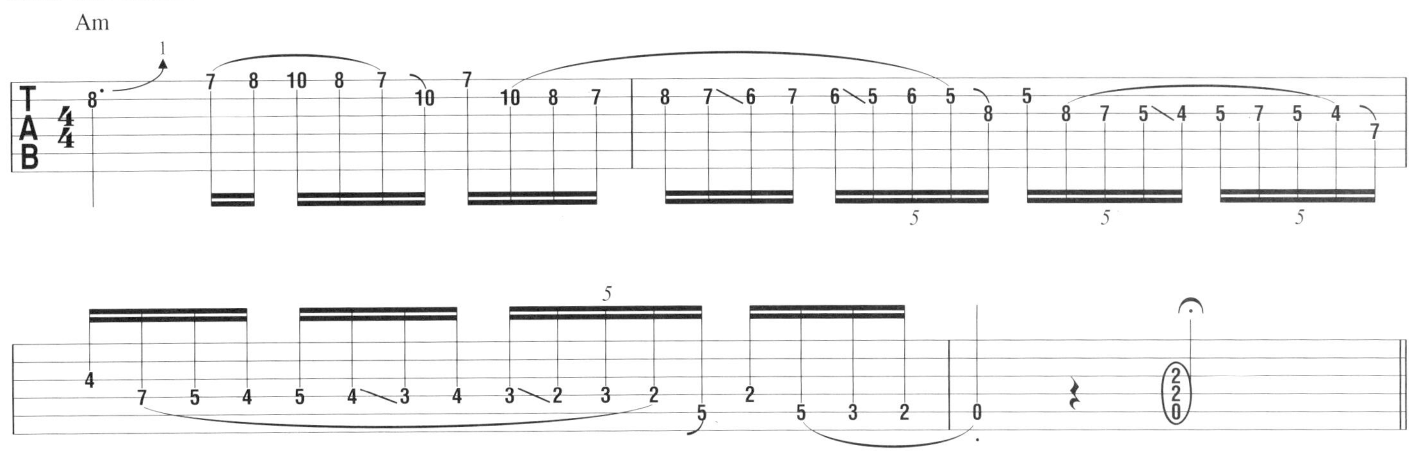

### 223: Screamer

Dm

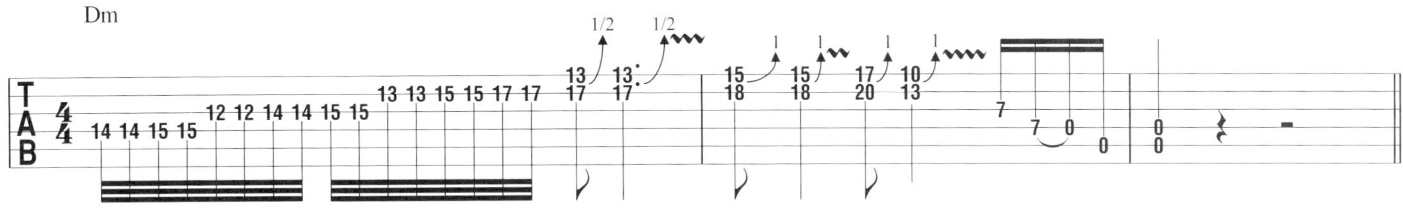

### 224: Scale Shred

Em

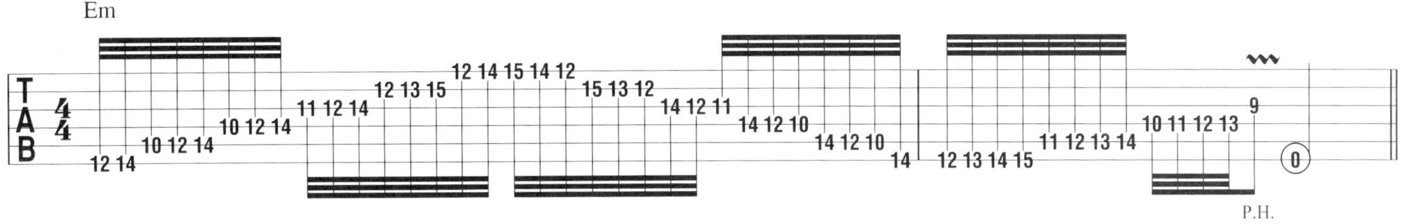

### 225: Rippin' Blues

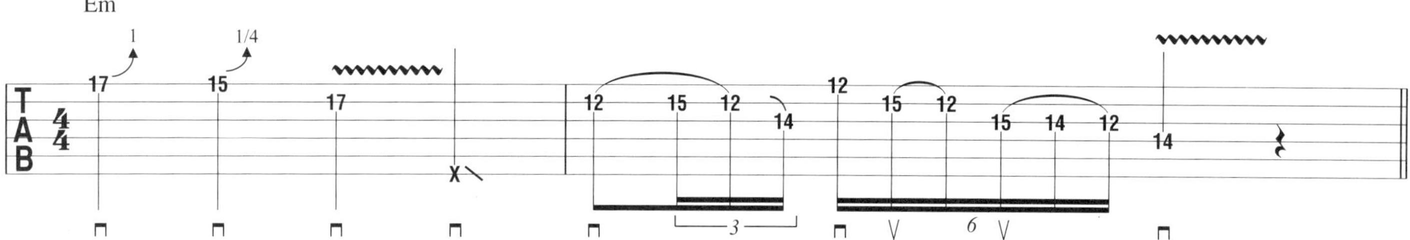


### 226: Triplet Twist

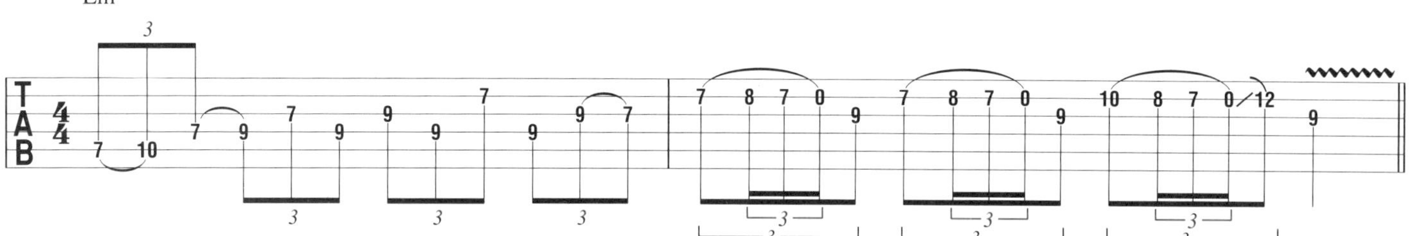


### 227: Tritone Blues

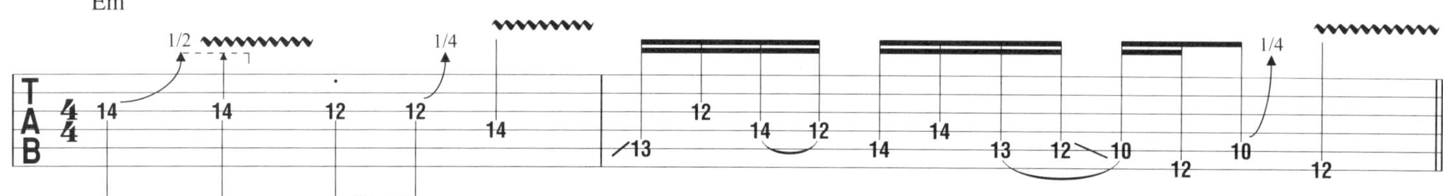


### 228: Unleash the Fury

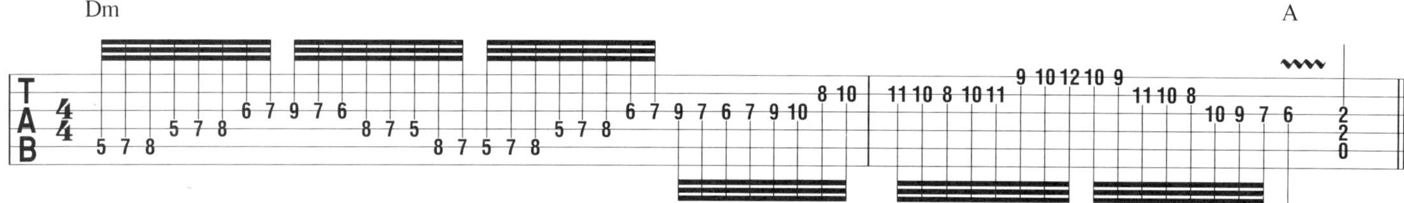


### 229: Killer Bends

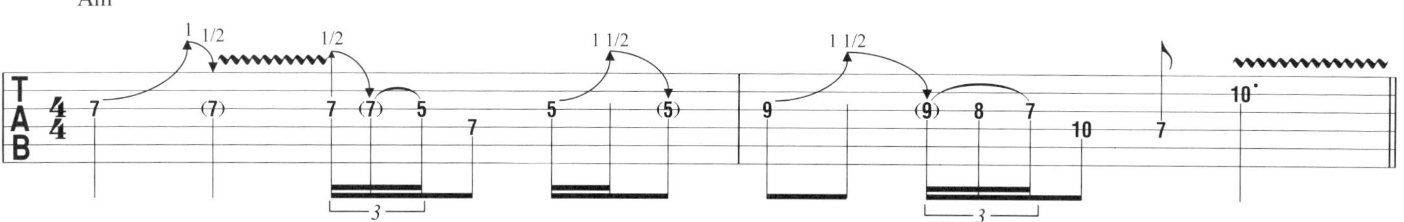


### 230: Rockin' Blues

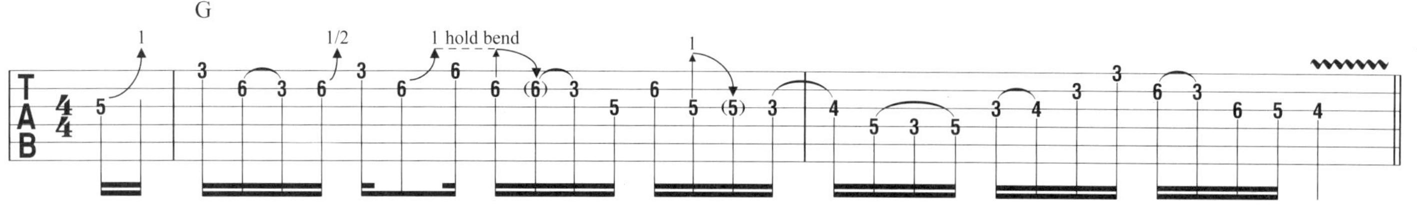


### 231: Minor/Major

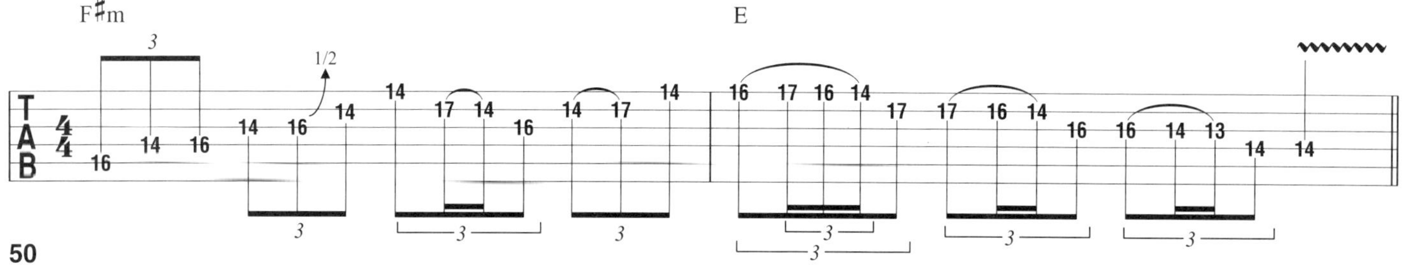

### 232: Elastic Thrash

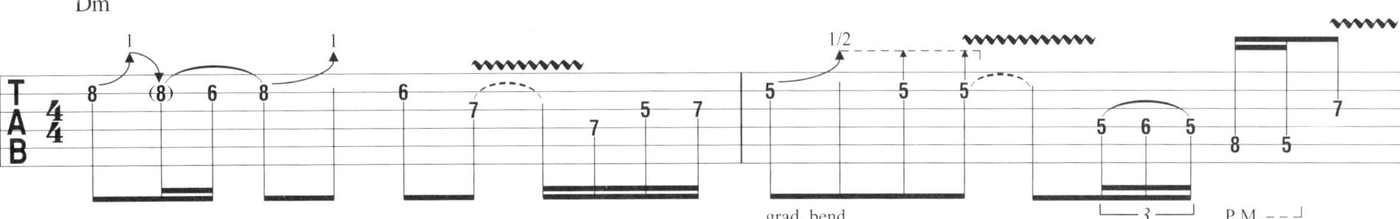


### 233: Tensity

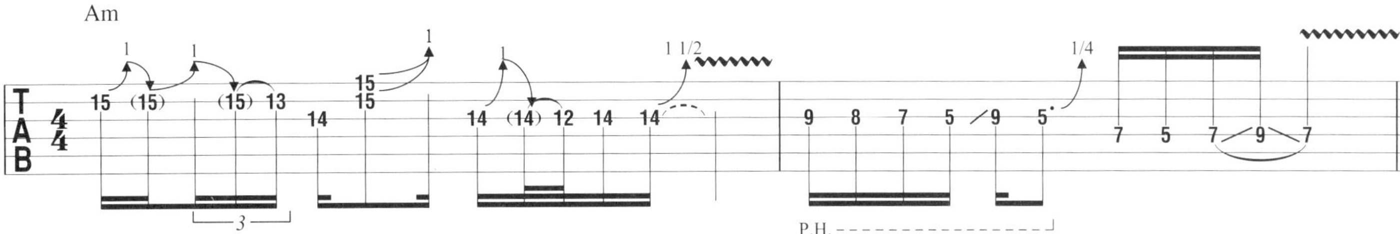


### 234: Palmistry

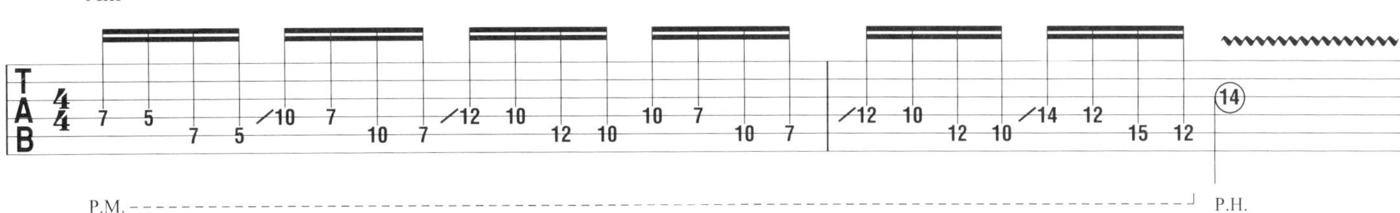


### 235: Blues Twist

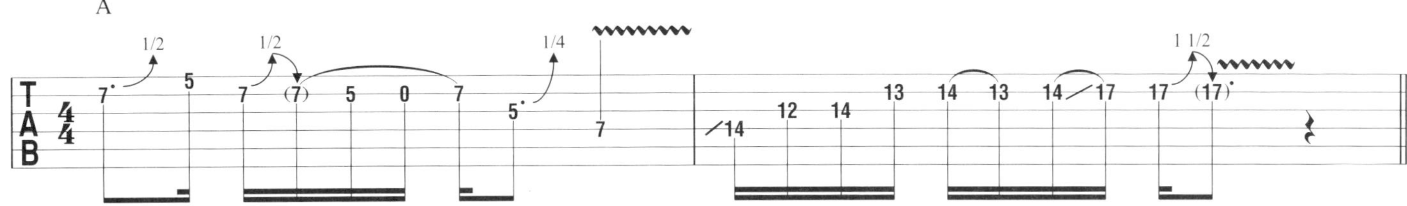


### 236: Melodic Metal

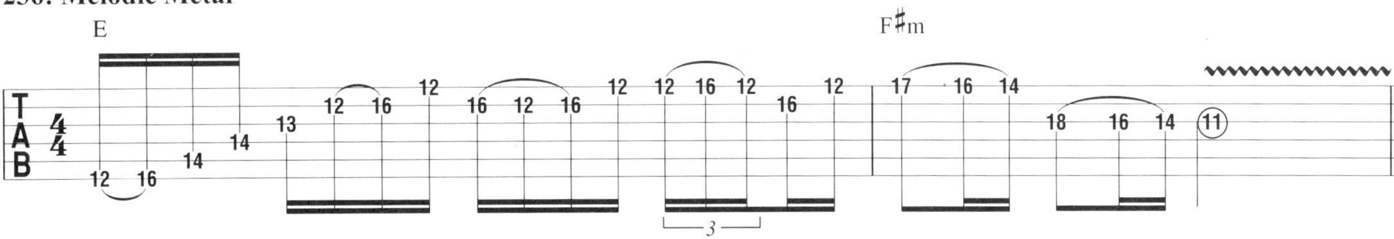


### 237: Total Ambiguity

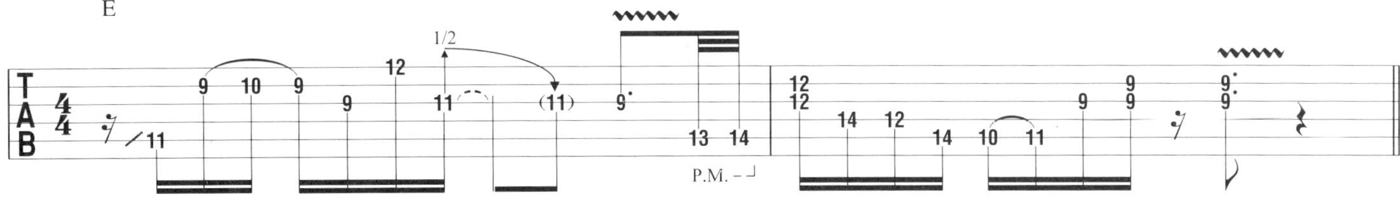


### 238: Doublestop Rock

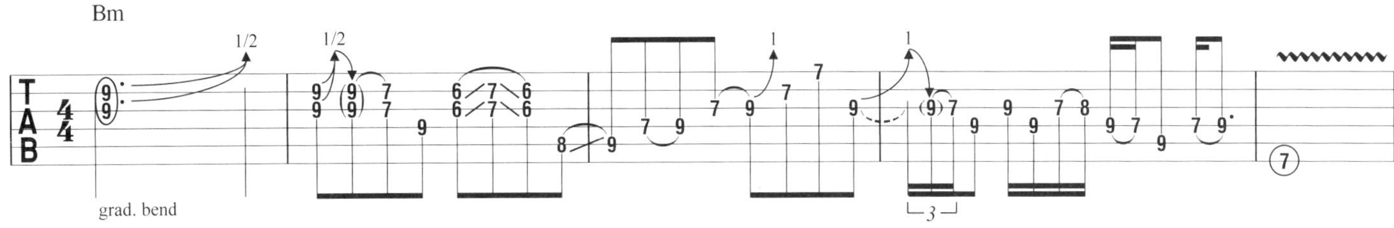

## 239: Speed Repeater

Am

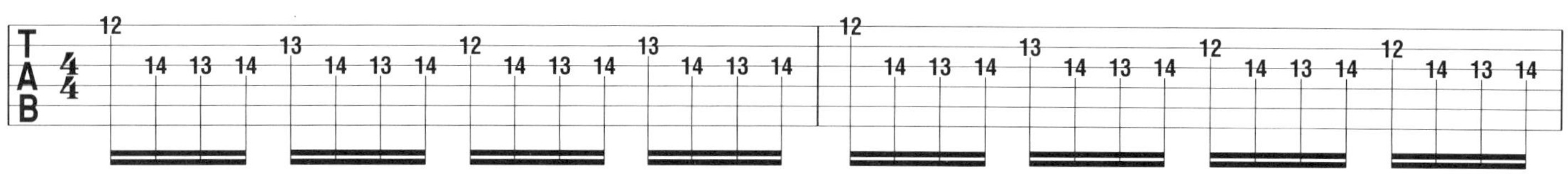

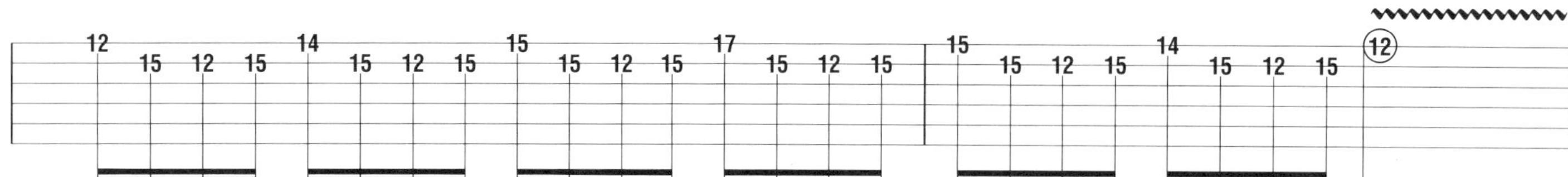

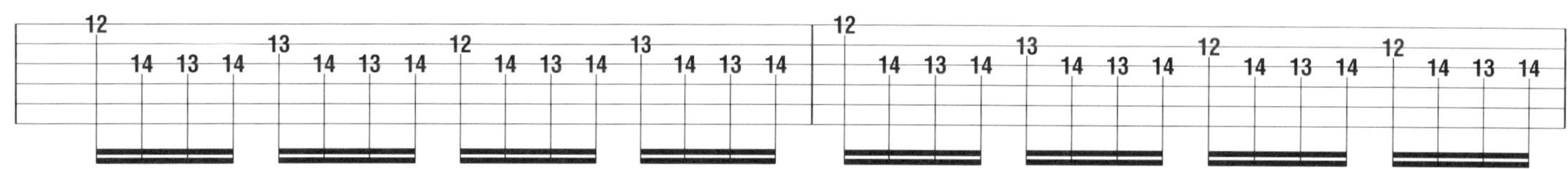

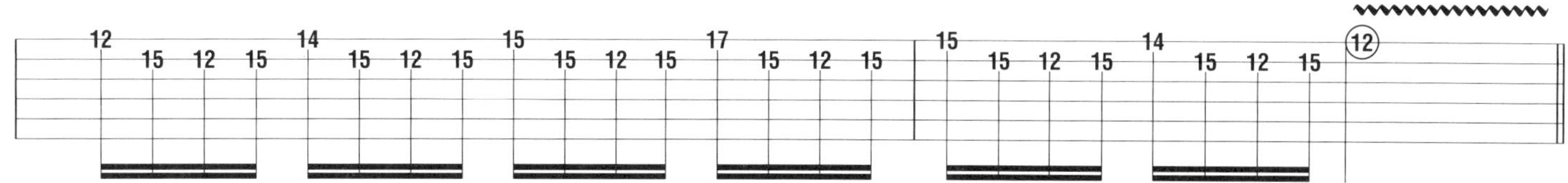

## 240: Gettin' Randy

Em

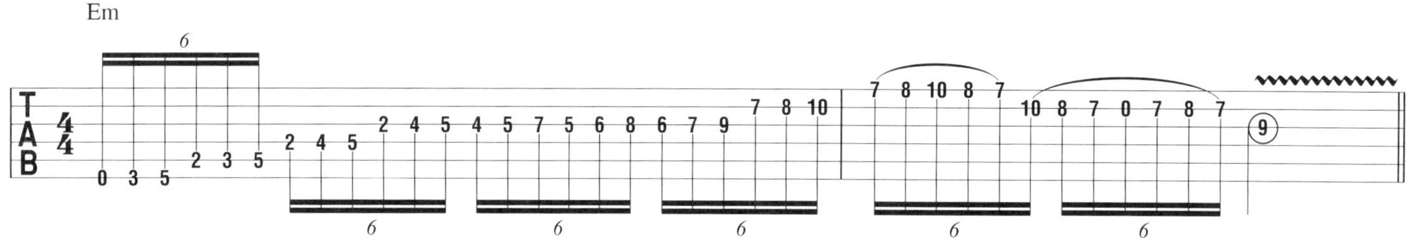

## 241: Off the Rails

Em

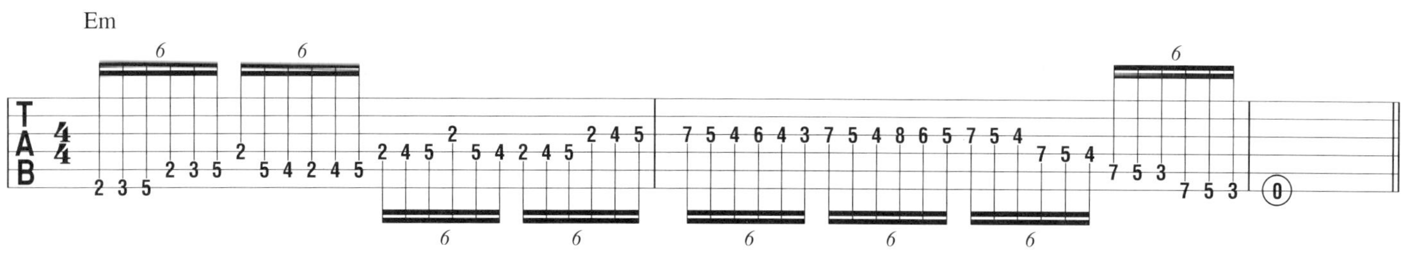

## 242: Gilbert-Inspired

Am

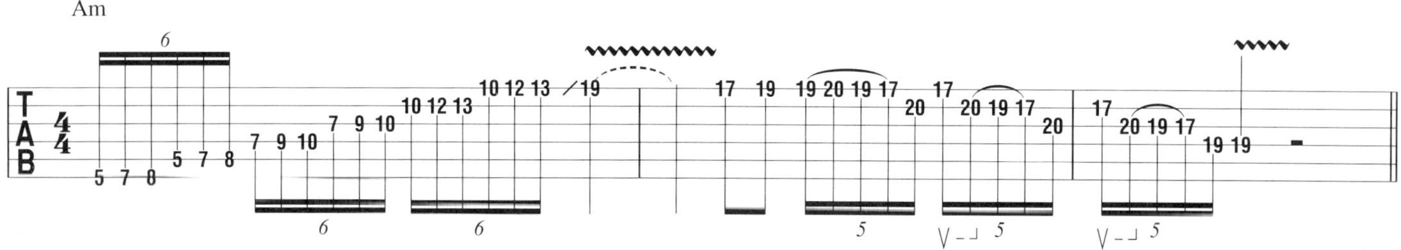

### 243: Open Onslaught

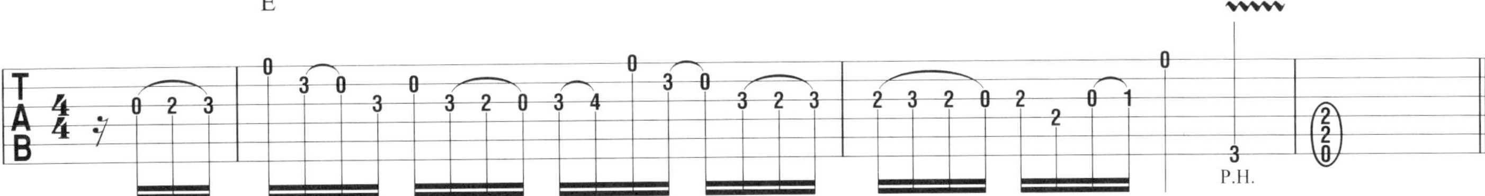


### 244: Speed Blues

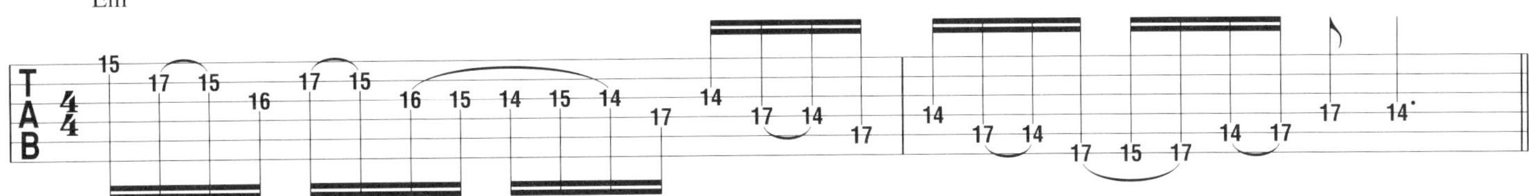


### 245: Displacer

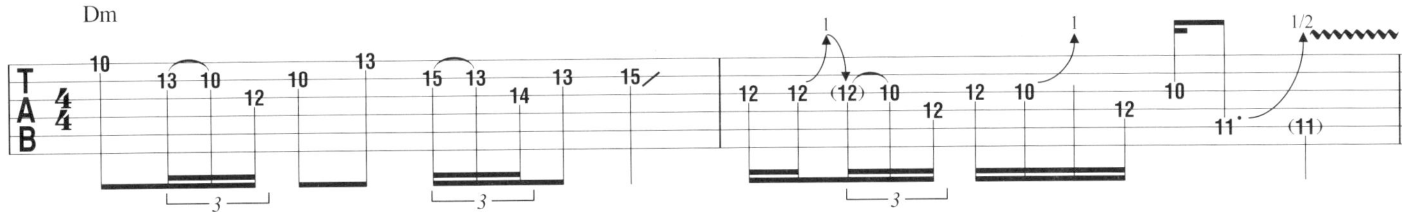


### 246: Floating Phrase

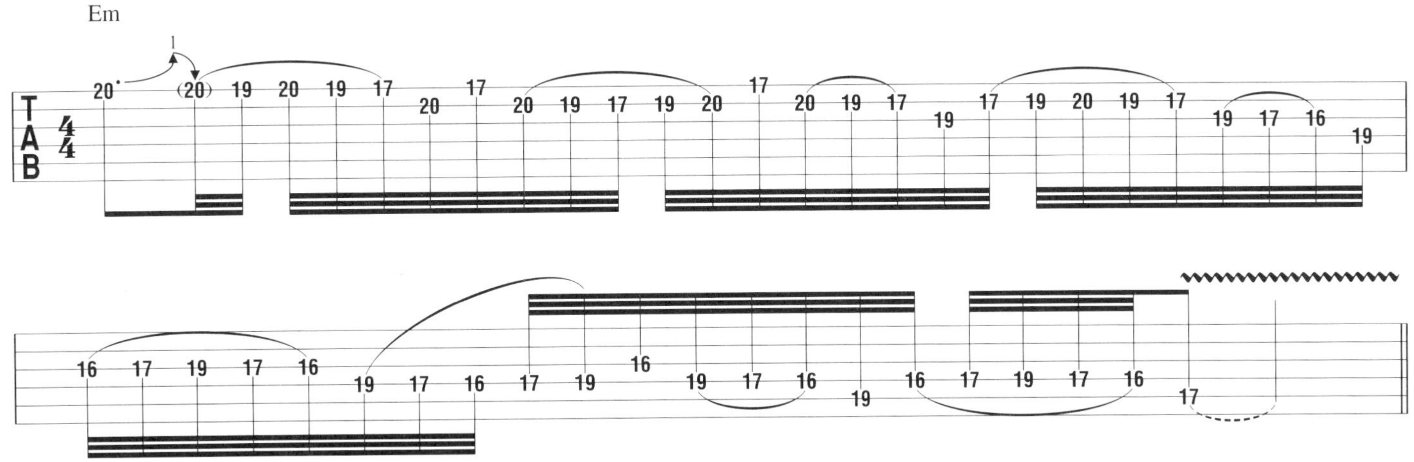


### 247: What the Fret?

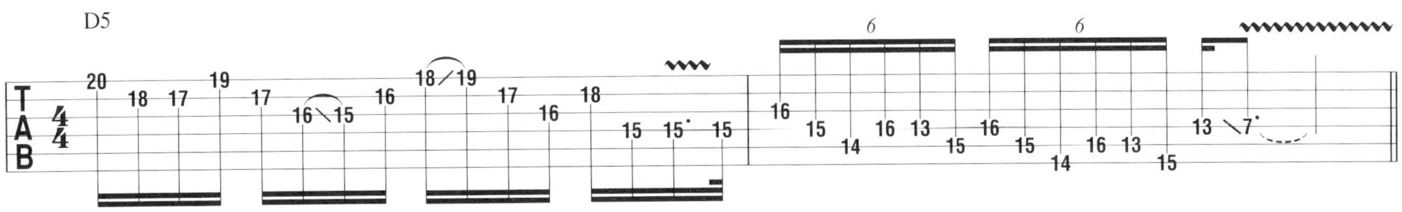


### 248: Spanish Shred

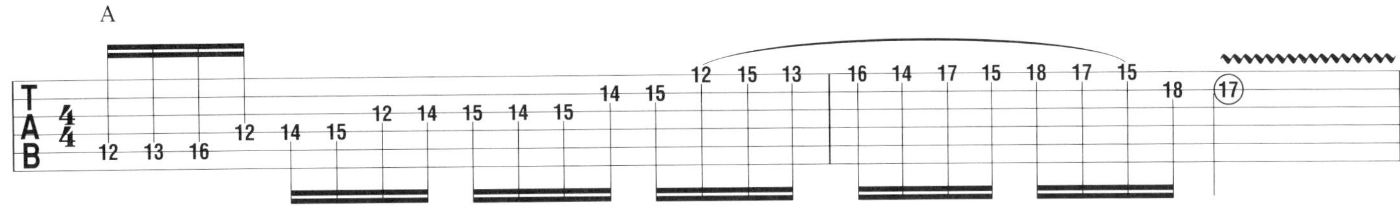

## 249: Sick Riff

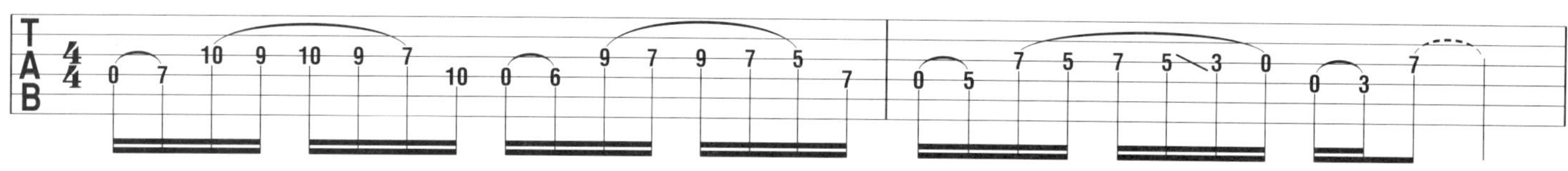


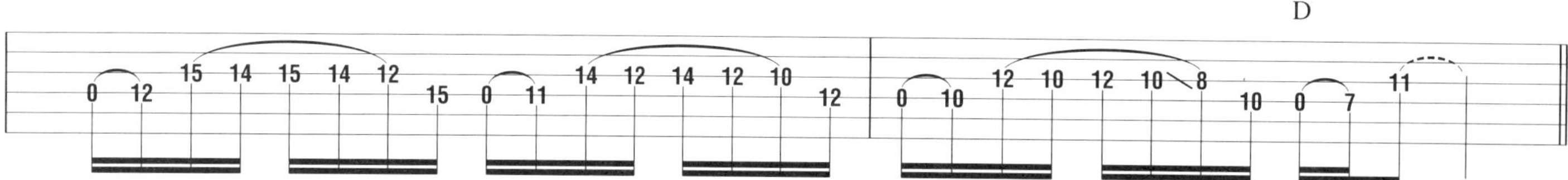


## 250: Sweep-Tap

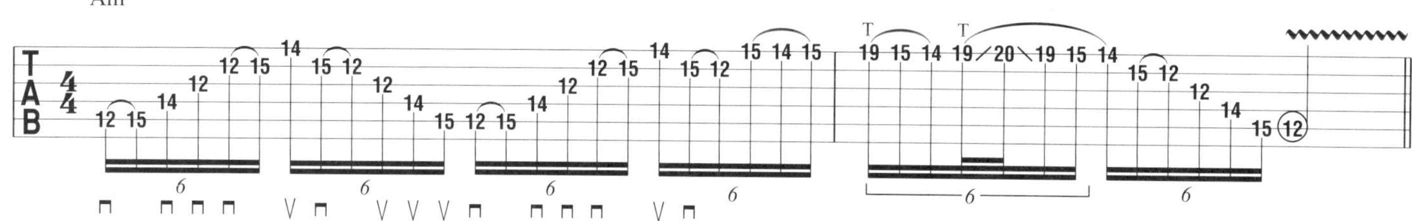


## 251: Melodic Motif

Swing feel

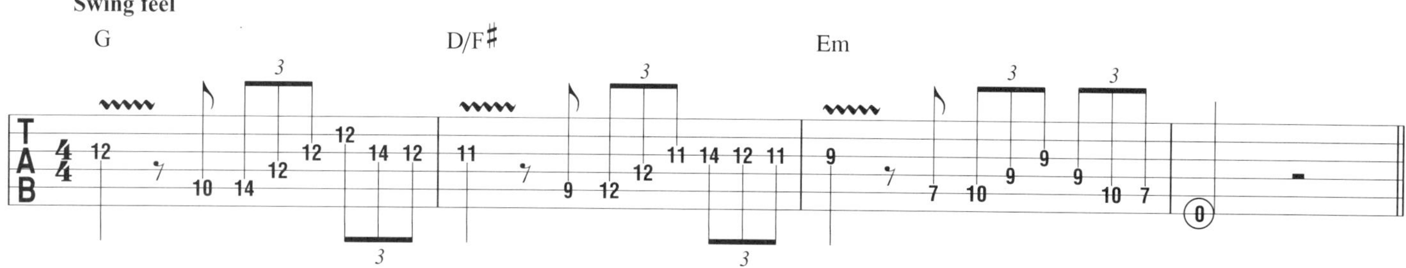


## 252: Accent It

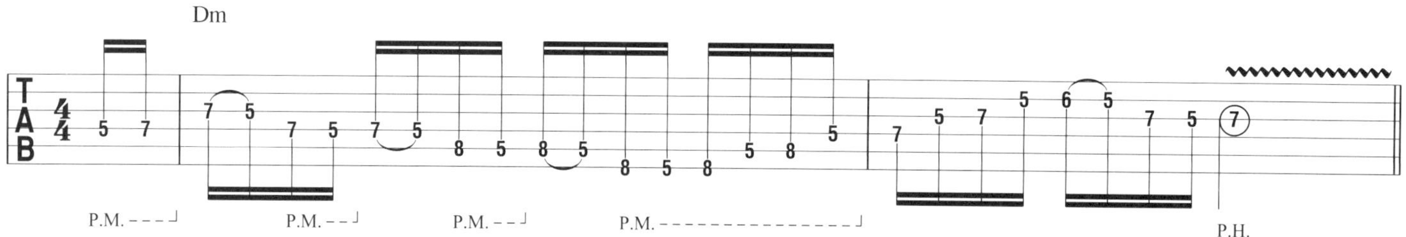


## 253: Pick Lick

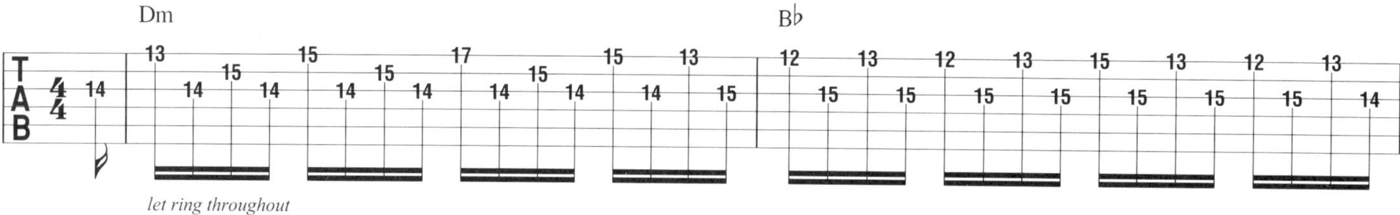


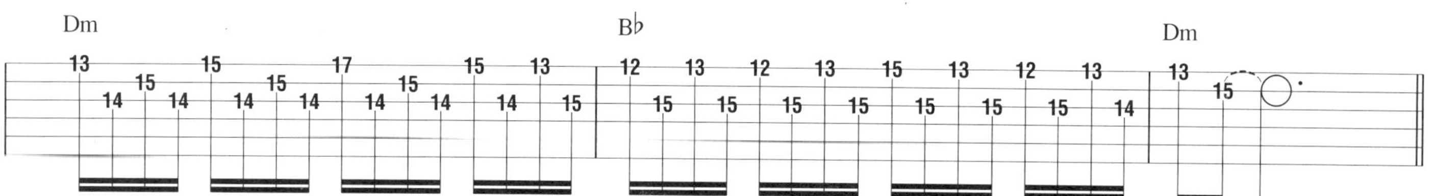

## 254: Legato Riff

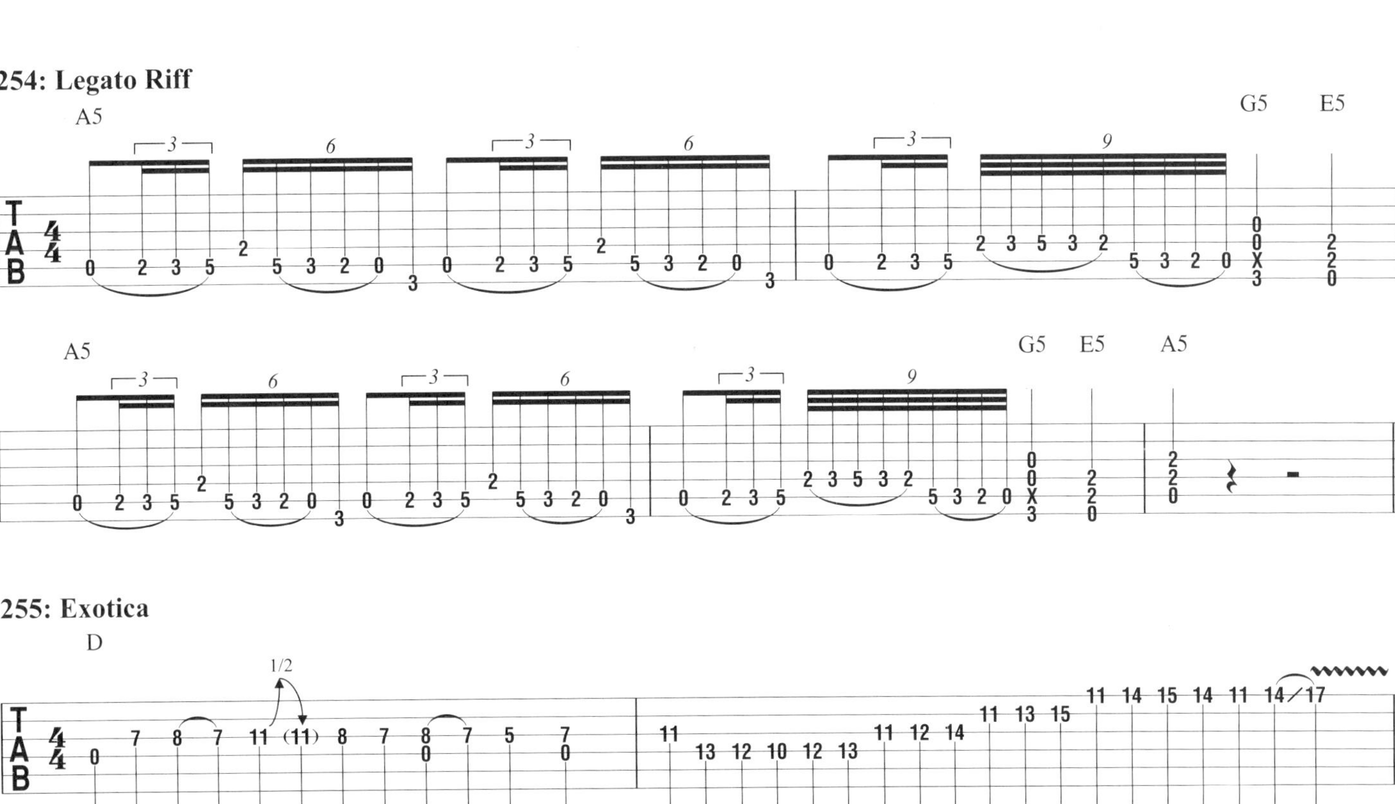


## 255: Exotica

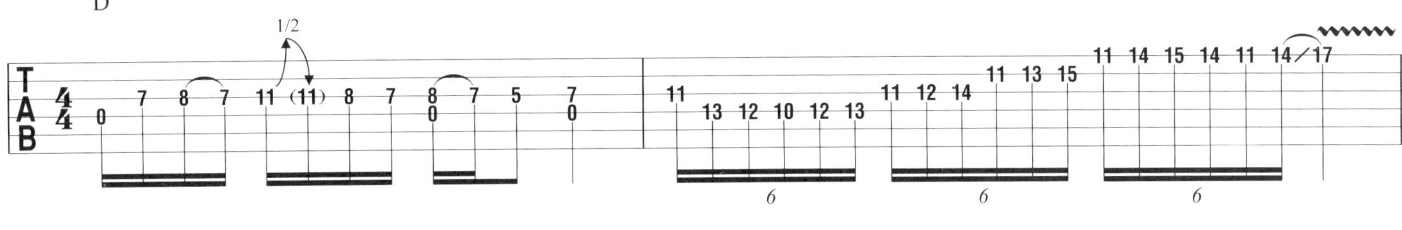


## 256: Power Rocker

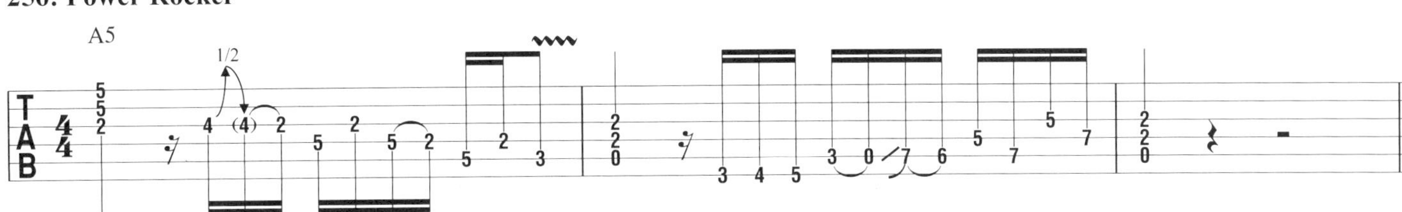


## 257: Pick-Tap

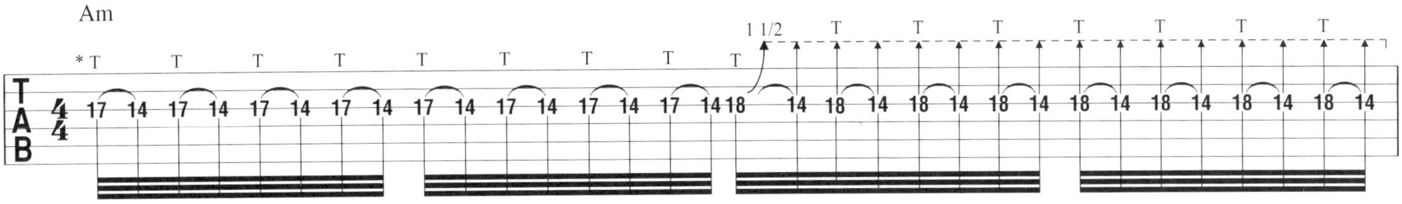

Am

*Tap w/ edge of pick throughout.

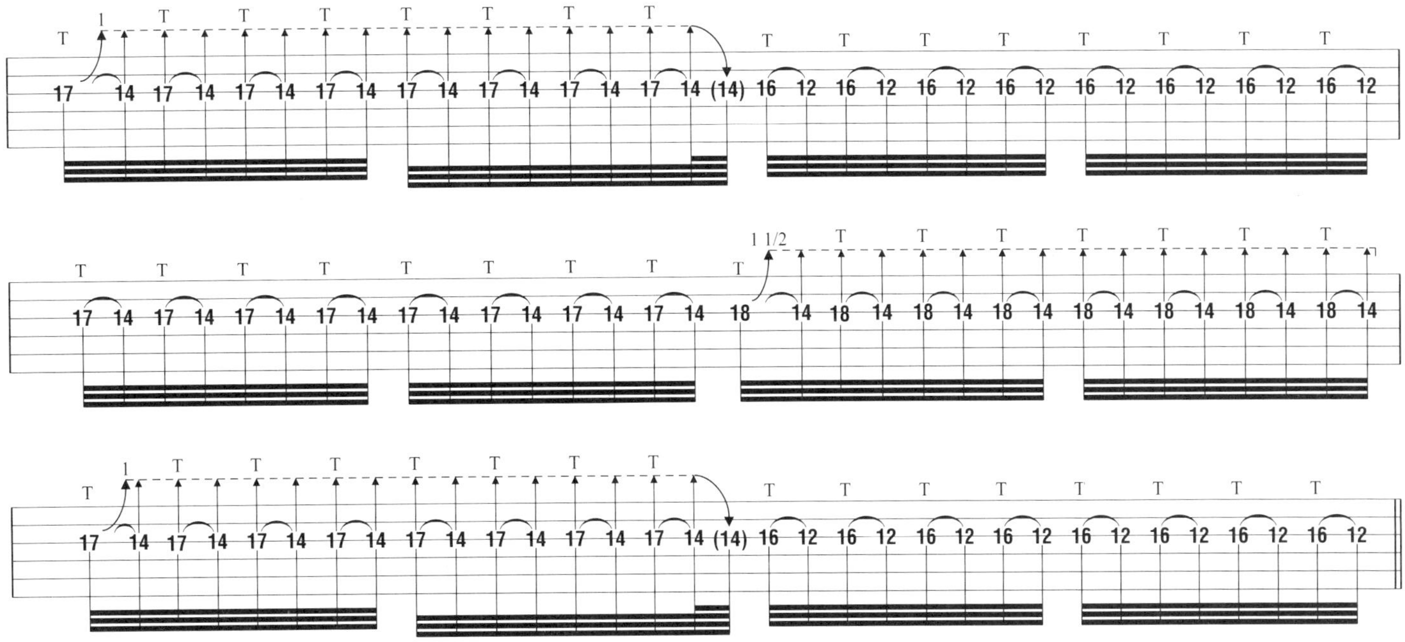

**258: Lydian Satch**

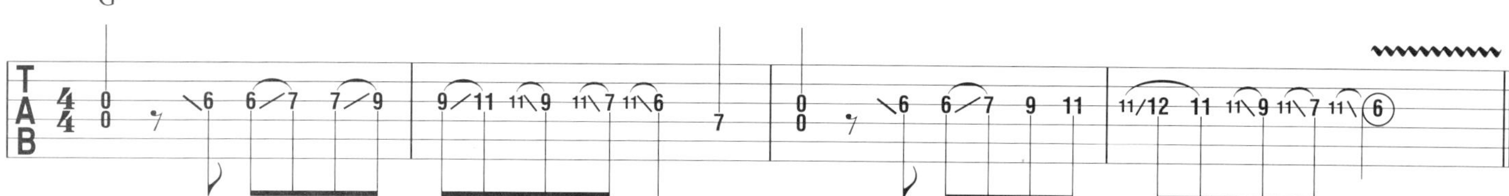


**259: Mixo-Rhythmic**

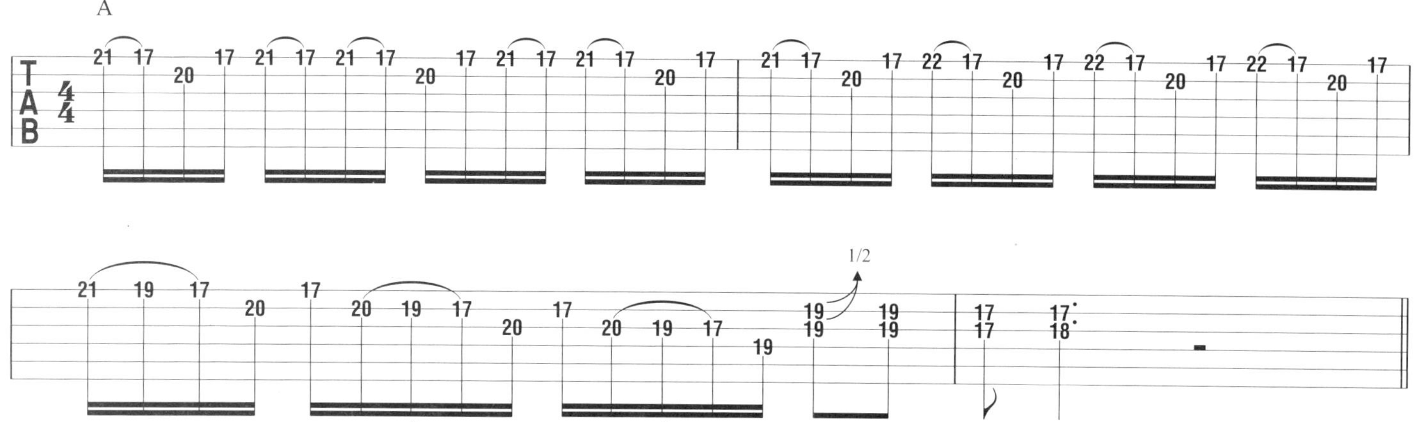


**260: Perfectly Disturbed**

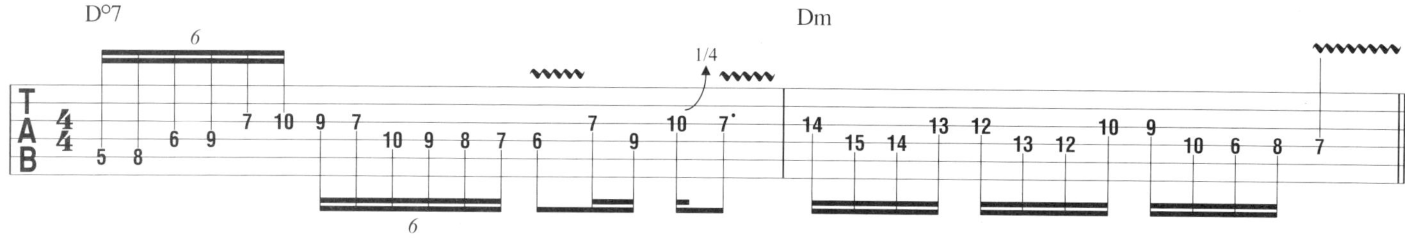


**261: Quirky Leaps**

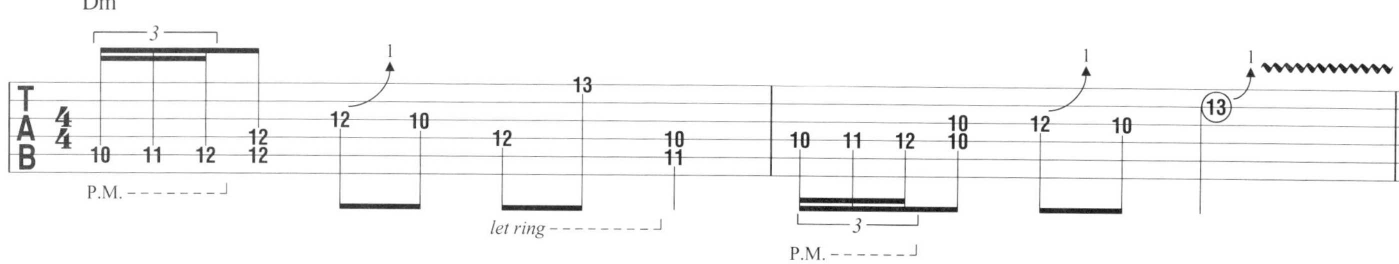


**262: Staccato-Legato**

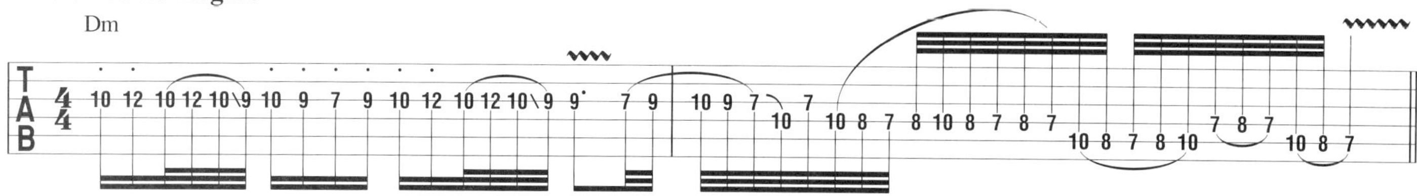


**263: EVH Tapping**

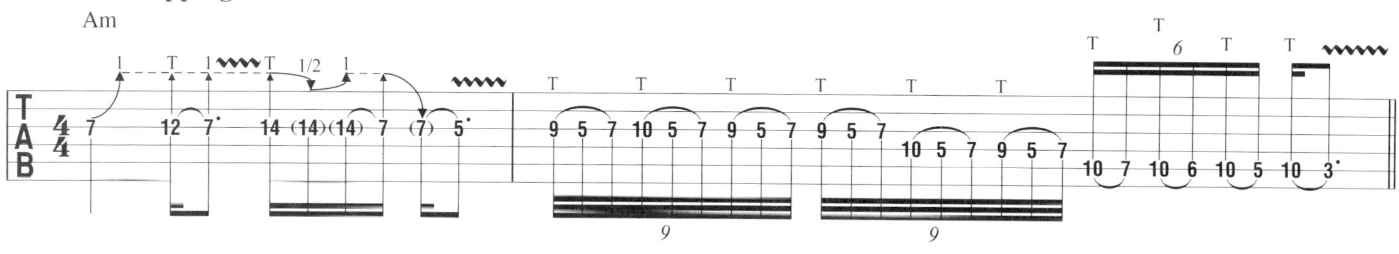

**264: Tapped Harmonics**

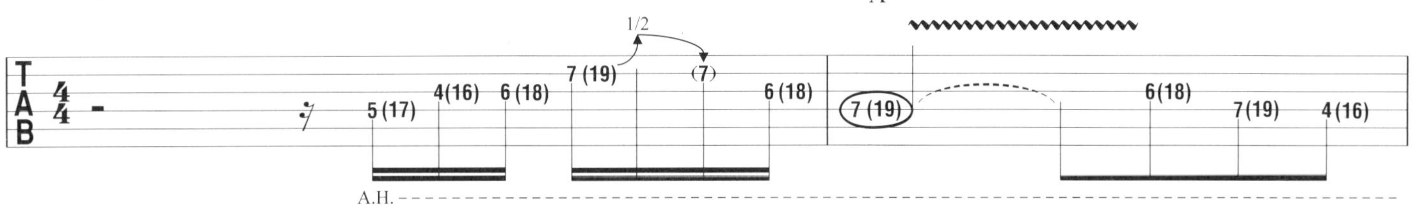


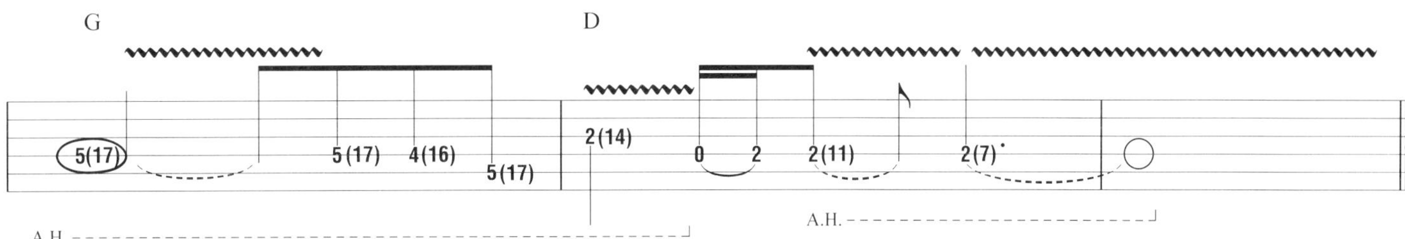


**265: Soaring Phrygian**

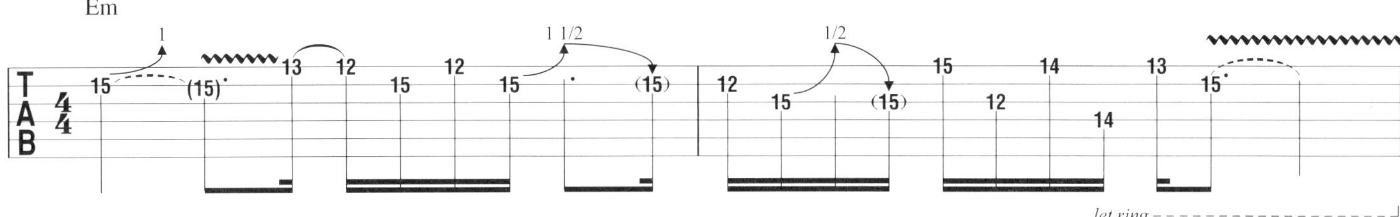


**266: Tonal Doubt**

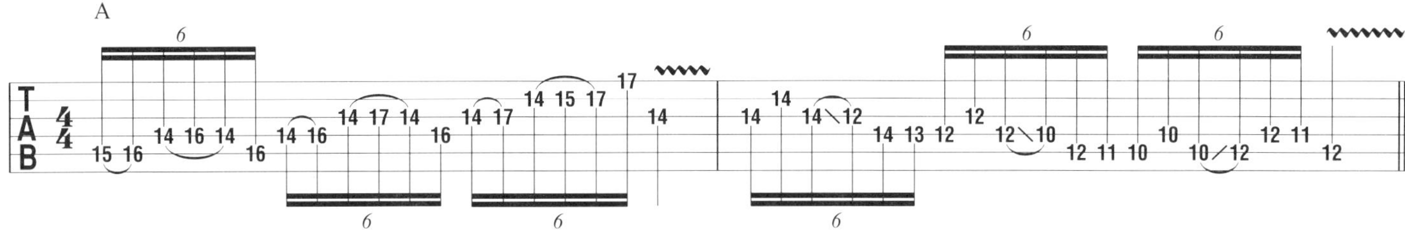


**267: Doublestop Heaven**

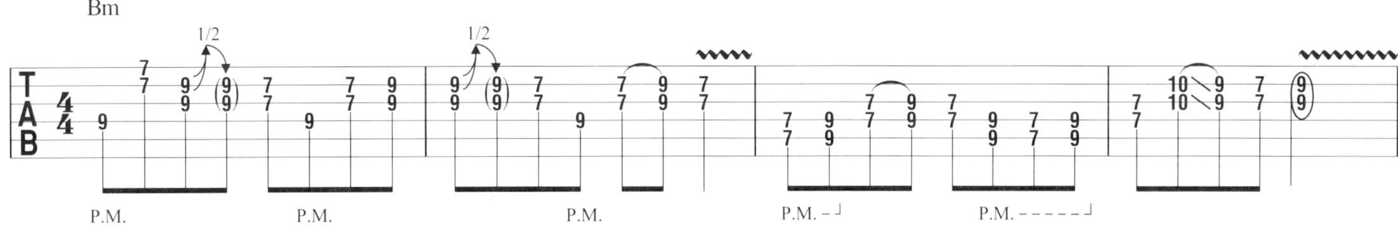


**268: Shredlicious**

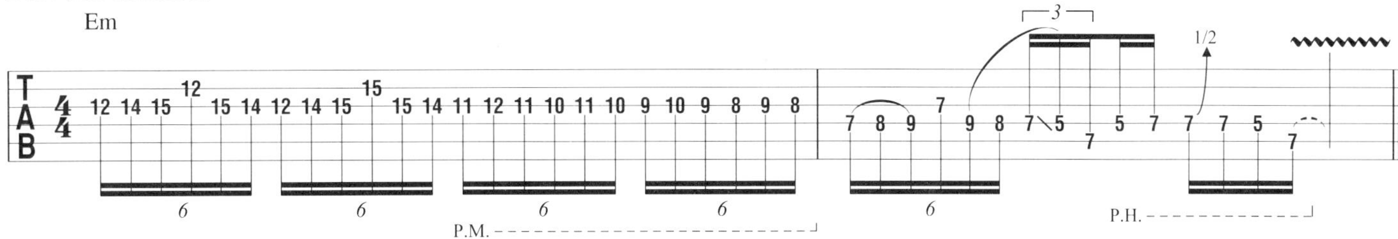


**269: Wild Overbends**

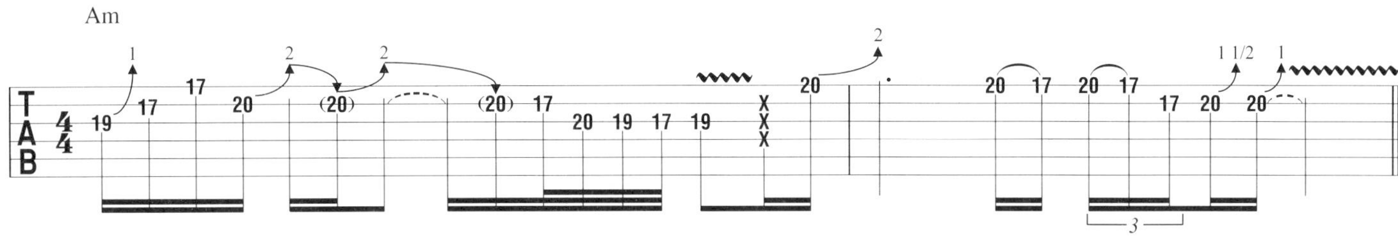

### 270: Phrygian Fantasy

Bm

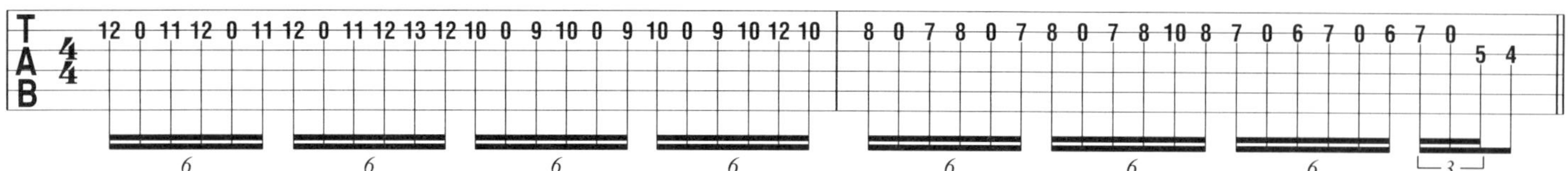

### 271: Diminished Doom

D°7

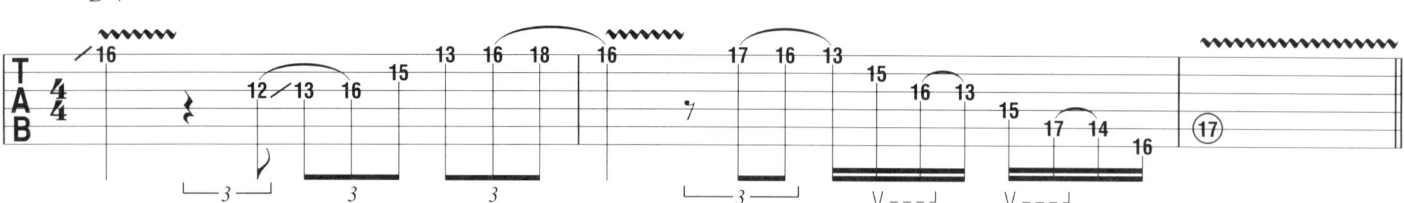

### 272: Sweeps It!

E°7

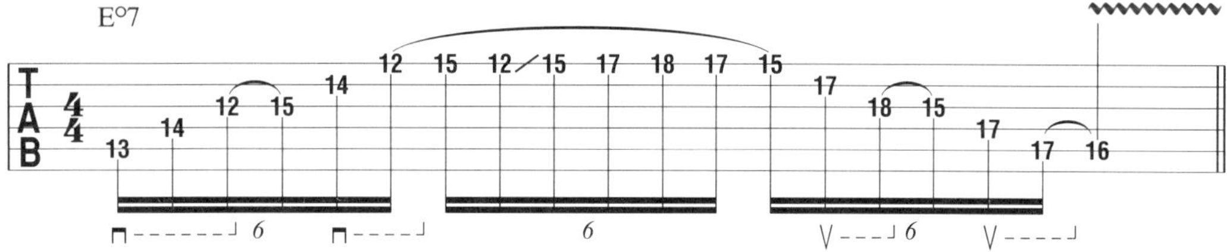

### 273: Silky Smooth

Em

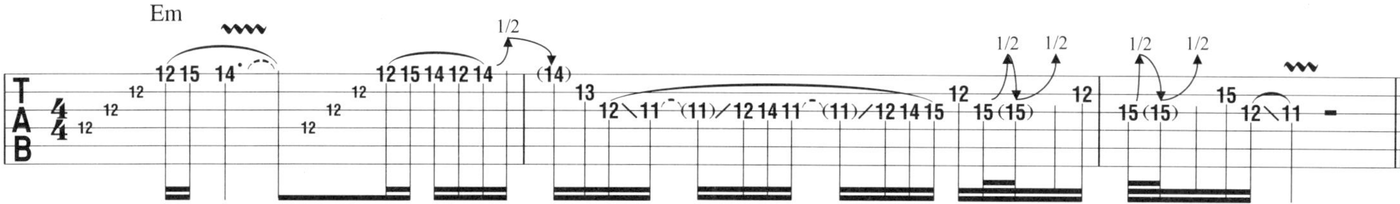

### 274: Blazing Phrasing

Dm

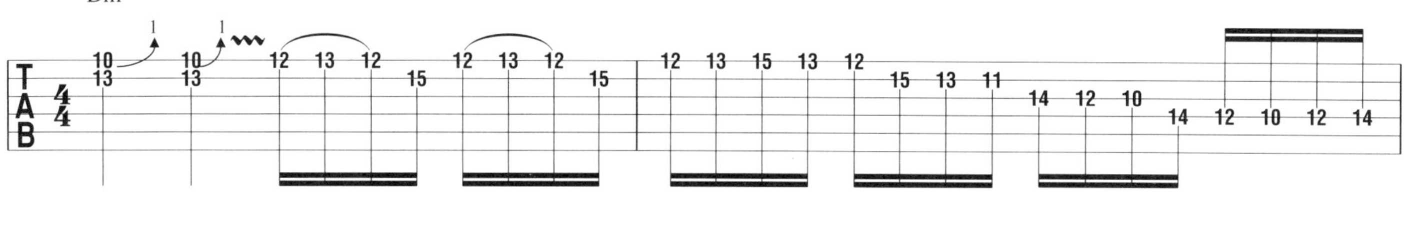

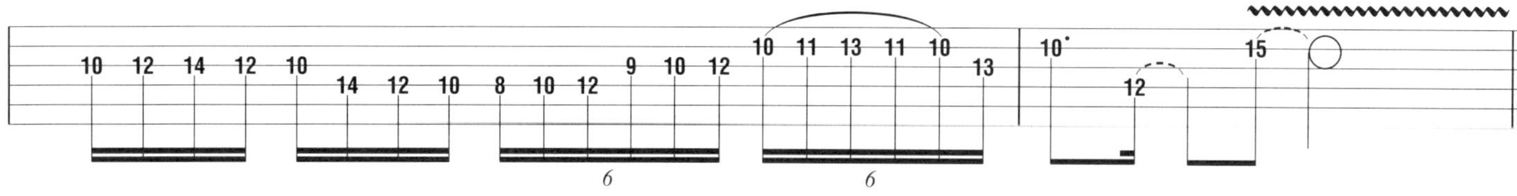

### 275: Minor Sequence

Dm

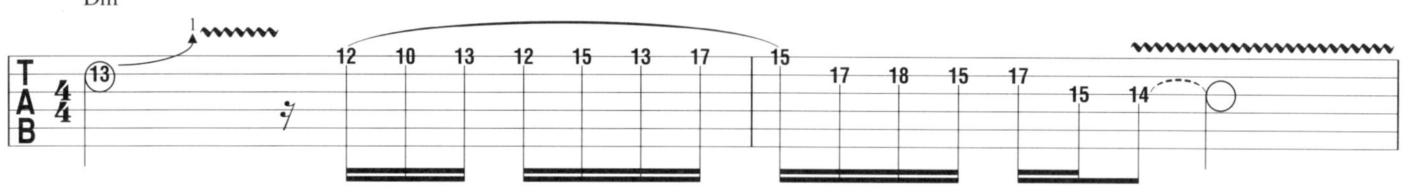

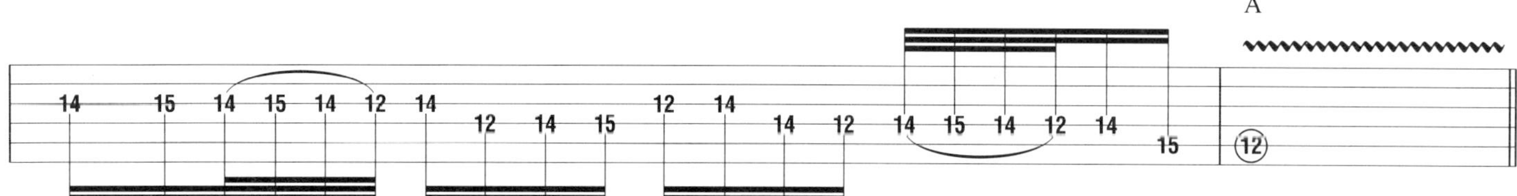

**276: Stop-Time Rock**

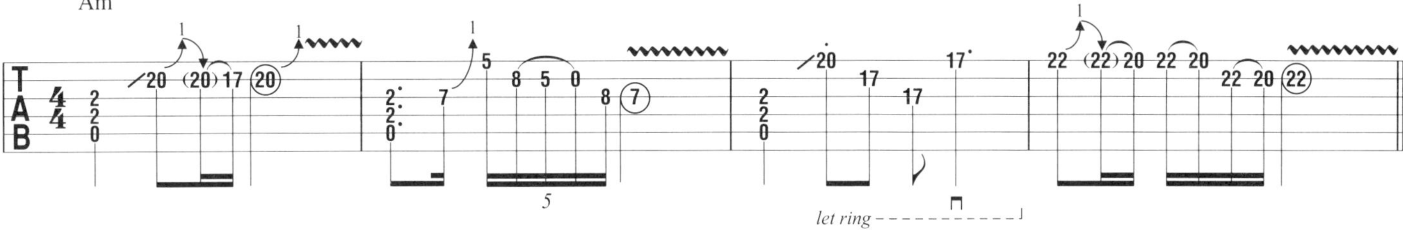


**277: Complex Tap**

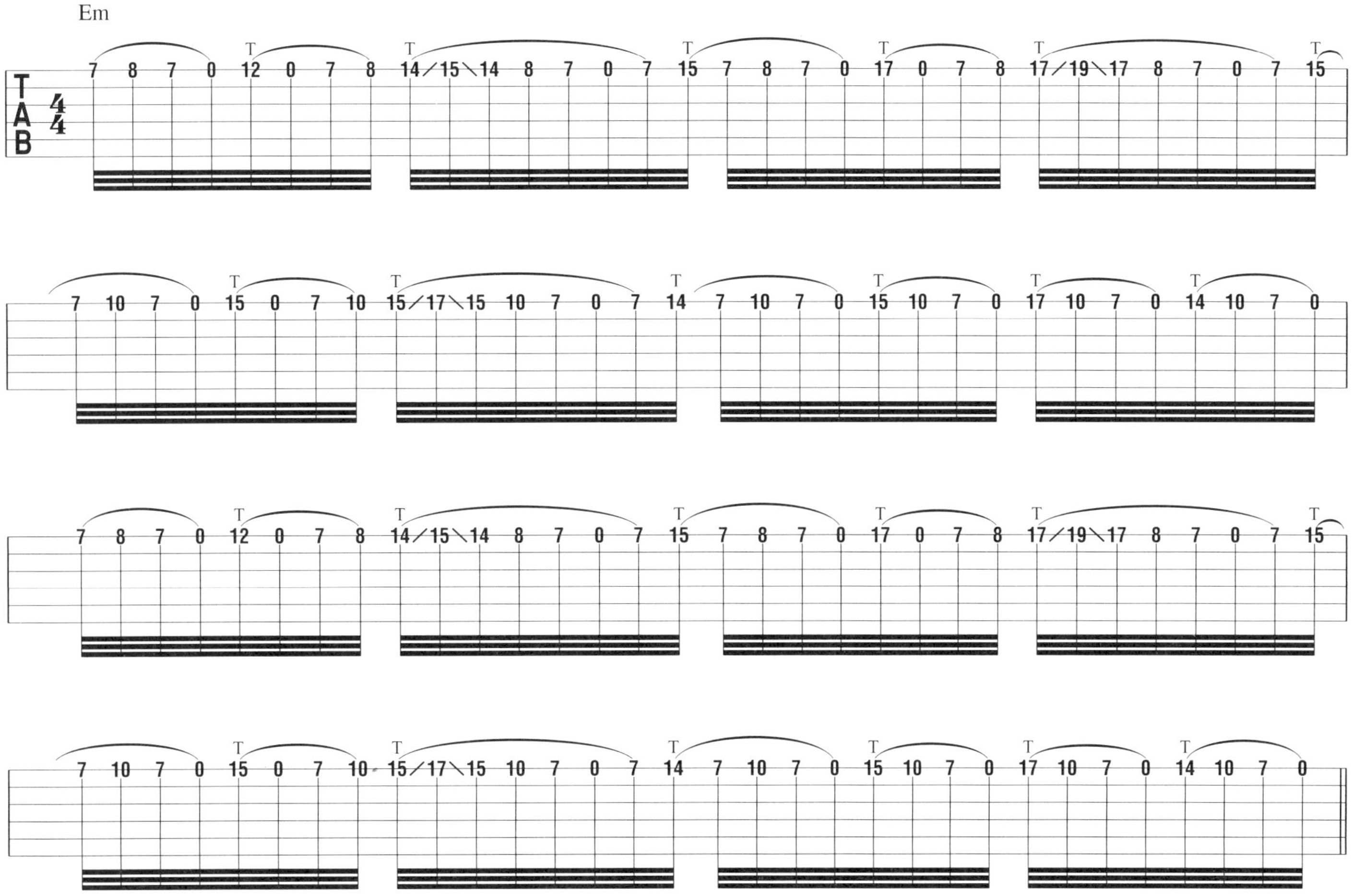

Em

**278: Death Tap**

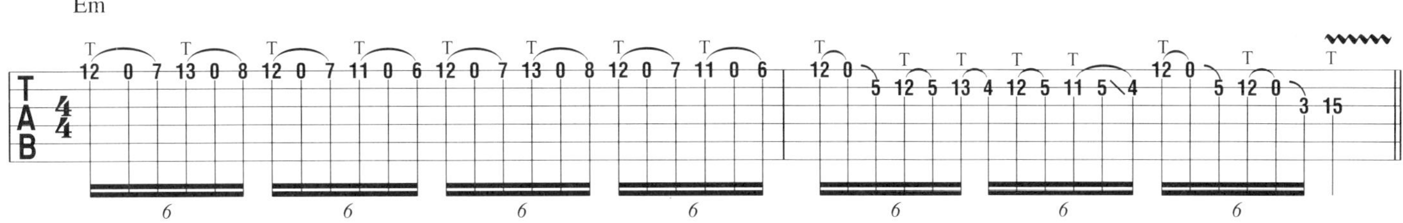


**279: Minor Sweep**

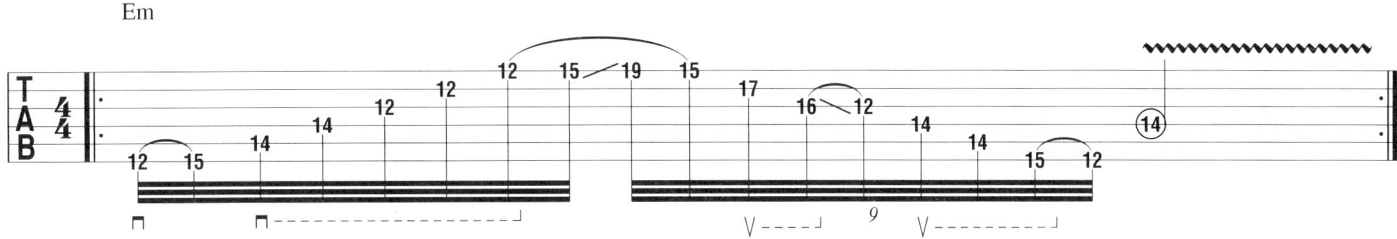

### 280: Aggro-Run

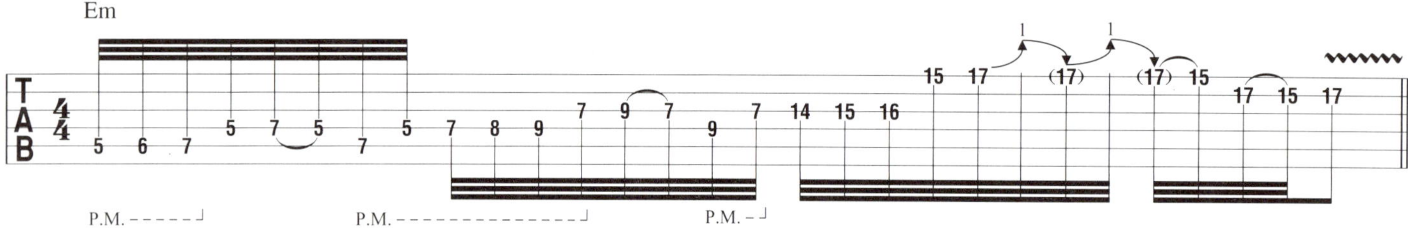


## Instructor: Greg Harrison

### 281: Hybrid Shred

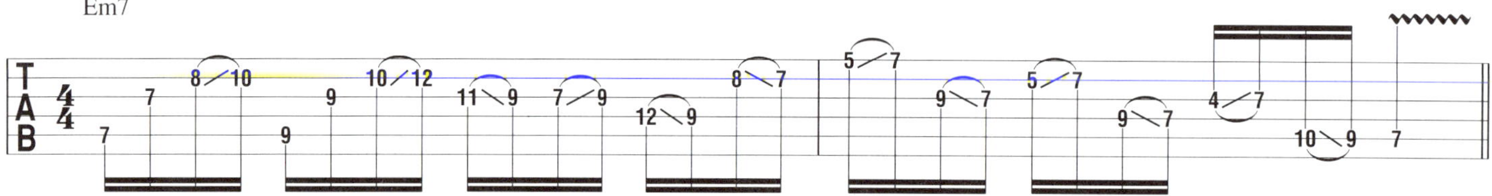


### 282: Stretch & Skip

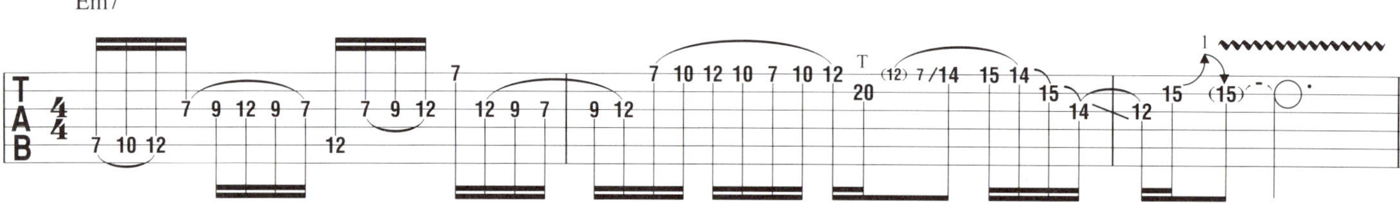


### 283: Speedy Sweep

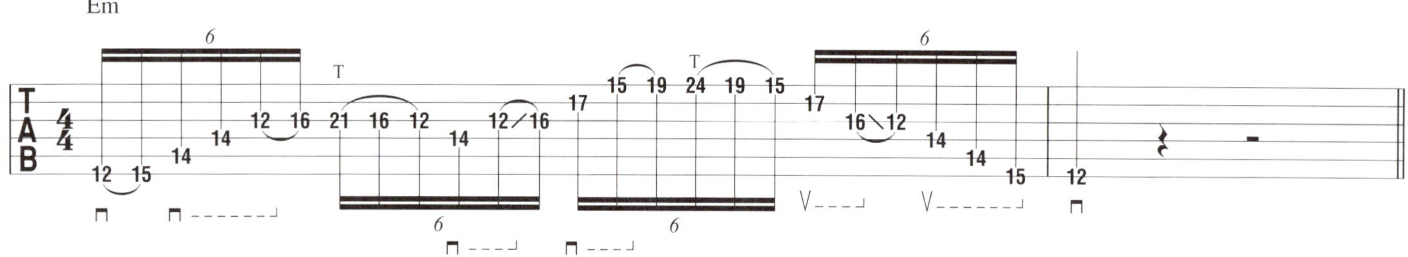


### 284: Don't Blink

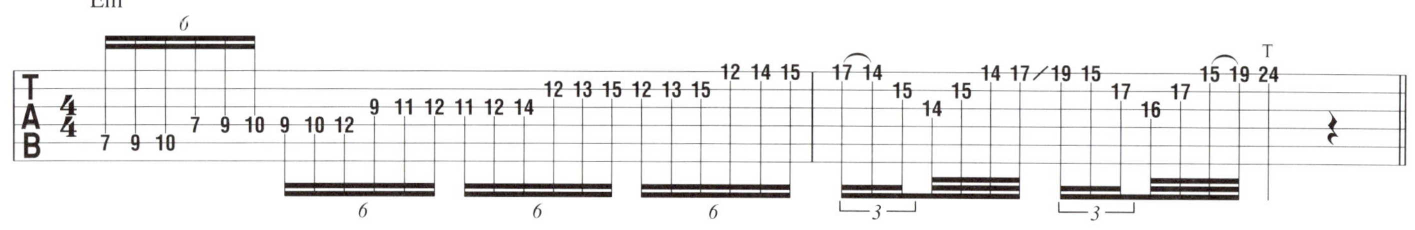


### 285: Chord Sweeper

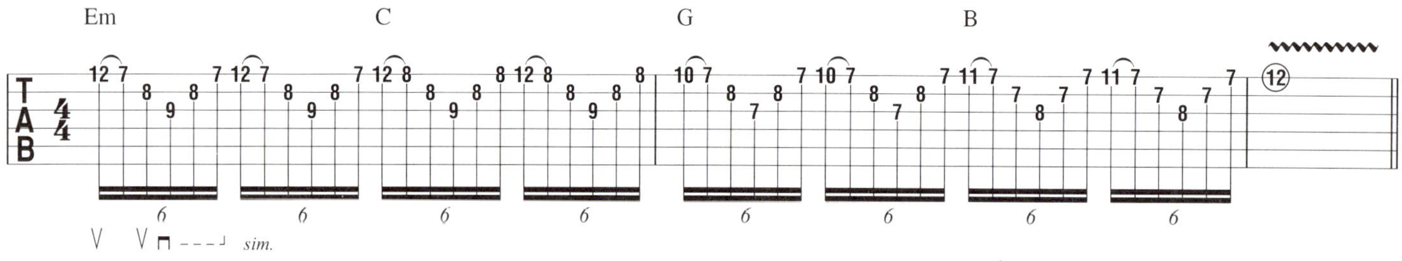

**286: Accelerant**

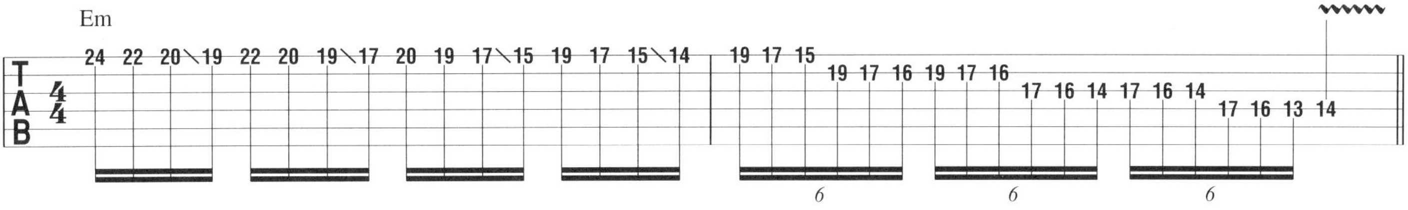

Em

**287: Sweep and Stretch**

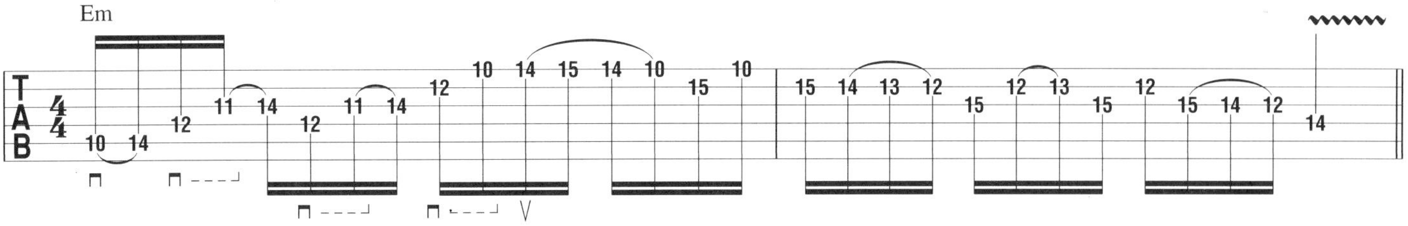

Em

**288: Killer Combo**

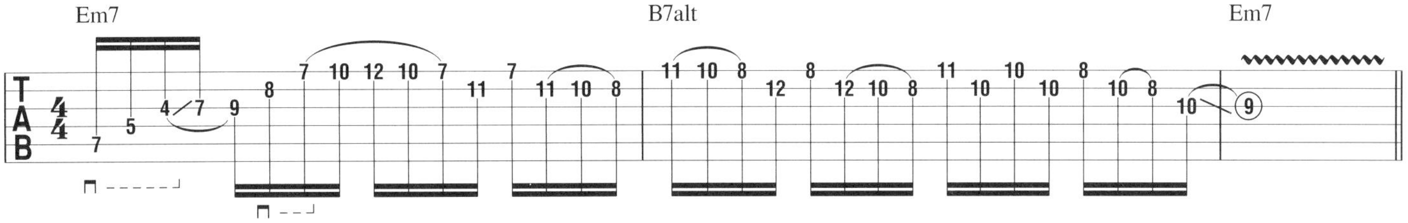

Em7 B7alt Em7

**289: Penta-Pedal**

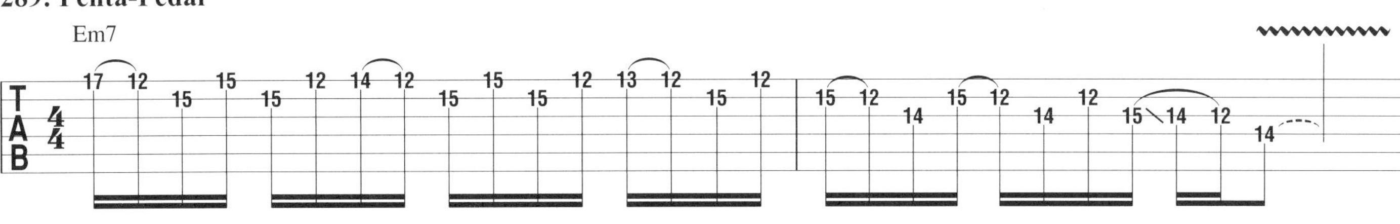


**290: Fancy Fretwork**

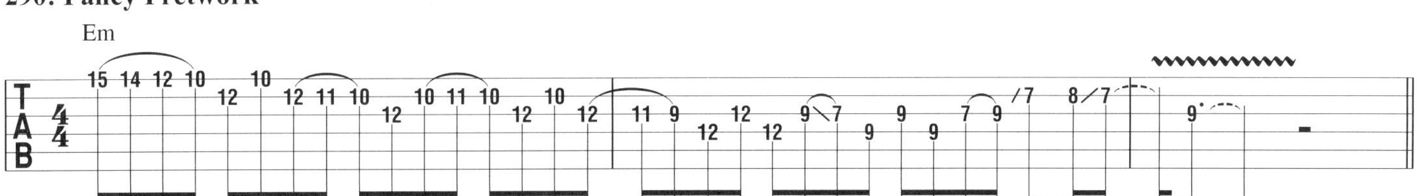


**291: Blazing Arps**

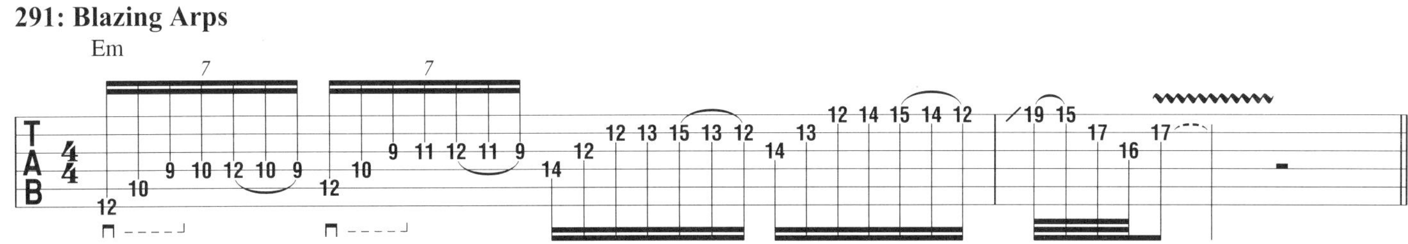


**292: Eye Opener**

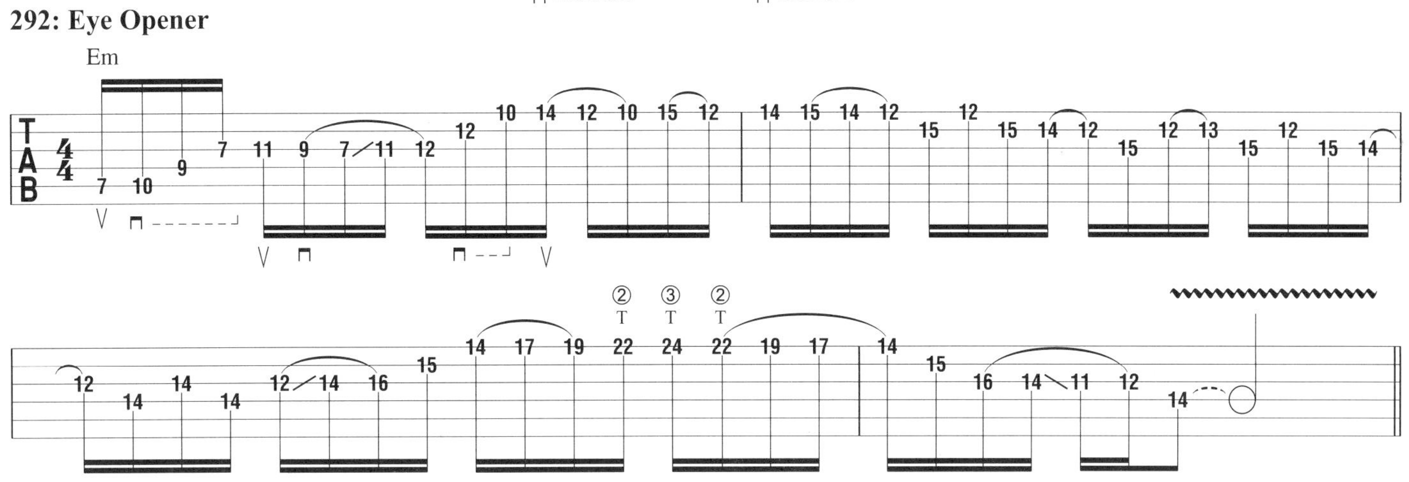

**293: Neo-Classic**

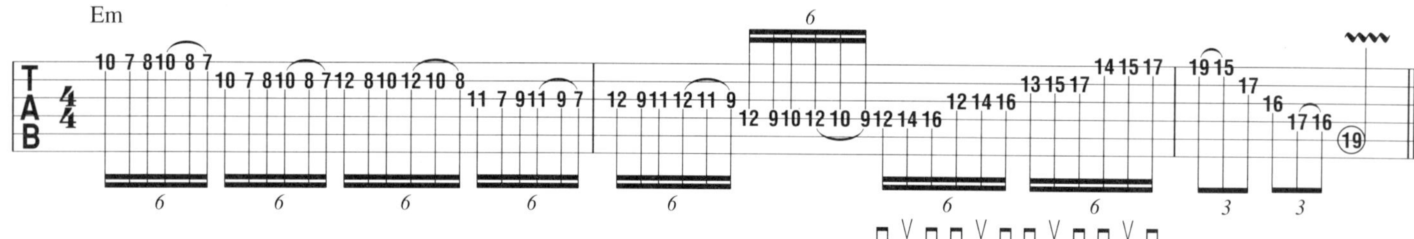


**294: Hybrid Peddler**

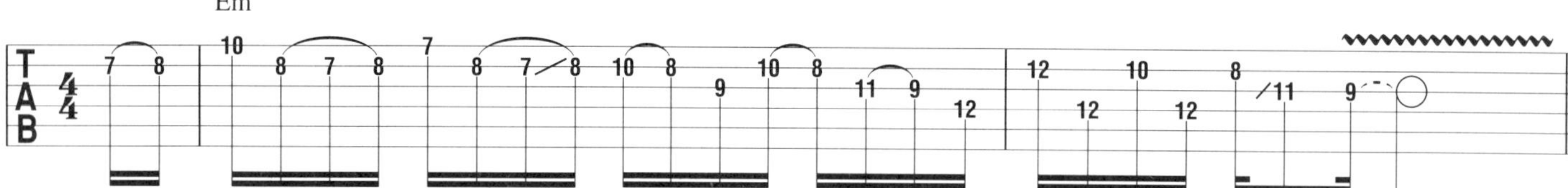


**295: Legato Power**

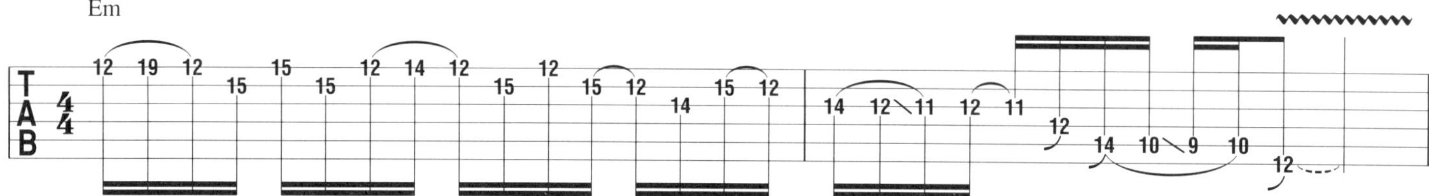


**296: Dimebag Flavor**

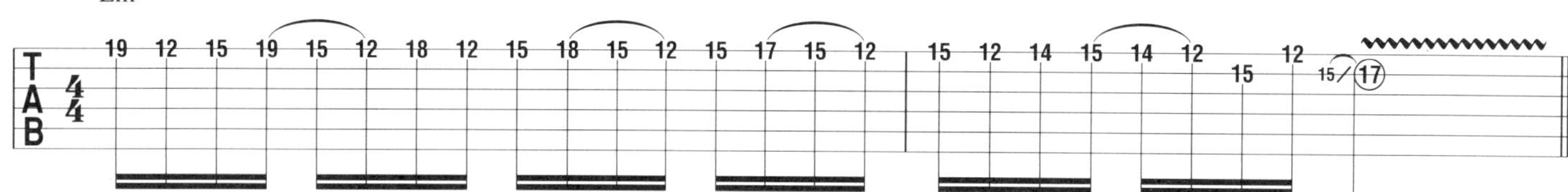


**297: Gambale Gunfire**

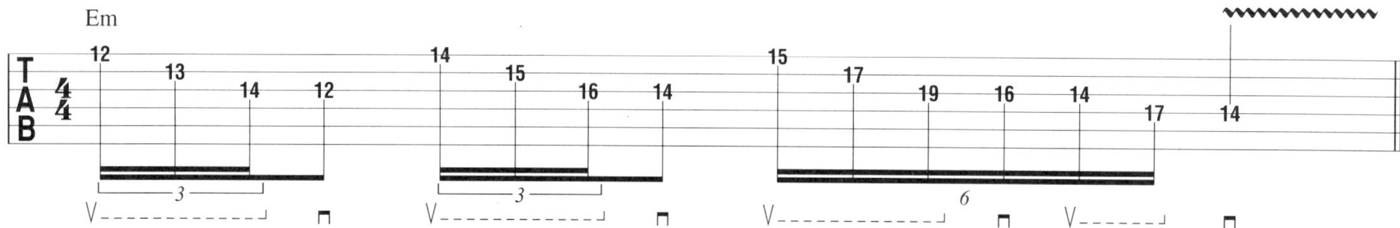


**298: Jaw Dropper**

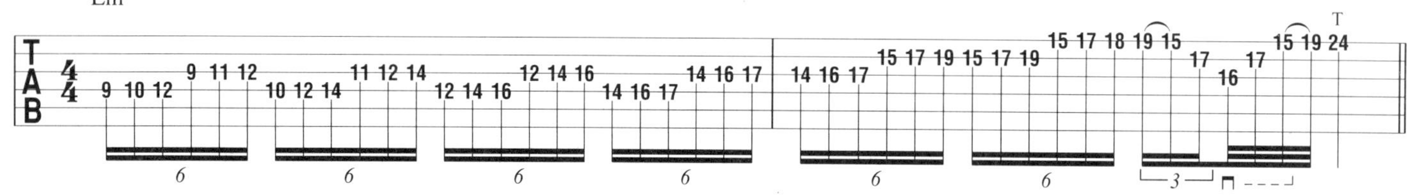


**299: Gambale Sweeps**

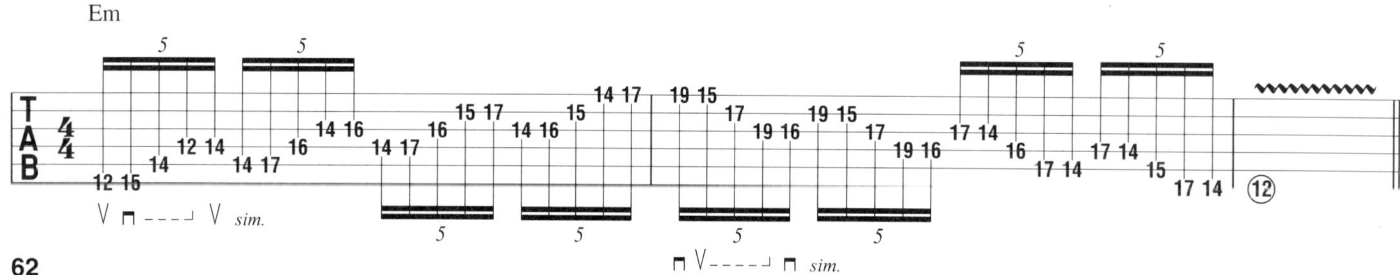

**300: Quintuple Chaos**

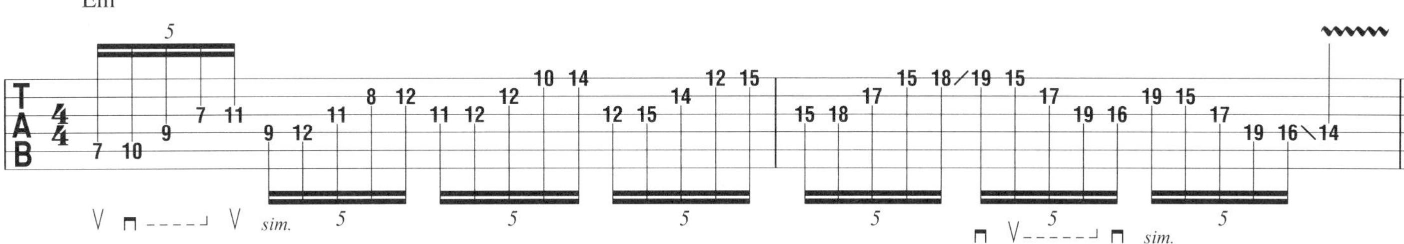


**301: Lydian Blues**

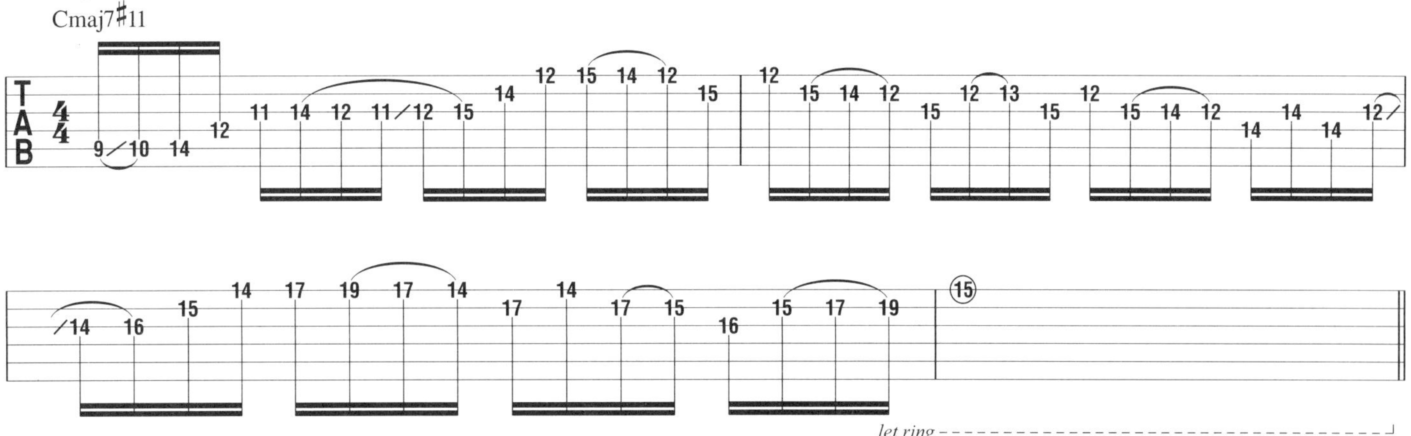


**302: Lydian Ascent**

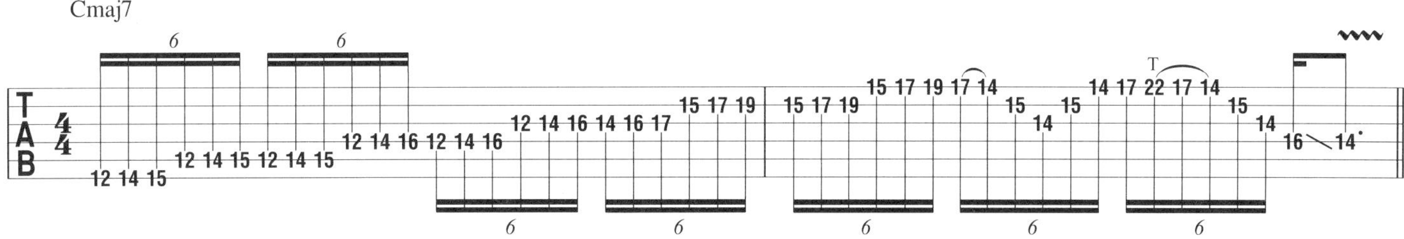


**303: Lydian Metal**

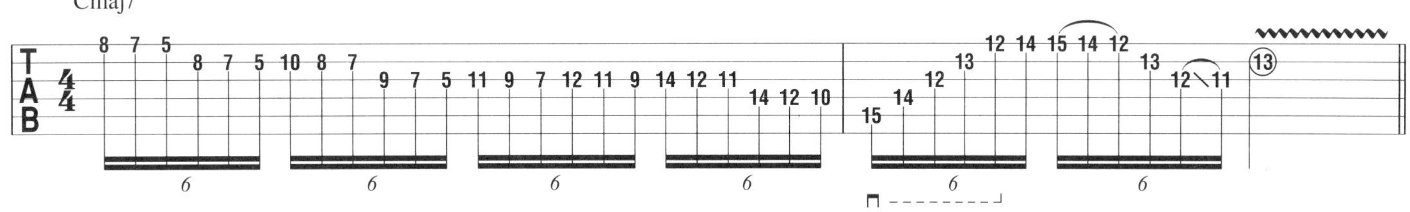


**304: Lydian Surprise**

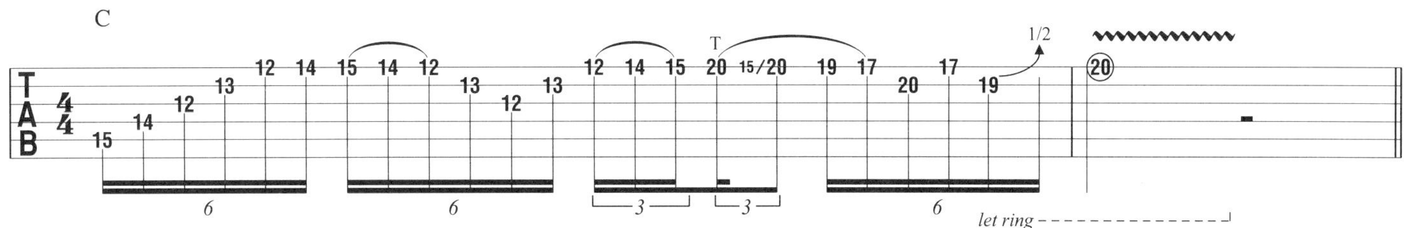


**305: Lydian Madness**

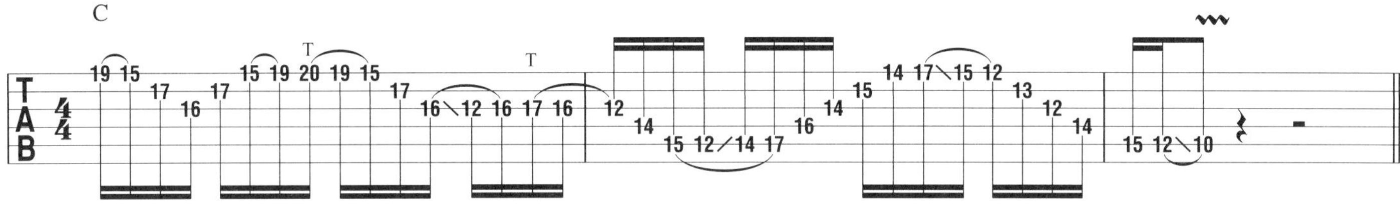

**306: Sweep & Descend**

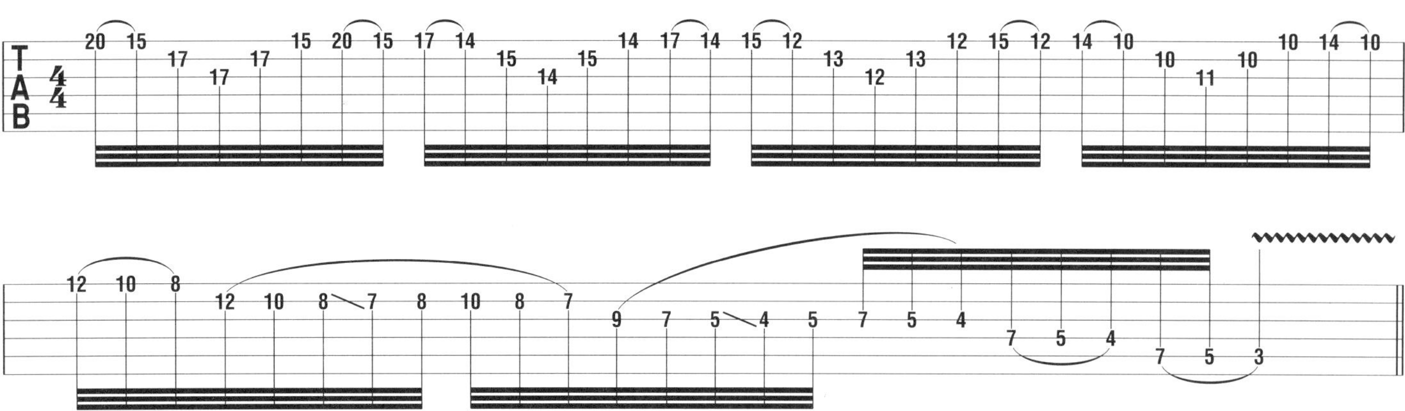


**307: Intervallic Shred**

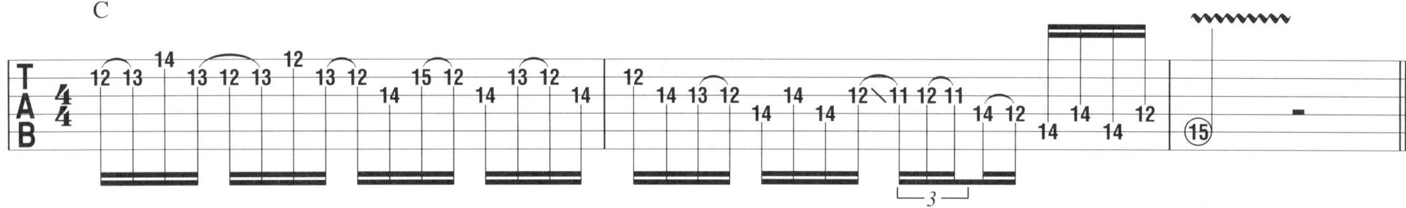


**308: Sequential Climb**

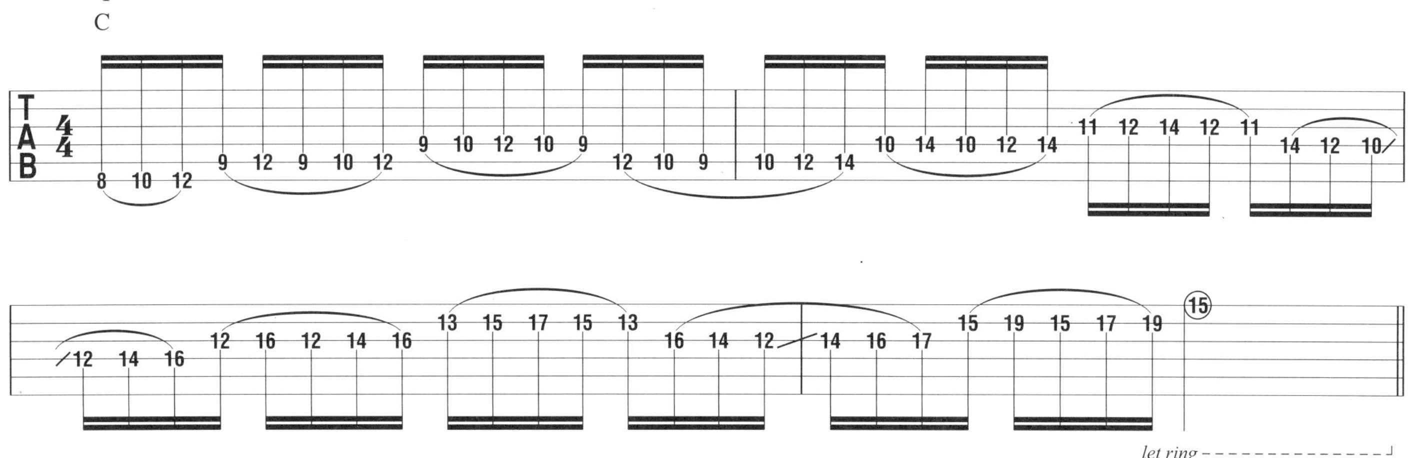


**309: Pedals of Dover**

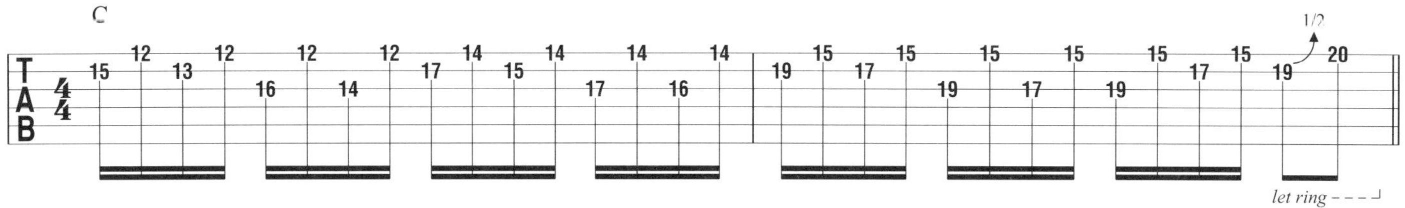


**310: 5ths Melody**

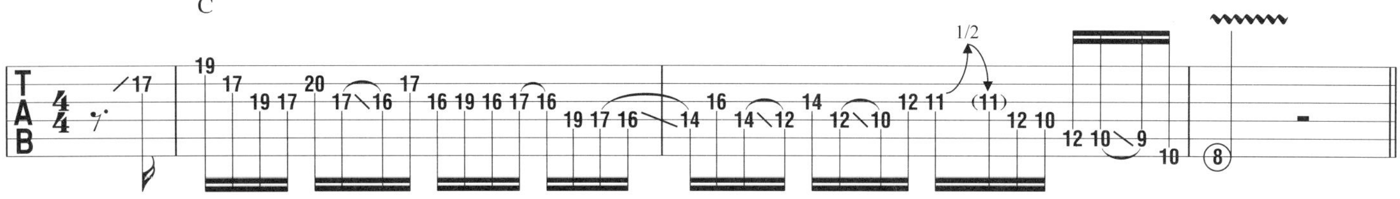

**311: Vai Slides**

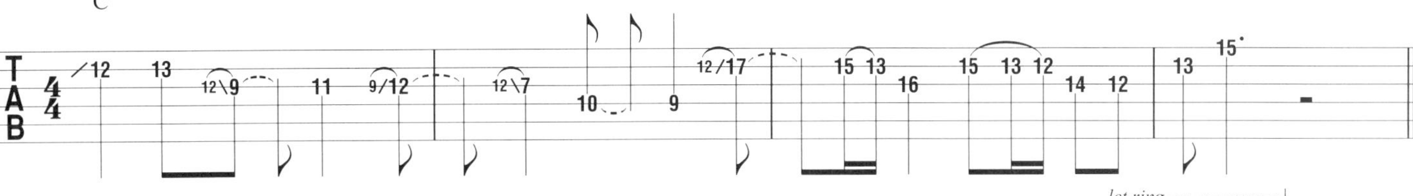


**312: Legati Satriani**

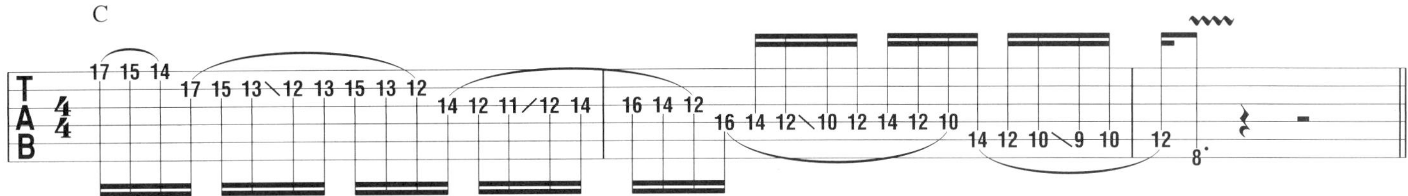


**313: Intervallica**

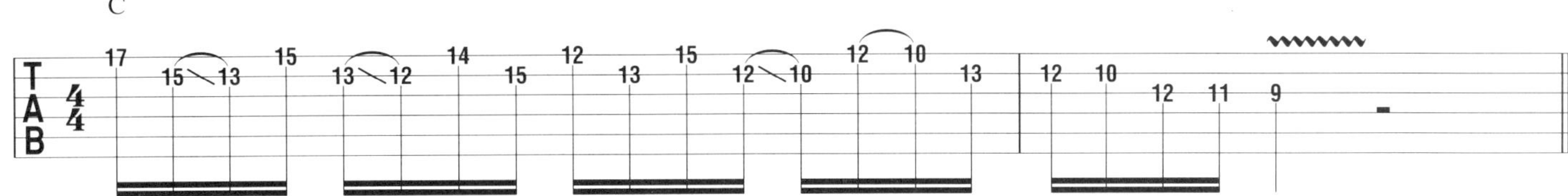


**314: Sliding Sequence**

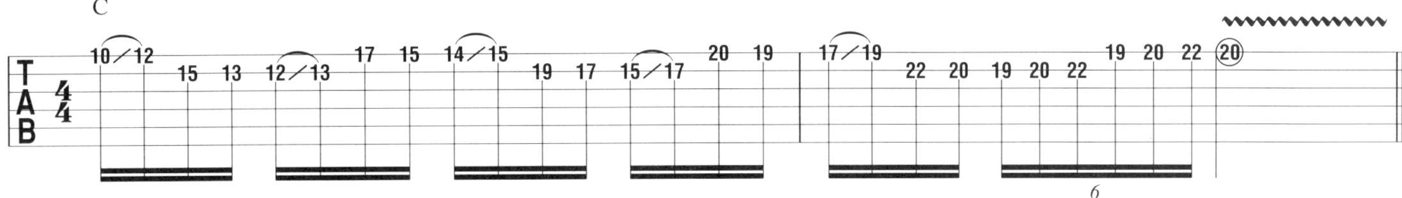


**315: Serpentine 6ths**

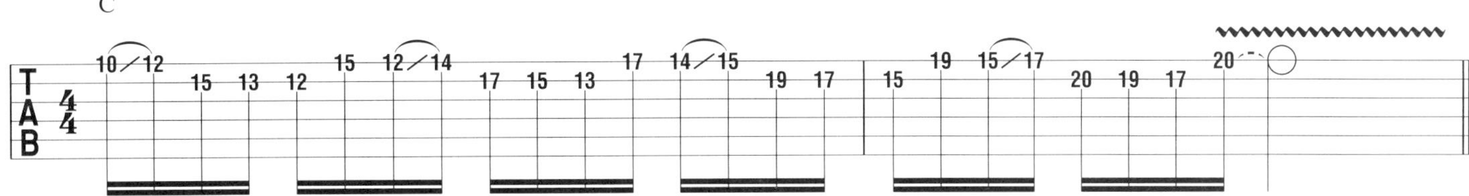


**316: Fretboarding**

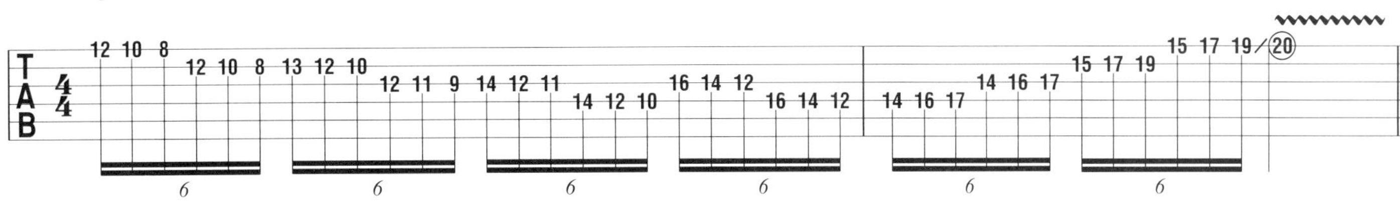


**317: Swept Away**

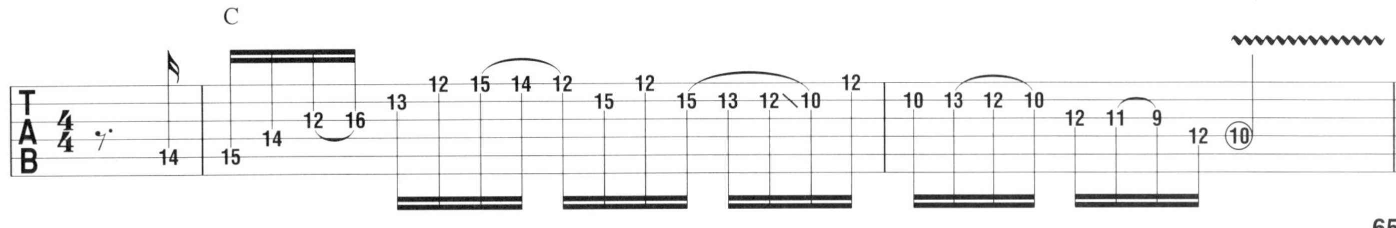

### 318: All Praise Gilbert

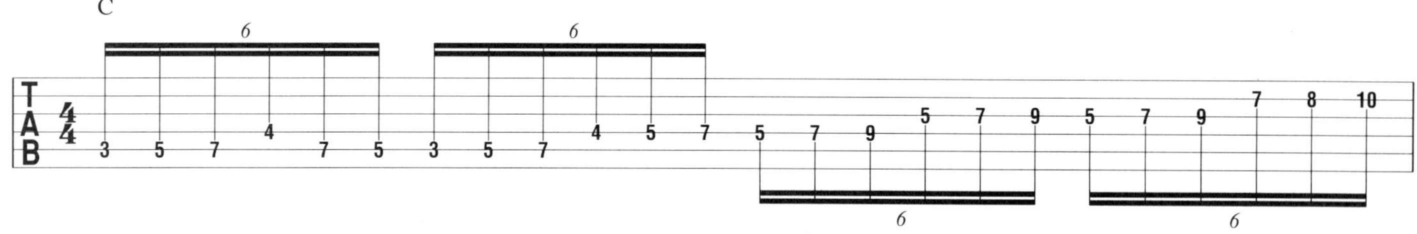


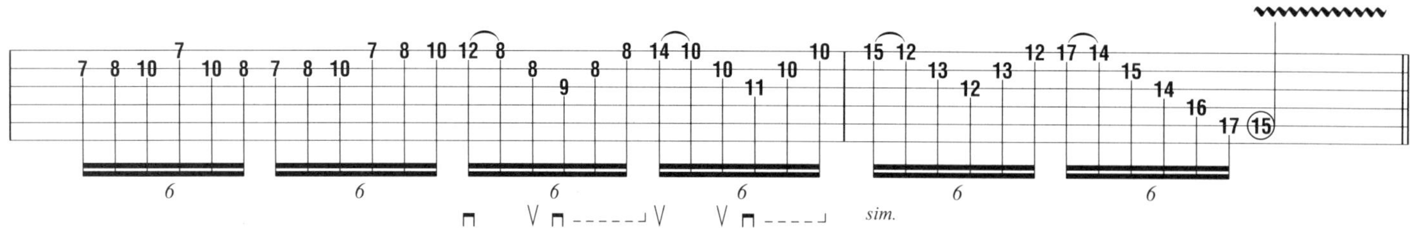


### 319: Fretboard Creeper

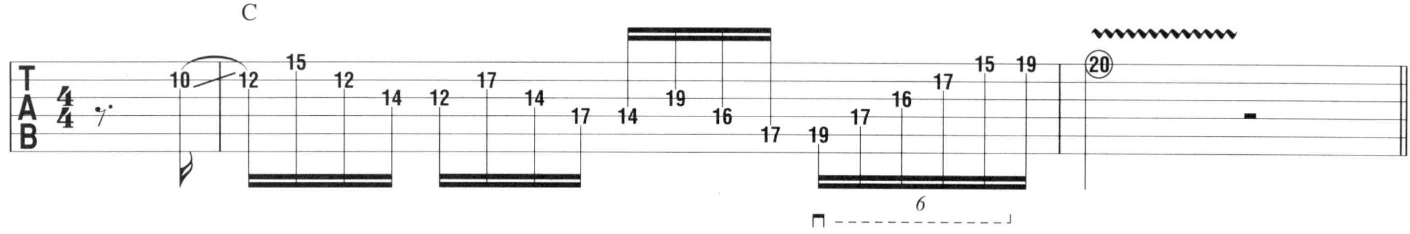


### 320: Pick, Skip, Repeat

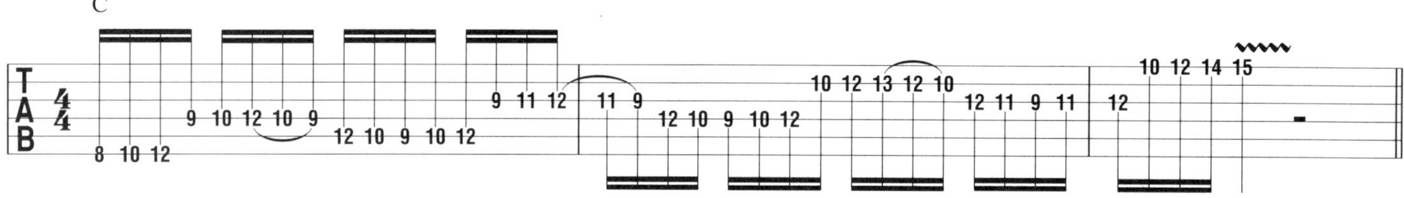


### 321: Mixo-Melodic

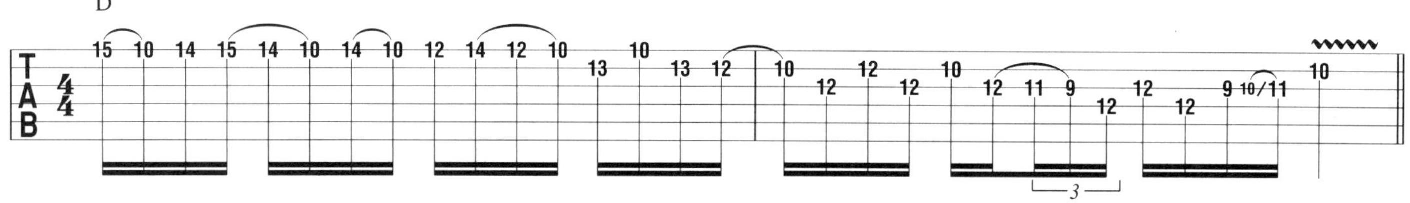


### 322: Outside the Box

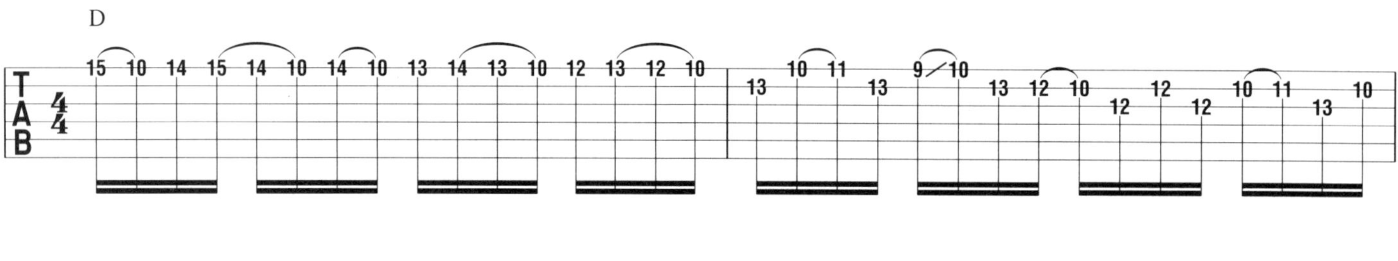


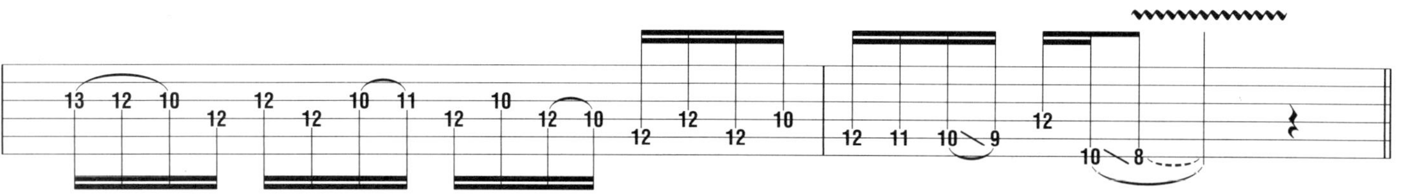

## 323: 3-Per-Stringer

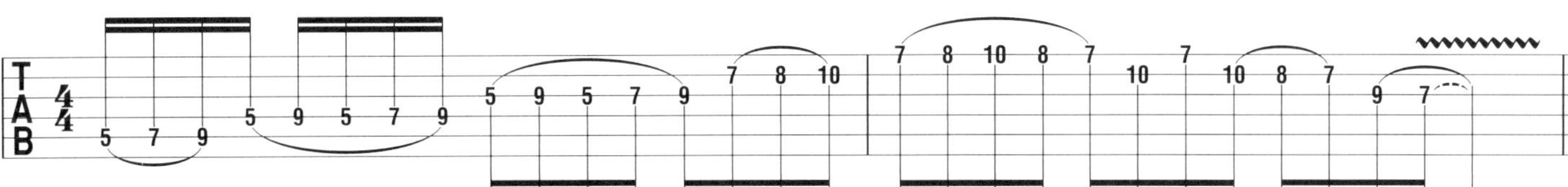

## 324: Melodic Climb

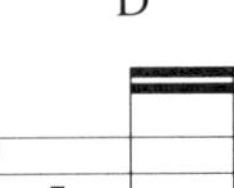

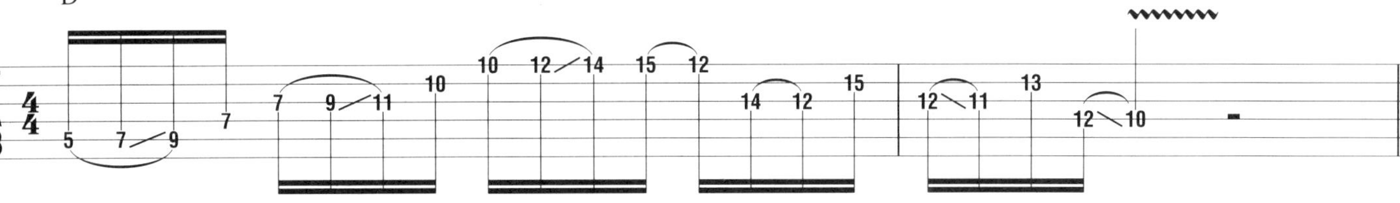

## 325: Speed Picker

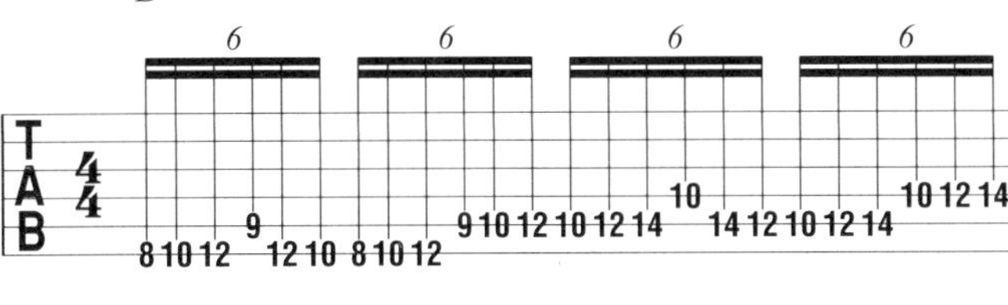

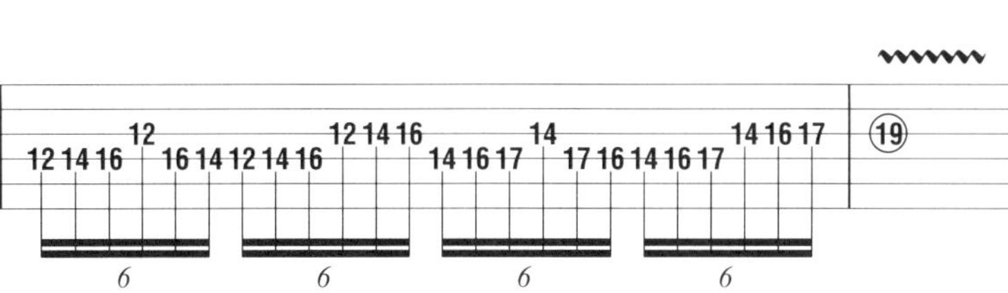

## 326: Triad Sweeps

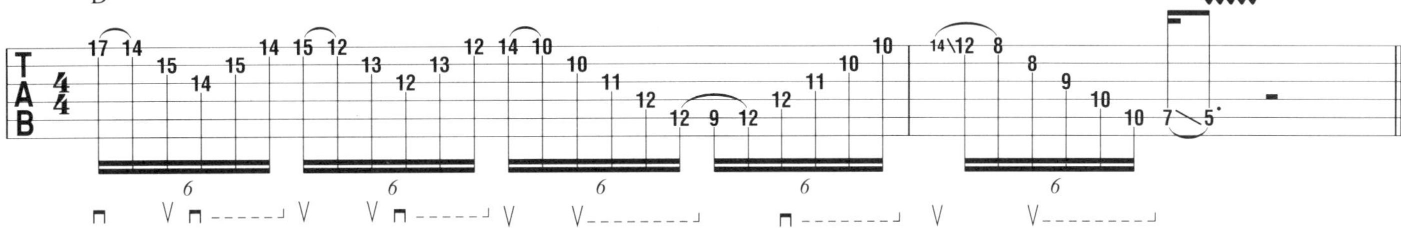

## 327: Fret Blazer

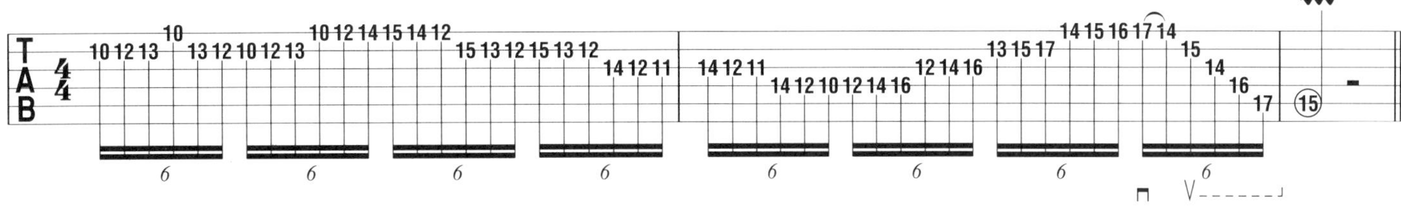

## 328: Legato Tap

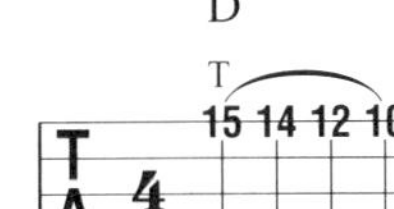

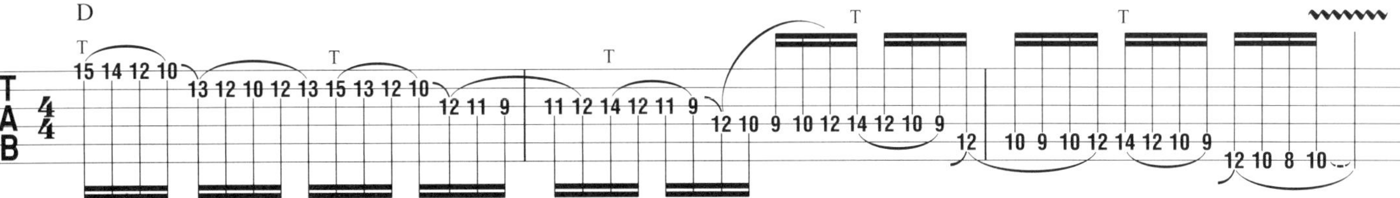

## 329: Mixo-Shred

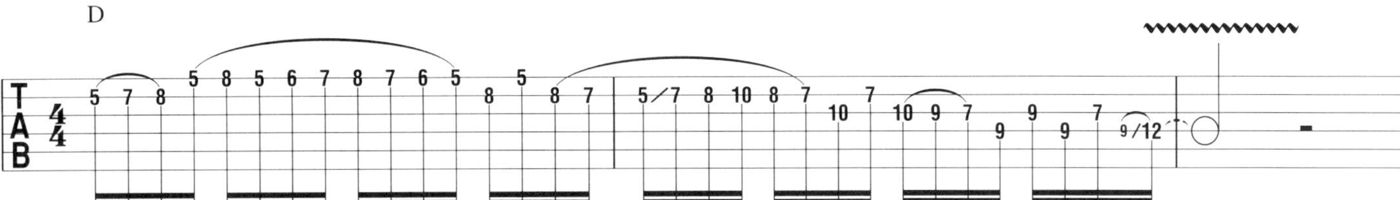

### 330: God Sweep

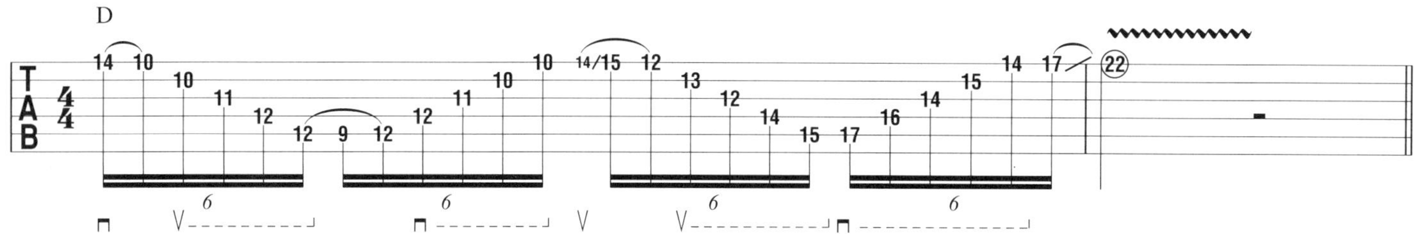


### 331: Penta-Wow

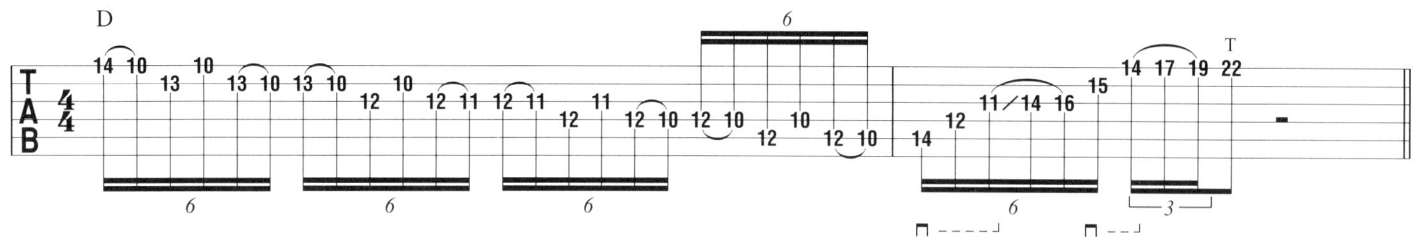


### 332: Hybrid Legato

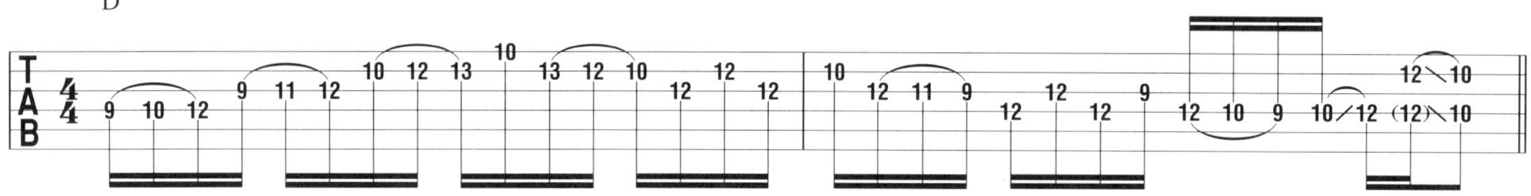


### 333: Sliding Intervals

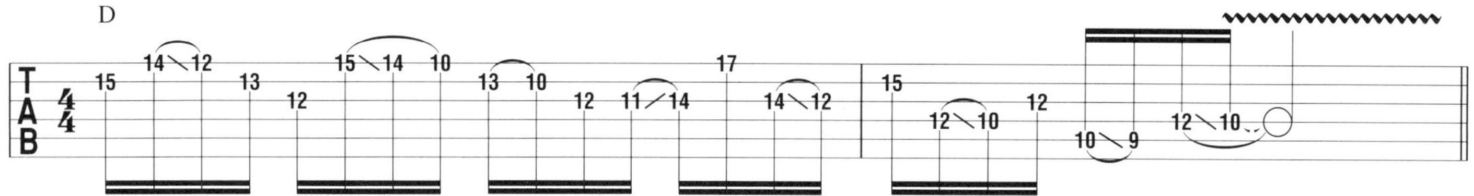


### 334: Dual Sequencer

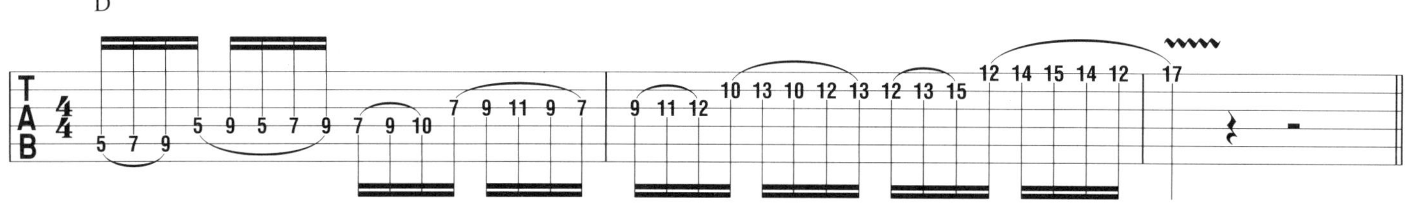


### 335: Cooley Quints

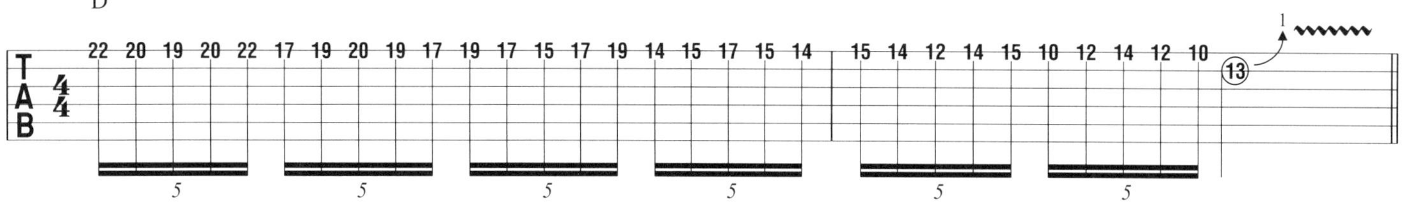


### 336: Bluesy Shred

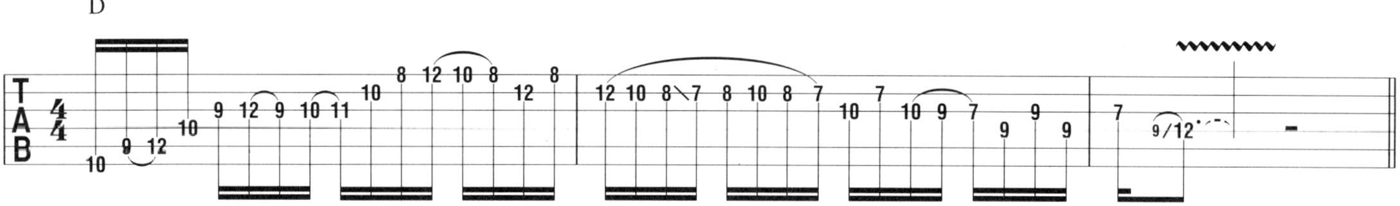

**337: Inside Picking**

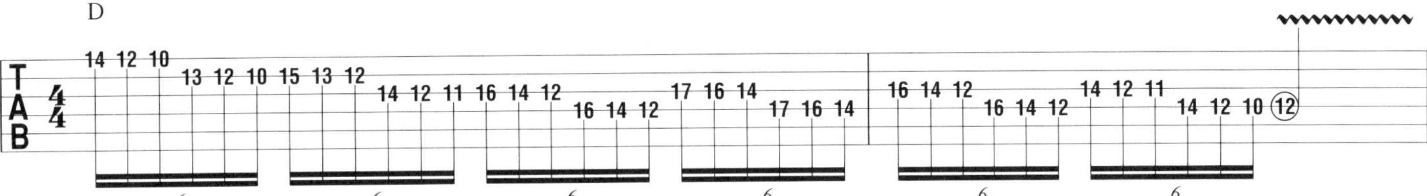


**338: Shred-Tastic**

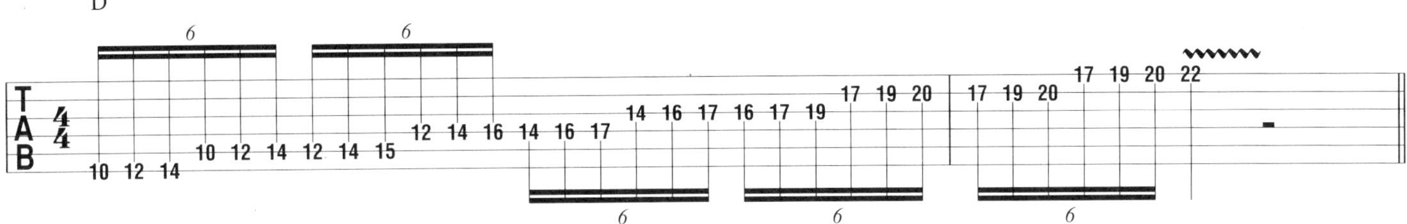


**339: Quintuplet Climb**

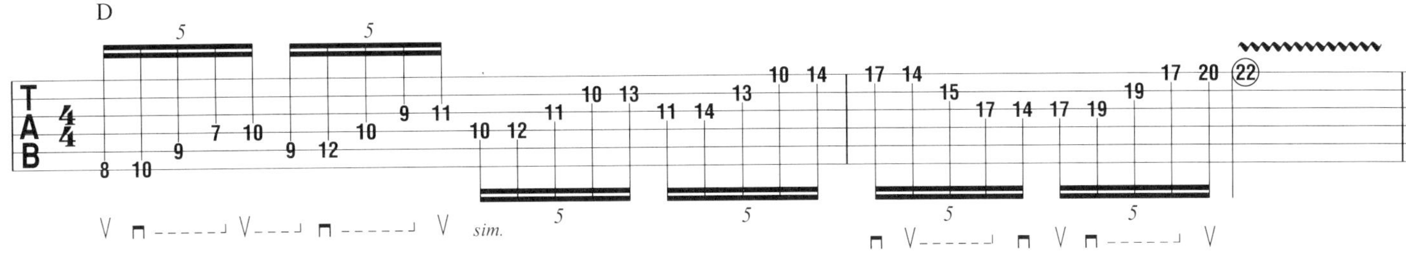


**340: Dorian Shred**

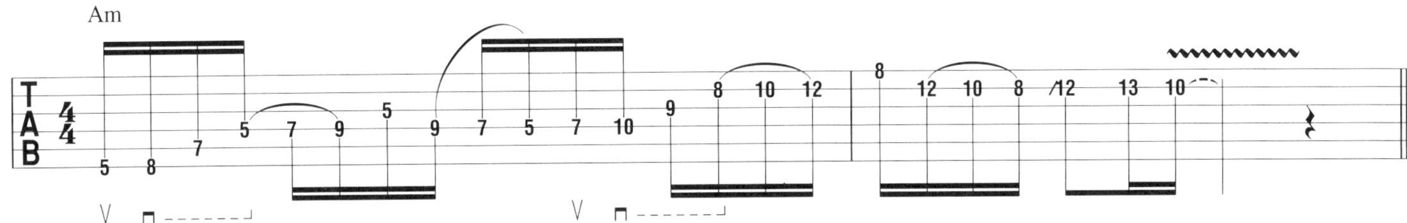


**341: Arpeggio Ascent**

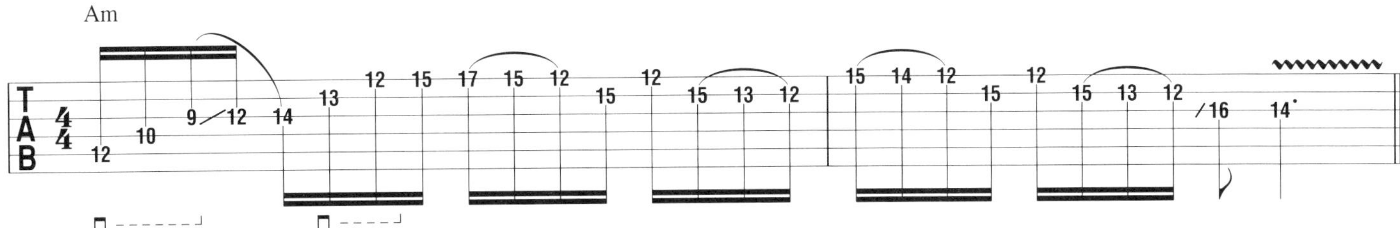


**342: Dorian Sequence**

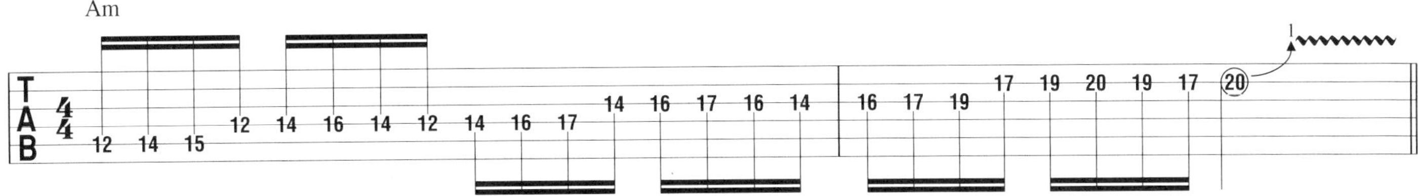


**343: Sliding Dorian**

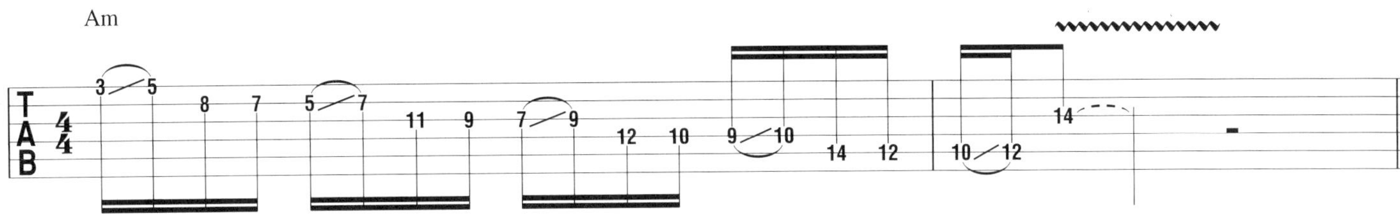

### 344: Gilbert Sequence

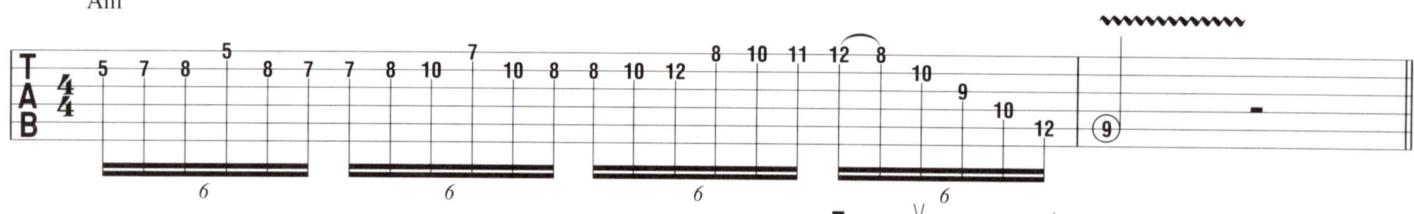

### 345: Dorian Thrash

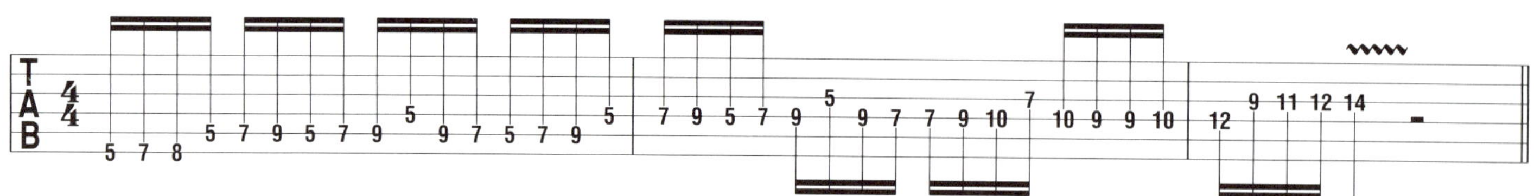

### 346: Sweep & Alternate

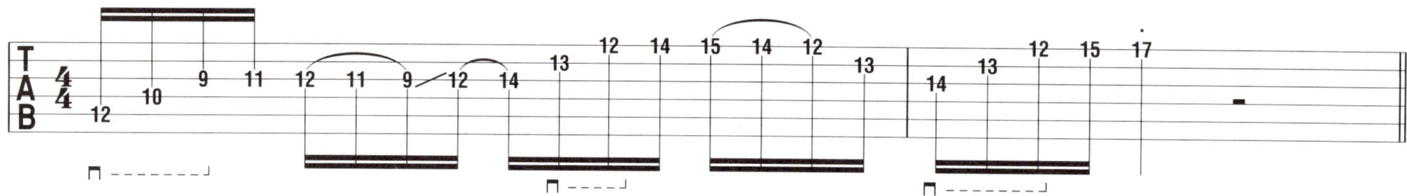


### 347: Fret Anarchy

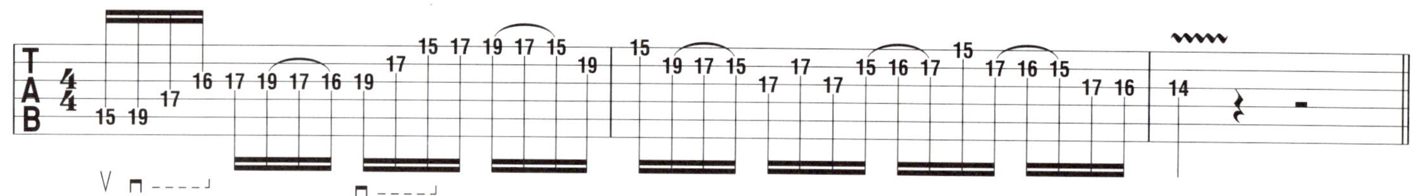

### 348: Yngwie Sequencer

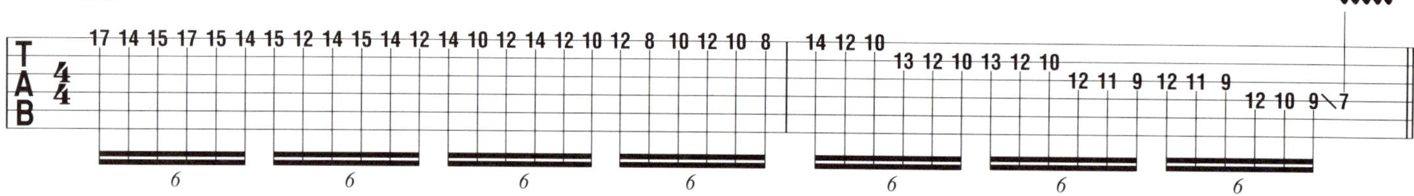


### 349: Speed Kills

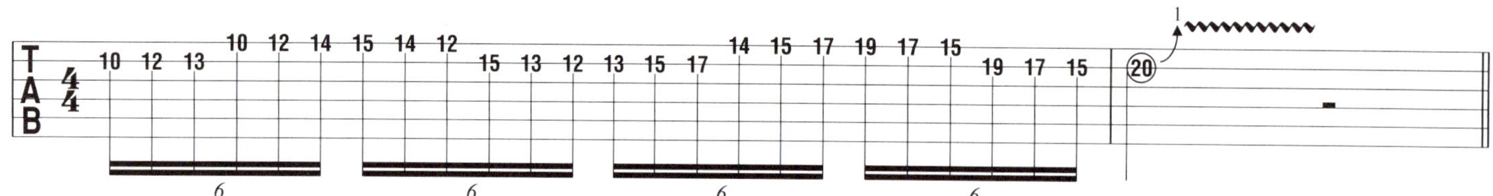


### 350: Phrygian Dominance

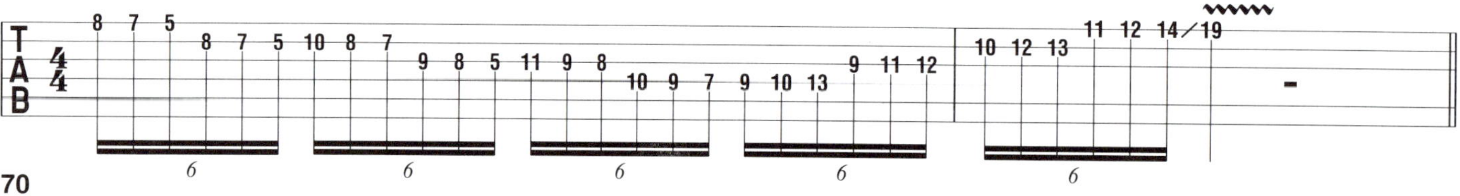

### 351: Fretboard Inferno

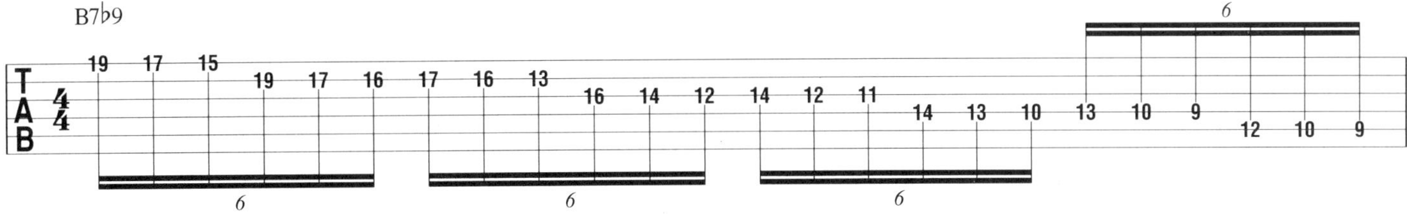


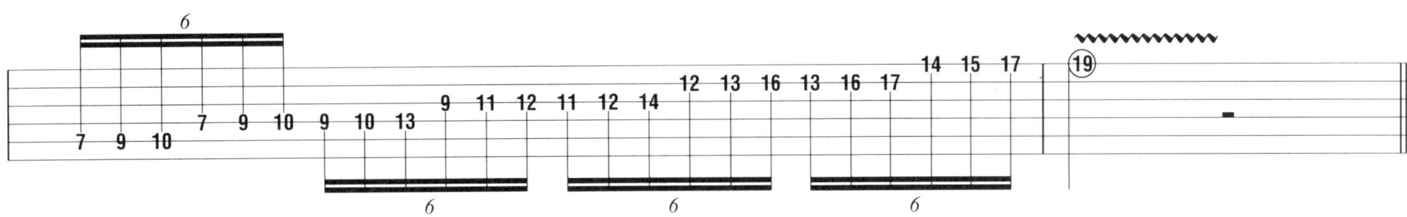

### 352: Frets Possessed

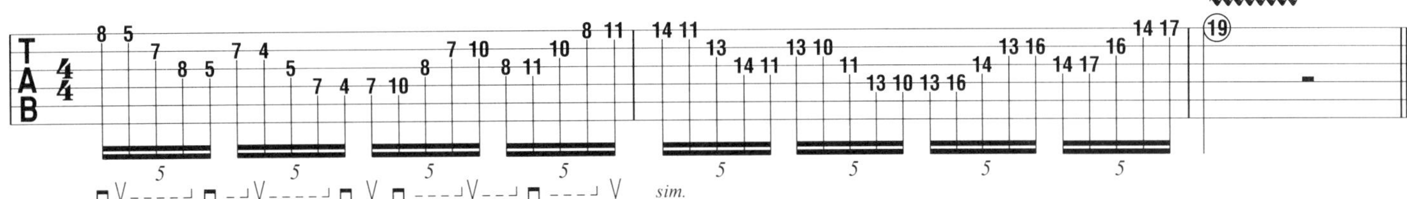


### 353: Phrygian Fire

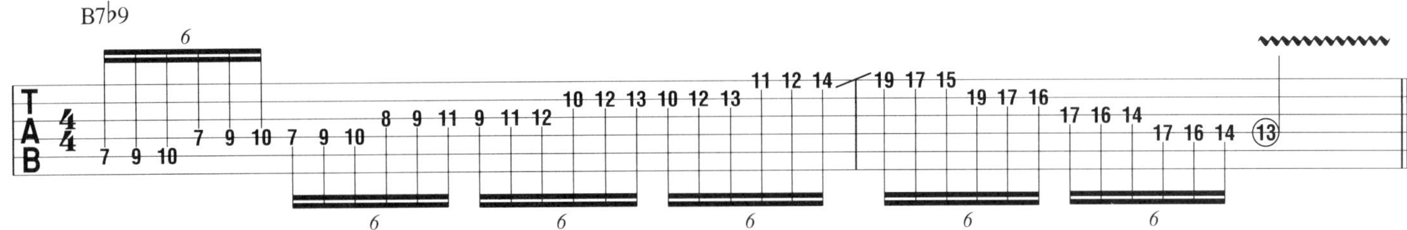


### 354: Diminished Ascent

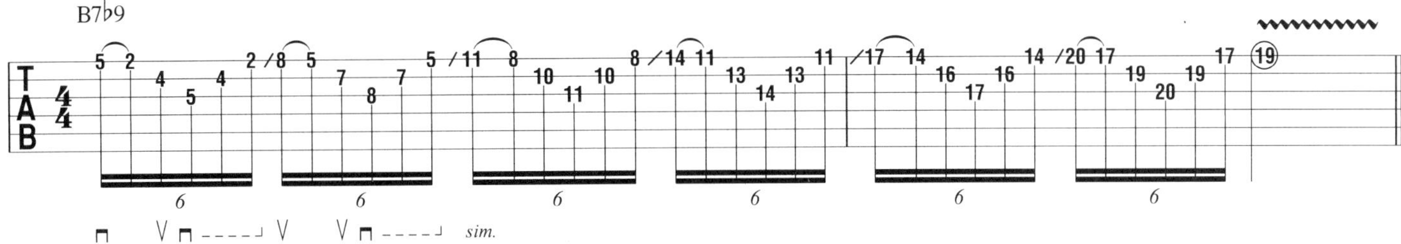


### 355: Bach Sequence

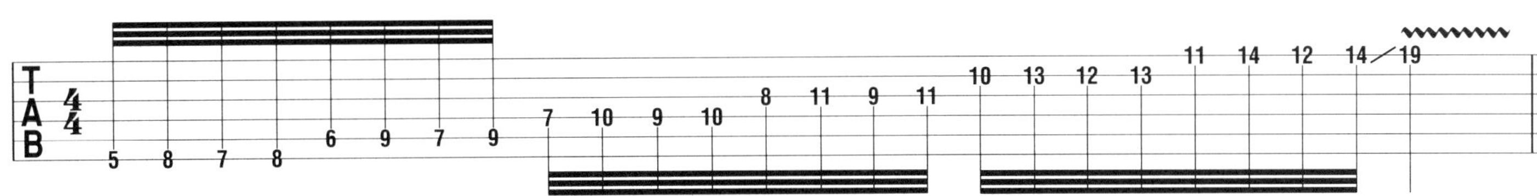


### 356: Classical Beast

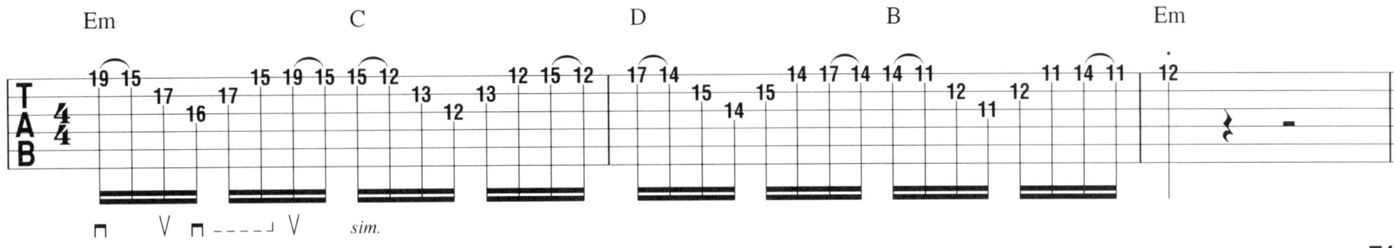

### 357: Quintastic

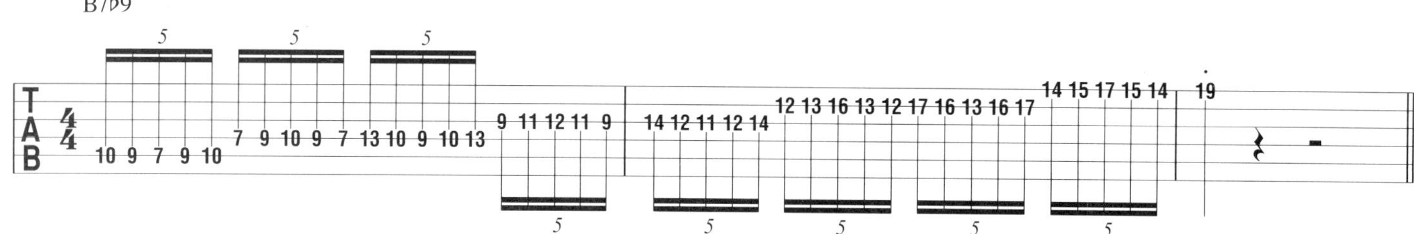


### 358: Double-Noting

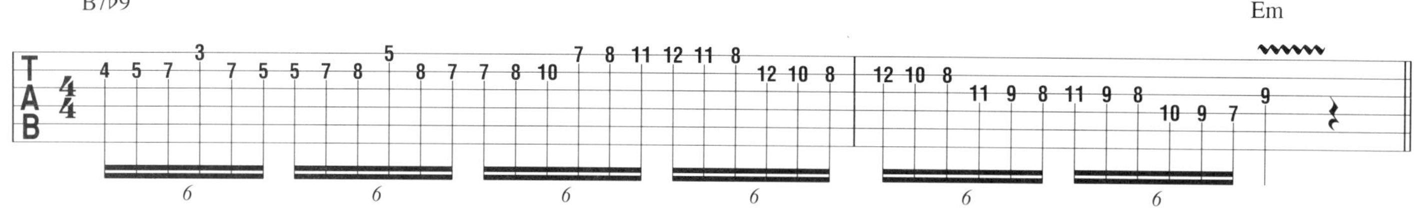


### 359: Classical Madness

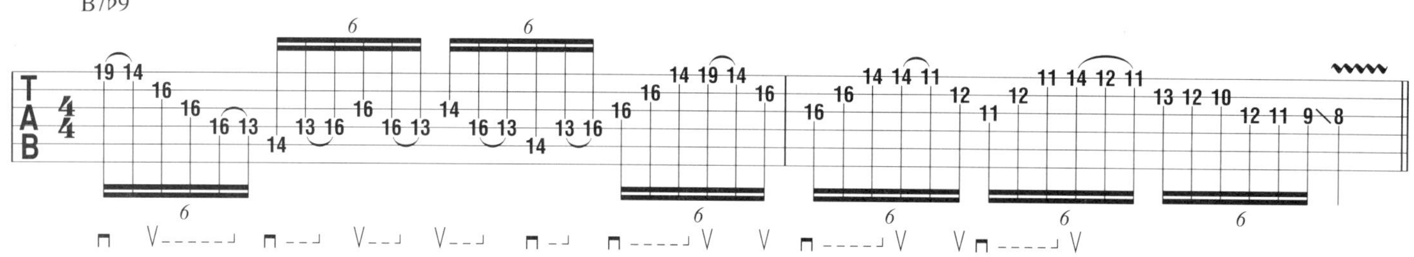


### 360: Shredology

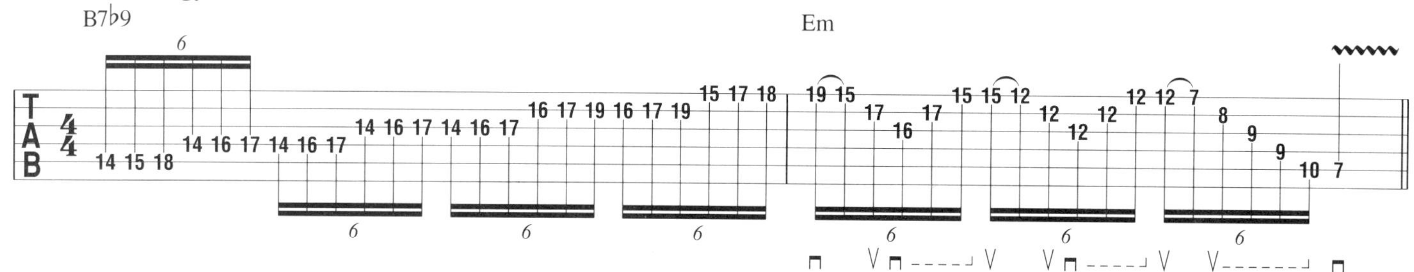


## Instructor: Matthew Schroeder

### 361: Pick Muting

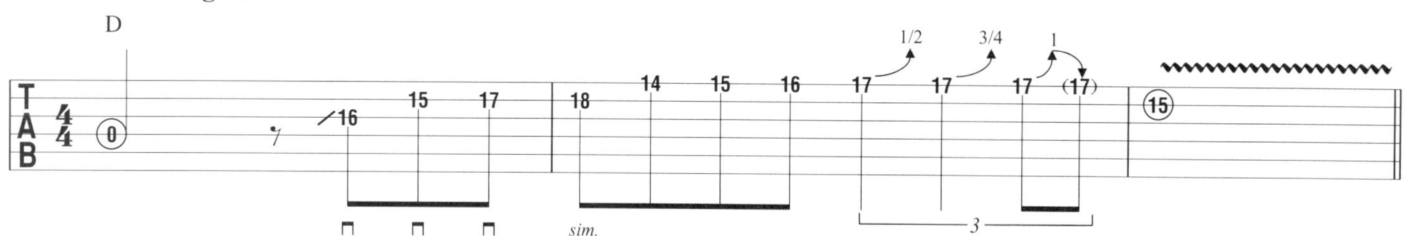


### 362: Sweep & Roll

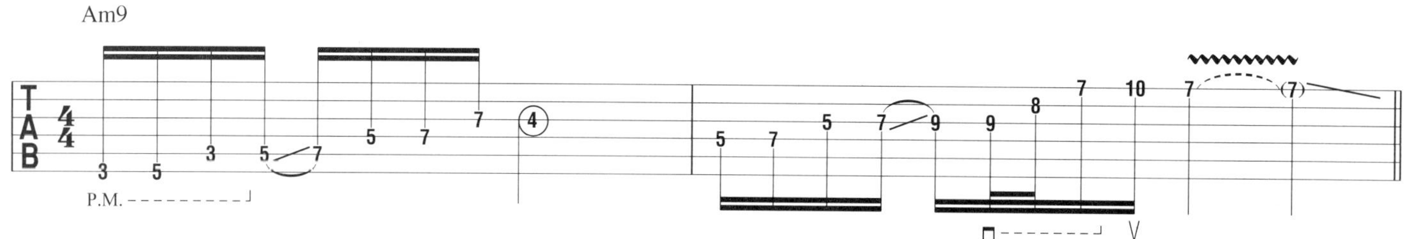

### 363: Classic Campbell

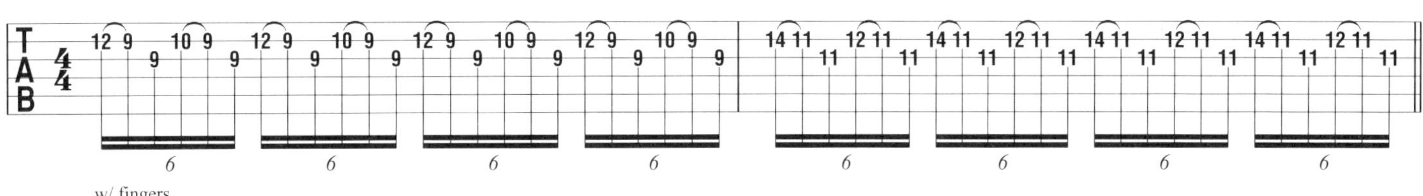


### 364: Chromatic Bends

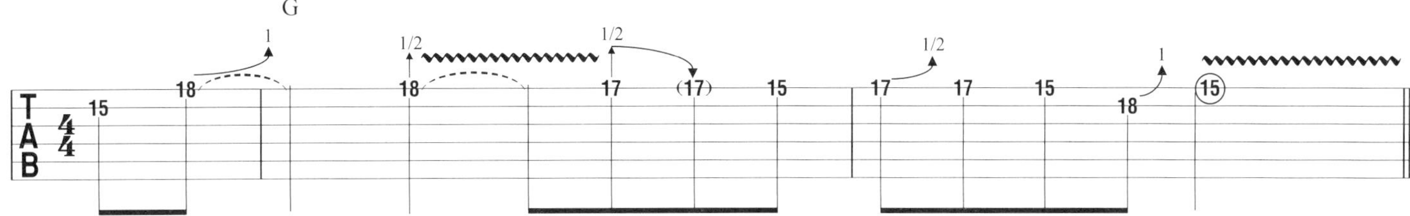


### 365: Classic Doublestops

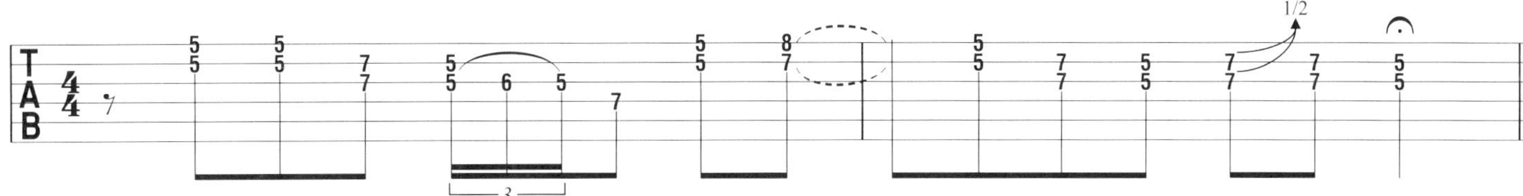

### 366: Open Pull-Offs

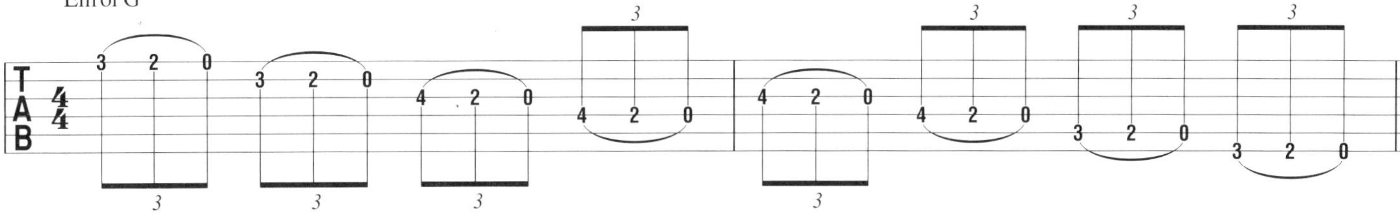

### 367: Minor Rake

Am

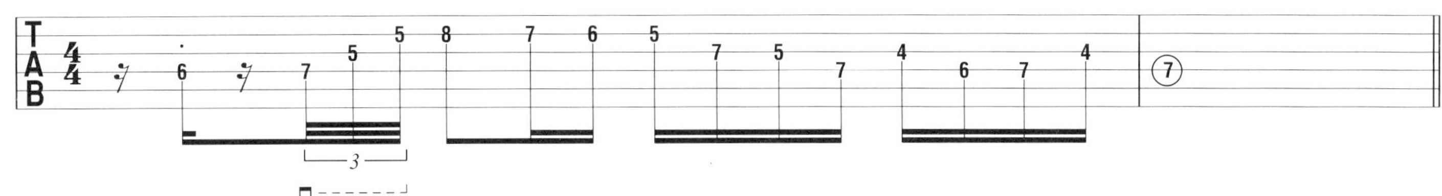

### 368: Slip & Slide

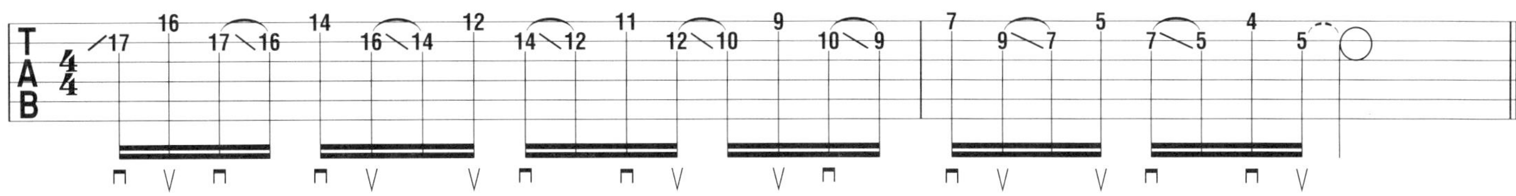

### 369: Off the Rhoad

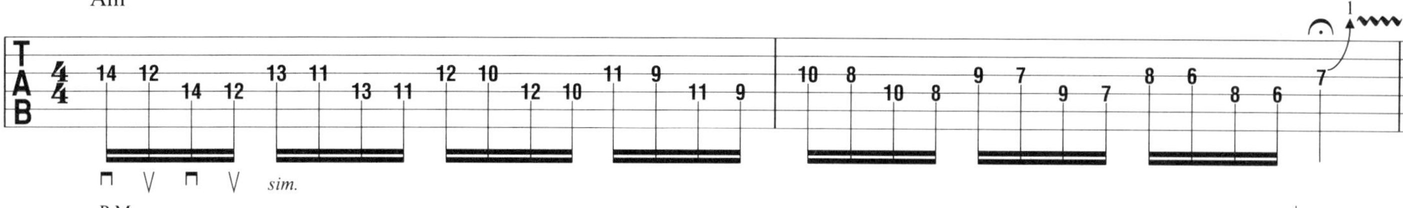


### 370: Blues Rockin'

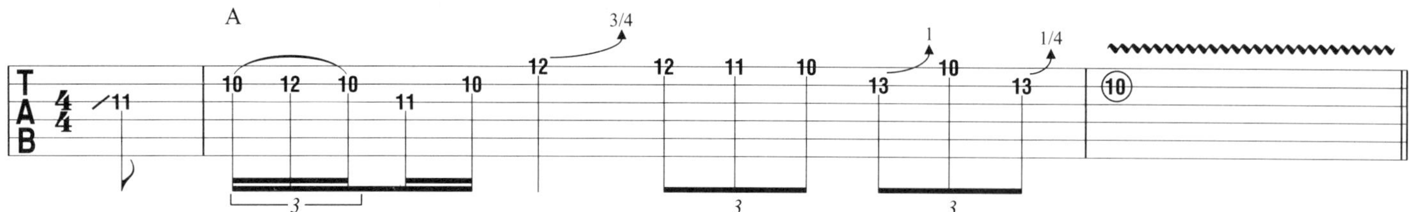


### 371: Penta-Tap

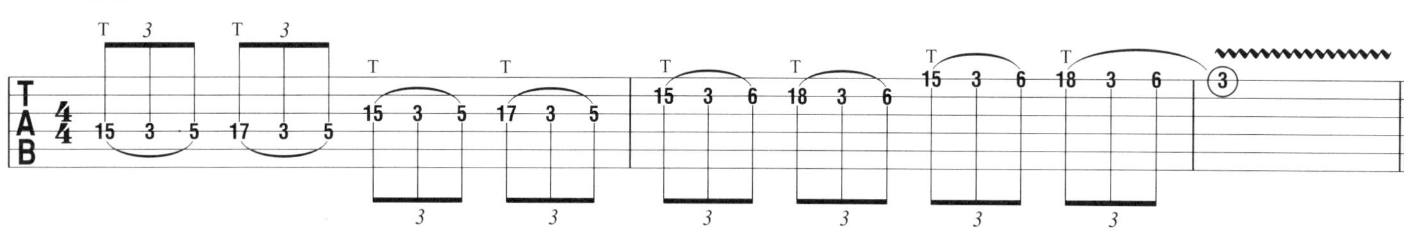


### 372: EVH Descent

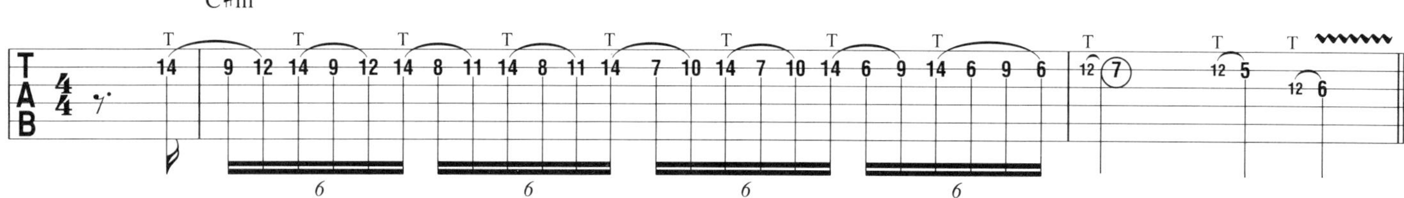


### 373: Tapped Bends

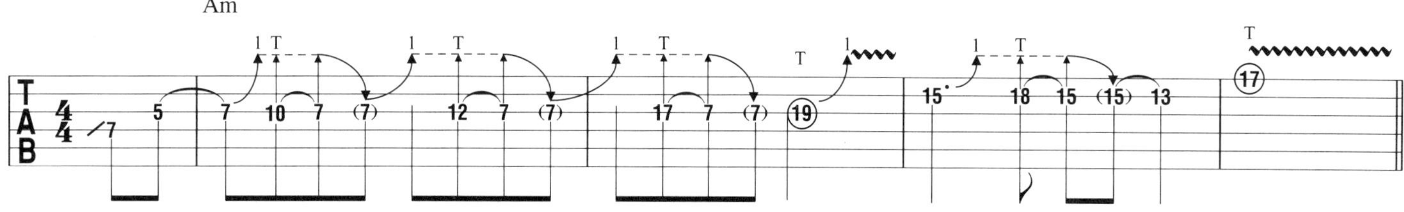


### 374: Dorian Rock

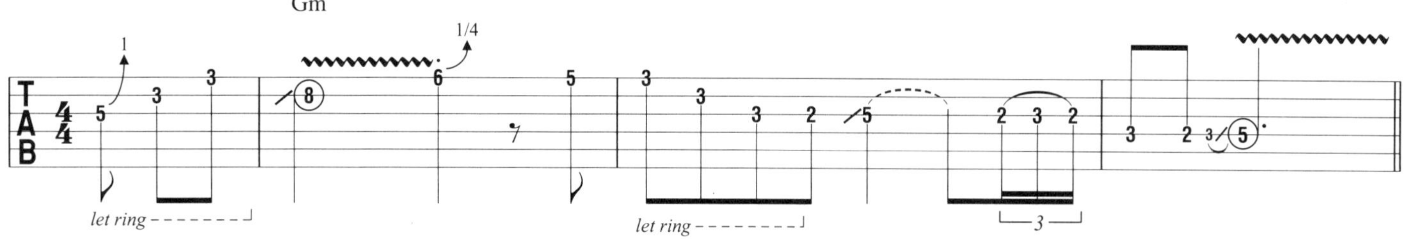


### 375: Honky Bends

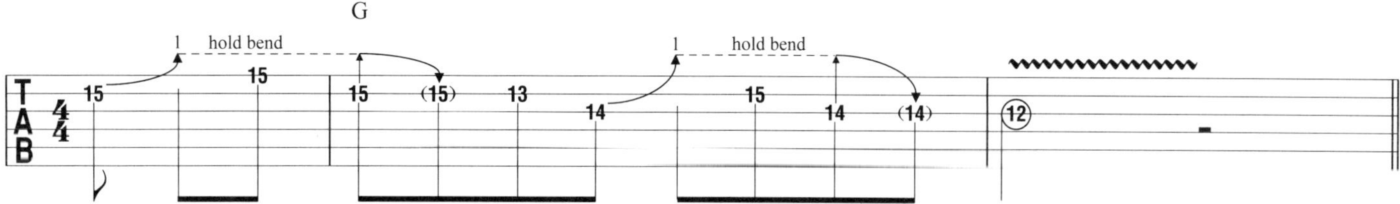

## 376: Get Bent

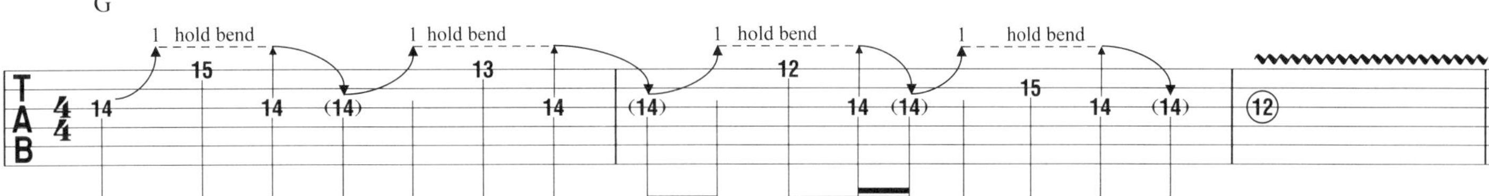


## 377: Pedalstops

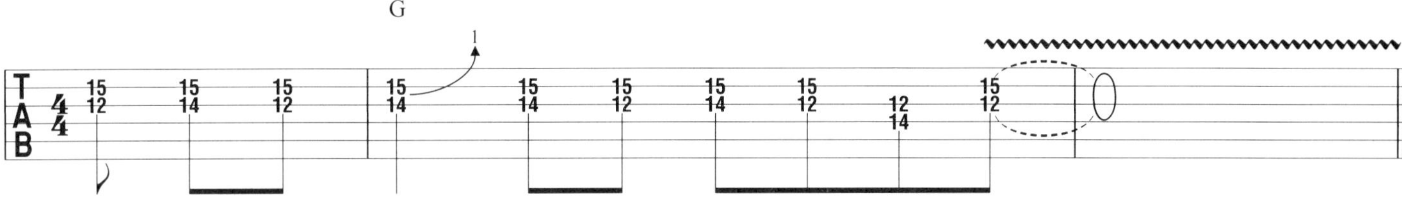


## 378: Climb-Ax

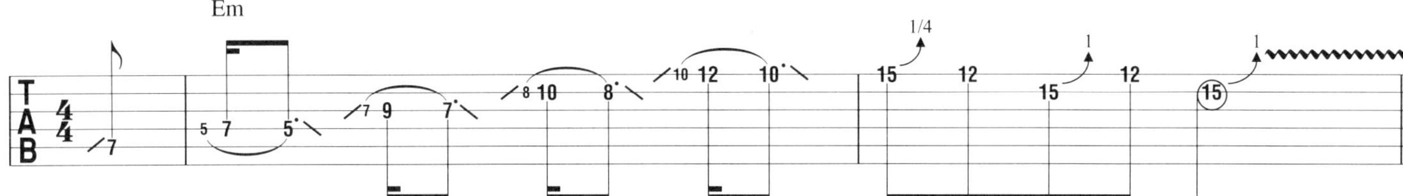


## 379: Double-Picker

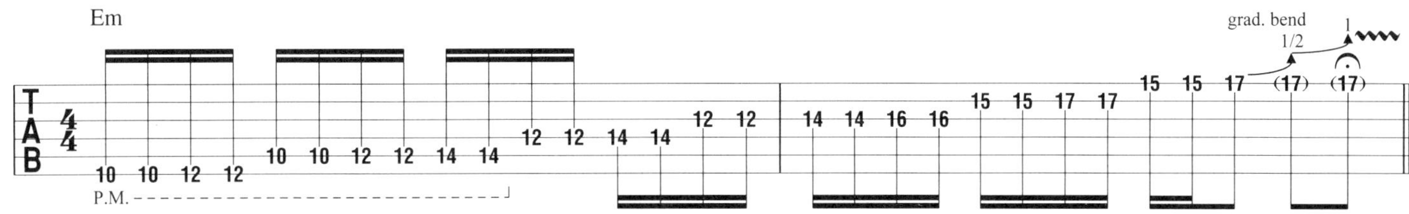


## 380: Double It

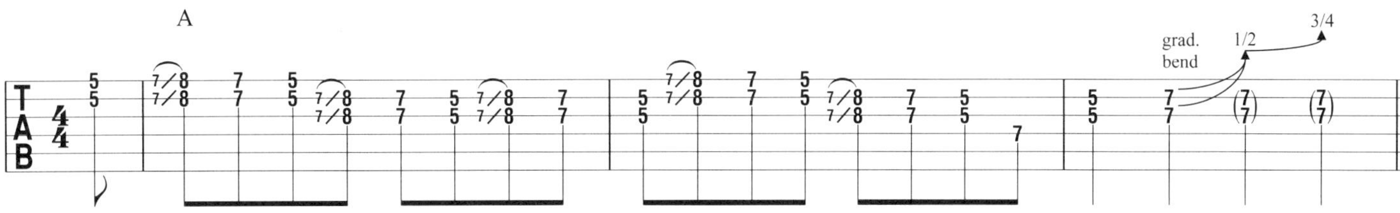


## 381: Sharp 4 Rock

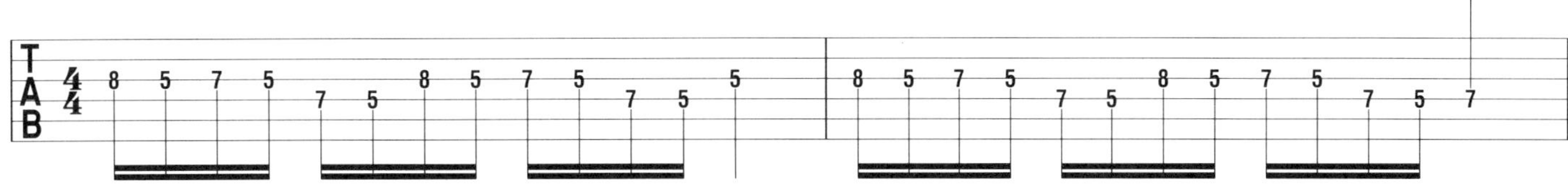


## 382: Rock Classic

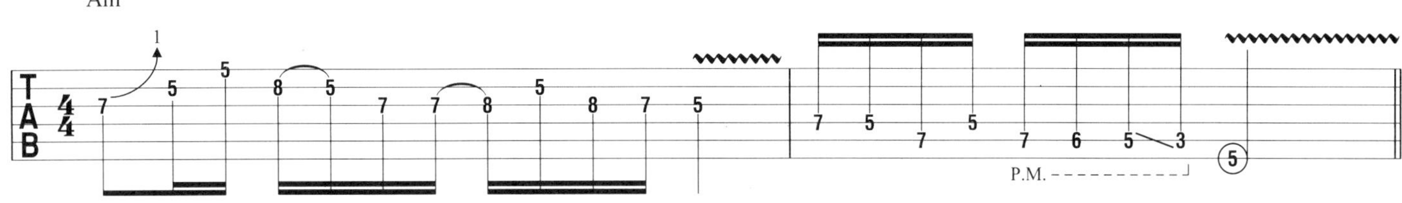

### 383: Bluesy Edge

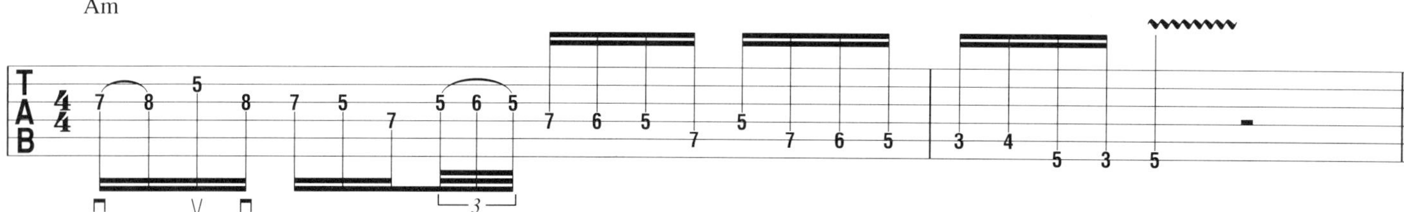


### 384: Penta-Chromatic

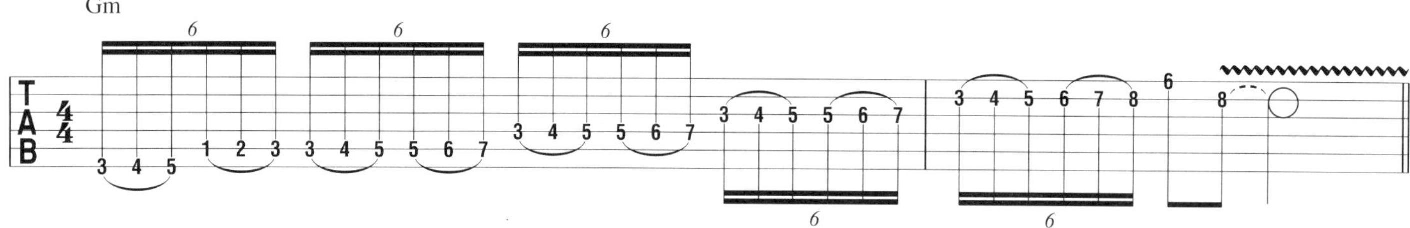


### 385: Major Hammers

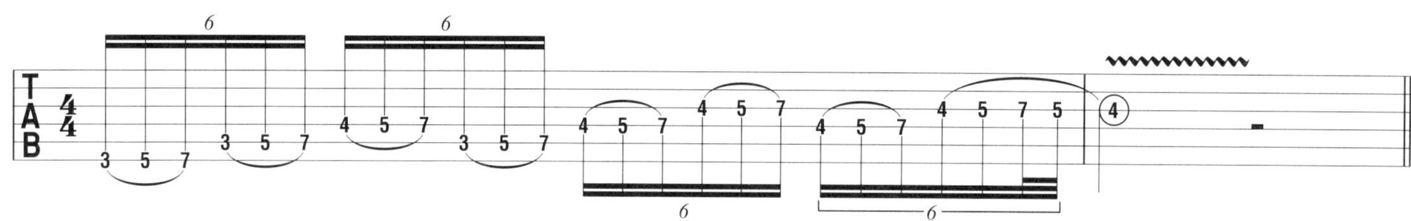


### 386: Minor Melody

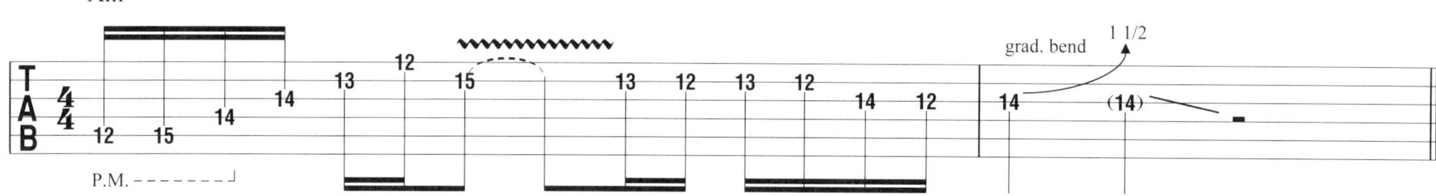


### 387: Diminished Sweep

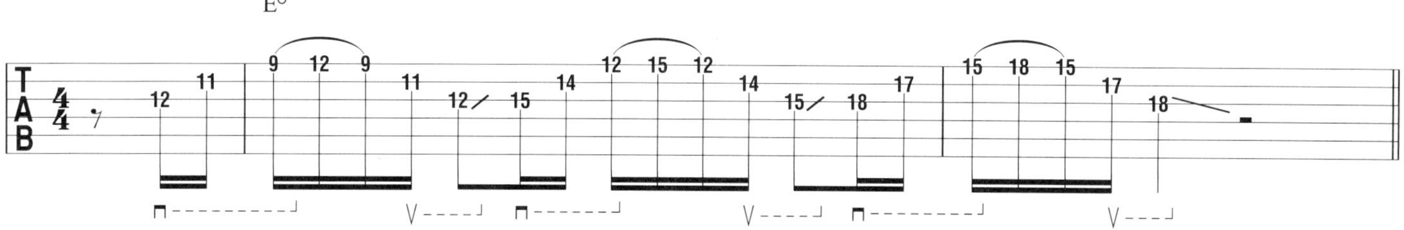


### 388: 5 Against 4

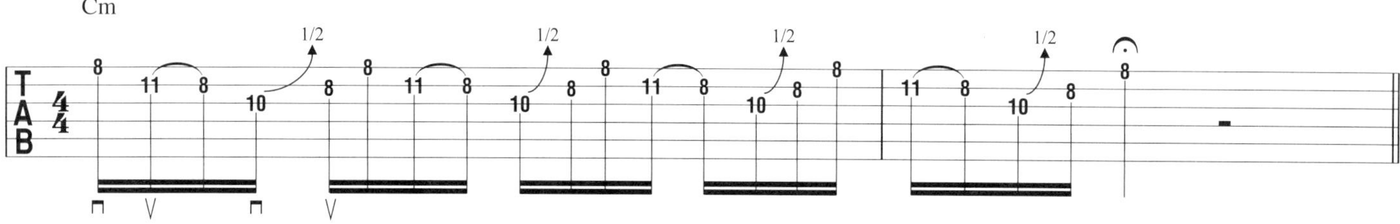


### 389: Reverse Bend

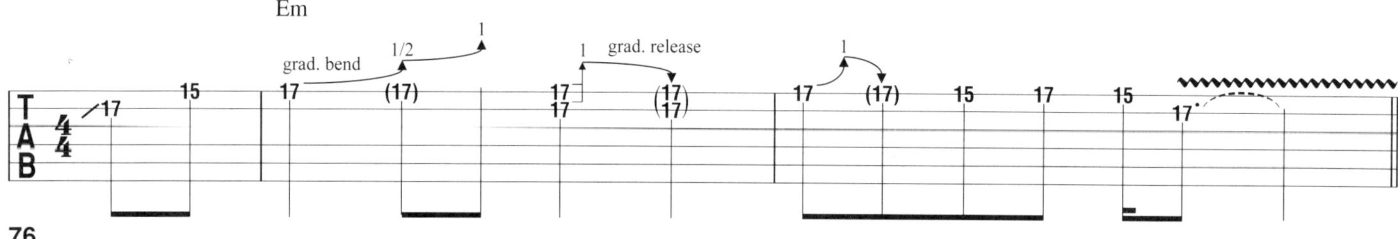

### 390: Triumph Triplets

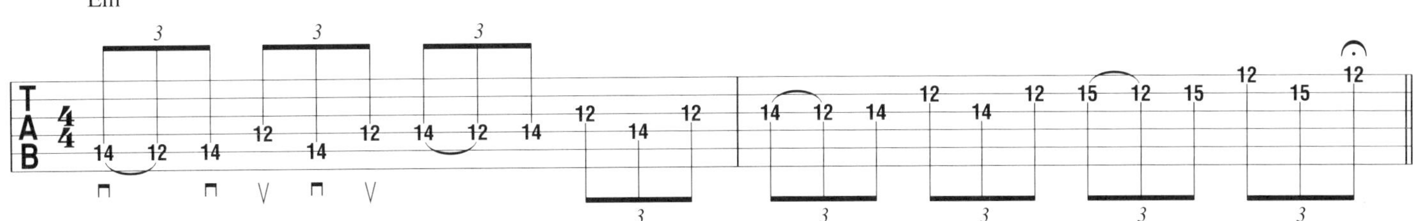


### 391: Classic Chuck

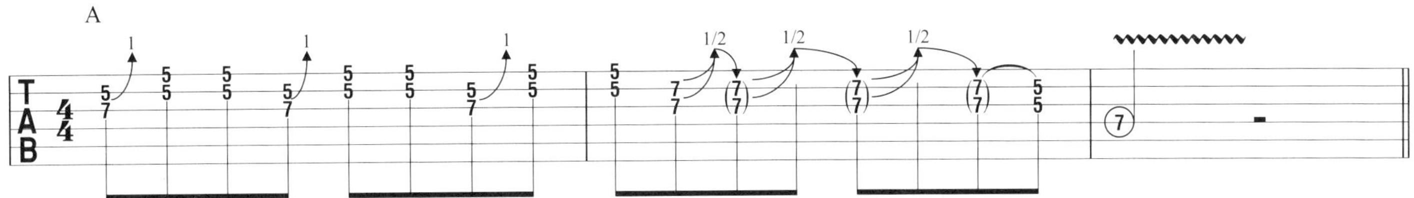


### 392: '70s Rocker

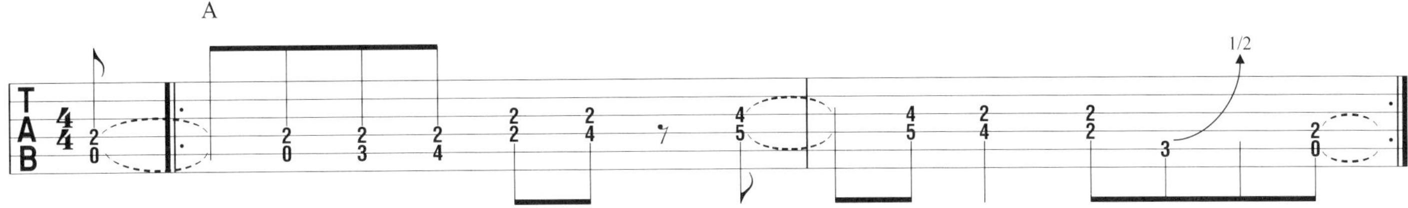


### 393: KISS It

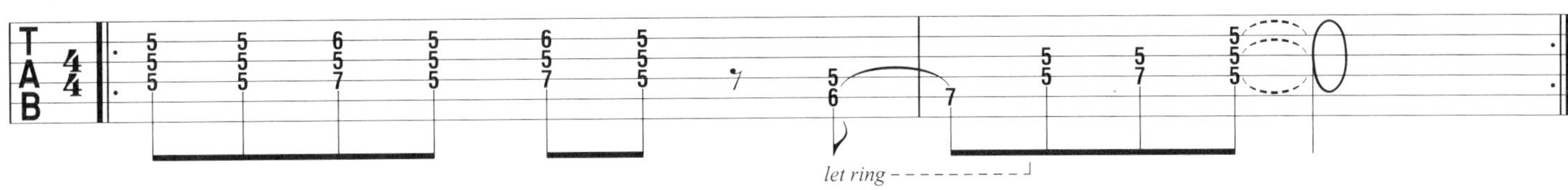


### 394: Rolling Riff

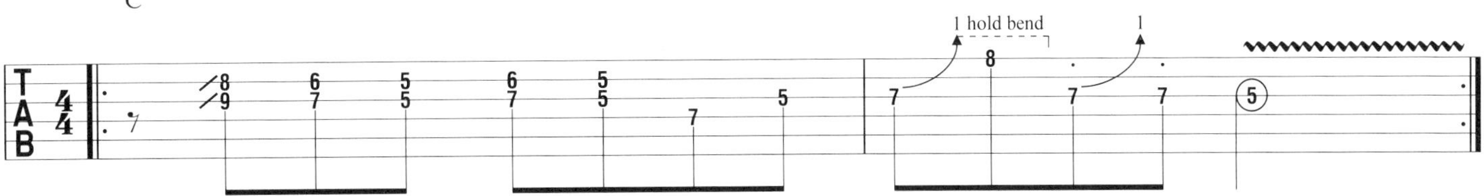


### 395: 3-Octave Climb

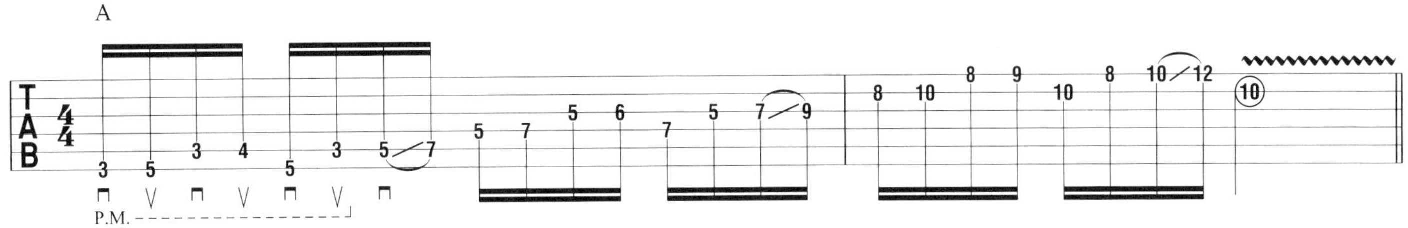


### 396: Syncopated 16ths

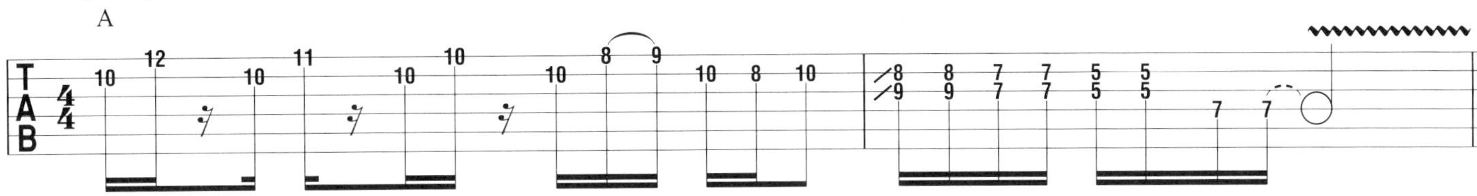

### 397: Rhythm & Harmony

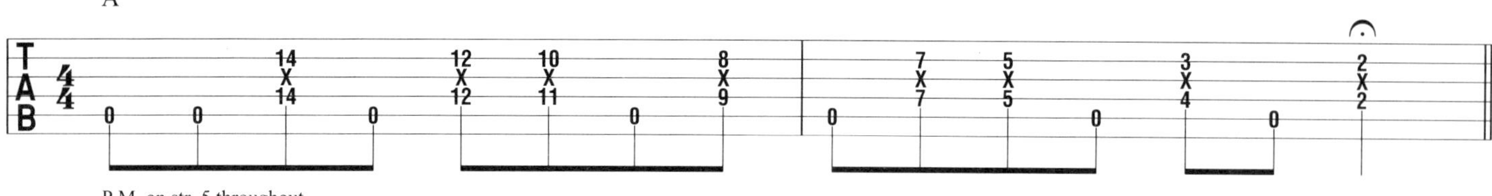


### 398: Box Sequence

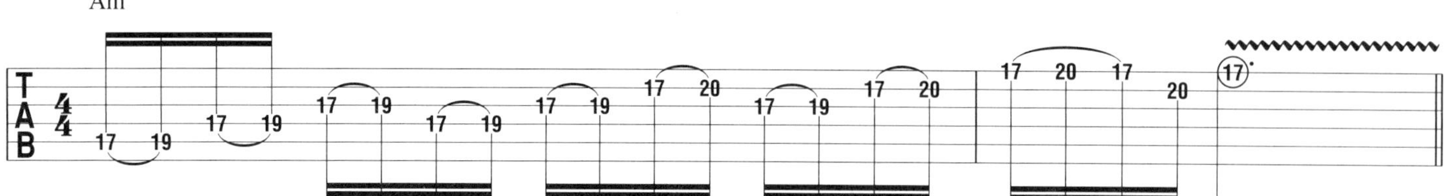


### 399: Minor Linear

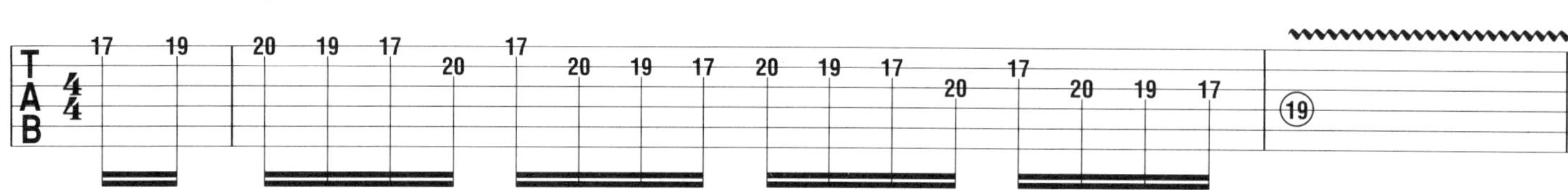


### 400: Cadenza Lick

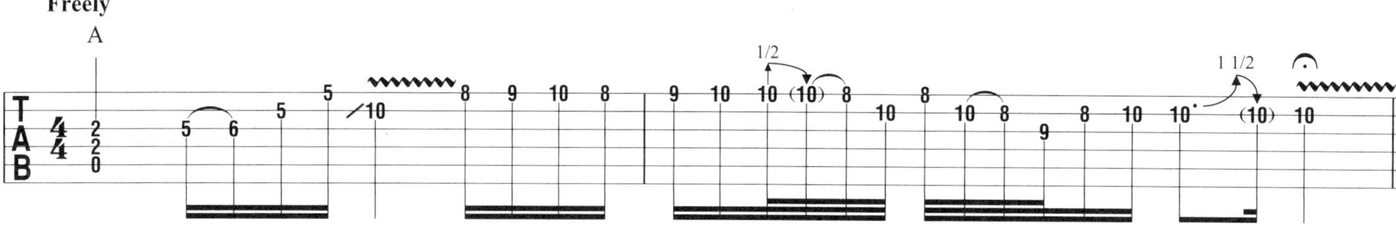

# ACOUSTIC LICKS

## Instructor: Matthew Schroeder

### 401: Open D Blues

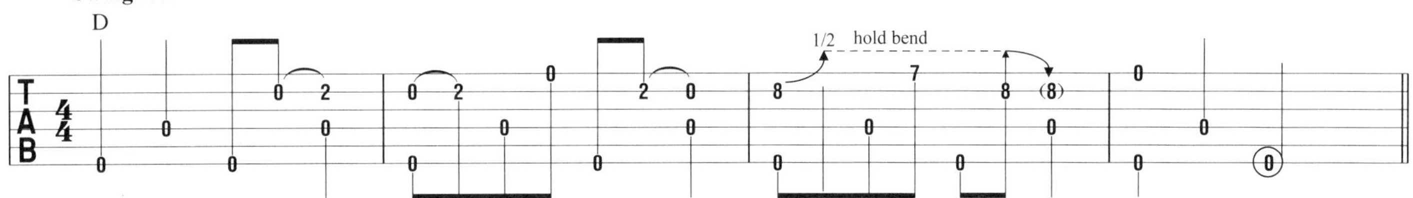


### 402: Doublestop Blues

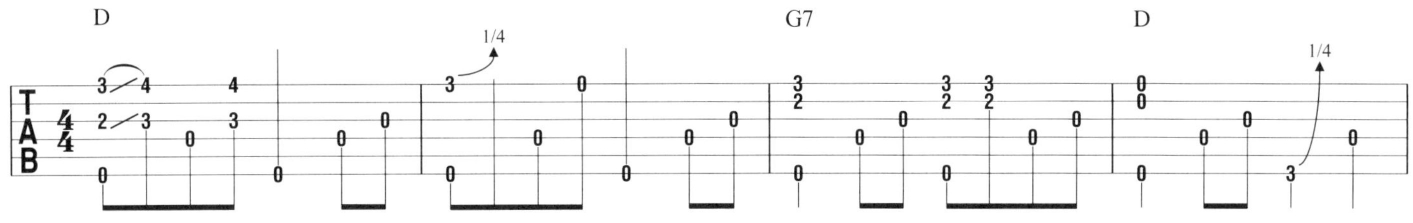


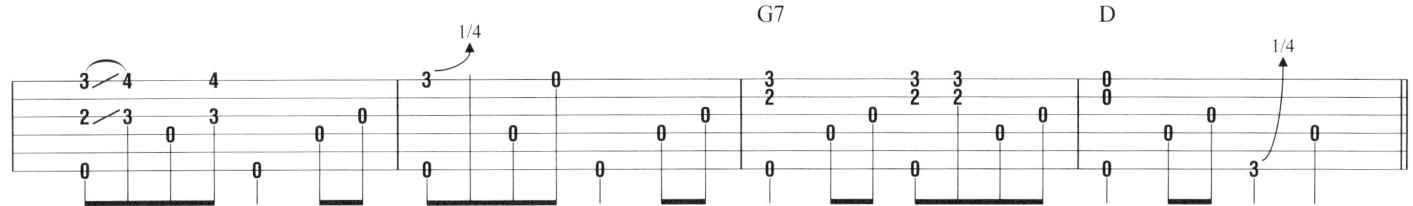


### 403: Blind Blues

D-A-D-F♯-A-D

Swing feel

D

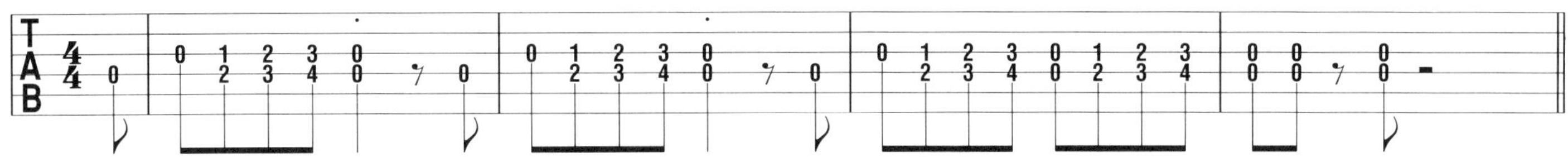

### 404: Turnaround Sub

D-A-D-F♯-A-D

Swing feel

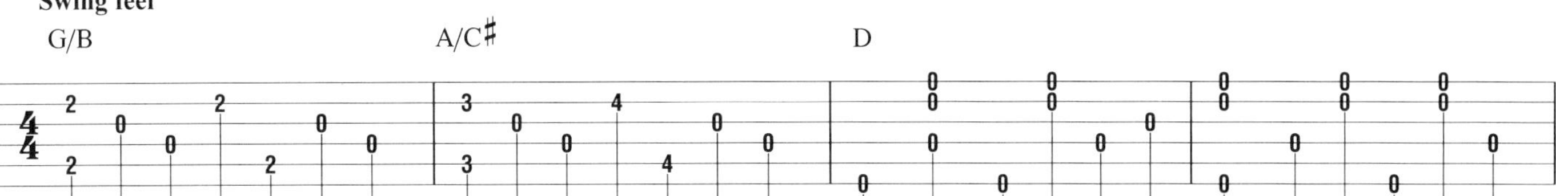


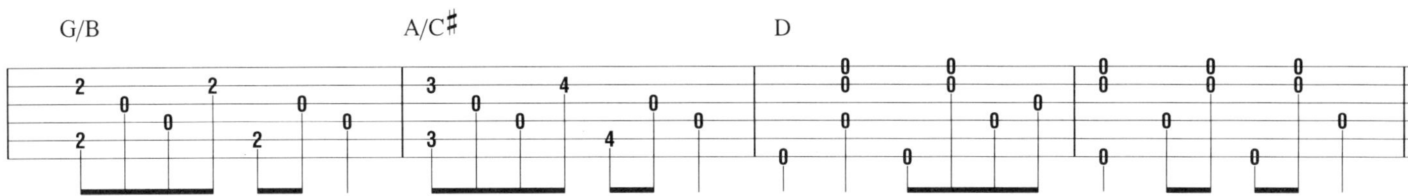

## 405: Fiddle Line

**D-A-D-F♯-A-D**

D

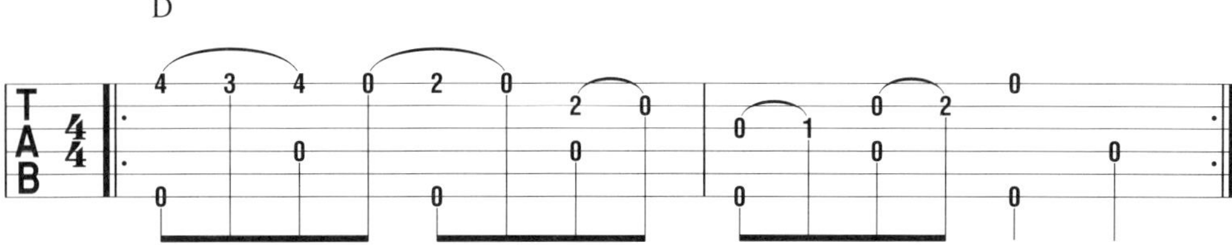

## 406: Noon Harmonics

***B-E-B-E-G♯-B**

E(G)

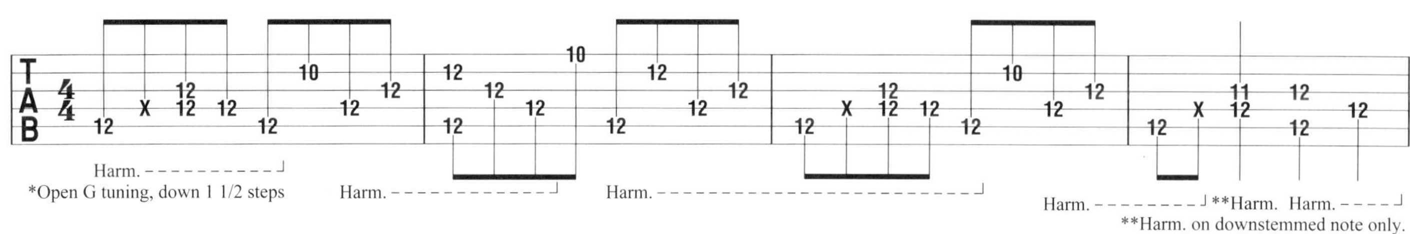


*Open G tuning, down 1 1/2 steps

**Harm. on downstemmed note only.

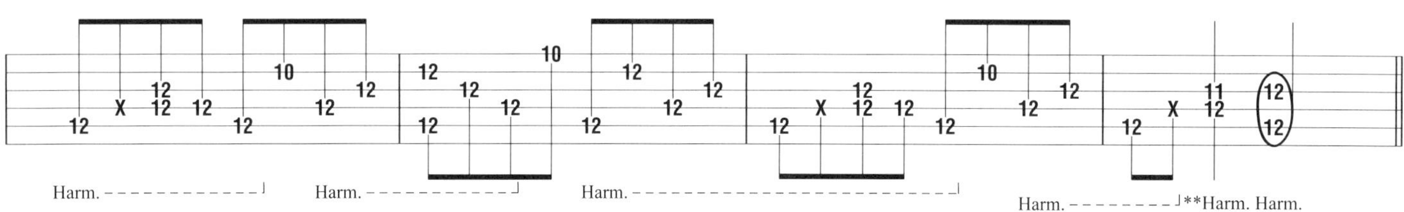


## 407: Fahey Pattern

**D-A-D-G-A-D**

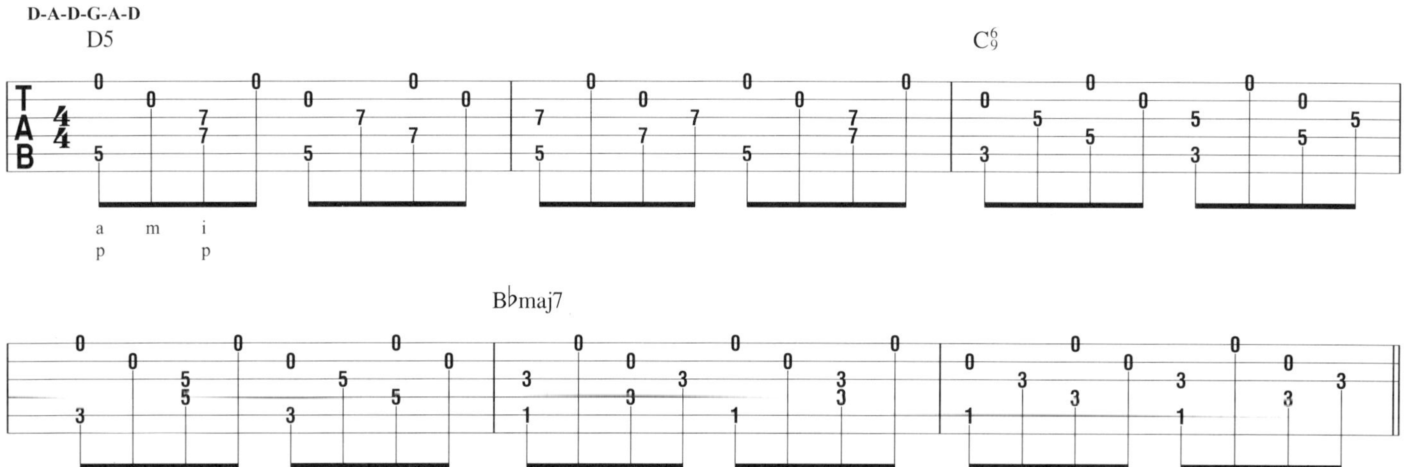


## 408: Chromatic Fahey

**D-A-D-G-A-D**

N.C.(D5)

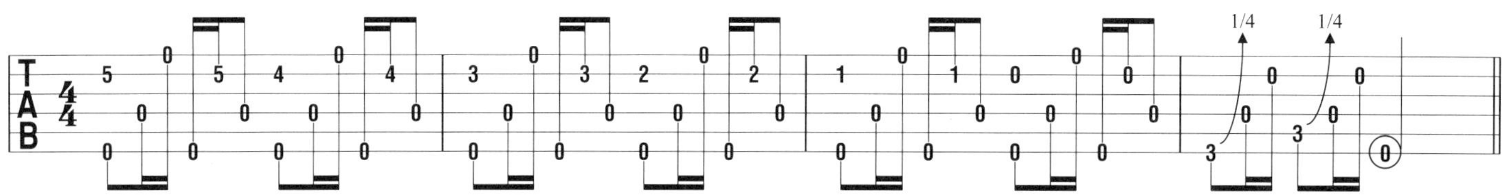

## 409: Old-Timey

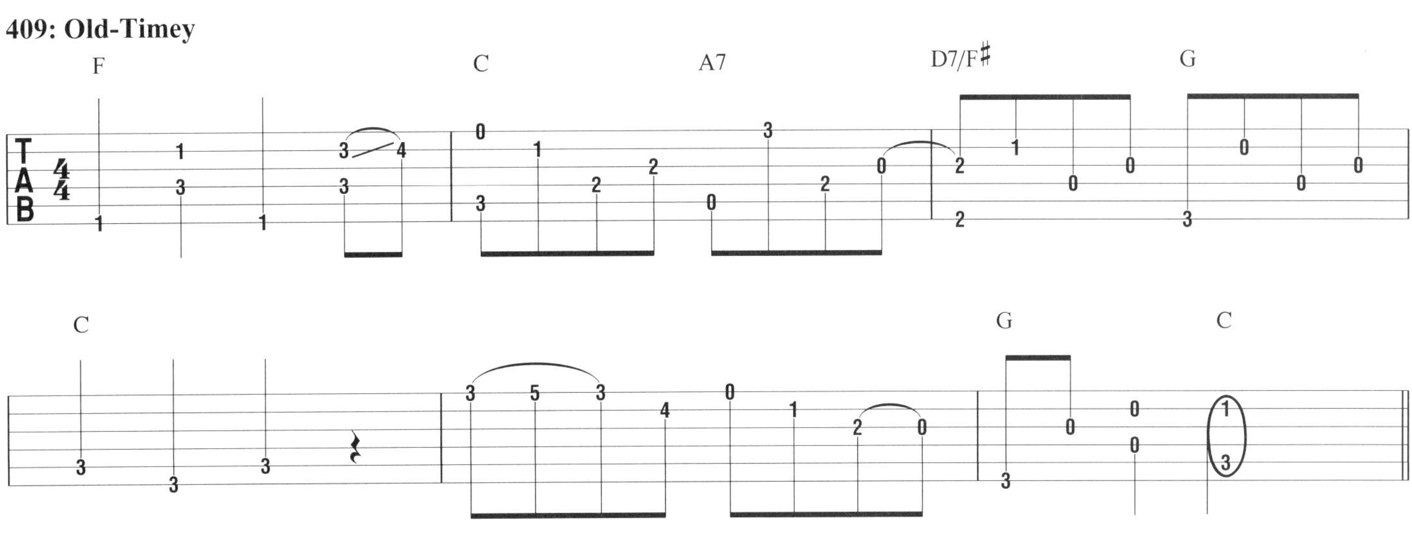


## 410: Bring It Around

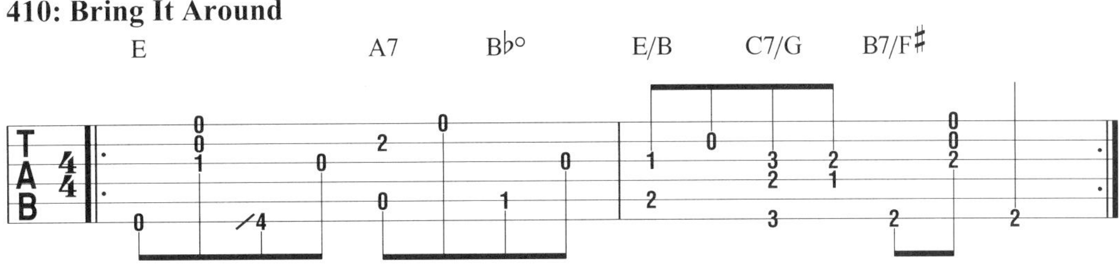


## 411: Pass the Lemonade

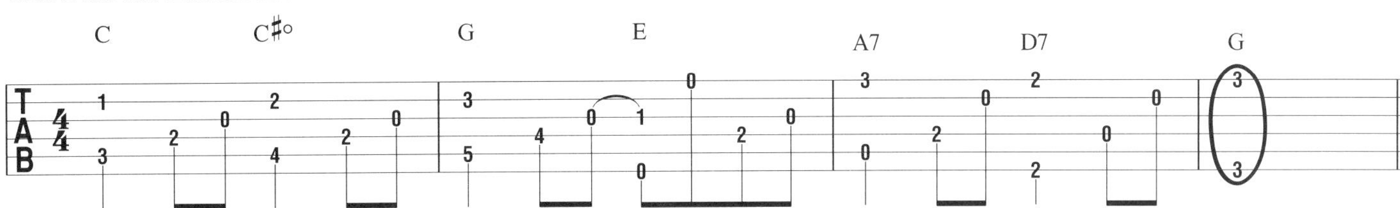


## 412: Travis Turnaround

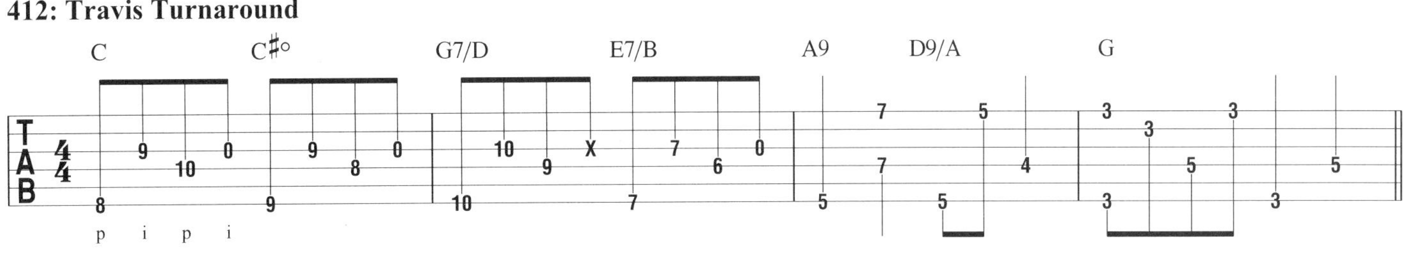


## 413: Chet's House

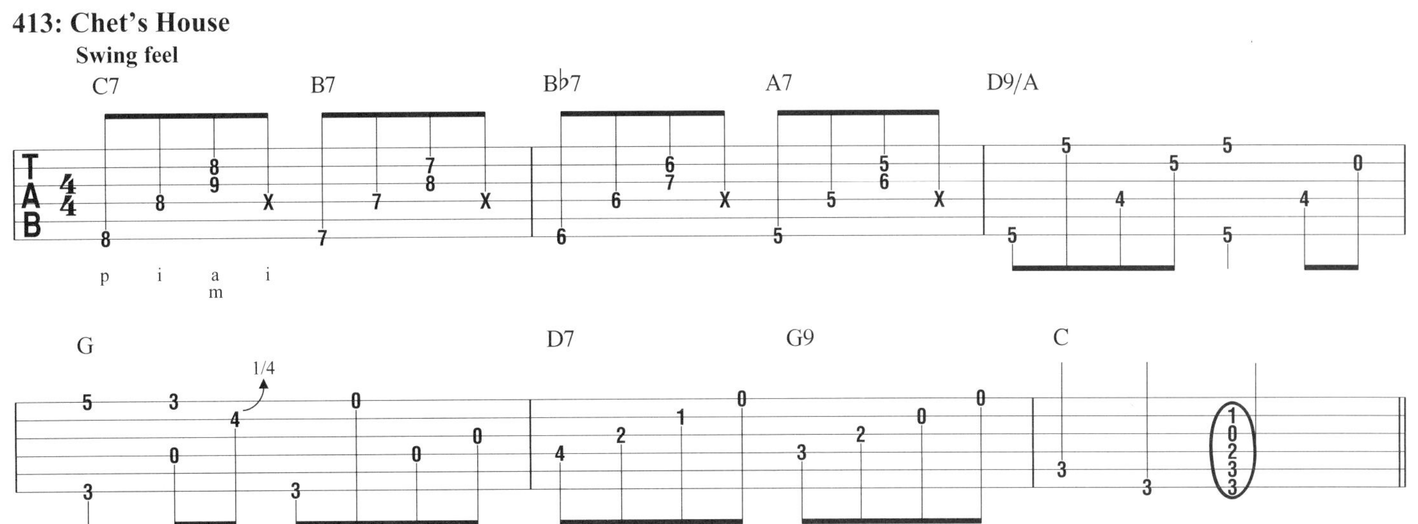

## 414: Blues Walk

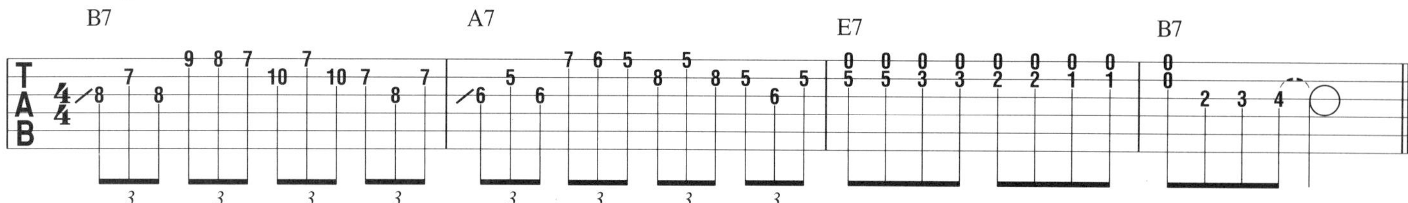


## 415: Blues Ending

Swing feel

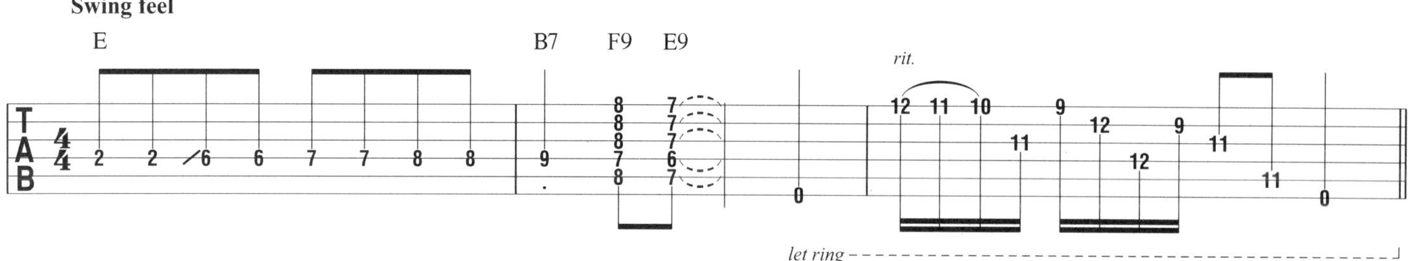


## 416: 6ths Turnaround

Swing feel

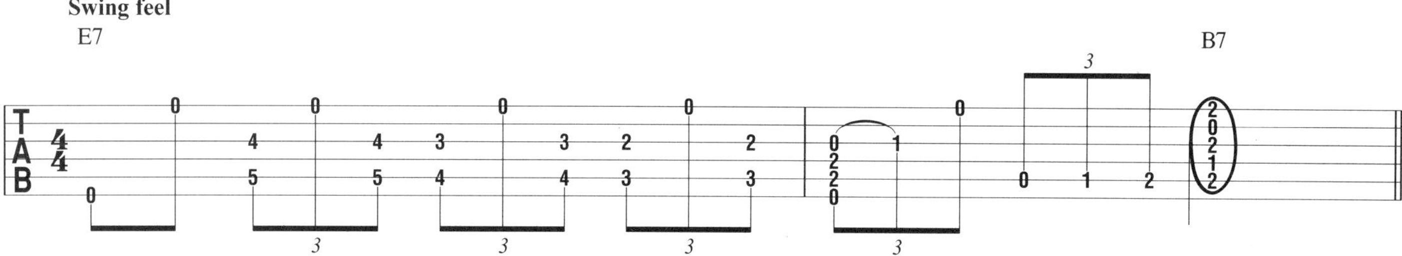


## 417: Classic I-V

Swing feel

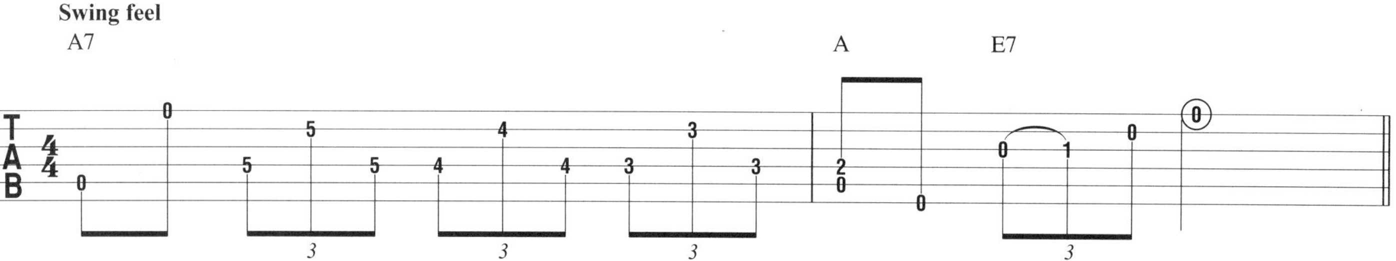


## 418: Triplet Ending

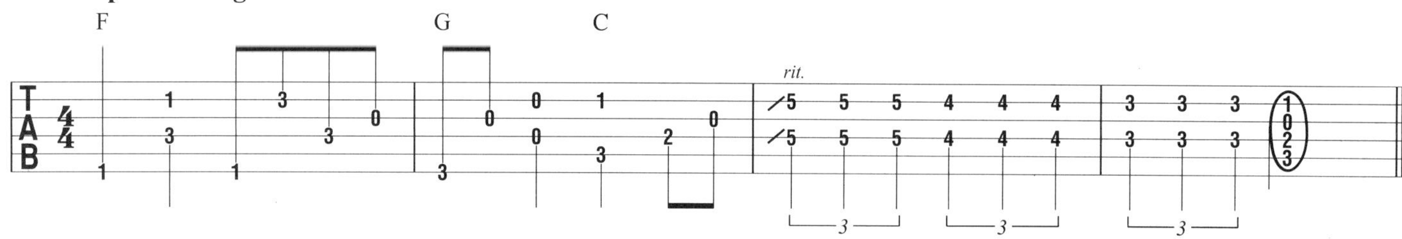


## 419: Hammer the IV

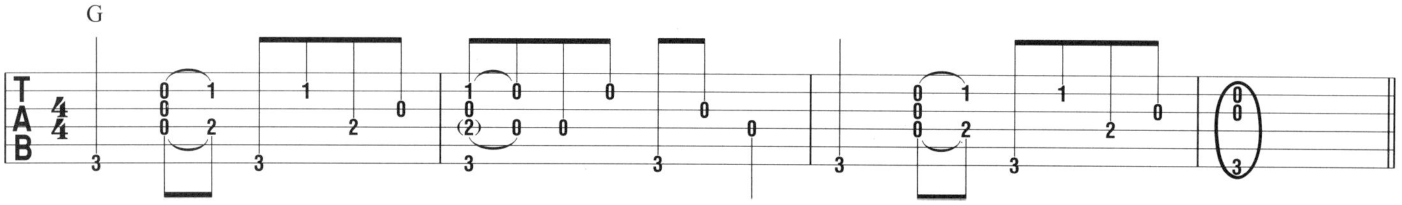

**420: Train Pattern**

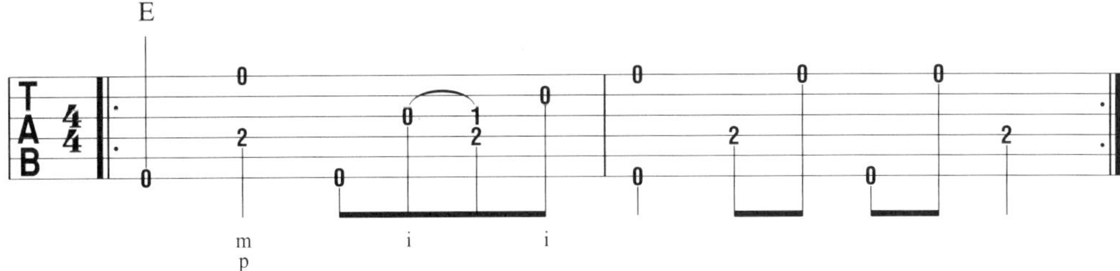


**421: Merle Picking**

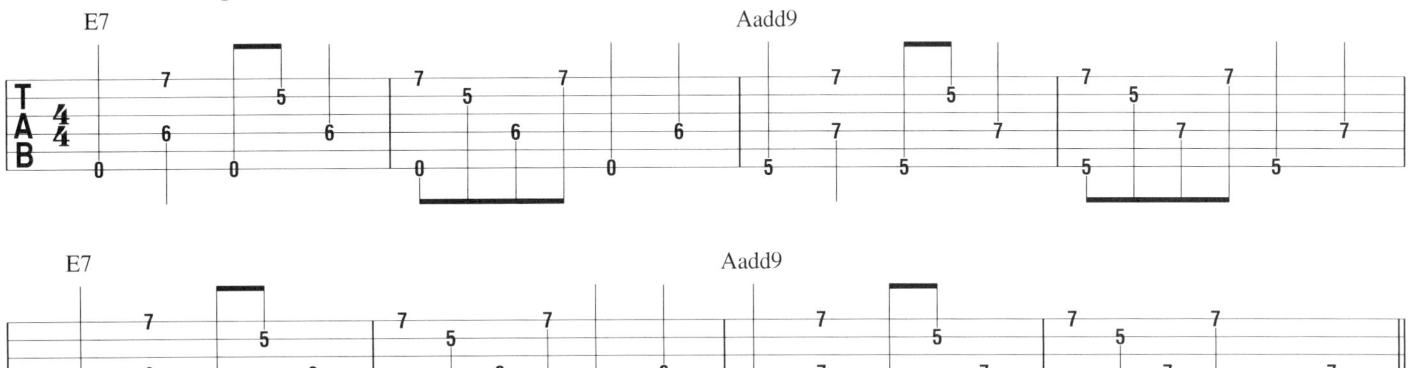


**422: Doc Ditty**

**Swing feel**

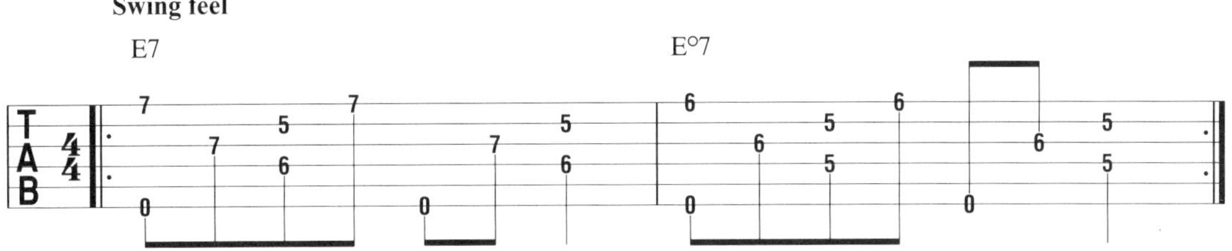


**423: McGee Blues**

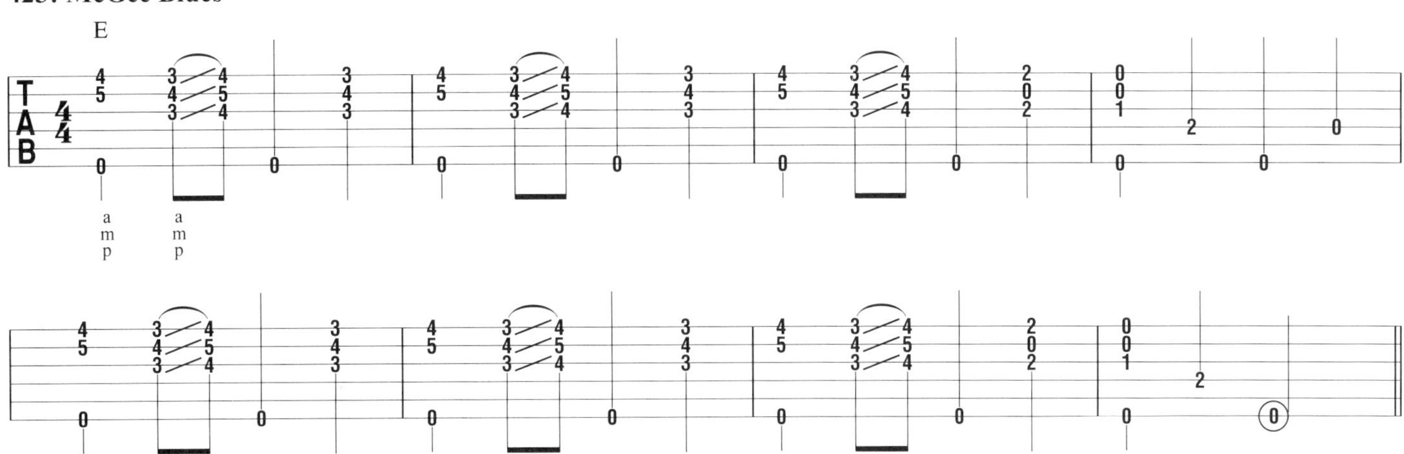


**424: Bossa Pattern**

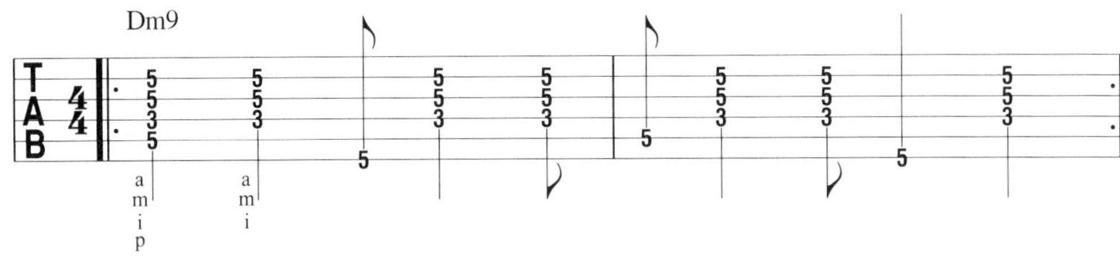

## 425: Shout Toward Leo

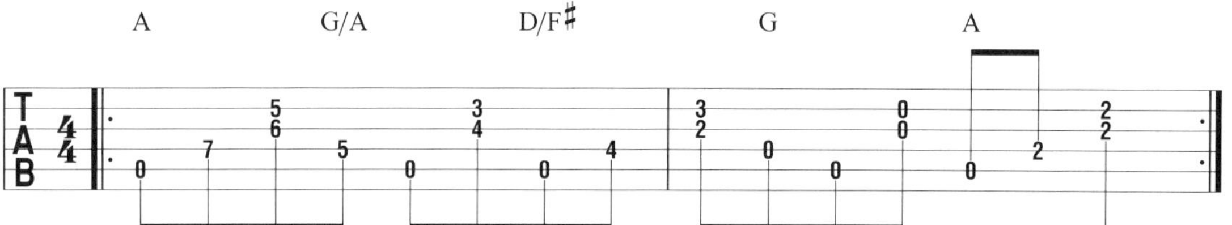


## 426: Chordal Riff

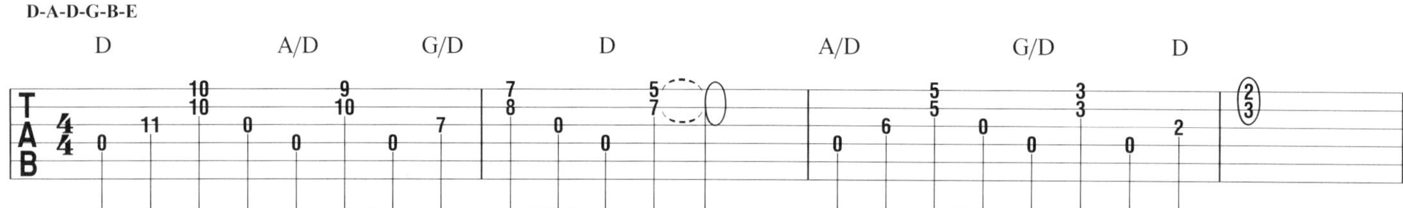


## 427: Kottke Bliss

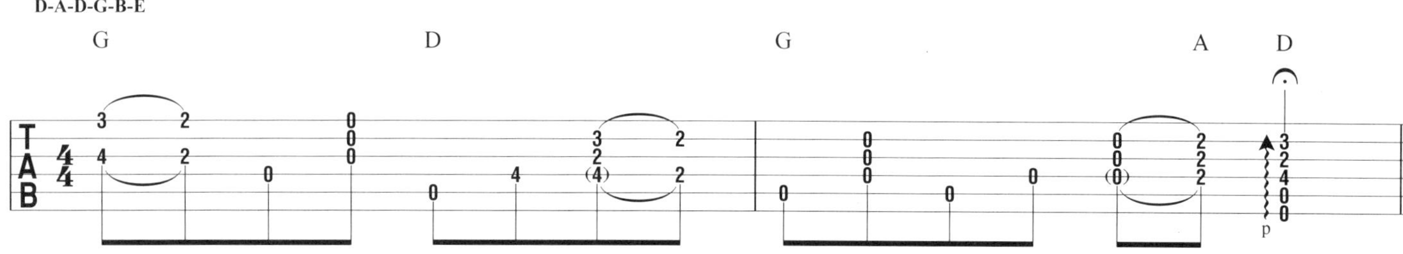


## 428: Harmonic Slides

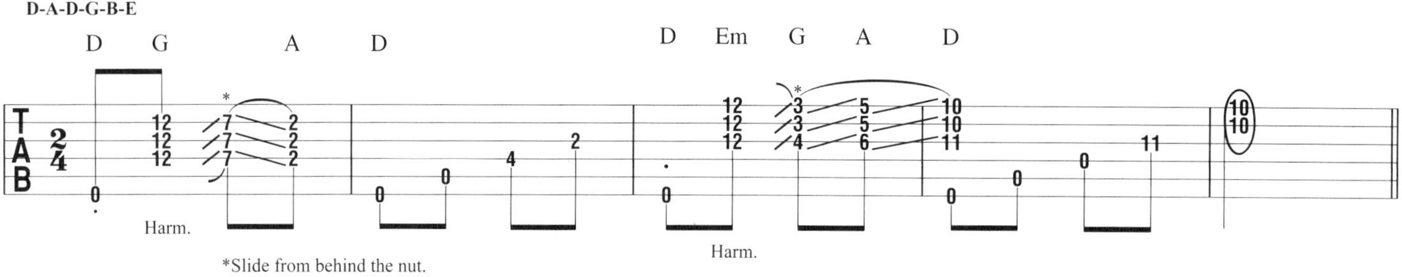


## 429: Chime Time

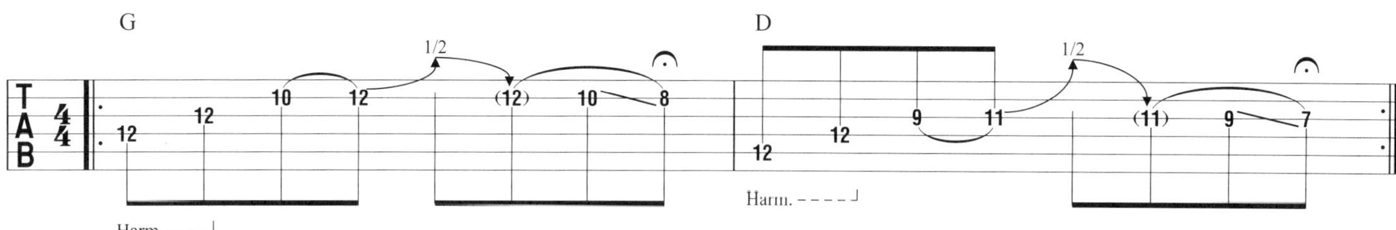


## 430: Slow Handed

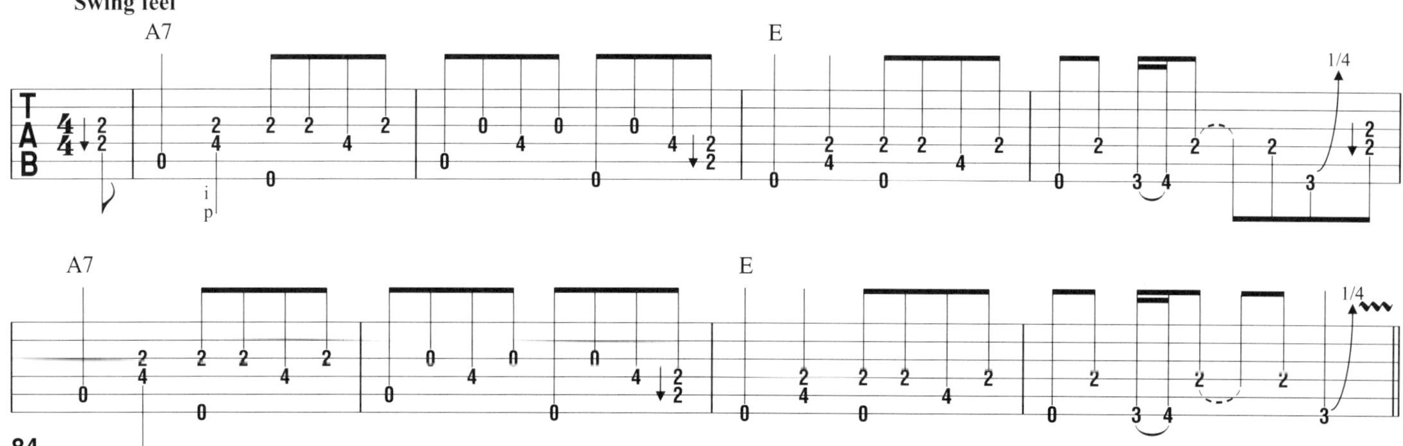

## 431: Graham Groove

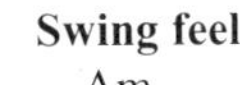


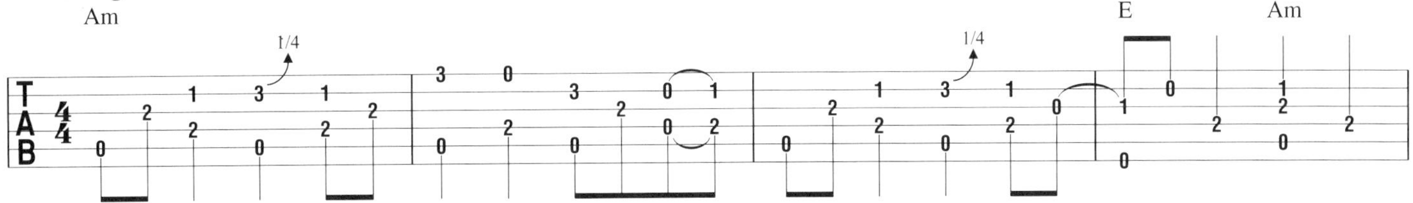


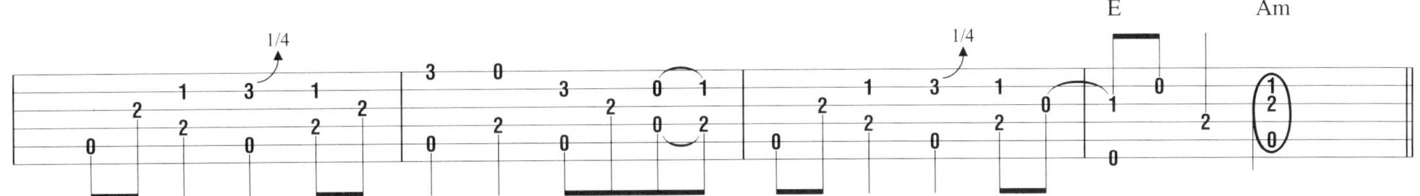


## 432: Travis Groove

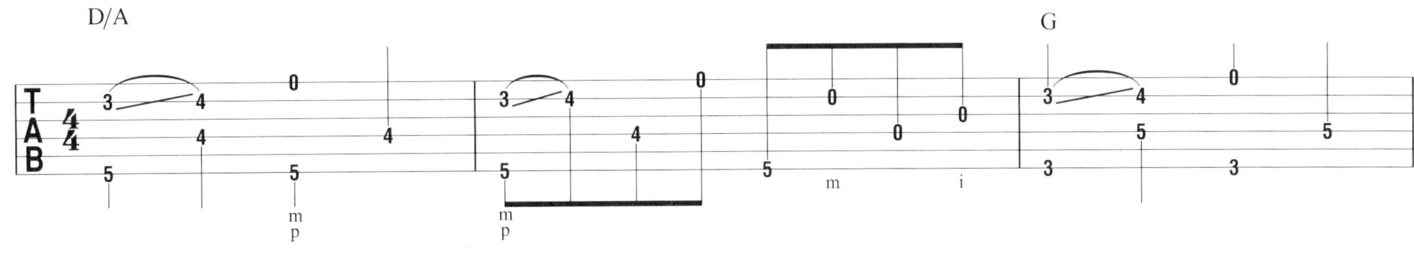


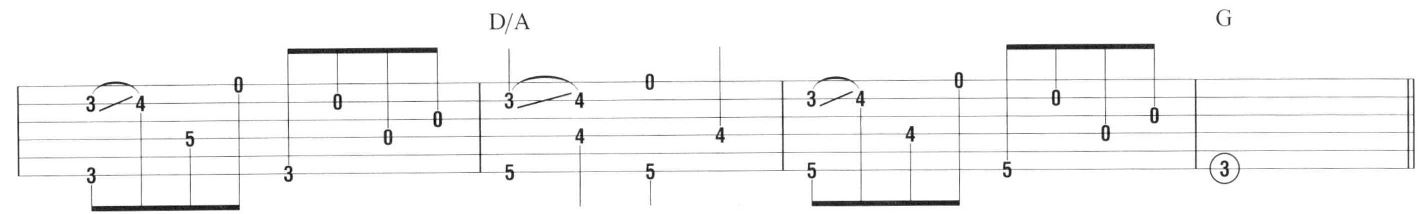


## 433: Chordal Walkdown

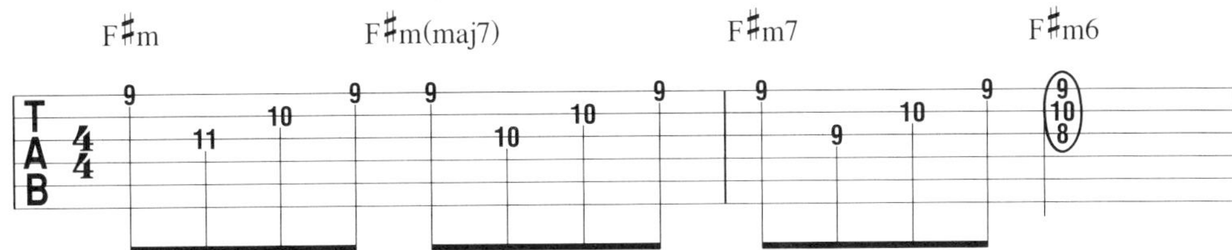


## 434: 10ths Walkdown

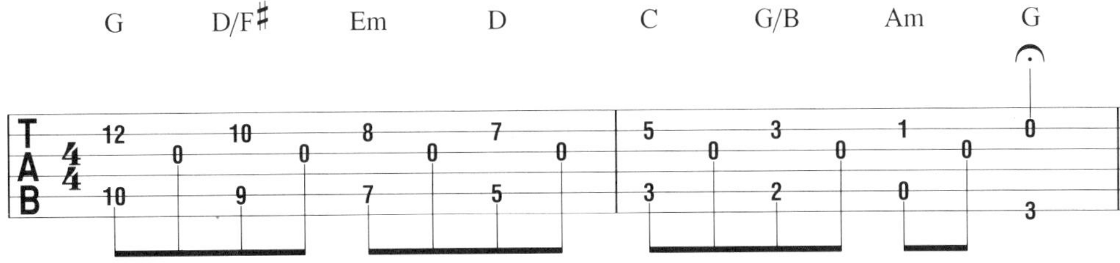


## 435: Diminished Ditty

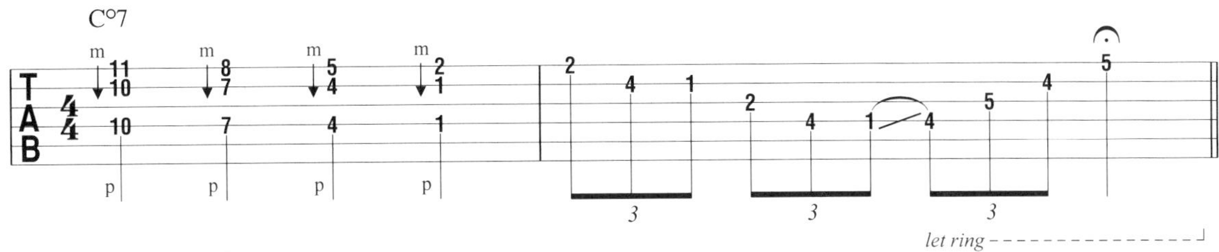

## 436: Arpeggio Garden

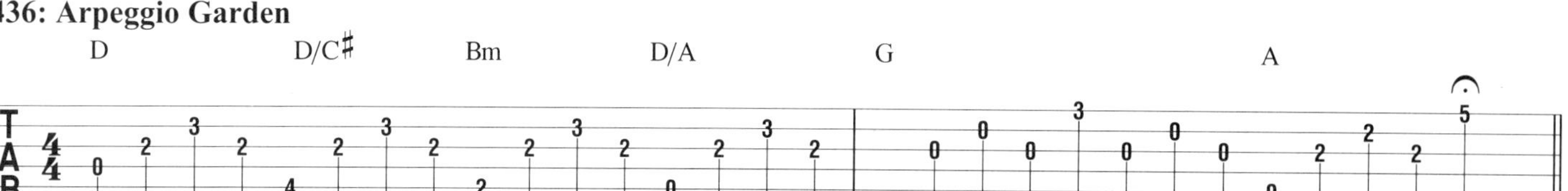


## 437: Blake Blues

D-A-D-G-B-E

Swing feel

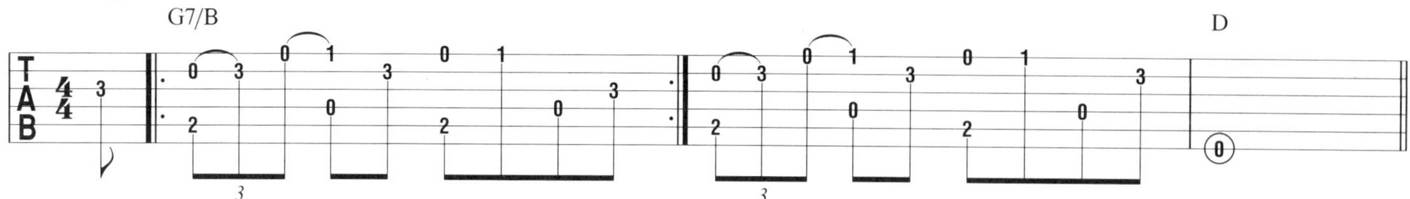


## 438: Blues Bender

D-A-D-G-B-E

Swing feel

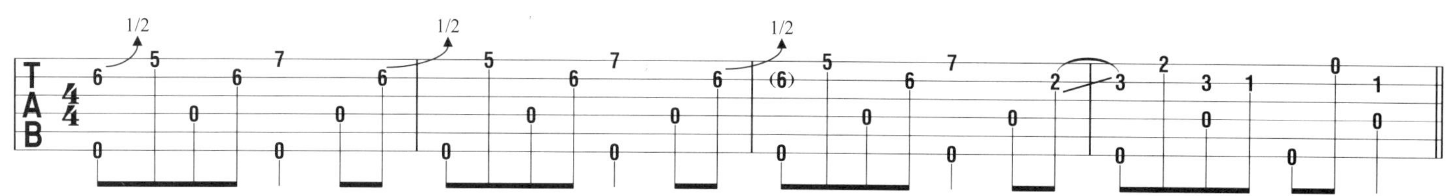


## 439: Melodic Chromatic

D-A-D-G-B-E

Swing feel

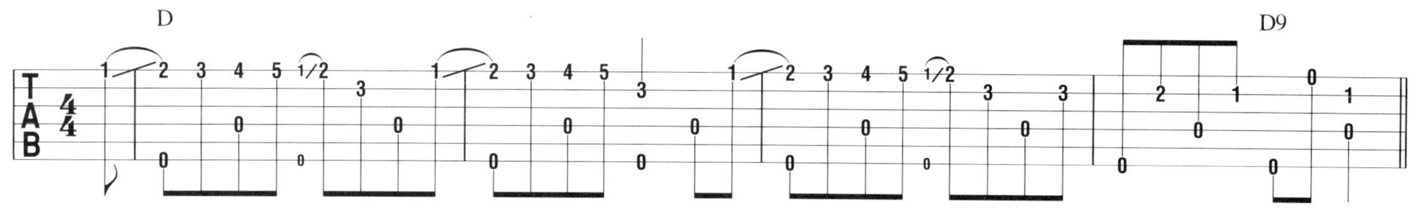


## 440: Classic V-IV-I

D-A-D-G-B-E

Swing feel

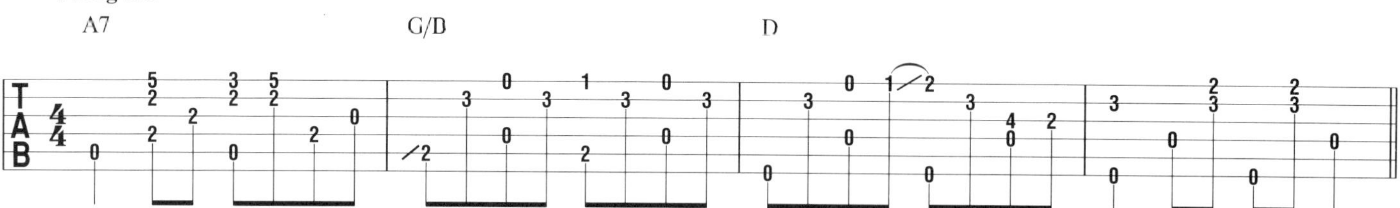


## 441: Train Groove

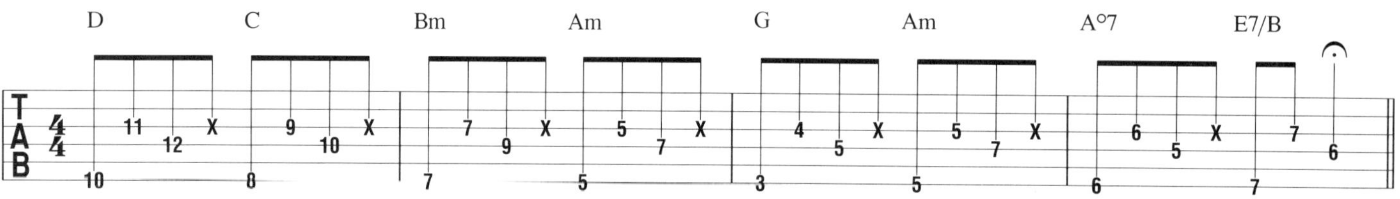

**442: Fast Break**

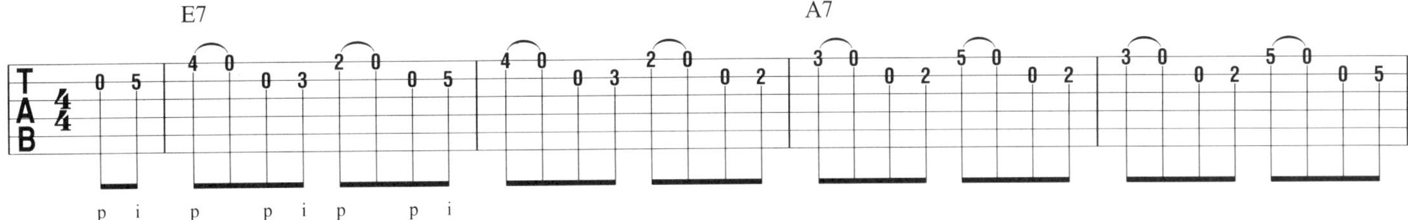


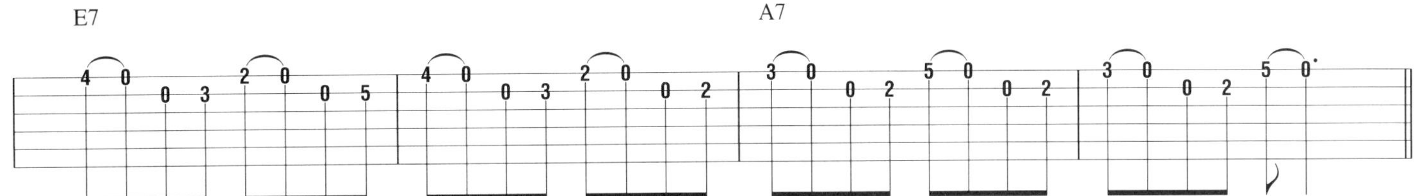


**443: Slow Blues**

Swing feel

E7

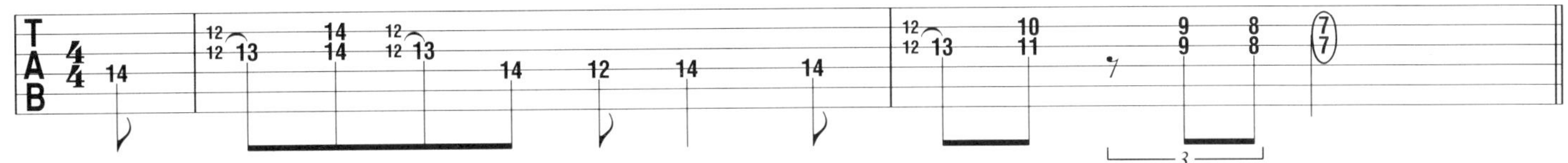


**444: Classic Triplets**

Swing feel

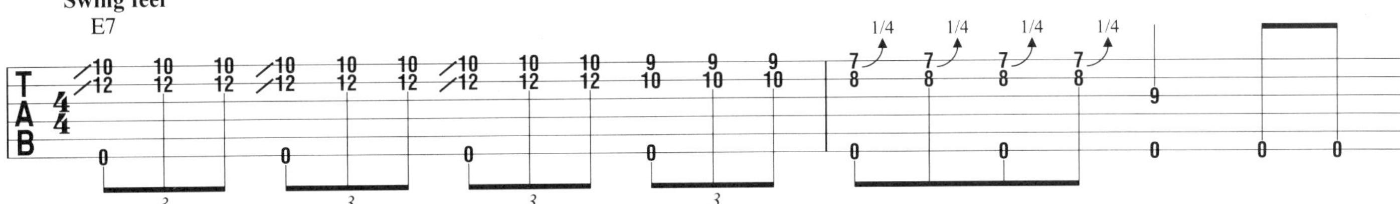


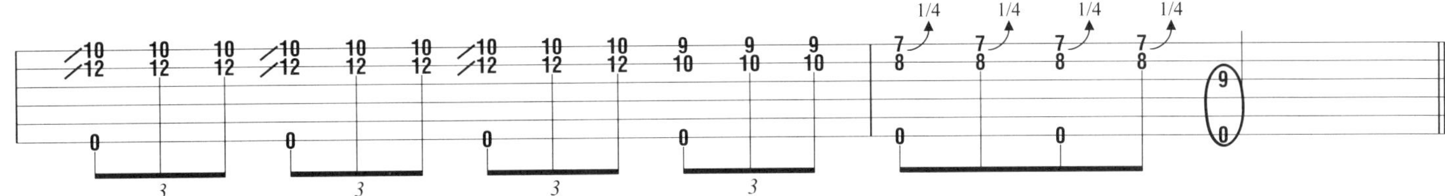

**445: Cledus Classic**

A

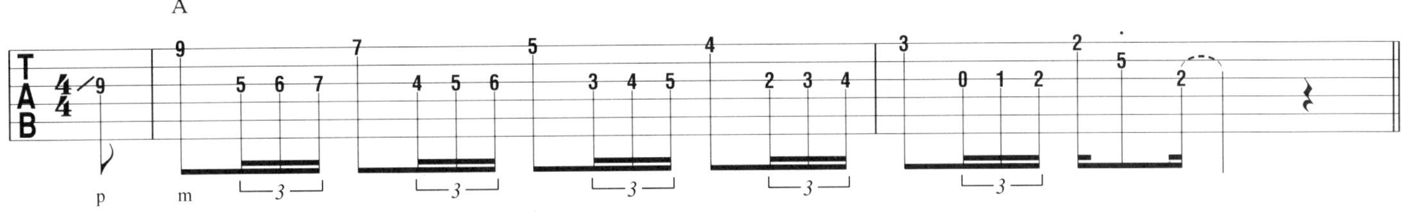


**446: Hendrixian Bliss**

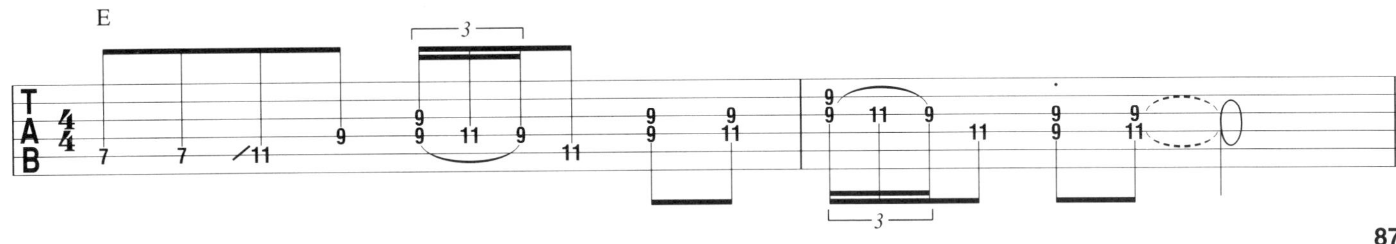

## 447: Pentatonic Pivot

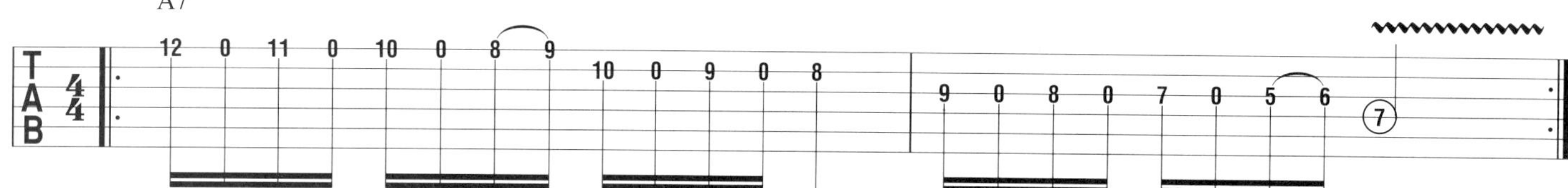


## 448: All-Purpose Lick

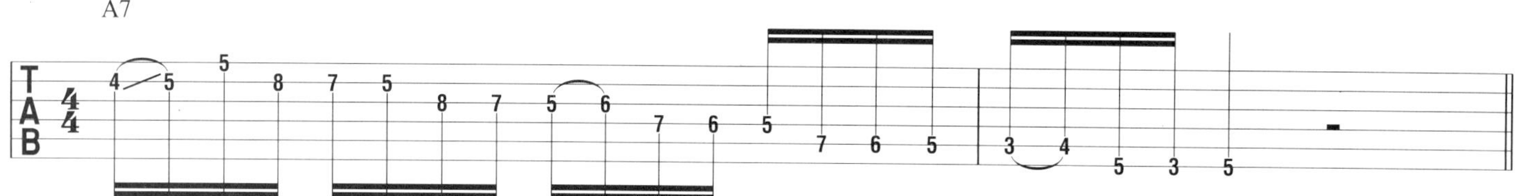

## 449: Chordal Break

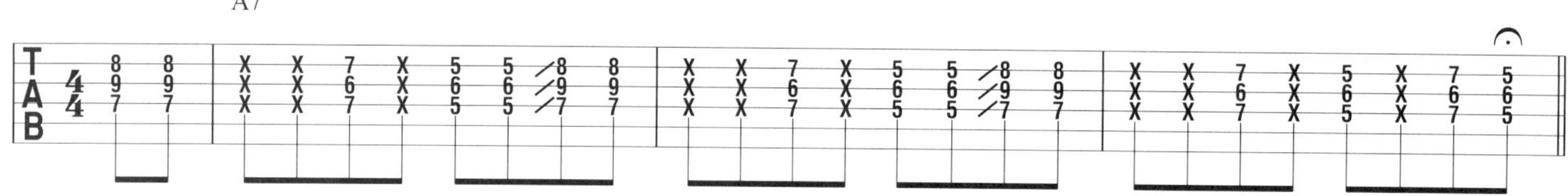


## 450: Melodic Sequence

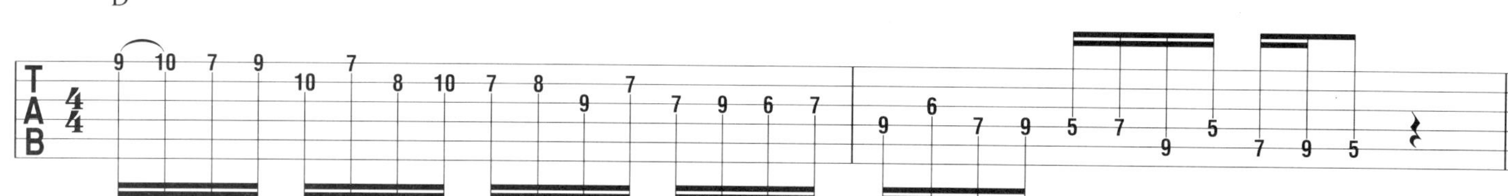


## 451: Single-Note Blues

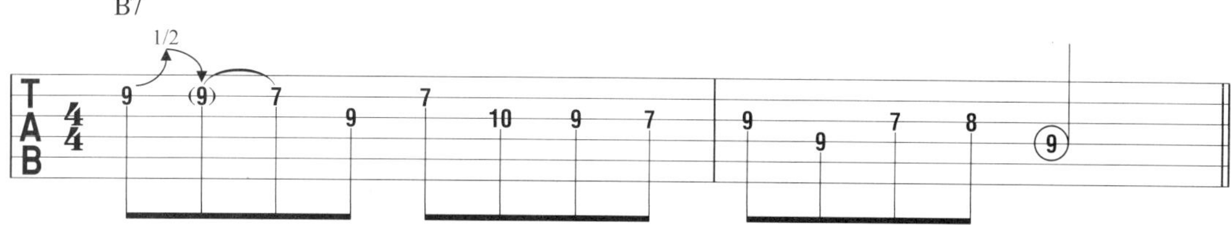


## 452: Bending Line

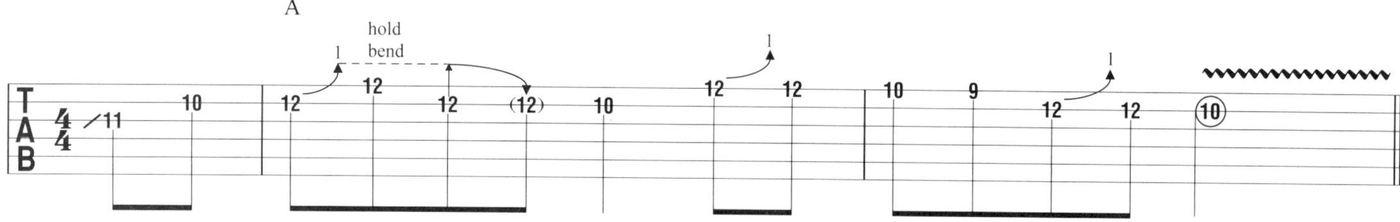


## 453: Sweet Resolve

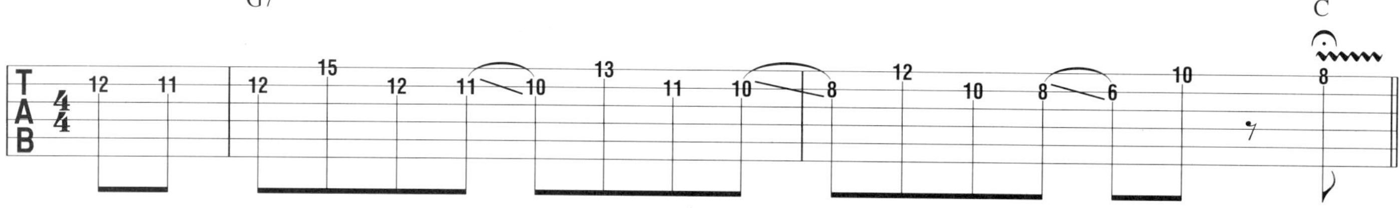

## 454: Hopscotch

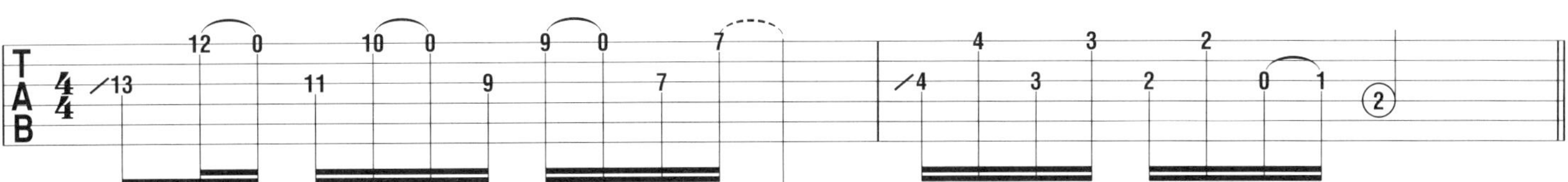

## 455: Rake It

Dm

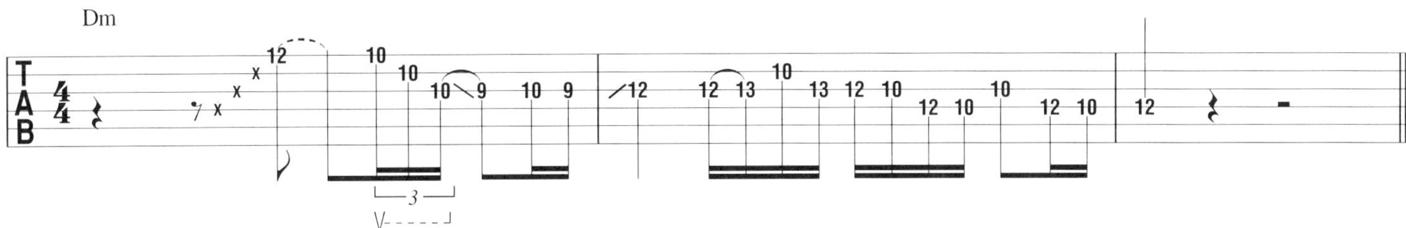

## 456: Doublestoppin'

A7

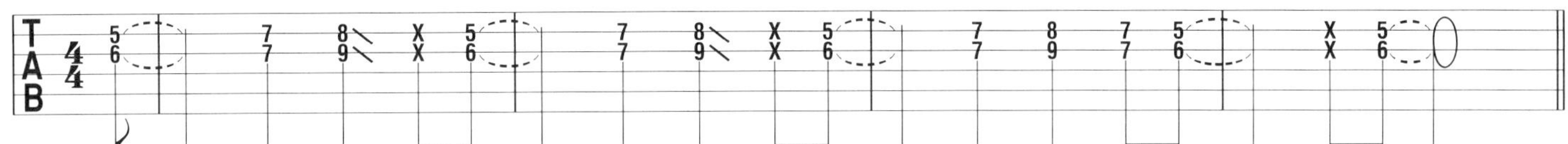

## 457: Riffin' Blues

A7

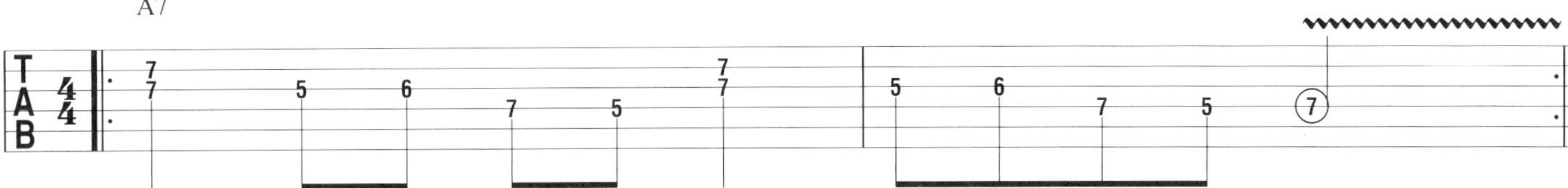

## 458: Channeling Chuck

A

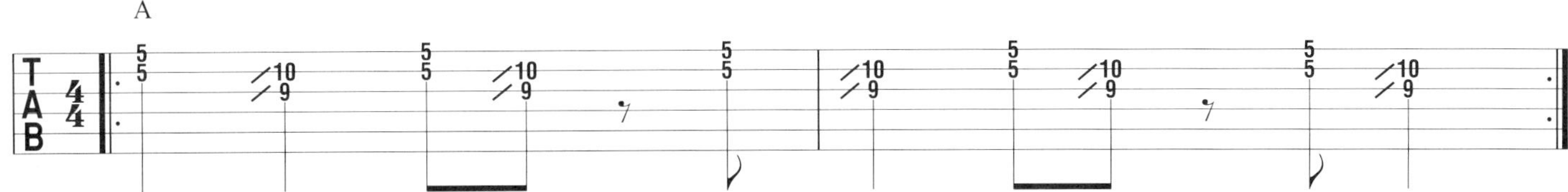

## 459: Triplet Country

G7

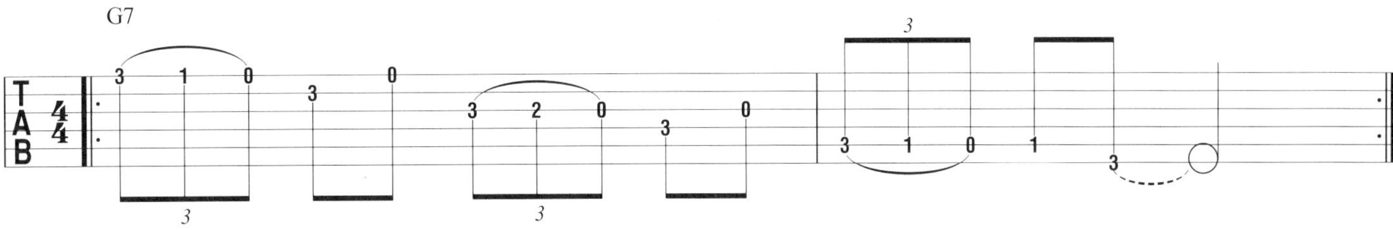

## 460: Flatt Fingered

G

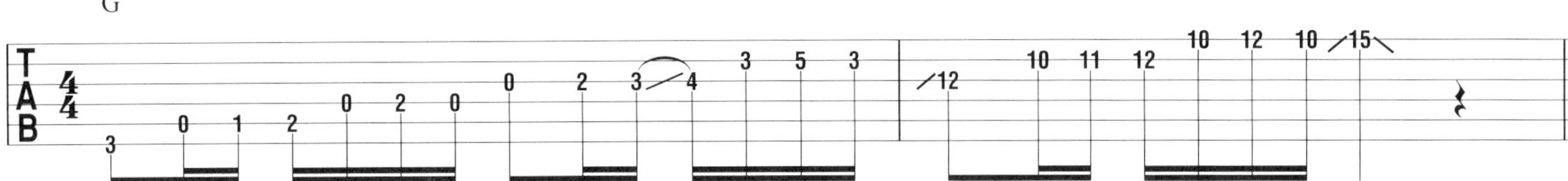

## 461: Country Line

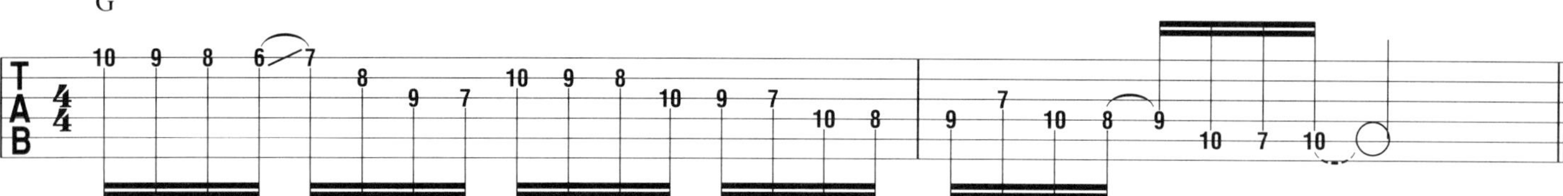


## 462: Staccato Slide

D-G-D-G-B-D

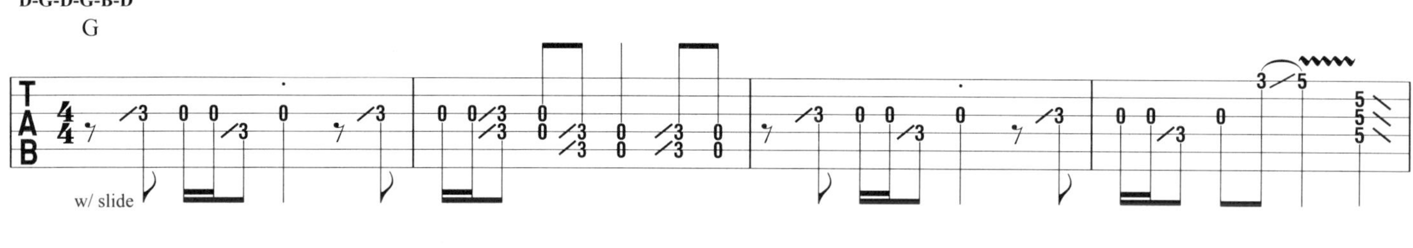


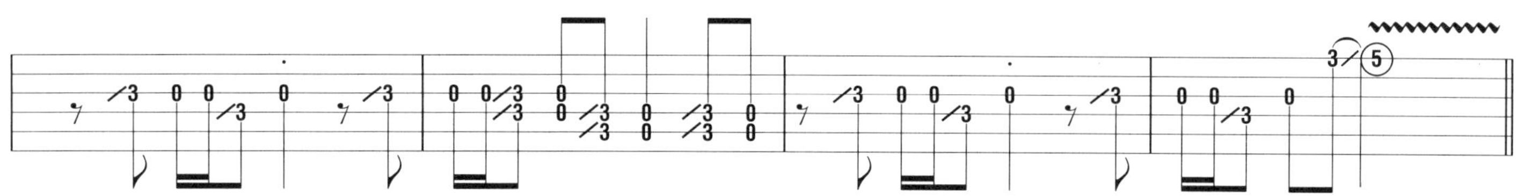

## 463: 12-String Slide

*B-E-B-E-G♯-B

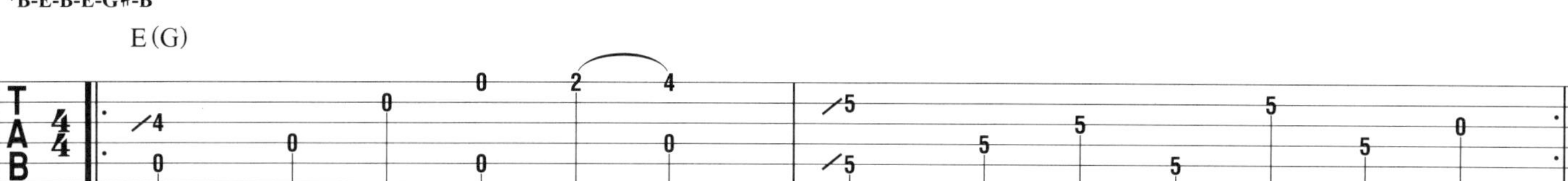


*Open G tuning, down 1 1/2 steps

## 464: Slide Turnaround

D-G-D-G-B-D

**Swing feel**

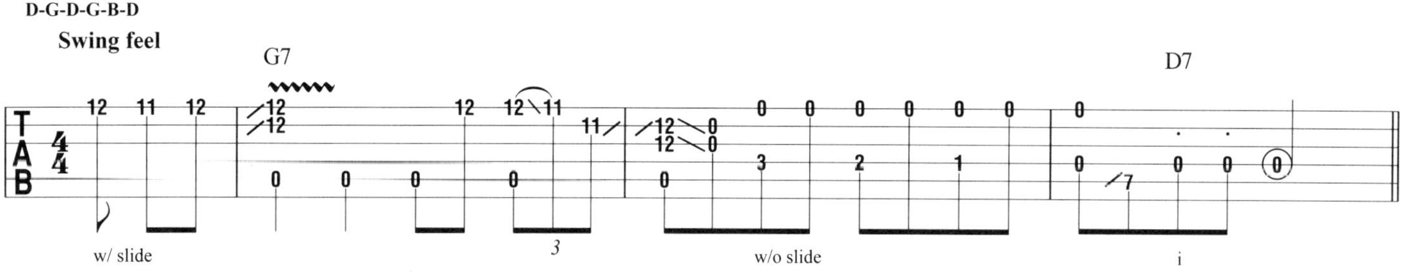


## 465: Slide Ending

D-G-D-G-B-D

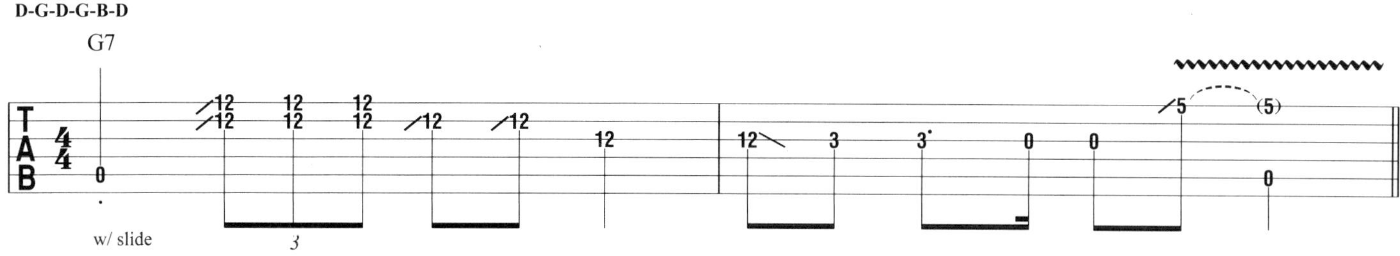

## 466: Slide Riff

D-G-D-G-B-D

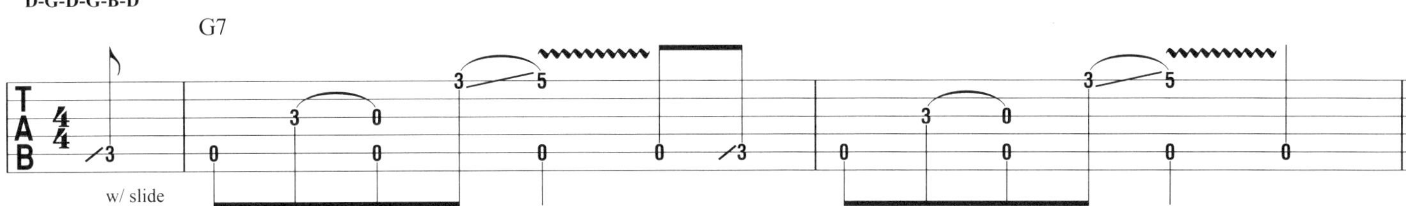


## 467: Aloha 12-String

*B-E-B-E-G♯-B

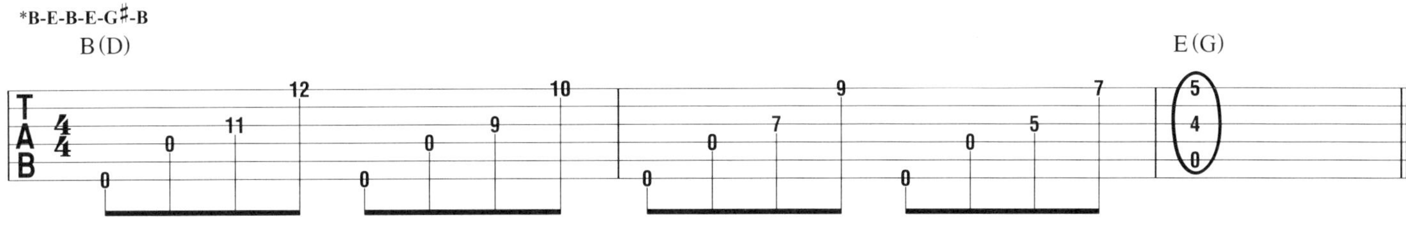


*Open G tuning, down 1 1/2 steps

## 468: Leo Bass Run

*B-E-B-E-G♯-B

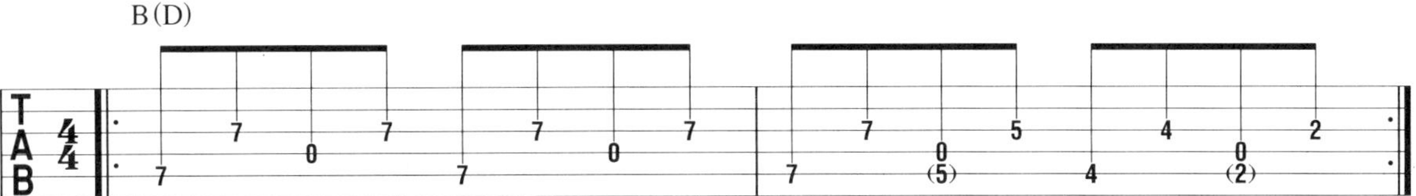


*Open G tuning, down 1 1/2 steps

## 469: Harp Harmonics

D-G-D-G-B-D

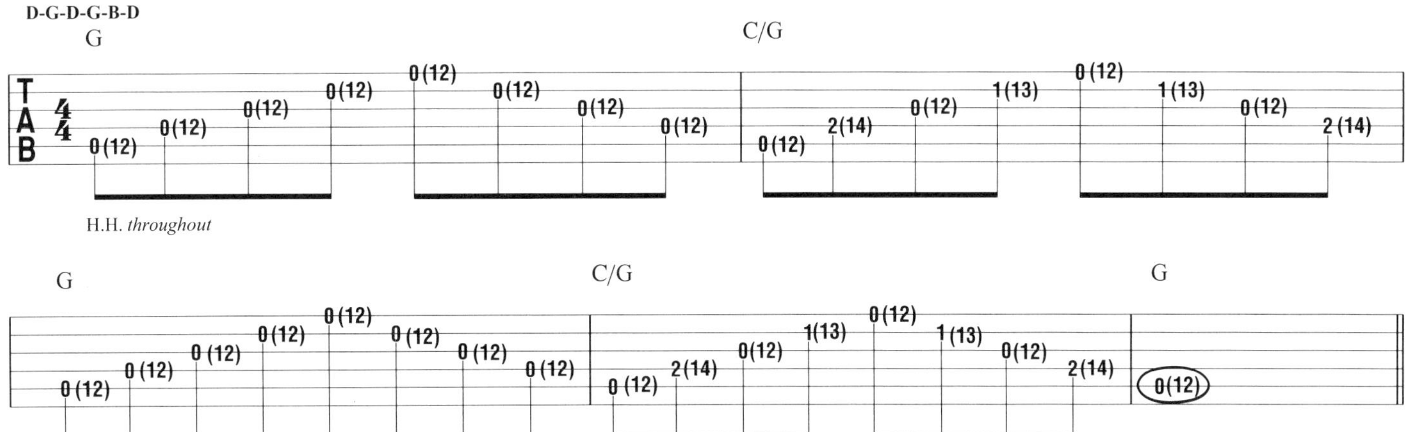


## 470: Slap Harmonics

D-A-D-G-C-F

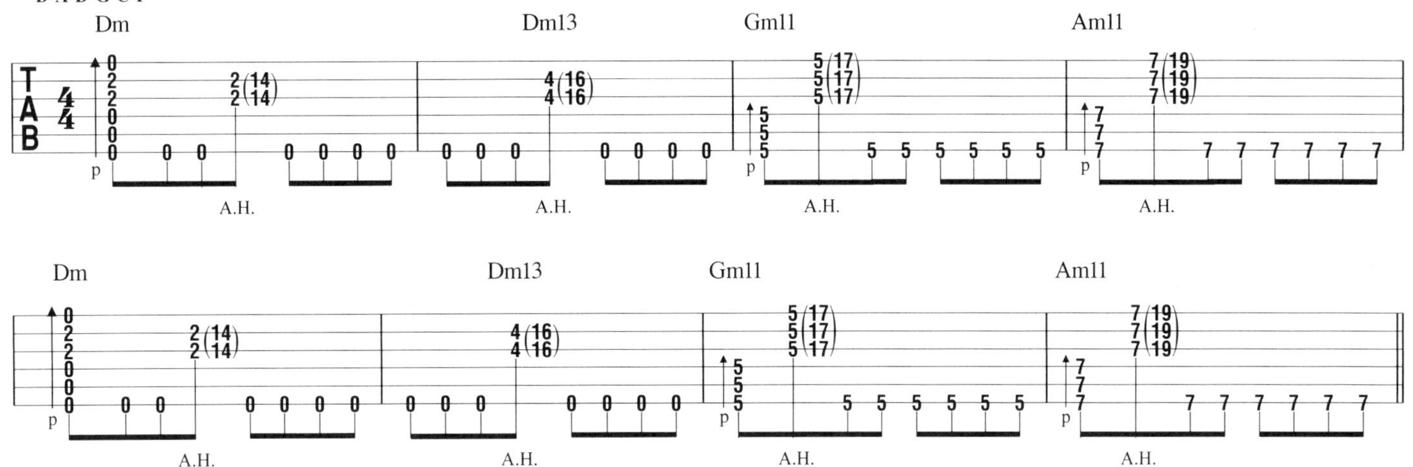

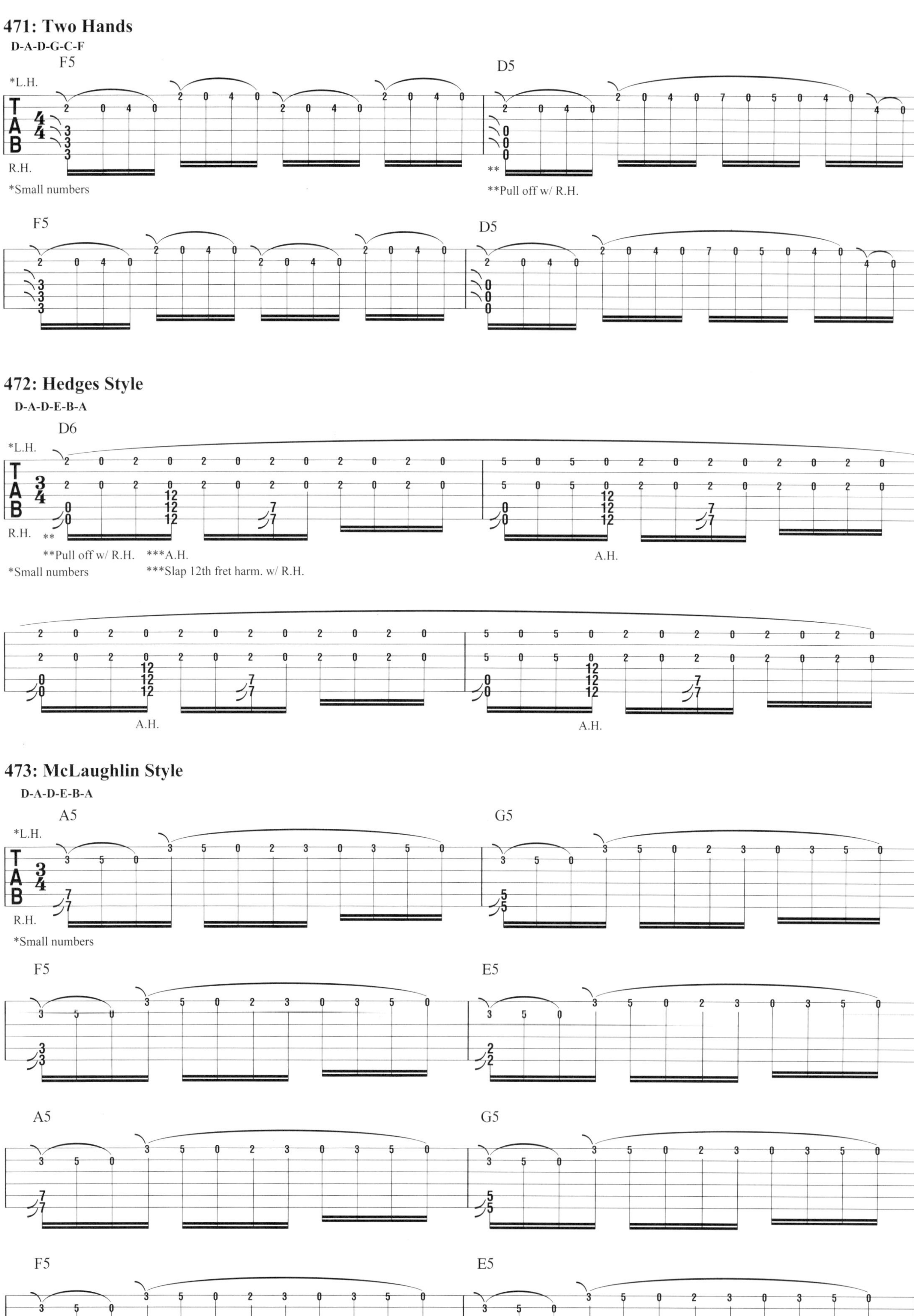
471: Two Hands
D-A-D-G-C-F
F5
D5
*L.H.
R.H.
*Small numbers
**Pull off w/ R.H.
472: Hedges Style
D-A-D-E-B-A
D6
*L.H.
R.H.
**Pull off w/ R.H.
***A.H.
*Small numbers
***Slap 12th fret harm. w/ R.H.
A.H.
473: McLaughlin Style
D-A-D-E-B-A
A5
G5
*L.H.
R.H.
*Small numbers
F5
E5

## 474: Satriani Style

D-A-D-E-B-B

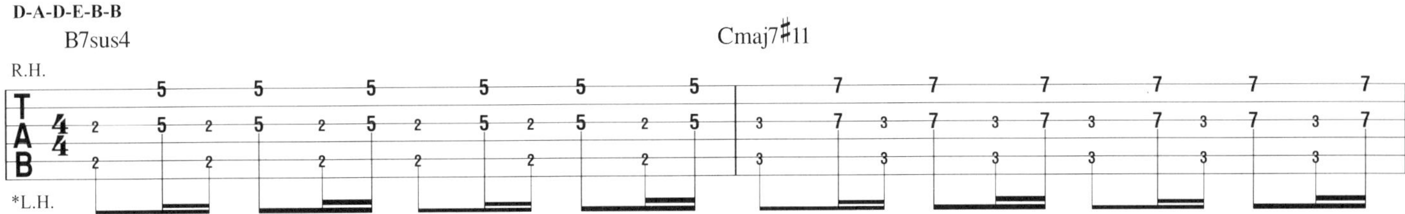


*L.H.: small numbers
All notes articulated with either L.H. or R.H. hammer-ons.

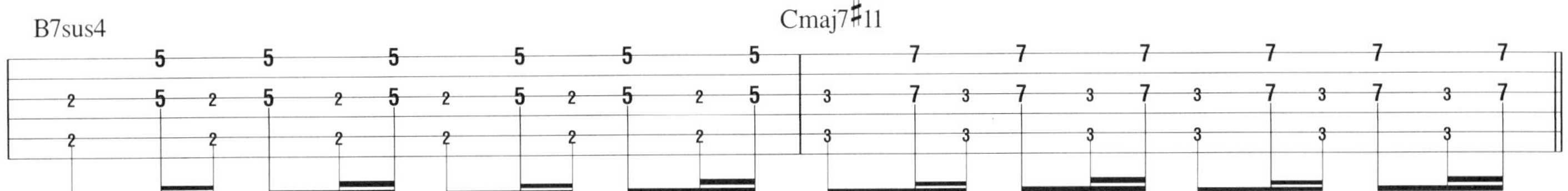


## 475: Fretboard Dancing

D-A-E-A-B-E

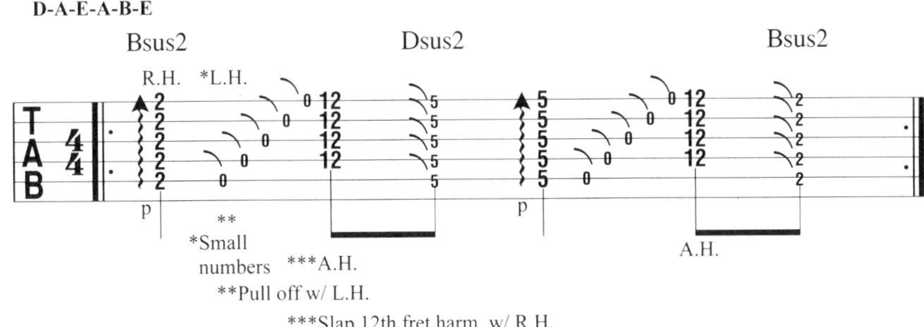


*Small numbers
***A.H.
**Pull off w/ L.H.
***Slap 12th fret harm. w/ R.H.

# Instructor: Ben Woolman

## 476: Bahama Walk

D-A-D-G-B-E

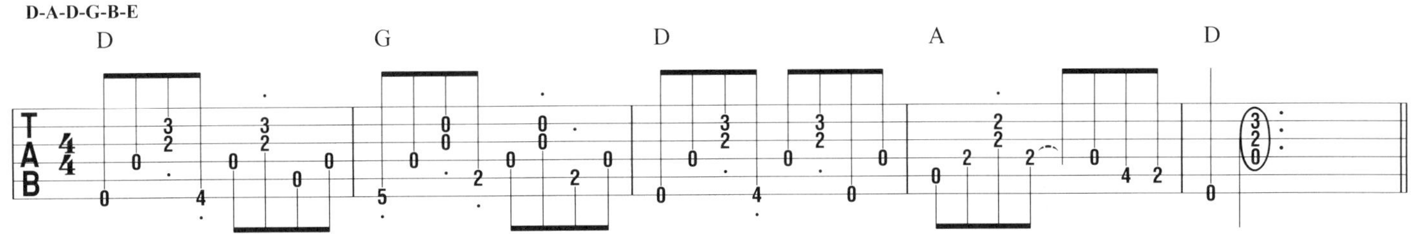


## 477: Chump Variation

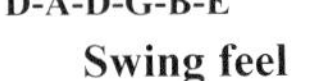


**Swing feel**

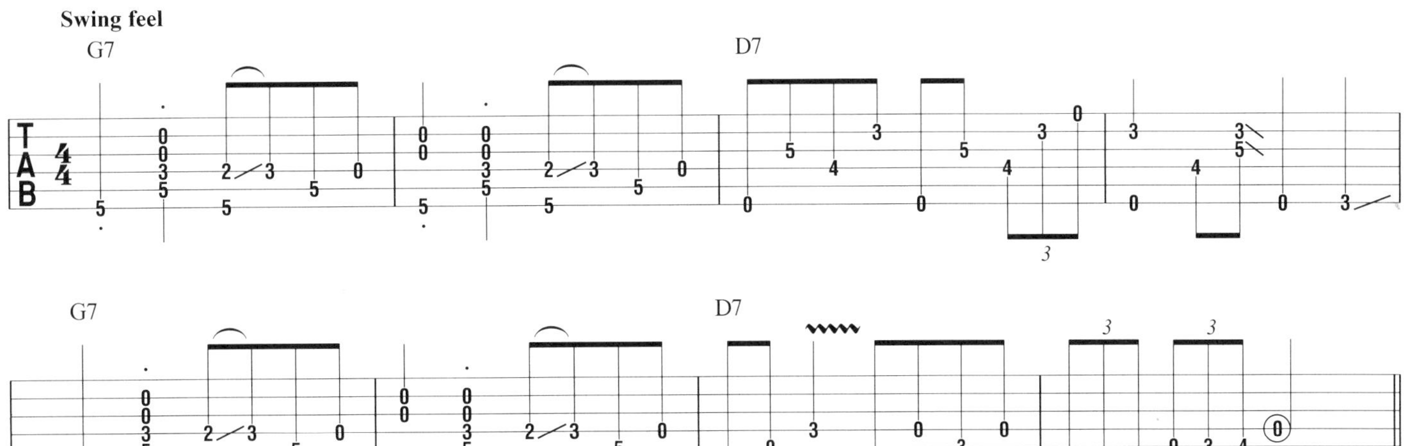

## 478: Rasgueado Groove

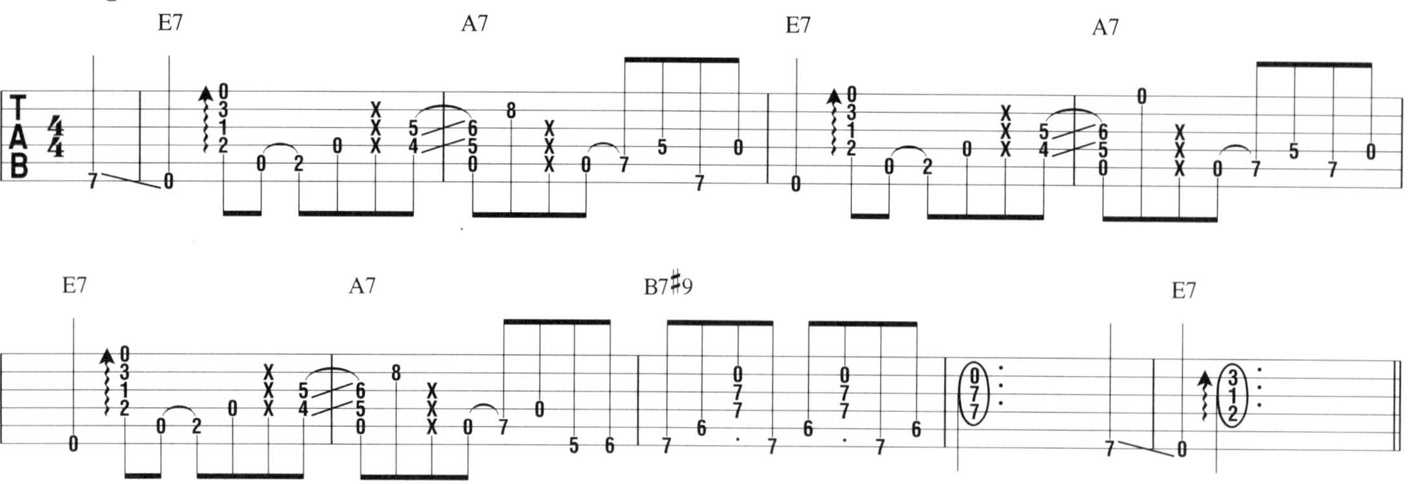


## 479: Dirty Slide

C-G-C-G-C-E

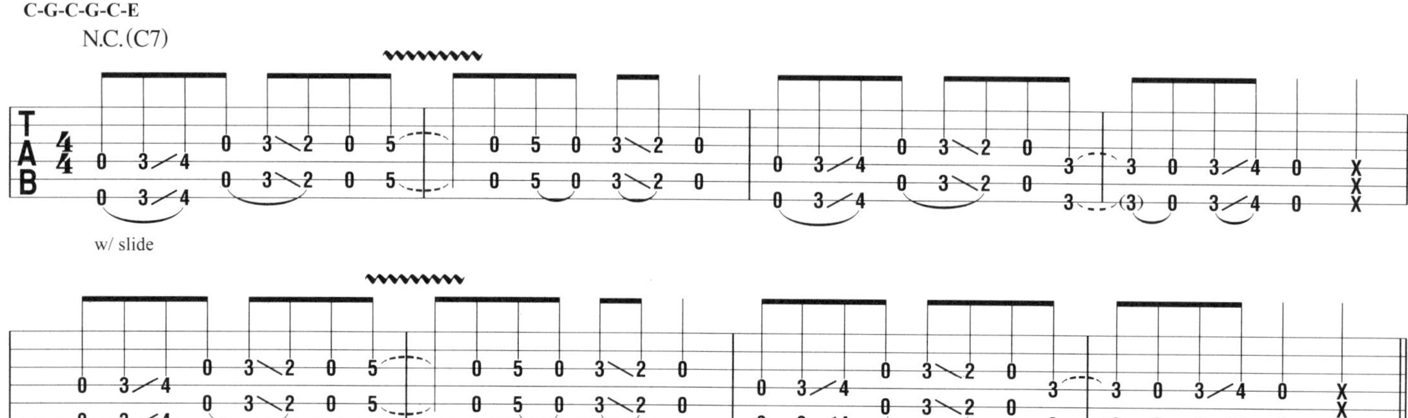


## 480: Texture Groove

C-G-C-G-C-E

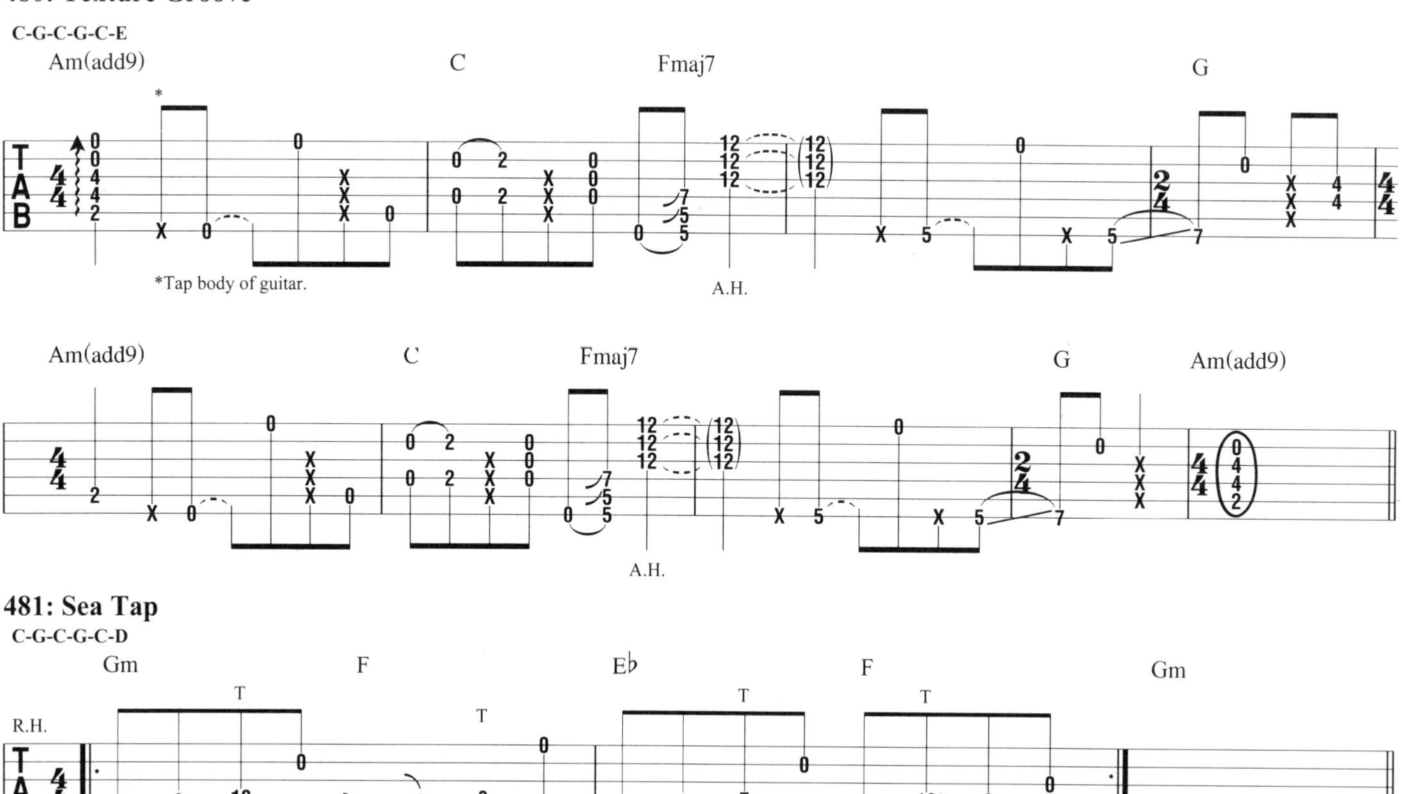


## 481: Sea Tap

C-G-C-G-C-D

### 482: Sea Bass Groove

C-G-C-G-C-D

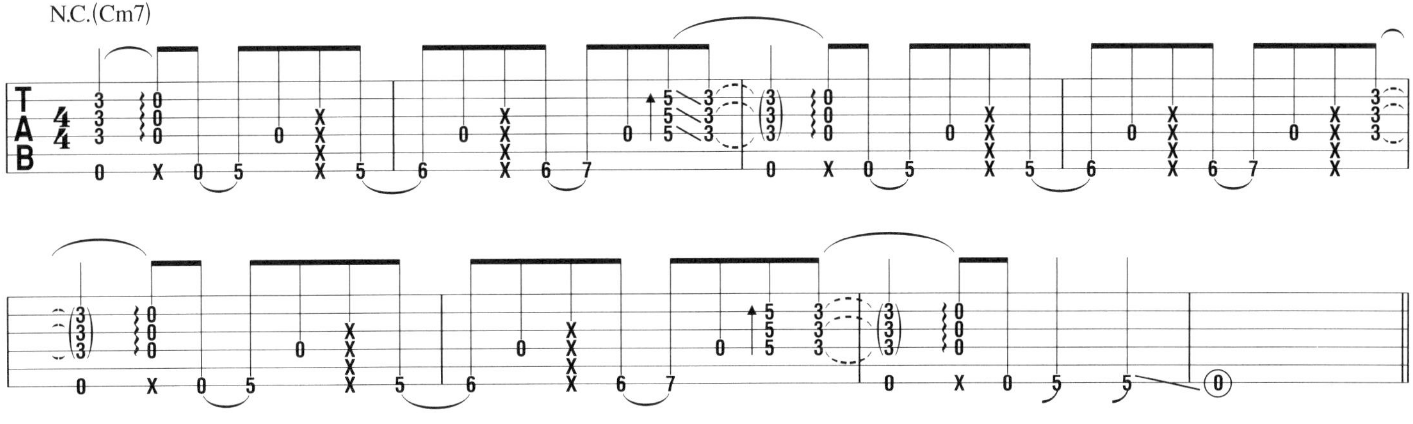


### 483: Basic Percussion

C-G-C-G-C-D

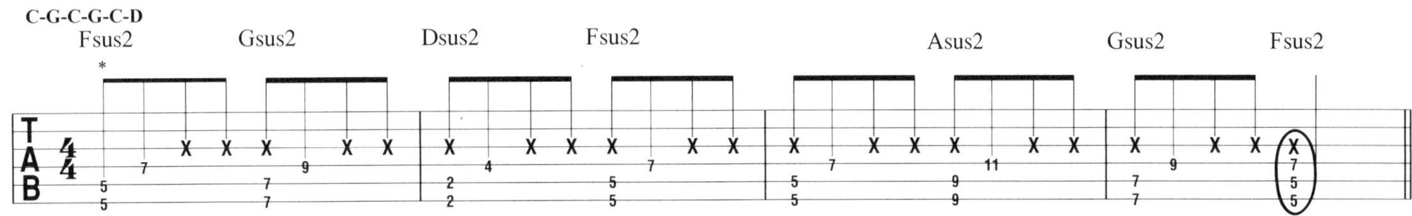


*All small notes hammered on by L.H.
All black notes executed by tapping body of guitar w/ R.H.

### 484: Celtic Frail

C-G-C-G-C-D

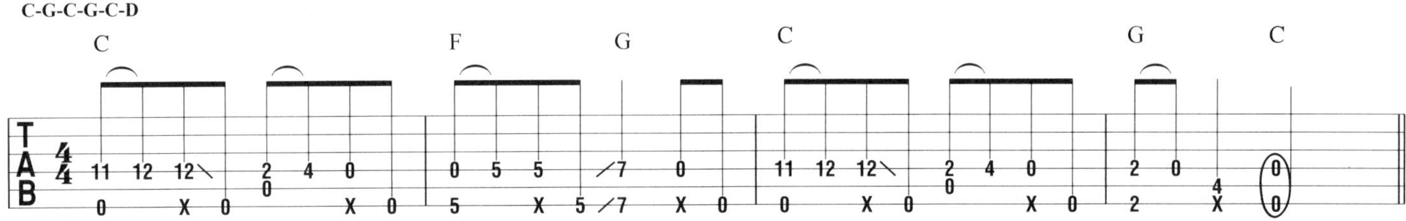


### 485: Synco-Boogie

C-G-D-G-B-E

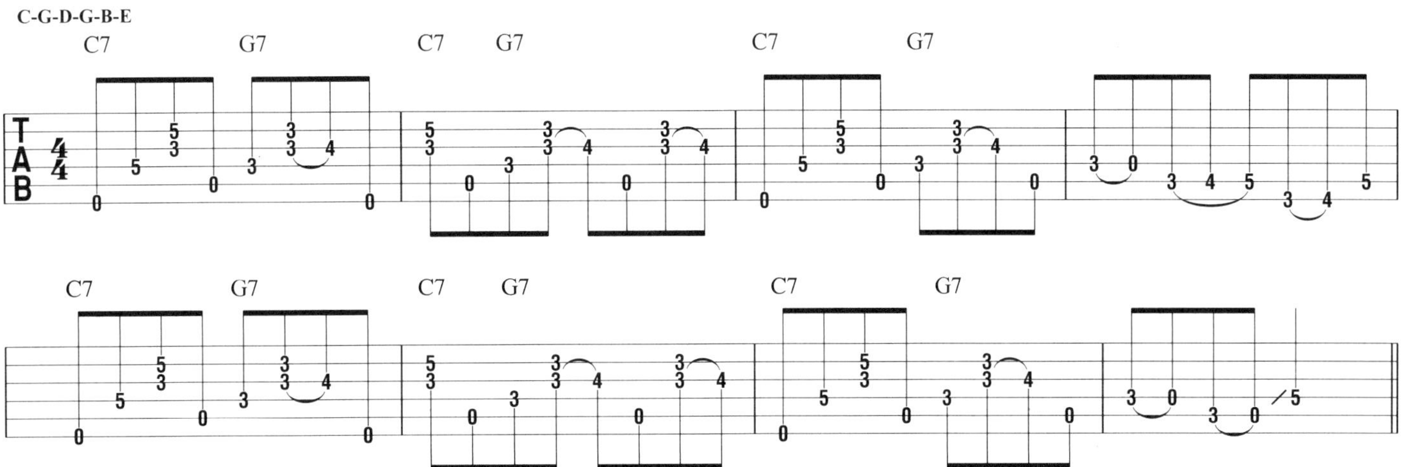


### 486: Bass Walk

Swing feel

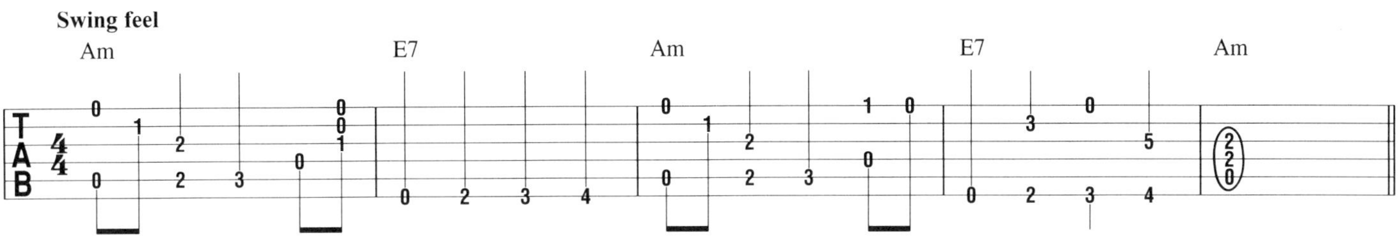

## 487: Cross String

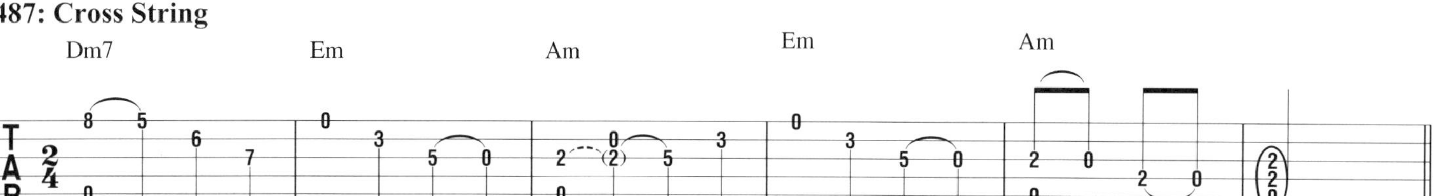


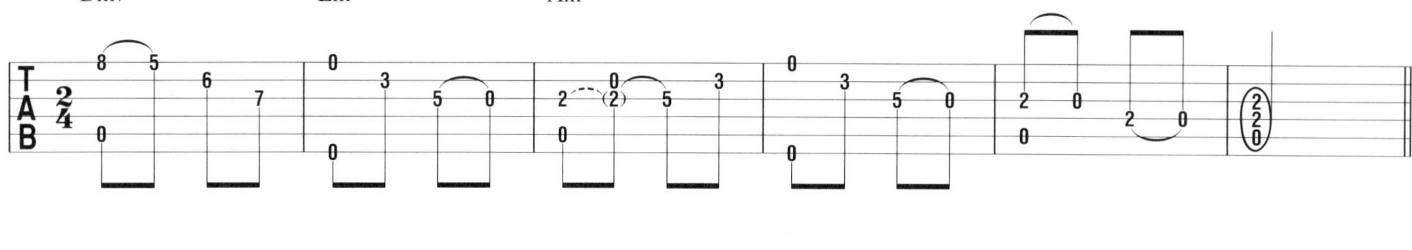

## 488: Floating Arpeggios

**Capo IV (strings 2–6 only)**

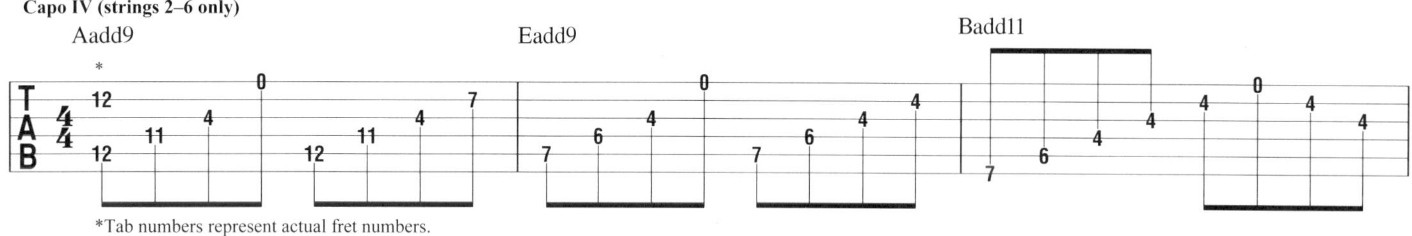


*Tab numbers represent actual fret numbers.
Capoed fret is 4 on strings 2–6.

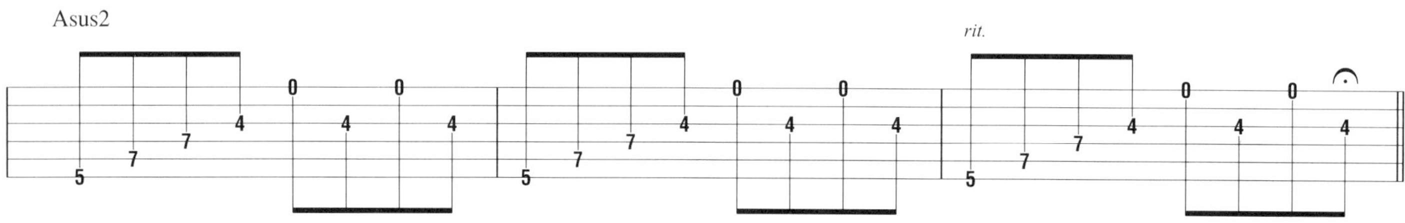


## 489: Organ Groove

**Swing feel**

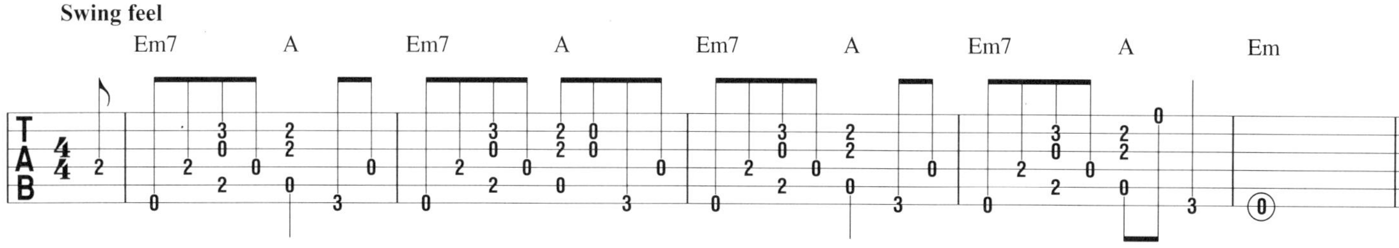


## 490: Tap Dance

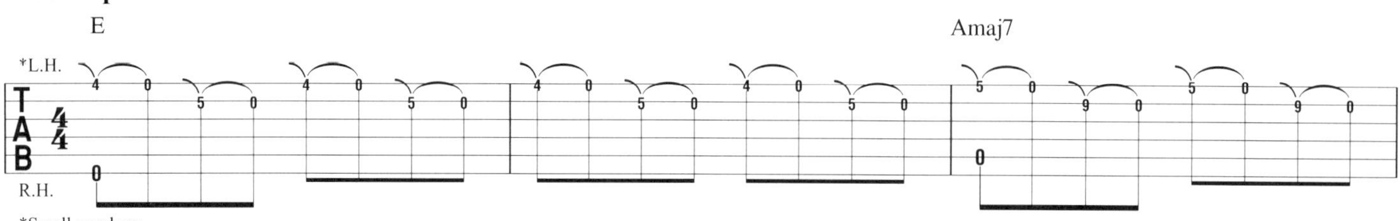


*Small numbers

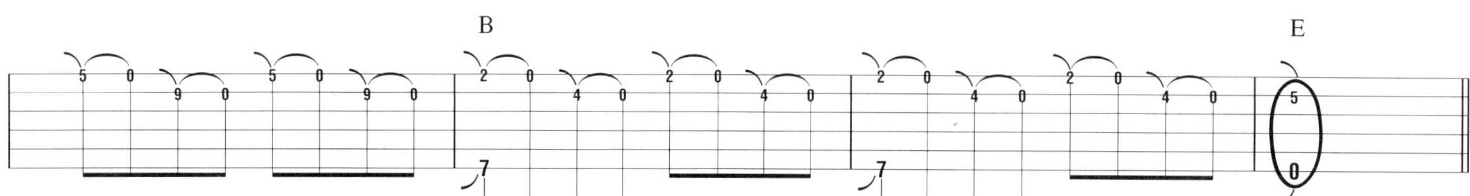

## 491: Bass & Drums

D-A-D-G-B-D

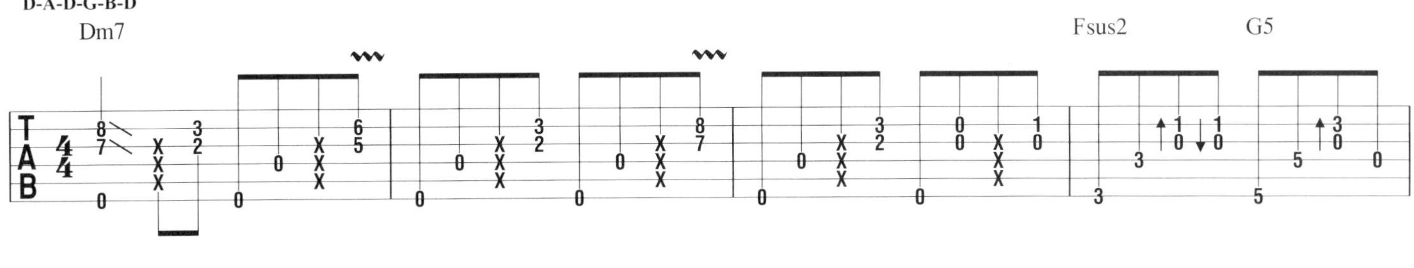


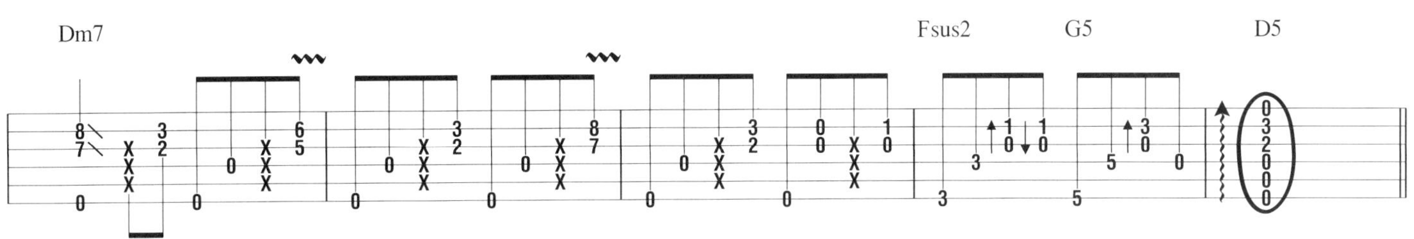


## 492: Hammer Bass

D-A-D-G-B-D

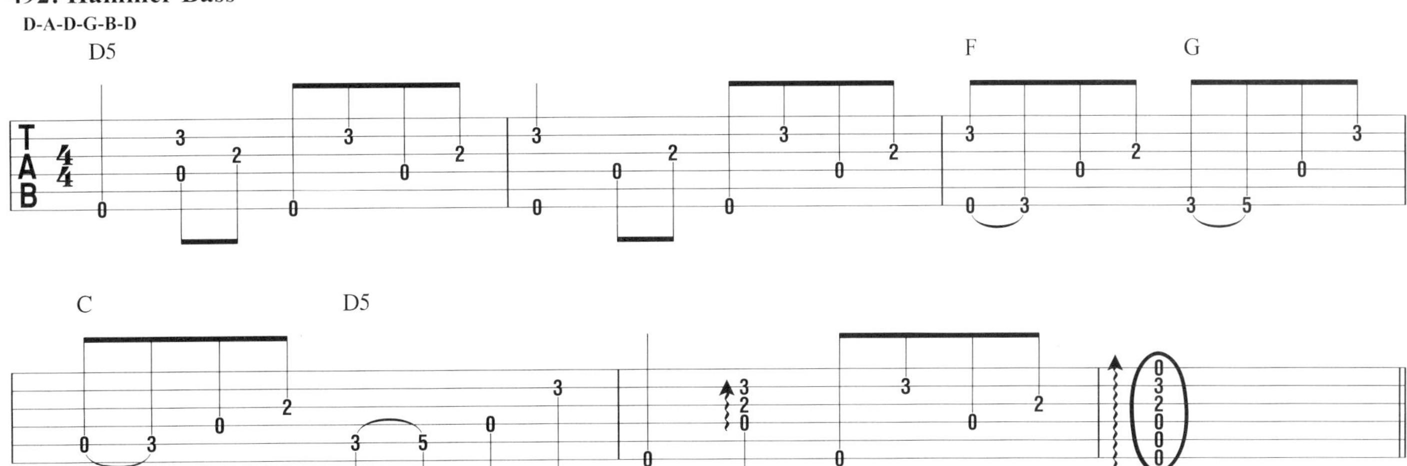


## 493: Pop Fingerstyle

Capo II (strings 2–6 only), D-A-D-G-B-E

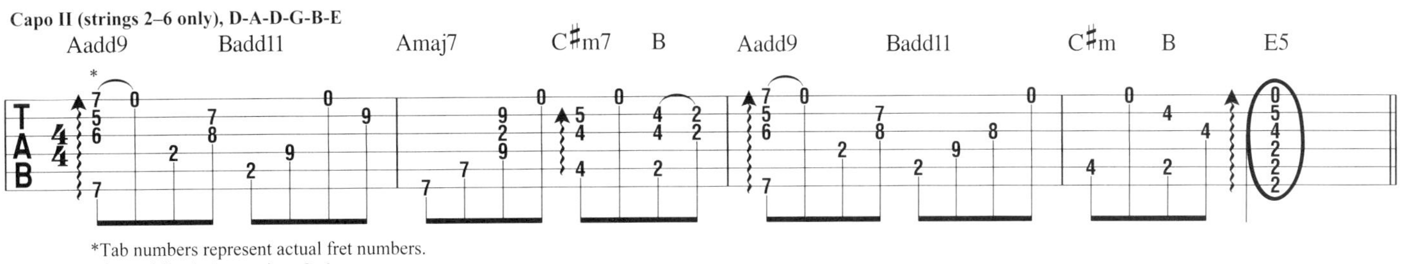


*Tab numbers represent actual fret numbers. Capoed fret is 2 on strings 2–6.

## 494: Celtic Dance

Capo II, D-A-D-G-A-D

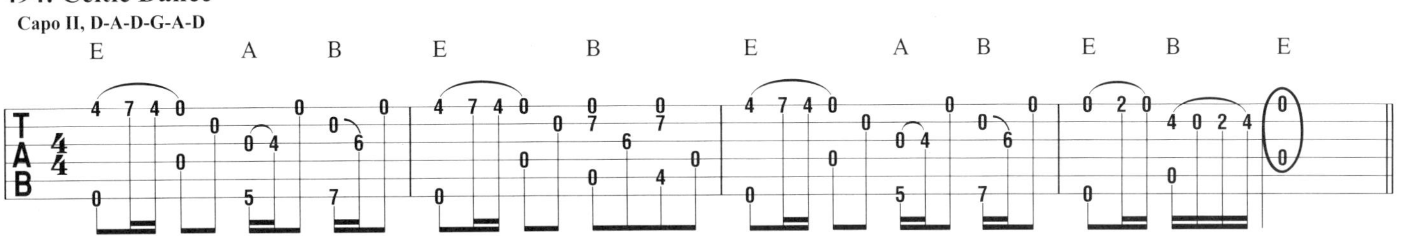

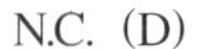

### 495: Slap Tap

Capo II, D-A-D-G-A-D

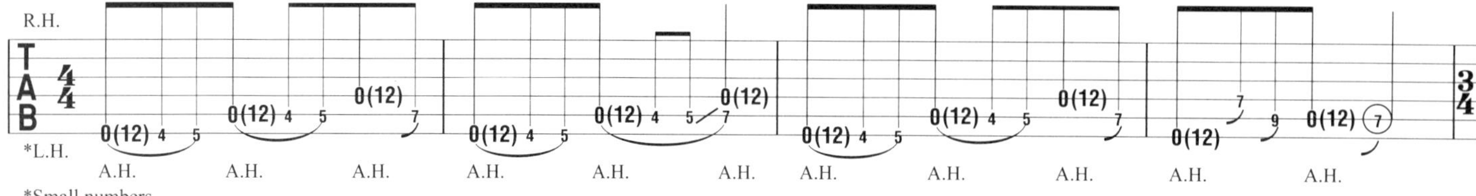


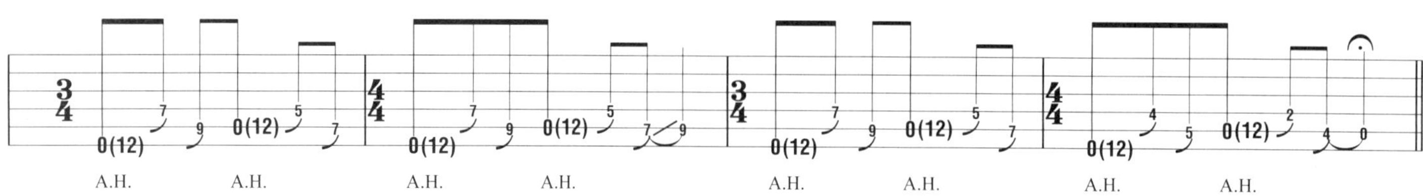


### 496: Bass-Slur Sync

Capo II, D-A-D-G-A-D

Swing feel

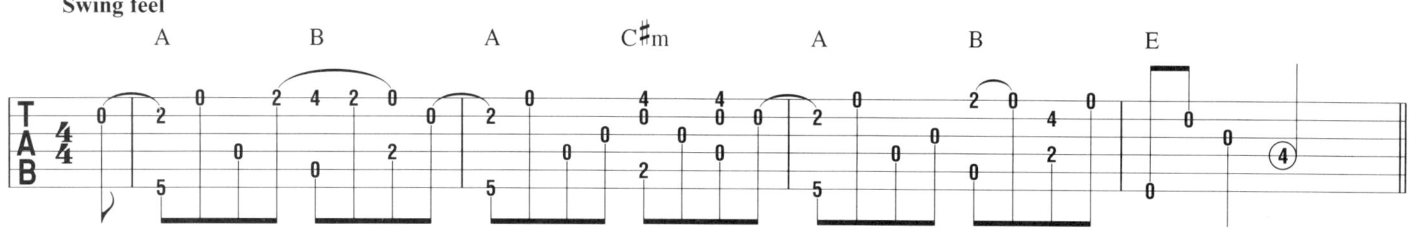


### 497: Country Folk

D-G-D-G-B-D

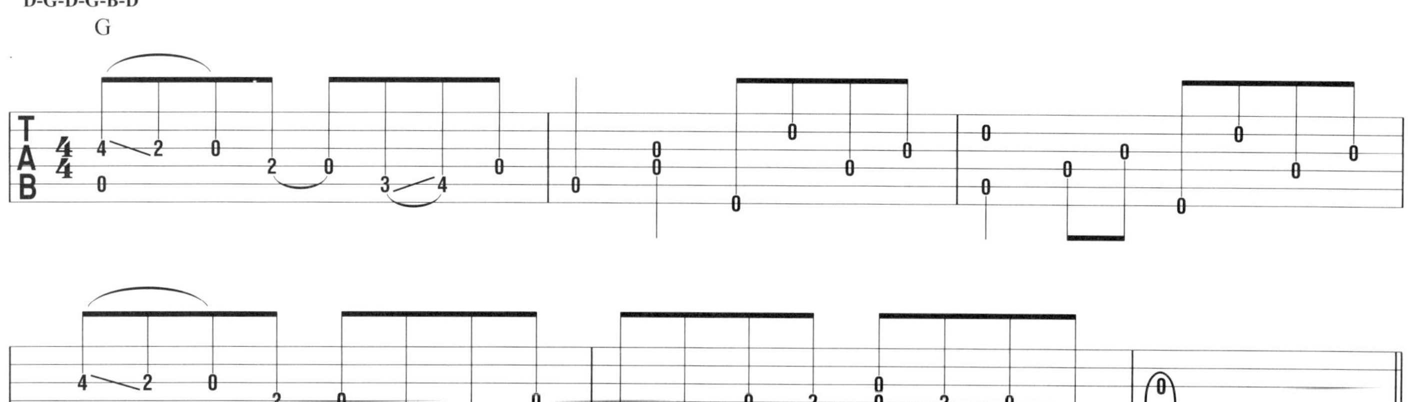


### 498: Melodic Vamp

D-G-D-G-B-D

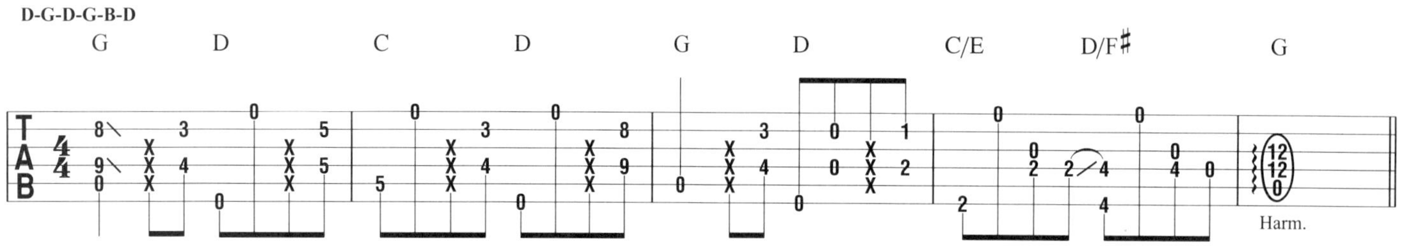

### 499: Harmonic Melody

D-G-D-G-B-D

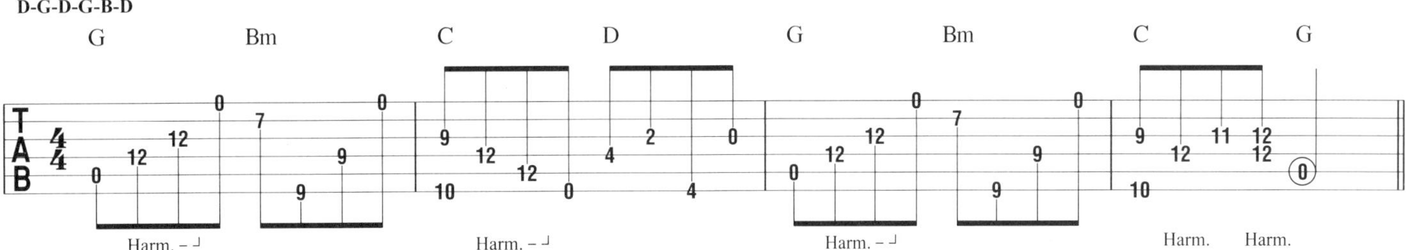


### 500: Open G Breakdown

D-G-D-G-B-D

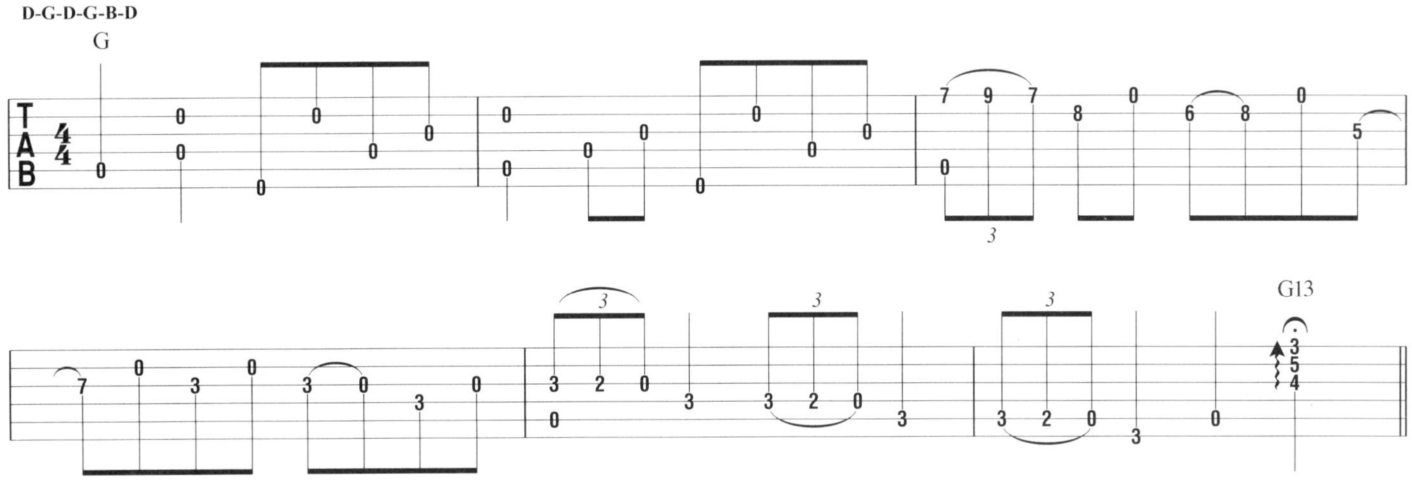


### 501: Pretty DADGAD

Capo II, D-A-D-G-A-D

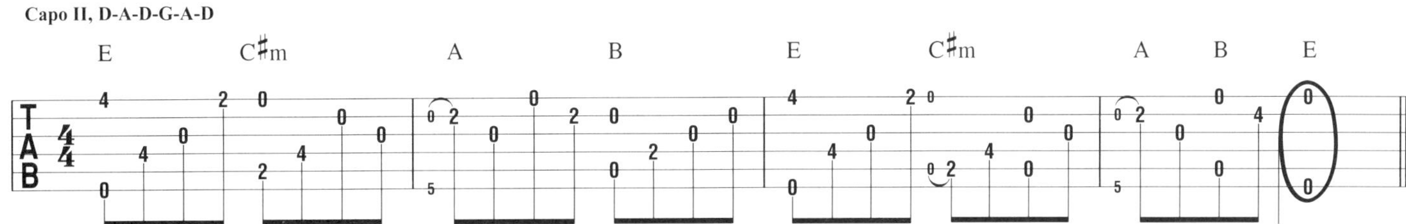


### 502: Smooth Octaves

Capo II, D-A-D-G-A-D

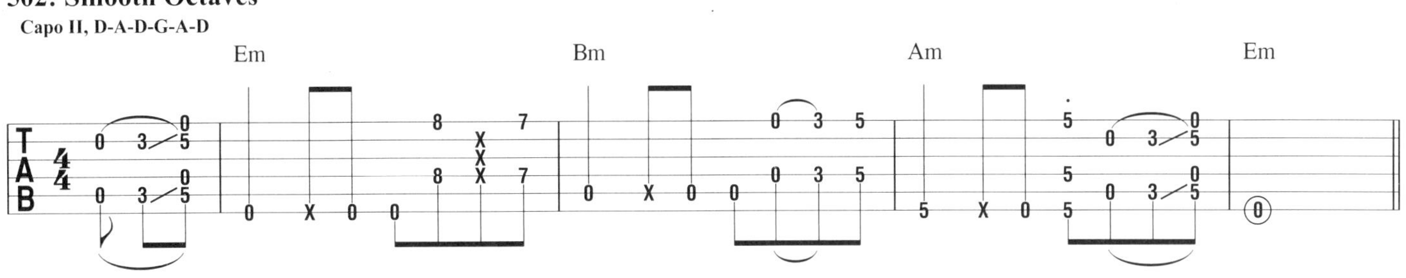


### 503: DADGAD Frail

Capo II, D-A-D-G-A-D

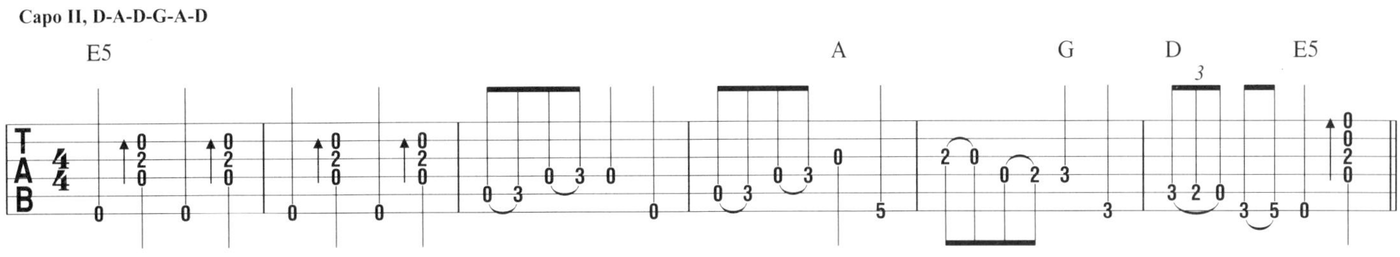

## 504: Textures & Moods

**D-G-D-G-B♭-D**

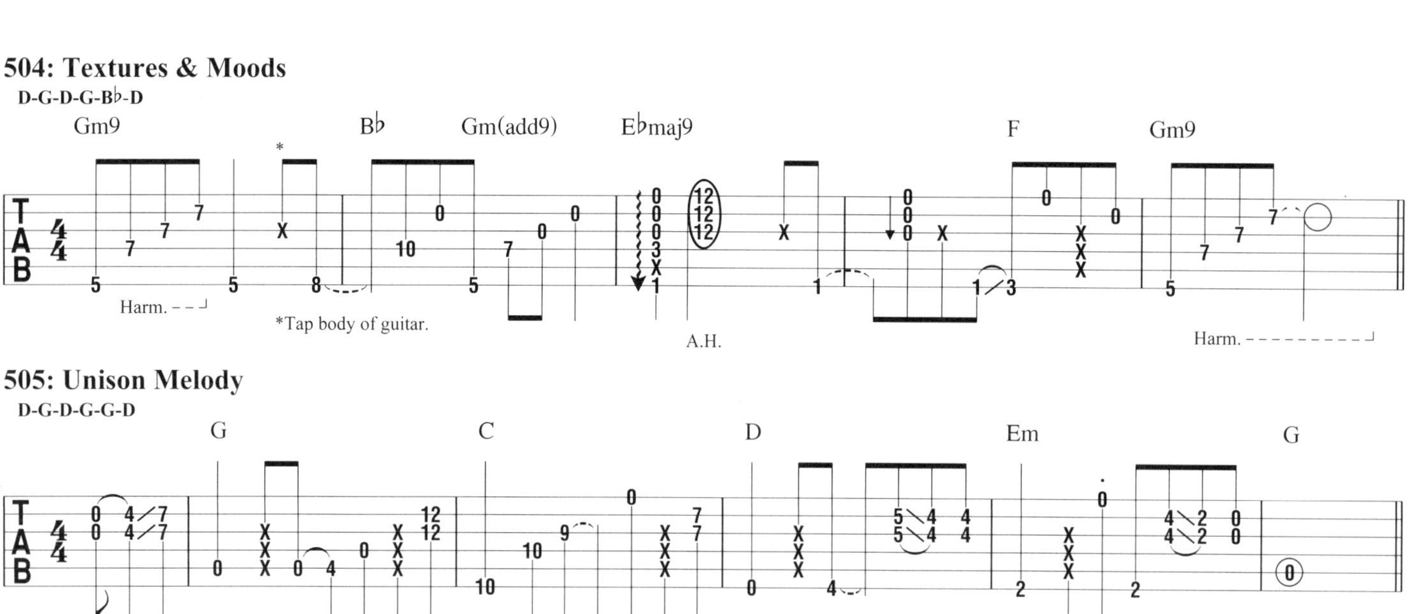


## 505: Unison Melody

**D-G-D-G-G-D**

## 506: Sweep Harmonics

**D-G-C-G-C-D**

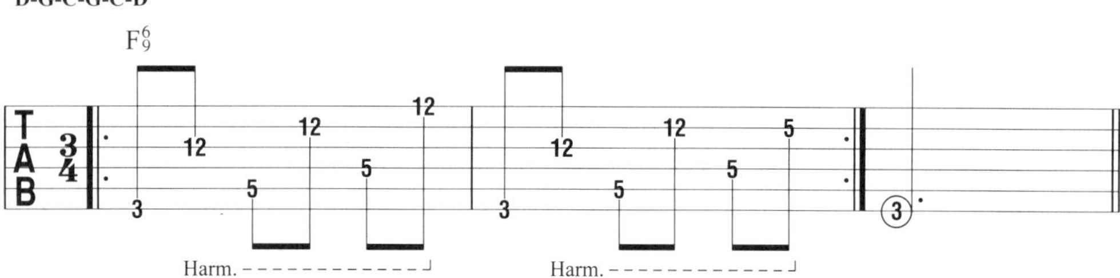


## 507: Moody Tap

**C-G-C-G-C-D**

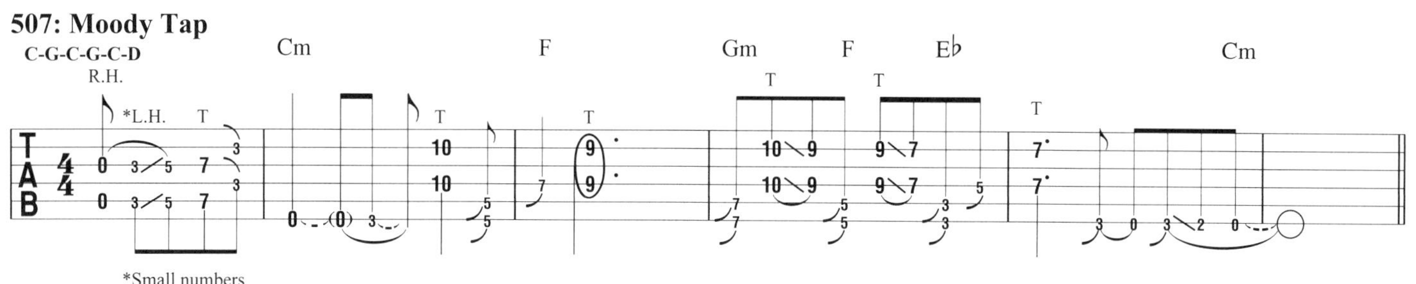

## 508: Country Groove

**Capo II, C-A-C-G-A-C**

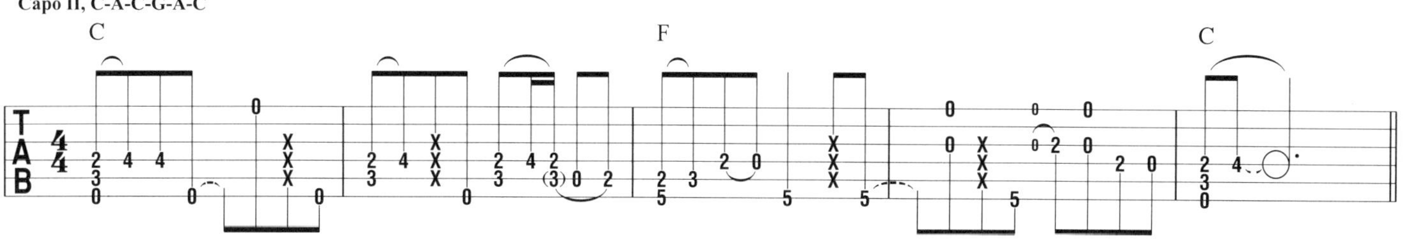


## 509: Standard Celtic

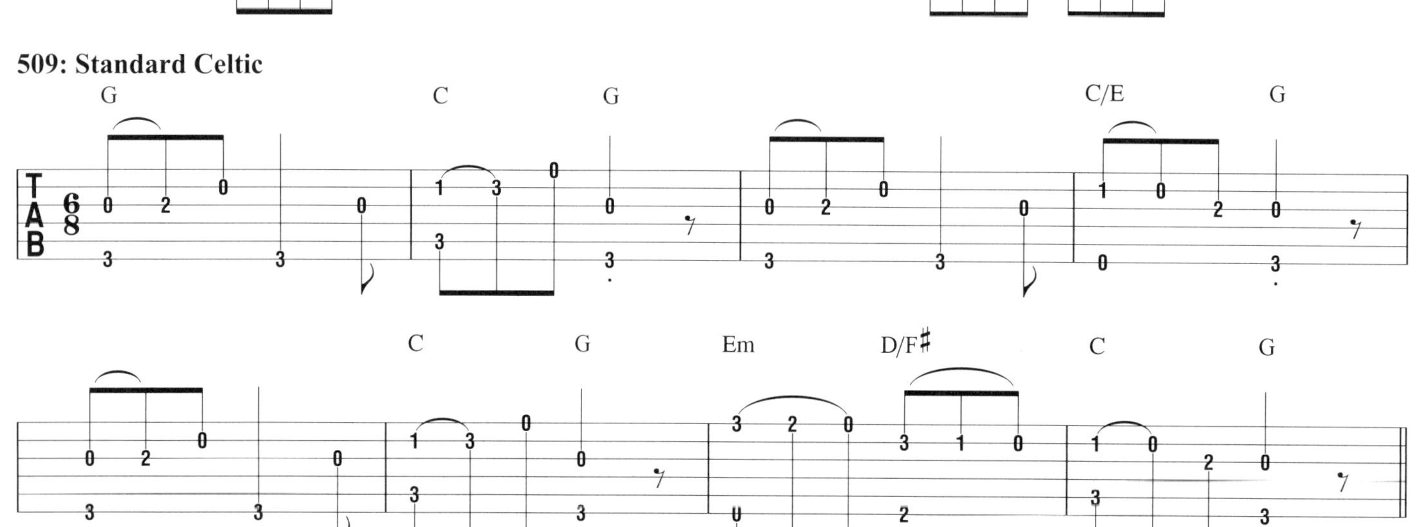

## 510: Mixolydian Shuffle

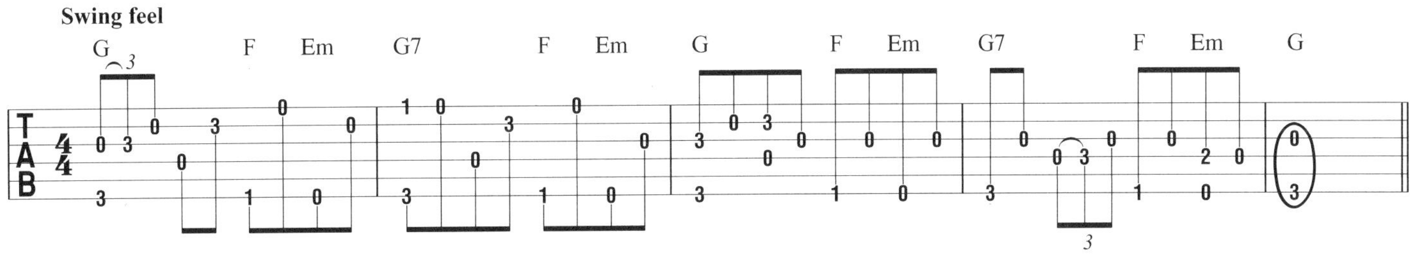


## 511: Tap & Pluck

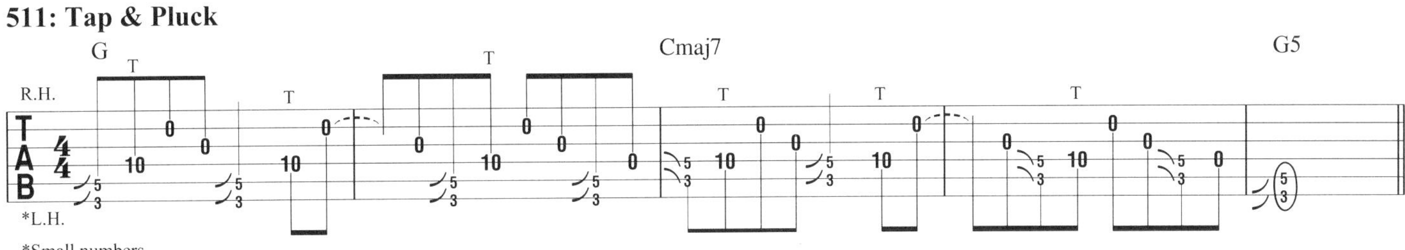


## 512: Thumb Ostinato

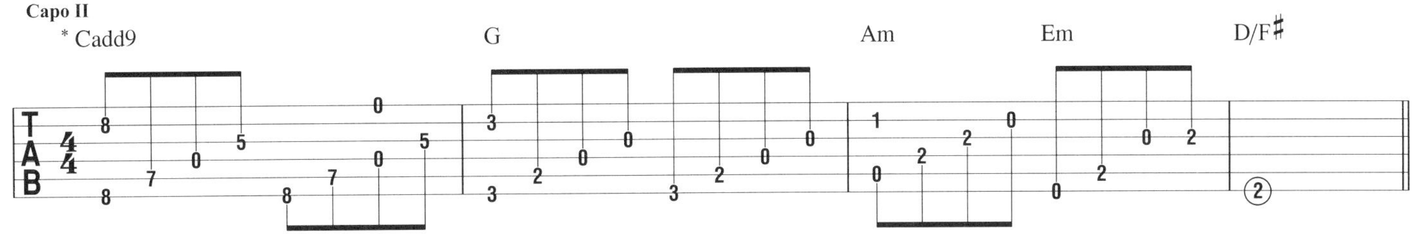


*Chord symbols relative to capoed gtr. and do not reflect actual sounding pitch.

## 513: Distant Chimes

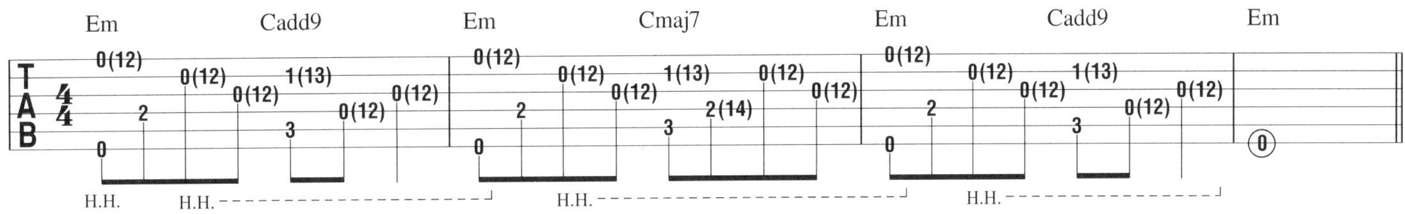


## 514: Blue Groove

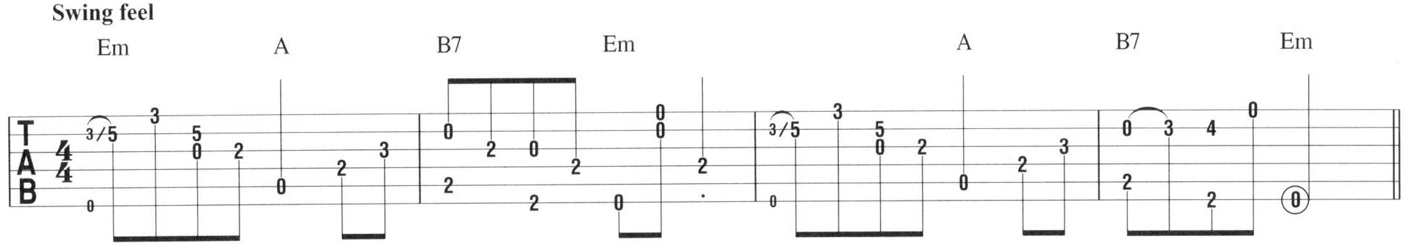


## 515: 3/4 Bass Ascent

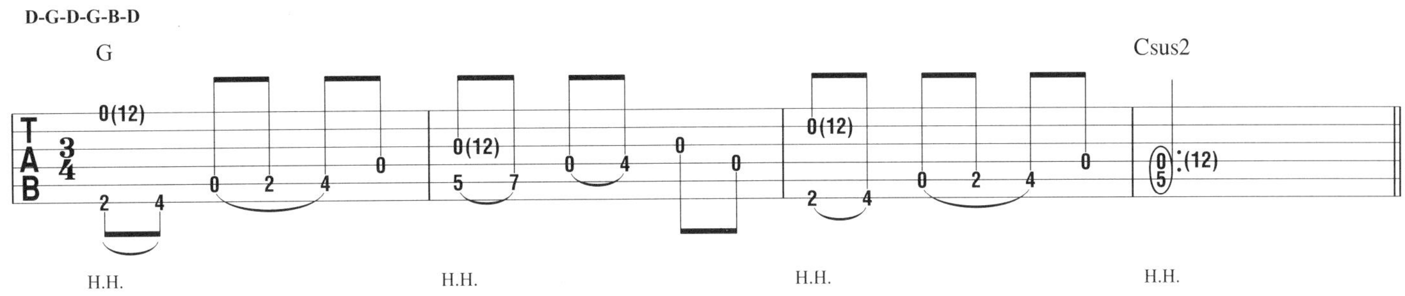

## Instructor: Peter Roller

### 516: Drop D Descent

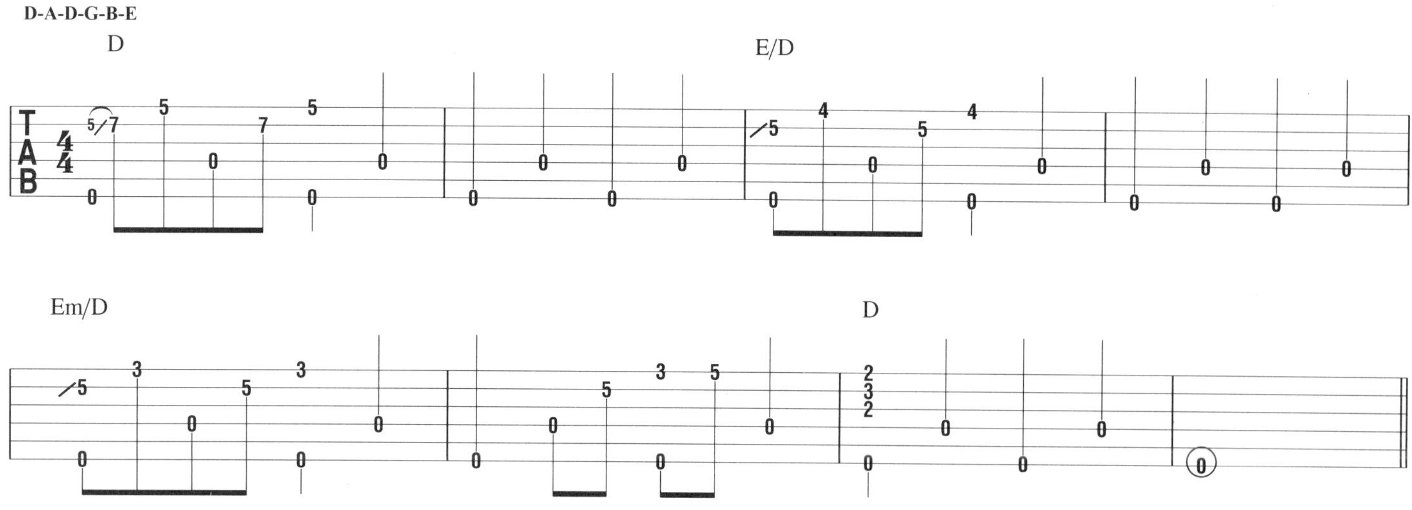


### 517: Lydian Mood

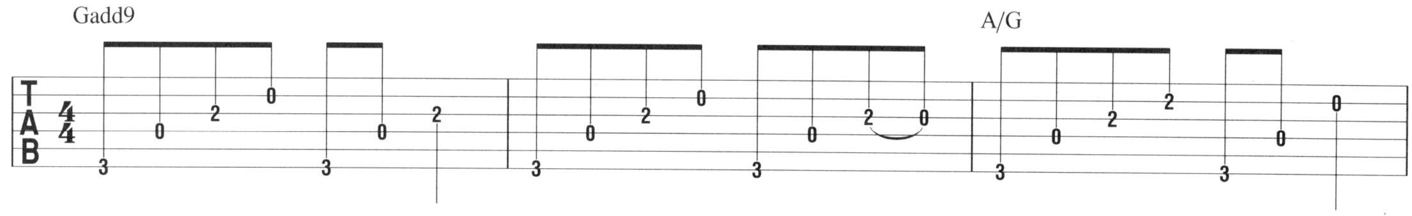


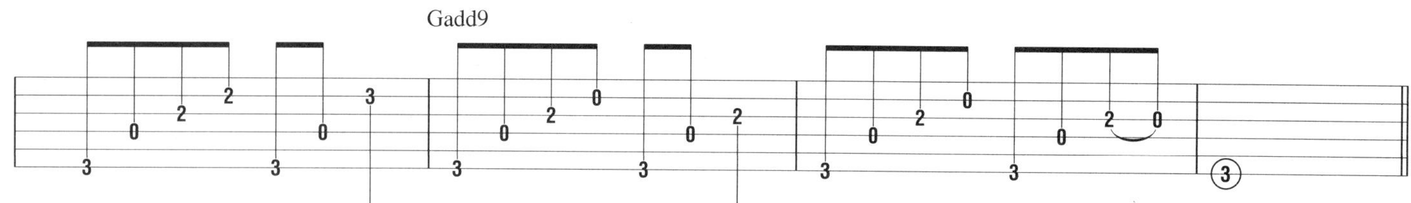


### 518: Celtic Cadenza

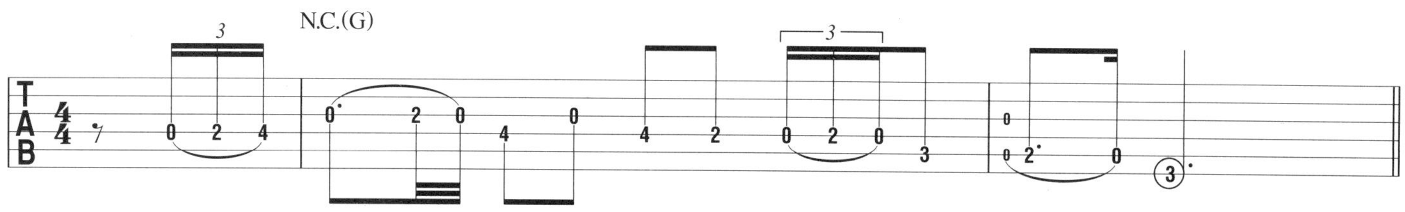


### 519: Talking Blues

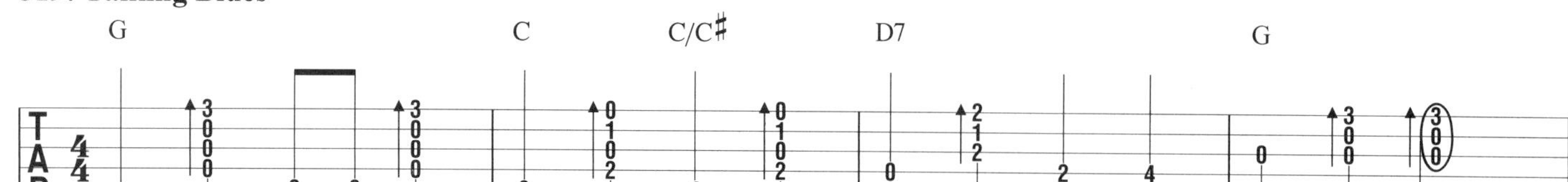


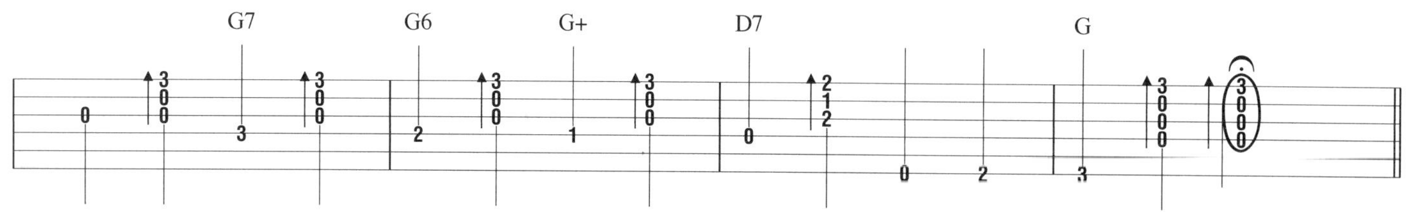

### 520: Country Blues

**Swing feel**

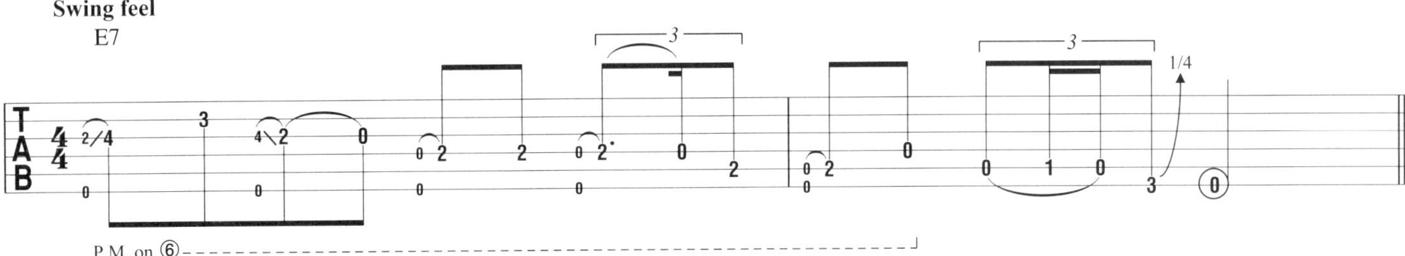


### 521: I-V Turnaround

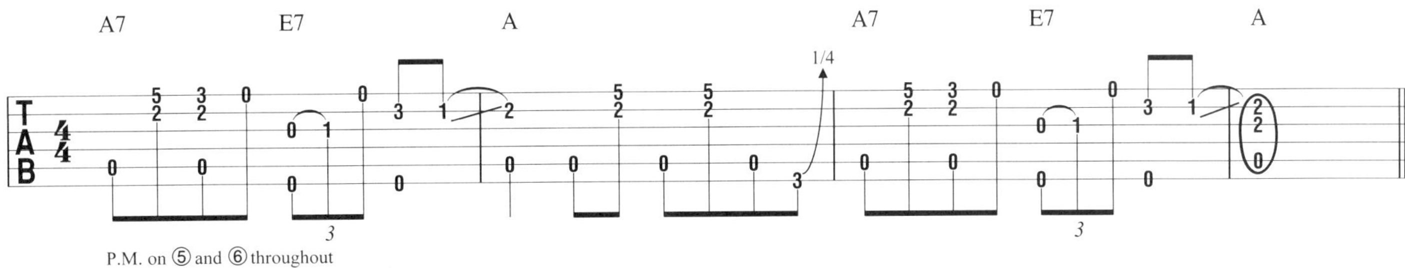


### 522: Delta Groove

**Swing feel**

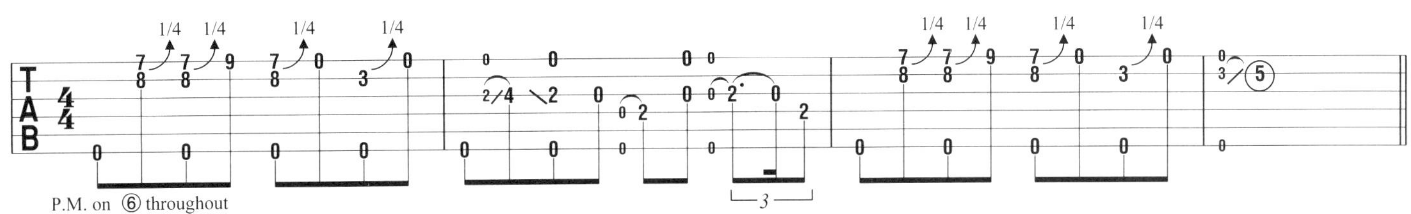


### 523: Ragtime Blues

**D-A-D-G-B-E**

**Swing feel**

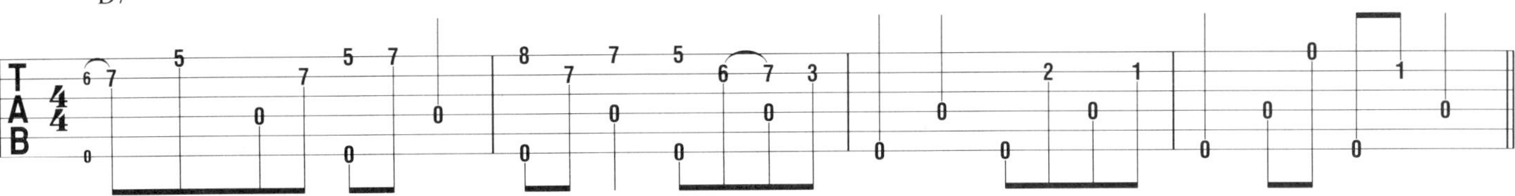


### 524: Mud Slide

**Swing feel**

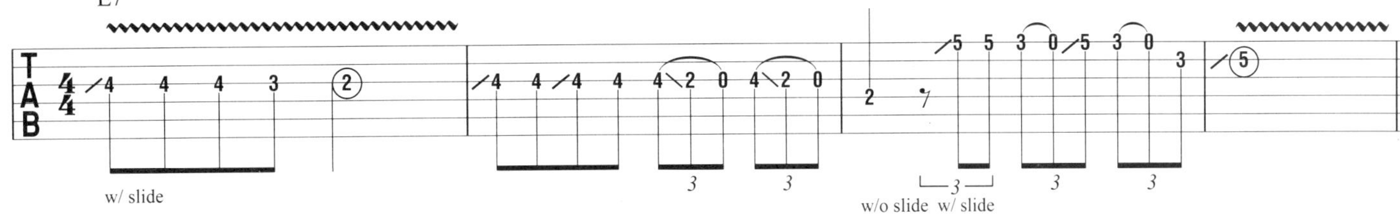

### 525: Open D Groove

D-A-D-F♯-A-D

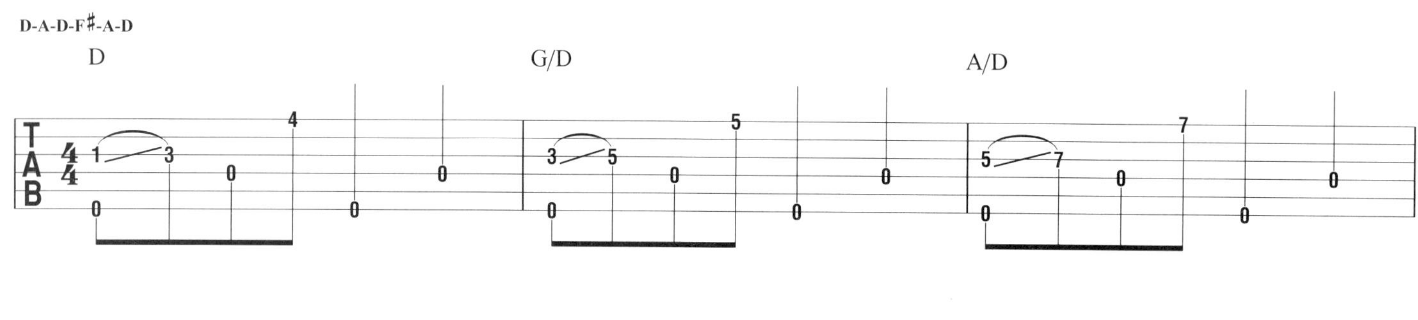


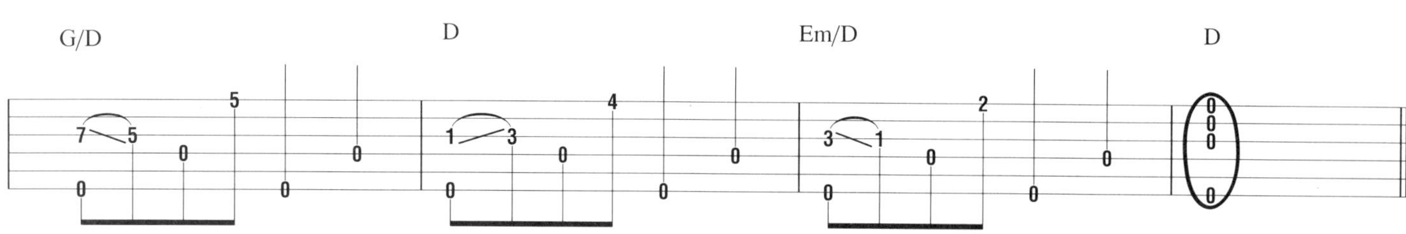


### 526: Open D Strum

D-A-D-F♯-A-D

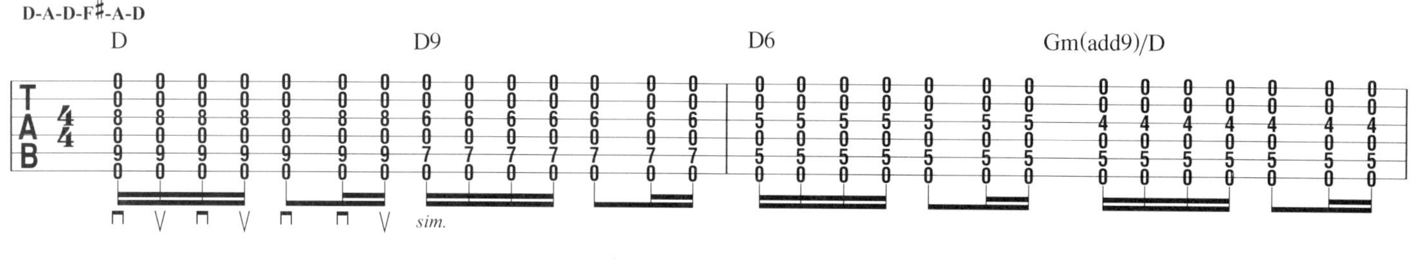


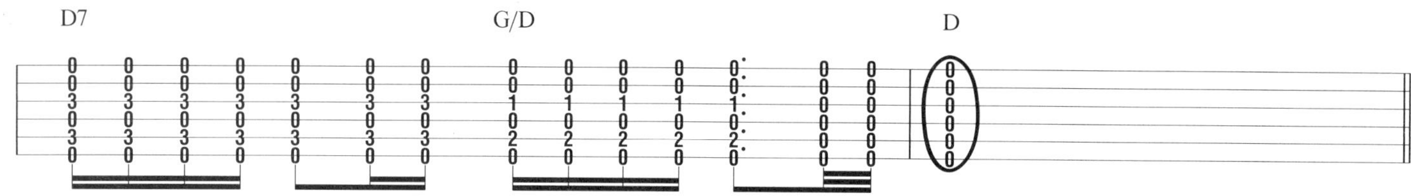


### 527: Slide Blues

D-A-D-F♯-A-D

Swing feel

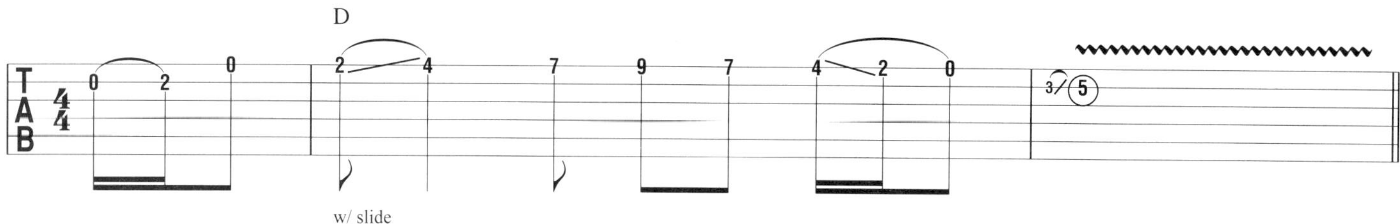


### 528: Gospel Slide

D-A-D-F♯-A-D

Freely

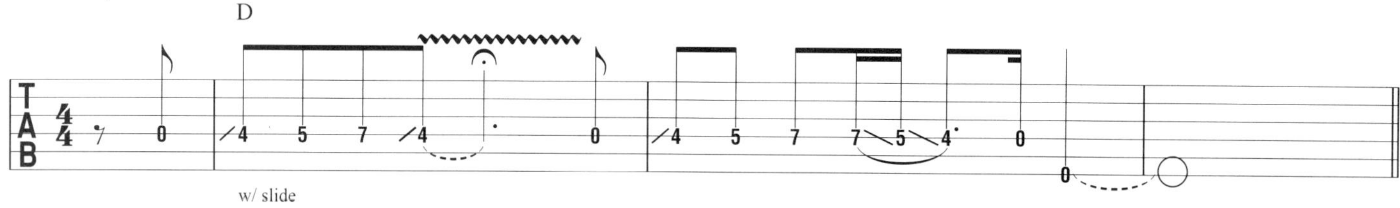

## 529: Fahey Slide

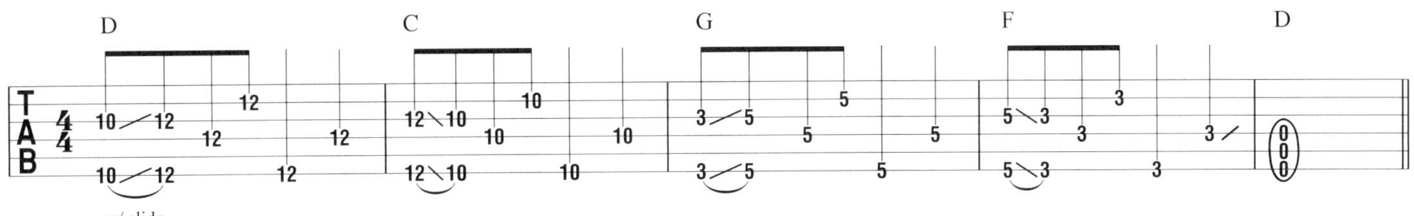


## 530: Delta Slide

D-A-D-F♯-A-D

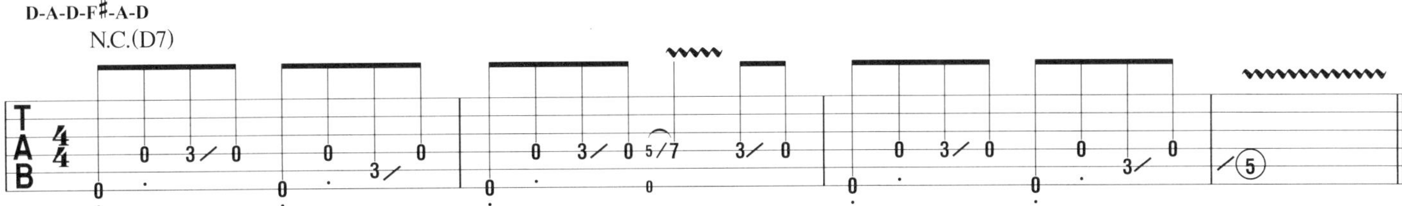


## 531: McDowell Slide

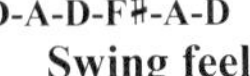


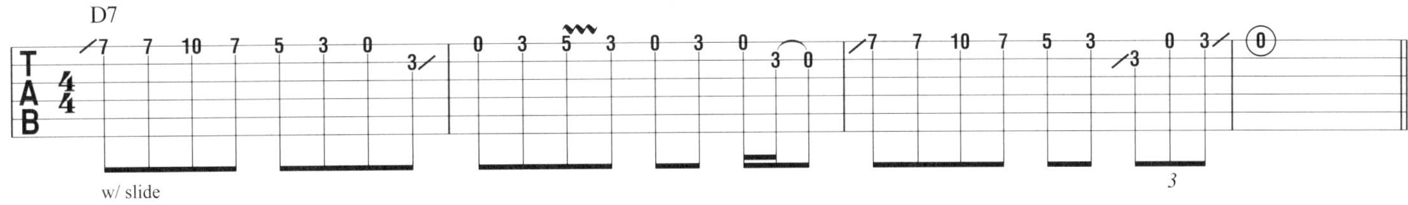


## 532: Bluesy Hula

Swing feel

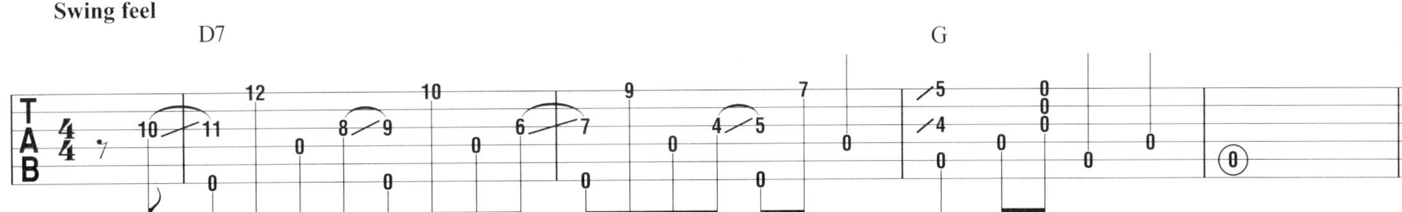


## 533: Slack Turnarounds

D-G-D-G-B-D

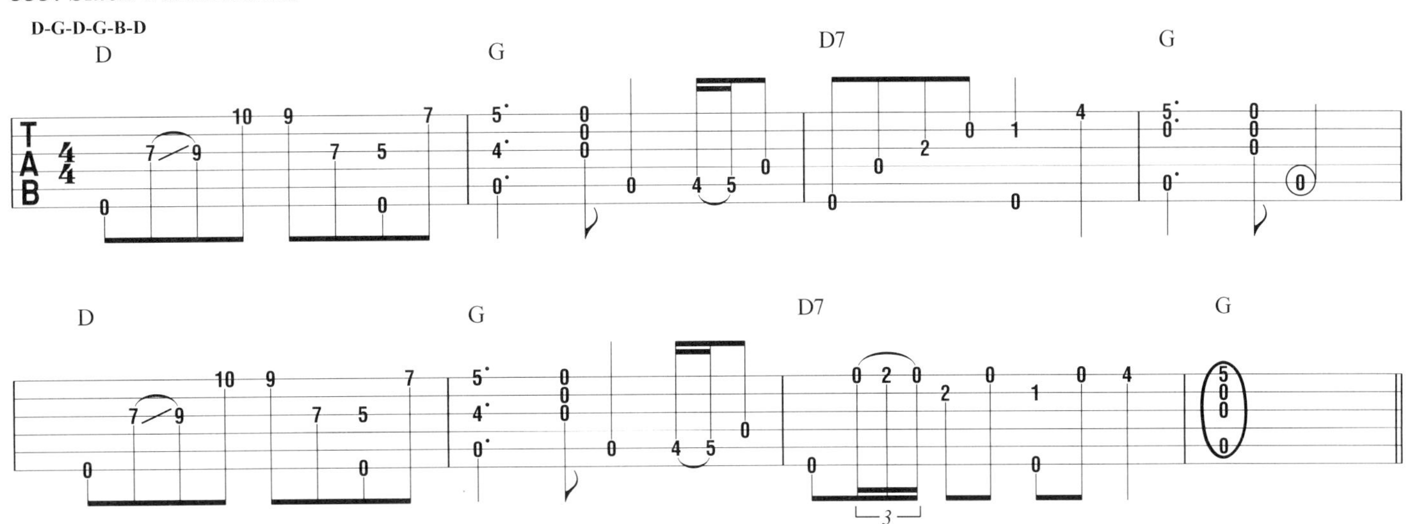

## 534: Drop C Slack Key

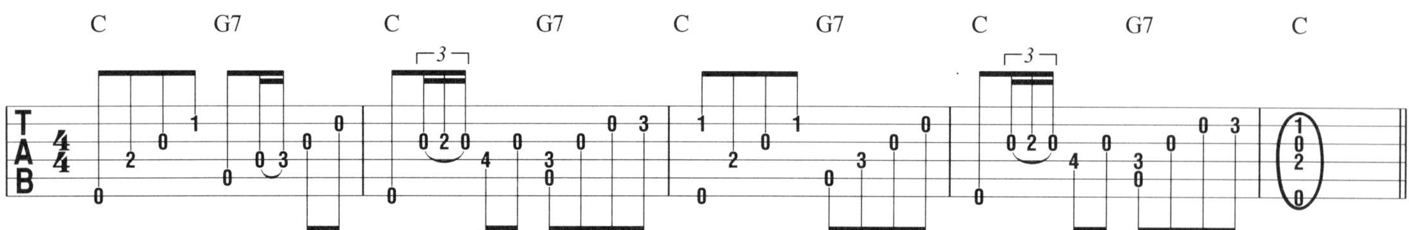


## 535: Delta Riff

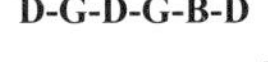


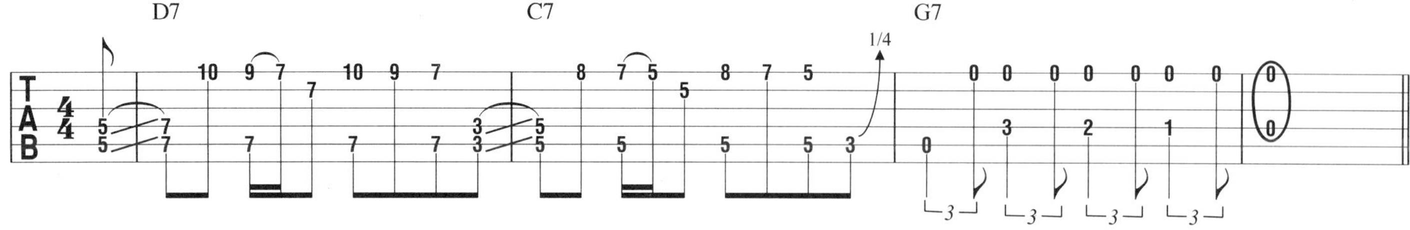


## 536: Lap Slide

D-G-D-G-B-D

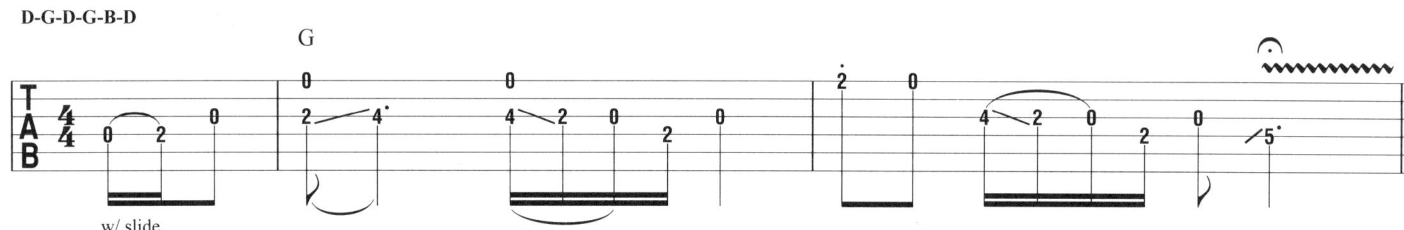


## 537: Country Slide

D-G-D-G-B-D

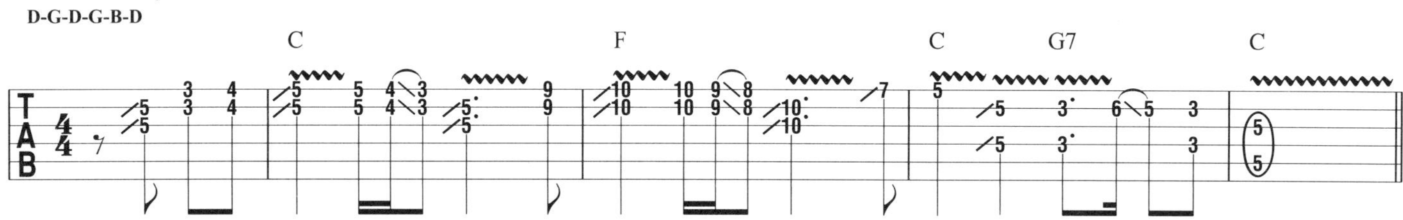


## 538: Lap Time

D-G-D-G-B-D

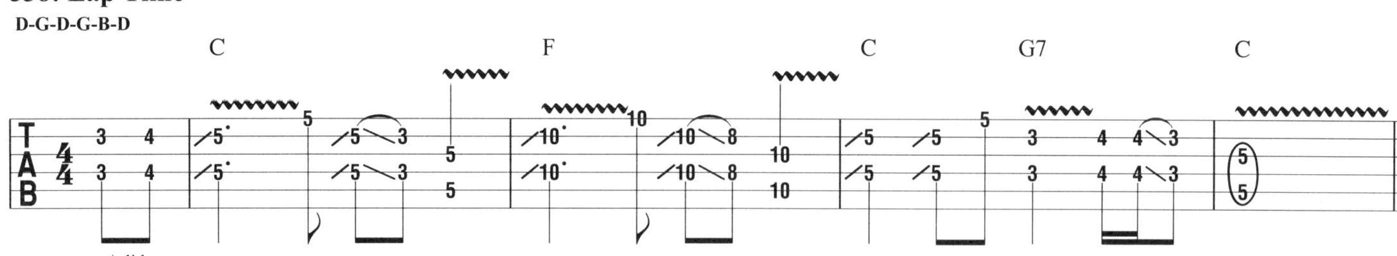


## 539: Slide Melody

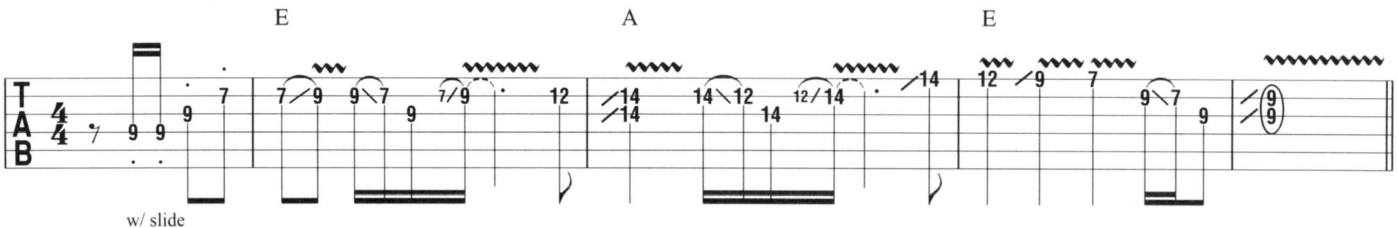

### 540: Steel-Drivin' Slide

D-G-D-G-B-D

Swing feel

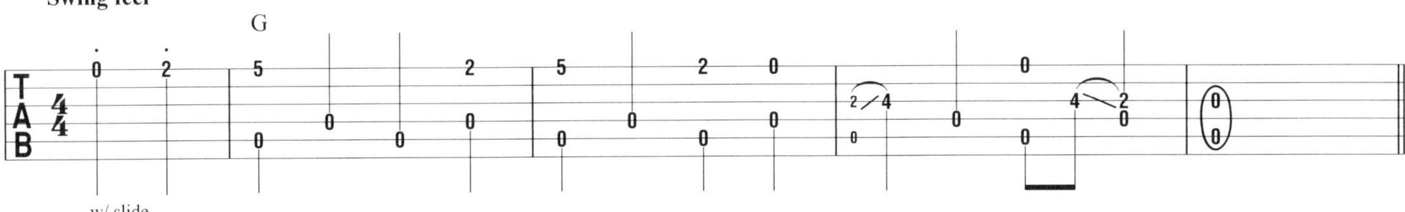


### 541: Sliding Scale

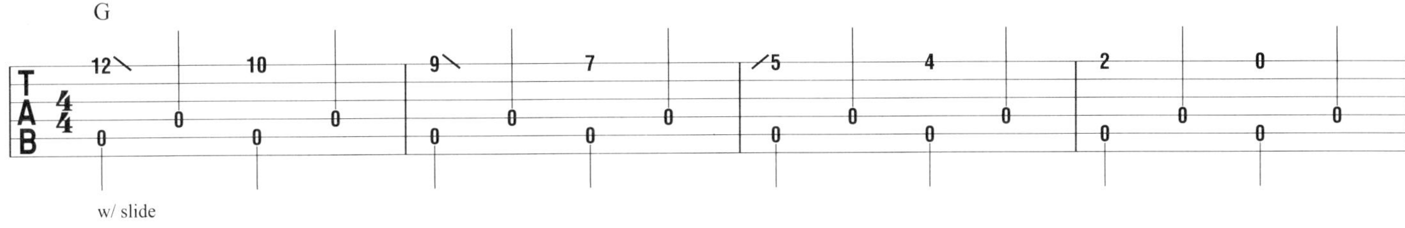


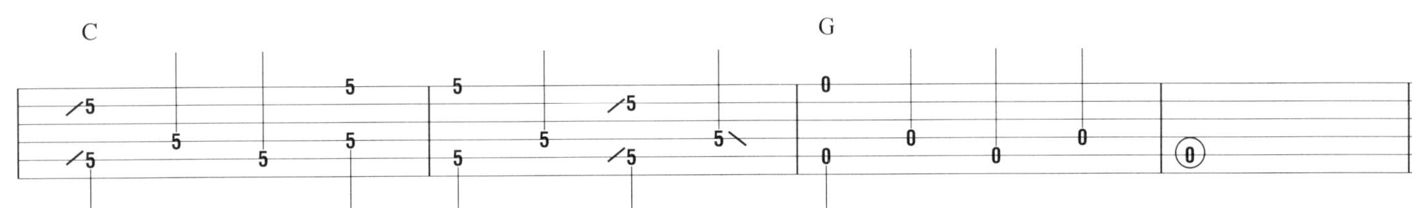


### 542: Bass Slide

D-G-D-G-B-D

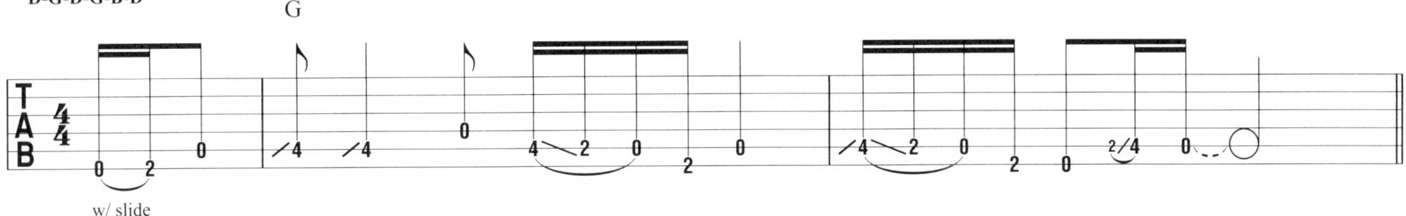


### 543: Crossroad Slide

D-G-D-G-B-D

Swing feel

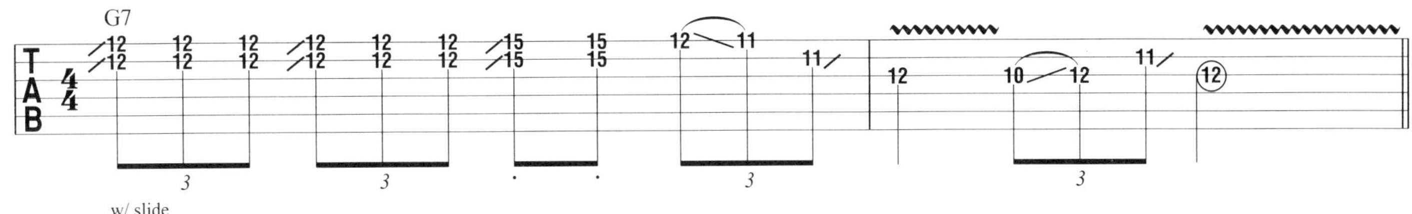


### 544: Mississippi Slide

D-G-D-G-B-D

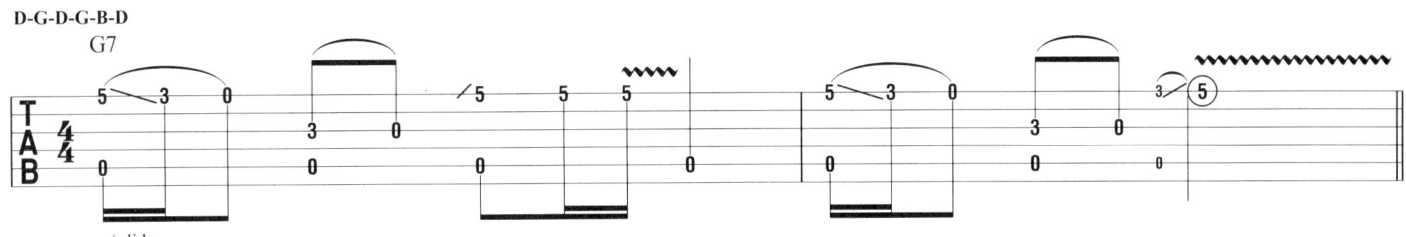


### 545: 12-Bar Intro

D-G-D-G-B-D

Swing feel

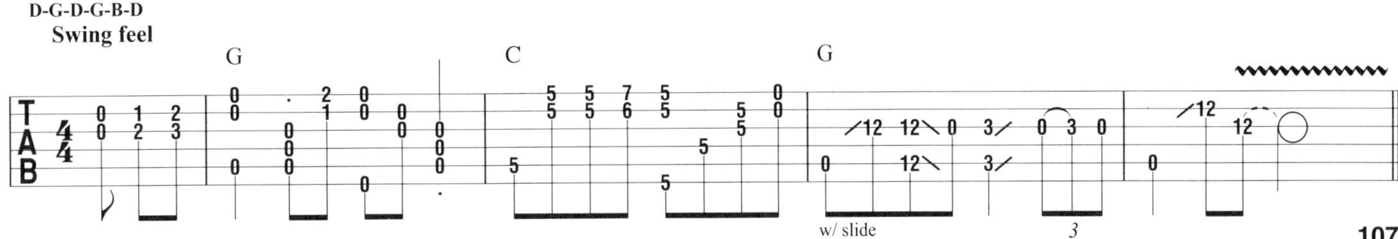

## 546: Moving Harmony

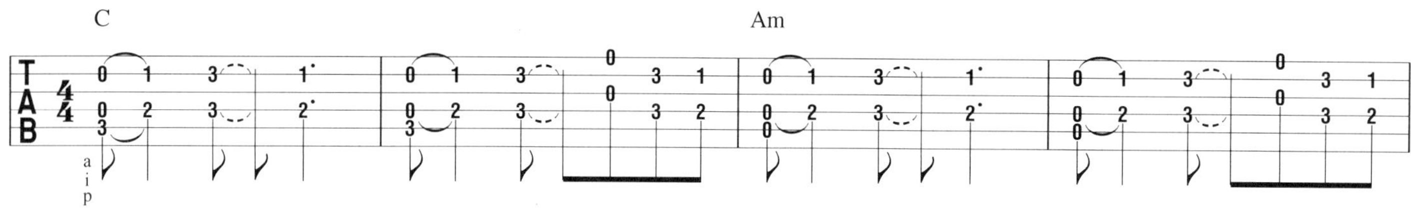


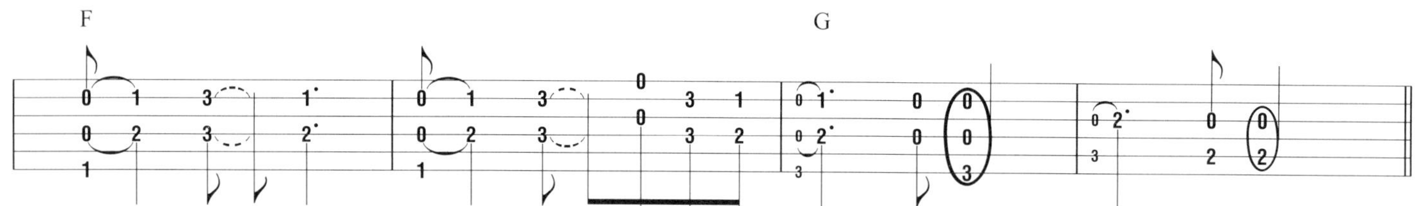


## 547: Early Hawaii

D-G-D-G-B-D

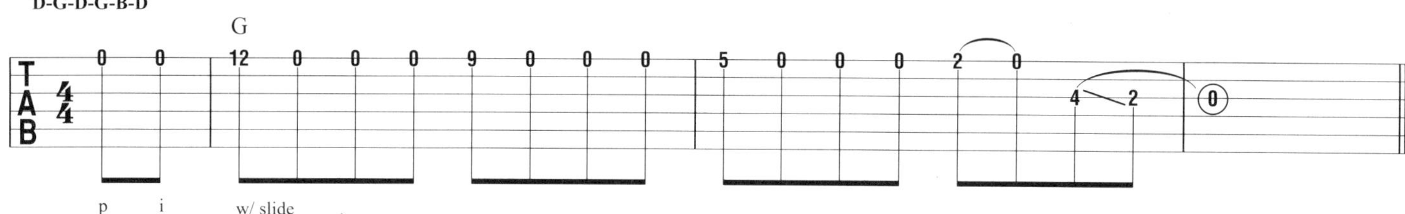


## 548: Comic Slide

D-G-D-G-B-D

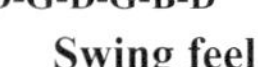


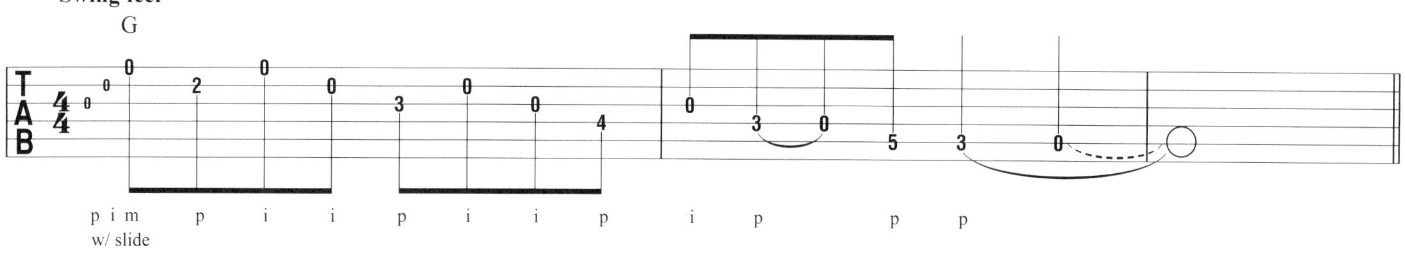


## 549: Overlap Blues

D-G-D-G-B-D

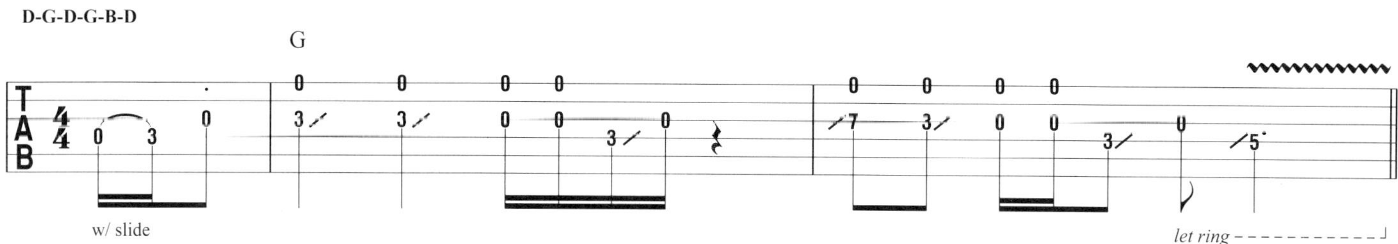


## 550: Cannon Slide

D-G-D-G-B-D

Swing feel

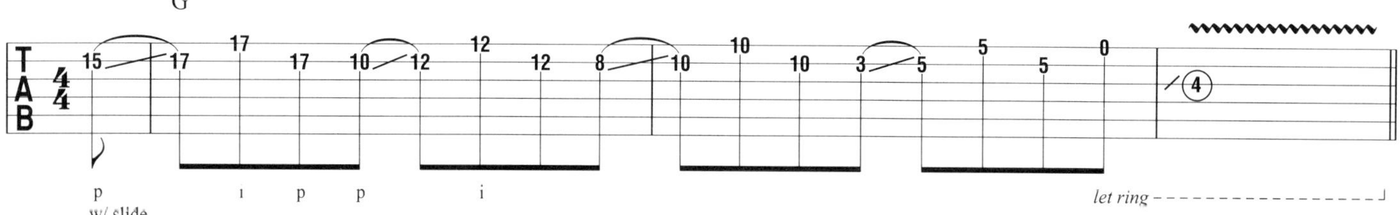

## Instructor: Colin O'Brien

### 551: Chordal Outline

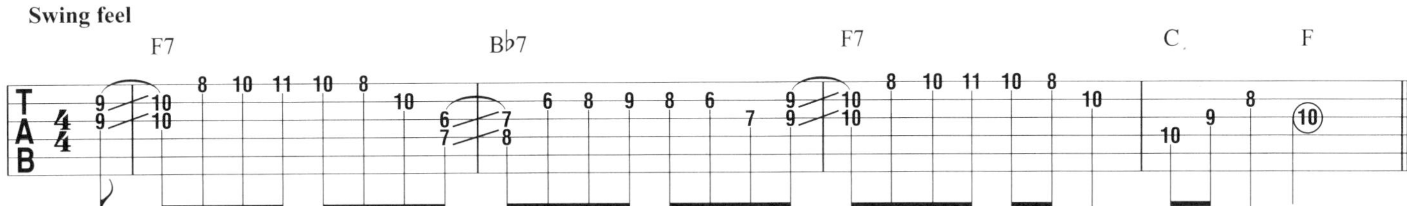


### 552: Double Tag

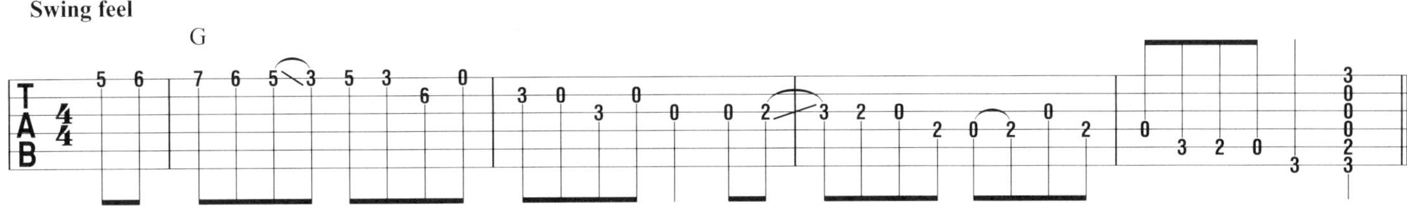


### 553: Arpeggio Statement

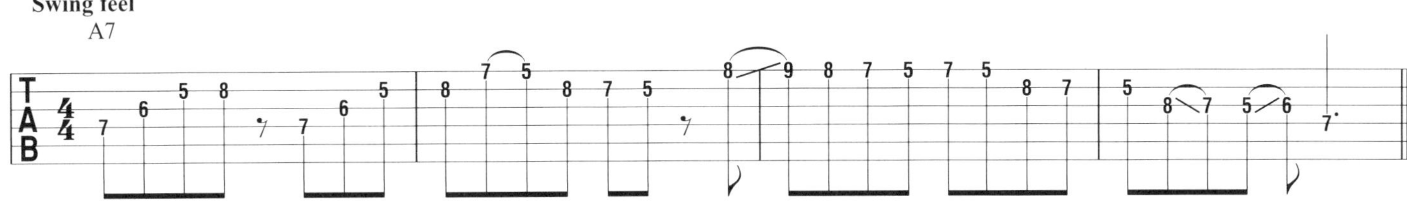


### 554: Backpedalin'

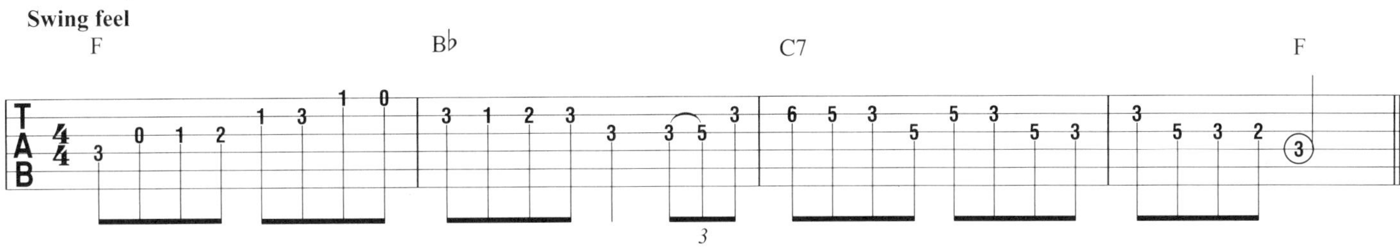


### 555: Bluegrasser

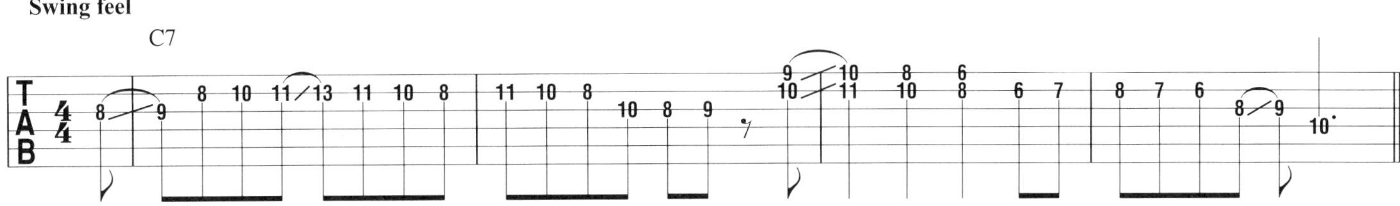


### 556: Classic Ending

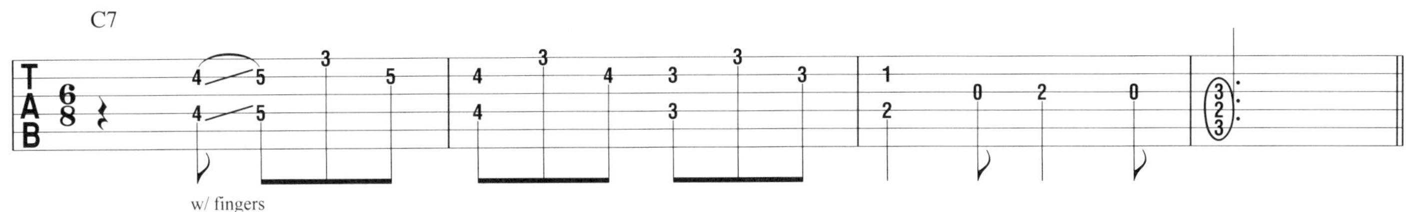

## 557: Finger It

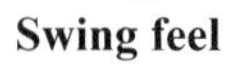

Swing feel

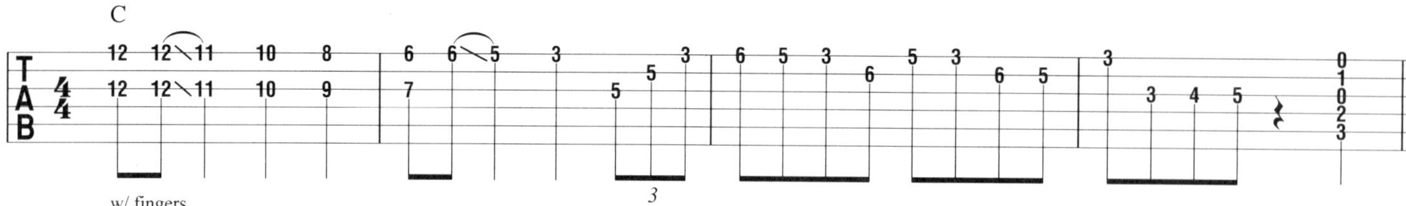


## 558: Flatt Run

Swing feel

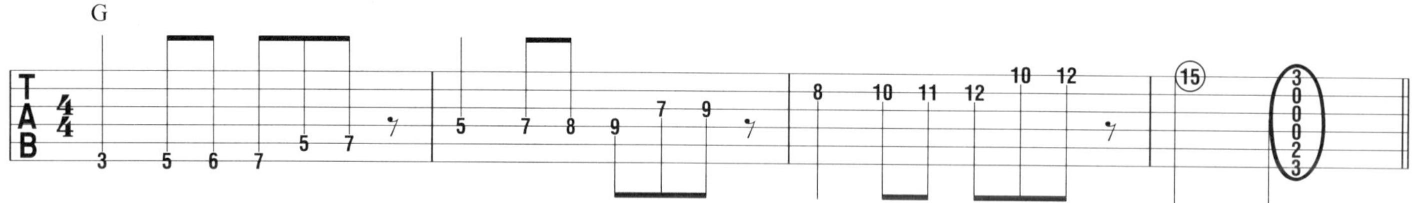


## 559: Chromatic Runs

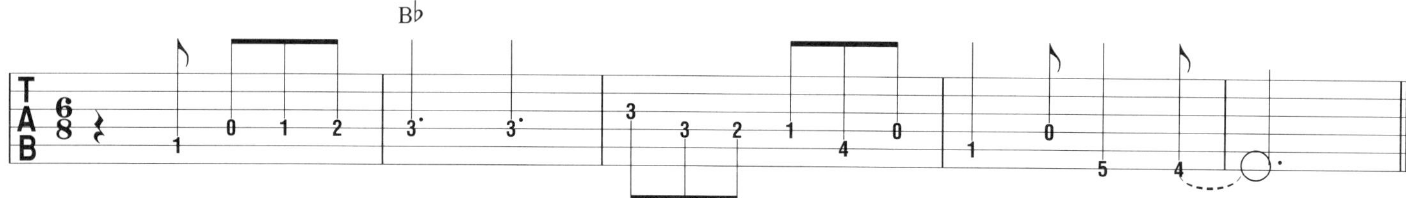


## 560: Shapes & Colors

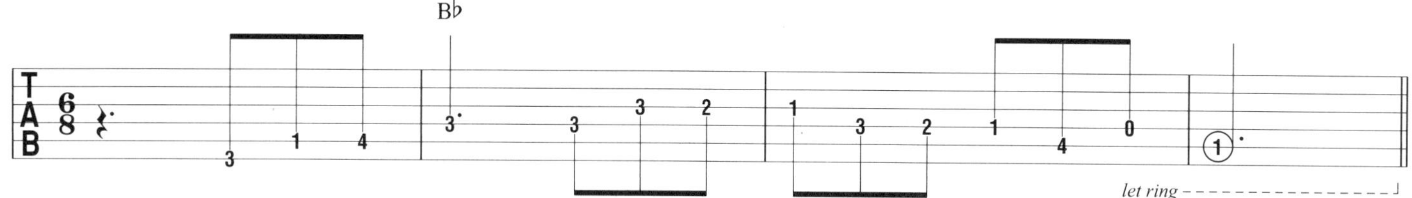


## 561: Answer Me

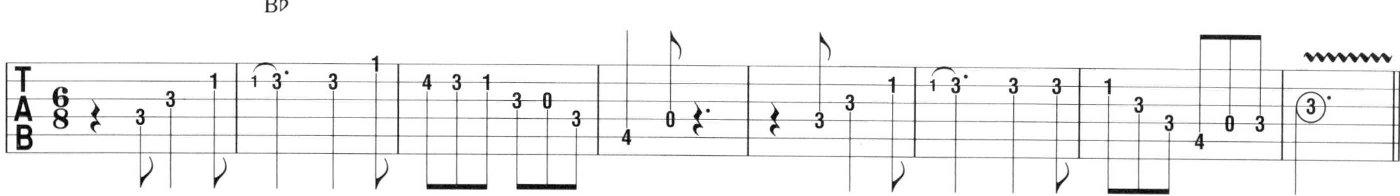


## 562: Minor Line

Swing feel

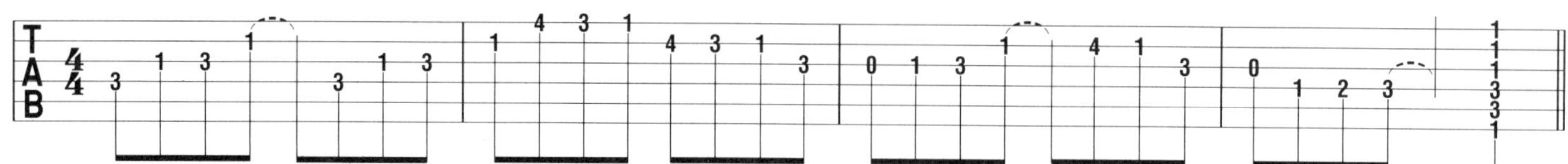


## 563: I-VI-V-I Melody

Swing feel

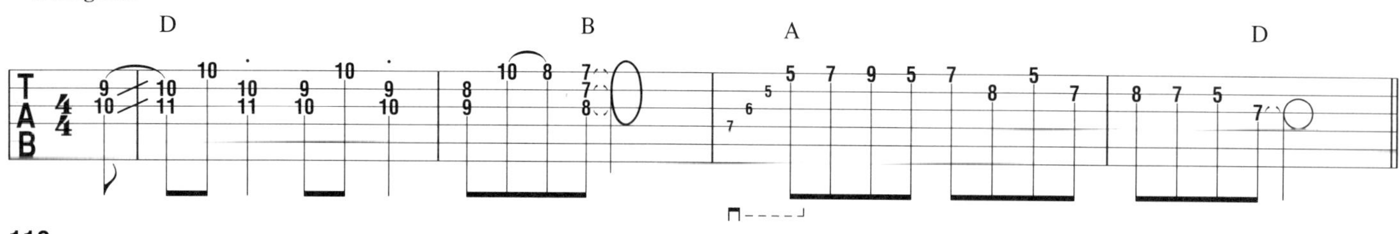

### 564: Cartoon Lick

Swing feel

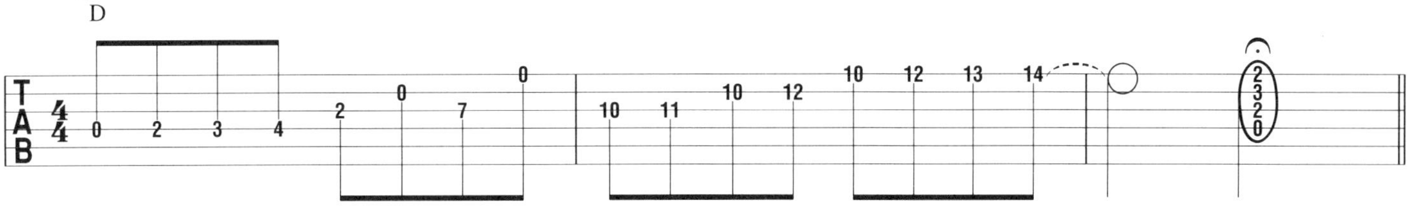

D

### 565: Cross Pickin'

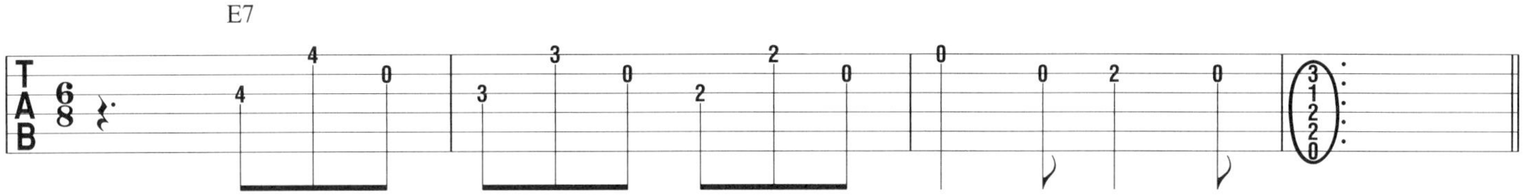

E7

### 566: Boogie Woogie

Swing feel

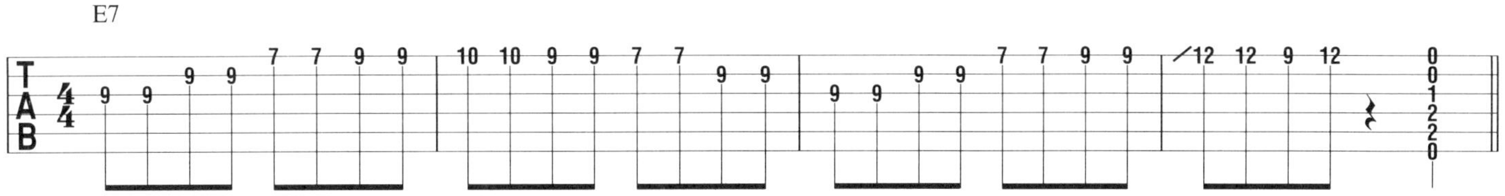

E7

### 567: Bluegrass Lead-In

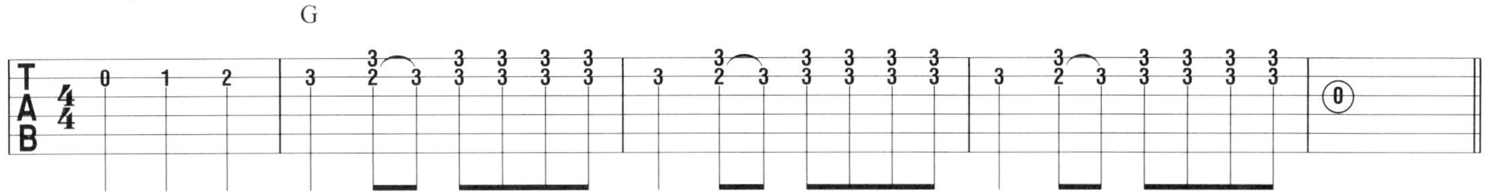

G

### 568: Chromaticism

Swing feel

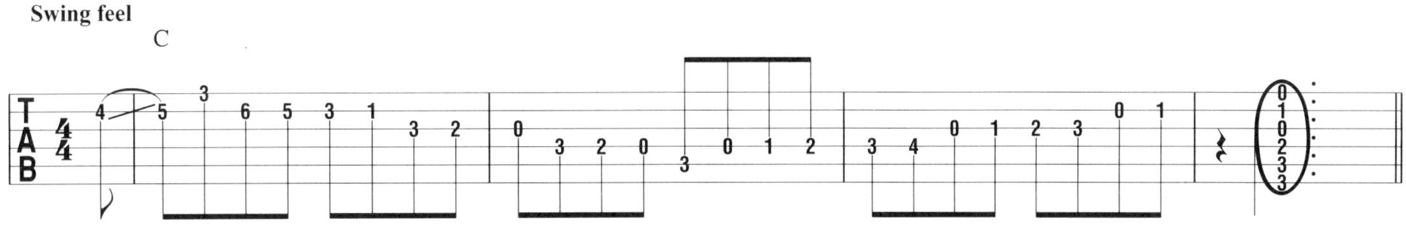

C

### 569: Carter Style

G

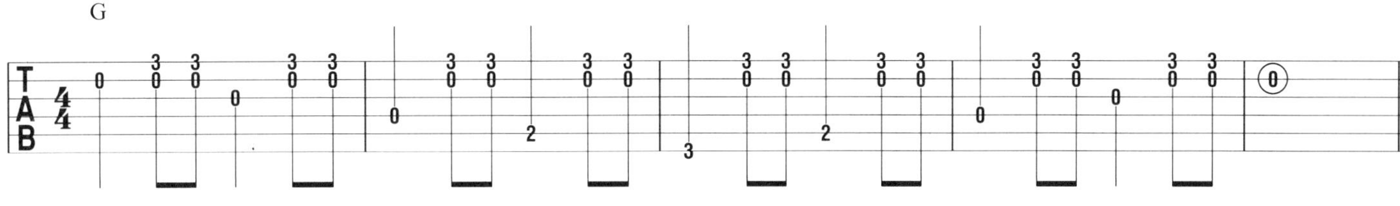

### 570: Bluegrass Strum

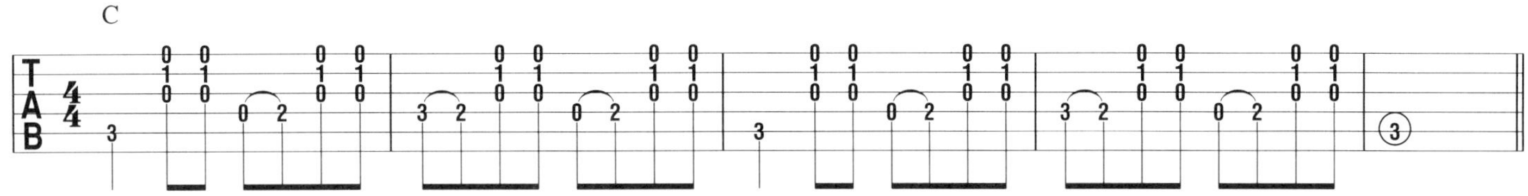

C

### 571: Dyad Climb

**Swing feel**

F
B♭
C
F
w/ fingers

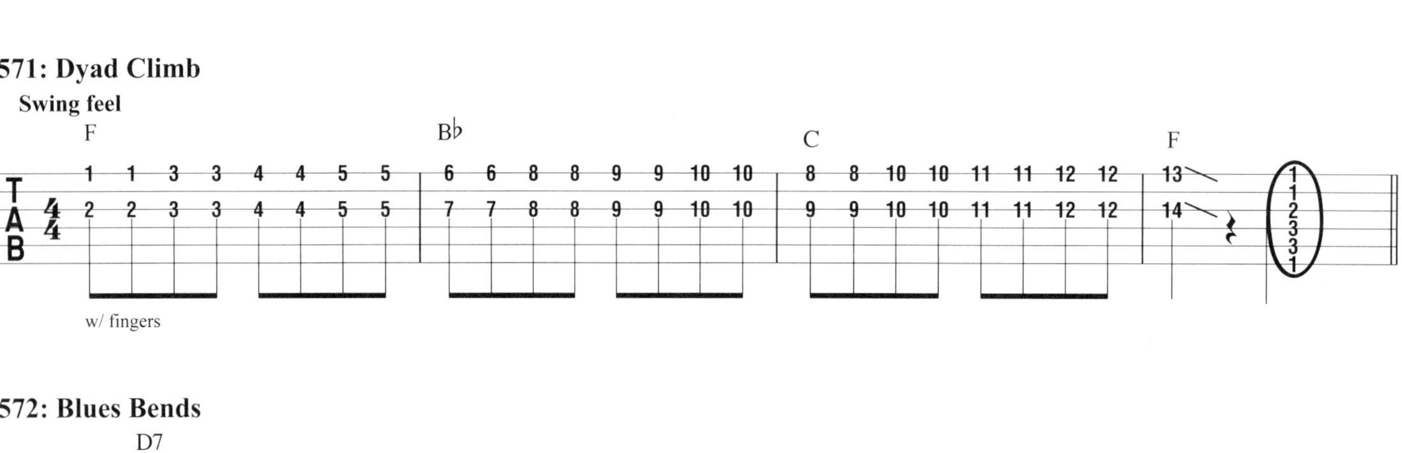

### 572: Blues Bends

D7
1/4 hold bend
1/4 hold bend
1/4 hold bend

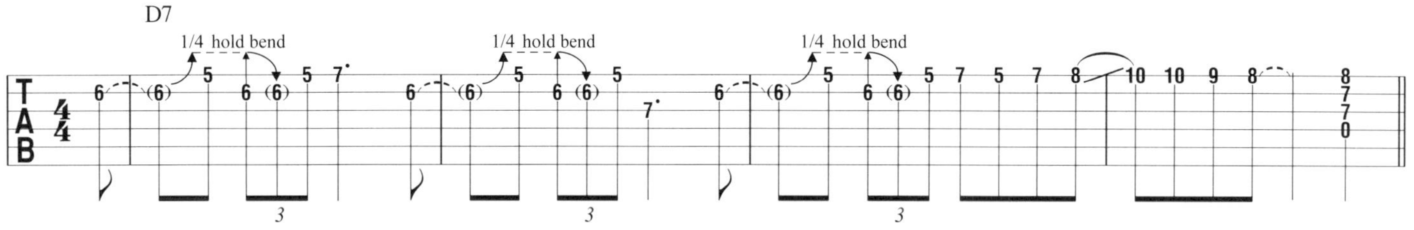

### 573: Chromatic Swing

**Swing feel**

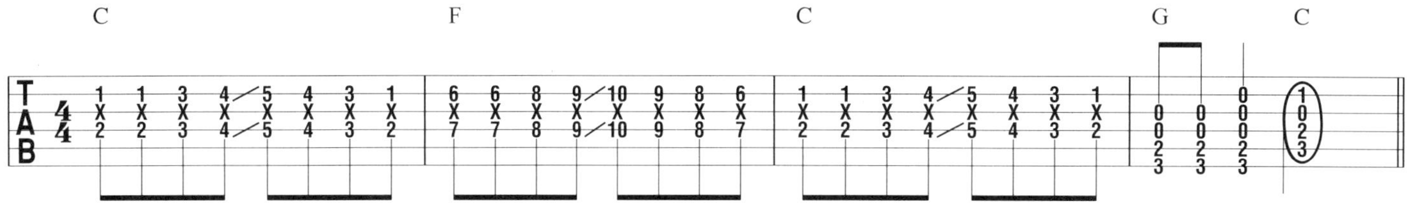

C
F
C
G
C

### 574: Lick Americana

**Swing feel**

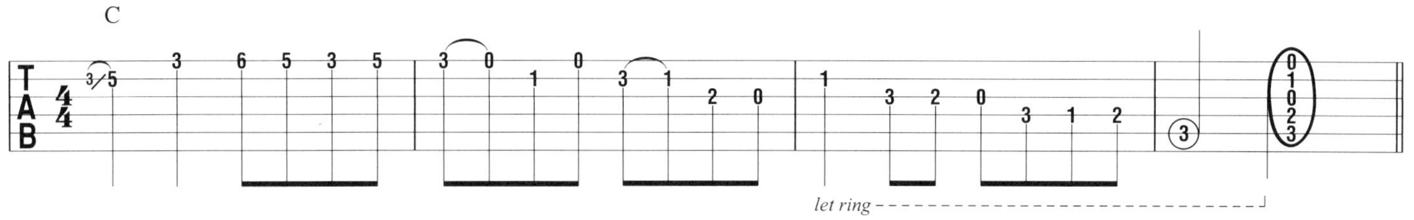

C
let ring

### 575: Melody Within

C
G
C
G
C
G
C

### 576: Bluegrass Pattern

G
D
G

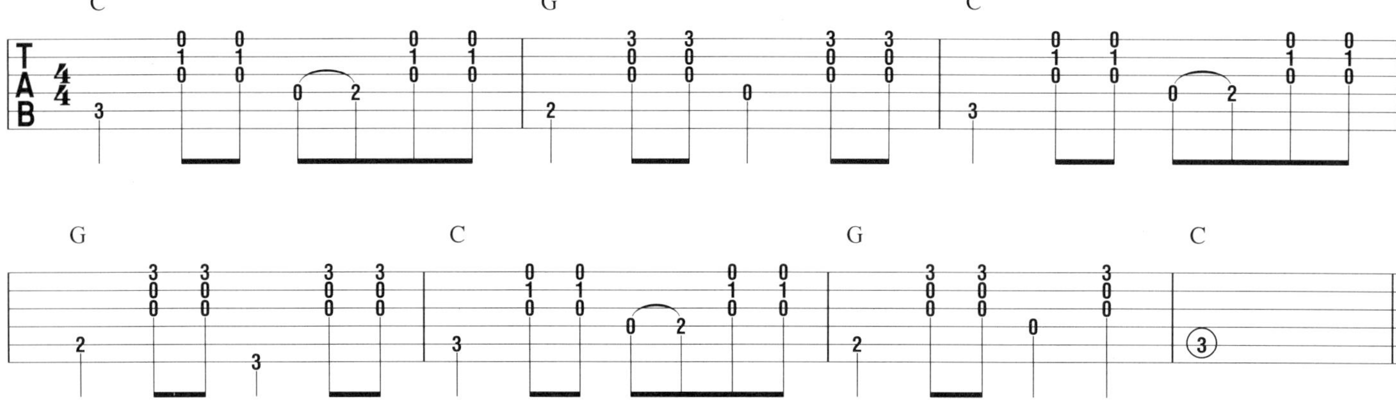

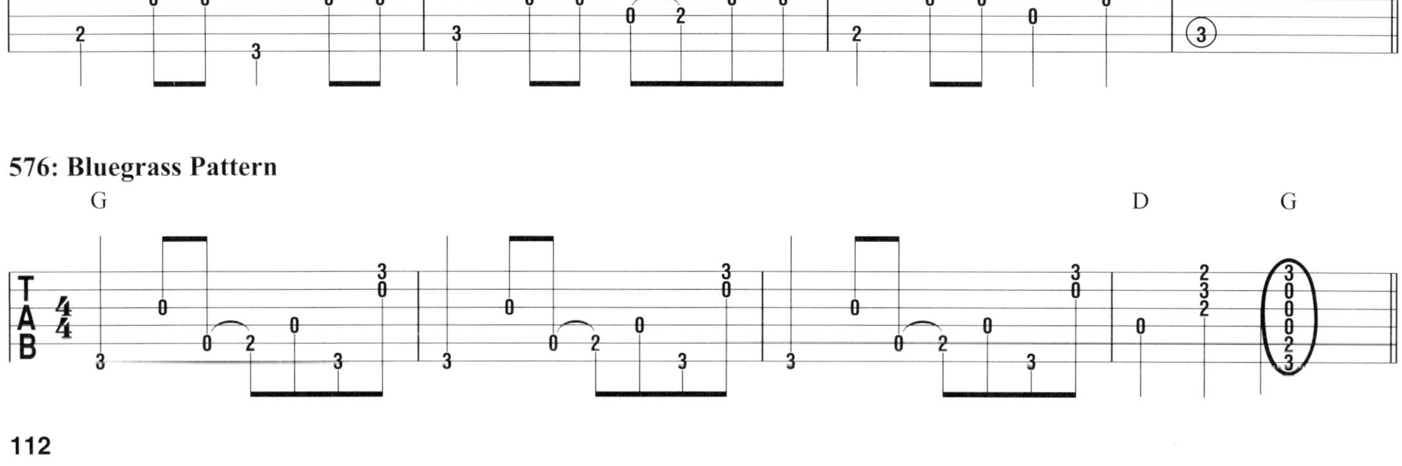

577: Busy Pinky

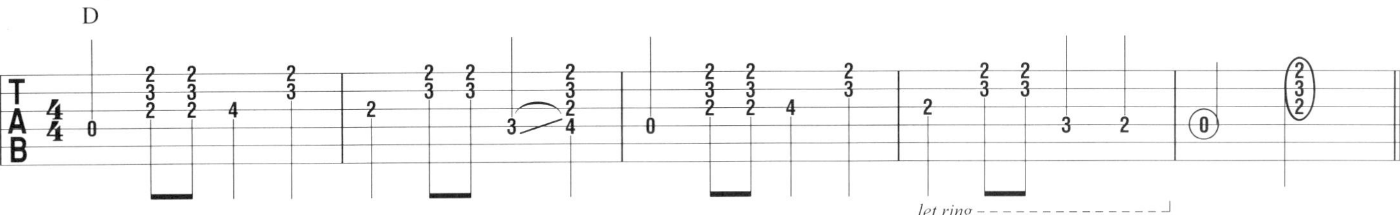
D
let ring

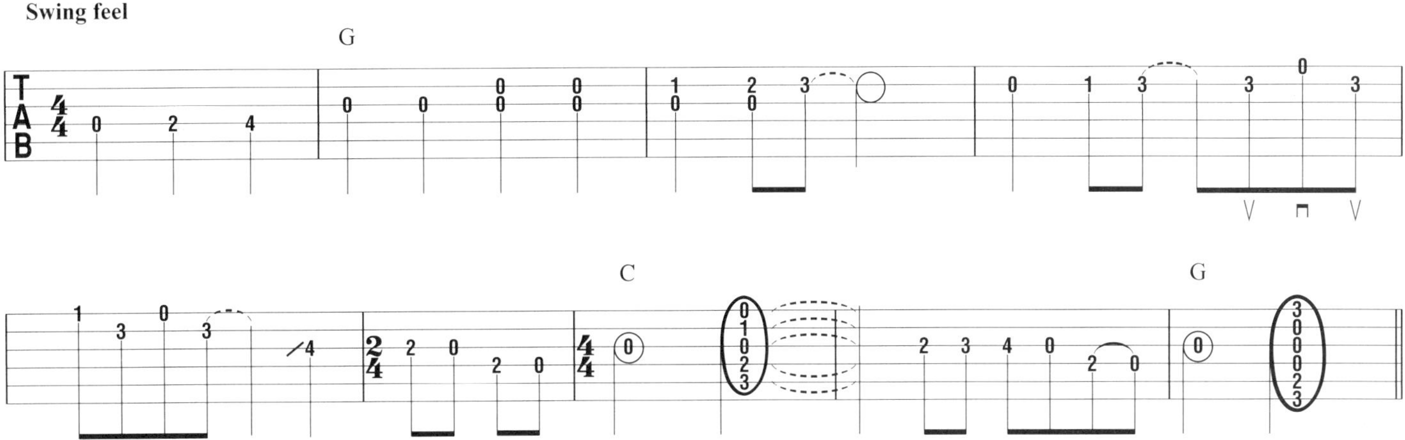
578: Chubby Time
Swing feel
G
C
G

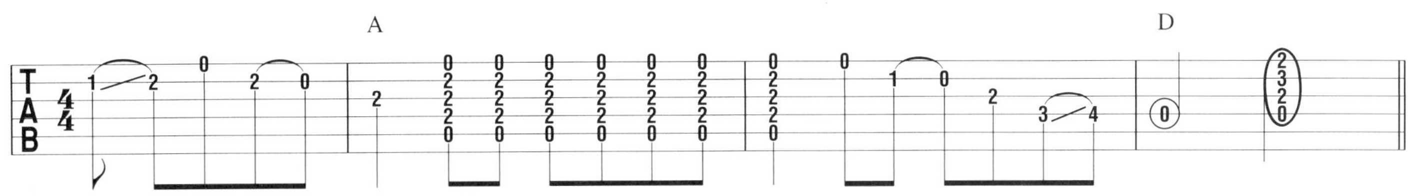
579: I-IV Fills
A
D

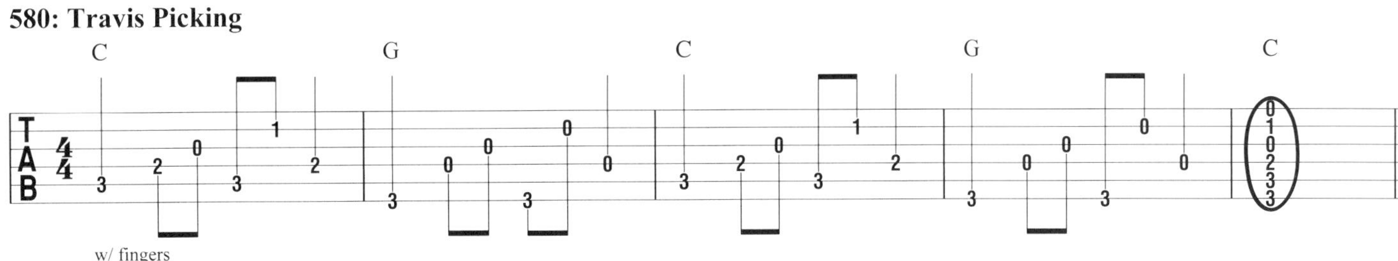
580: Travis Picking
C
G
C
G
C
w/ fingers

581: Travis Variation

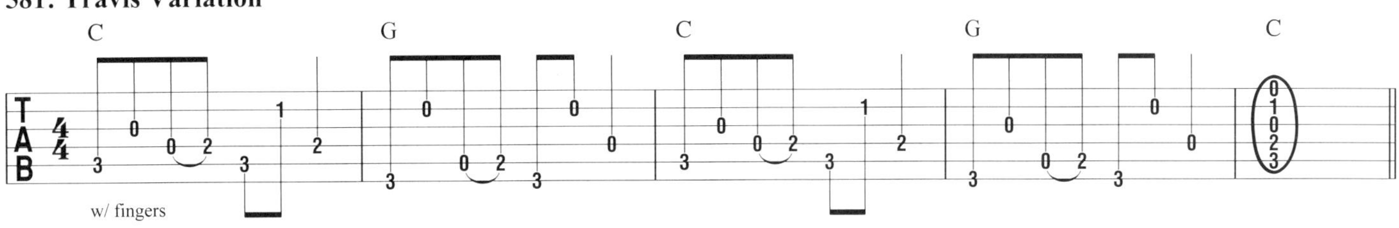
C
G
C
G
C
w/ fingers

582: Smooth Groove

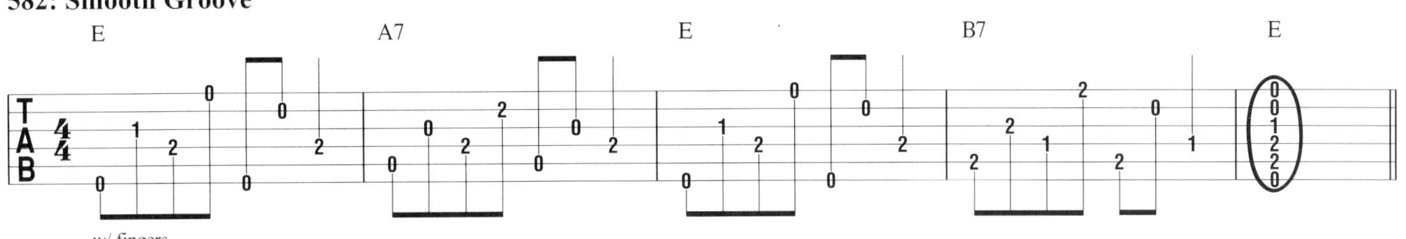
E
A7
E
B7
E
w/ fingers

## 583: 7th Chord Groove

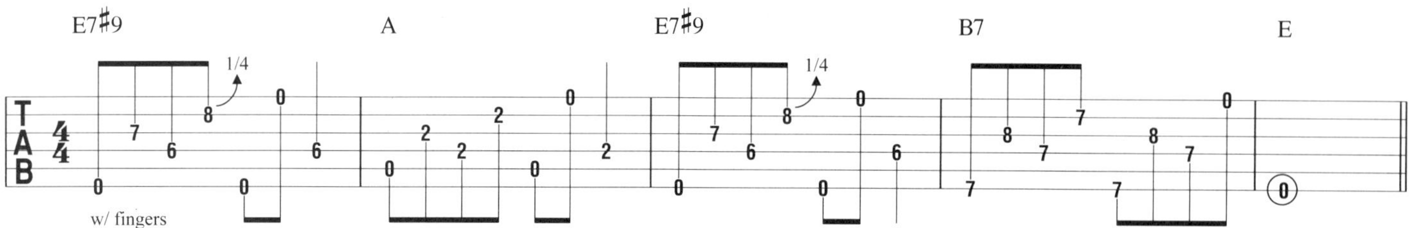


## 584: Dovetail Pattern

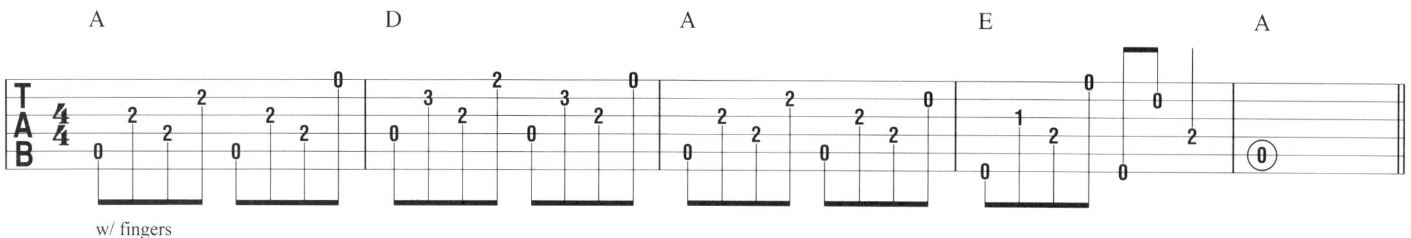


## 585: Bluesy Rubs

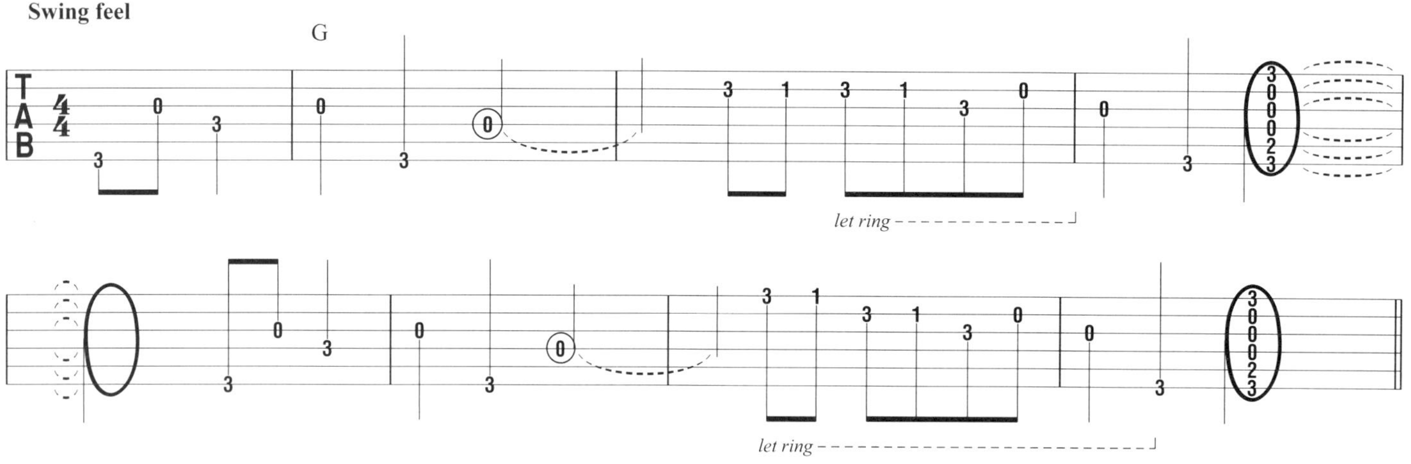


## 586: Bluegrass Break

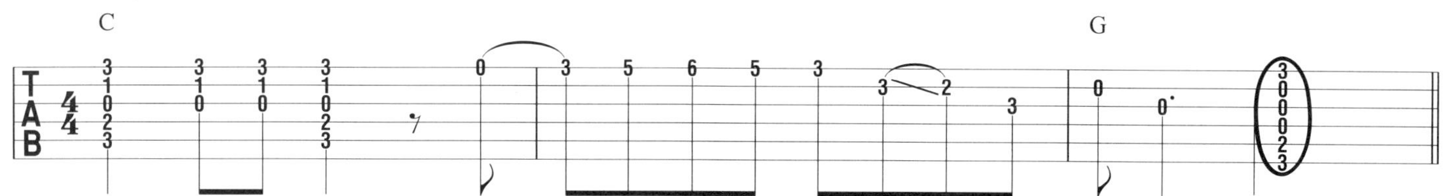


## 587: Happy Porch

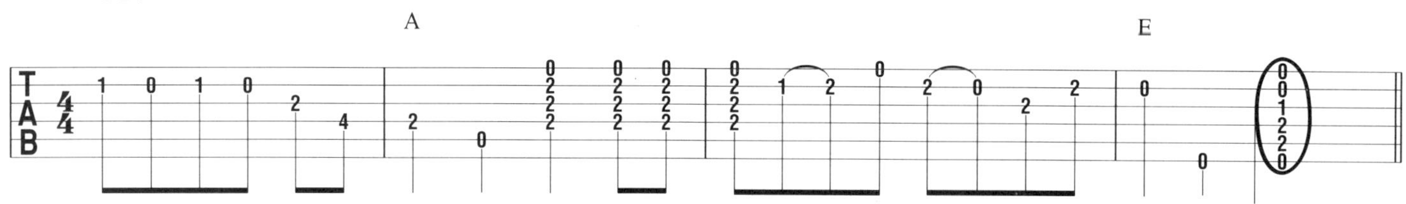


## 588: Drop D Delight

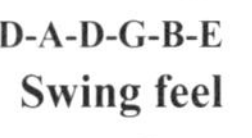


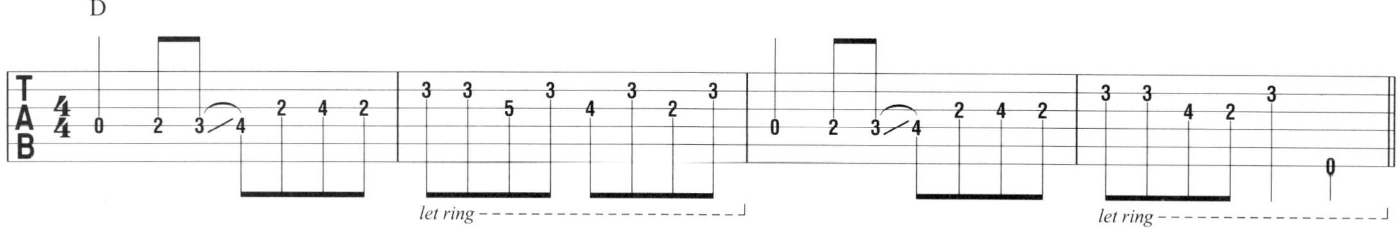

## 589: Drop D Blues

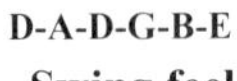

D-A-D-G-B-E

**Swing feel**

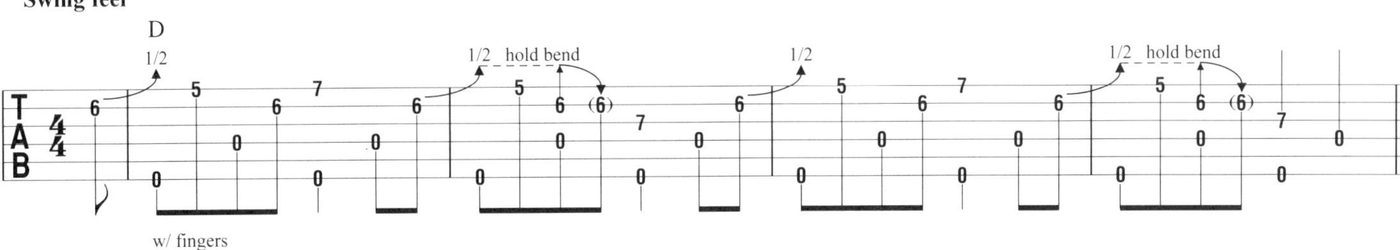


## 590: Blues Pattern

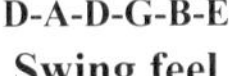

D-A-D-G-B-E

**Swing feel**

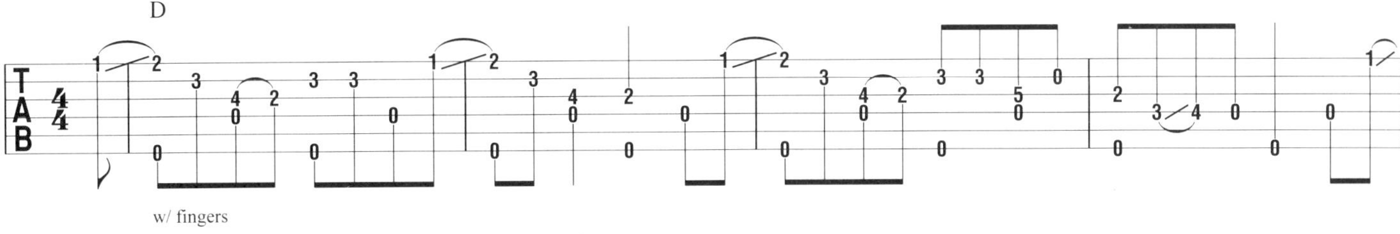


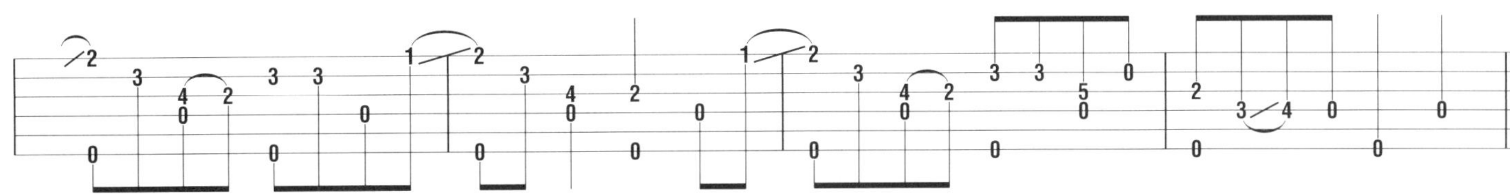

## 591: Blues Groove

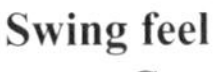

**Swing feel**

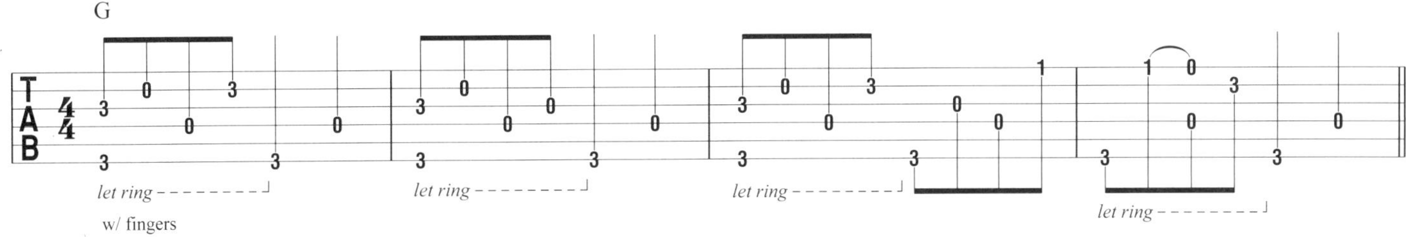


## 592: Good Time Blues

**Swing feel**

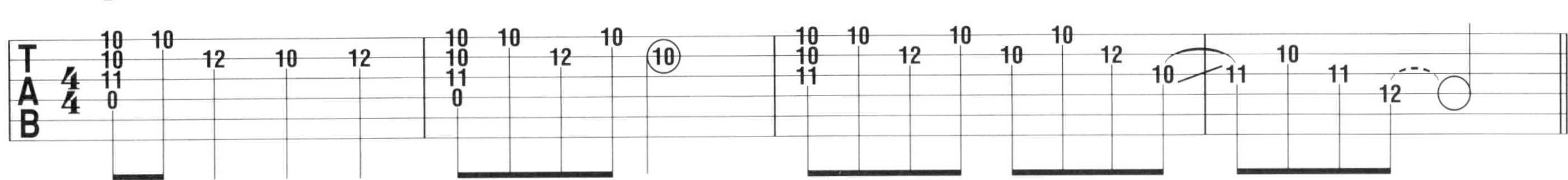


## 593: Sweet 6/8

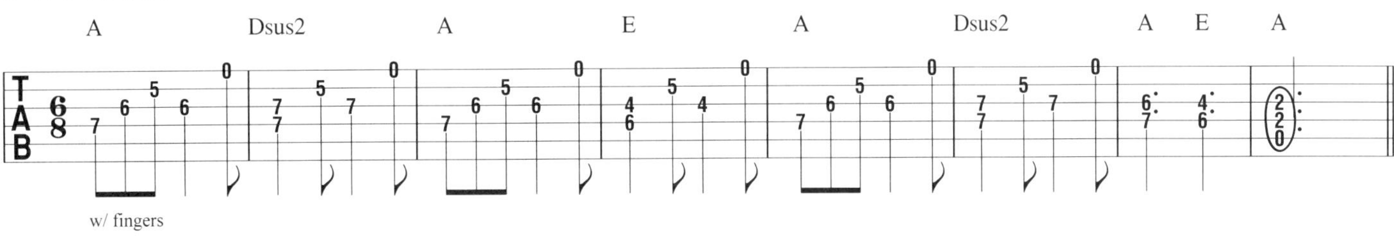

## 594: Monroe Style

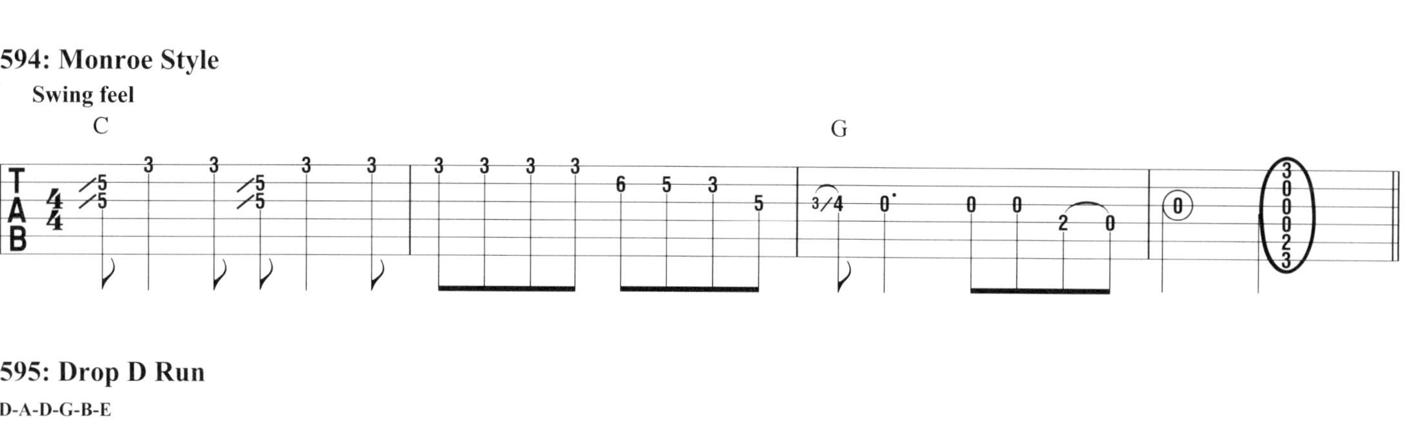


## 595: Drop D Run

D-A-D-G-B-E

Swing feel

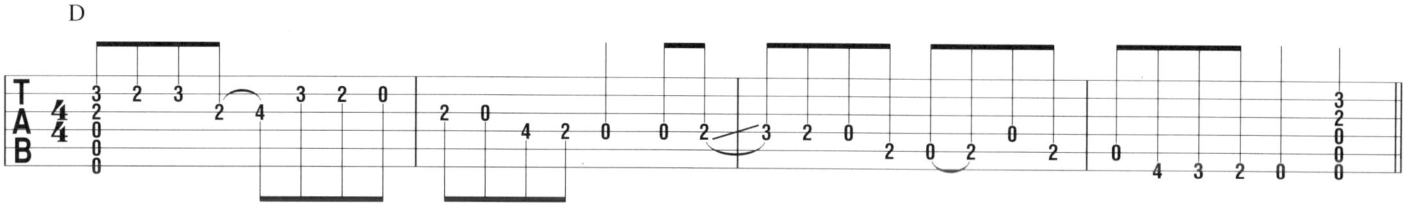

D

## 596: Fiddle-Inspired

Swing feel

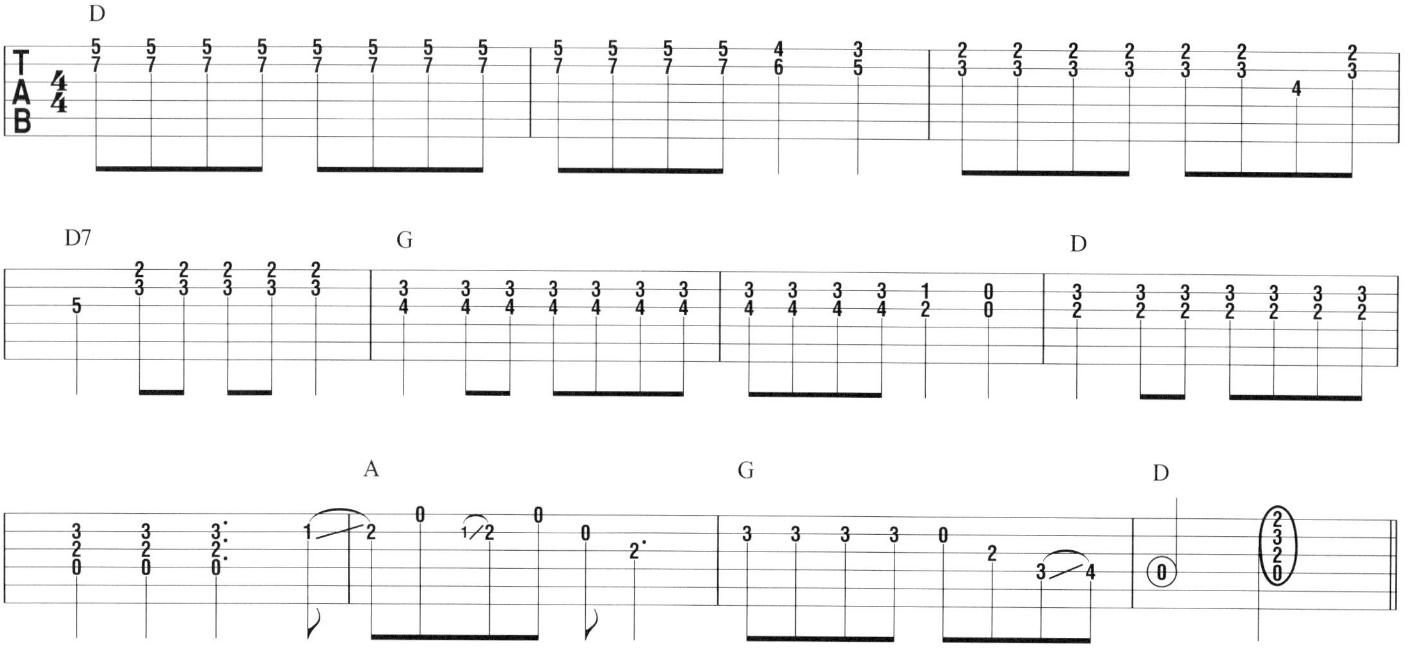

D

D7 G D

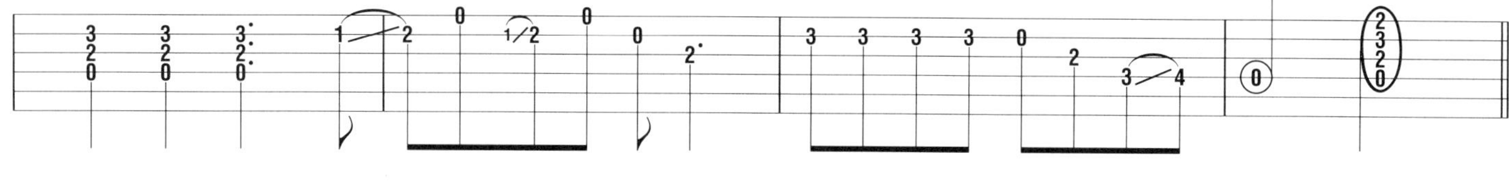


## 597: Doc Watson Style

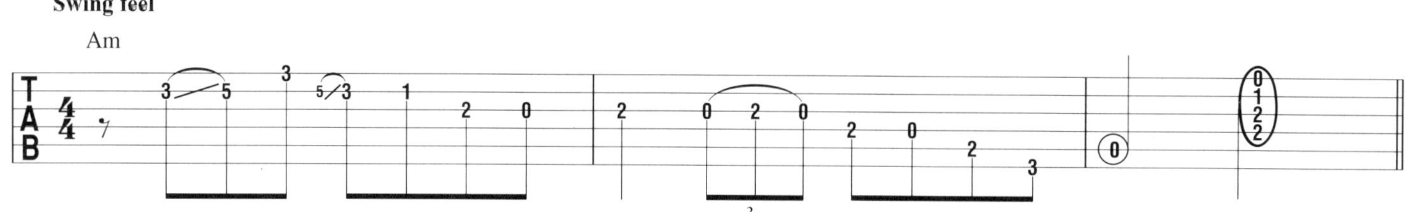


## 598: Happy Grass

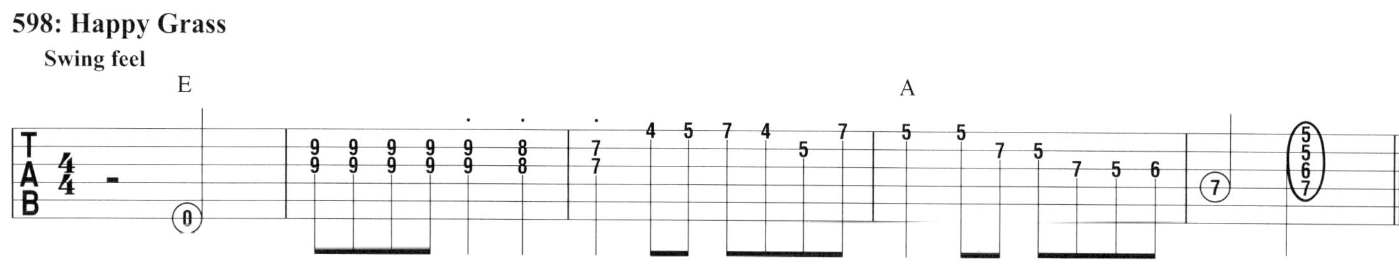

## 599: Chubby Run

**Swing feel**

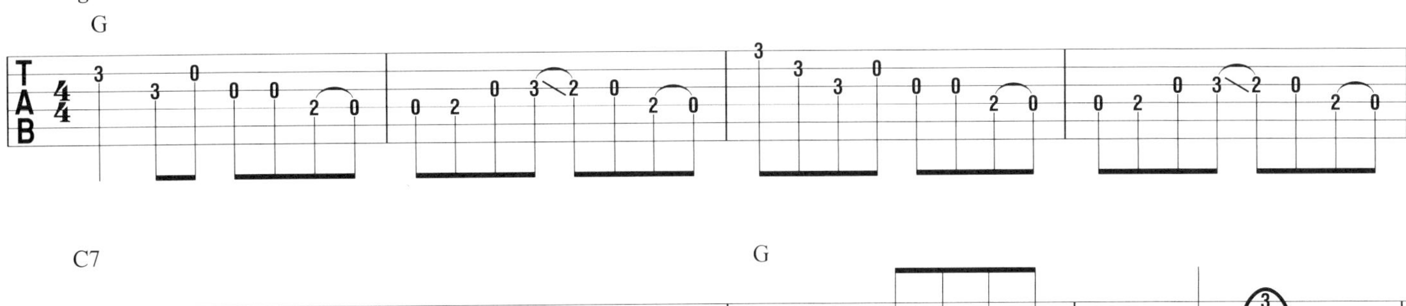


C7 G

## 600: V-I Resolve

**Swing feel**

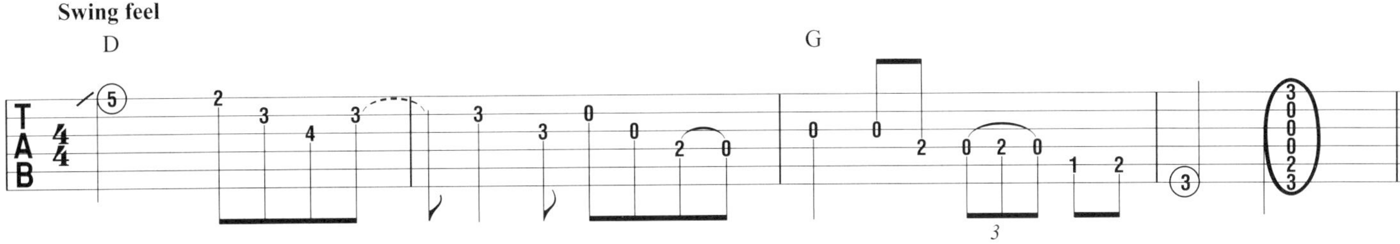

# COUNTRY LICKS

## Instructor: John Heussenstamm

### 601: Capturing Country

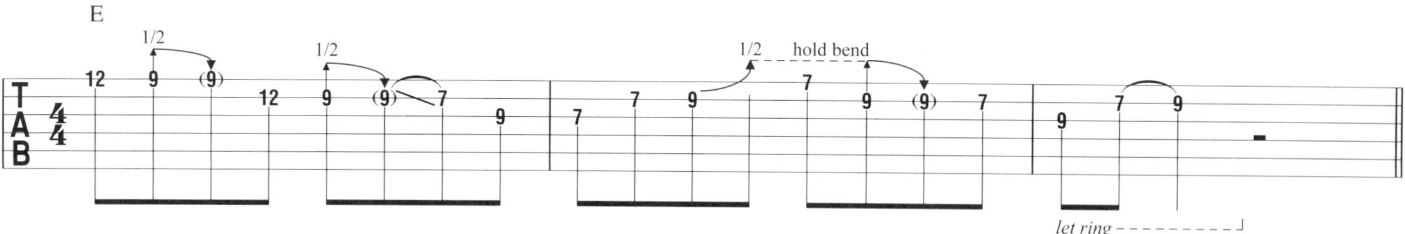


### 602: Doublestop Shop

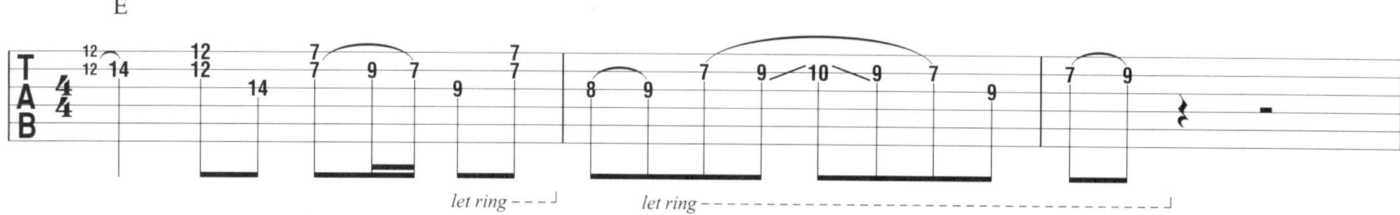


### 603: Sustained Bends

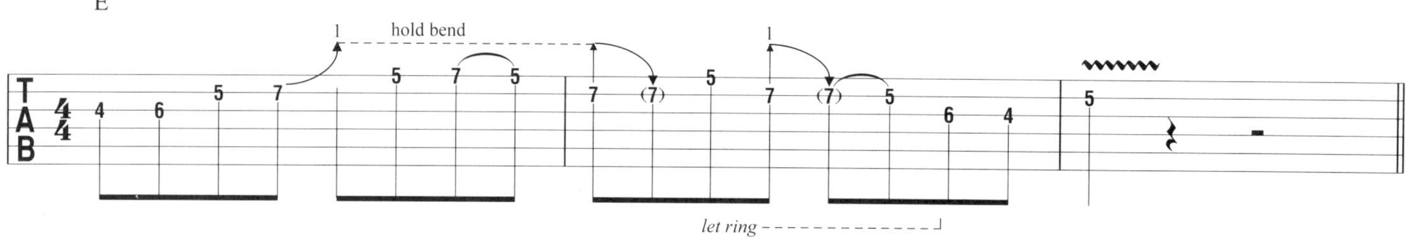


### 604: Smooth Slider

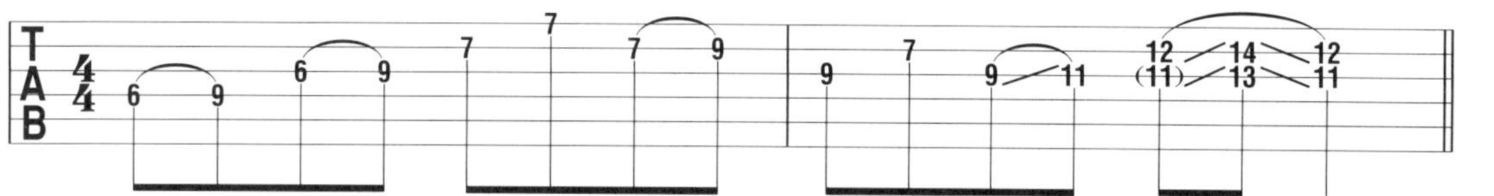


### 605: Major Resolve

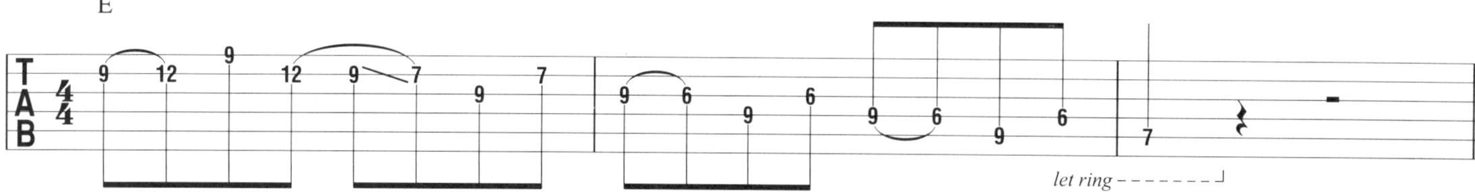


### 606: Legato Sequence

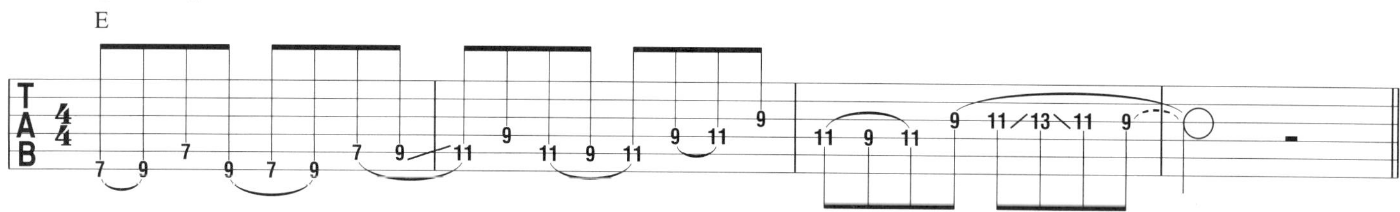

### 607: Grin & Barre It

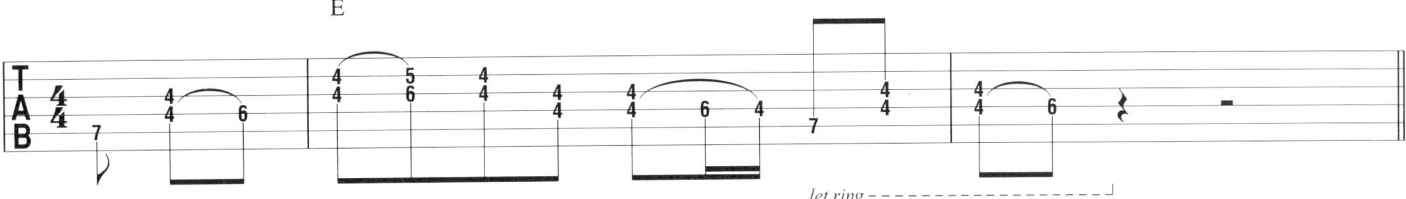


### 608: Close Intervals

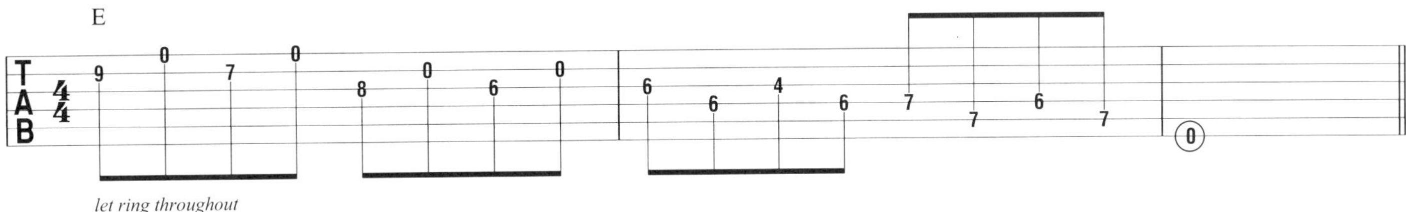


### 609: Melodic Style

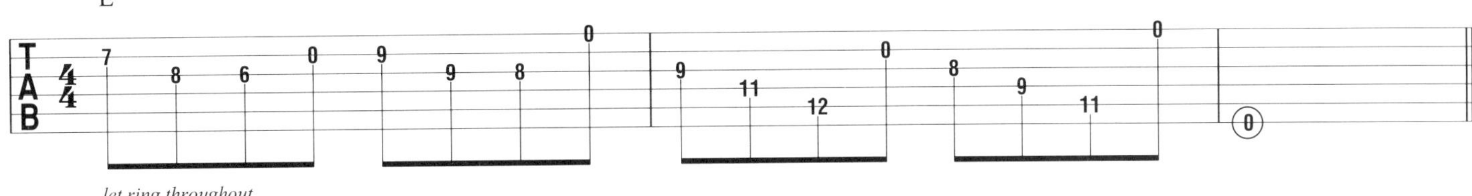


### 610: Twang It

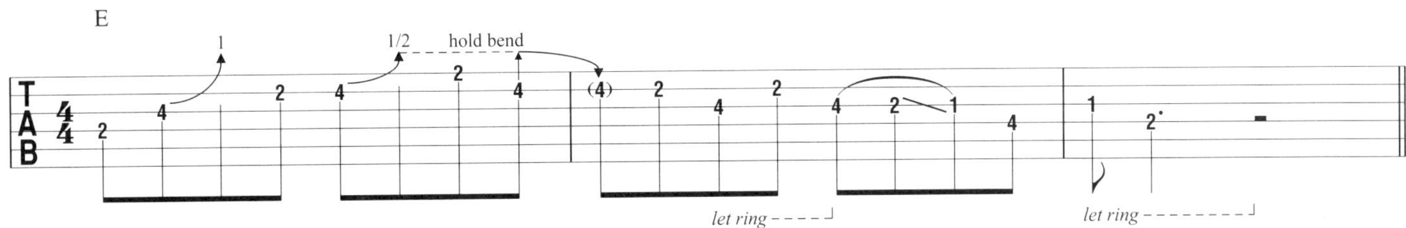


### 611: Sweet Barres

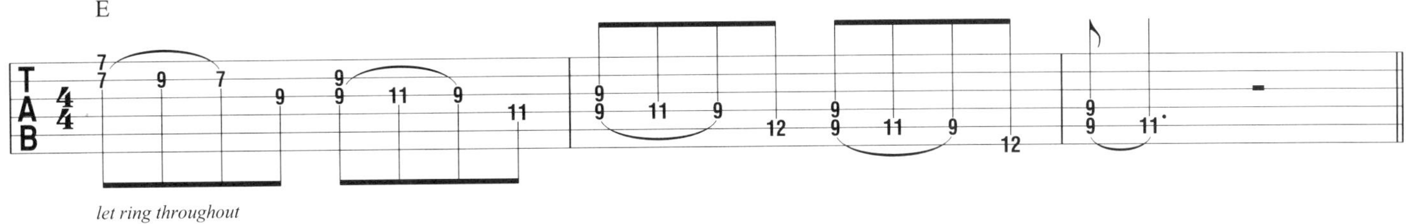


### 612: Major Box

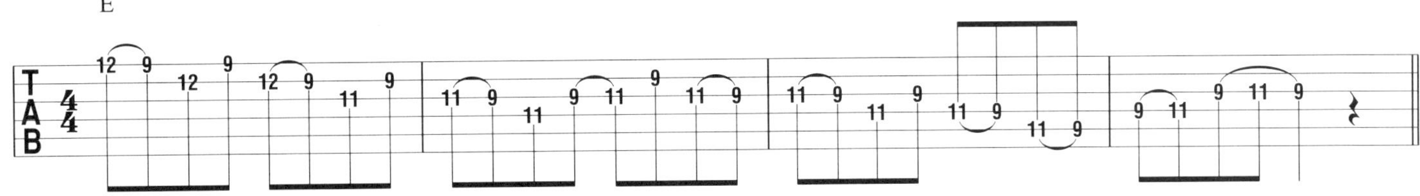


### 613: Twangy Ascent

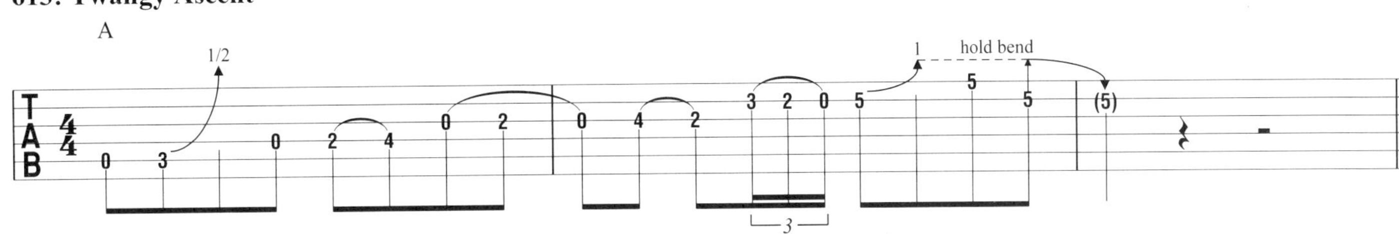

### 614: Classic Country

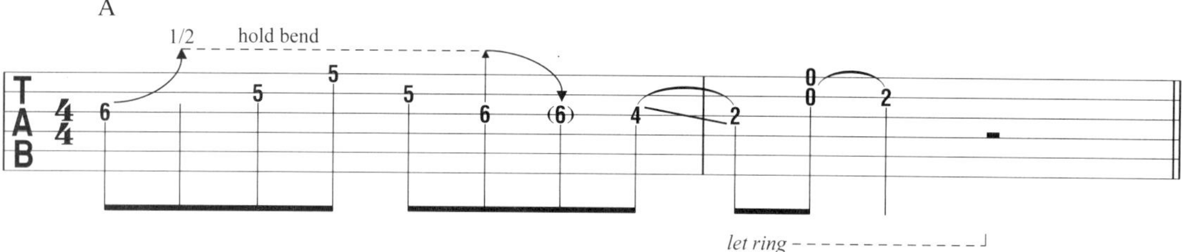


### 615: Legato Ascent

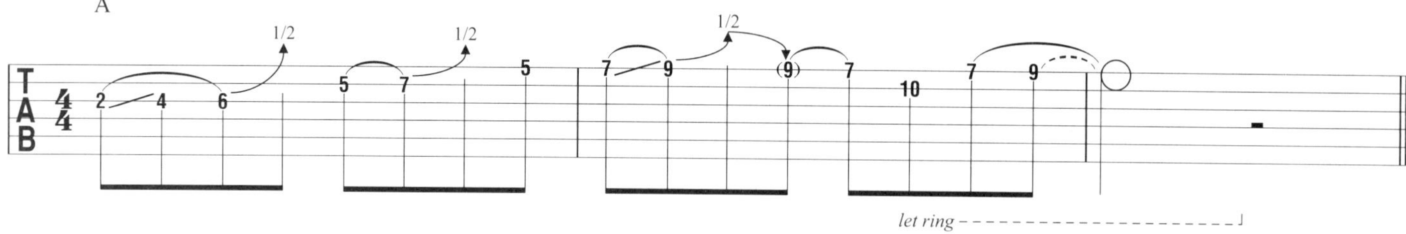


### 616: Redneck Bliss

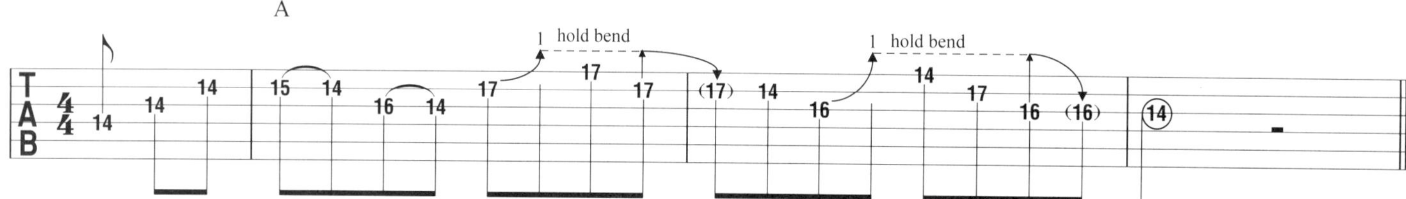


### 617: Country Blue

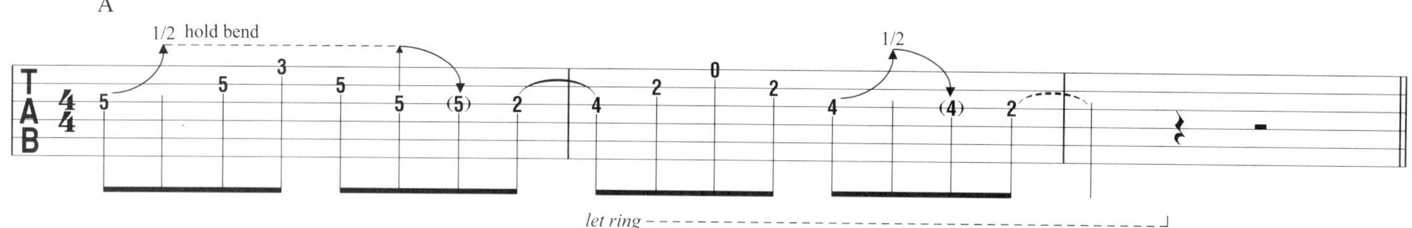


### 618: Country Delight

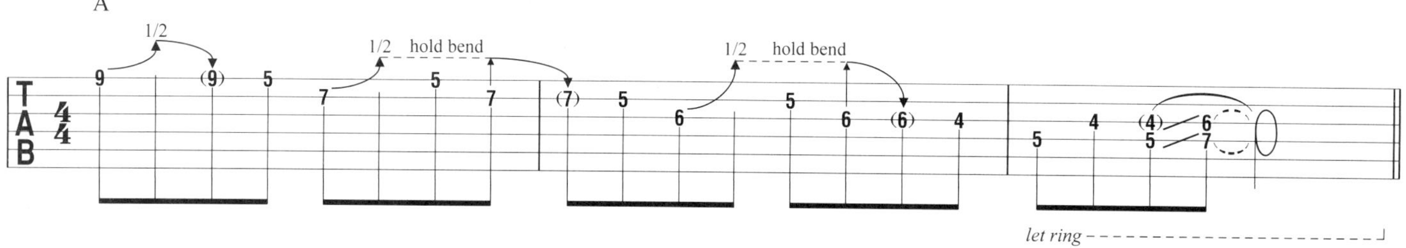


### 619: Sweet Sting

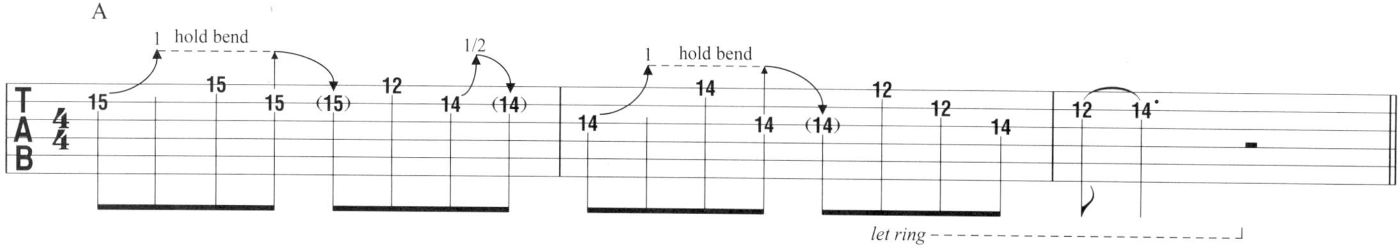


### 620: Country Rock

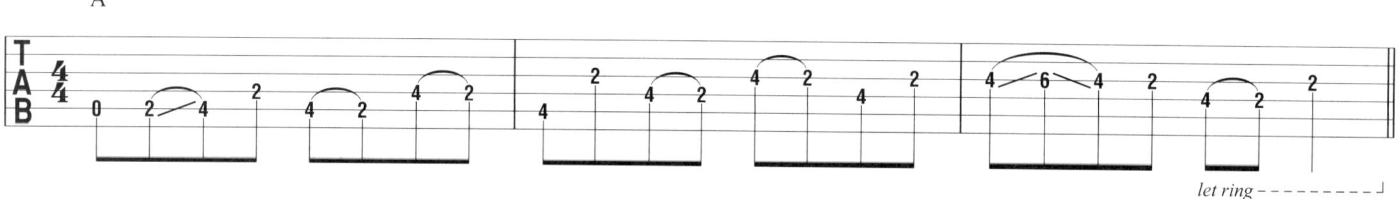

### 621: Droning Skipper

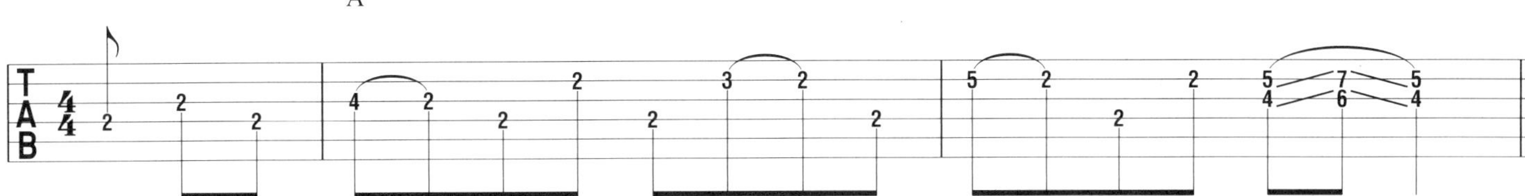


### 622: Two-Per-String

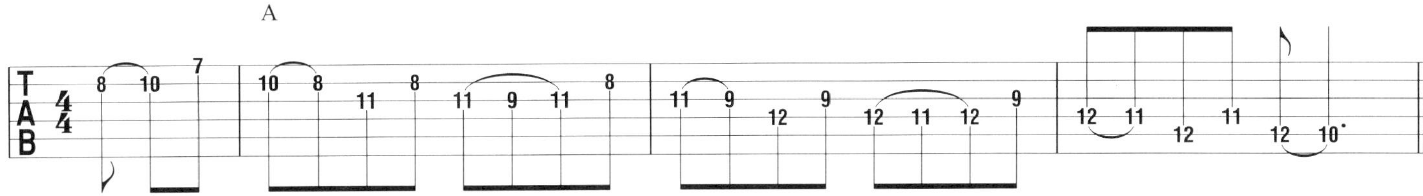


### 623: Pull-Off Sequence

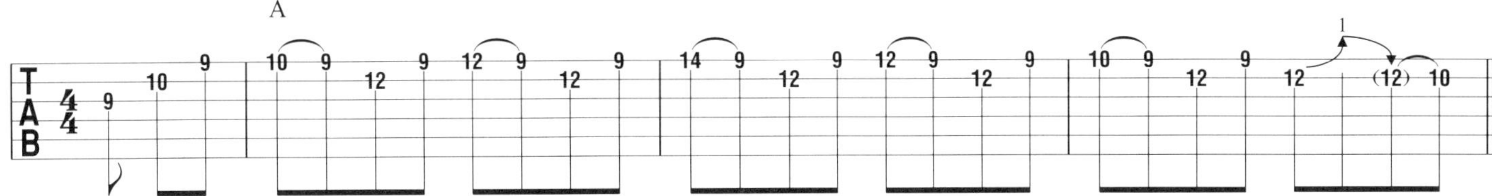


### 624: Bluegrassin'

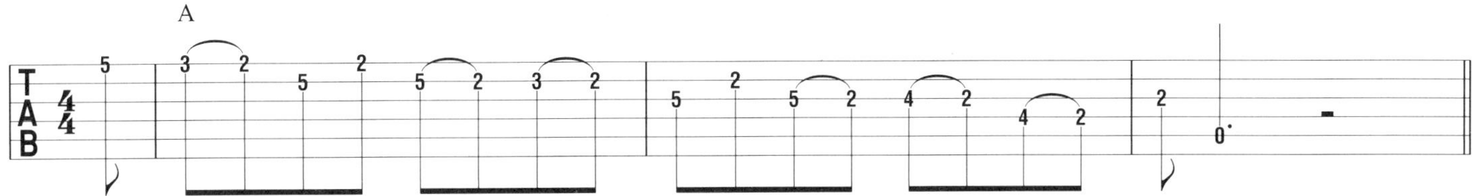


### 625: On a Bender

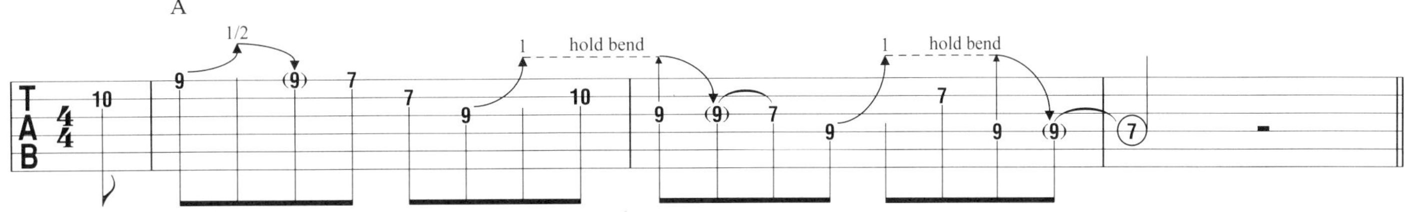


### 626: Mixolodious

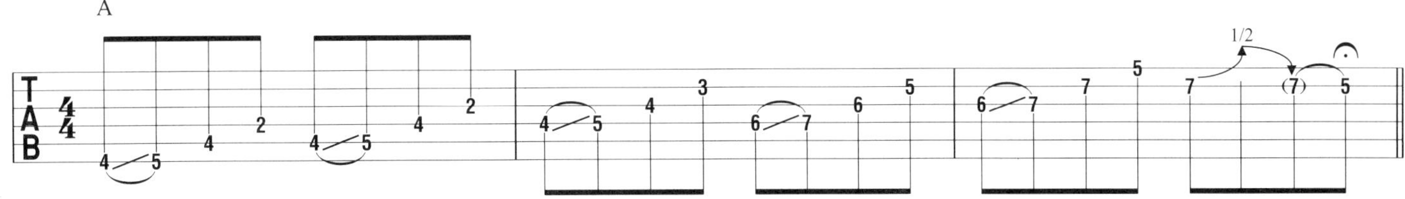


### 627: Doublestop Study

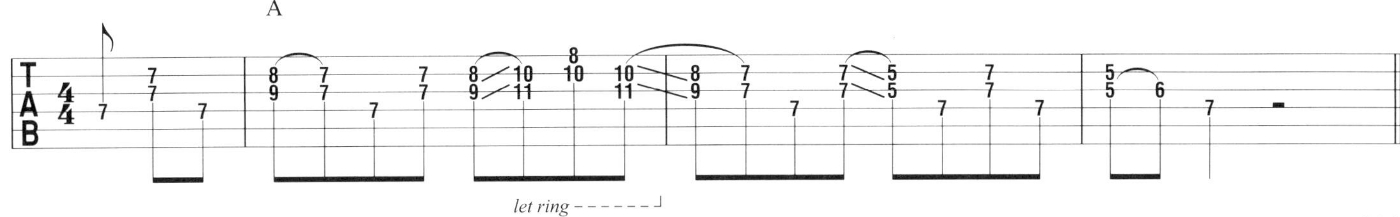

### 628: Chicken Pickin'

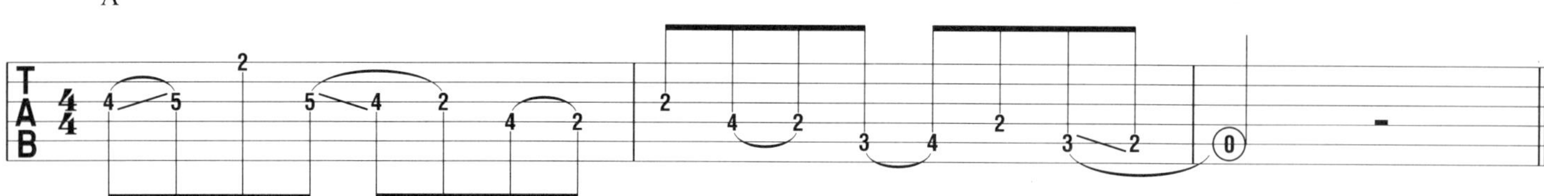


### 629: Moving 4ths

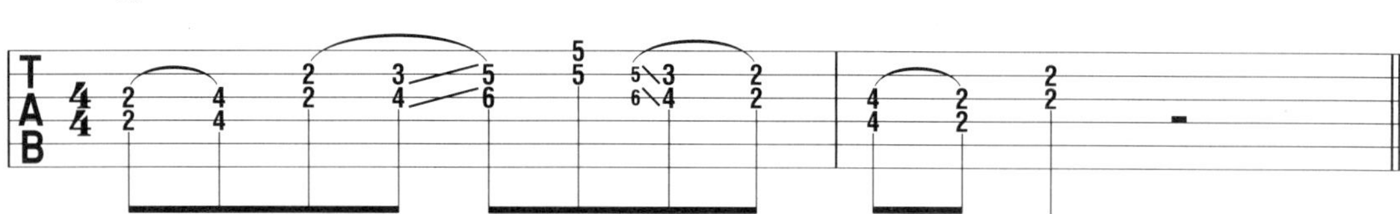


### 630: Southern Sustain

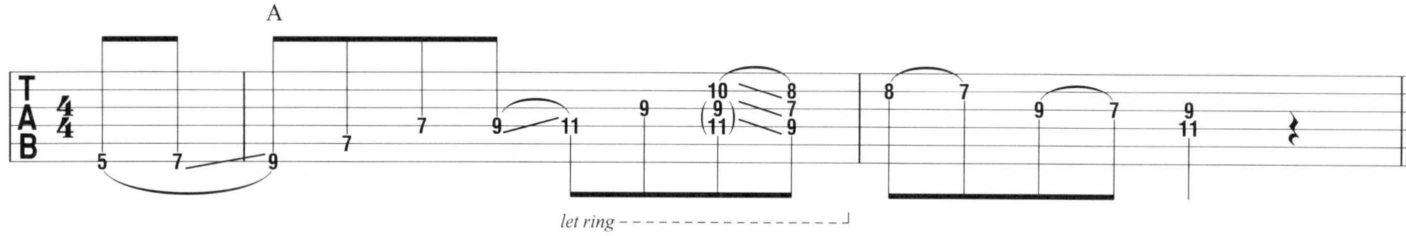


### 631: Blue Skies

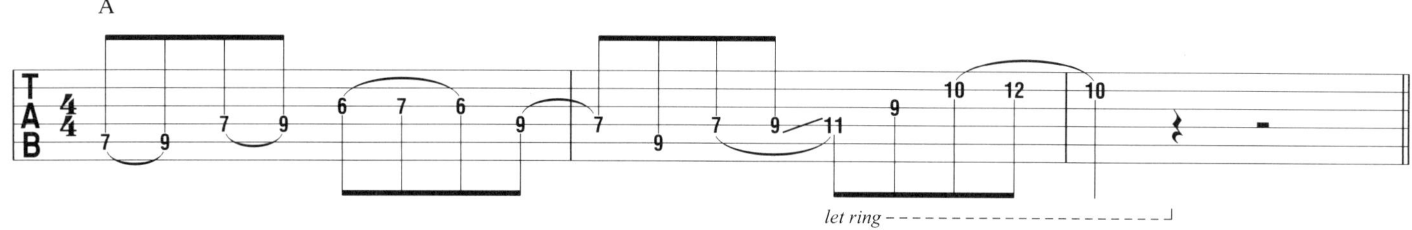


### 632: Farm Fresh

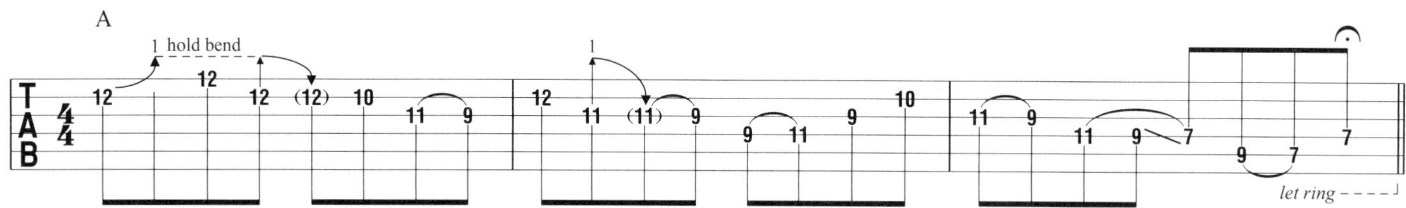


### 633: Pedal Steel

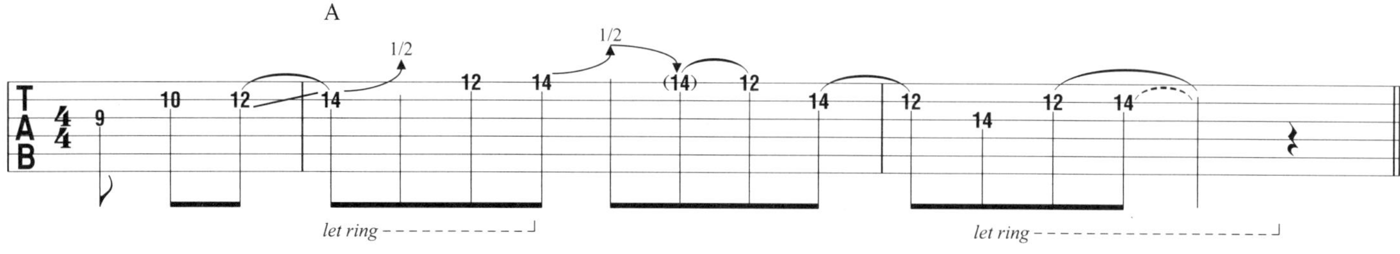


### 634: Hillbilly Delight

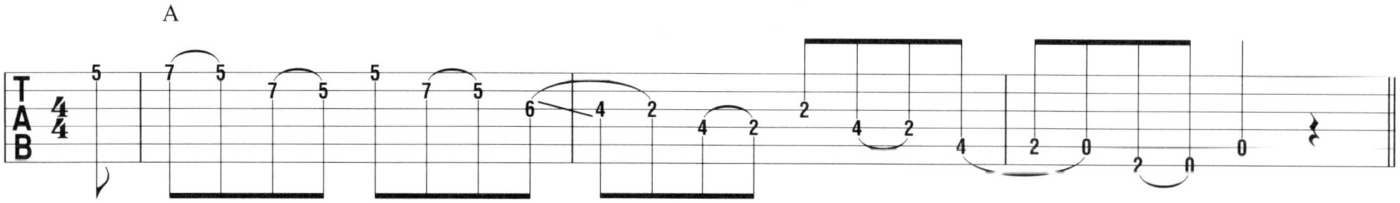

## 635: Penta-Flow

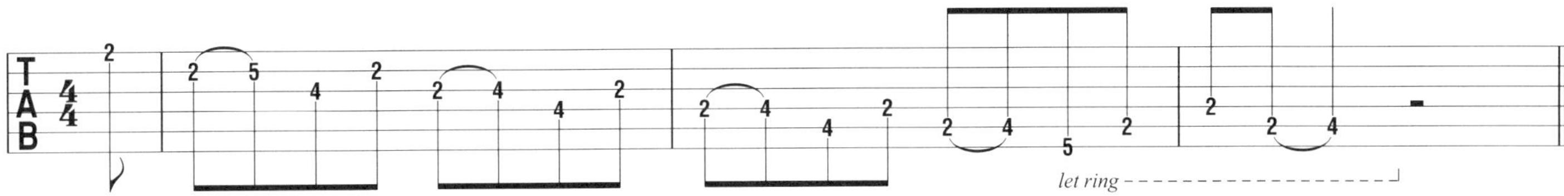


## 636: Steelin' Secrets

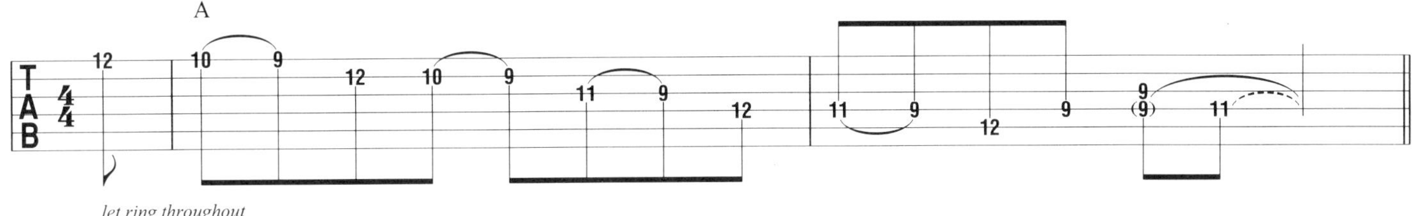


## 637: Country Concepts

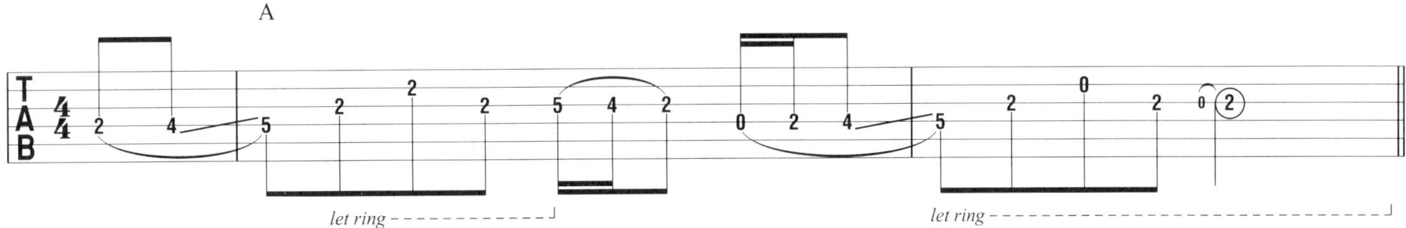


## 638: Bending Steel

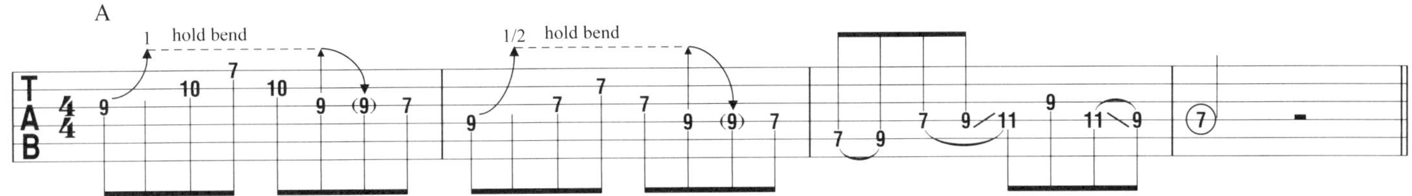


## 639: Neck Jumper

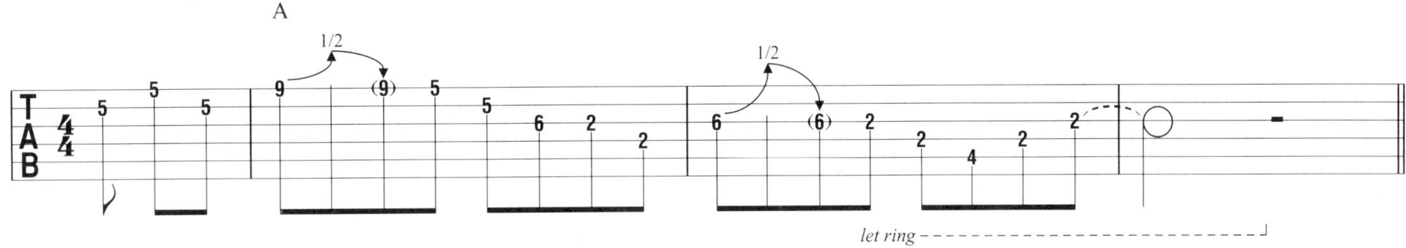


## 640: Trad Country

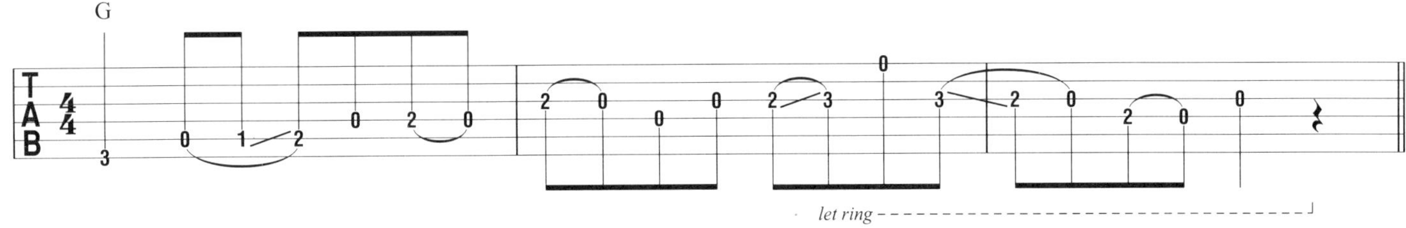


## 641: Pull 'Em Off

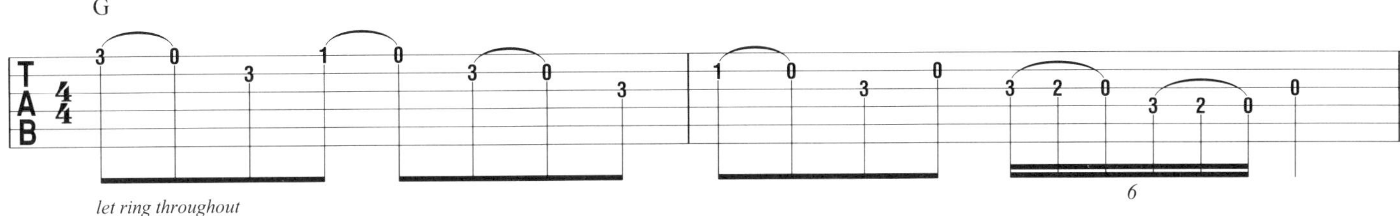

## 642: Triadic Ascent

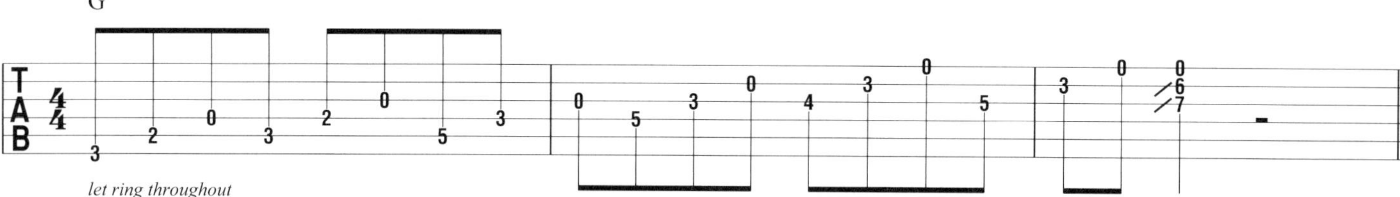


## 643: String Skippin'

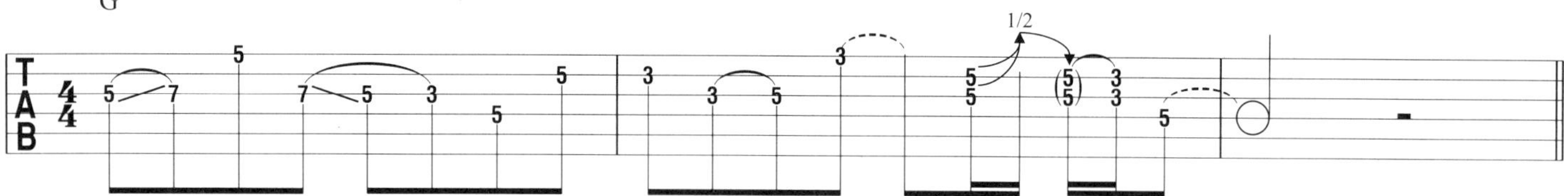


## 644: Open Strangs

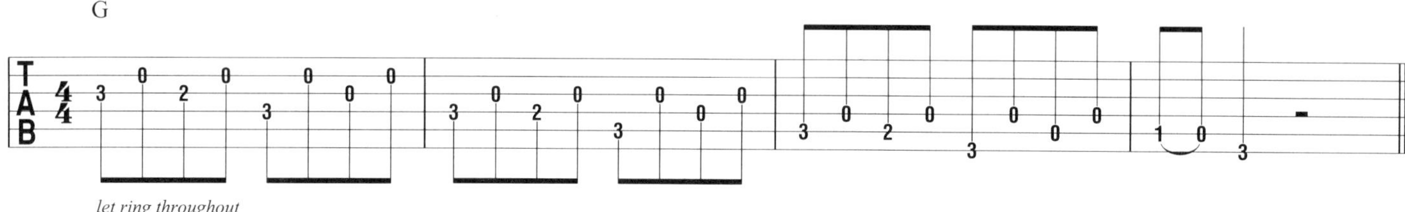


## 645: Banjo Roll

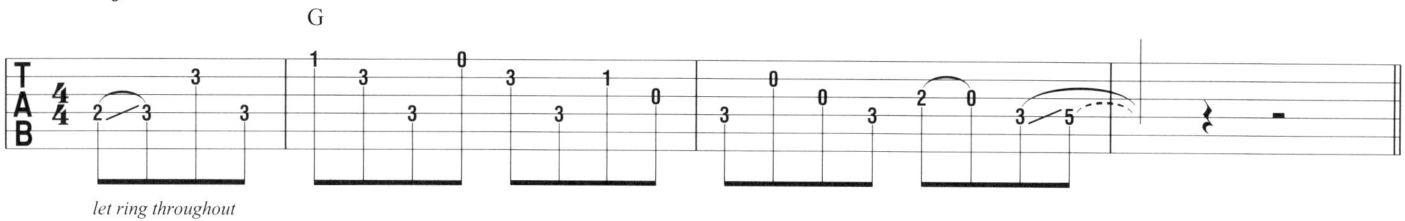


## 646: Dyad Peddler

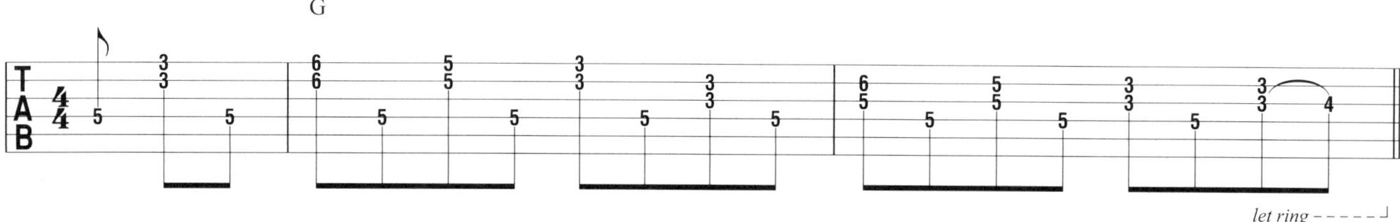


## 647: Up the Mountain

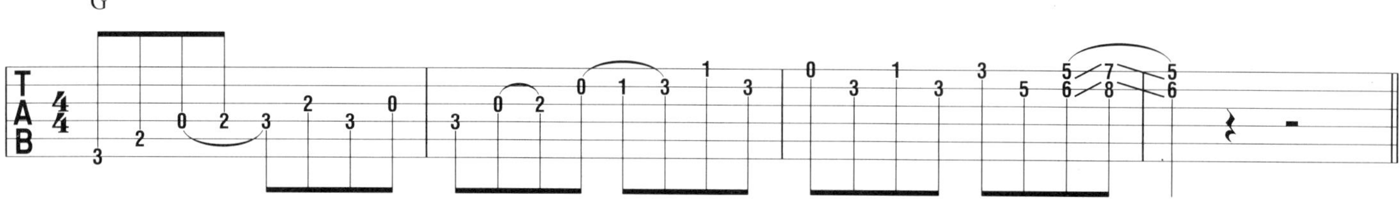


## 648: Southern Surprise

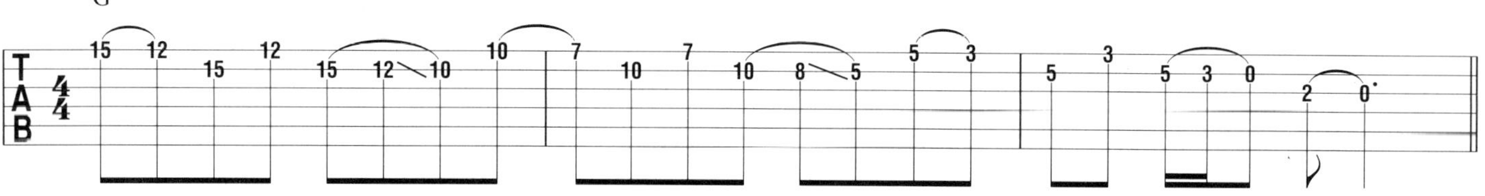

## 649: Let Ring

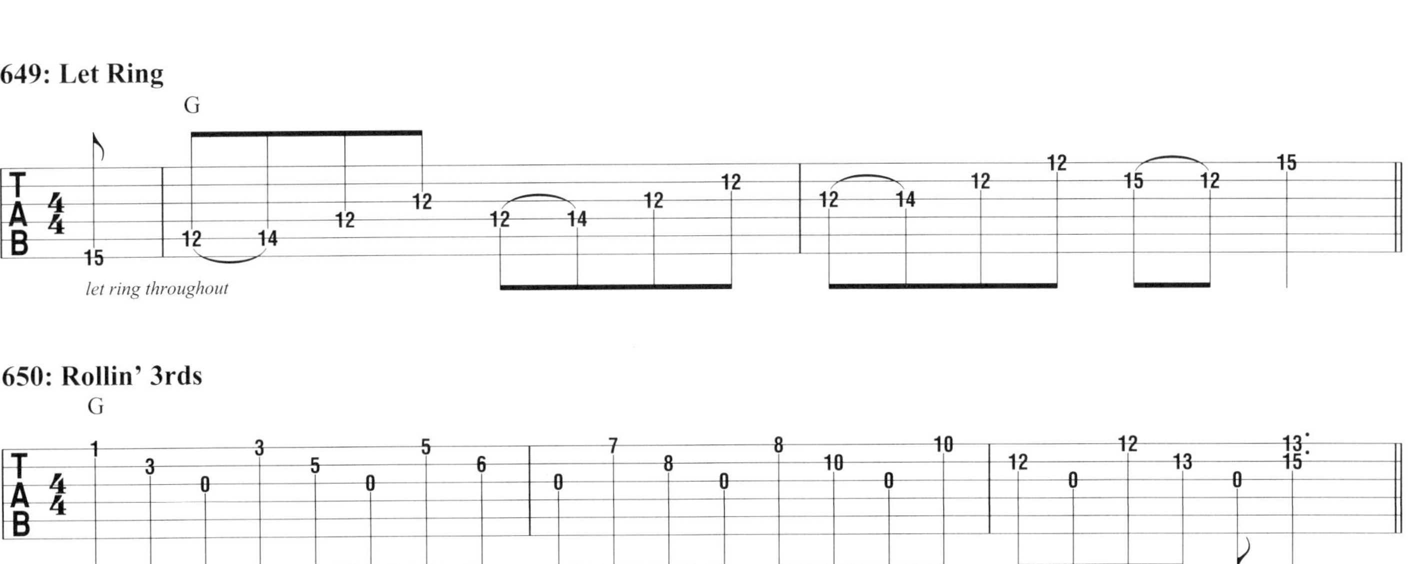


## 650: Rollin' 3rds

## 651: Smooth Twang

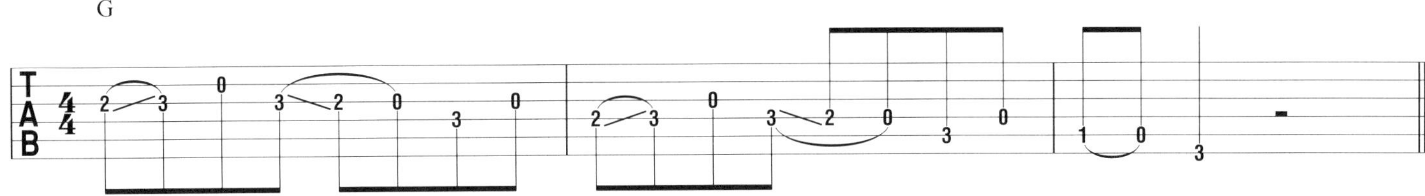


## 652: Pull-Off Riff

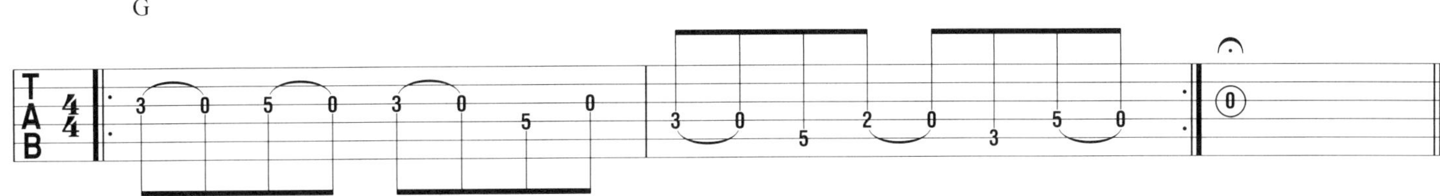


## 653: String Hopper

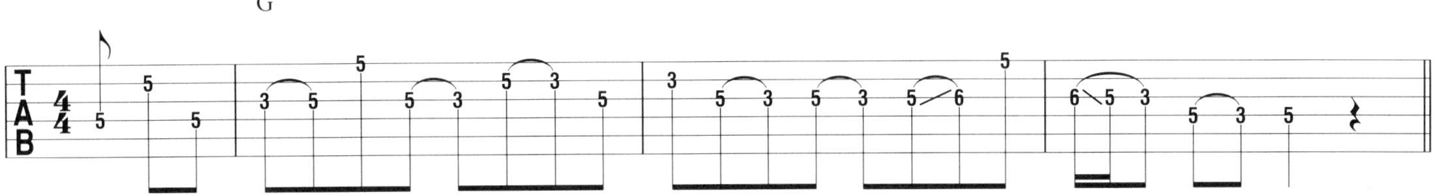


## 654: Southern Blues

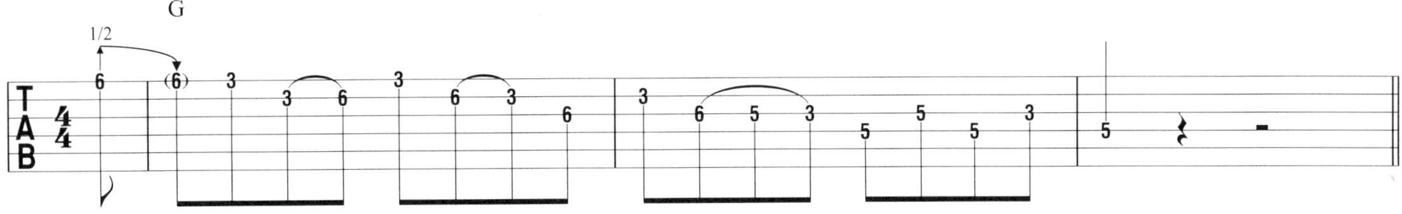


## 655: Wicked Bends

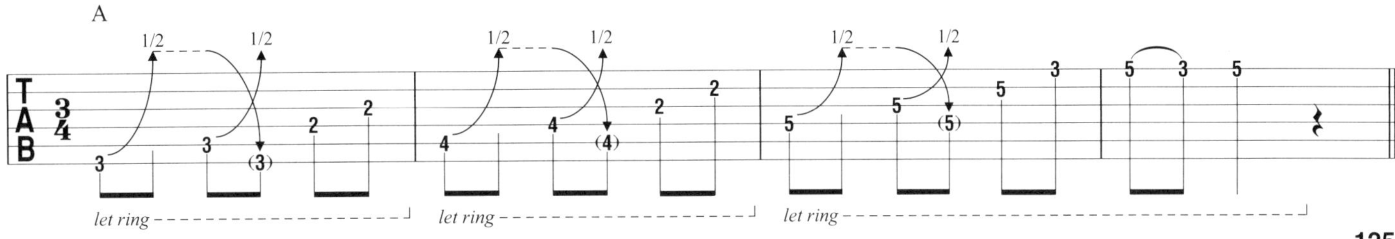

### 656: Country Ending

C

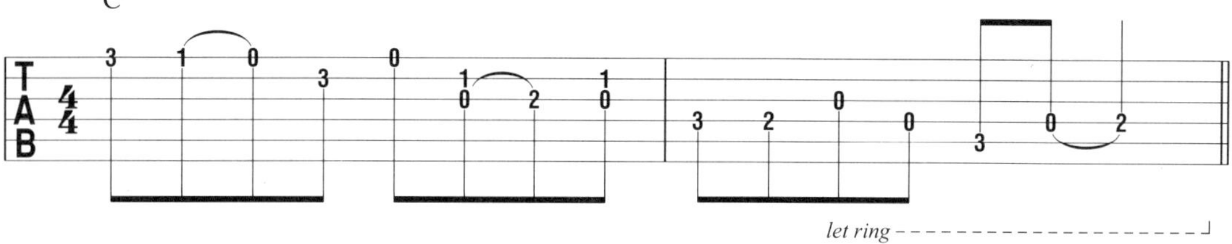


### 657: Pentatonic Burn

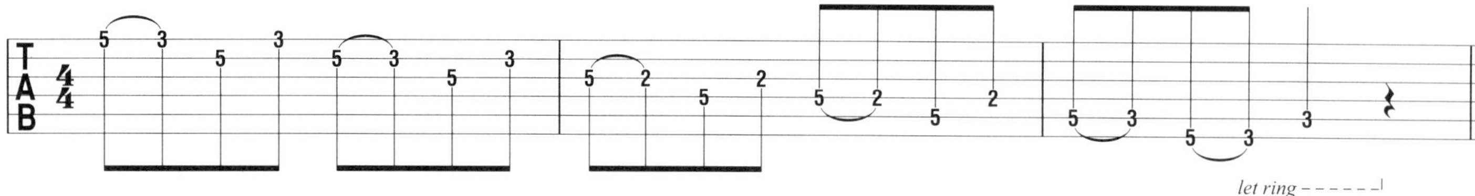


### 658: Hold Bends

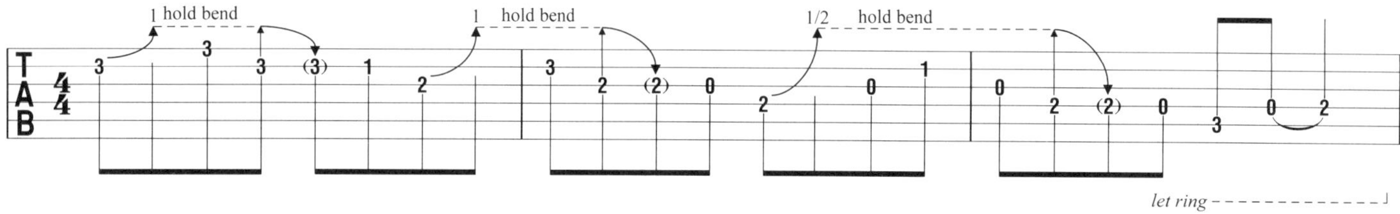


### 659: Bright Bends

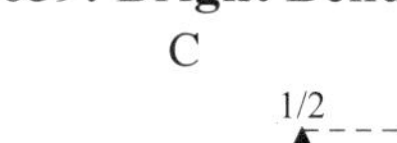


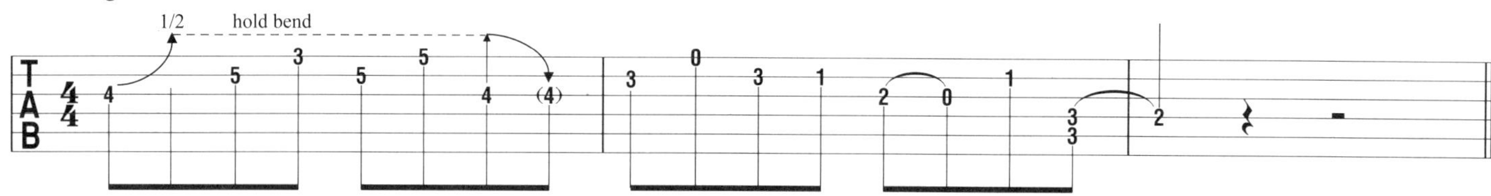


### 660: Country Turn

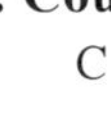


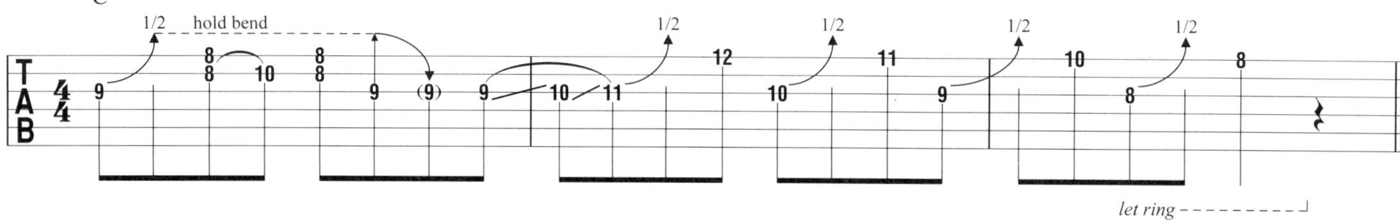


### 661: Pedal Bends

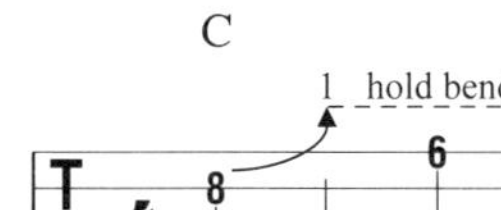


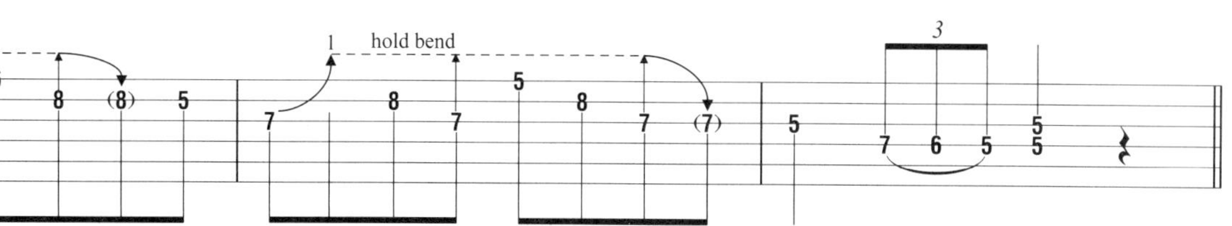


### 662: Sweet Corn

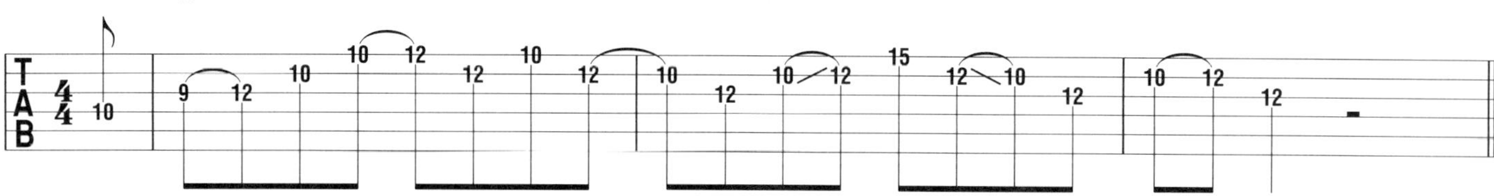

### 663: Sweet & Low

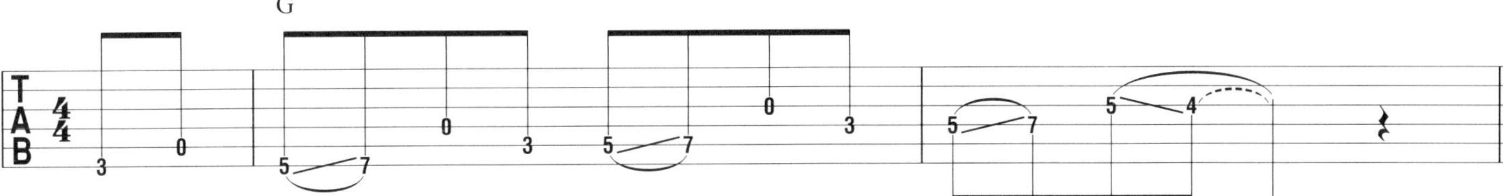


### 664: Open Descent

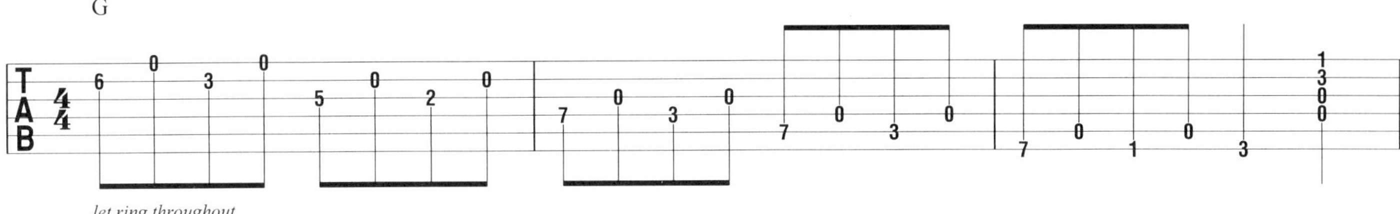


### 665: Open Cascade

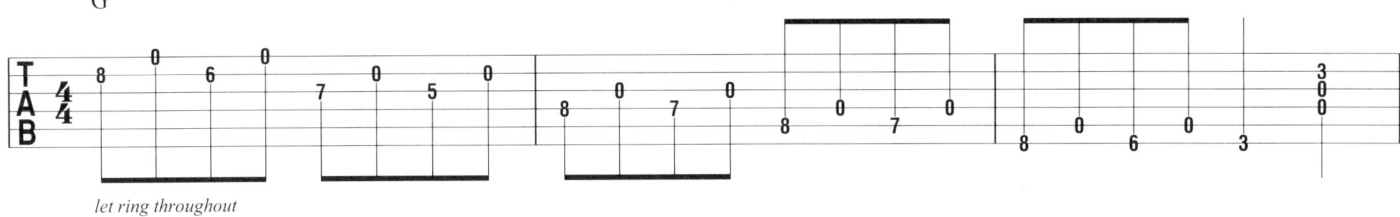


### 666: Cornbread Blues

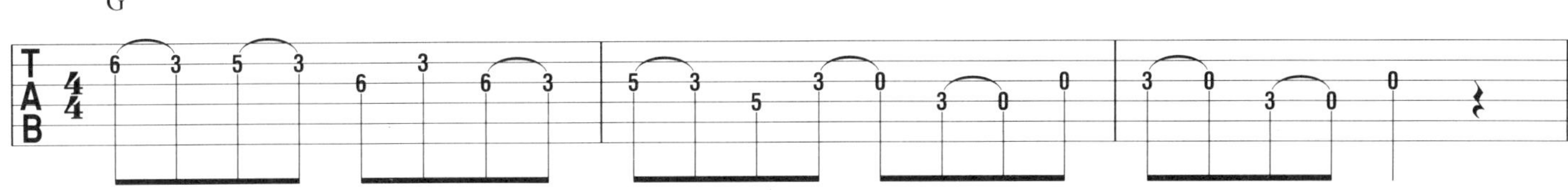


### 667: Double Pulls

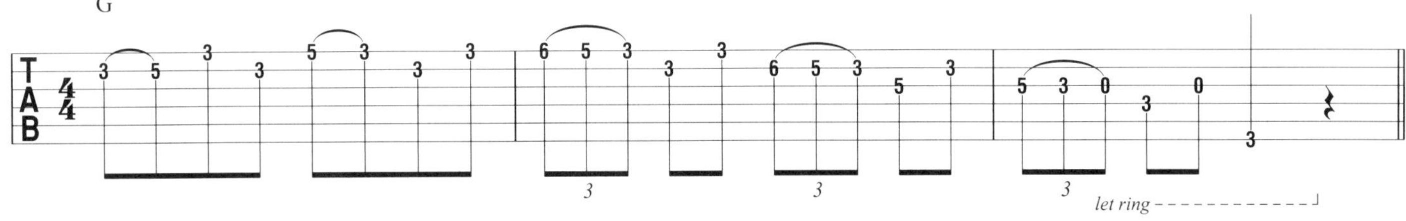


### 668: Boss Hogg

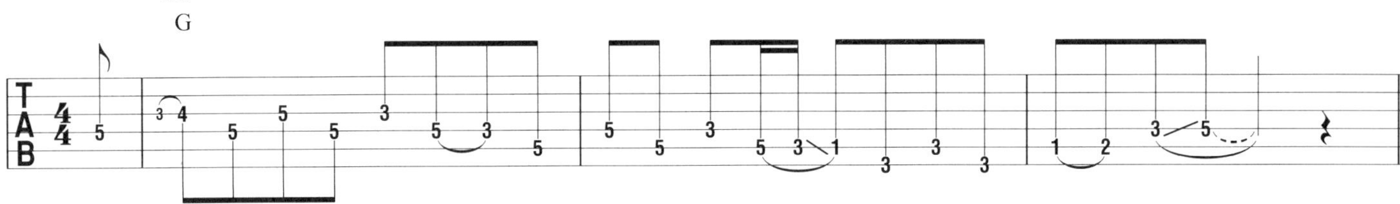


### 669: Country 6ths

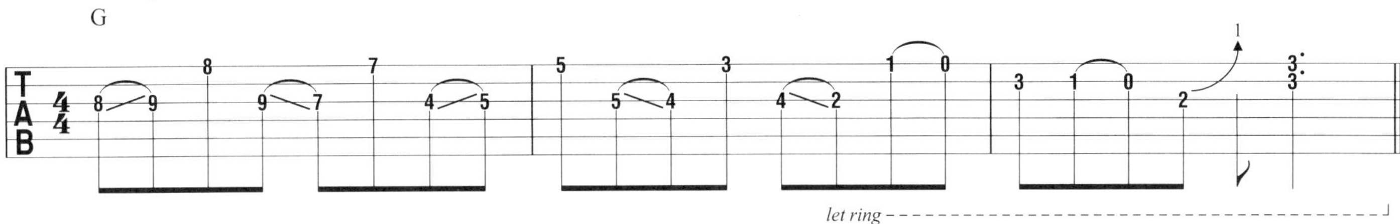

**670: Unison Run**

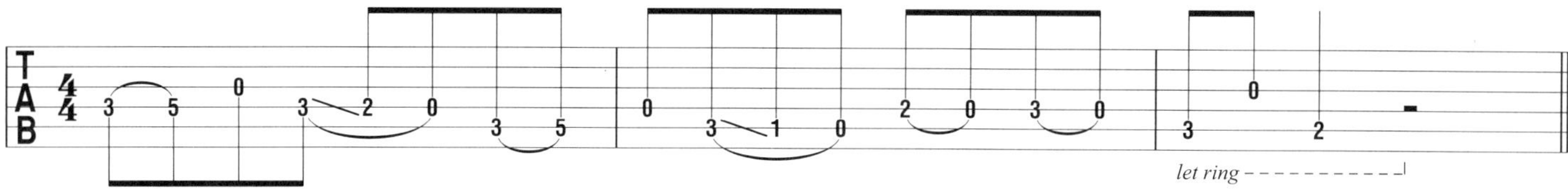


**671: Blues Biscuits**

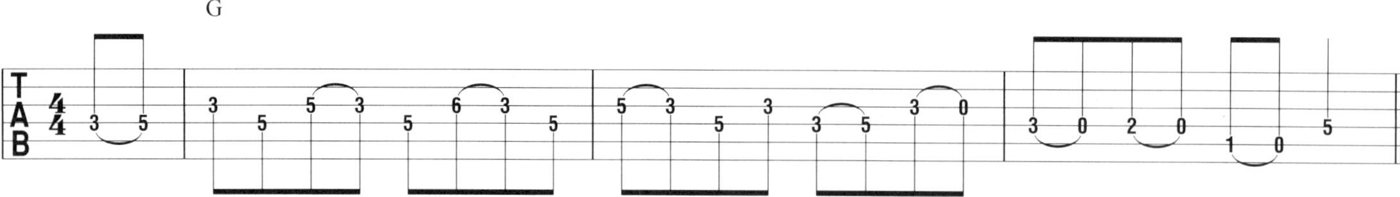


**672: Penta-Pulls**

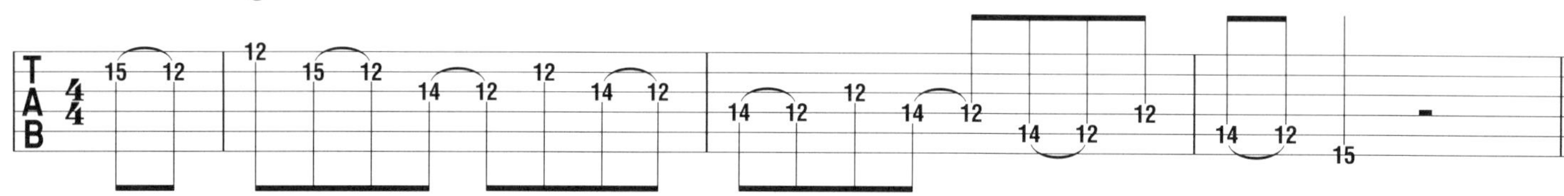


**673: String Jukin'**

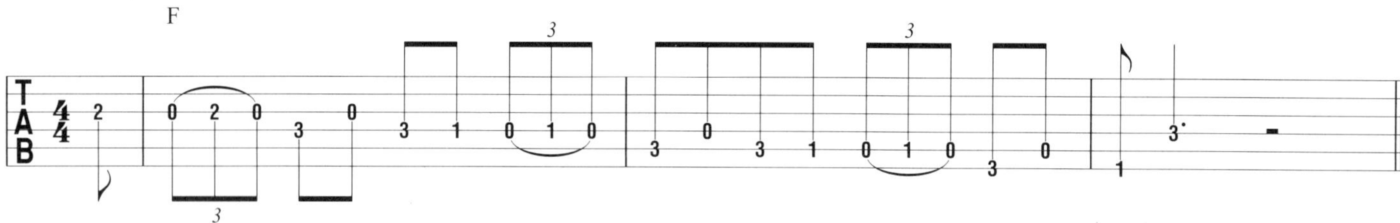


**674: Scalar Phrasing**

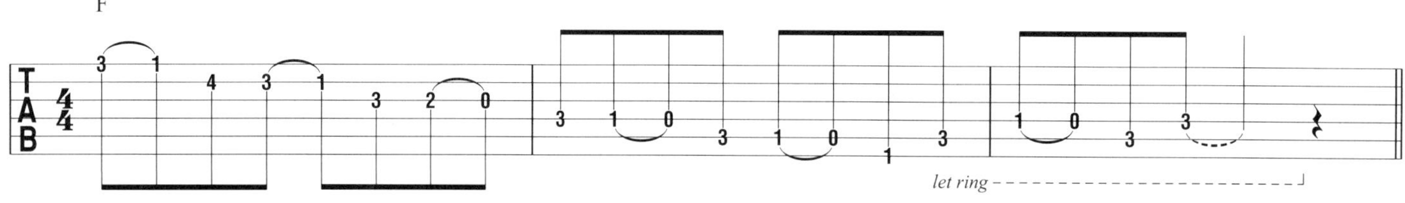


**675: It's All There**

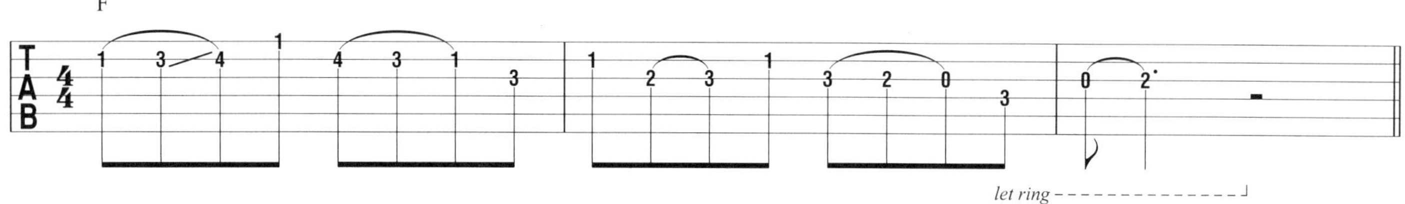


**676: Hammer & Bend**

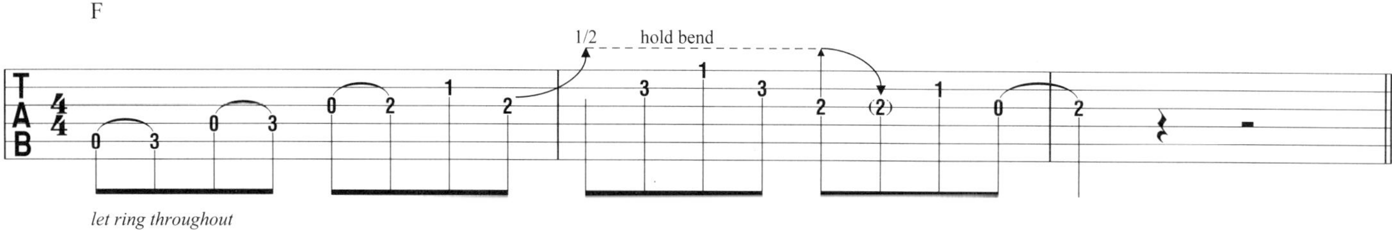

### 677: Penta-Stops

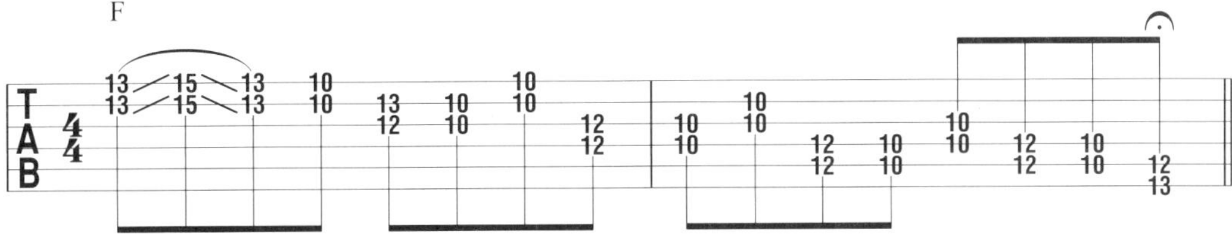


### 678: Open the Box

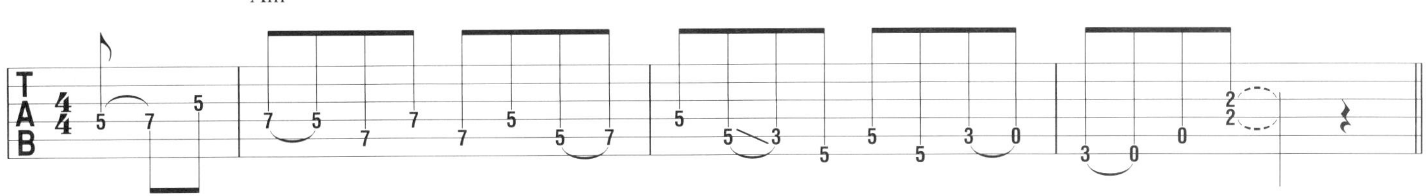


### 679: Simply Tasty

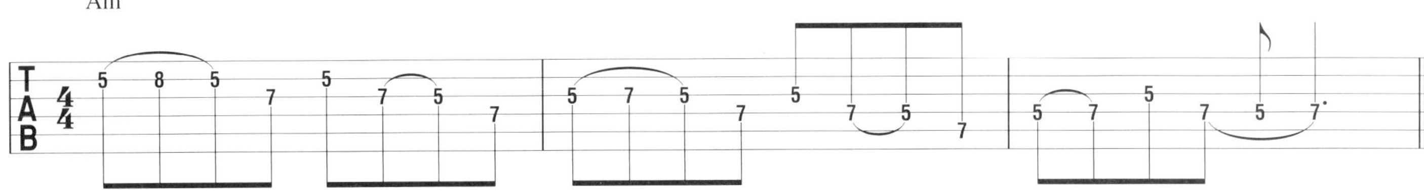


### 680: Penta-Shifter

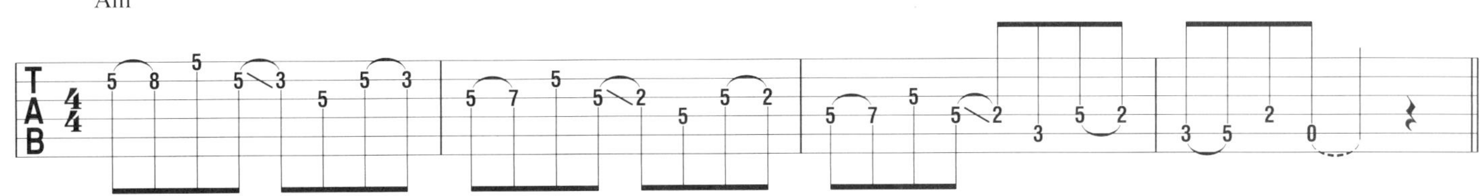


## Instructor: Josh Tovar

### 681: Old School Chimer

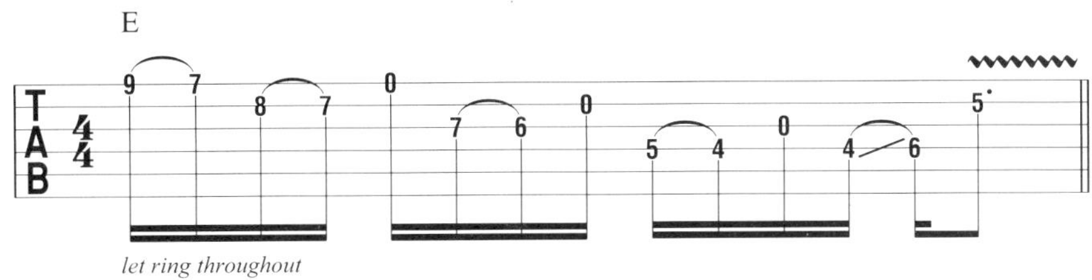


### 682: Pedal Steelin'

Swing feel

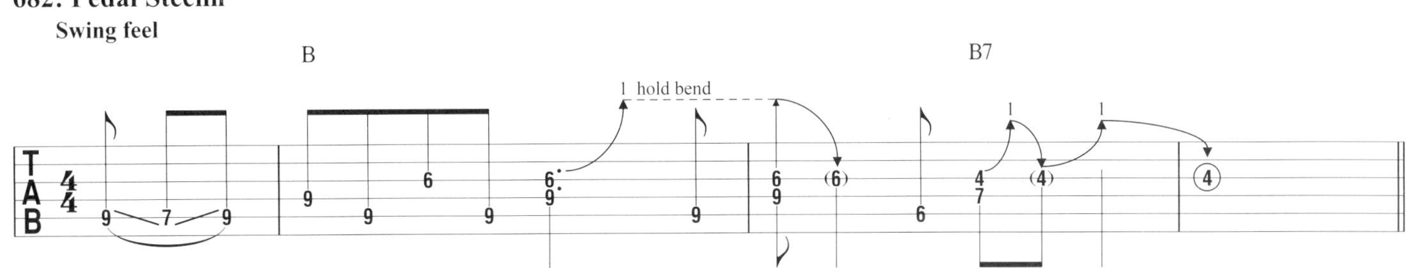

## 683: Sweet Grass

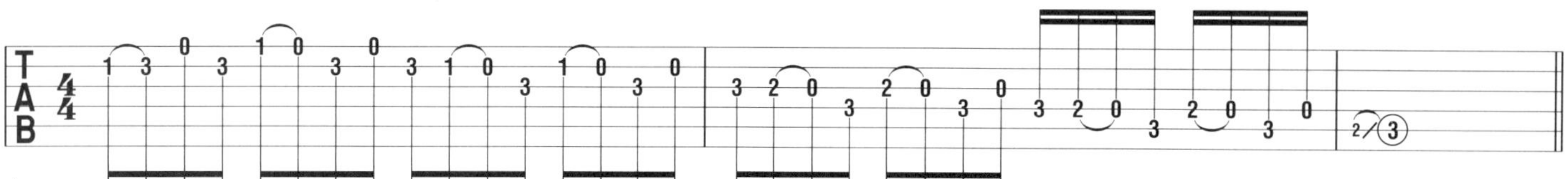

## 684: Speedy Stops

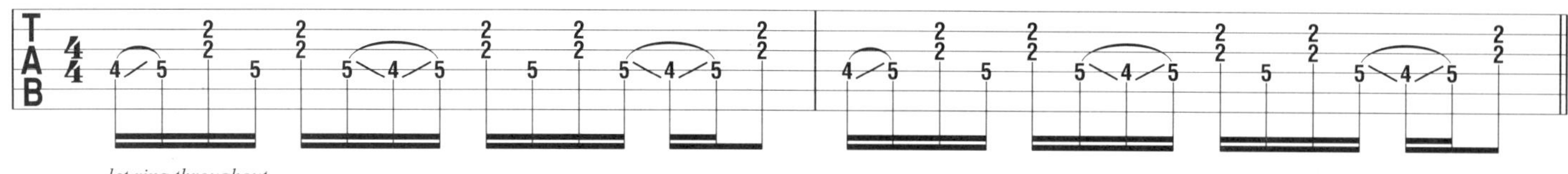


## 685: Reed to Gatton

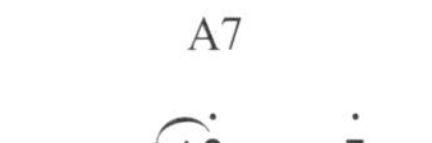


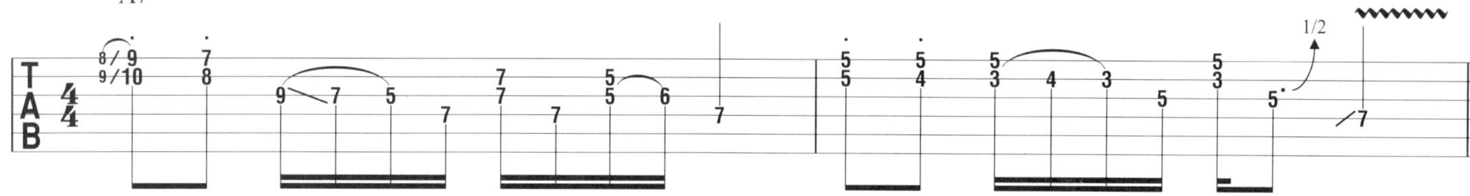

## 686: Pedal-Steel Banjo

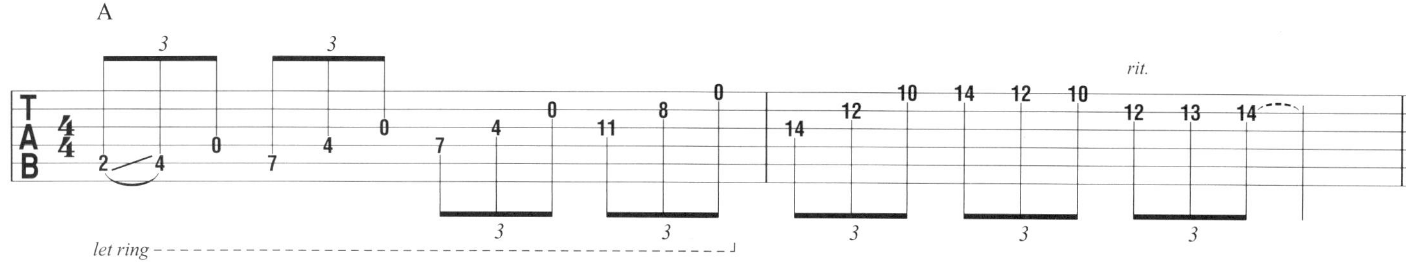


## 687: Cluck Pluck

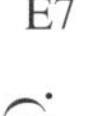


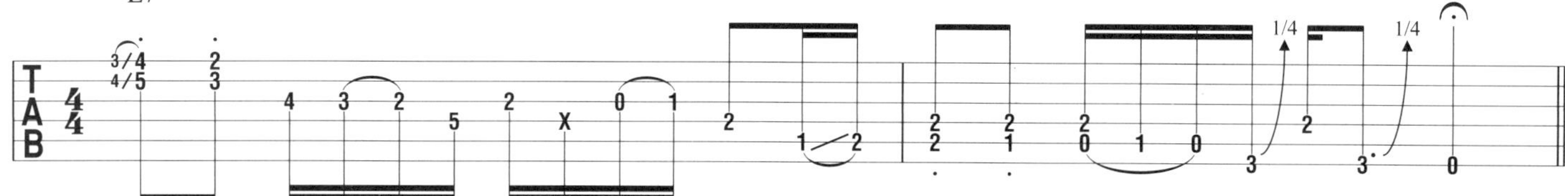

## 688: Doublestop Groove

A7

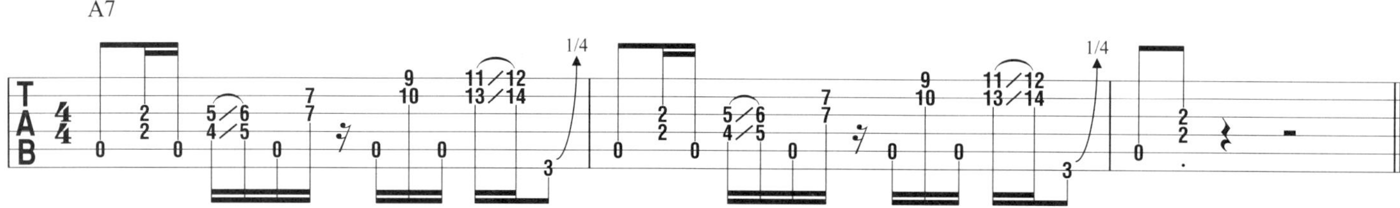

## 689: Pentatonic Descent

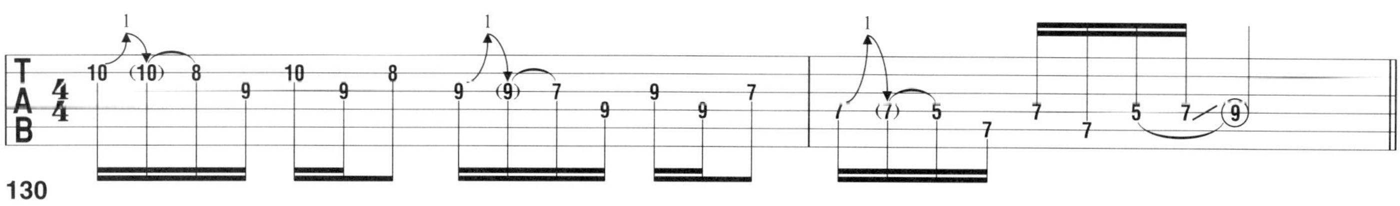

## 690: Waylon Tone

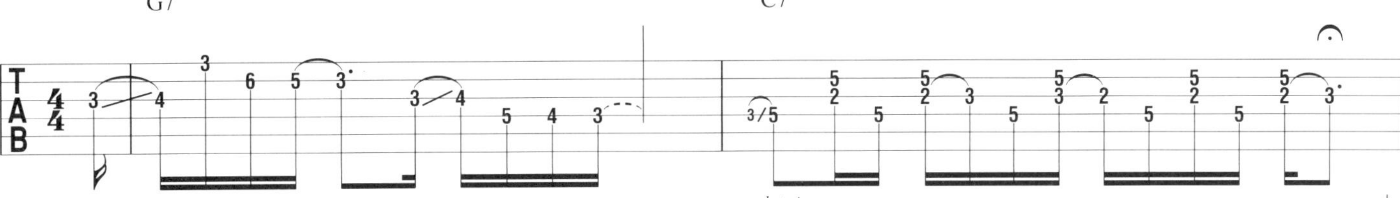


## 691: Steel Slidin'

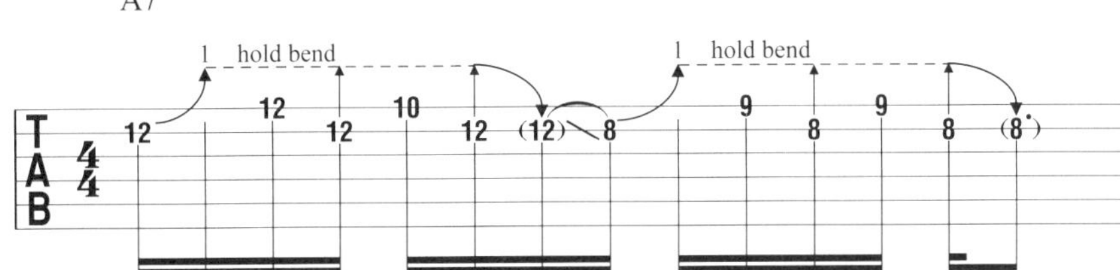


## 692: Plentiful Pre-Bends

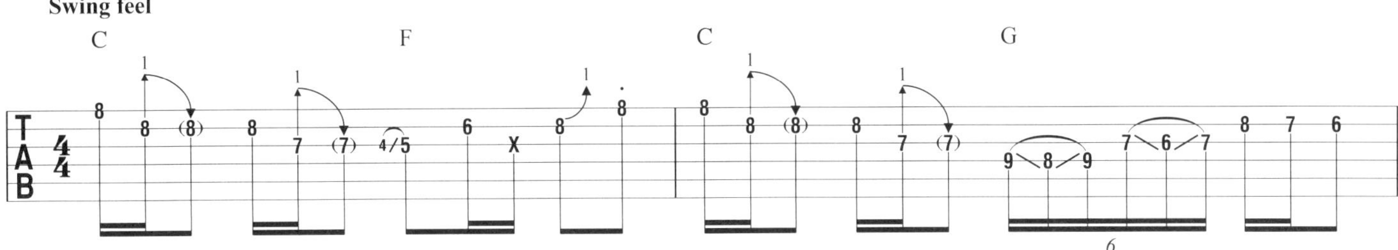


## 693: Arpeggiated Steel

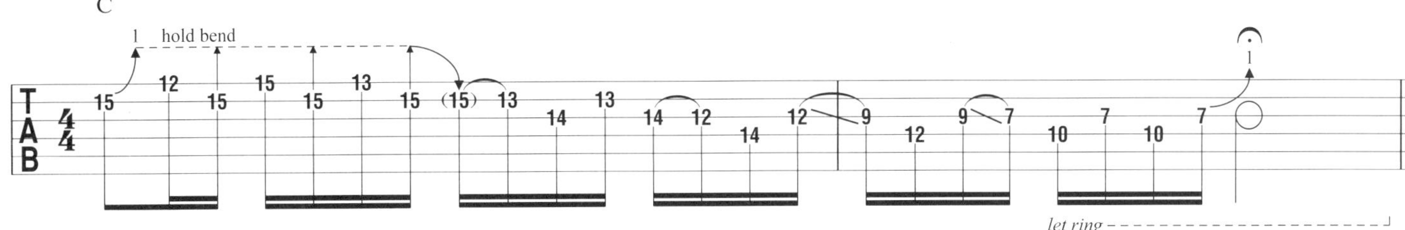


## 694: Roy Nichols Style

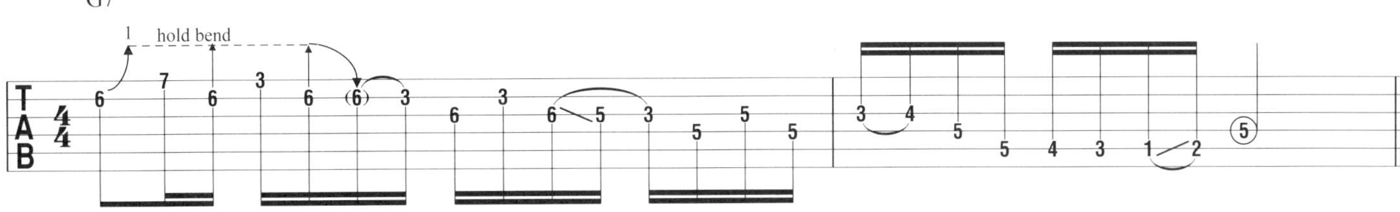


## 695: Triplet Exercise

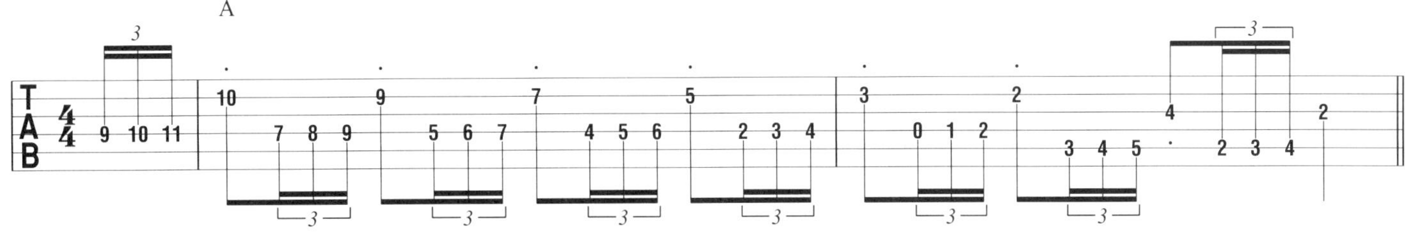


## 696: Steel-Bent Descent

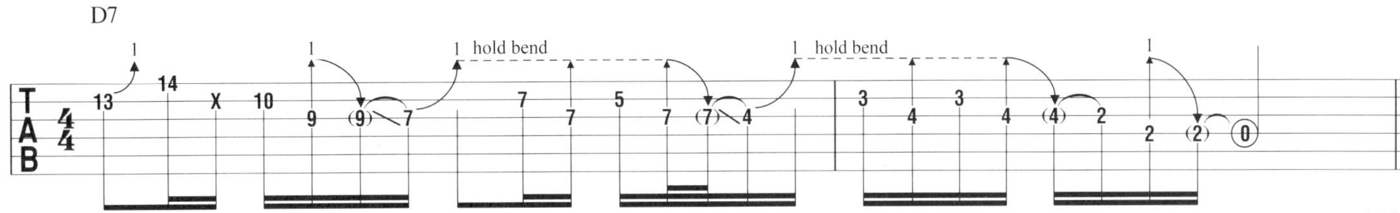

### 697: Chet Scale

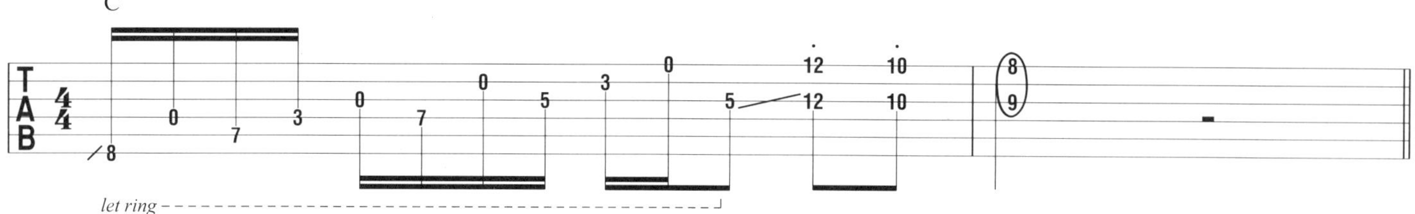


### 698: Biscuits & Gravy

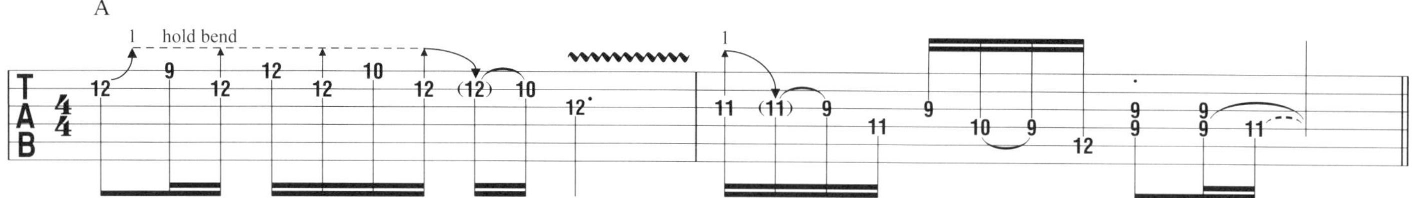


### 699: Southern Swing

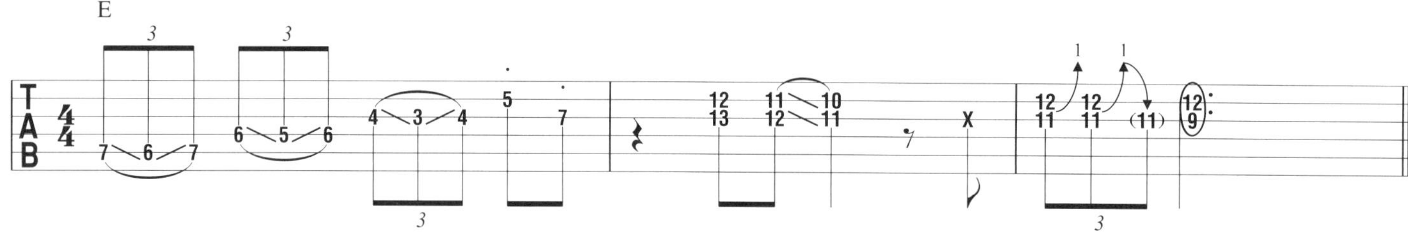


### 700: Honky Tonkin'

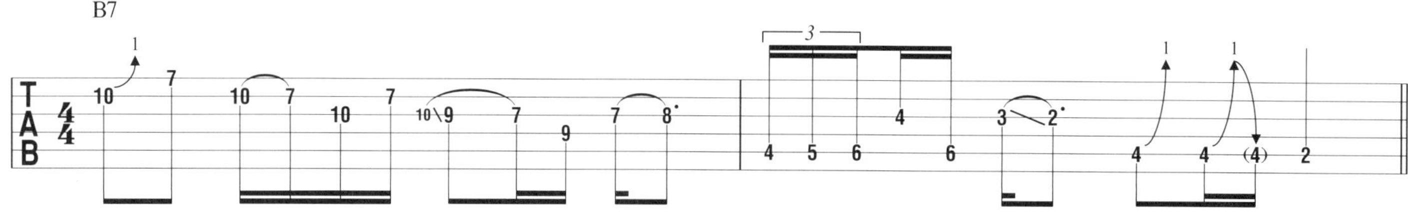


### 701: Tele Time

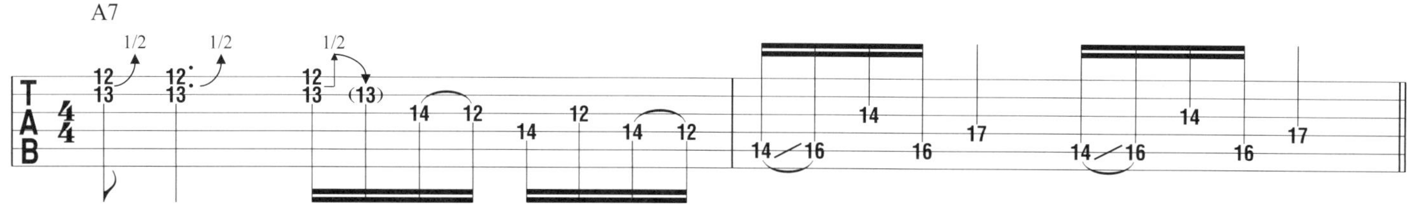


### 702: Funky Bends

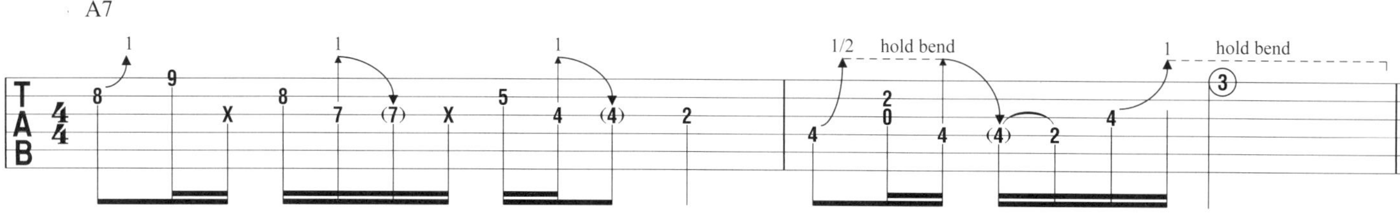


### 703: Country Fresh

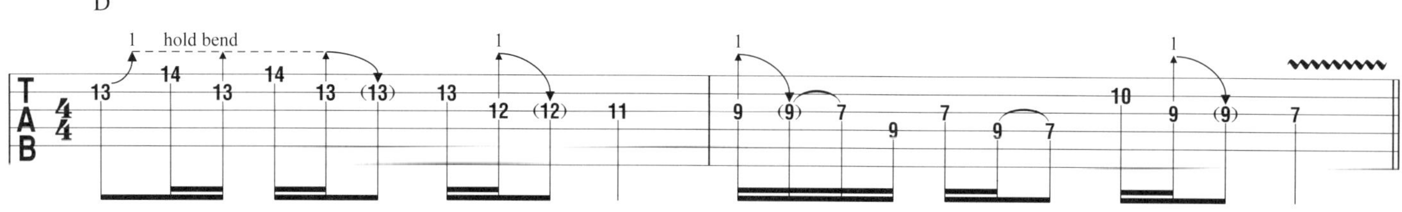

### 704: Southern Rock

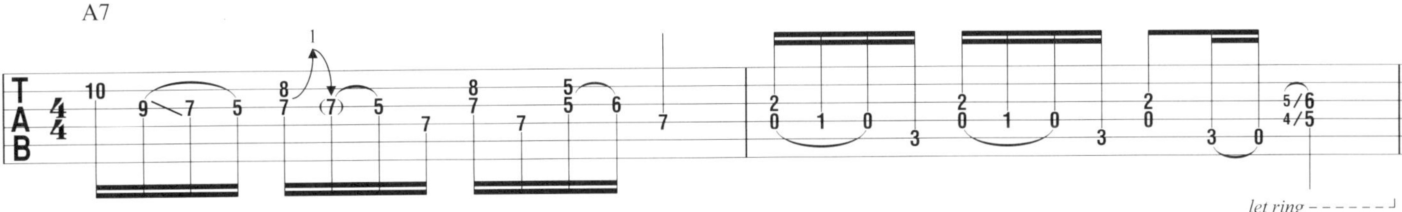


### 705: Chicken Picker

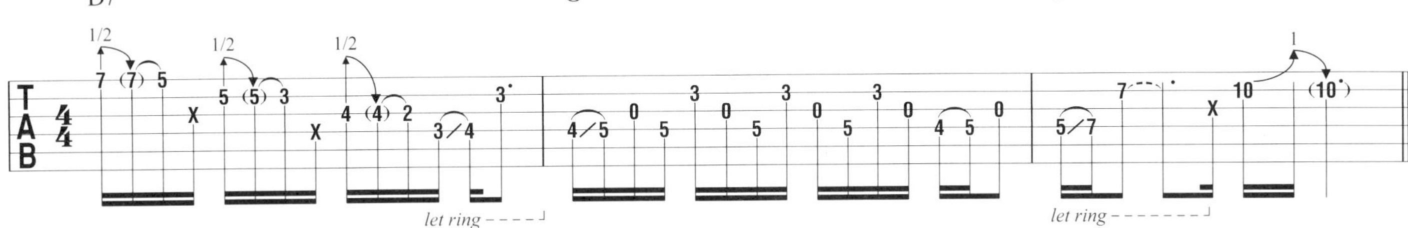


### 706: Volume Swells

A D A A6 A7

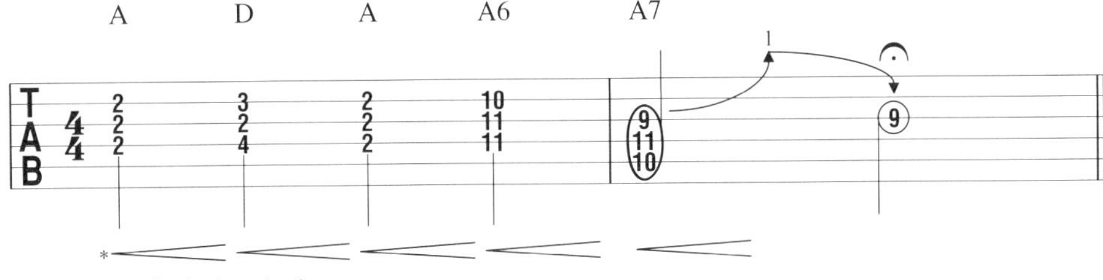

*Swell w/ volume knob

### 707: Walkin' Triplets

A

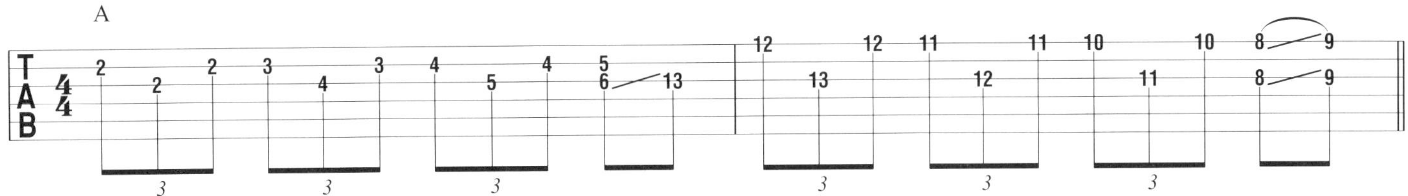

### 708: Hazzardous

E7

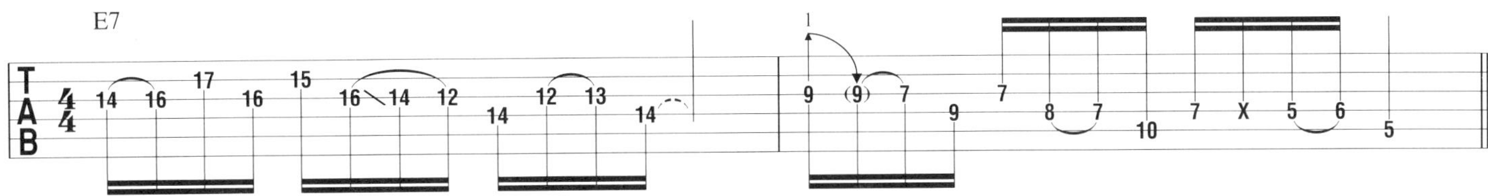

### 709: Honky Classic

E

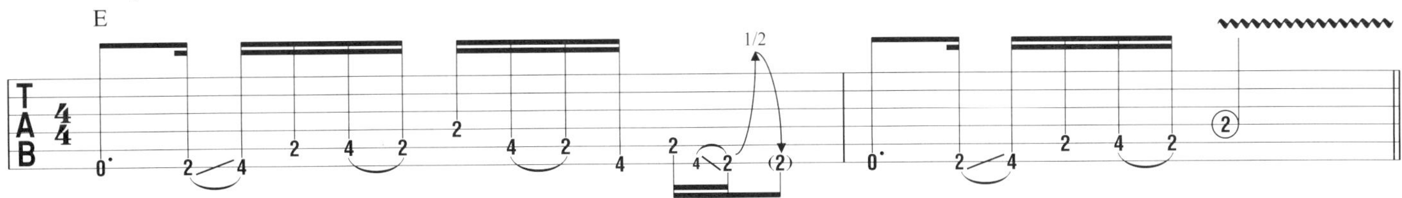

### 710: Country Creeper

E

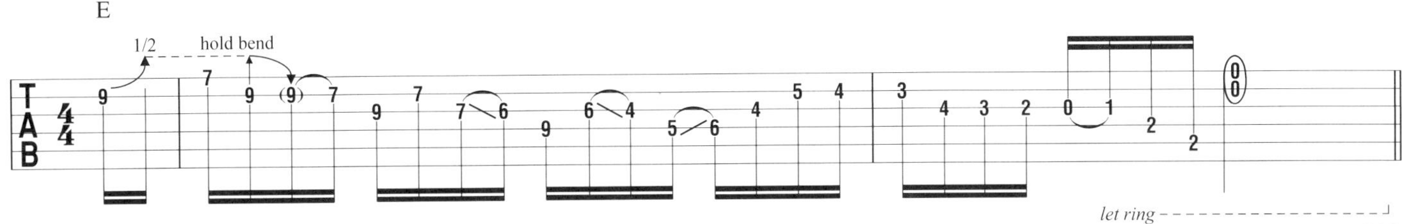

### 711: Steel Emulator

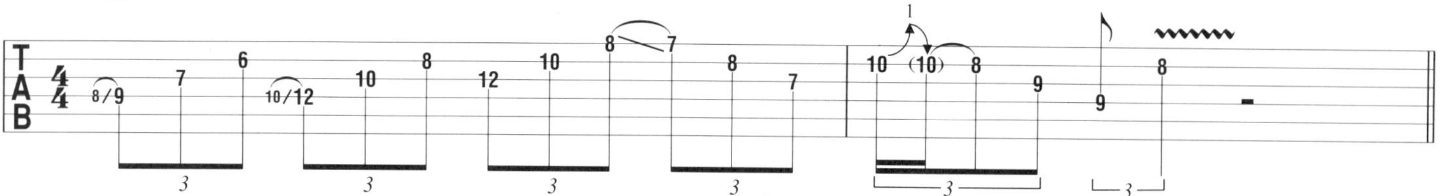

### 712: Bluegrass Tele

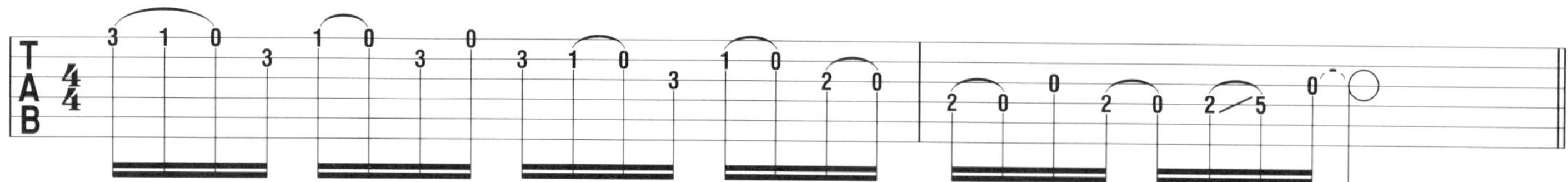

### 713: Sweet Steel

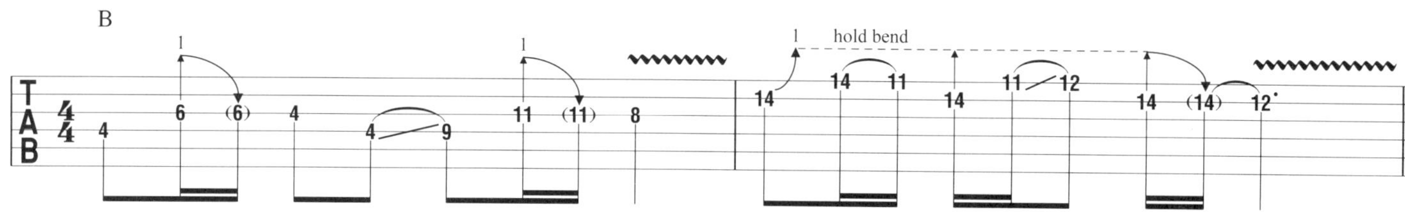


### 714: Mountain Bends

D

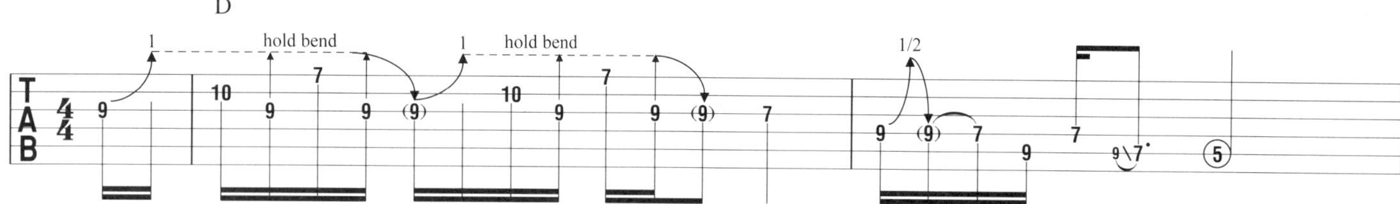


### 715: Chromatic Triplets

A

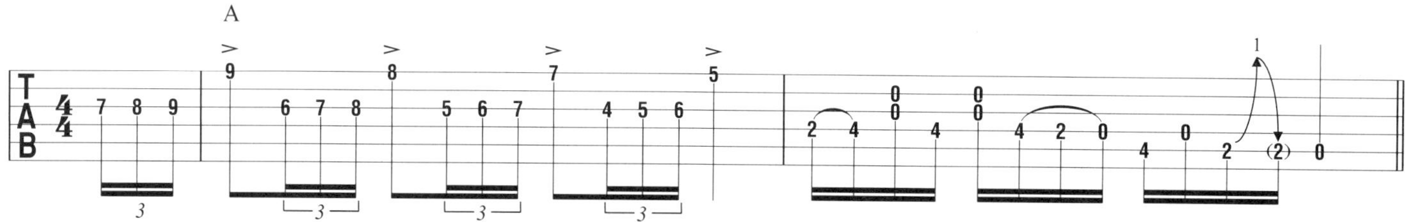

### 716: Open-String Roll

A7

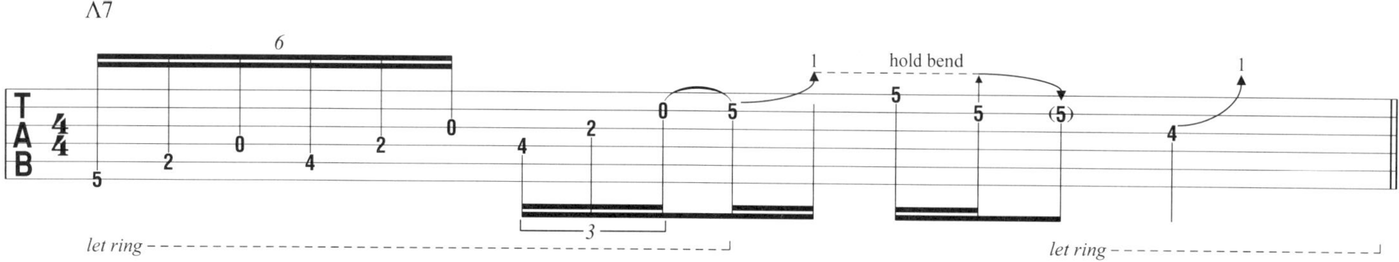


### 717: Pedal-Steel Swing

Am7 Fmaj7 Em7 Dm(maj7) C

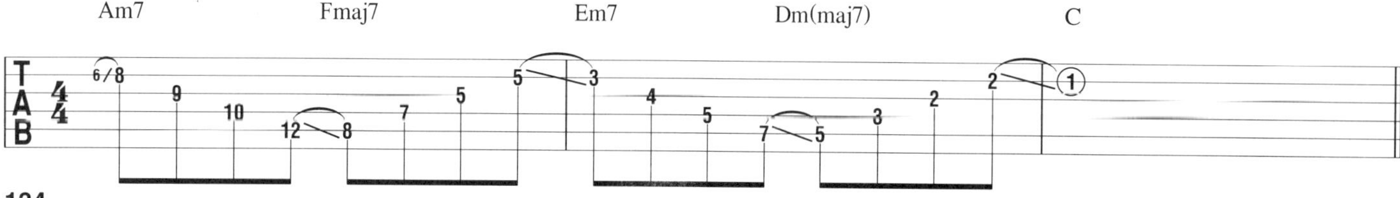

## 718: Swingin' Arps

Swing feel

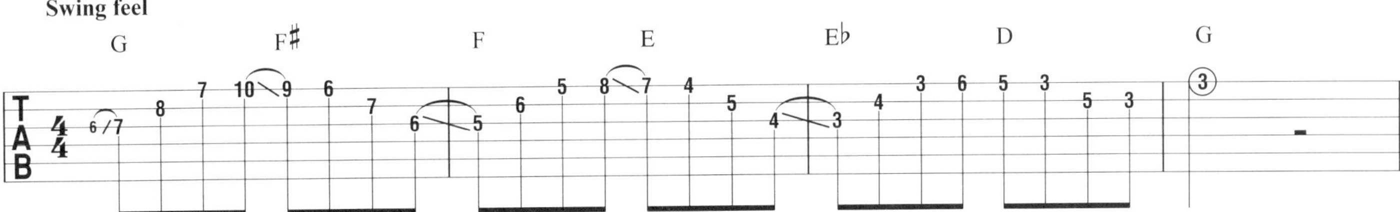


## 719: Fingerpickin' Good

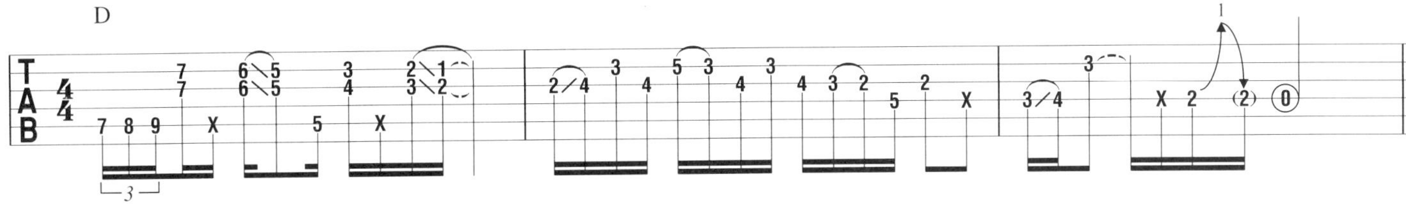


## 720: Albert Lee Rolls

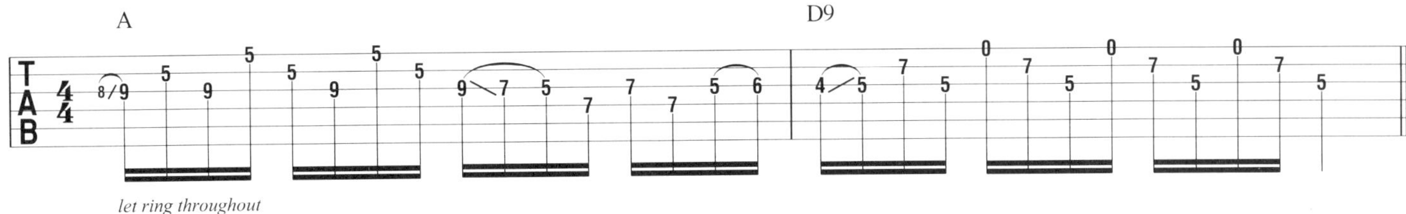


## 721: Steel Bends

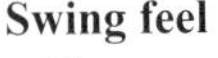


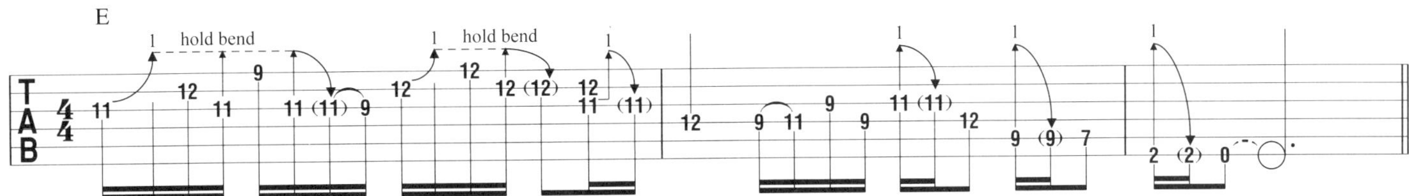


## 722: Western Swing

Swing feel

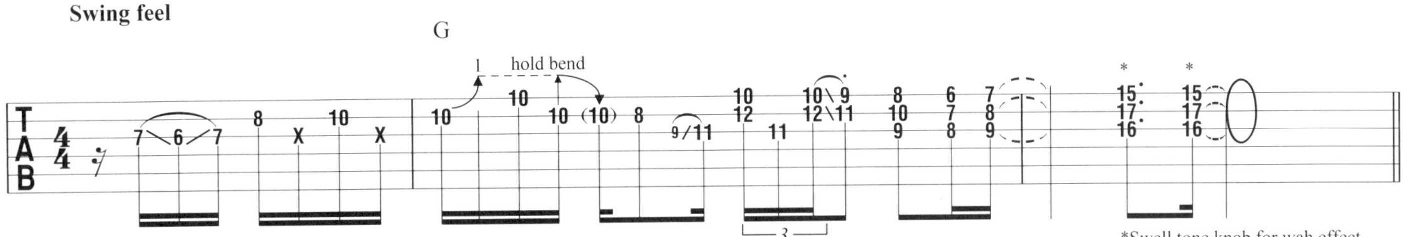

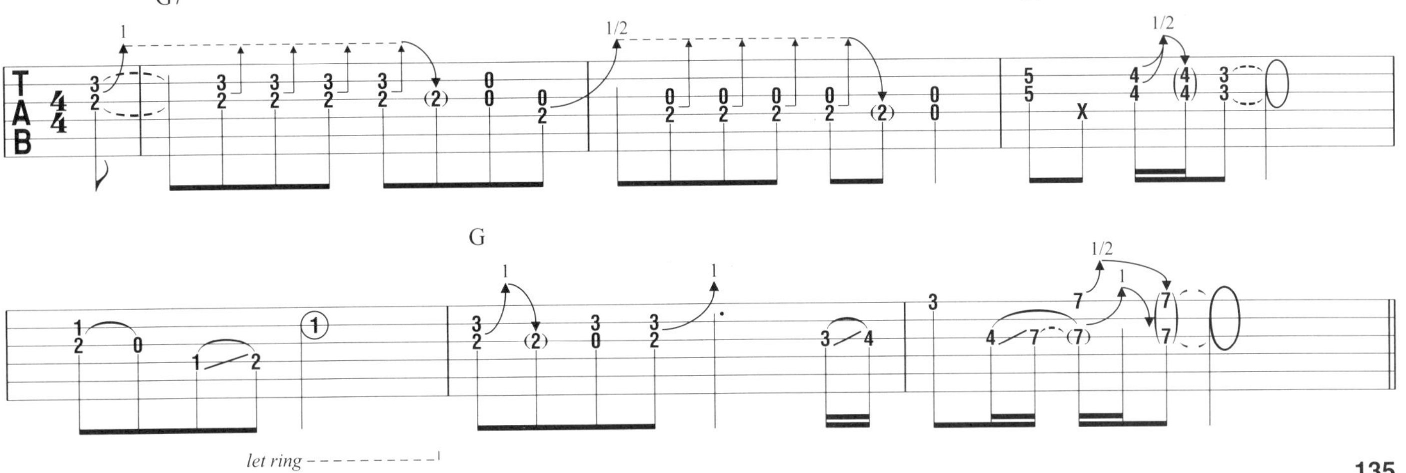

## 724: Country Phrasing

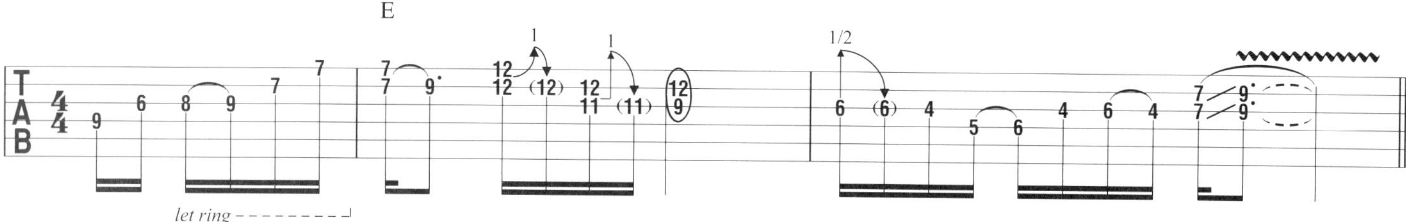


## 725: Country Melody

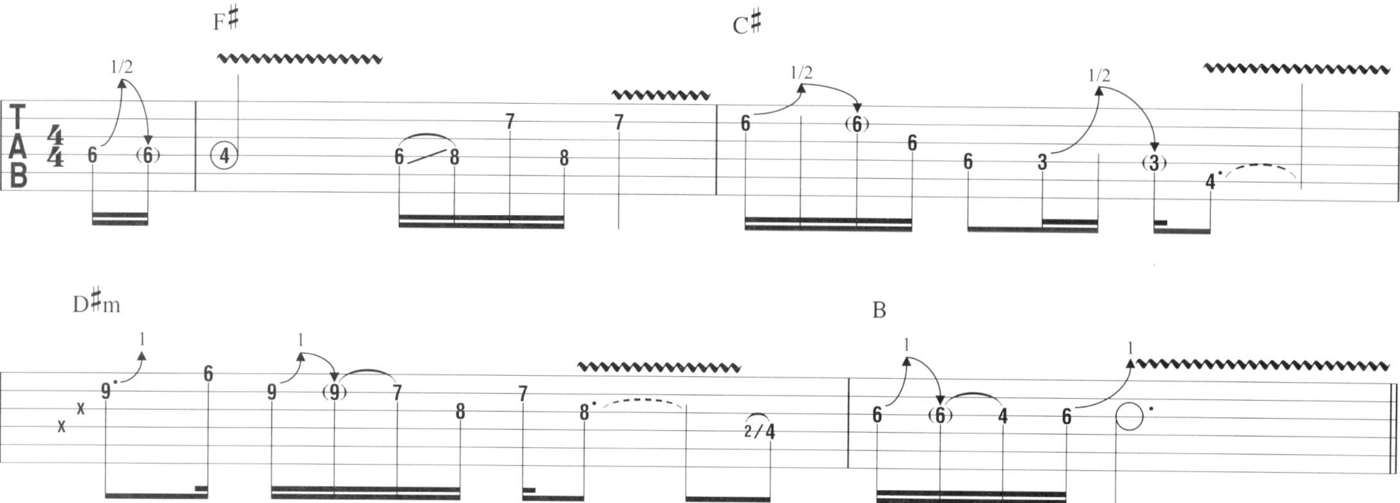


## 726: I-IV-I Twang

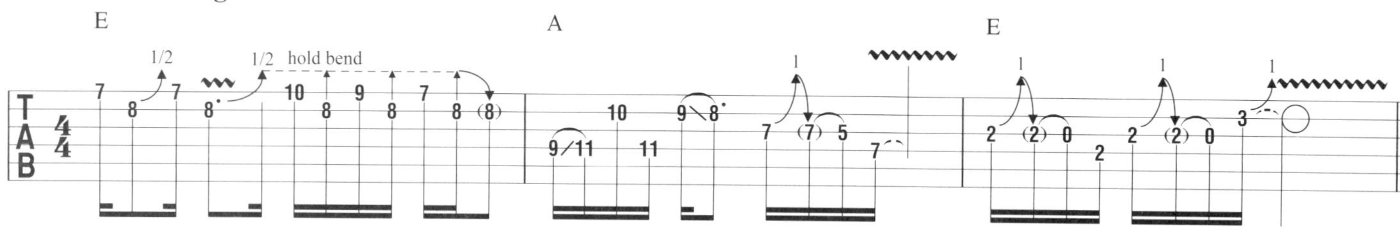


## 727: Paisley Pickin'

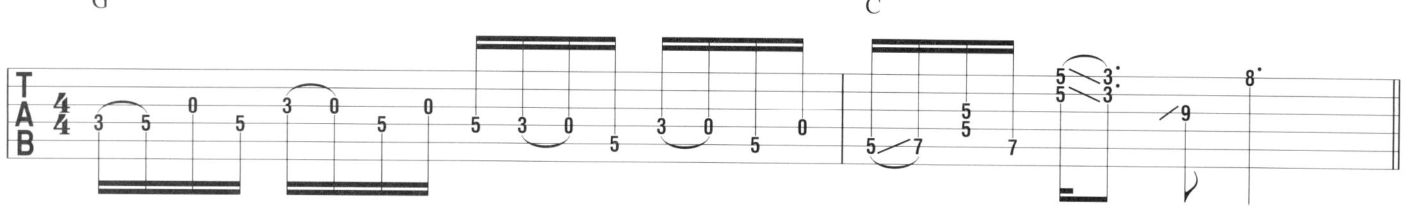


## 728: Rollin' Through

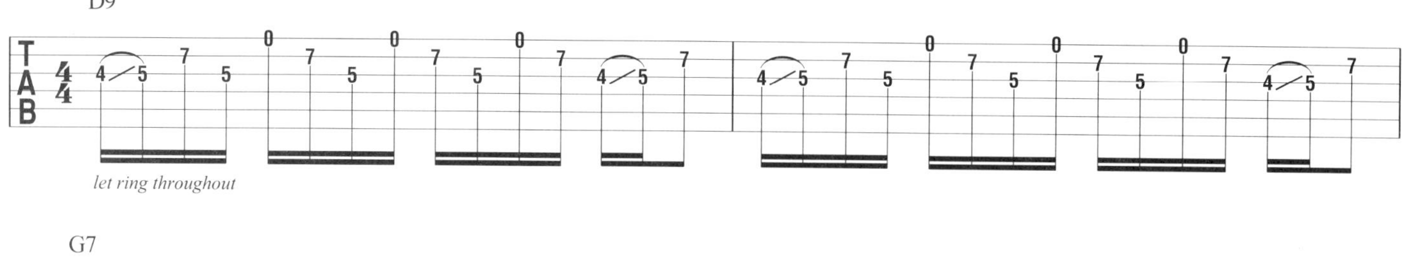


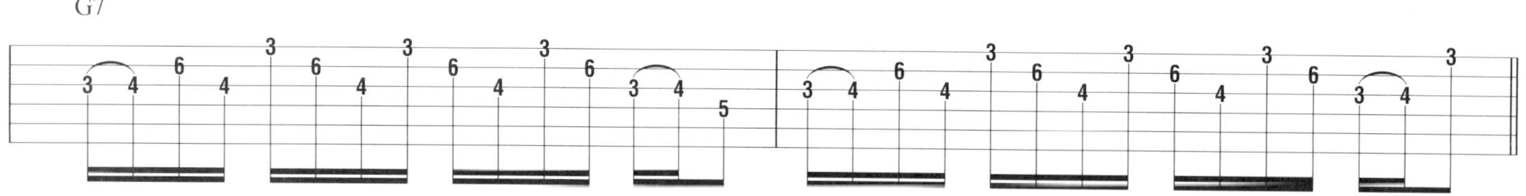

### 729: Redneck Romp

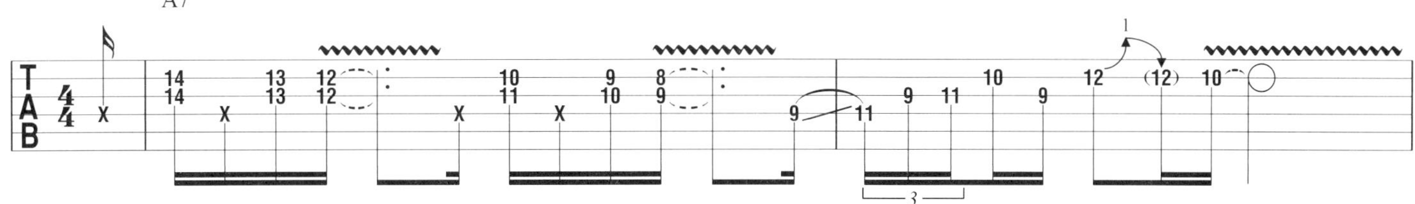


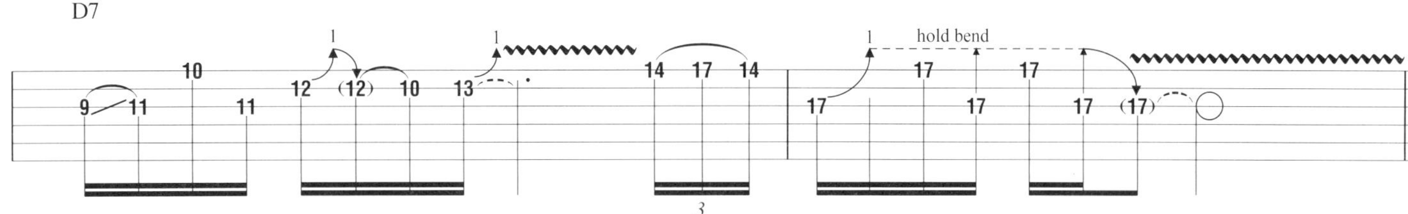


### 730: Harmonized Bends

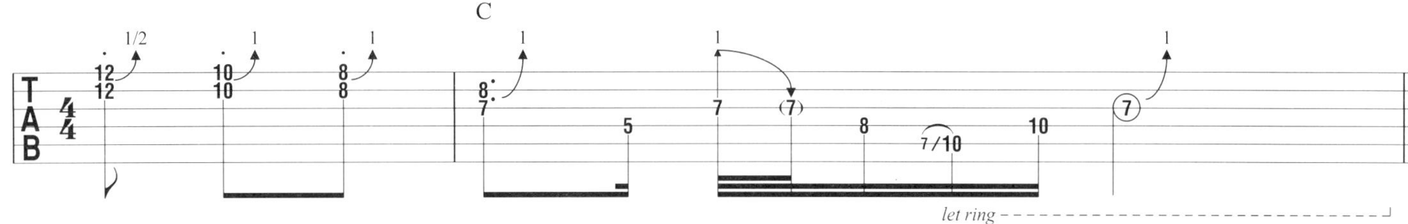


### 731: Pseudo Banjo

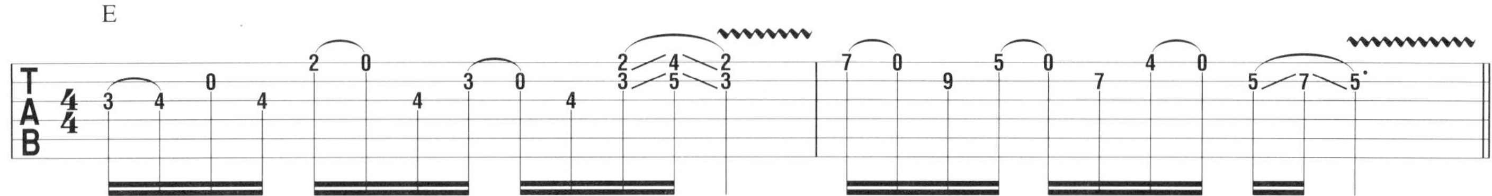


### 732: Atkins-Inspired

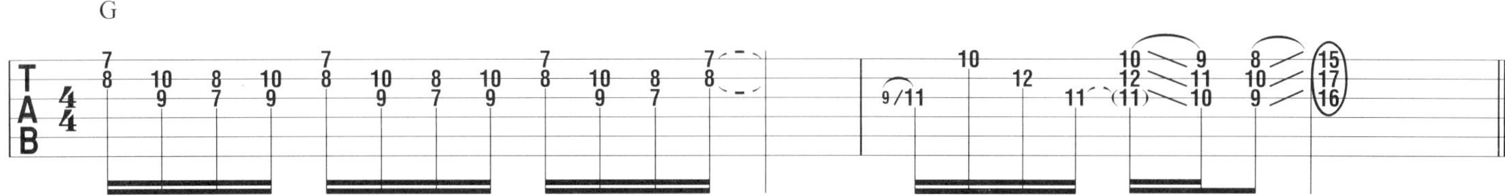


### 733: Chicken Delight

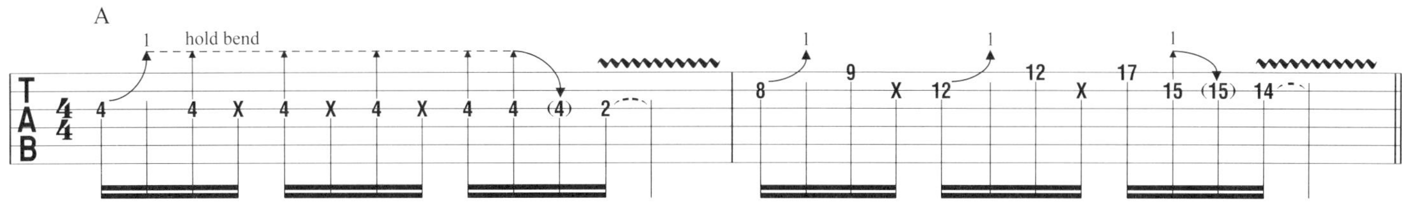


### 734: Pseudo Steel

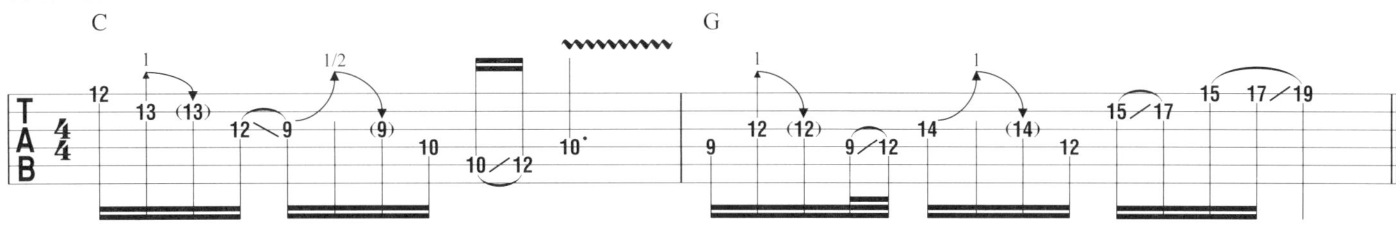

### 735: Nashville Approved

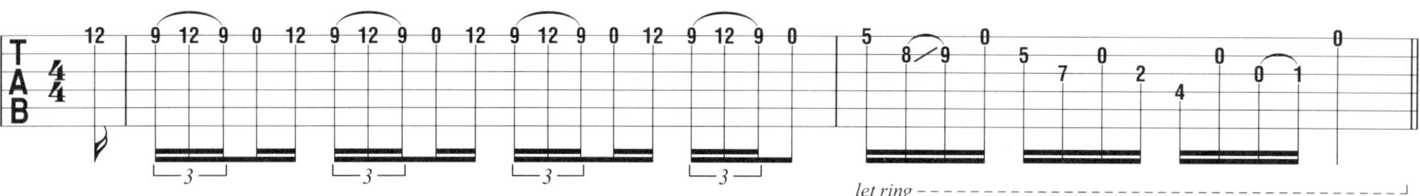


### 736: Real Perty

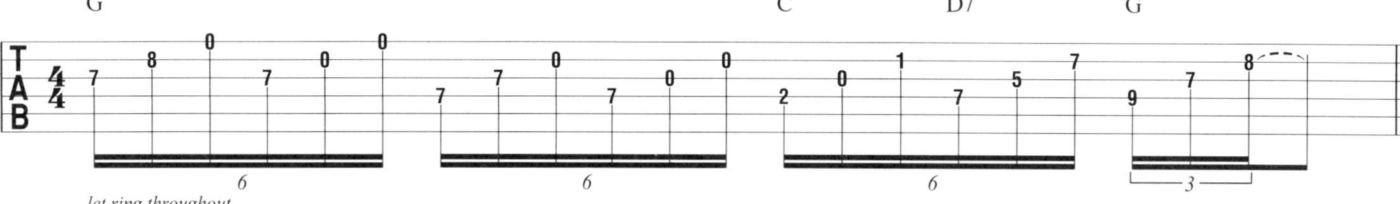


### 737: Swingin' 6ths

Swing feel

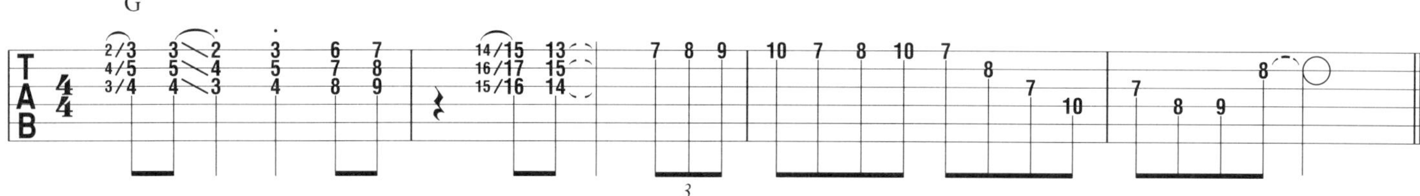


### 738: Southern Grit

B

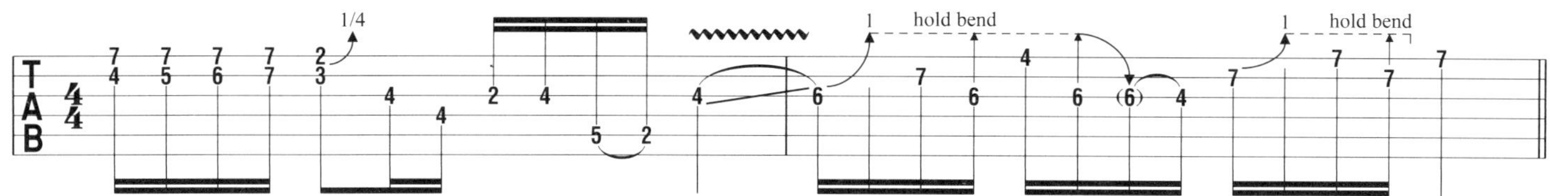


### 739: Redneck Blues

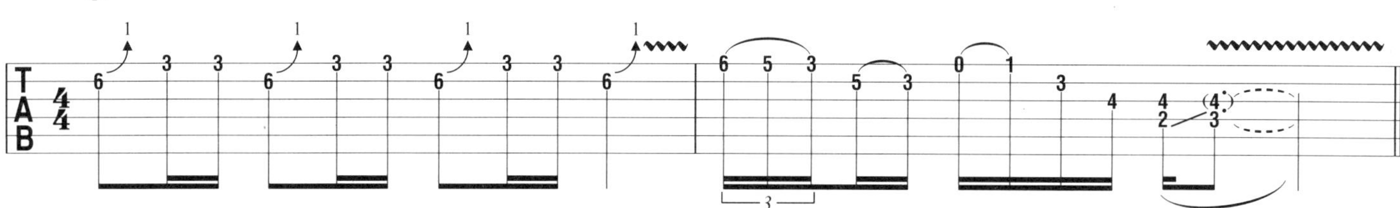

### 740: Country Crunch

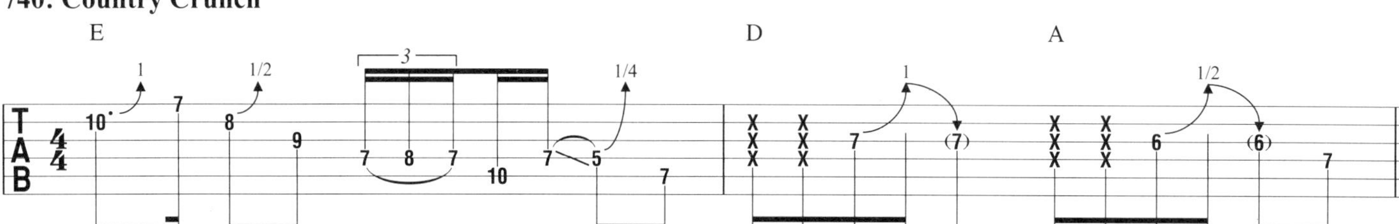


### 741: Garland Sequence

Swing feel

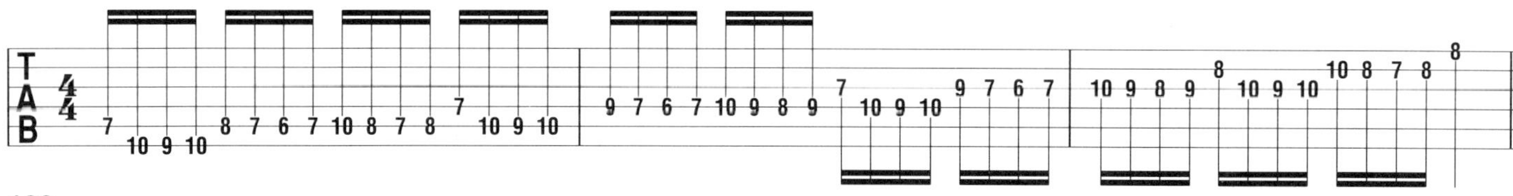

## 742: Deep Country

D-A-D-G-B-E

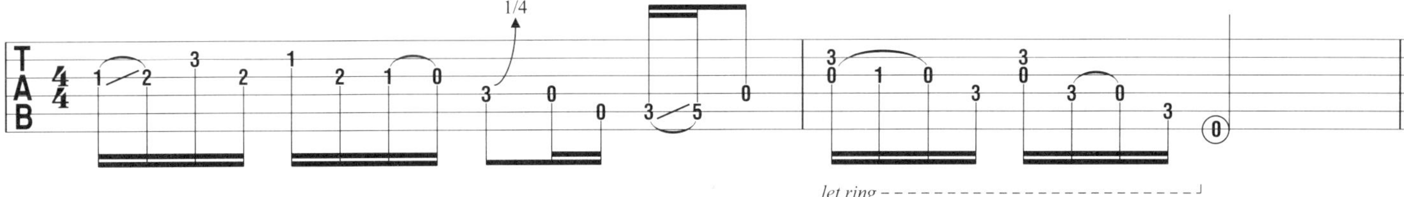


## 743: Muskeg Blues

D-A-D-G-B-E

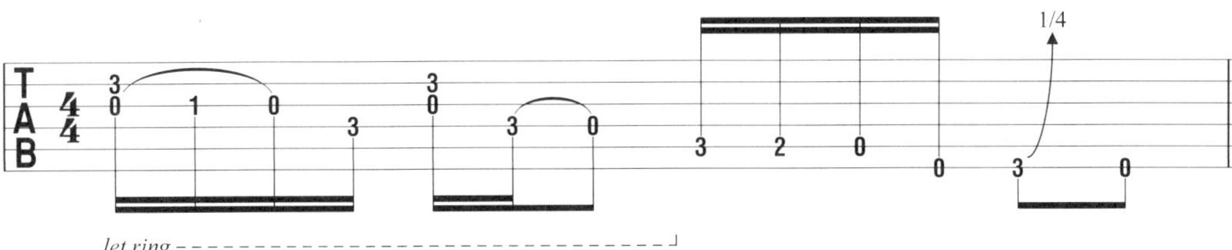


## 744: Drop D Swamp

D-A-D-G-B-E

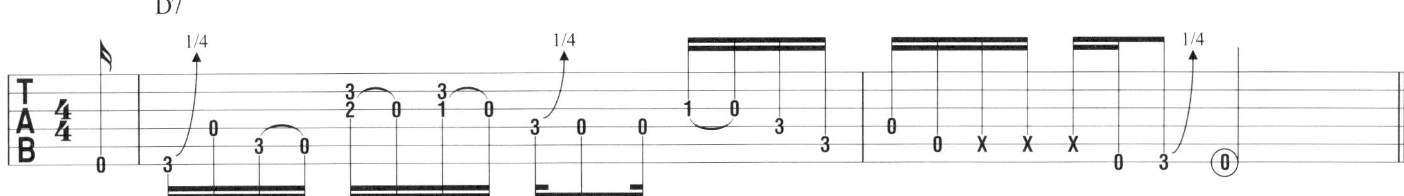


## 745: Fat Country

D-A-D-G-B-E

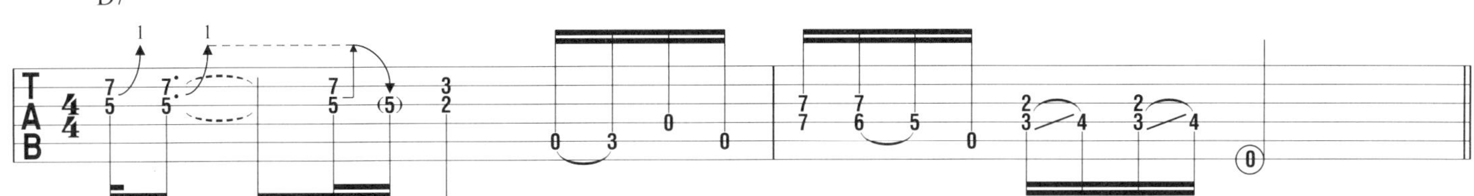


## 746: Chromatic Country

Swing feel

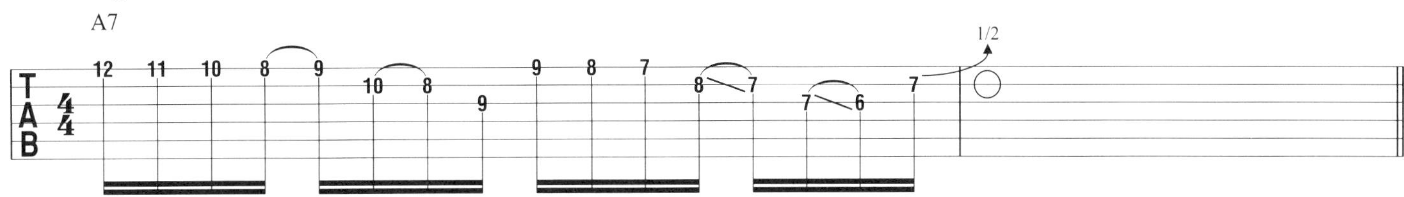


## 747: Barnyard Bliss

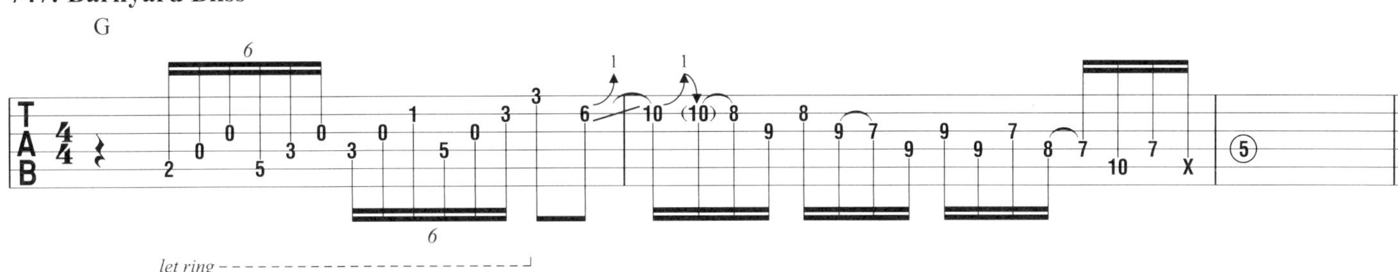

## 748: Bob Wills Swing

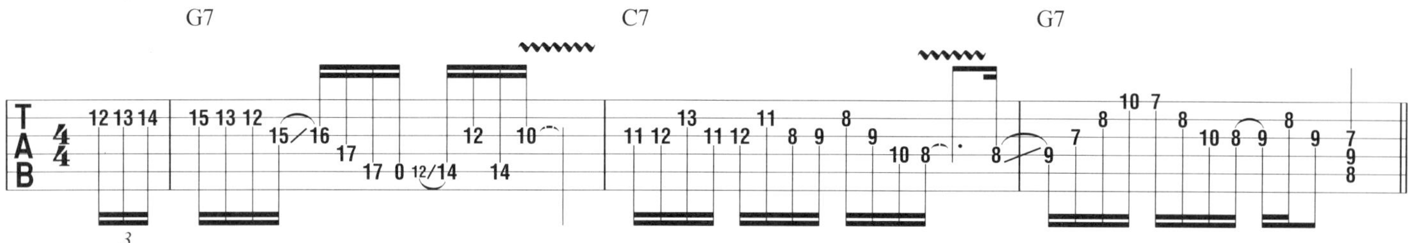


## 749: Smooth I-IV

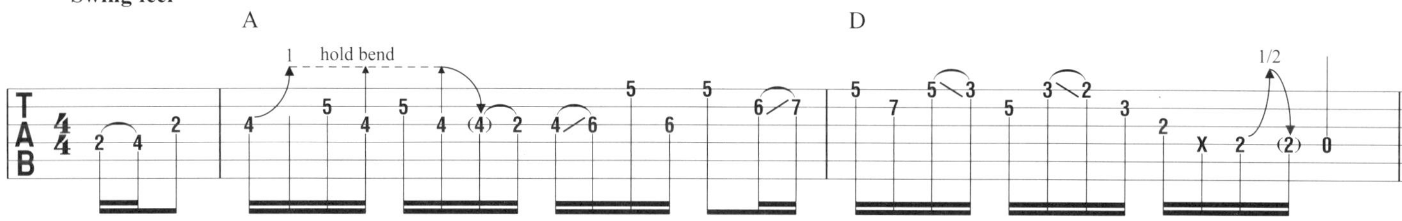


## 750: Country Theme

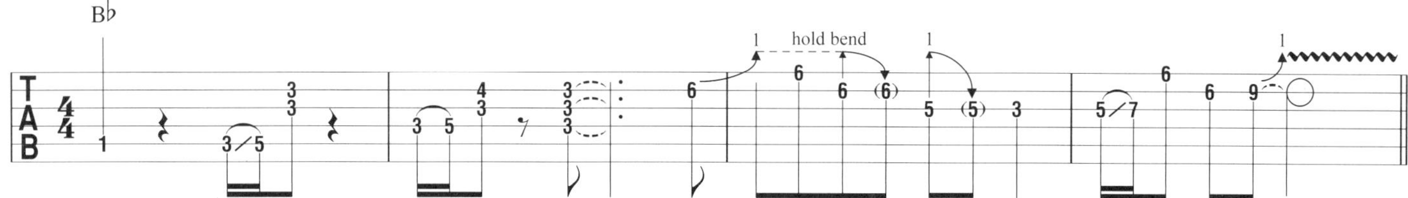


## 751: Doublestop Bends

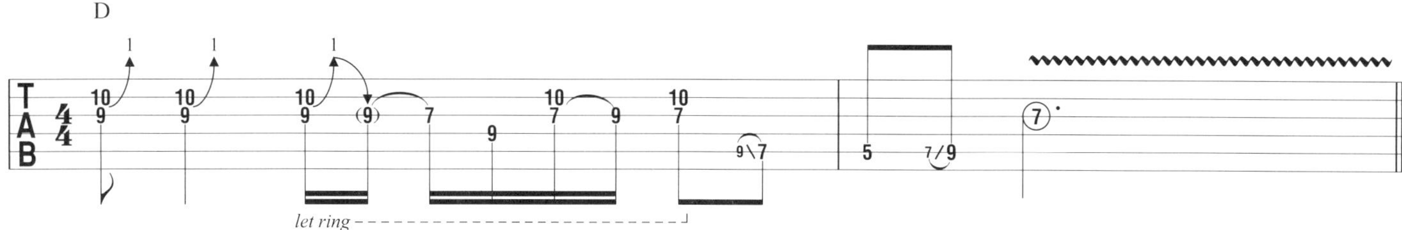


## 752: Bluesy Country

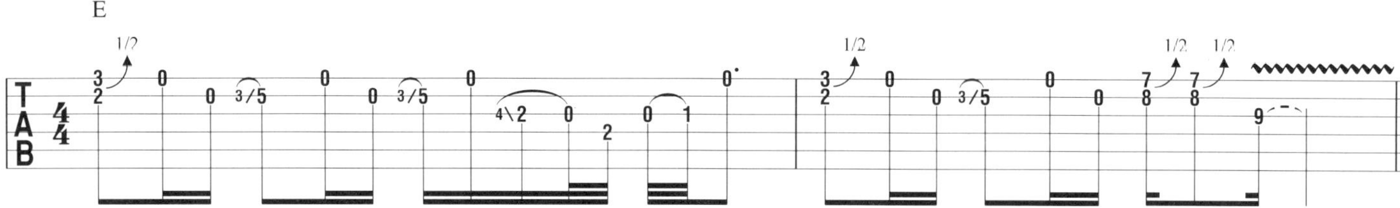


## 753: Triad Outline

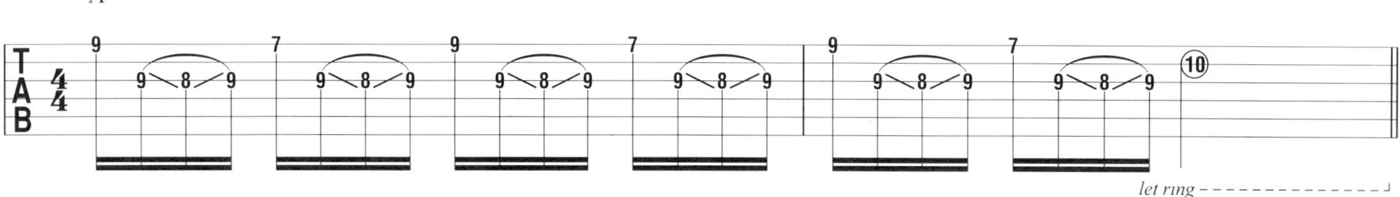

### 754: Jerry Reed Run

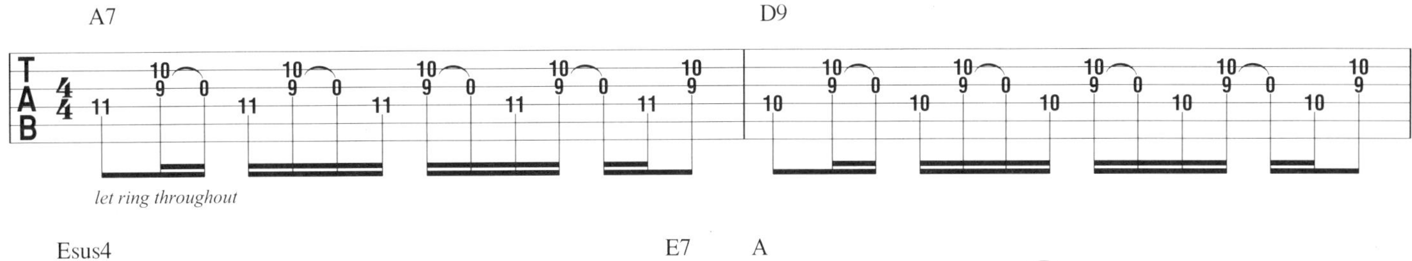


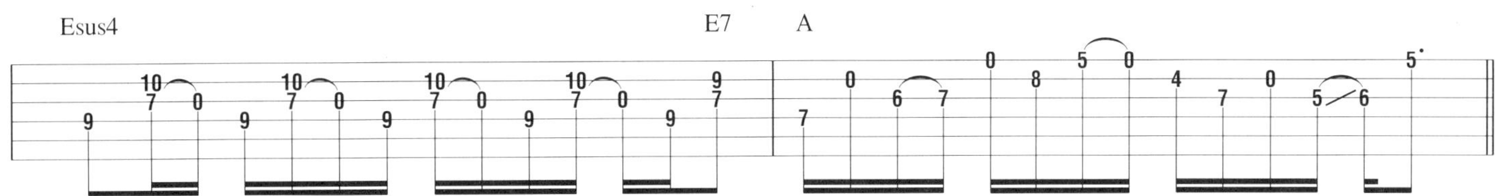


### 755: Bend Exercise

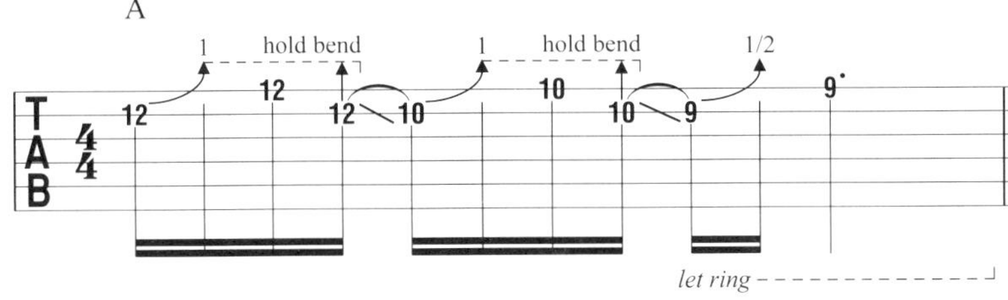


## Instructor: Chad Johnson

### 756: Country Composite

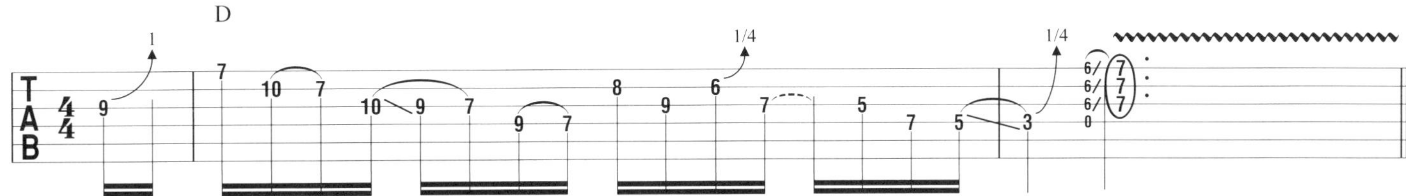


### 757: Modal Country

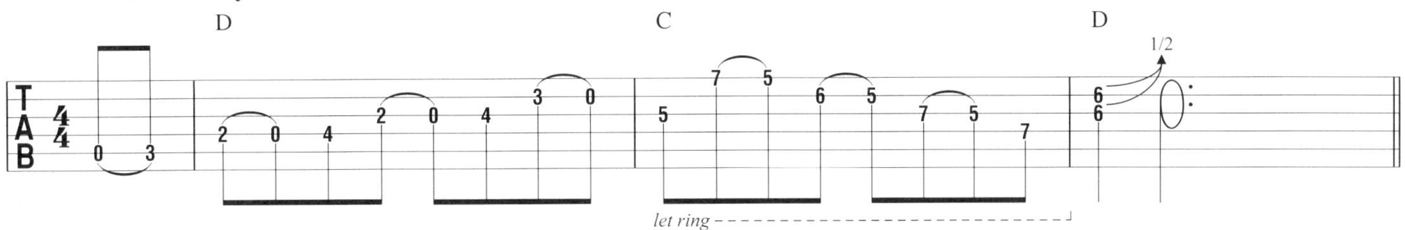


### 758: Steel Simulator

**Swing feel**

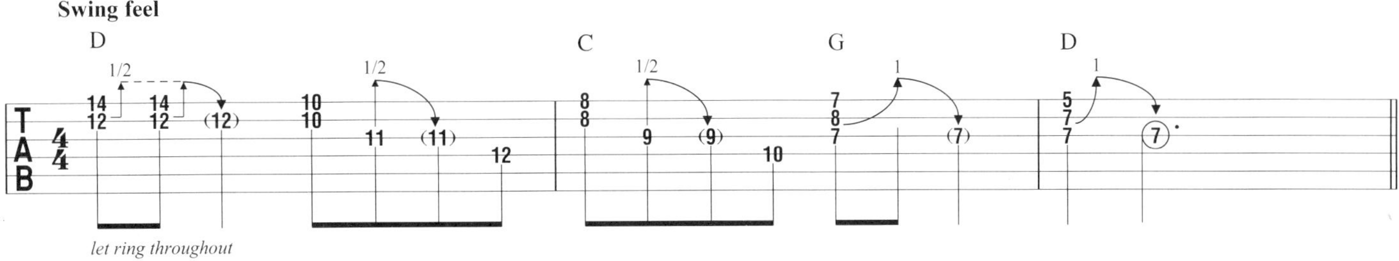


### 759: Barnyard Bends

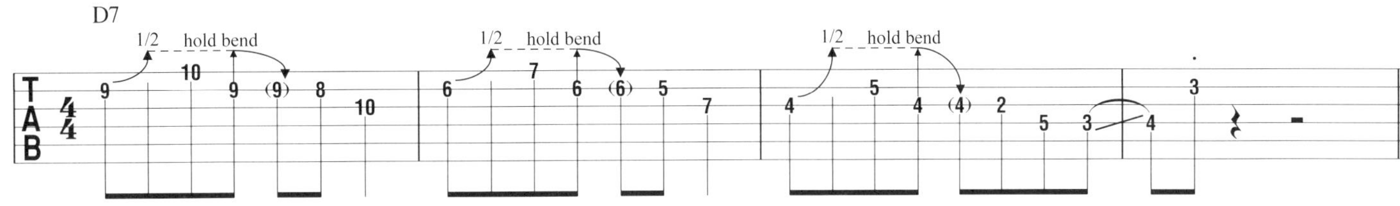

### 760: Bend Volley

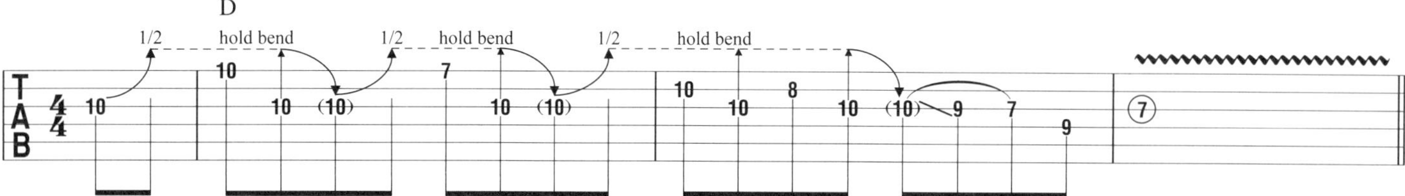


### 761: That's All Folks!

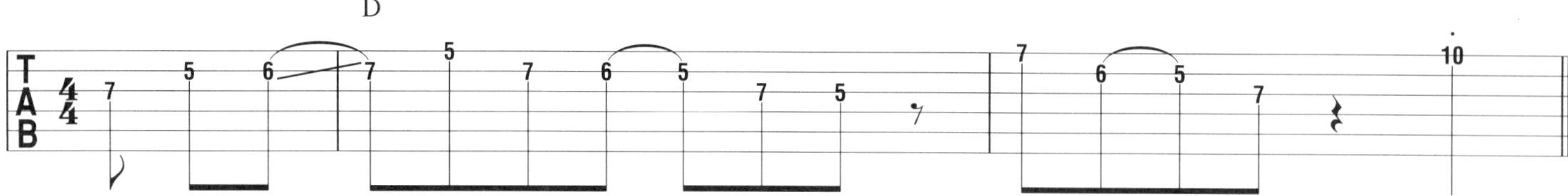


### 762: Jazzy Country

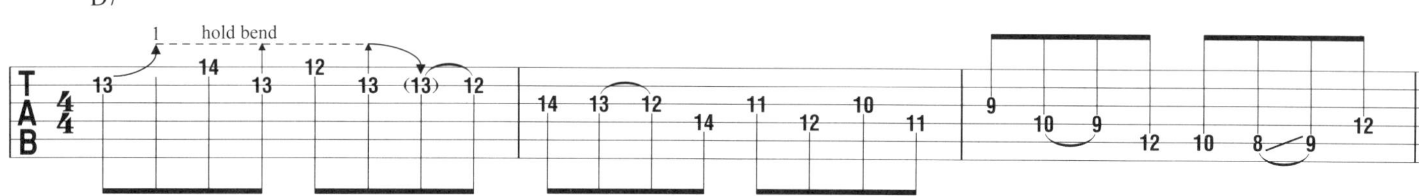


### 763: Twang Time

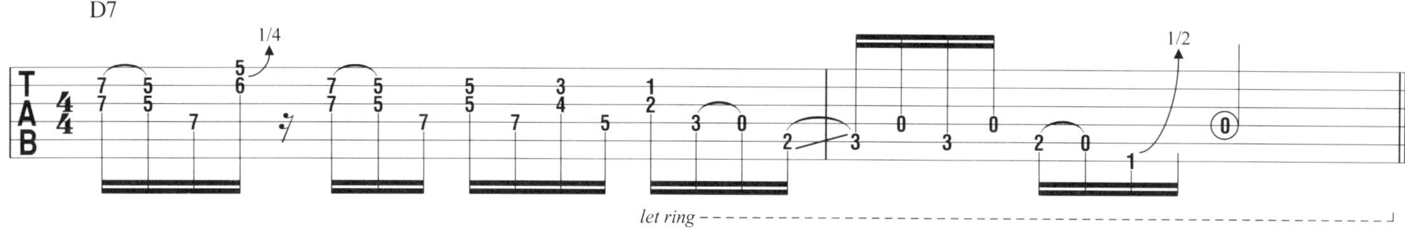


### 764: Slippery Mixolydian

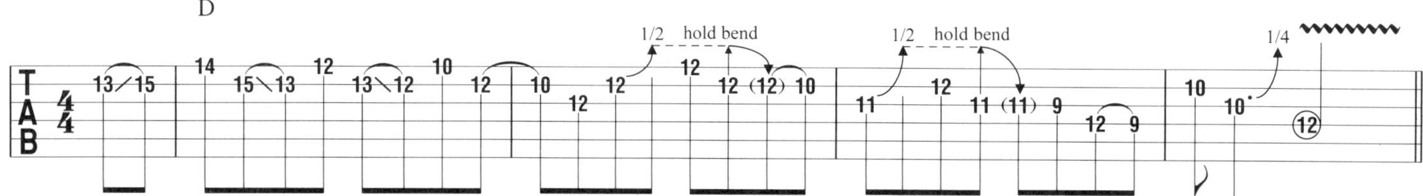


### 765: Swingin' West

**Swing feel**

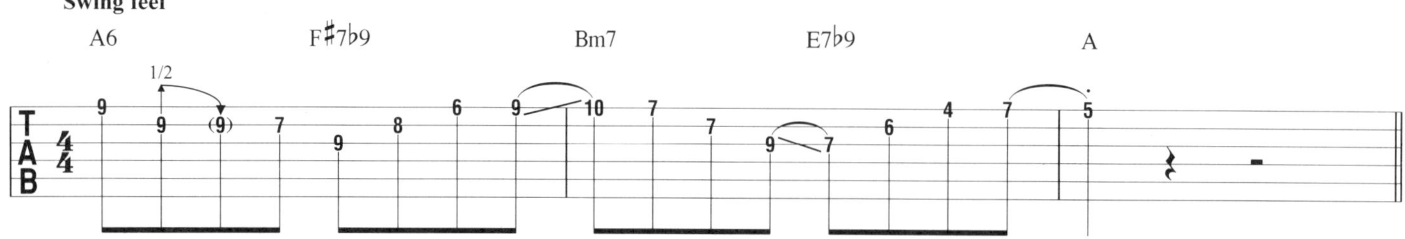


### 766: Climbing 3rds

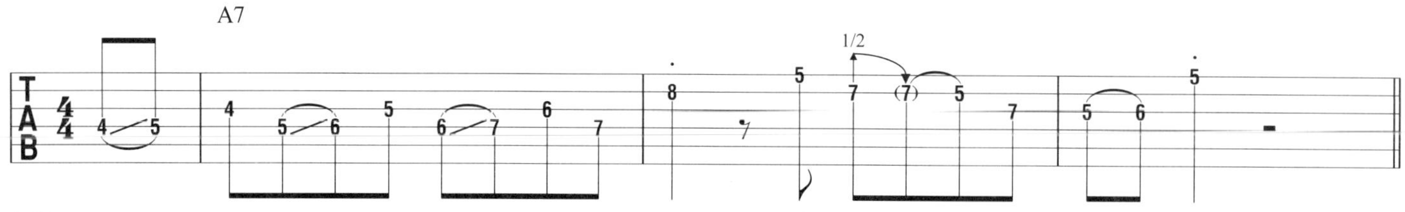

## 767: Arpin' Dominant

Swing feel

A7

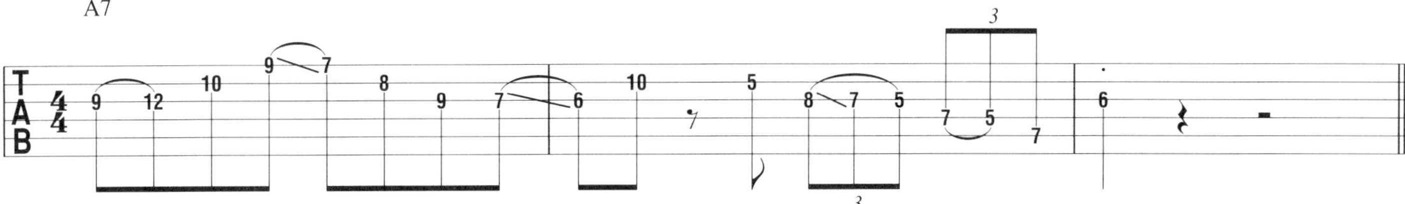

## 768: Western Twang

Swing feel

A7

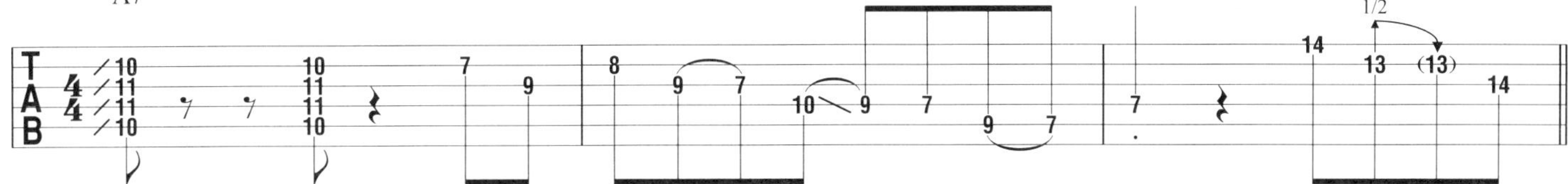


## 769: Syncopated Swing

Swing feel

A6

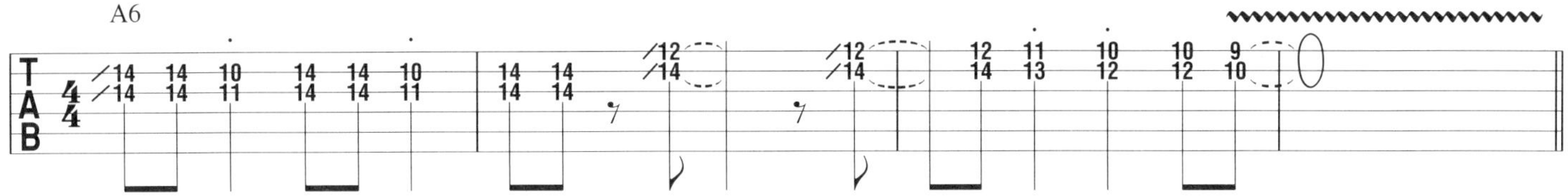

## 770: Southern Tart

Swing feel

A7

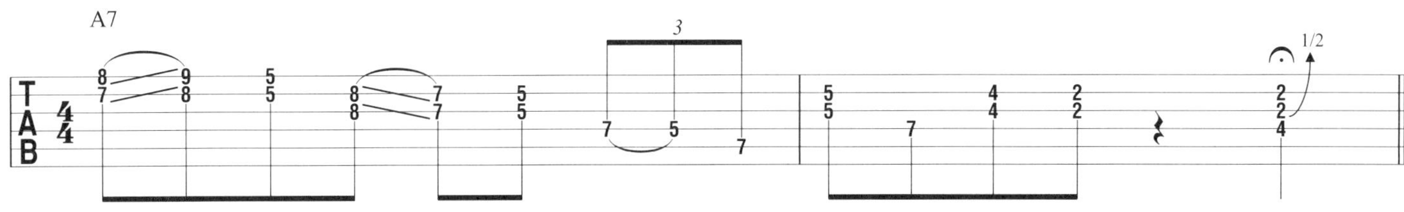


## 771: Transposing Lick

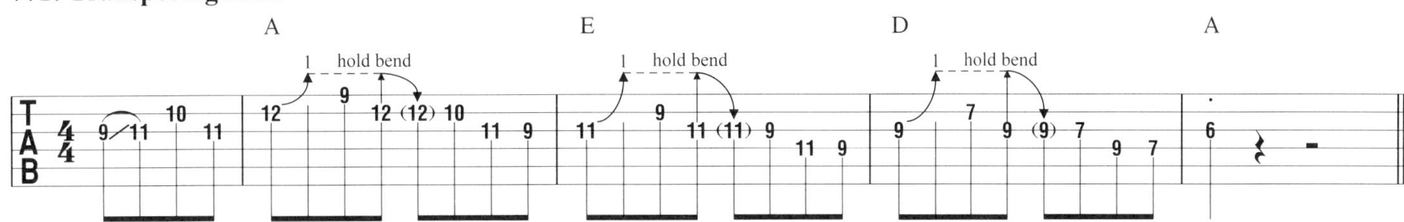


## 772: Y'all Come Back

A7

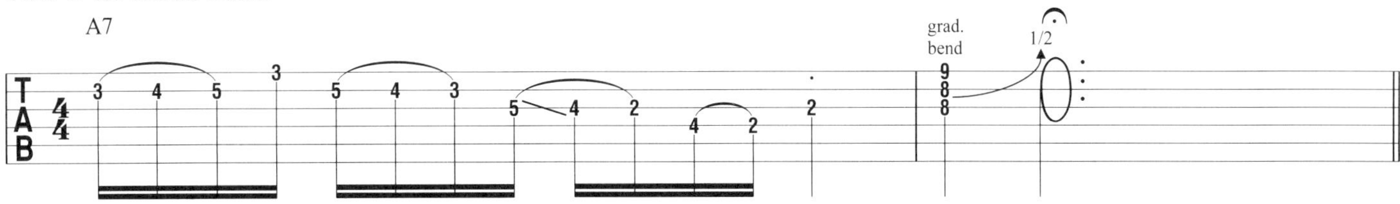


## 773: 3-Position Line

A

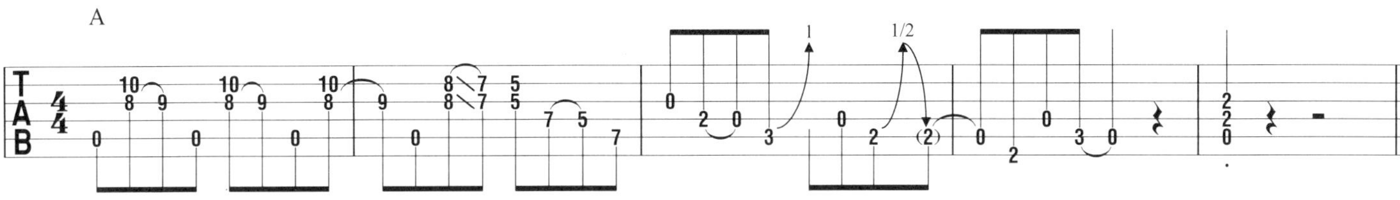

## 774: Doublestop & Pop

Swing feel

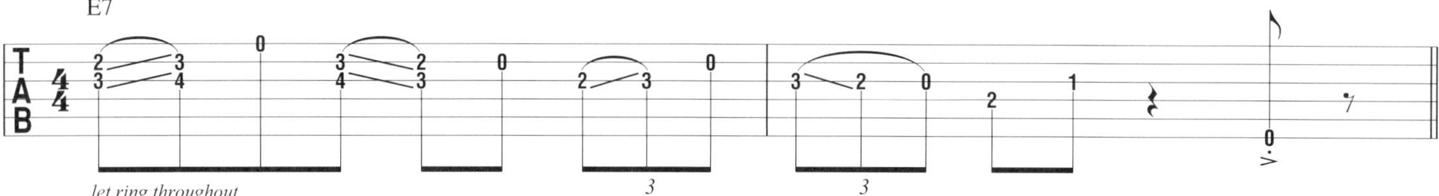


## 775: Sus4 Sass

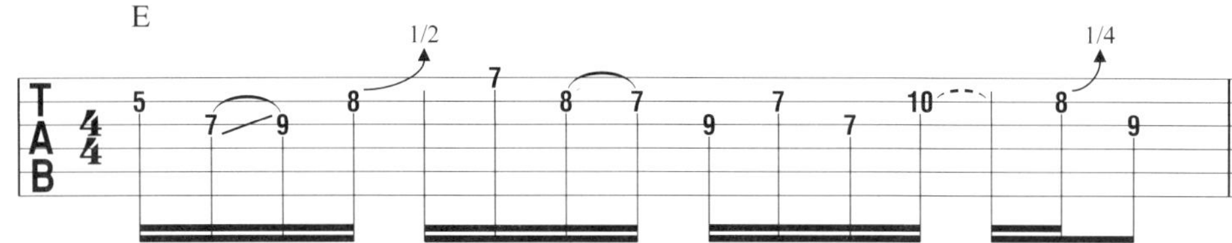


## 776: Strang Bendin'!

Swing feel

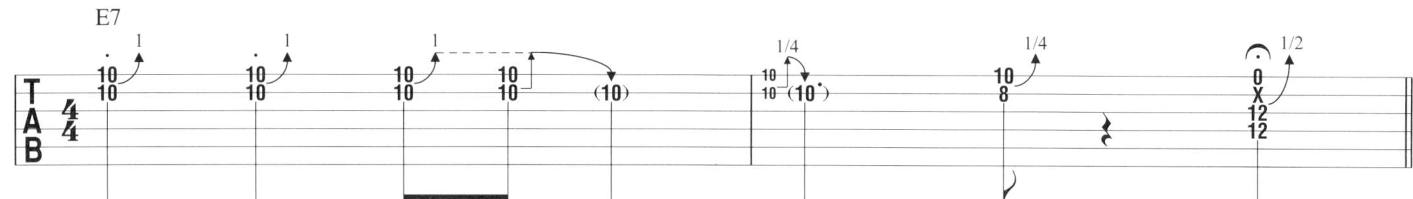


## 777: Behind the Nut

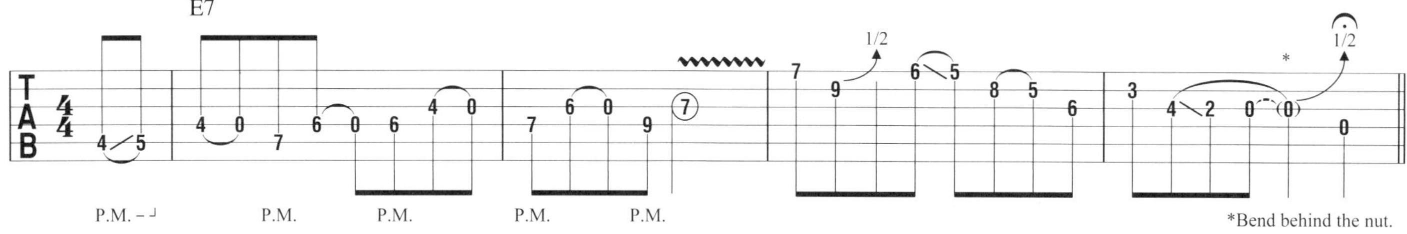


## 778: Pretzel Bend

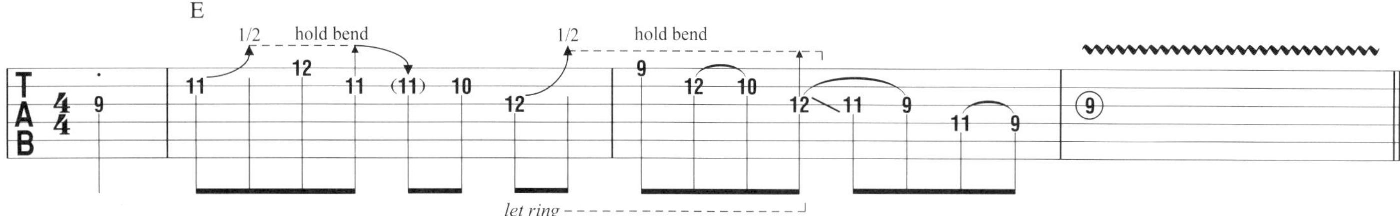


## 779: Great Wide Open

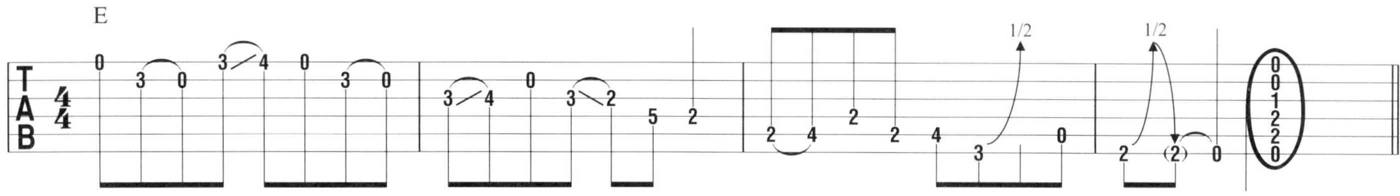


## 780: Pedal-Steel Precision

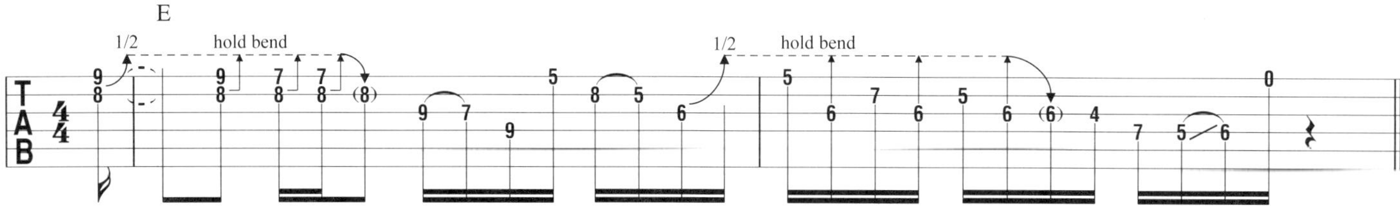

### 781: Authentic Steel

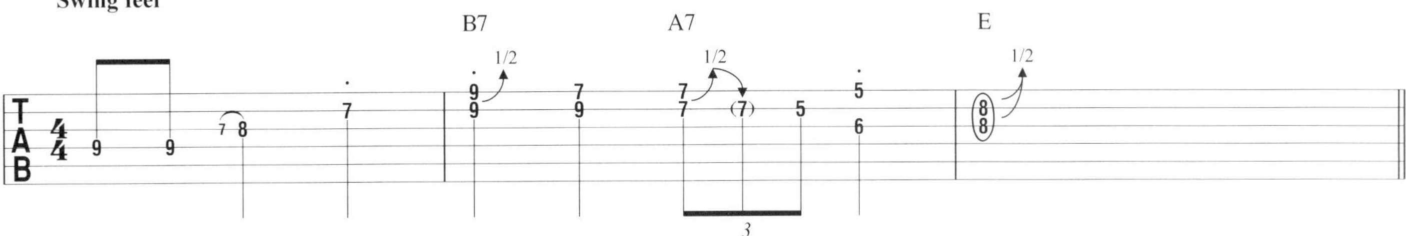


### 782: Hybrid Exercise

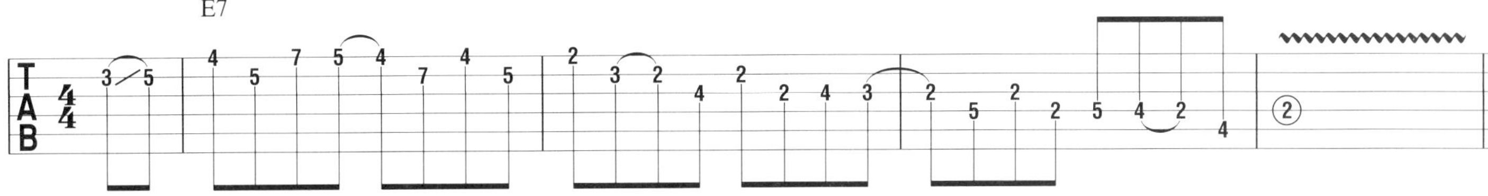


### 783: Tele Twang

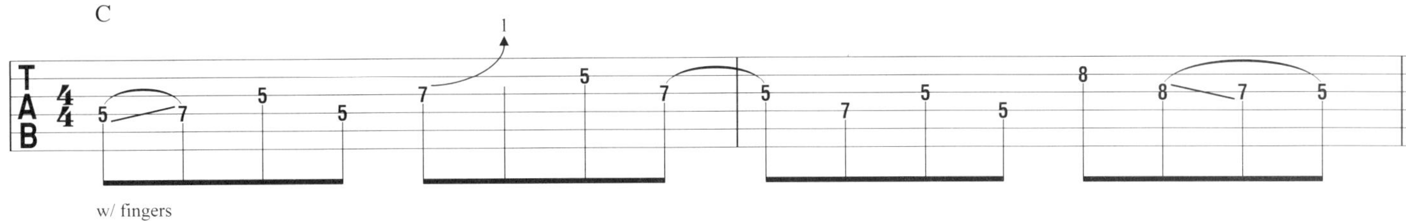


### 784: Hybrid Sequence

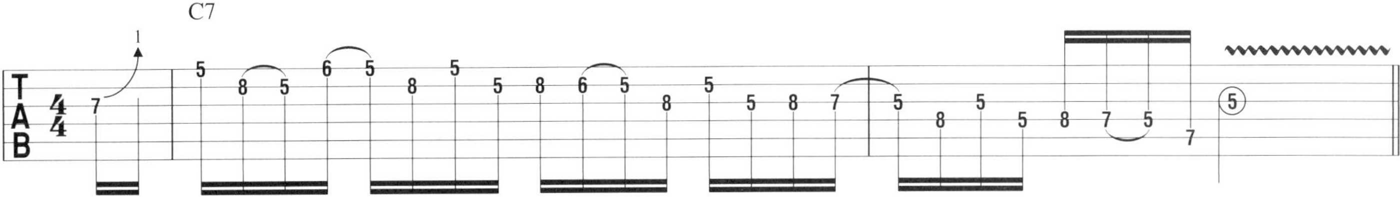


### 785: Redneckin'

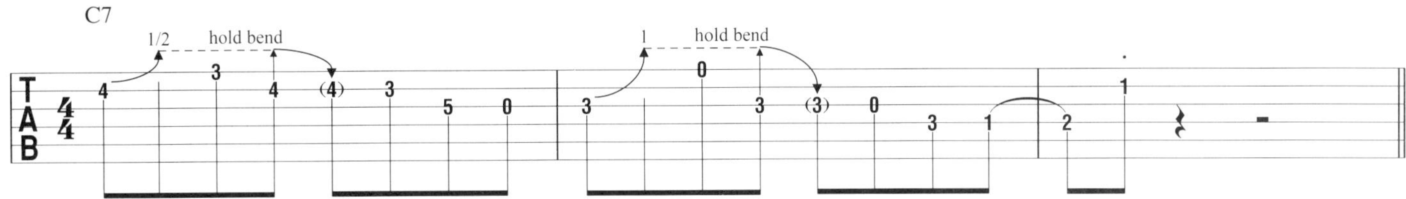


### 786: Half-Steppin'

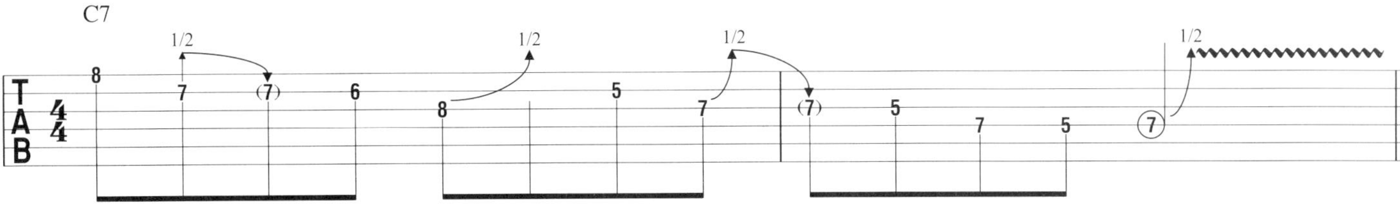


### 787: Falling 3rds

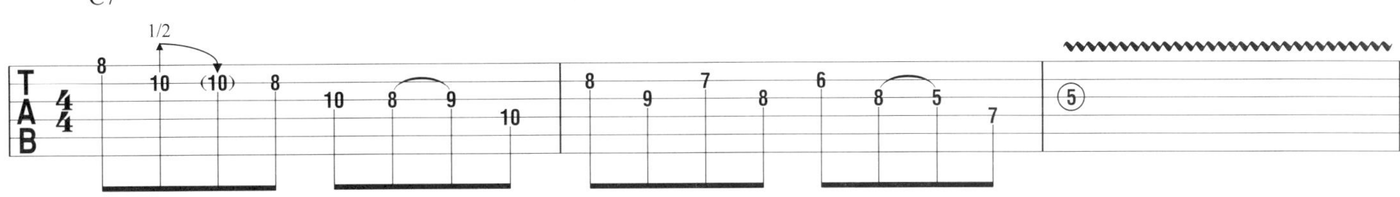

### 788: Scoopin'

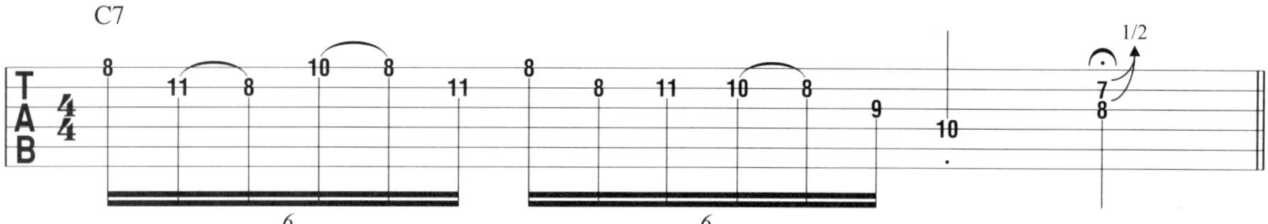


### 789: Country Harp

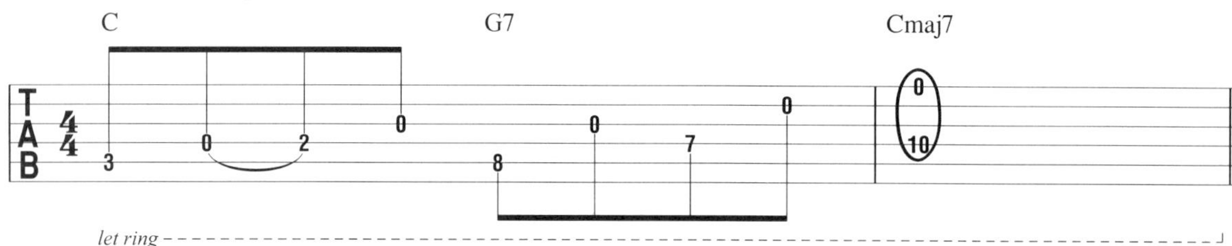


### 790: Stop-Time Lick

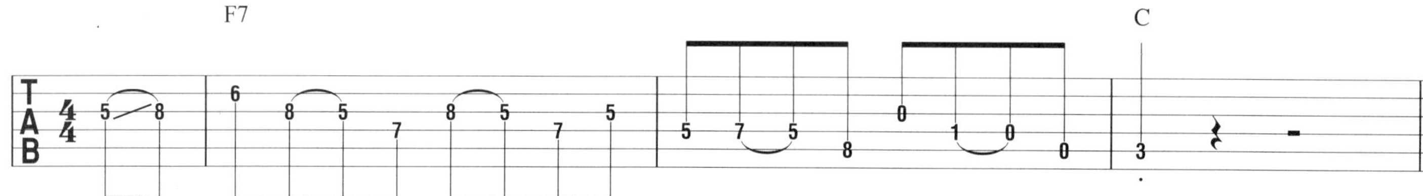


### 791: Tricky Bends

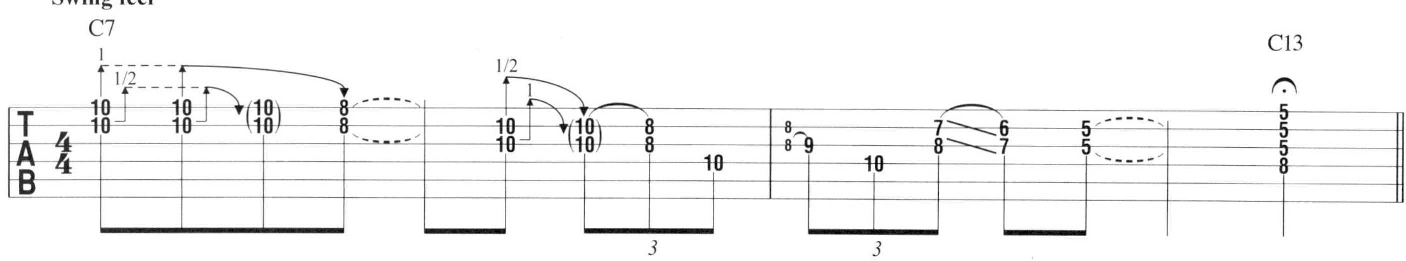


### 792: Hybrid Composite

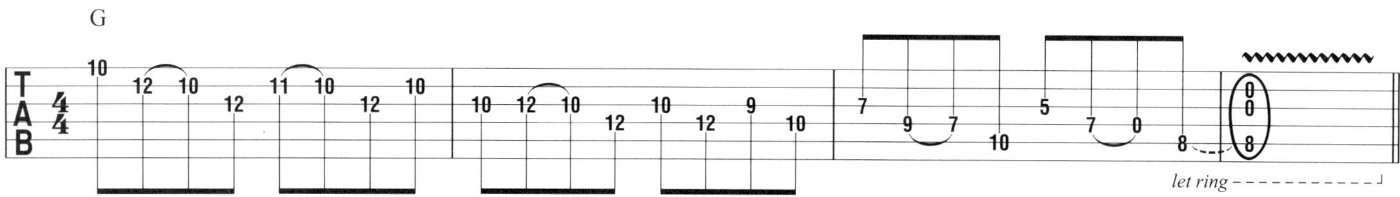


### 793: Composite Cascade

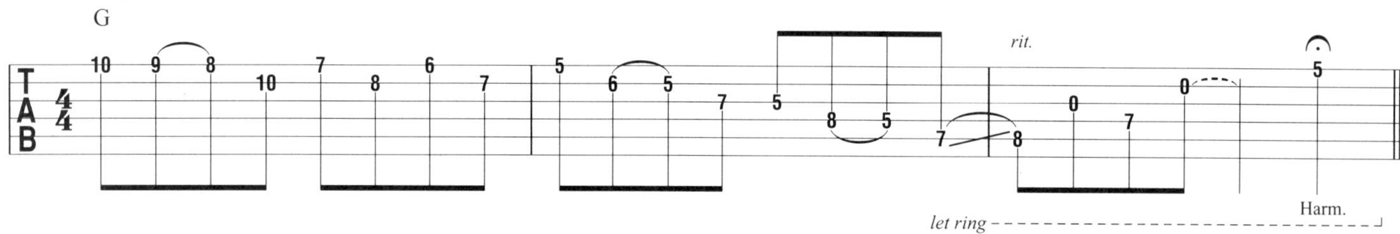


### 794: Legato Line

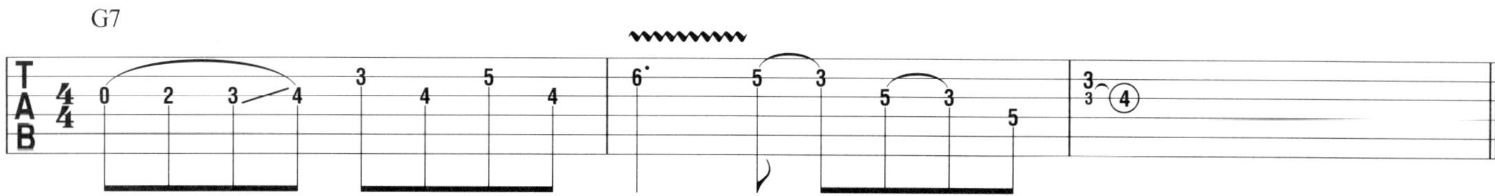

**795: Open Country**

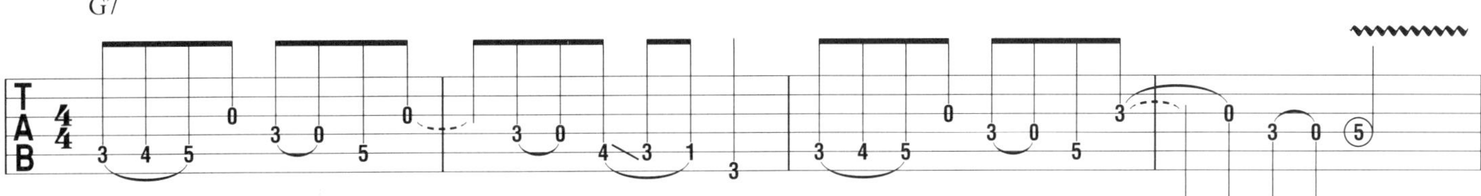


**796: Southern Funk**

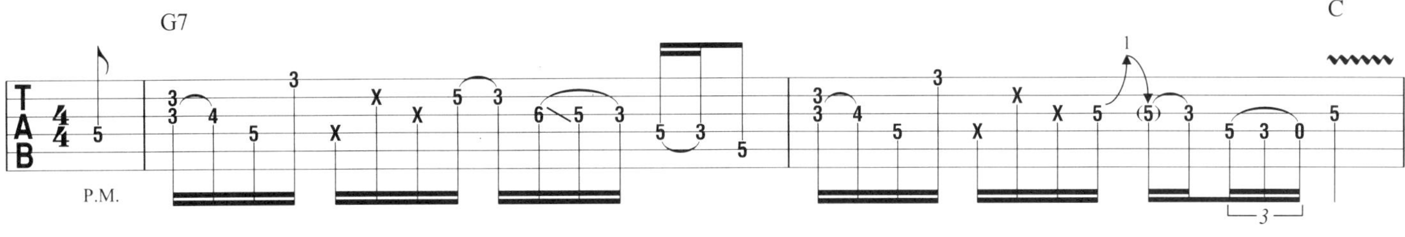


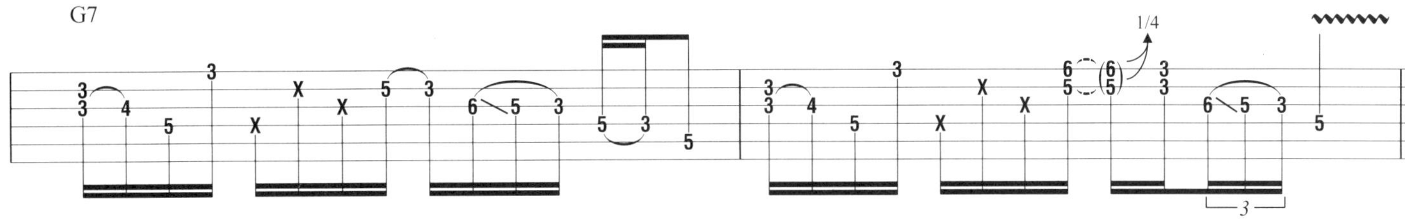


**797: I-♭VII-IV-I**

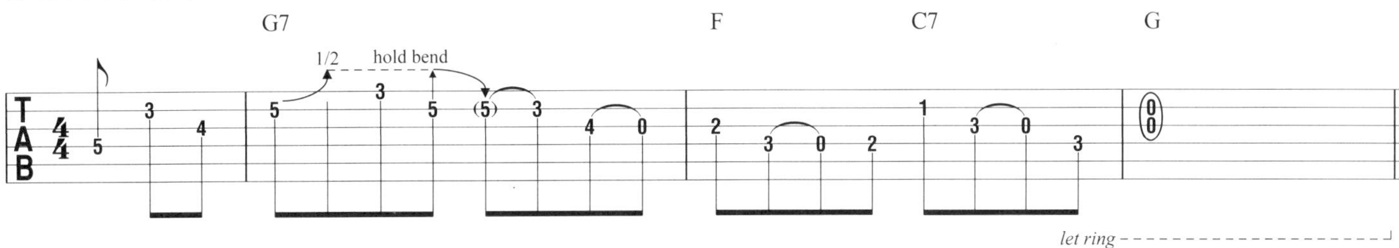


**798: Country Turnaround**

**Swing feel**

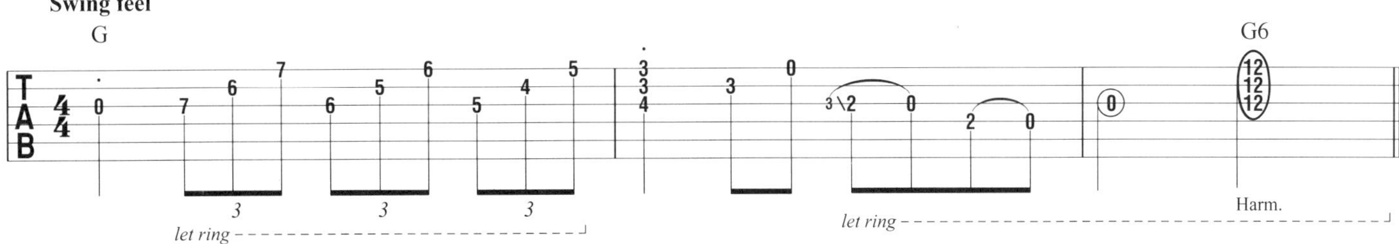


**799: Classic Intro**

**Swing feel**

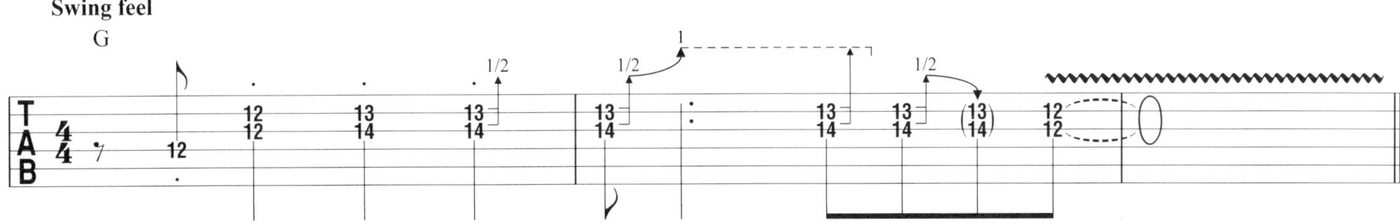


**800: Pedal Steel ii-V-I**

**Swing feel**

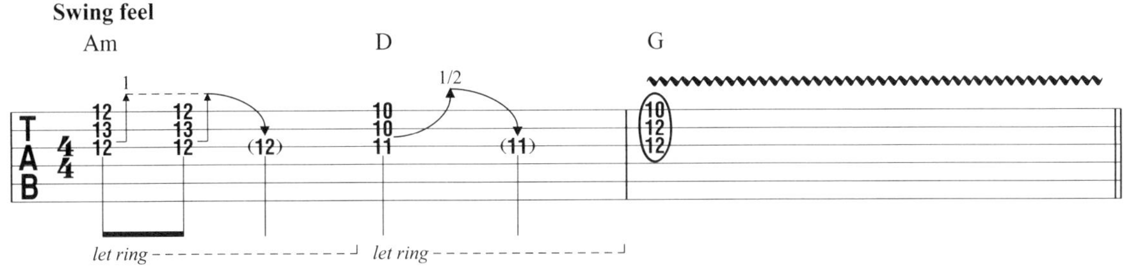

# JAZZ LICKS

## Instructor: Don Linke

### 801: Surround Sound

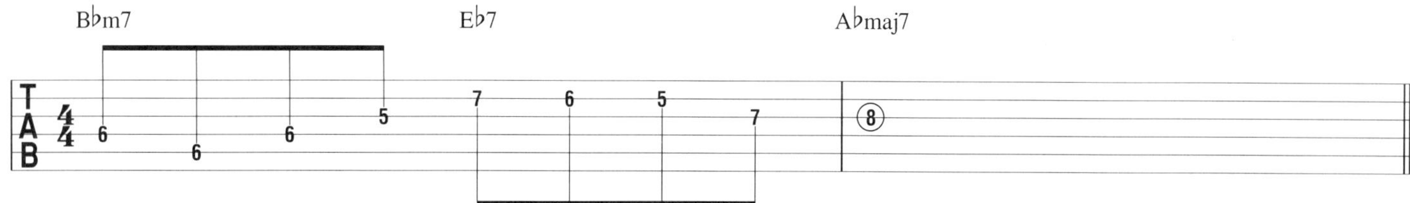


### 802: Sweet 16ths

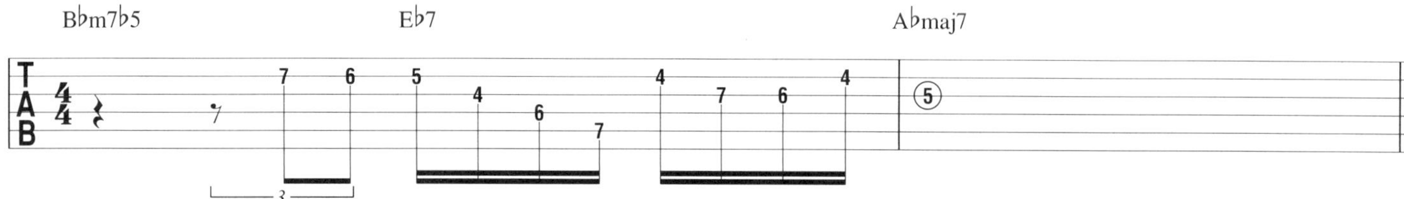


### 803: Pass It Around

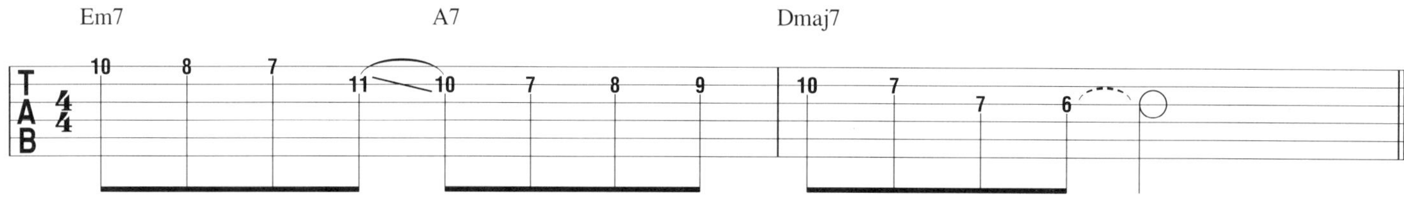


### 804: Bluesy Jazz

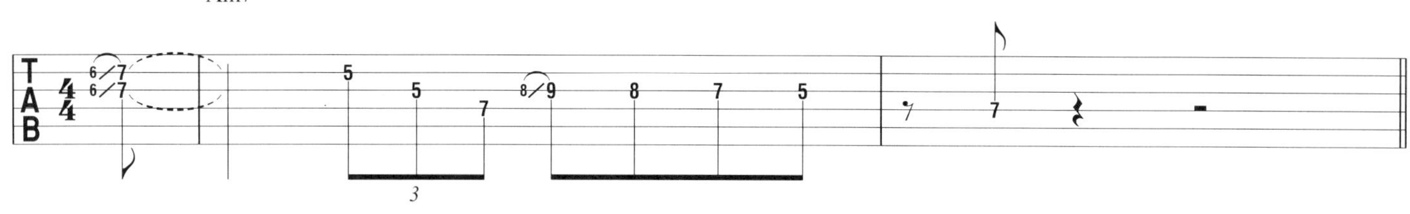


### 805: Spooky Jazz

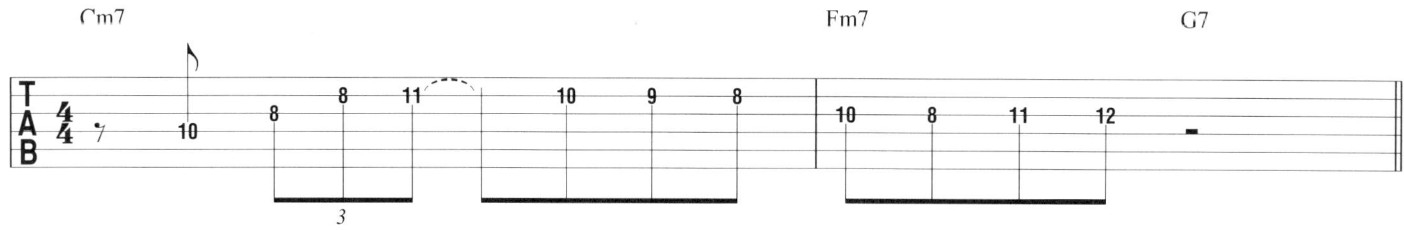


### 806: Motivic Sequence

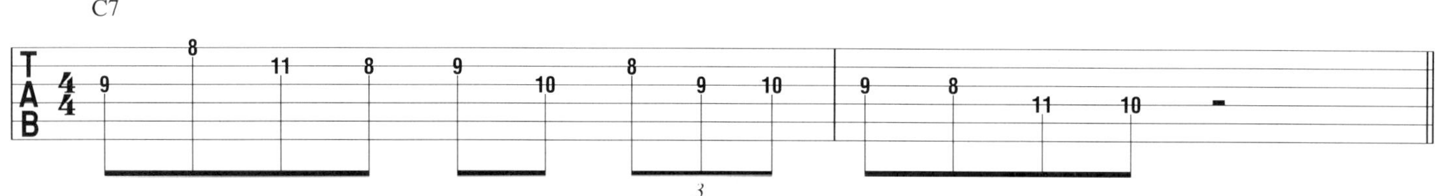

**807: Bebopper**

**808: Appoggiaturian**

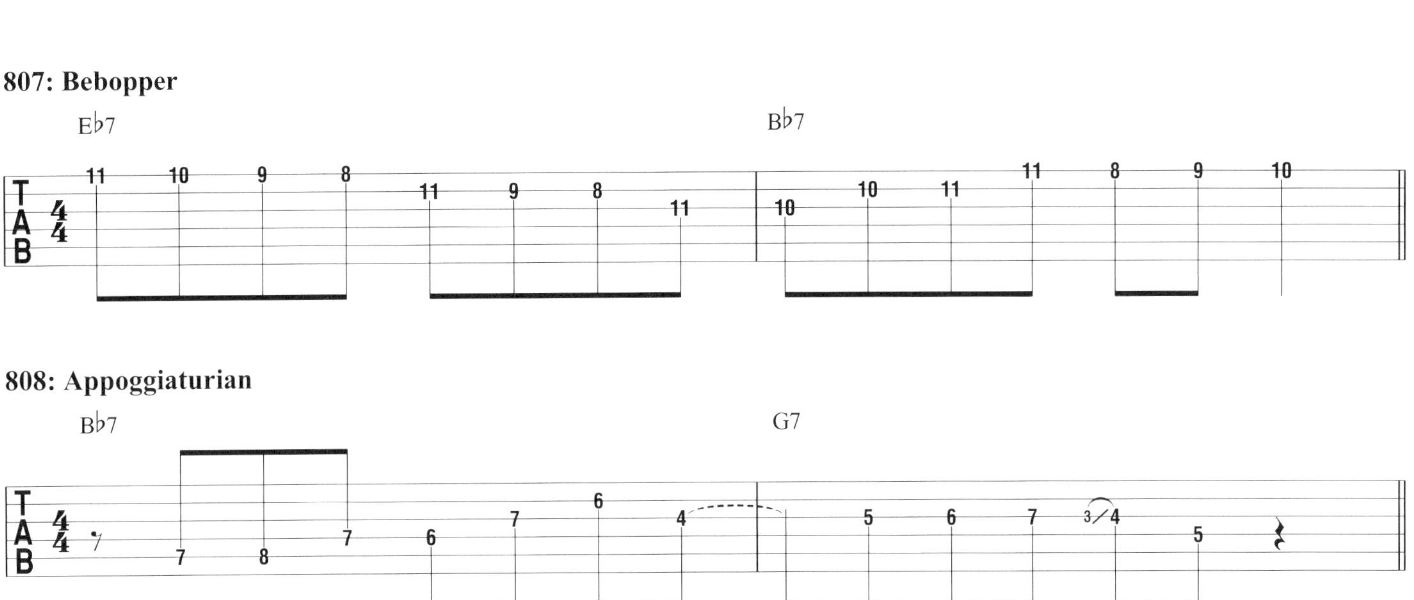


**809: Altered State**

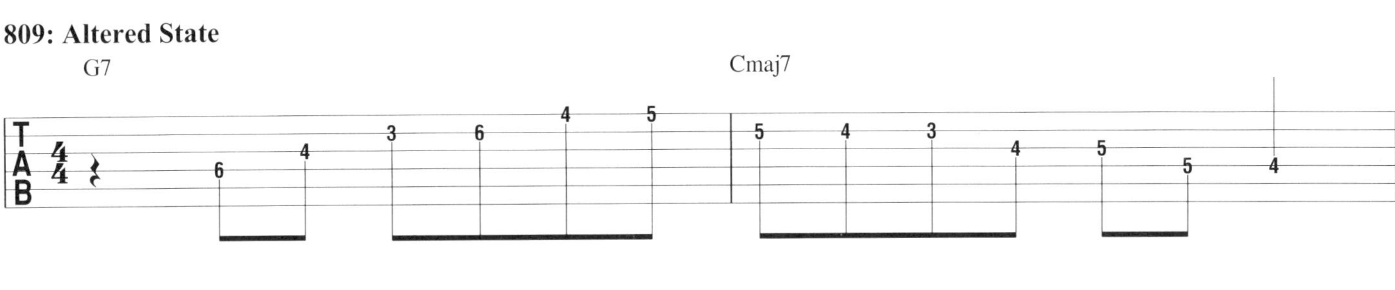


**810: Bop-Tastic**

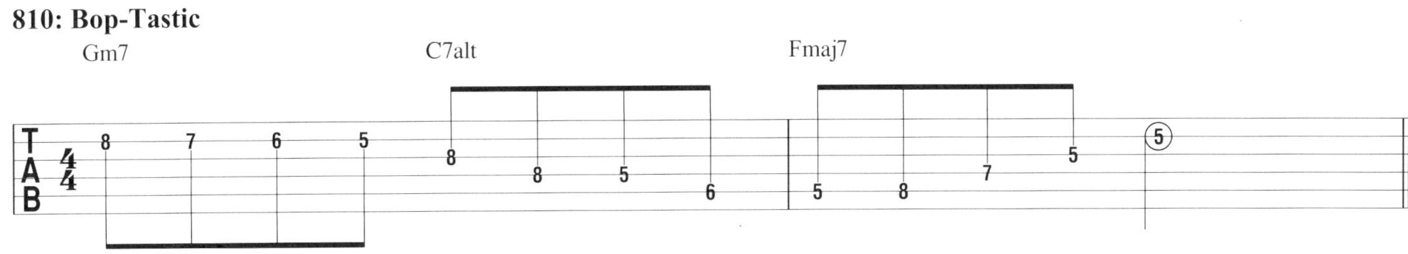


**811: Swing It**

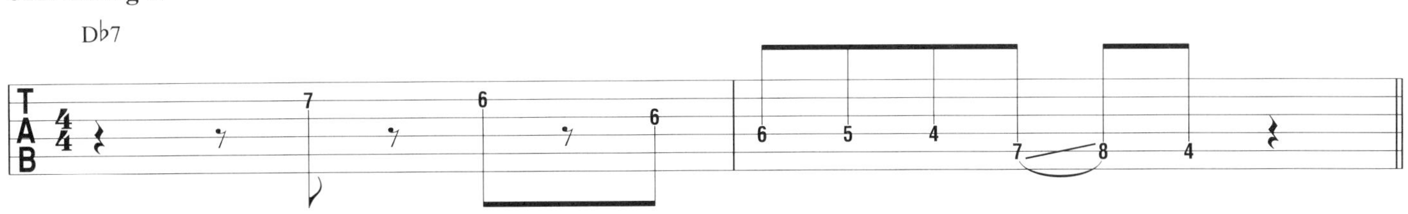


**812: Surround the 3rd**

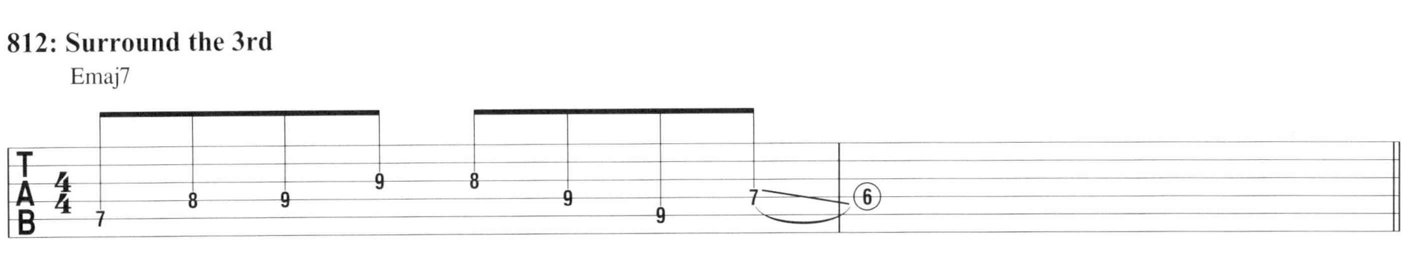


**813: Tasty Turnaround**

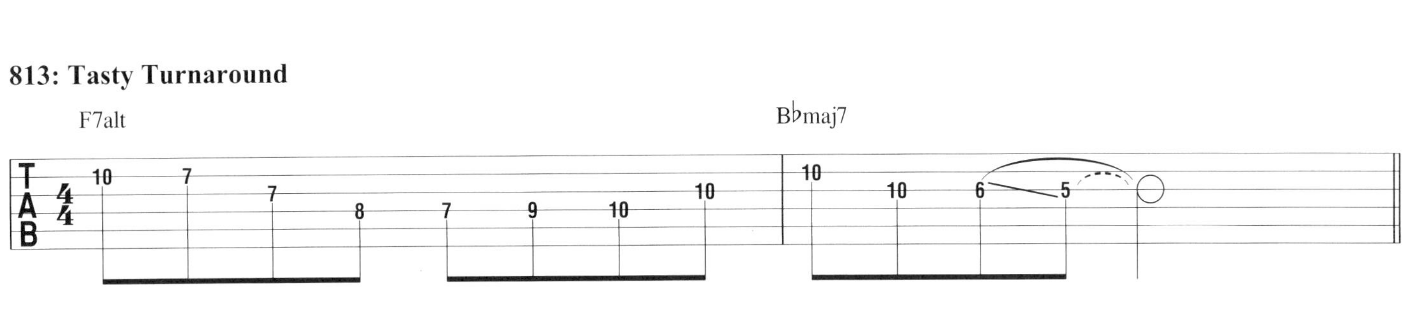

### 814: Short & Sweet

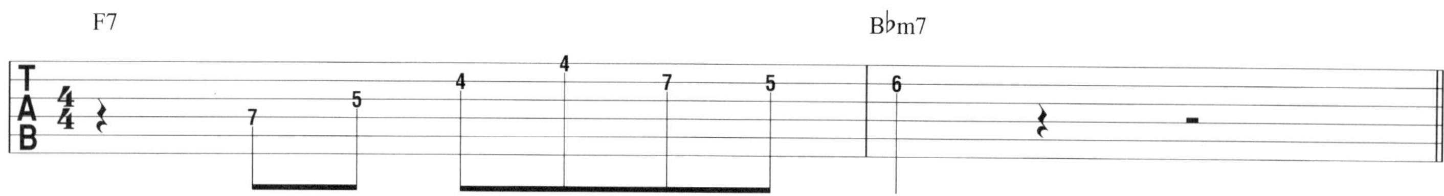


### 815: Dorian Descent

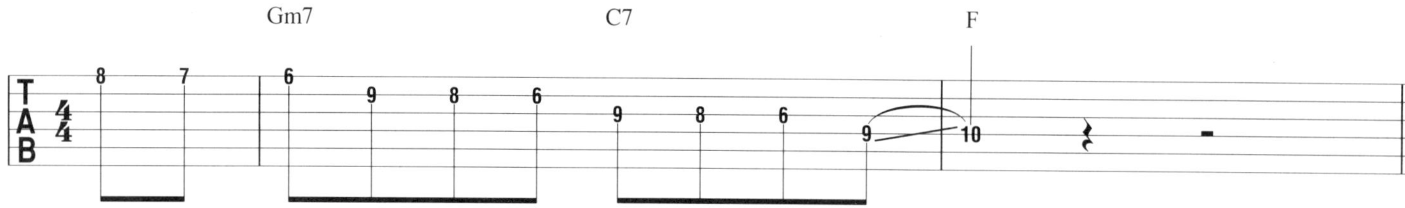


### 816: Mini-Barres

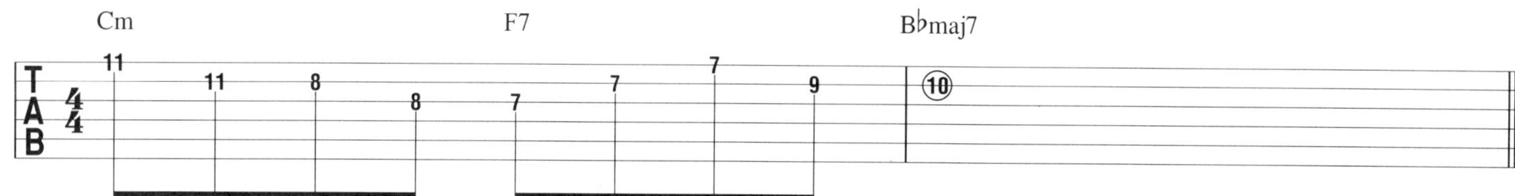


### 817: Arpeggiosity

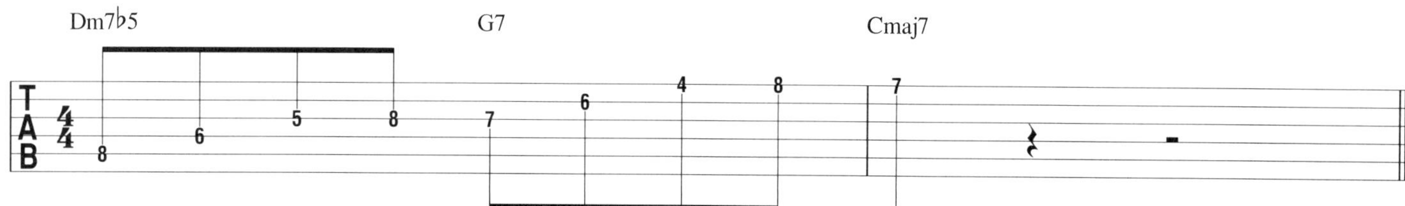


### 818: Hammer Up

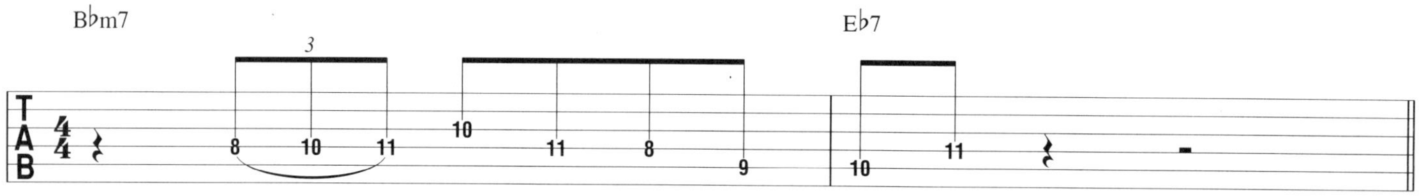


### 819: Minor Jazz

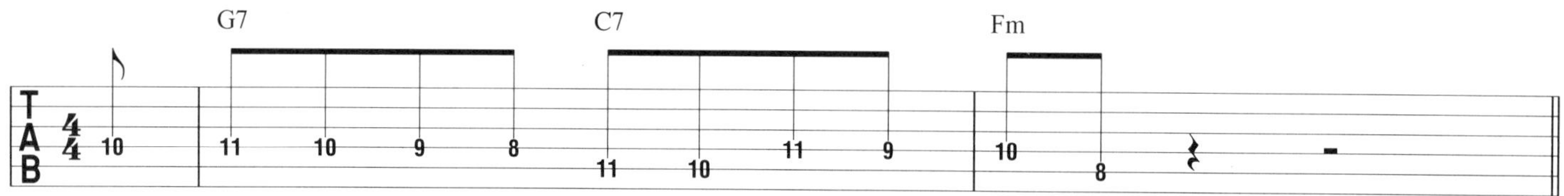


### 820: Restless Neighbors

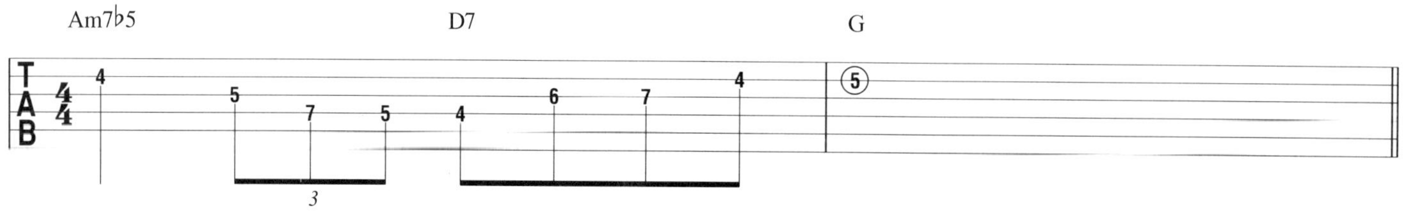

## 821: Mixolydian Romp

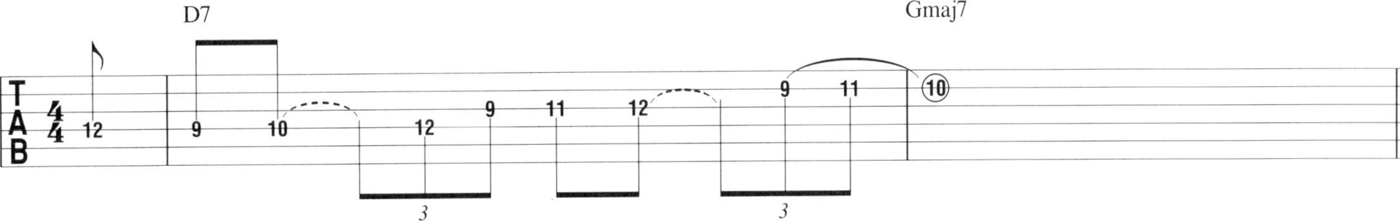


## 822: Dorian Delight

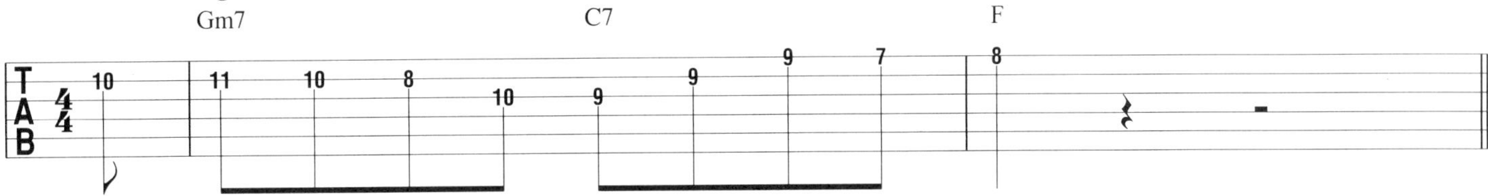


## 823: Chromatic Resolve

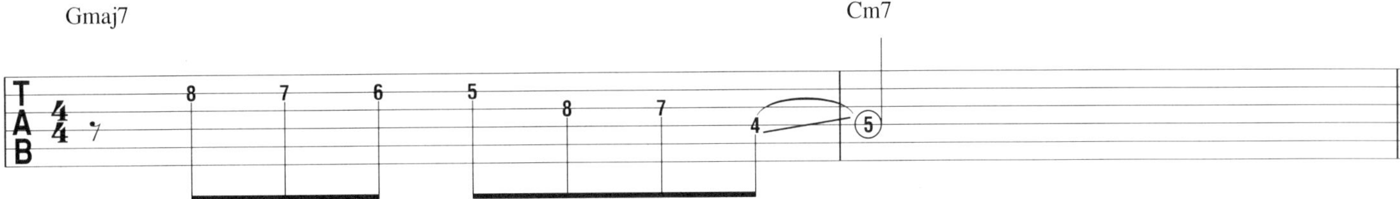


## 824: Angular Jazz

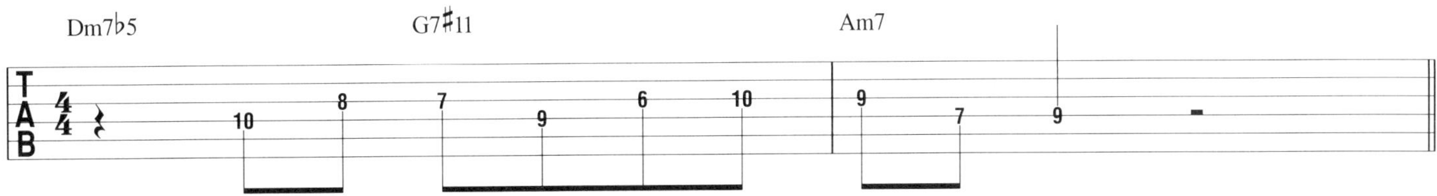


## 825: Upper Extent

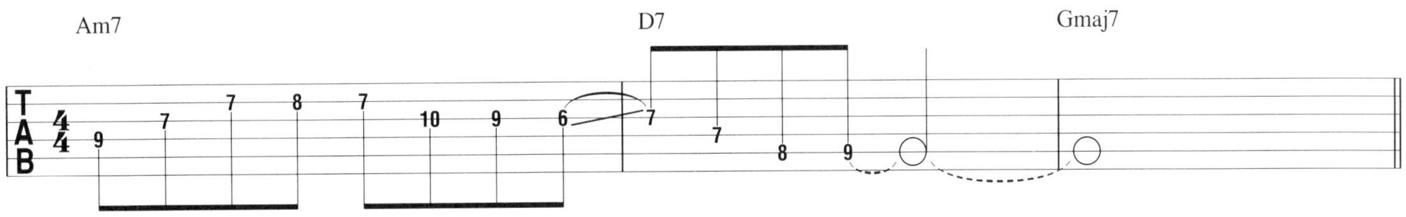


## 826: ii-V-I Me

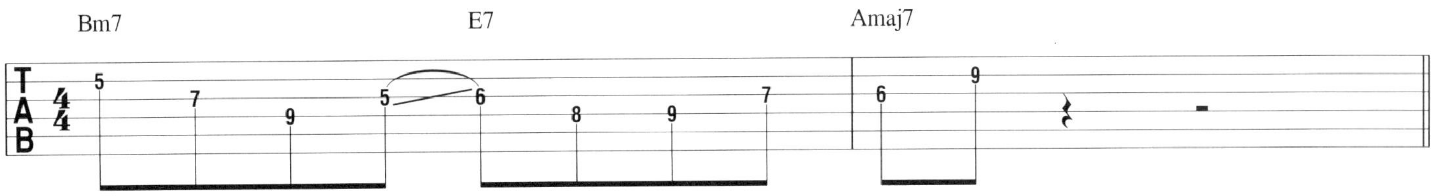


## 827: Half-Diminished

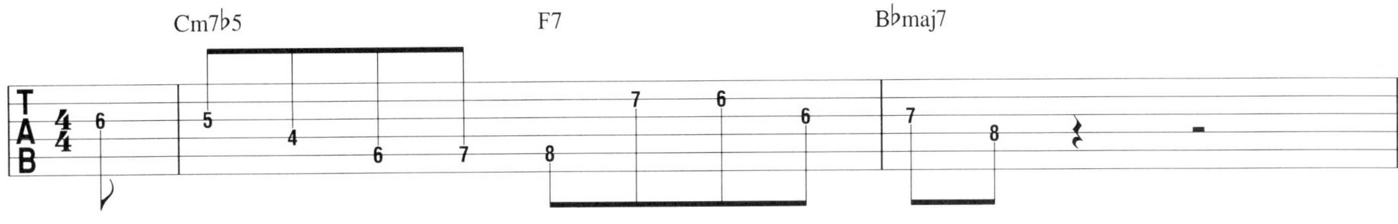

**828: Upbeat Swinger**

**829: Lucky 13**

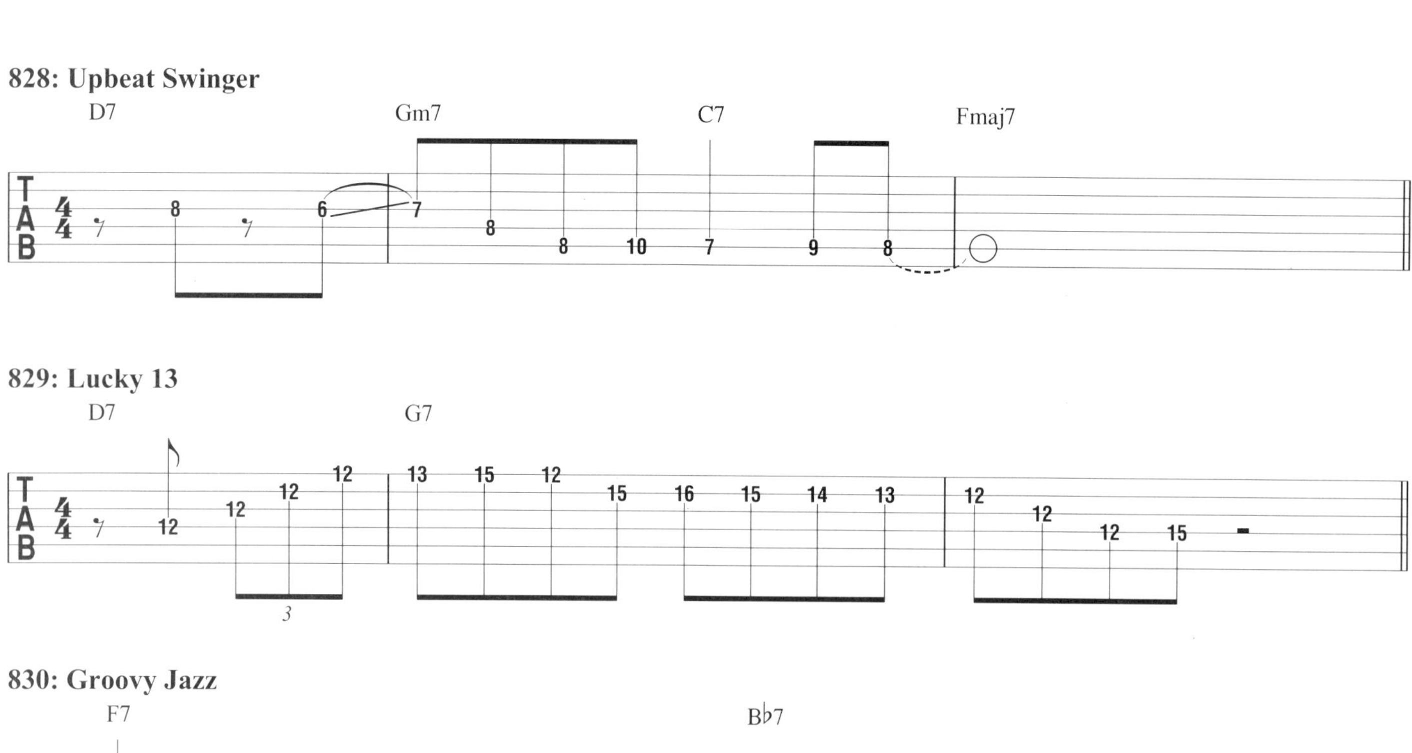


**830: Groovy Jazz**

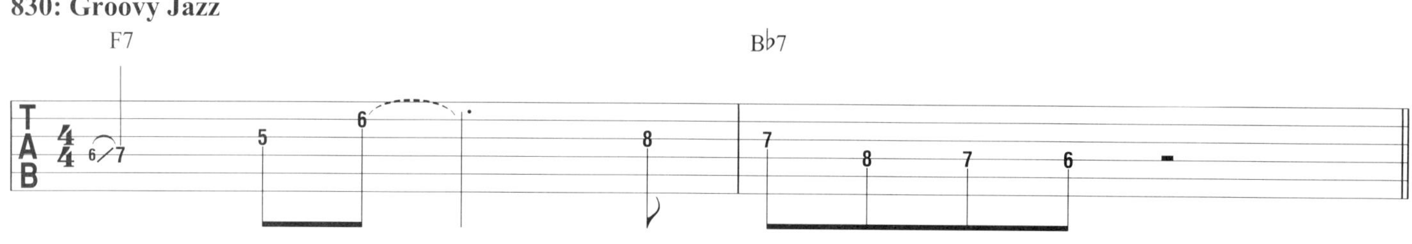


**831: Triplet Pickup**

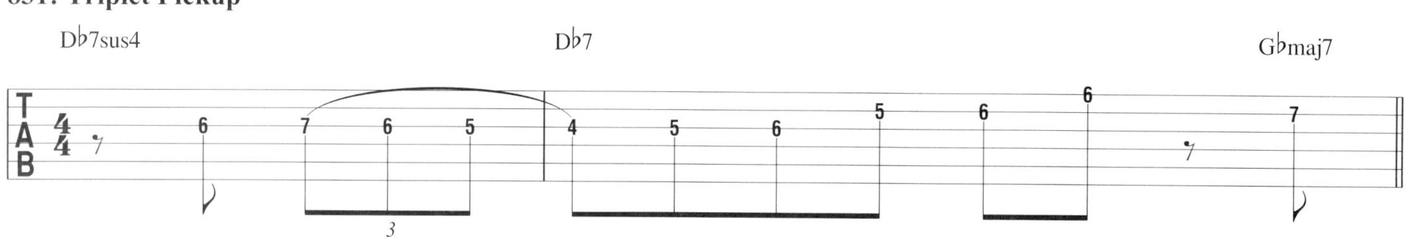


**832: ii-V-I Melody**

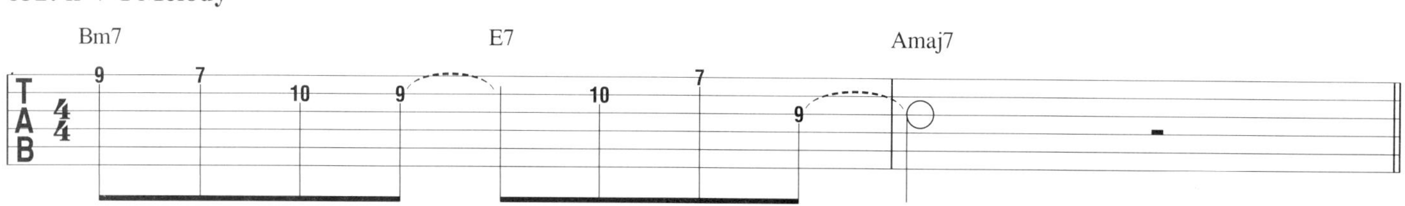


**833: Hip to That**

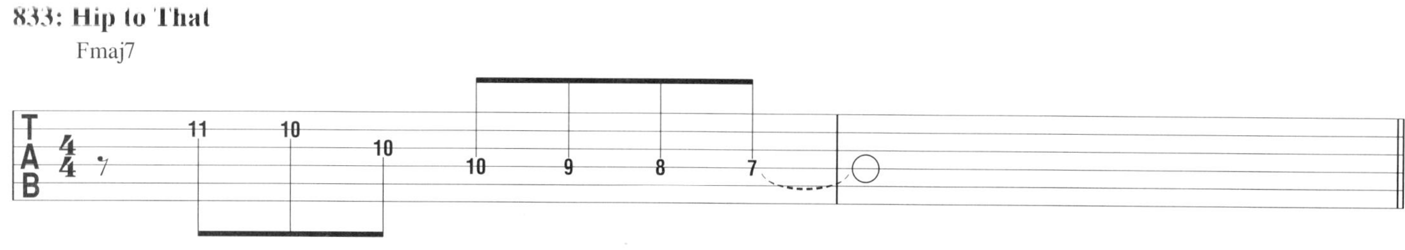


**834: Bop Climb**

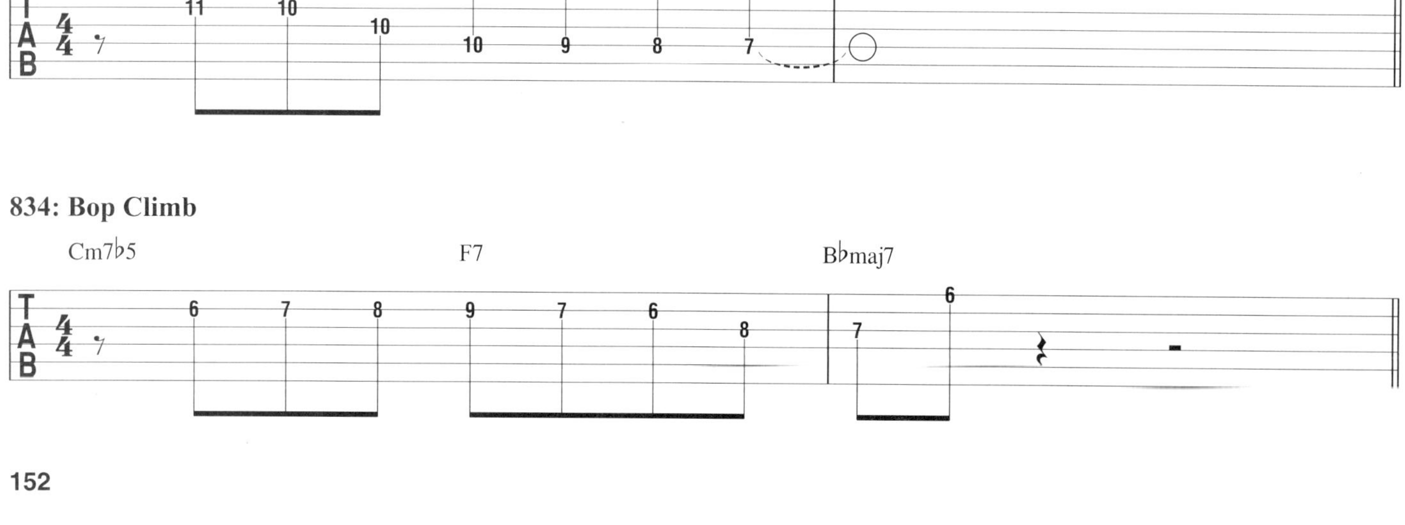

**835: Harp Arps**

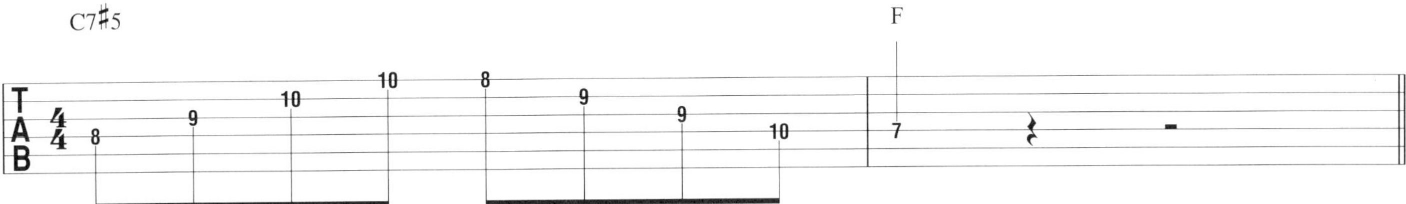


**836: Snaky Jazz**

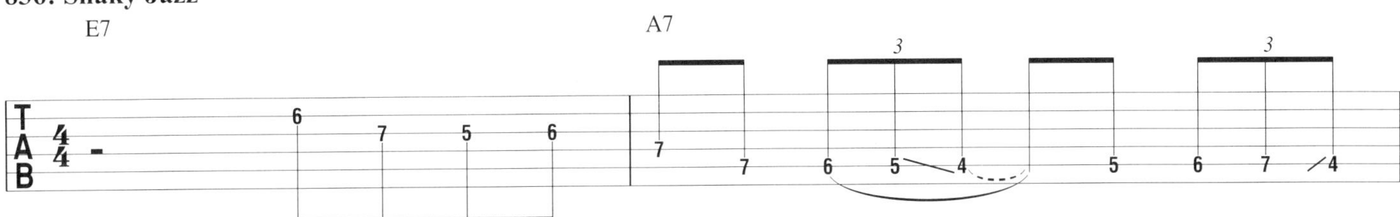


**837: Jazzy Juxtapose**

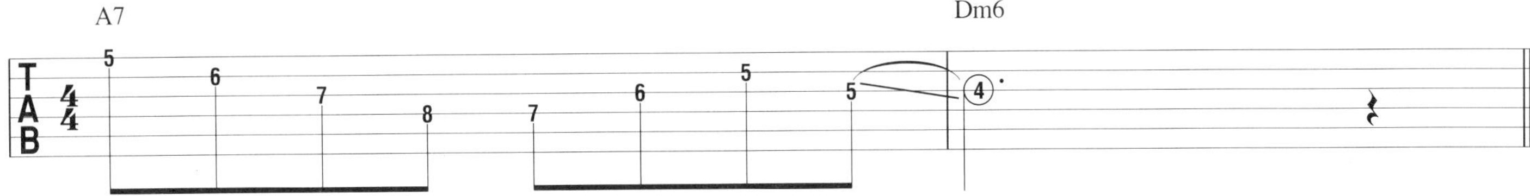


**838: Pure Minor**

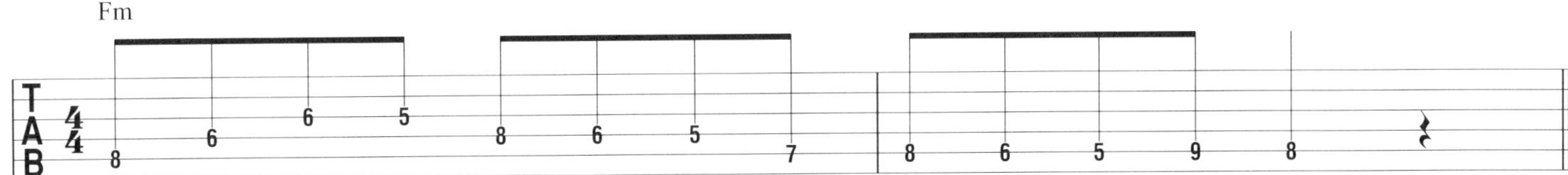


**839: Organic Jazz**

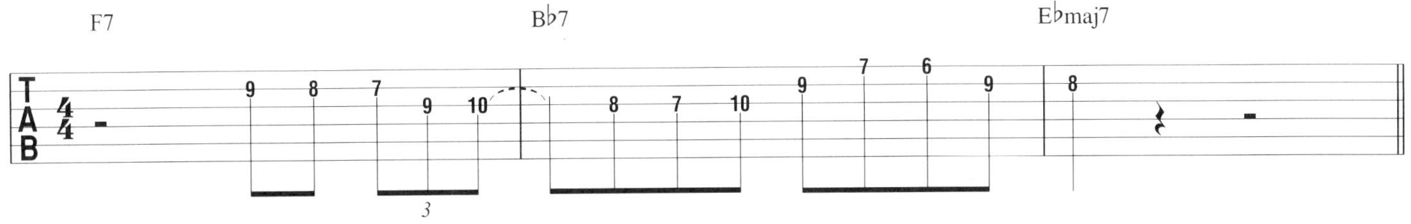


**840: Straight Up**

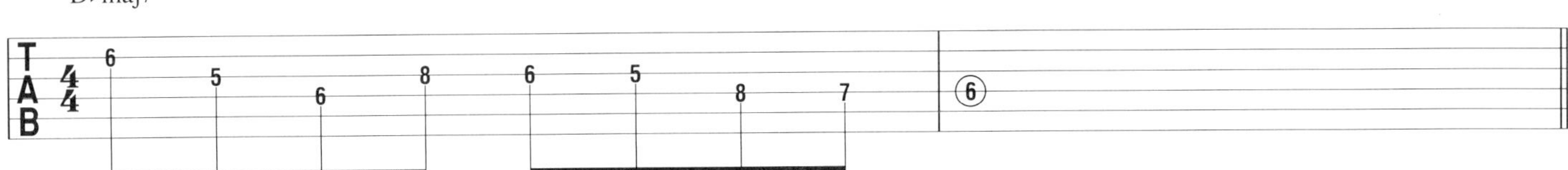


**841: Altered Dominance**

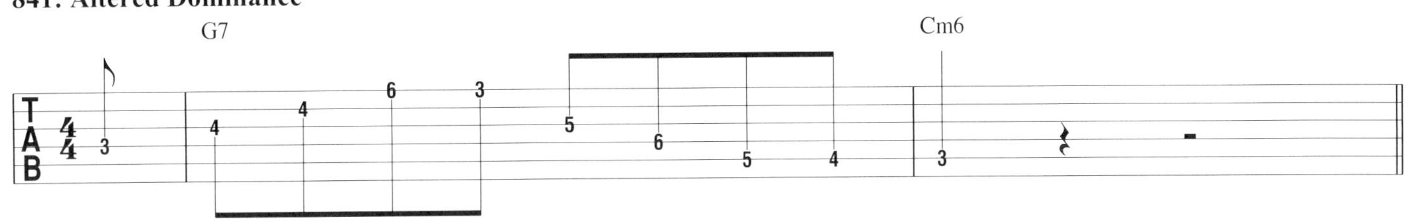

## 842: Cool Jazz

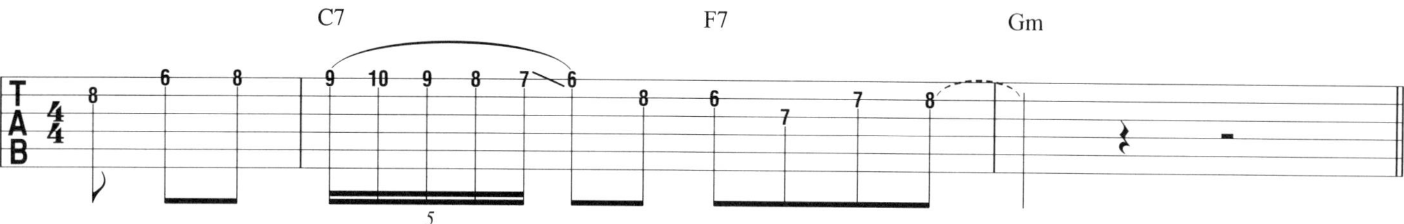


## 843: Jazz Hands

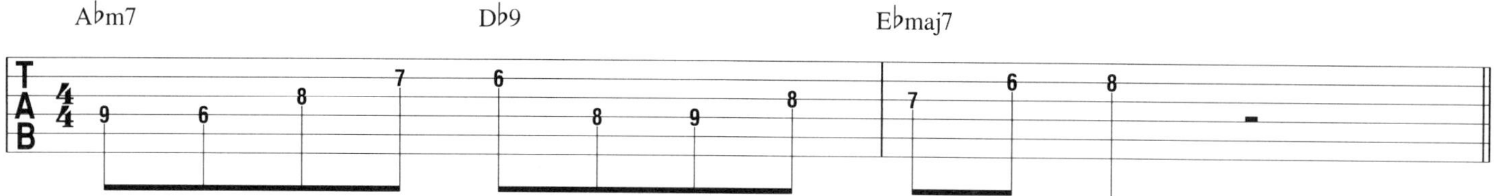


## 844: V-I Run

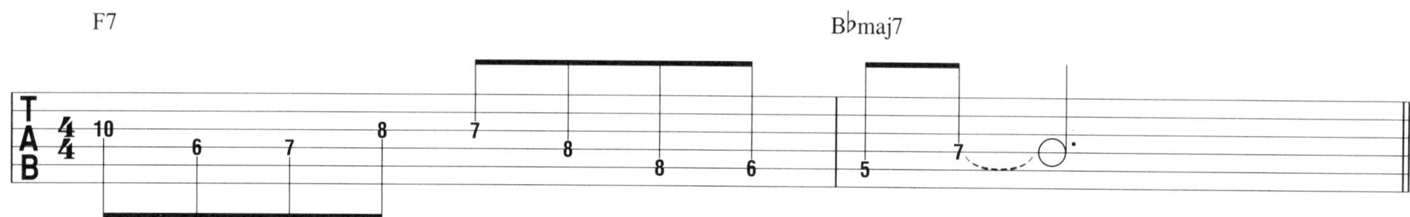


## 845: Chord-Tone Magic

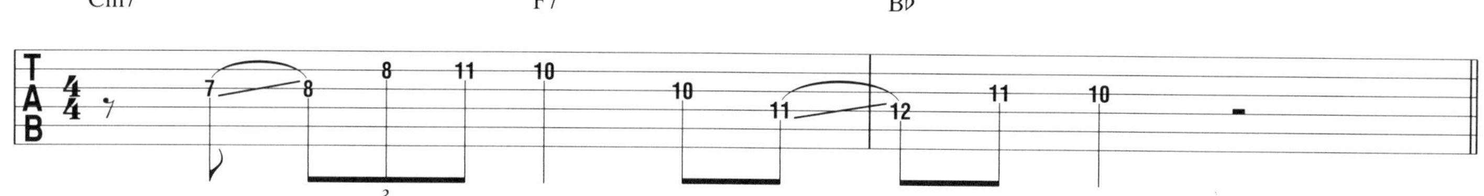


## 846: To the Tonic

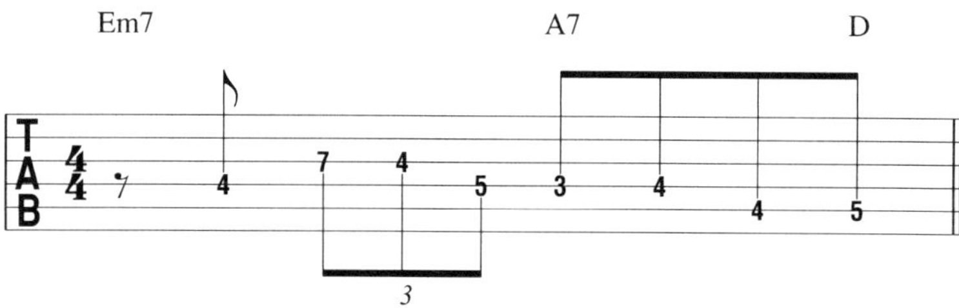


## 847: Cyc-Lick

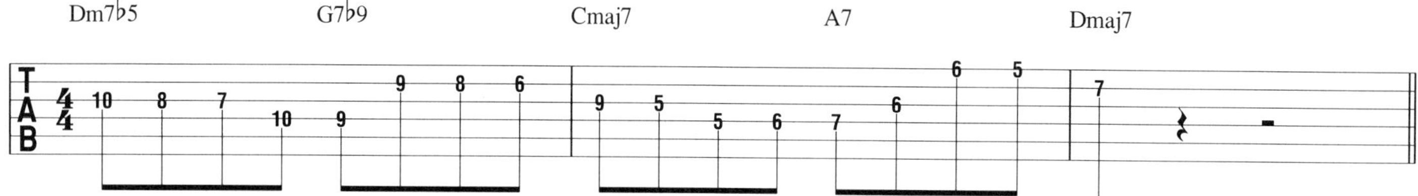


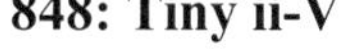

## 848: Tiny ii-V

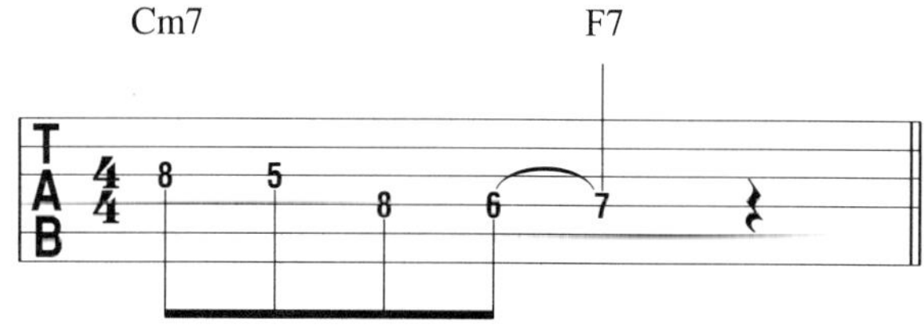

### 849: Dark & Smoky

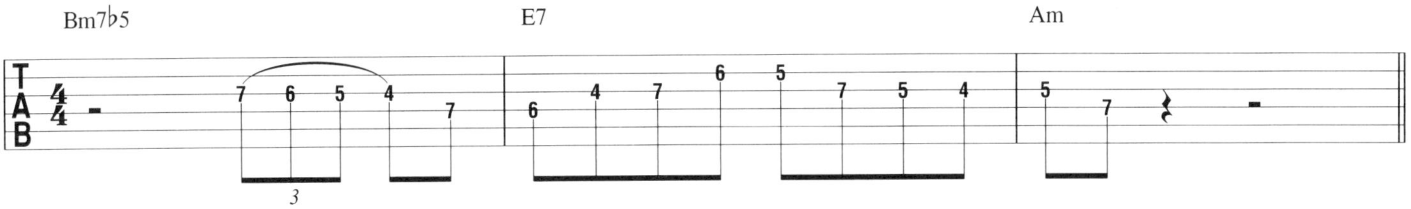

Bm7♭5 | E7 | Am

### 850: Classic ii-V-I

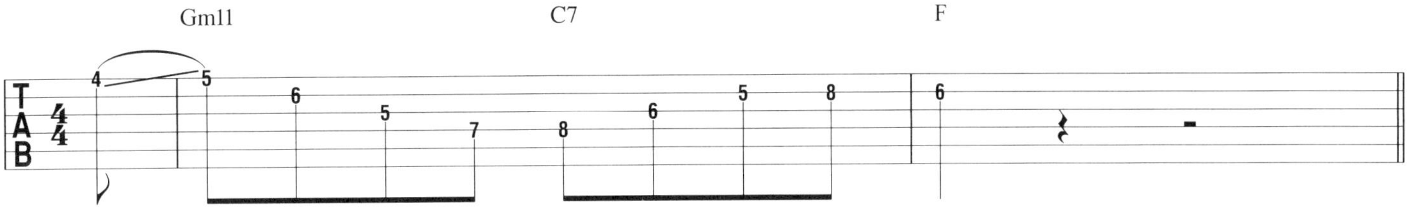

Gm11 | C7 | F

### 851: Gin & Tonic

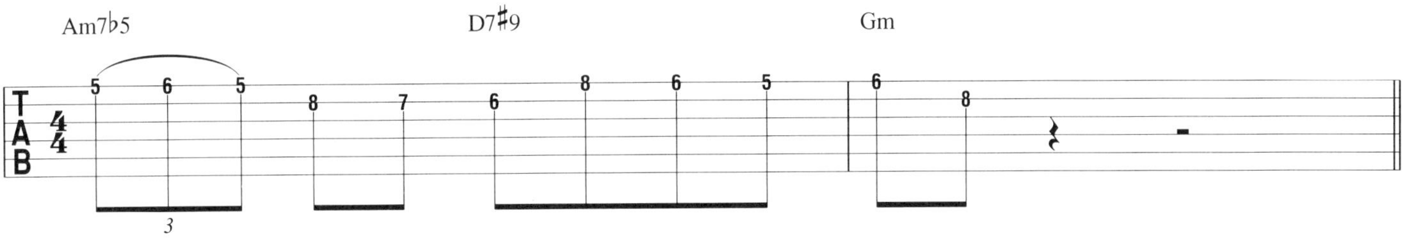

Am7♭5 | D7♯9 | Gm

### 852: Question & Answer

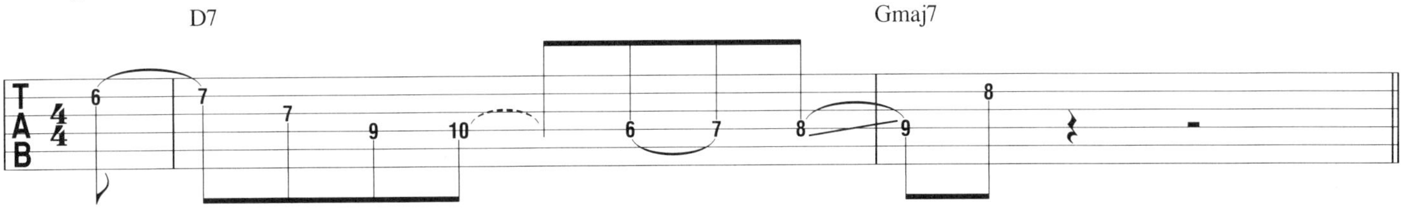

D7 | Gmaj7

### 853: Chromatic Surround

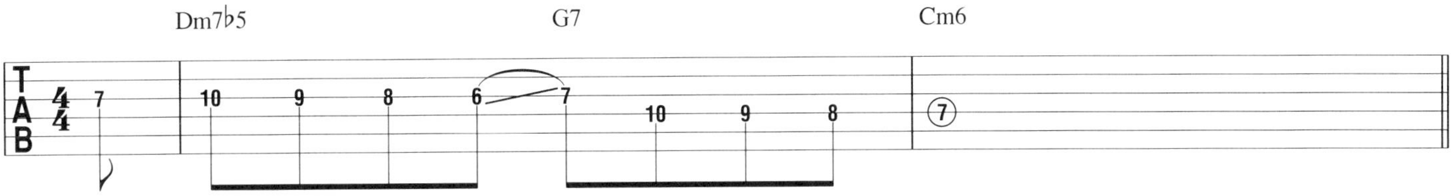

Dm7♭5 | G7 | Cm6

### 854: Half Steppin'

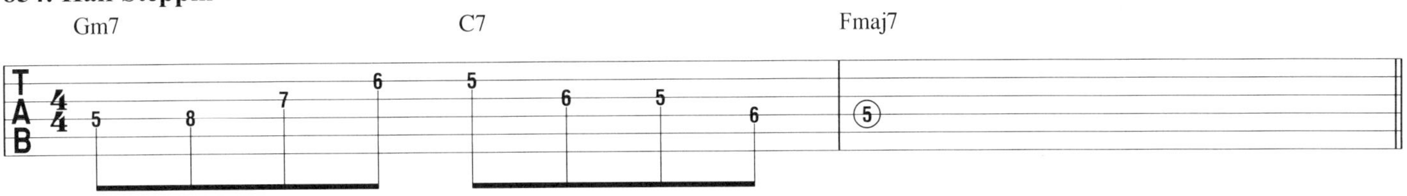

Gm7 | C7 | Fmaj7

### 855: Little Surround

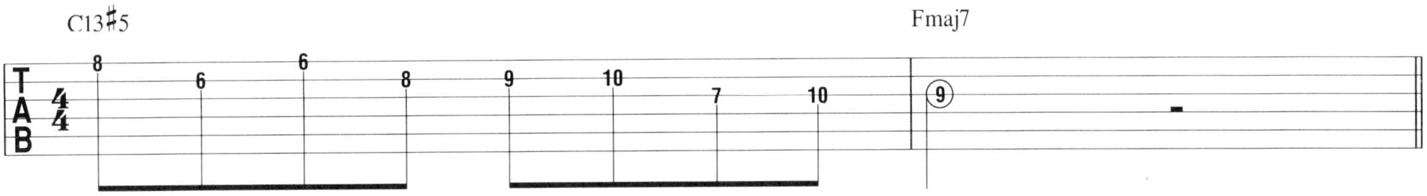

C13♯5 | Fmaj7

## 856: Dominant Run

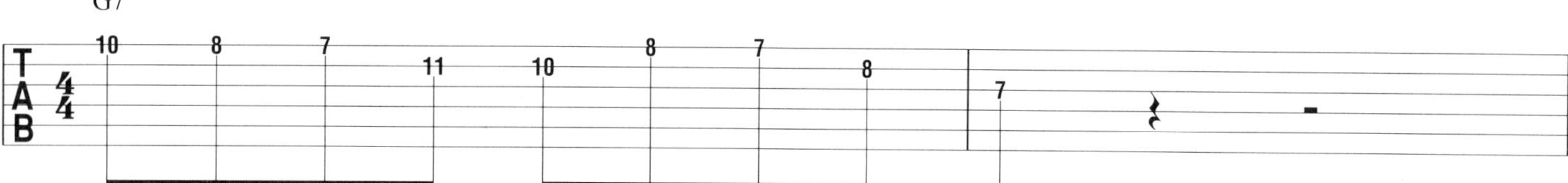


## 857: Smoky Barre

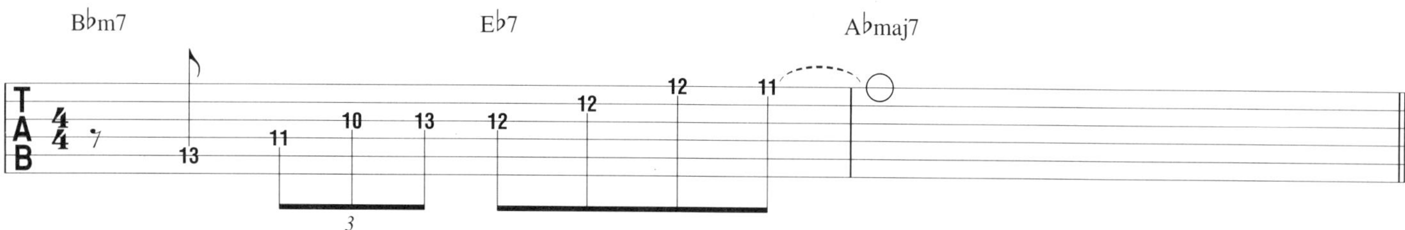


## 858: Arp It

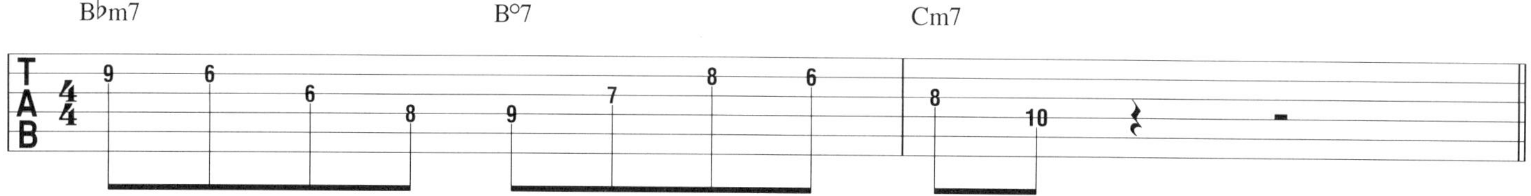


## 859: Altercation

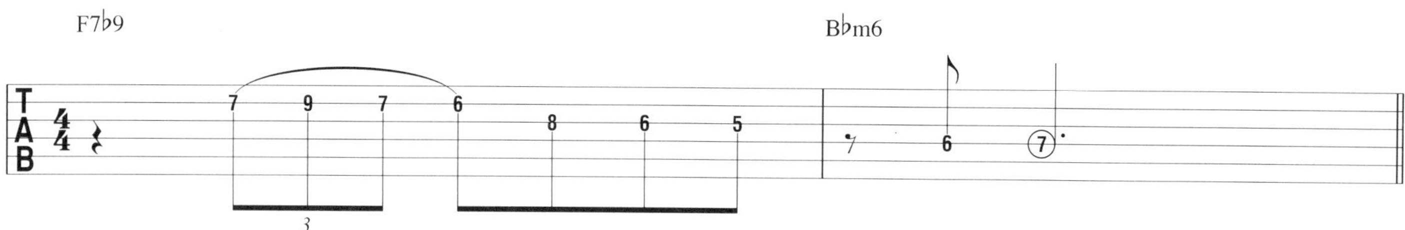


## 860: Major Line

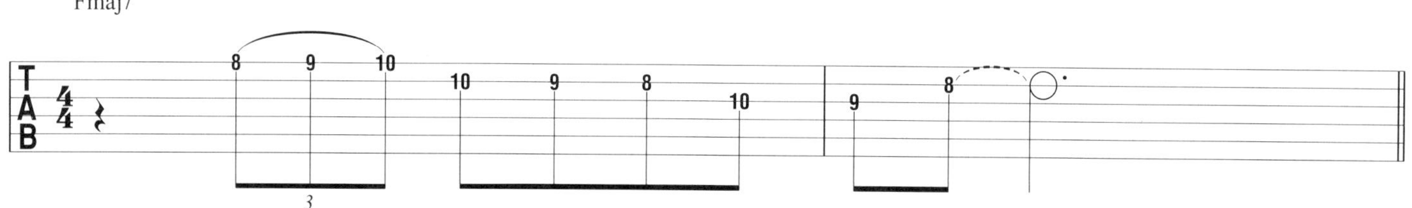


## 861: Punctuated

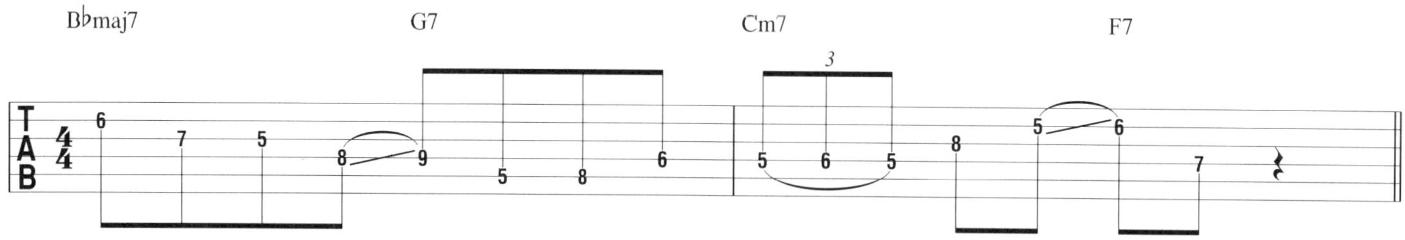


## 862: Classy Jazz

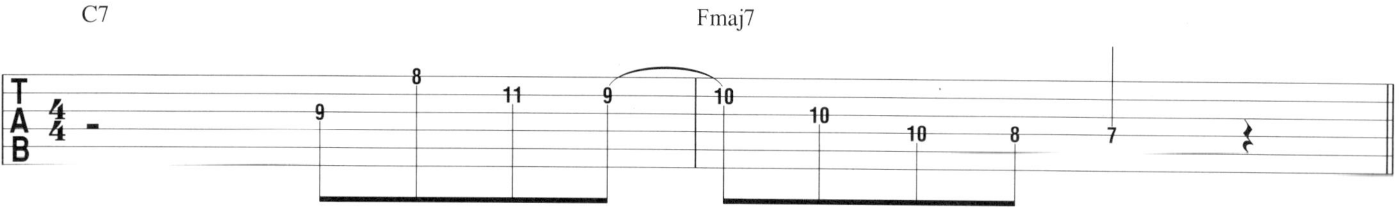

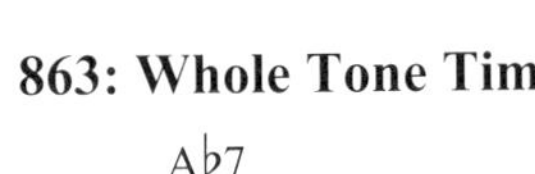

## 863: Whole Tone Time

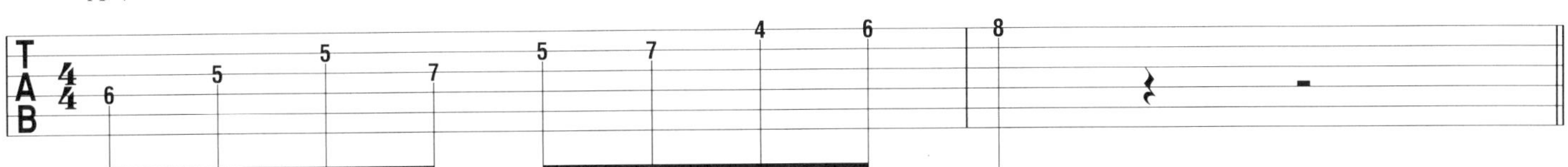


## 864: Tone Hole

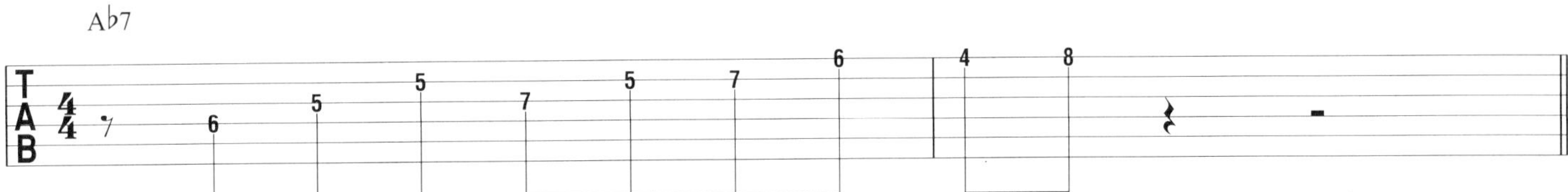


## 865: Whole Toning

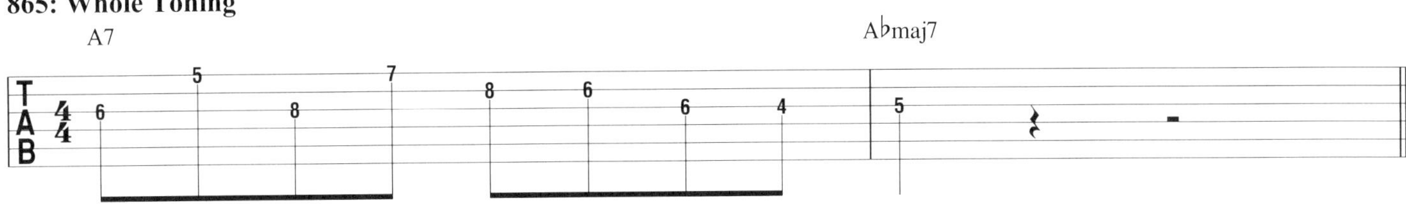


## 866: Waterfalling

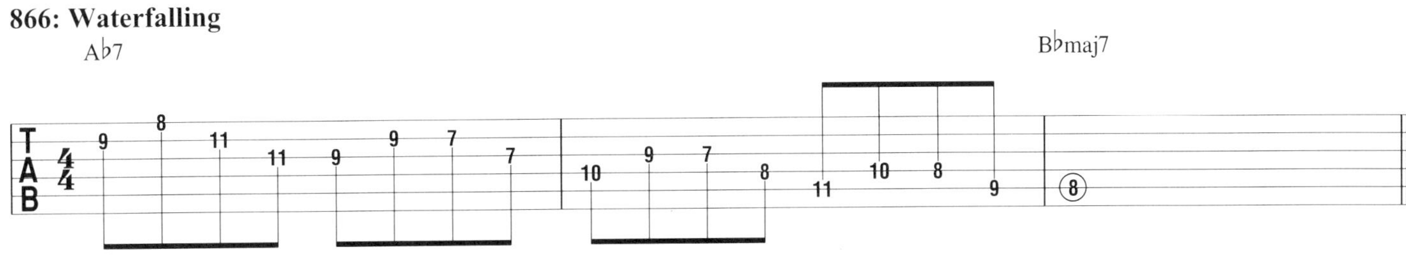


## 867: Firm Landing

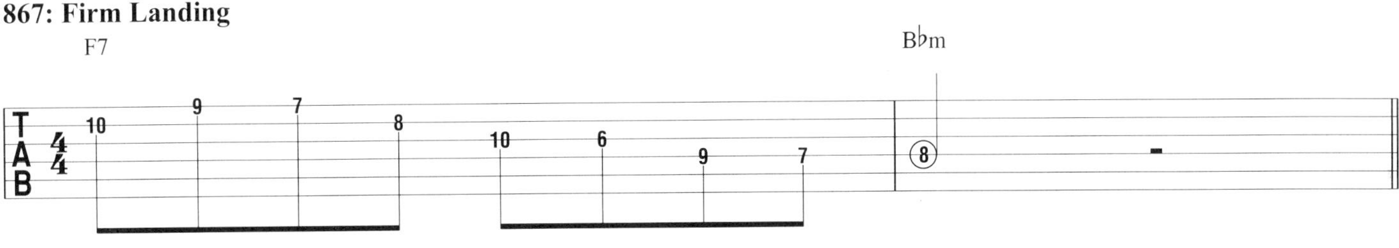


## 868: Major or Minor

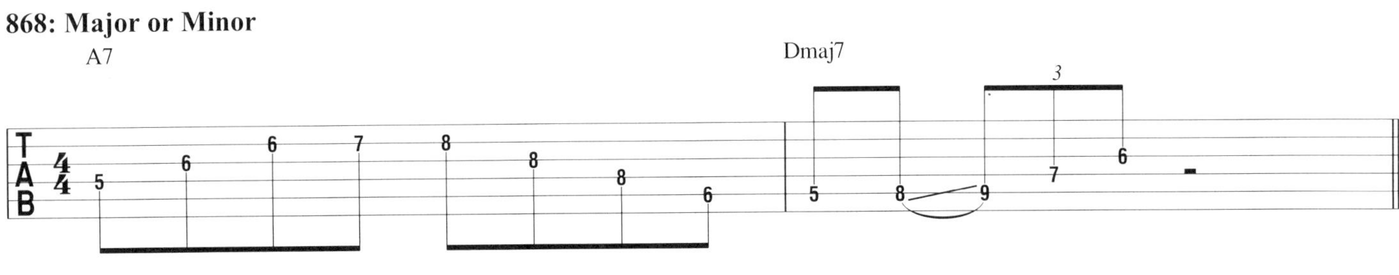


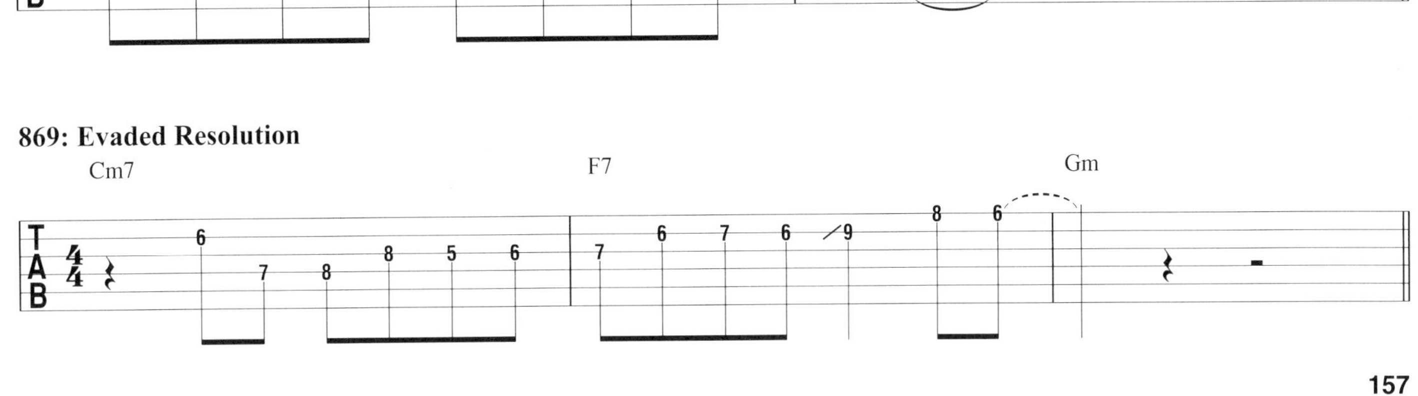

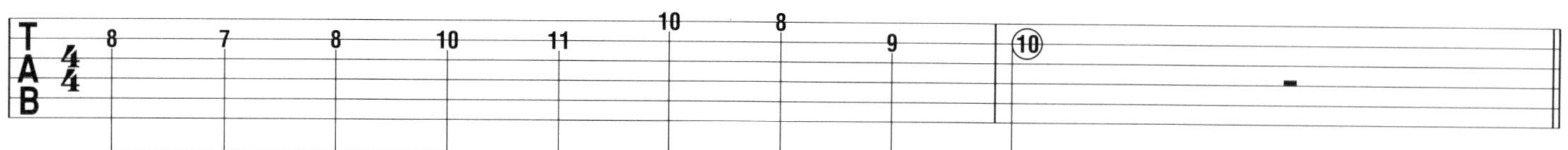


### 871: ii-V-I It

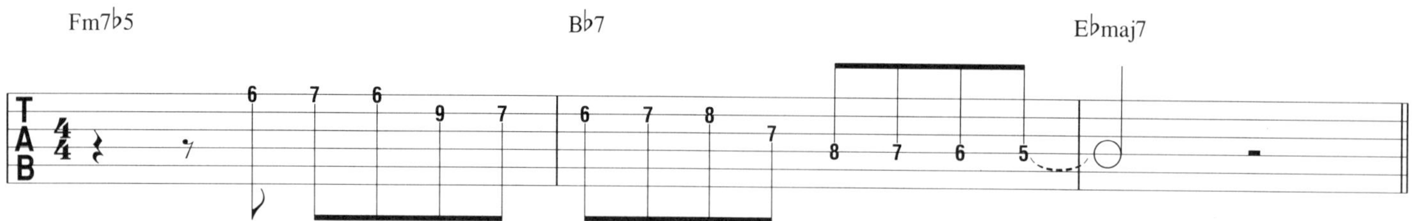


### 872: Major Surprise

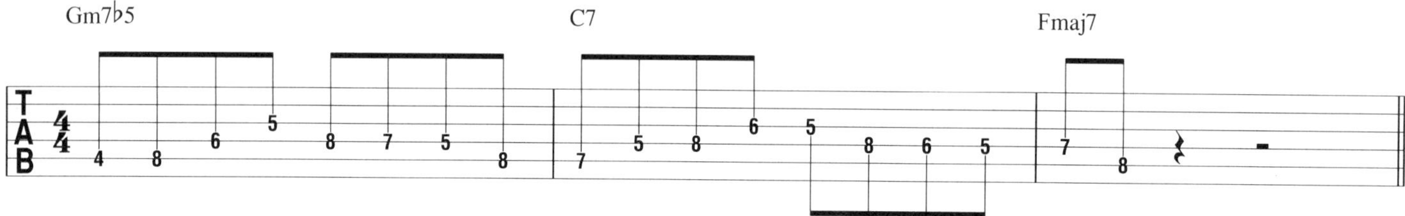


### 873: Minor Large

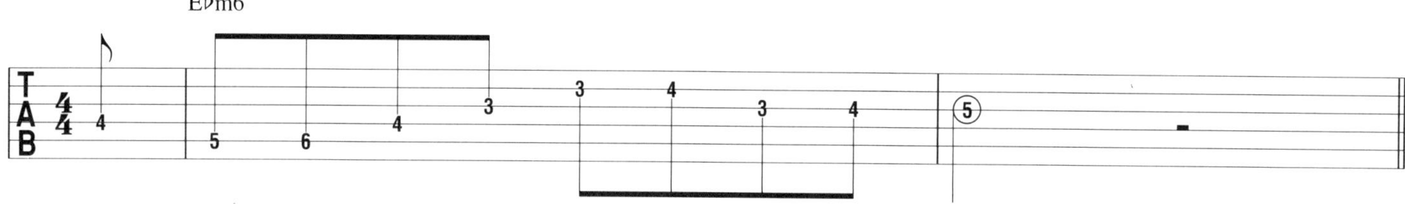


### 874: Altered Elegance

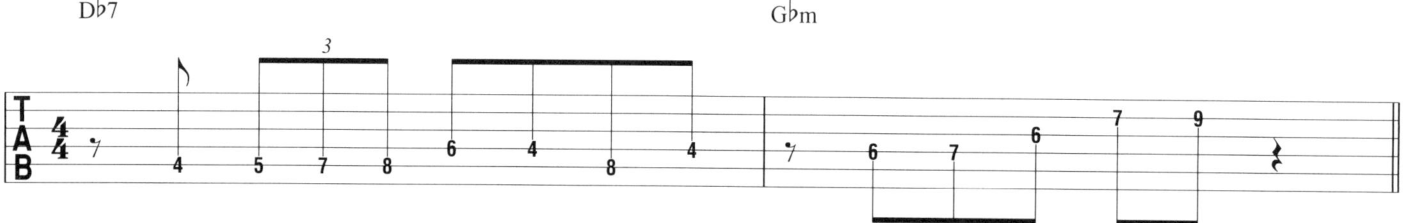


### 875: ii-V-VI

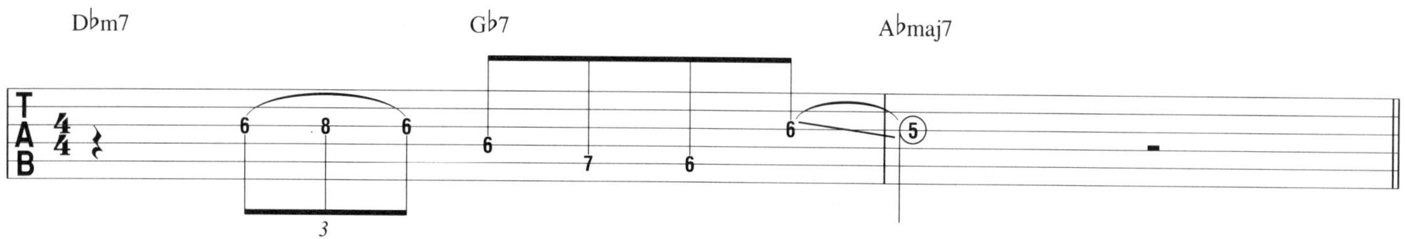

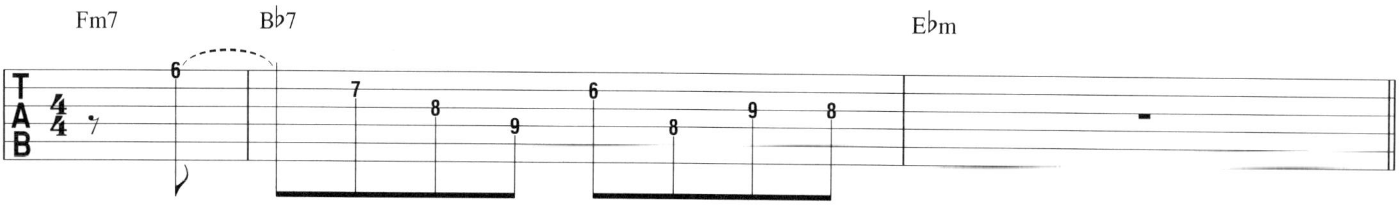

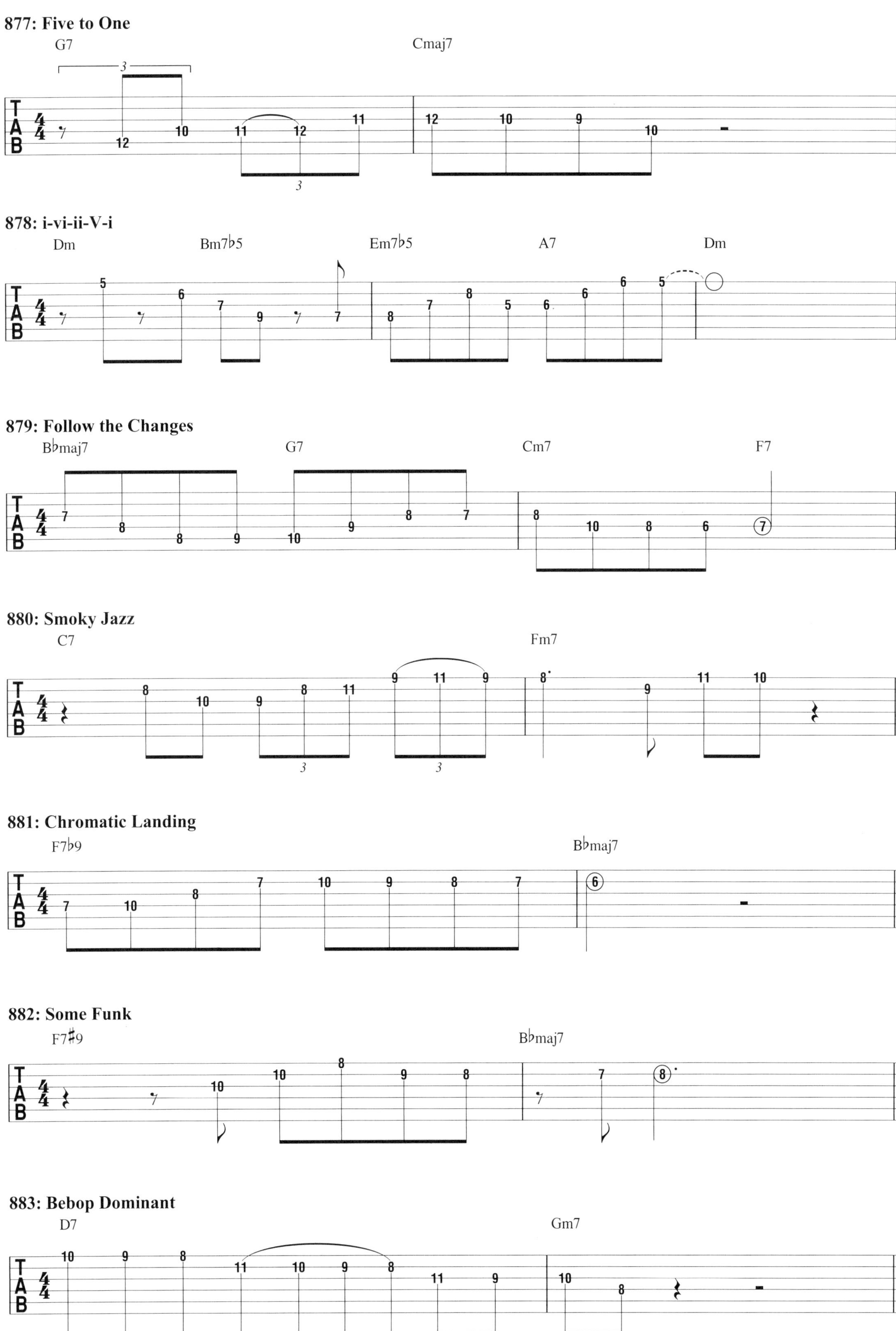
877: Five to One
G7
Cmaj7
878: i-vi-ii-V-i
Dm
Bm7♭5
Em7♭5
A7
Dm
879: Follow the Changes
B♭maj7
G7
Cm7
F7
880: Smoky Jazz
C7
Fm7
881: Chromatic Landing
F7♭9
B♭maj7
882: Some Funk
F7♯9
B♭maj7
883: Bebop Dominant
D7
Gm7

### 884: V-i

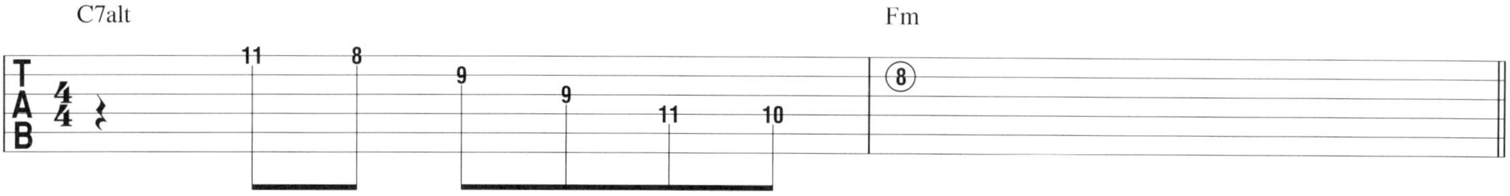

C7alt Fm

### 885: Arpology

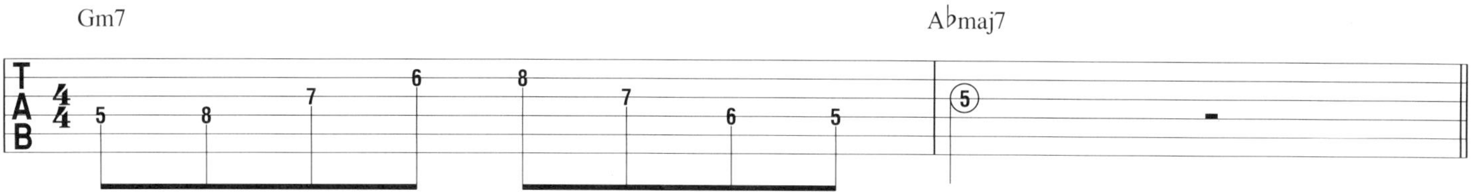

Gm7 A♭maj7

### 886: ii-V-I-VI

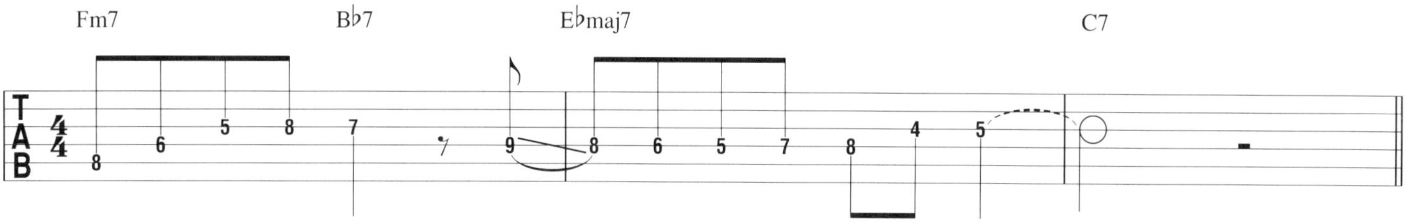

Fm7 B♭7 E♭maj7 C7

### 887: Borrowed Minor

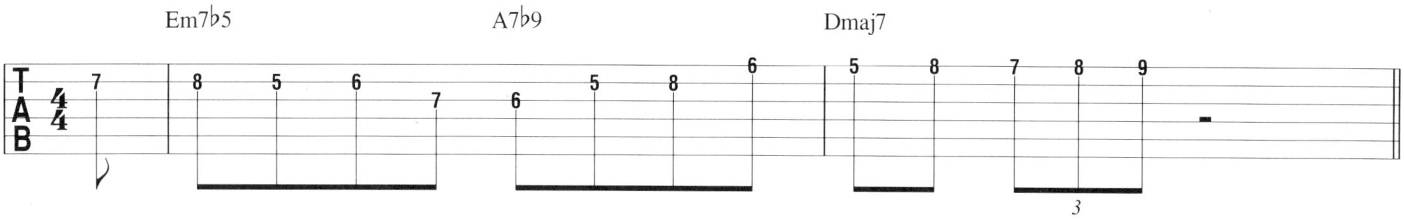

Em7♭5 A7♭9 Dmaj7

### 888: Exotic Melodic

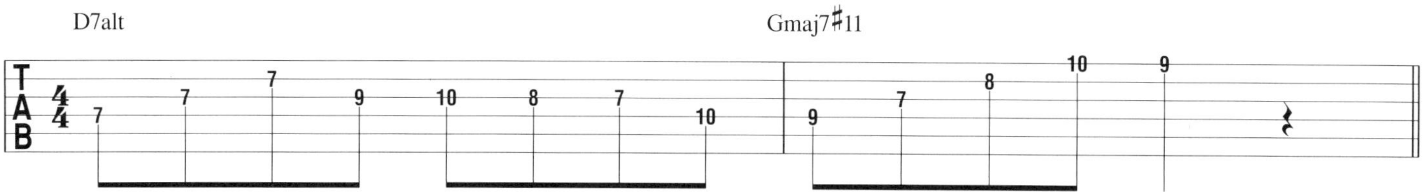

D7alt Gmaj7♯11

### 889: Expressing Dorian

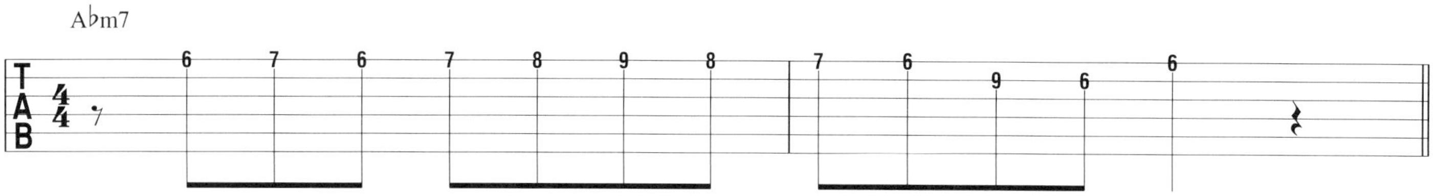

A♭m7

### 890: Phraseology

B♭7♯5 E♭maj7

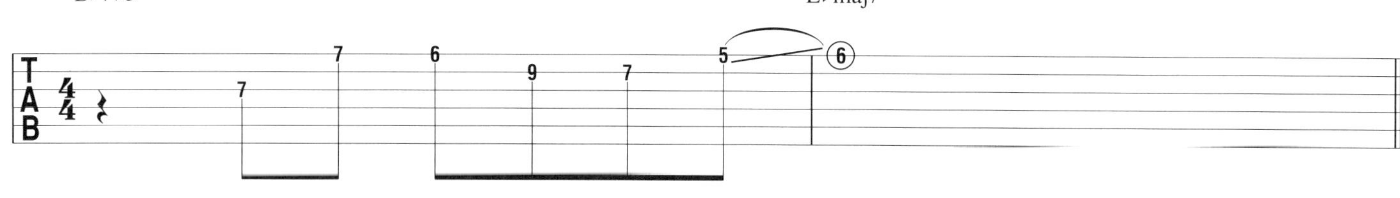

**891: Organic Melodic**

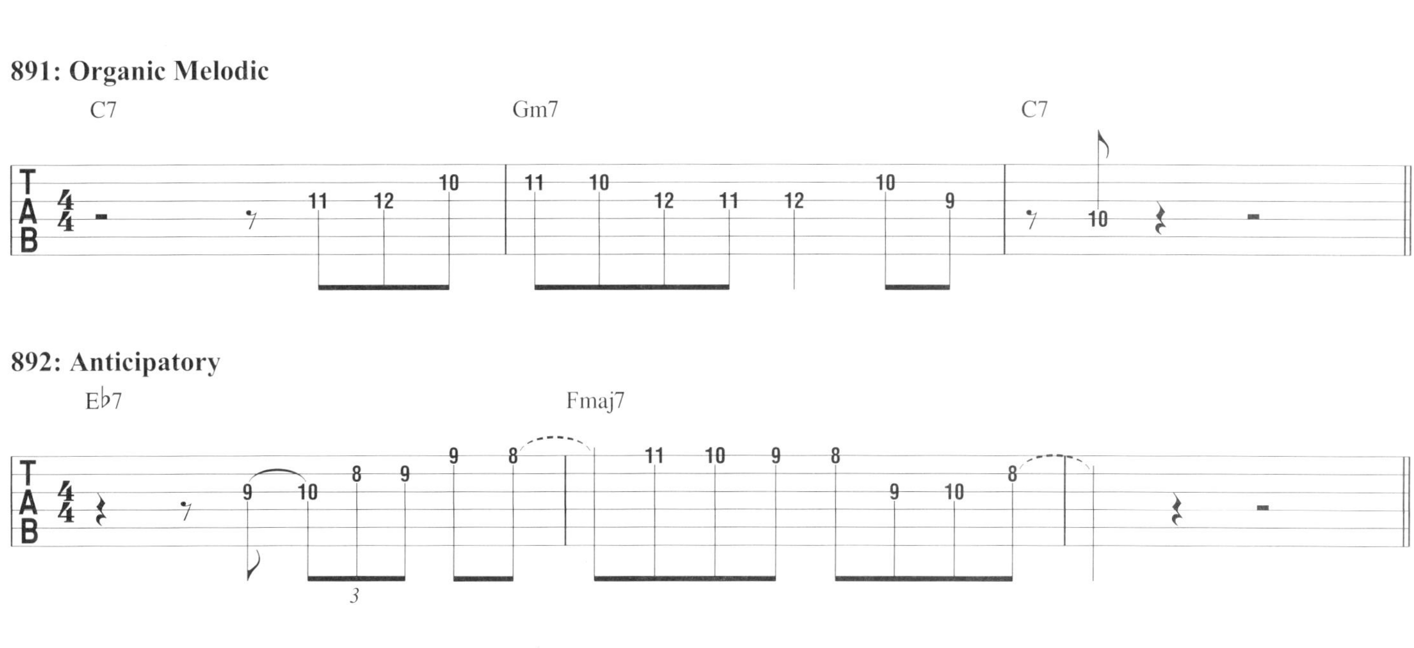


**892: Anticipatory**

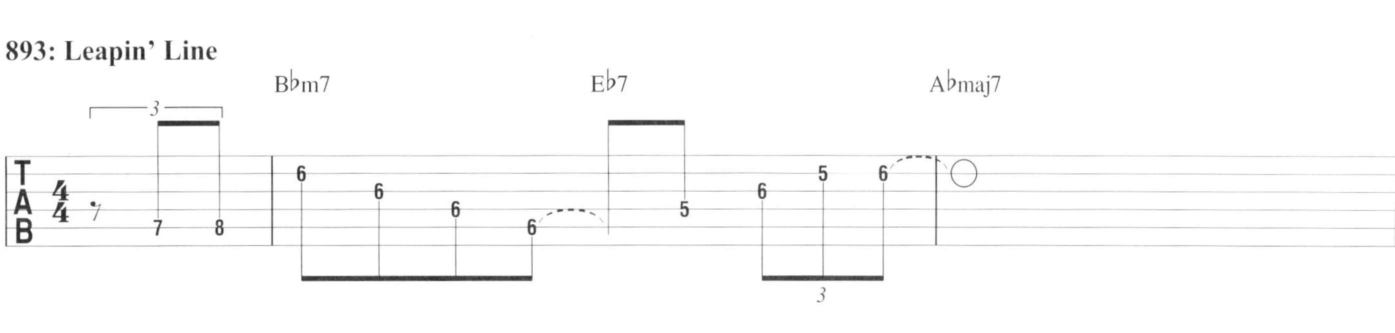


**893: Leapin' Line**

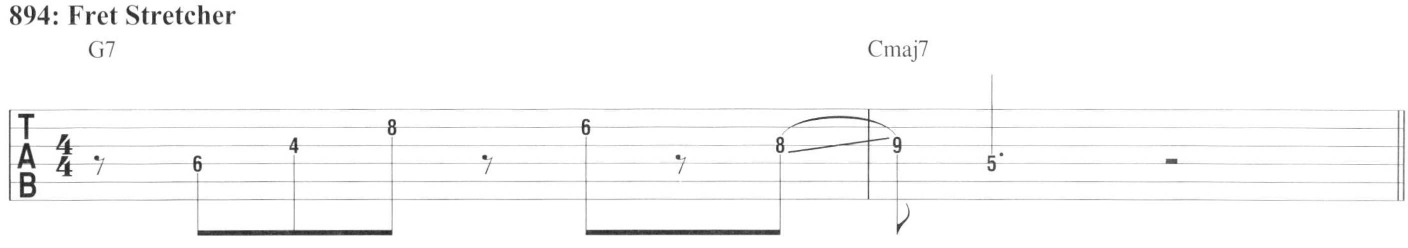


**894: Fret Stretcher**

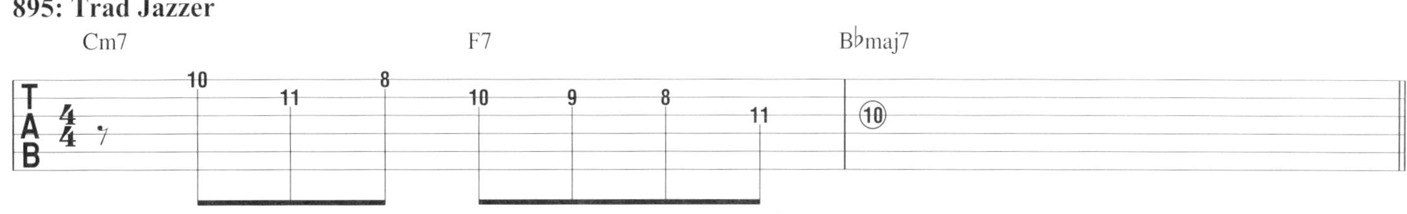


**895: Trad Jazzer**

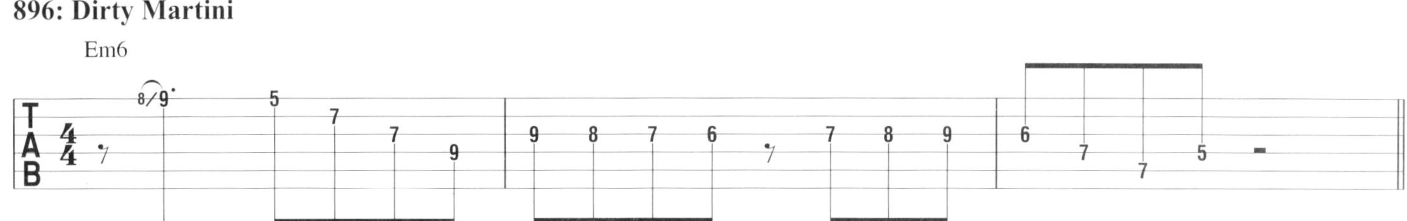


**896: Dirty Martini**

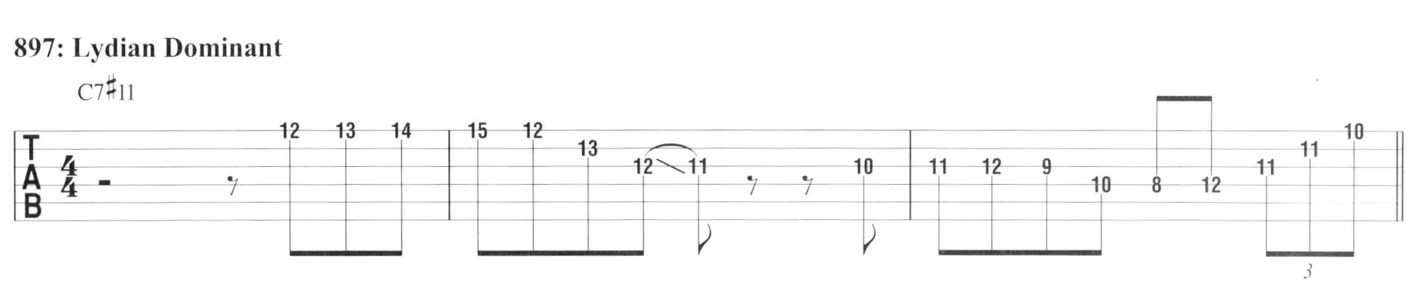


**897: Lydian Dominant**

### 898: Smokin' Bebop

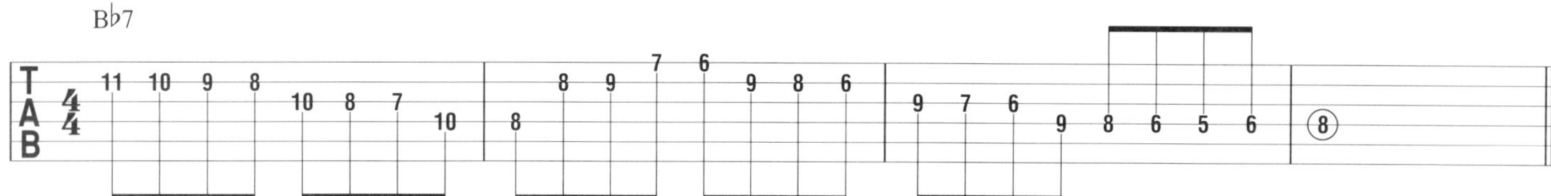


### 899: Penta-Dorian

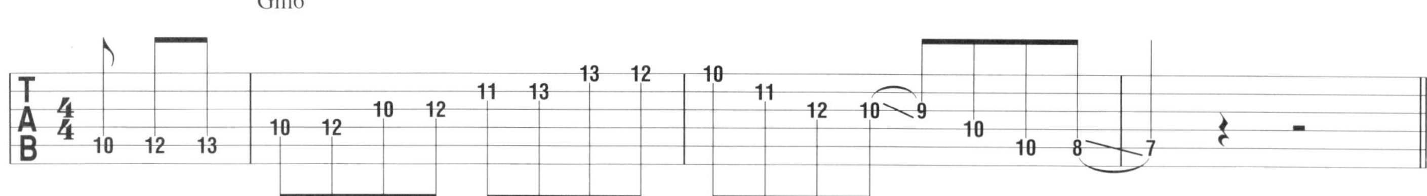


### 900: 6/9 to Lydian

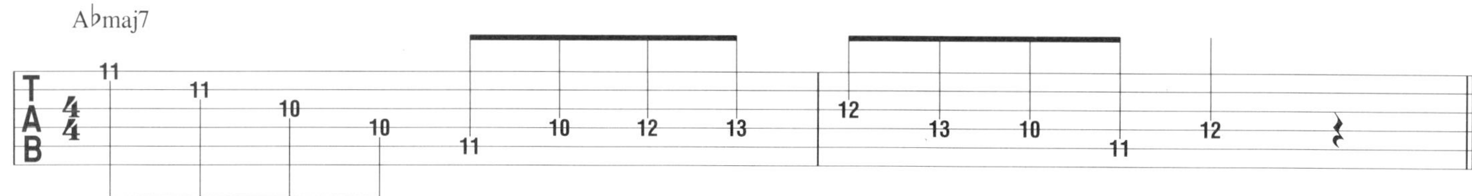


### 901: Altered Line

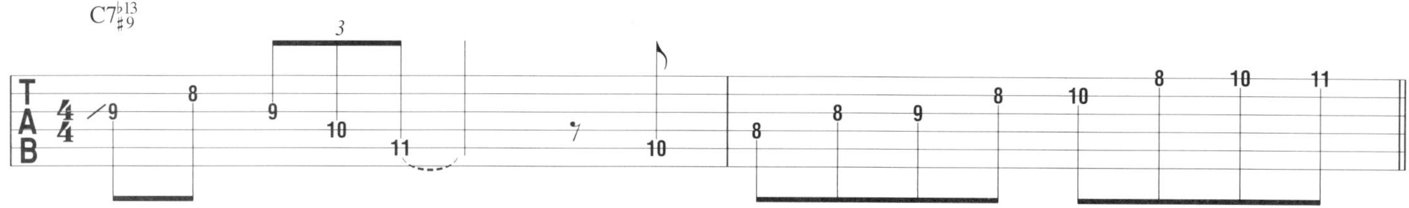


### 902: Half-Wholing

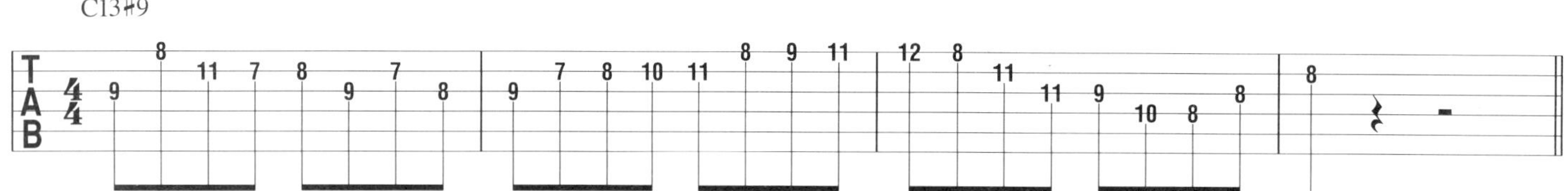


### 903: Cross-String Arpeggios

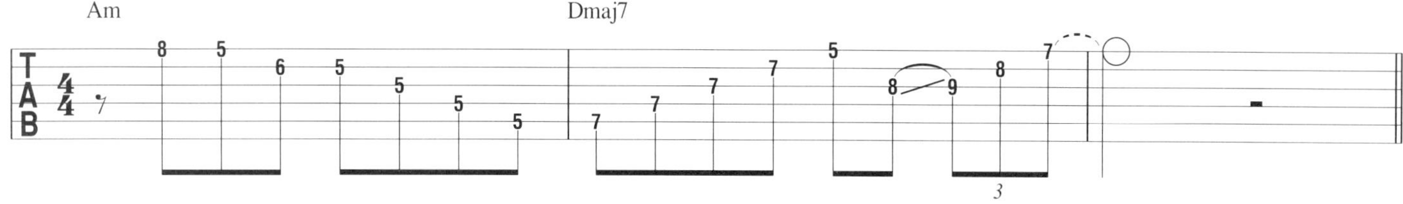


### 904: Dorian Flow

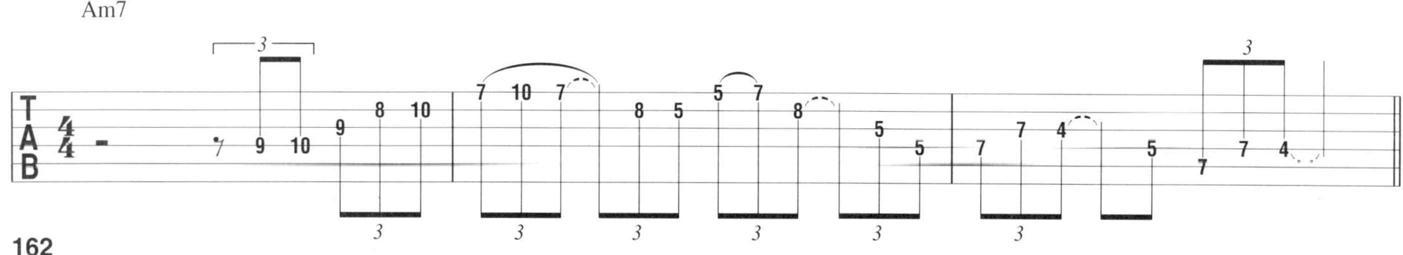

**905: Augmented**

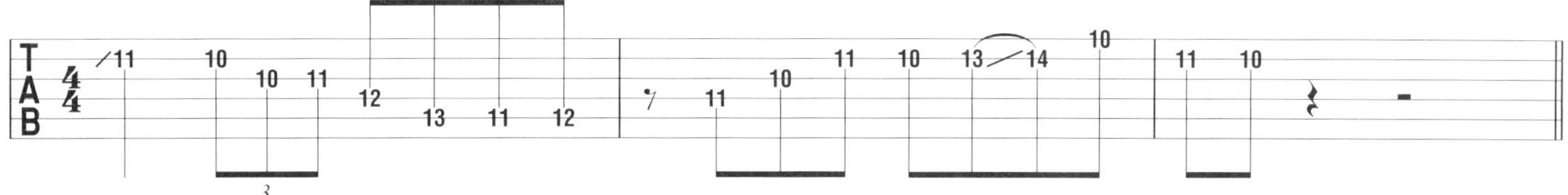

## Instructor: John Heussenstamm

**906: Major 7 Magic**

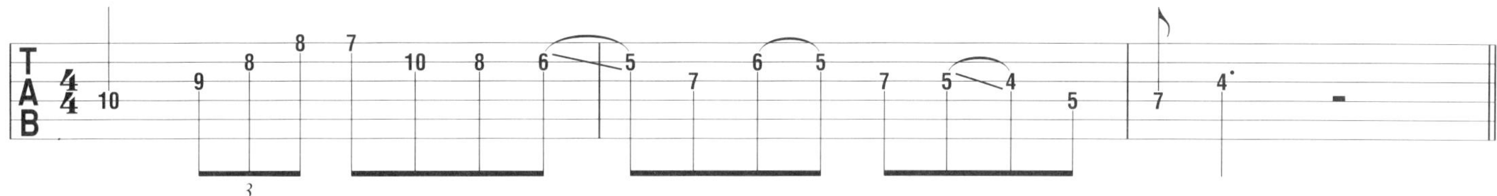

**907: Major Mileage**

Cmaj7

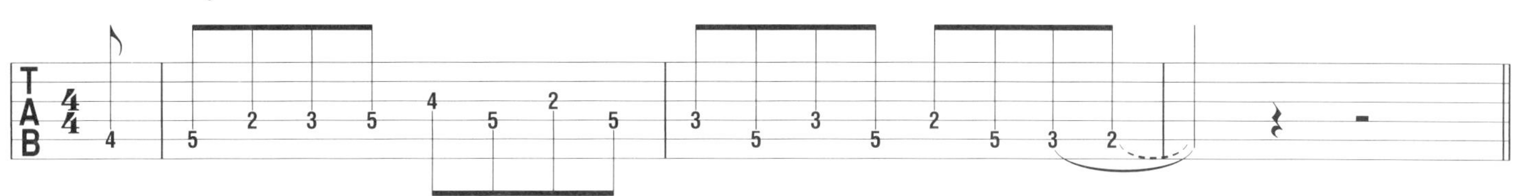

**908: Arp Sweeps**

Cmaj7

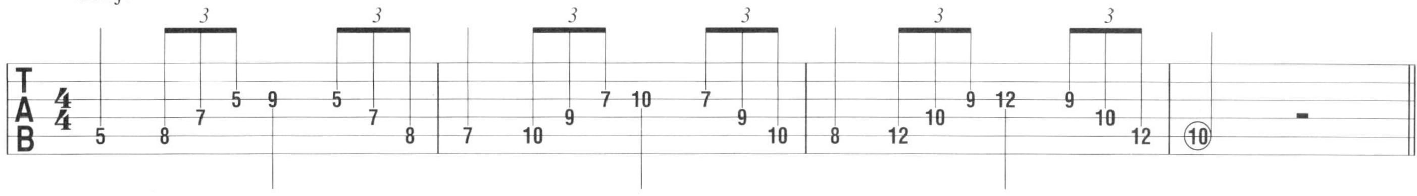

**909: Scalar Mixer**

Cmaj7

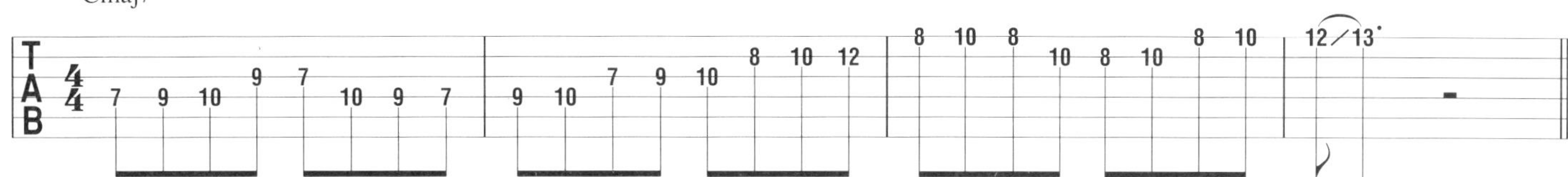

**910: Mini-Sweeps**

Cmaj7

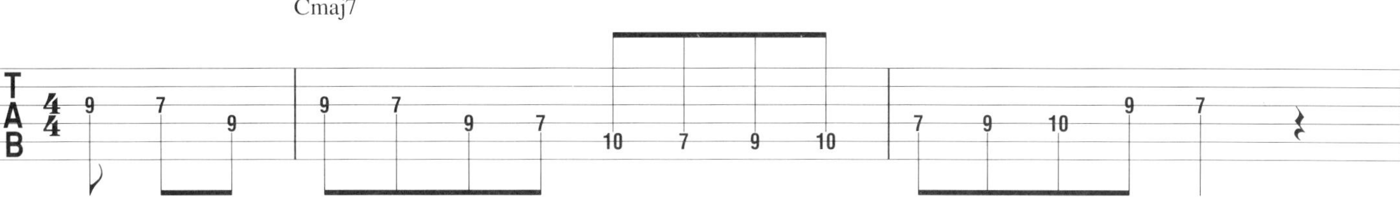

## 911: Tricky Ghosts

Cmaj7

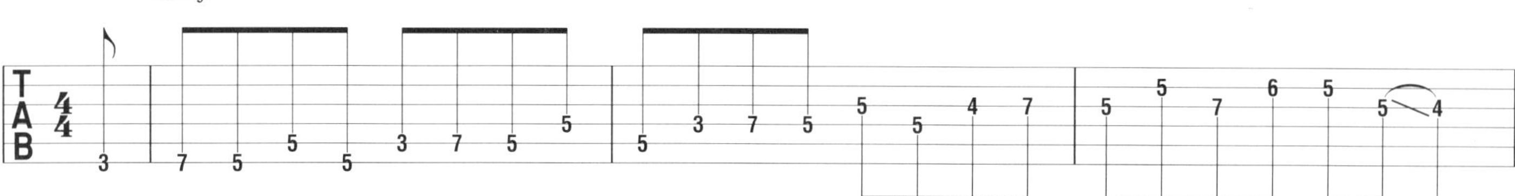

## 912: Changing Directions

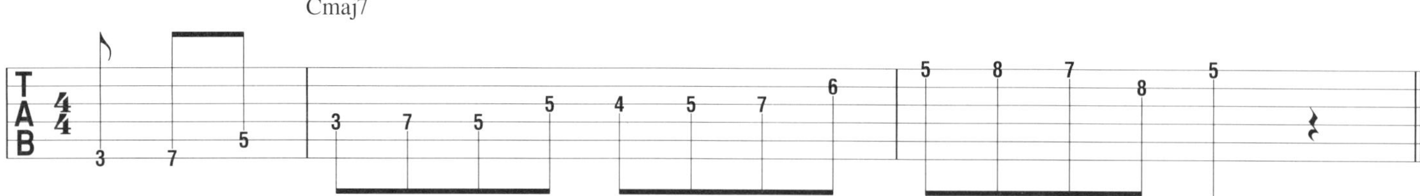


## 913: Jazz Fingers

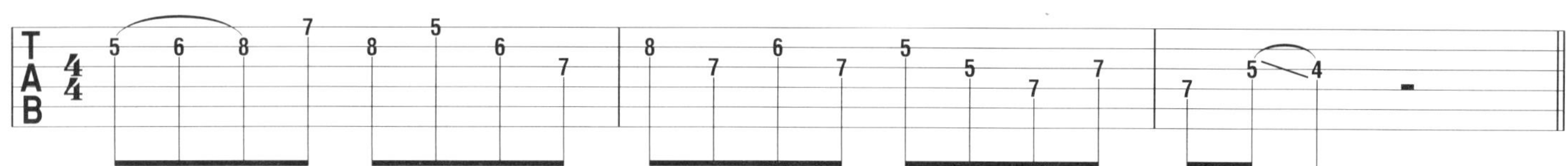

## 914: Smooth Angles

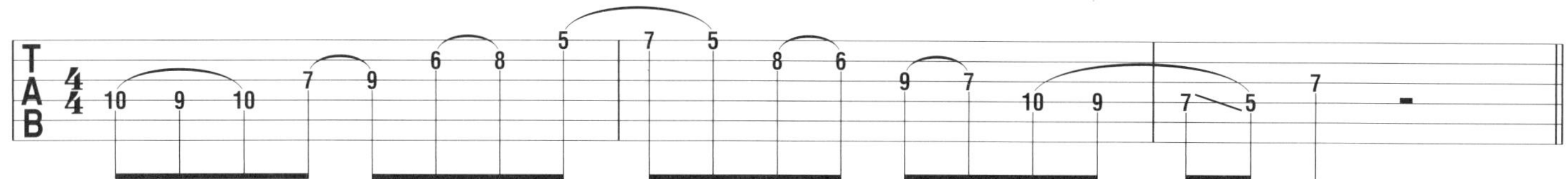

## 915: Legato Jazz

Cmaj7

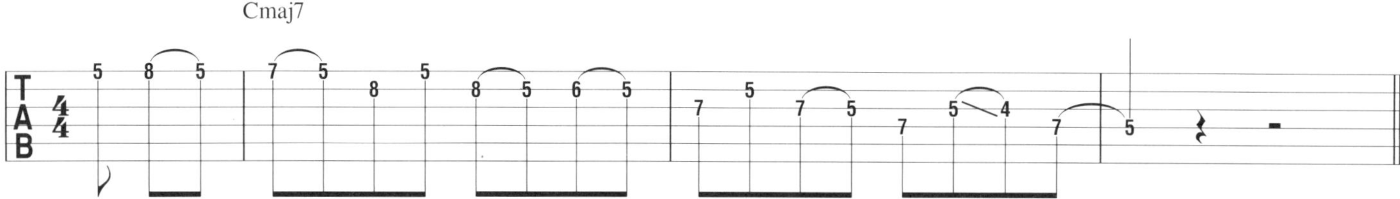

## 916: Mixo-Magic

A7

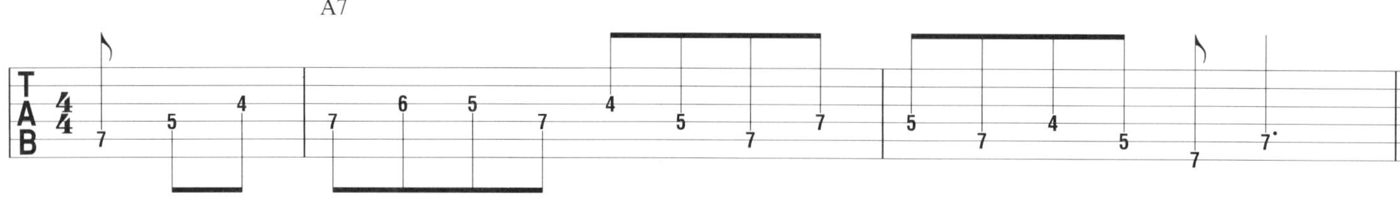

## 917: Zig-Zagger

A7

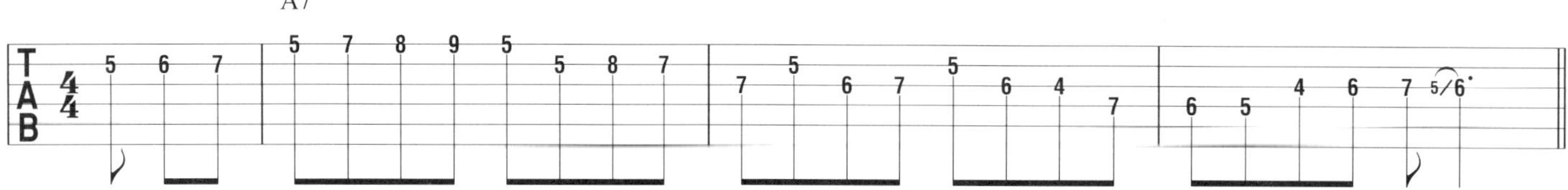

### 918: Jump Around

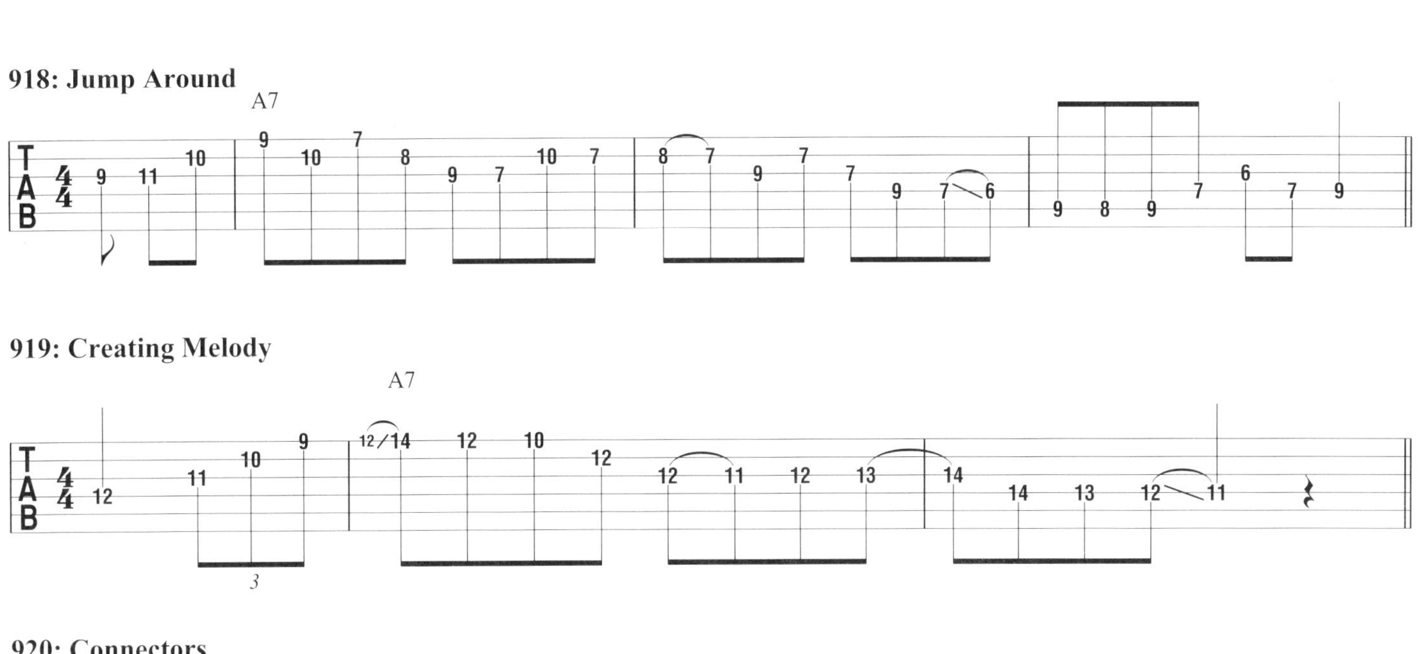


### 919: Creating Melody

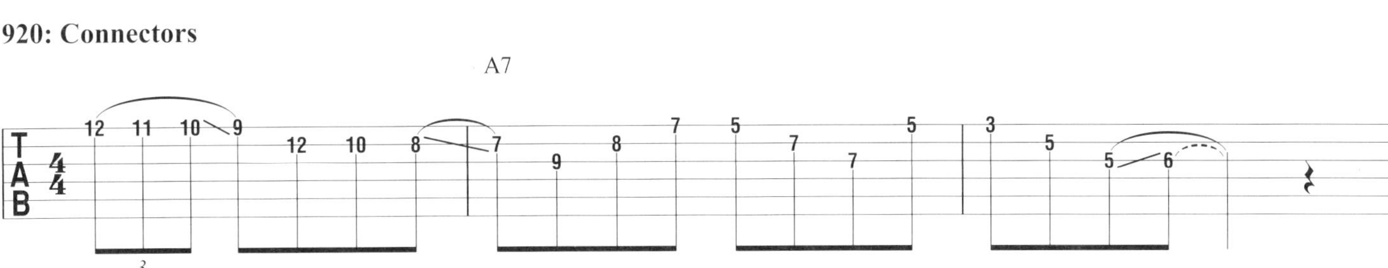


### 920: Connectors

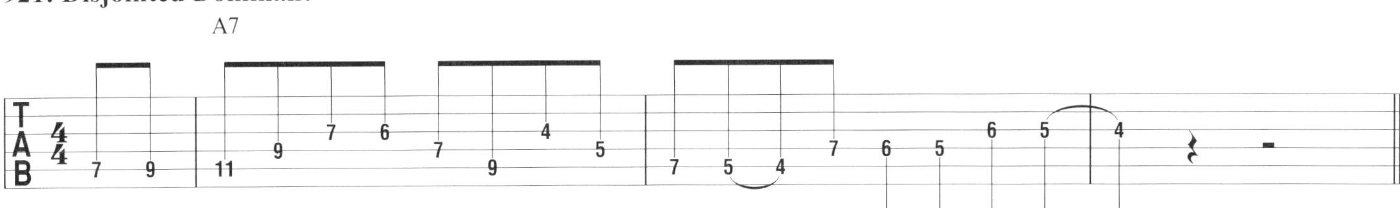


### 921: Disjointed Dominant

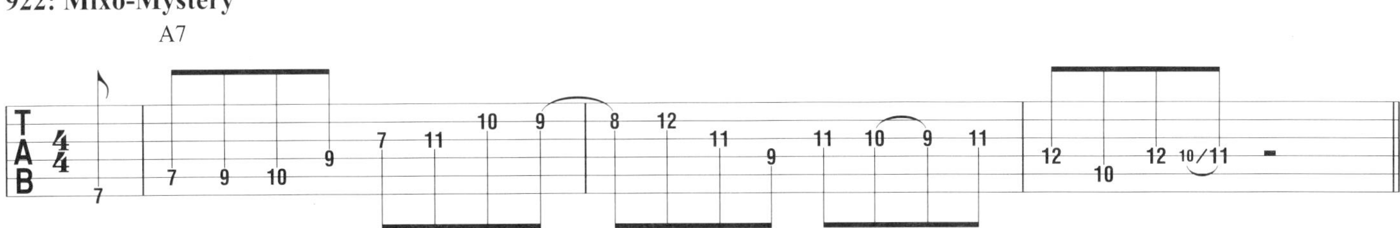


### 922: Mixo-Mystery

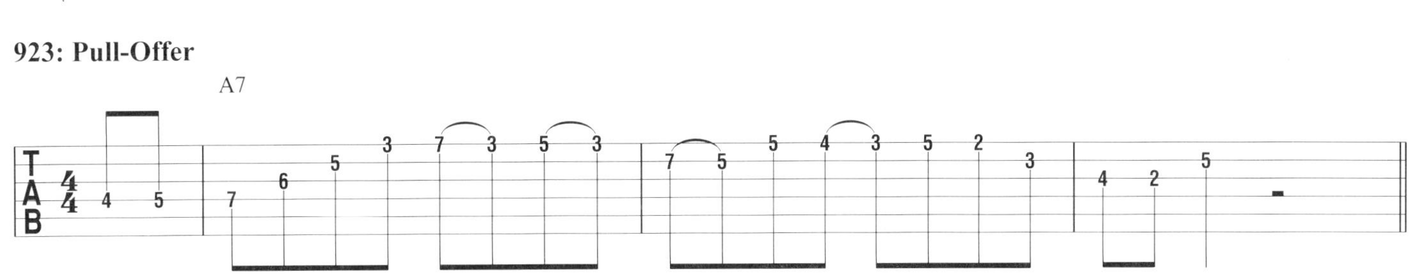


### 923: Pull-Offer

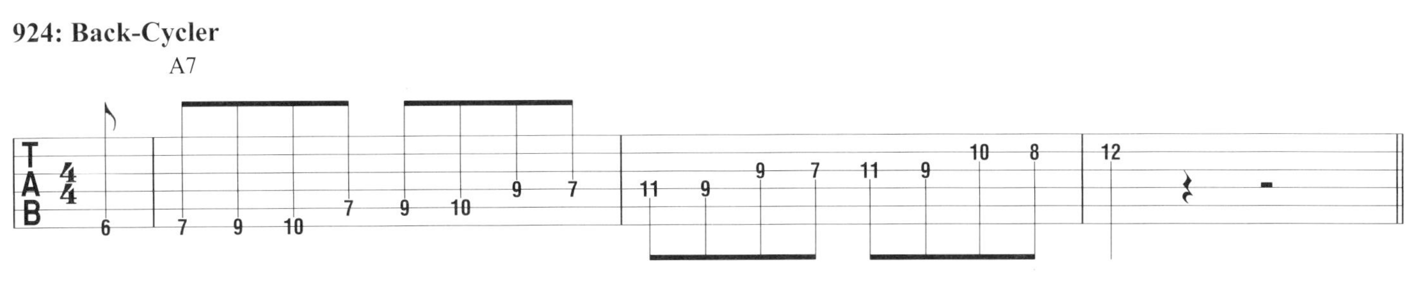


### 924: Back-Cycler

A7

### 925: Smokin' Series

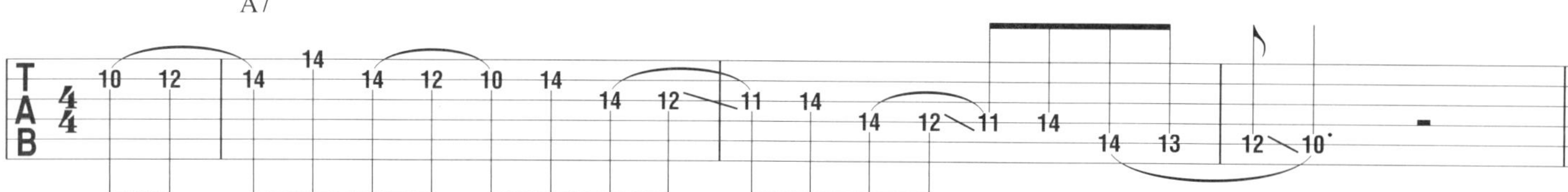


### 926: Harmonic Minor

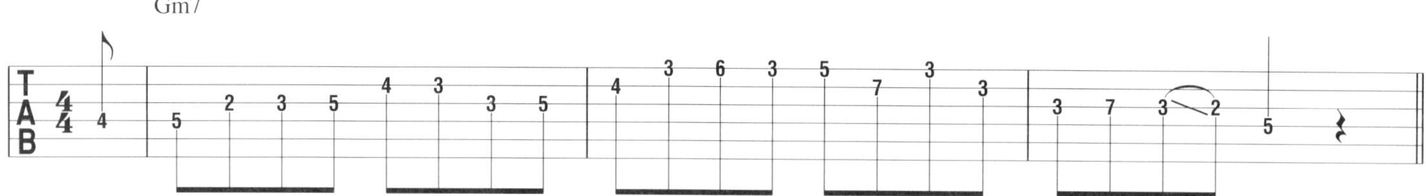


### 927: Classical Jazz

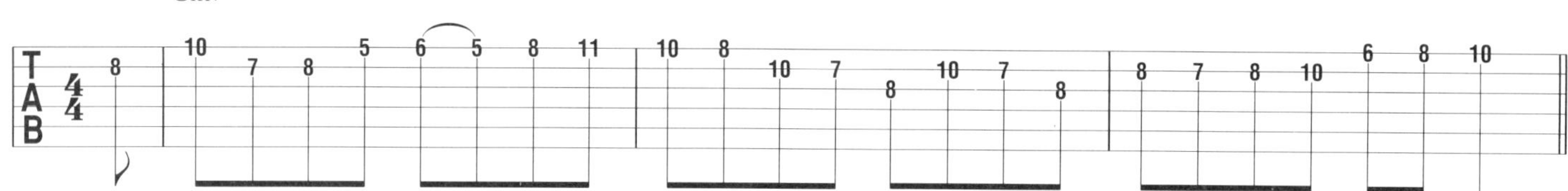


### 928: Gypsy Jazz

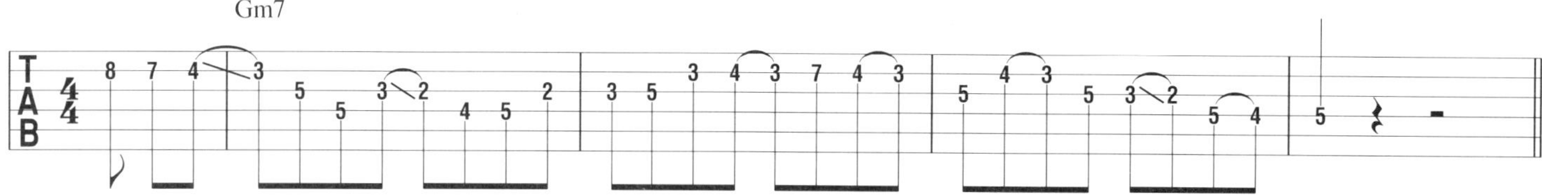


### 929: Cycle Climb

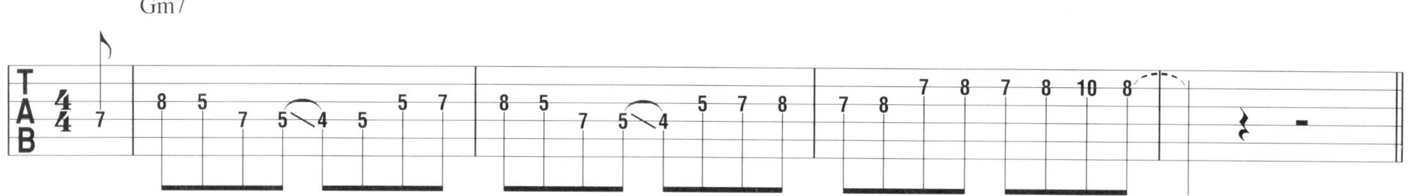


### 930: Django Time

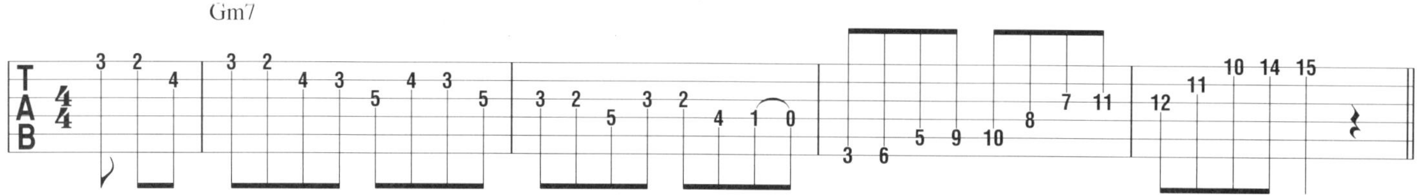


### 931: Diminished Blues

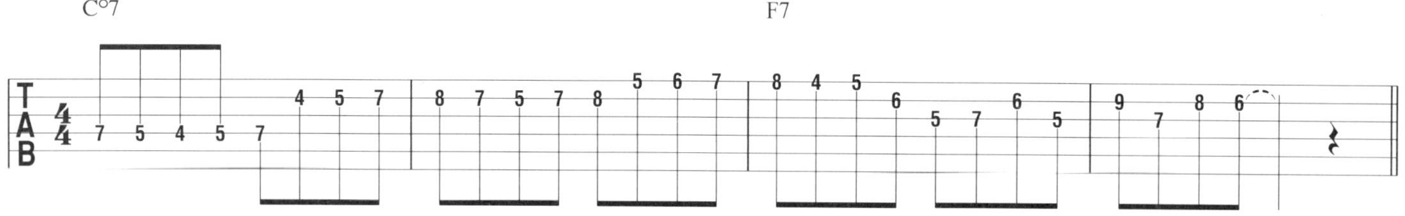

### 932: Jazz Blues

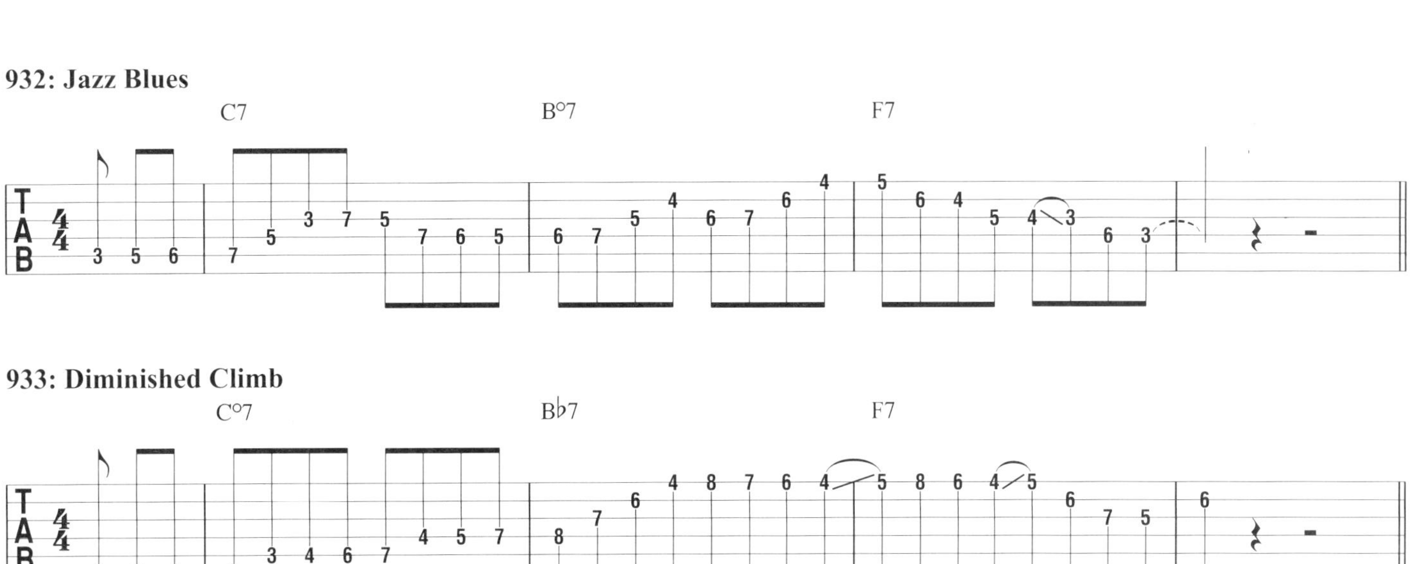


### 933: Diminished Climb



### 934: Half-Stepper

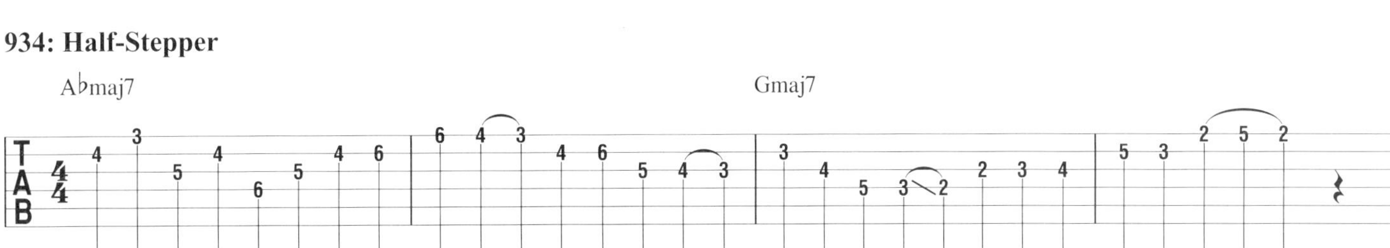


### 935: Chroma-Connect

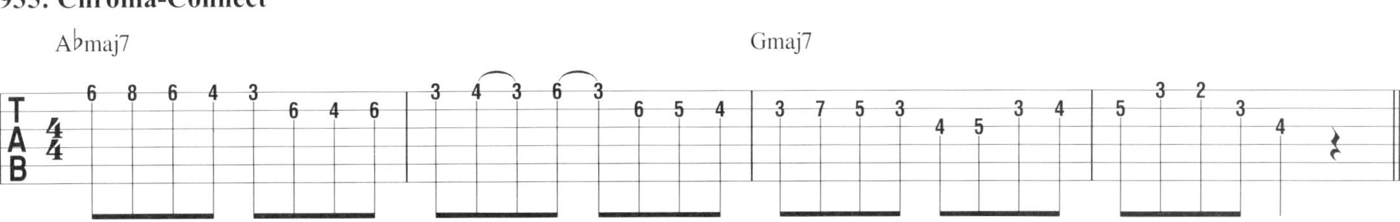


### 936: Dominant Melody

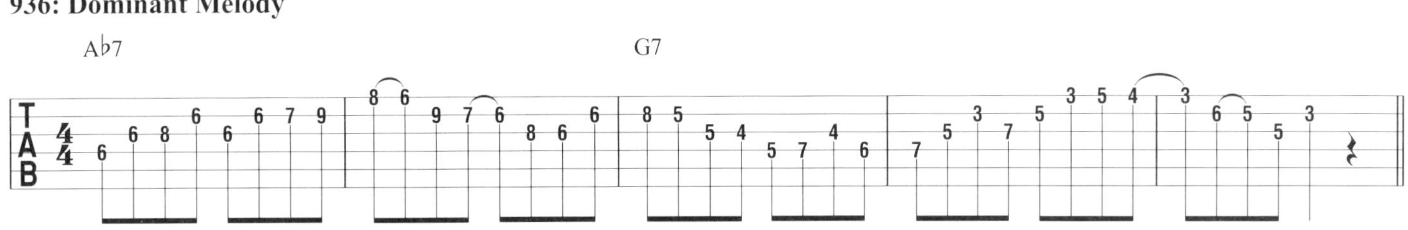


### 937: Up-Down Cycle

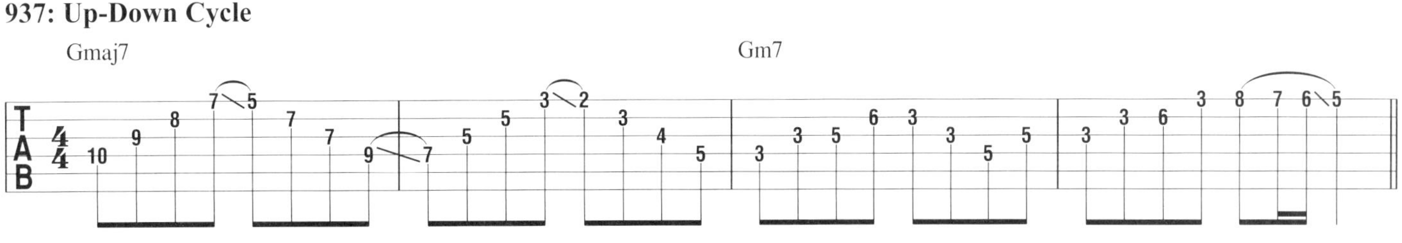


### 938: Major to Minor

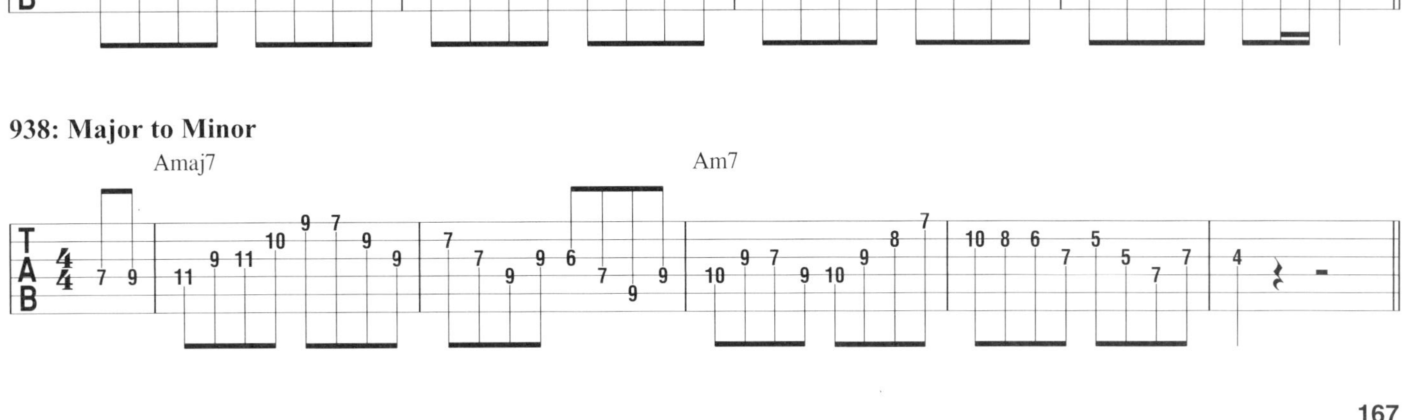

### 939: Dorian Resolve

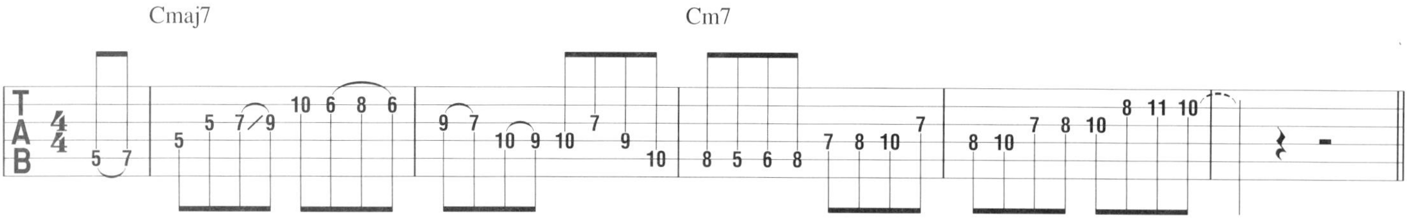

Cmaj7 Cm7

### 940: Minor 3rds

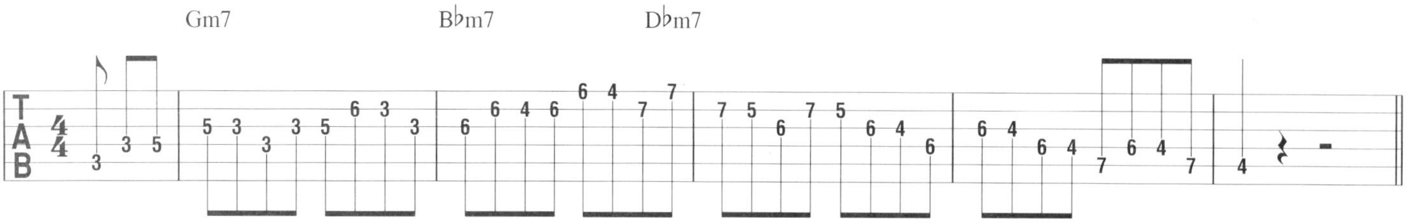

Gm7 B♭m7 D♭m7

### 941: Symmetry

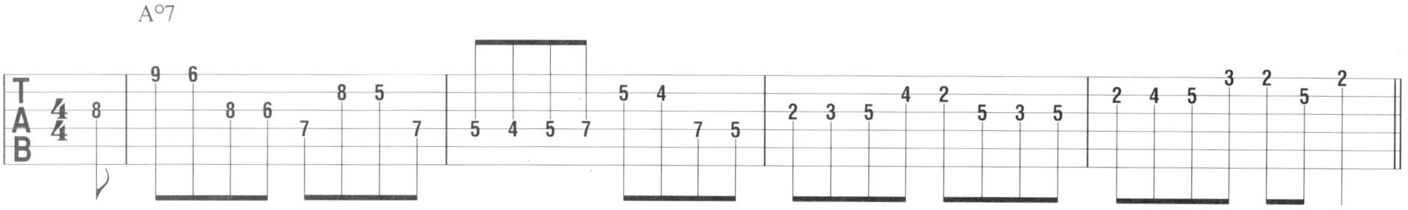

A°7

### 942: Diminished Shapes

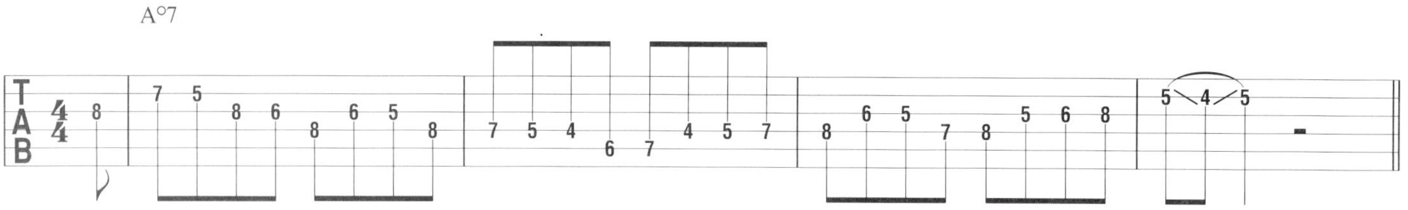

A°7

### 943: Smokin' Outside

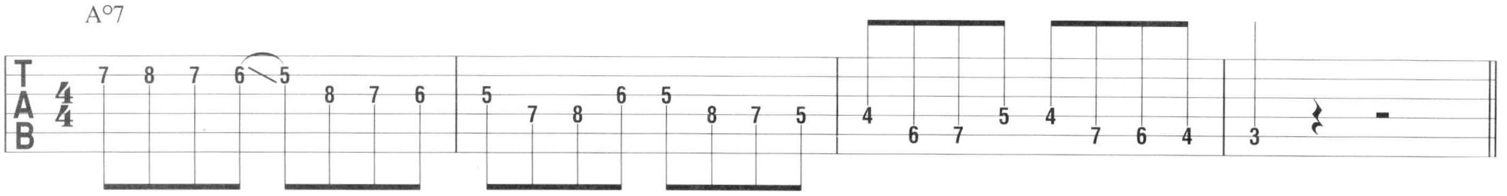

A°7

### 944: Minor 3rd Leaps

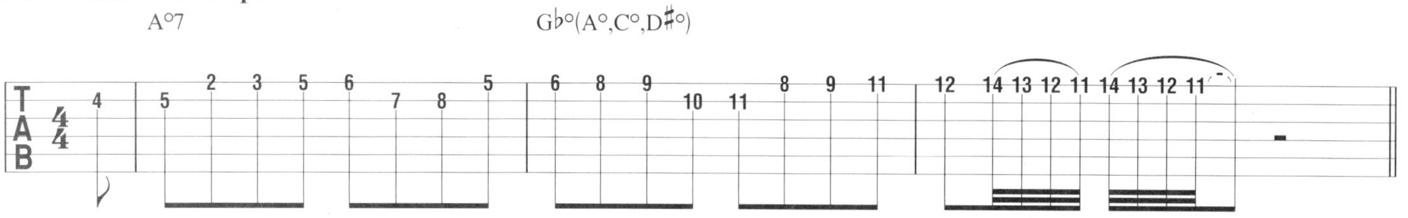

A°7 G♭°(A°,C°,D♯°)

### 945: Dorian Run

Gm7

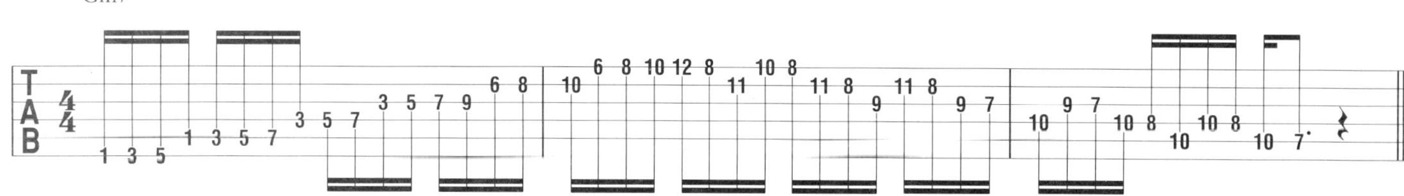

# Instructor: Paul Silbergleit

### 946: Bluesy Minor

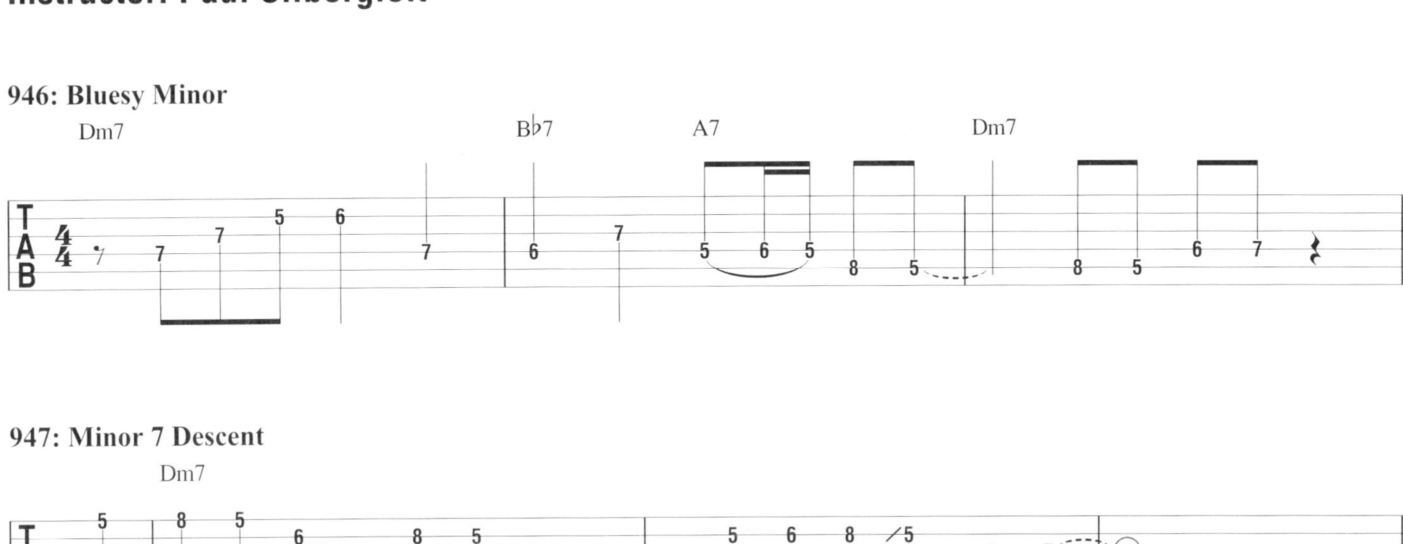


### 947: Minor 7 Descent

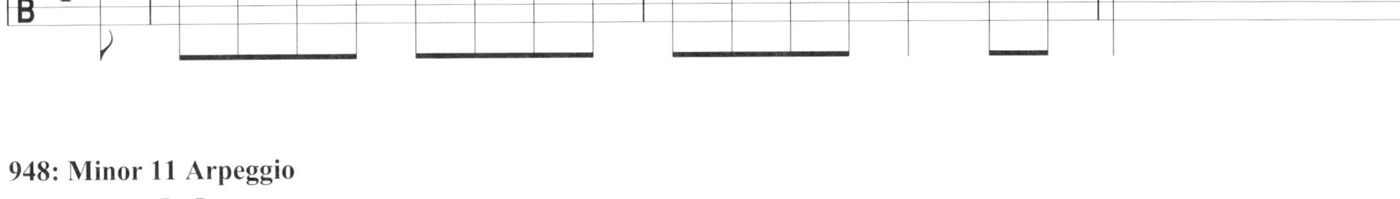


### 948: Minor 11 Arpeggio

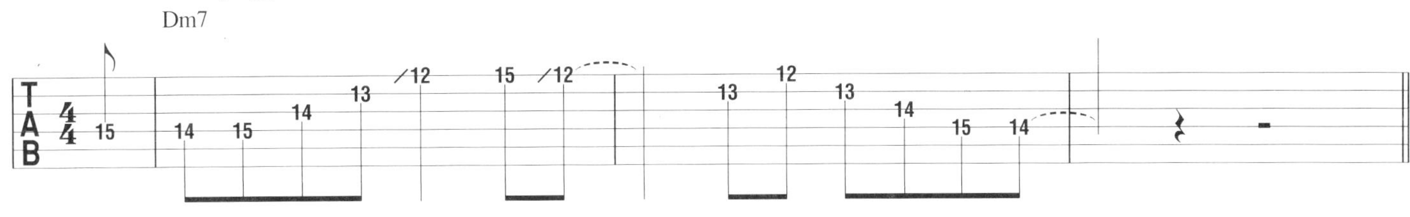


### 949: Perfect 4ths

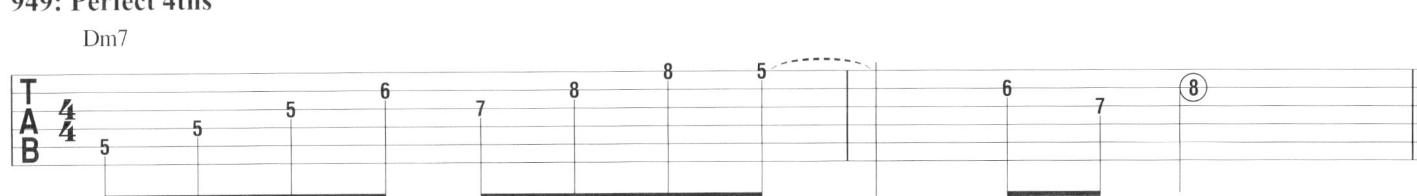


### 950: Chromatic Minor 7

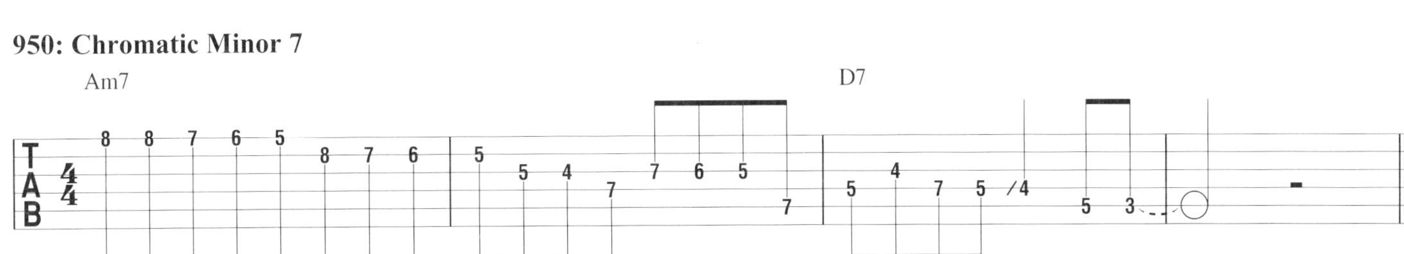


### 951: Power Minor 7

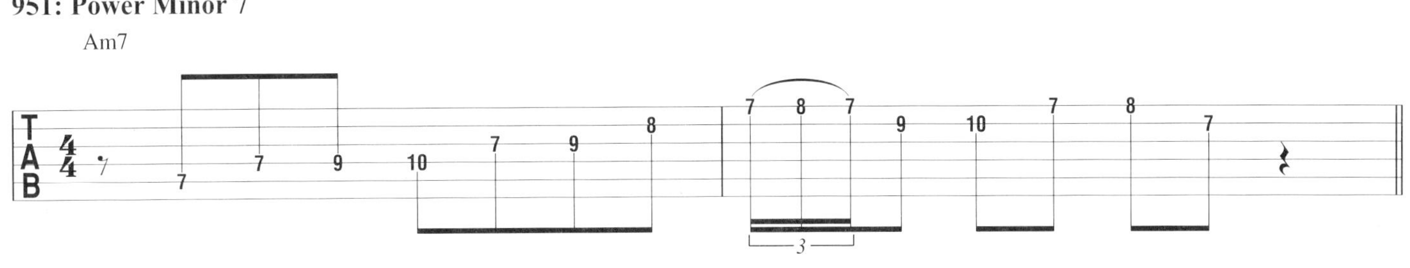

**952: Dramatic Melodic**

Am

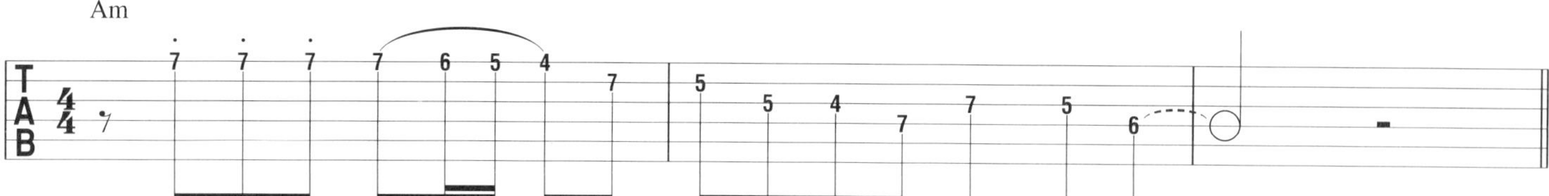

**953: Funky Grant**

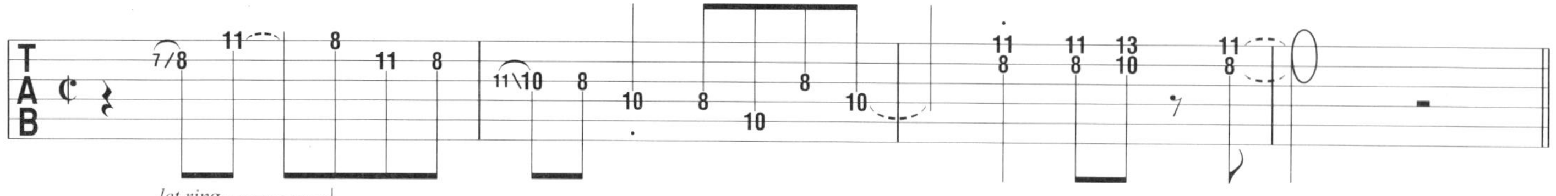


**954: 13 Chord Shape**

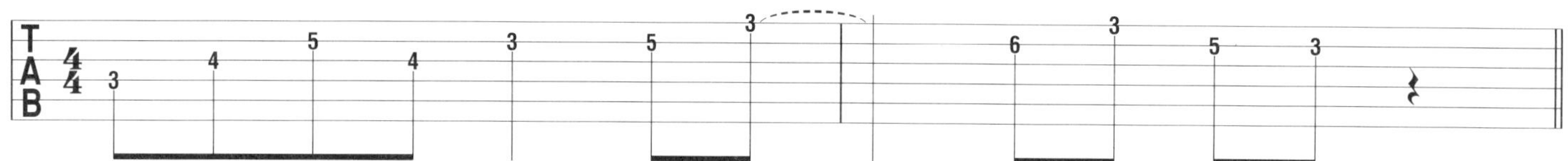

**955: Sharp 11 Shape**

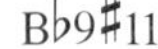


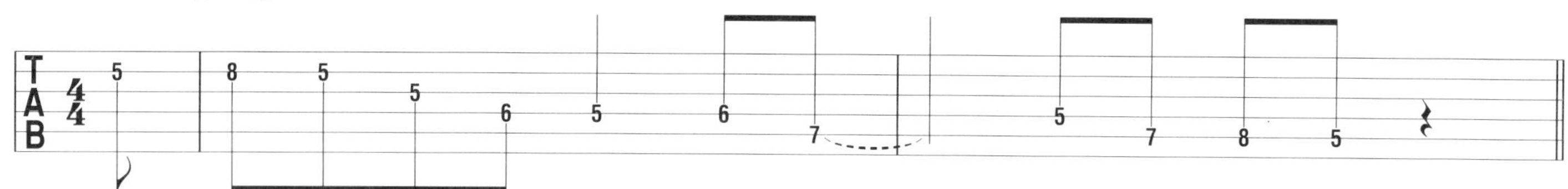

**956: Versatile Shape**

C7 F7

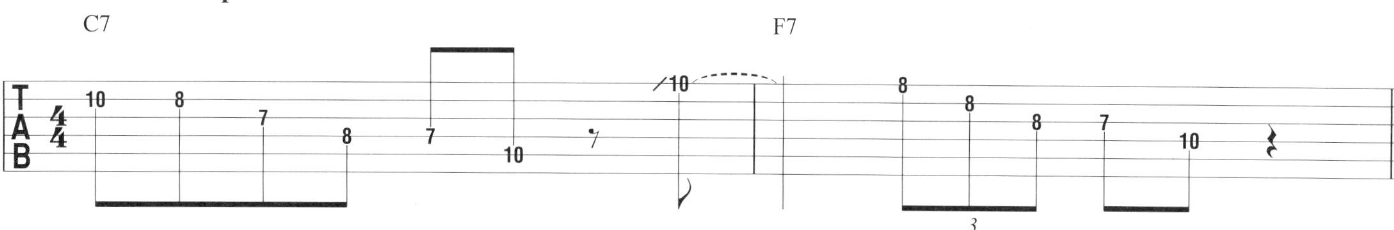

**957: Swingin' Hemiola**

B♭7

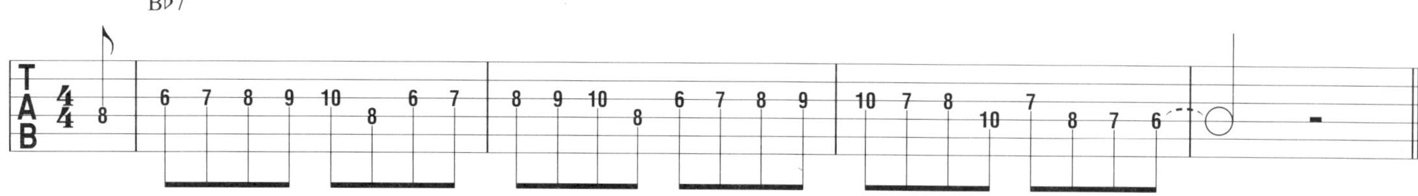

**958: Relaxin' in Major**

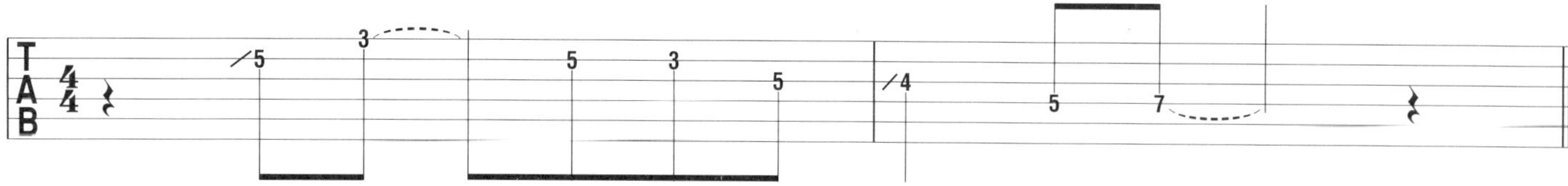

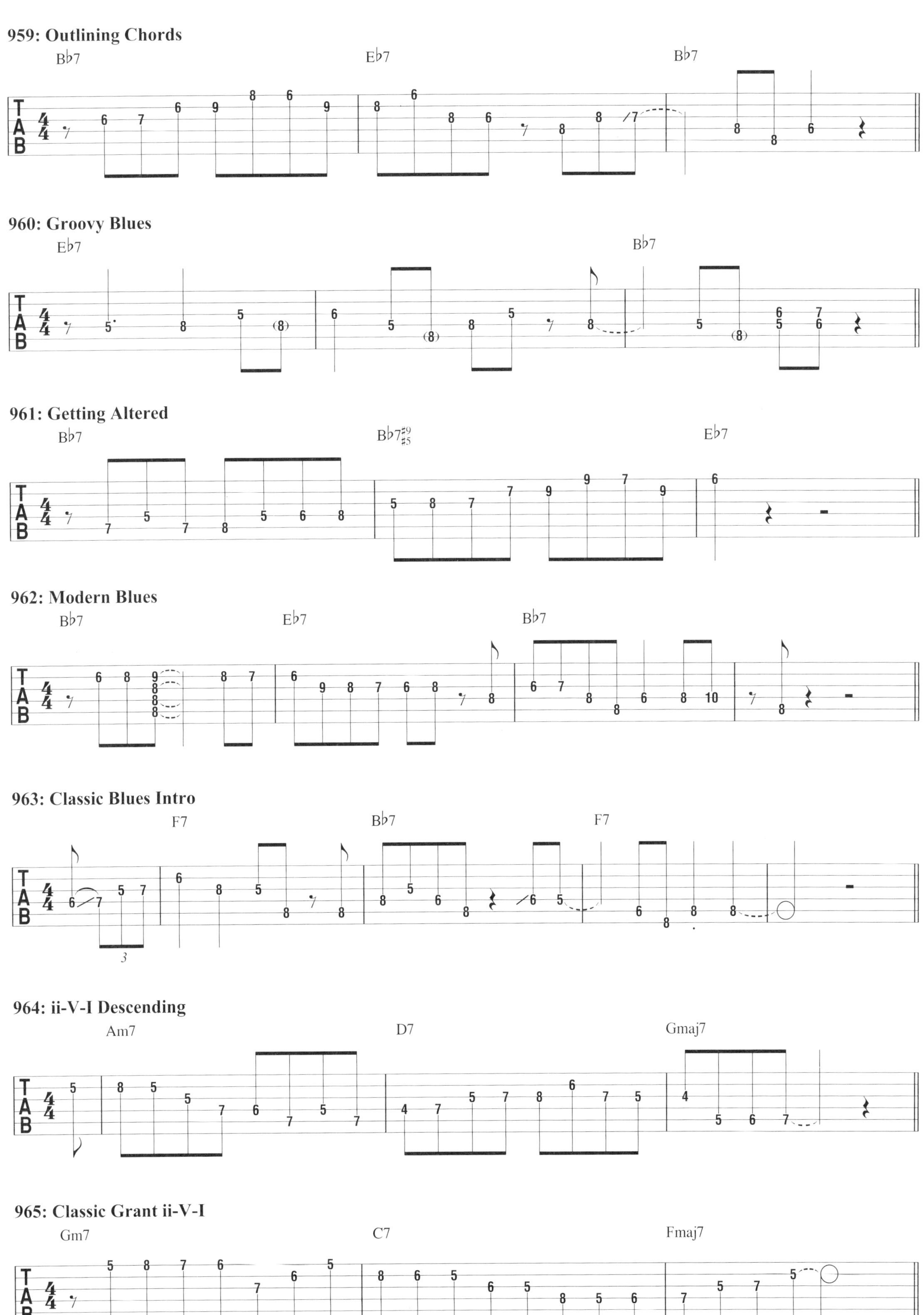
959: Outlining Chords
B♭7
E♭7
B♭7
960: Groovy Blues
E♭7
B♭7
961: Getting Altered
B♭7
B♭7♯9♯5
E♭7
962: Modern Blues
B♭7
E♭7
B♭7
963: Classic Blues Intro
F7
B♭7
F7
964: ii-V-I Descending
Am7
D7
Gmaj7
965: Classic Grant ii-V-I
Gm7
C7
Fmaj7

### 966: ii-V-I Scale Mix

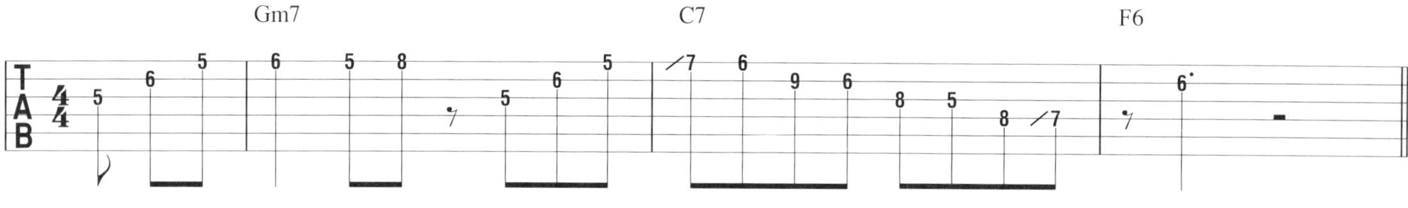


### 967: Metheny-ish ii-V-I

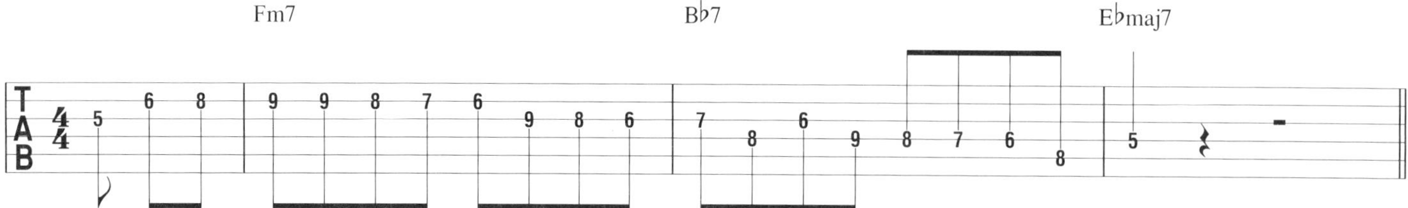


### 968: ii-V-I Tritone Sub

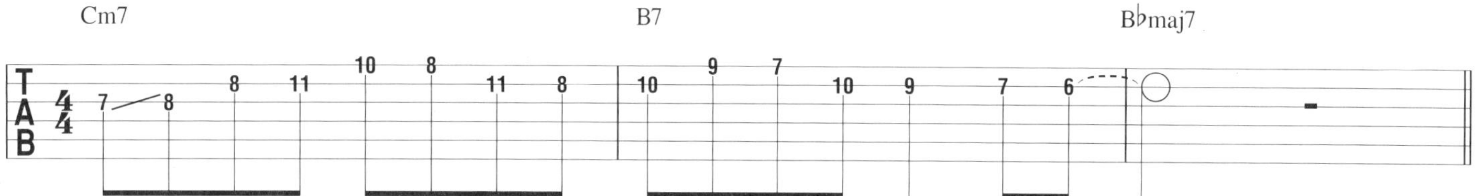


### 969: 2-Bar ii-V-I

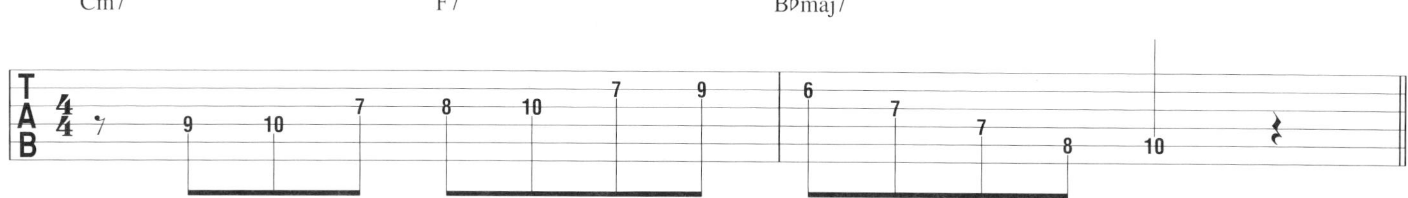


### 970: Bossa ii-V-I

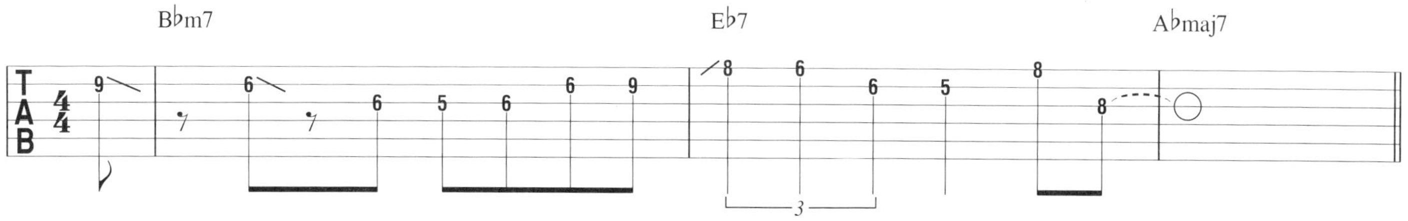


### 971: Minor ii-V-i

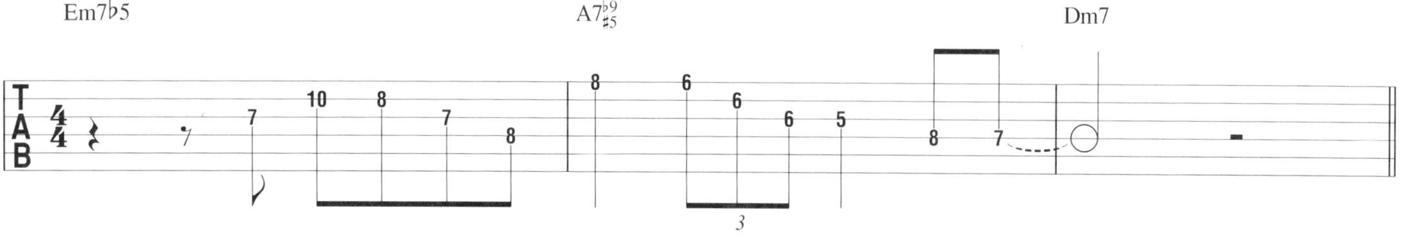


### 972: Grant Minor ii-V-i

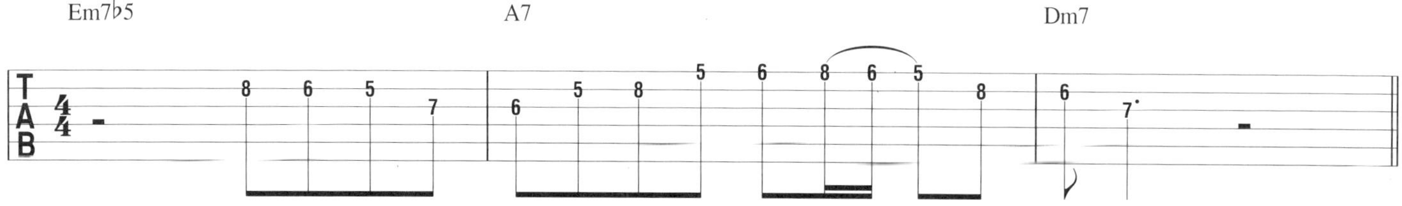

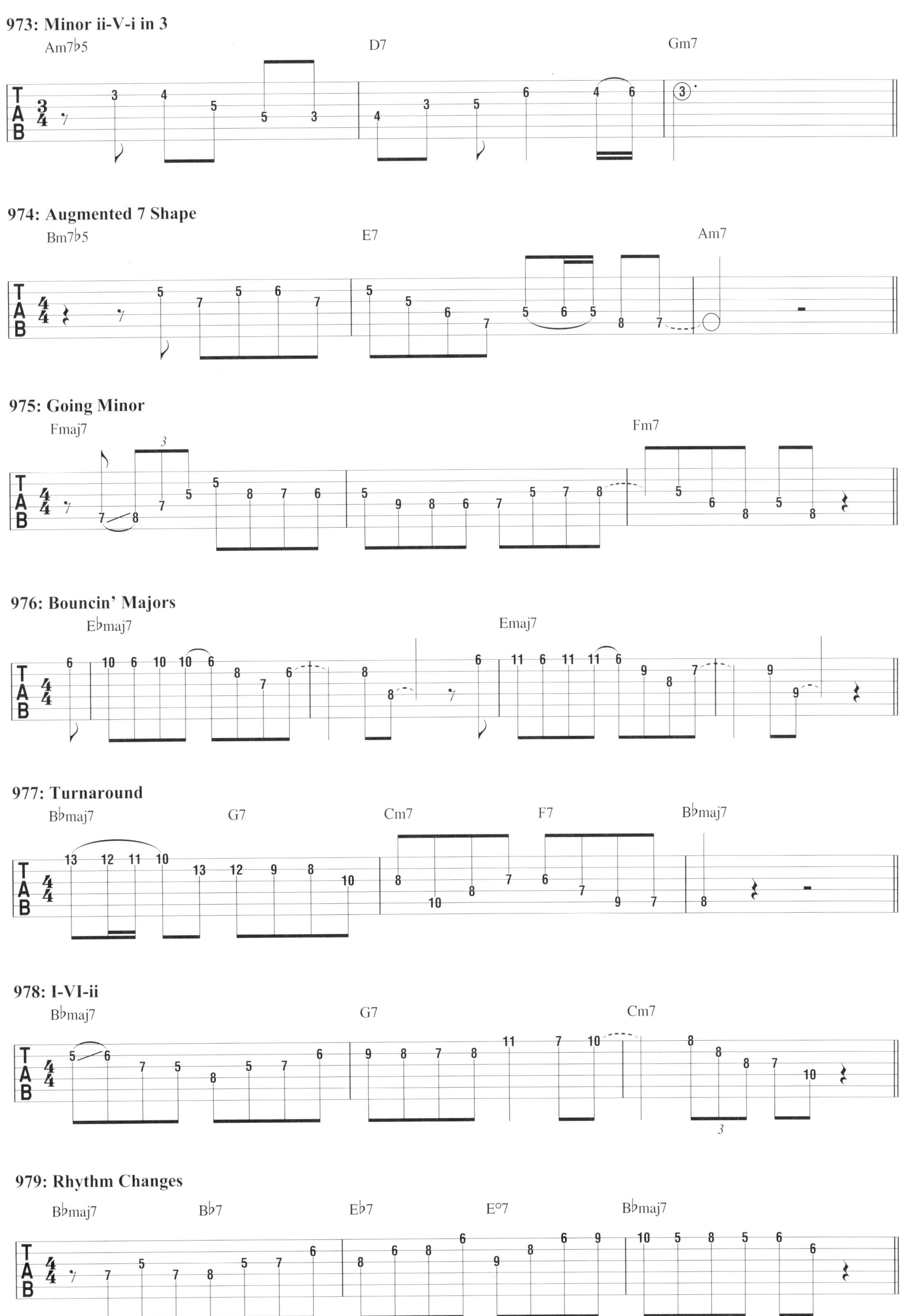
973: Minor ii-V-i in 3
Am7♭5
D7
Gm7
974: Augmented 7 Shape
Bm7♭5
E7
Am7
975: Going Minor
Fmaj7
Fm7
976: Bouncin' Majors
E♭maj7
Emaj7
977: Turnaround
B♭maj7
G7
Cm7
F7
B♭maj7
978: I-VI-ii
B♭maj7
G7
Cm7
979: Rhythm Changes
B♭maj7
B♭7
E♭7
E°7
B♭maj7

**980: Minor Variation**

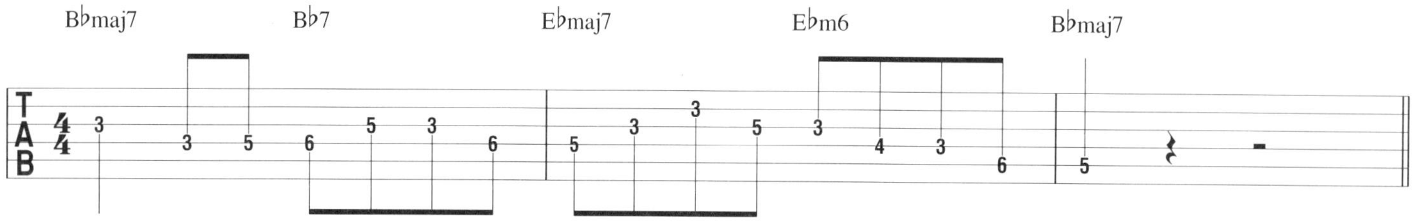

B♭maj7
B♭7
E♭maj7
E♭m6
B♭maj7

**981: Dramatic Major 7♯11**

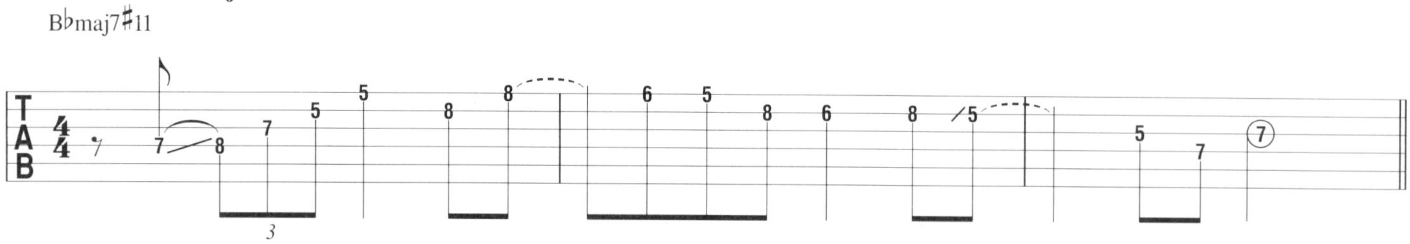

B♭maj7♯11

**982: Resolving Major 7♯11**

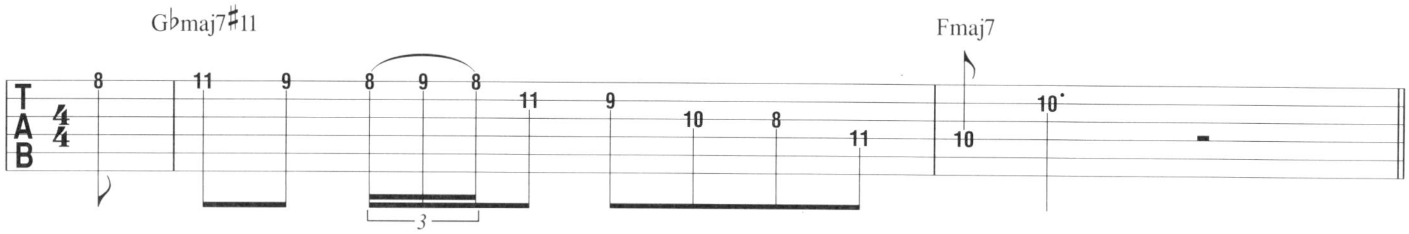

G♭maj7♯11
Fmaj7

**983: ii-iv**

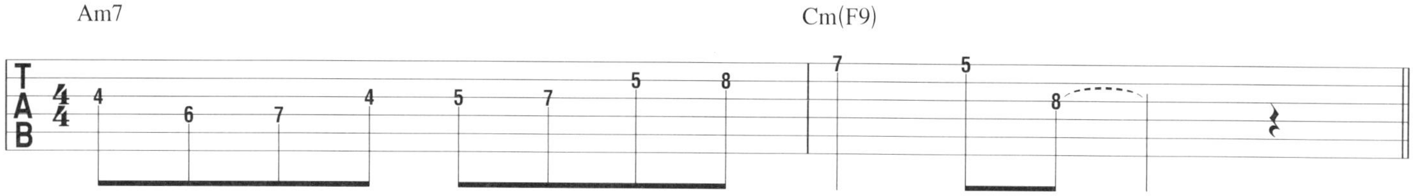

Am7
Cm(F9)

**984: Trane Arpeggios**

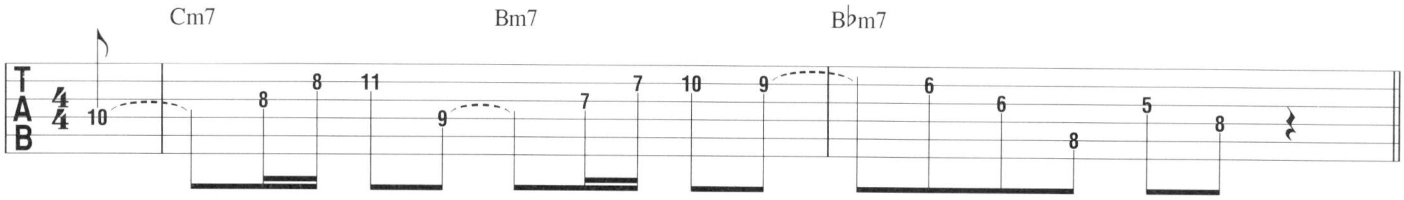

Cm7
Bm7
B♭m7

**985: ii-V-I Bop Subs**

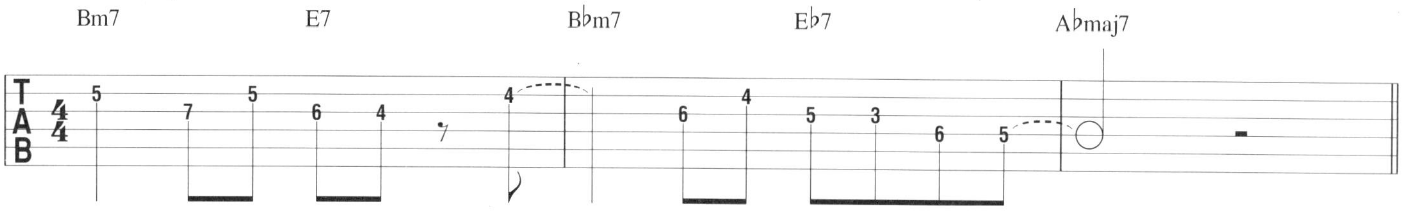

Bm7
E7
B♭m7
E♭7
A♭maj7

## Instructor: Bill Stone

**986: Altered Illusion**

F7alt
B♭m9

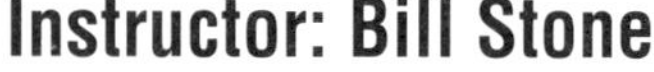

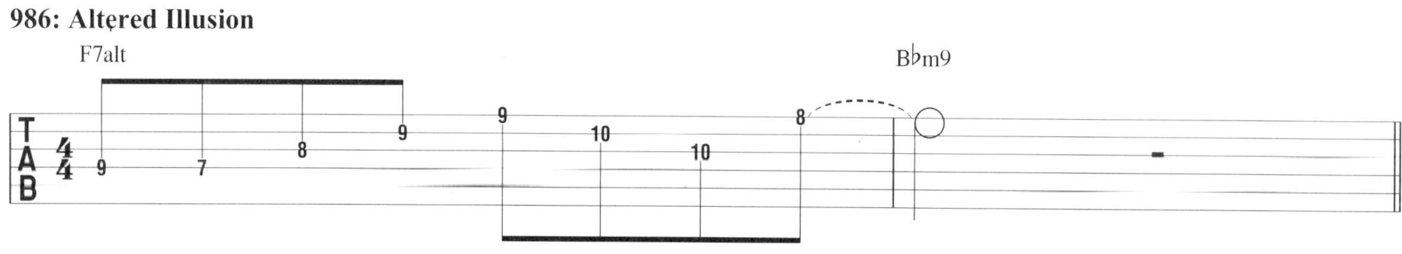

### 994: ii-V-I Descent

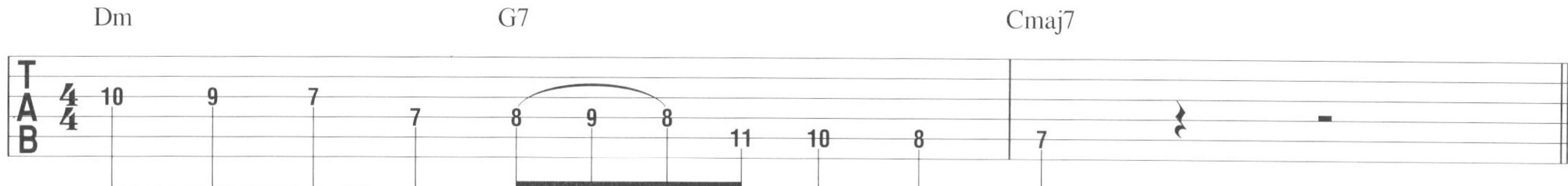


### 995: Chromatic Curve

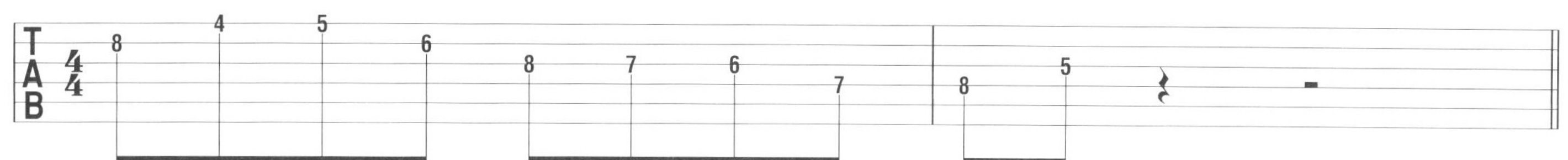


### 996: Triad Triplets

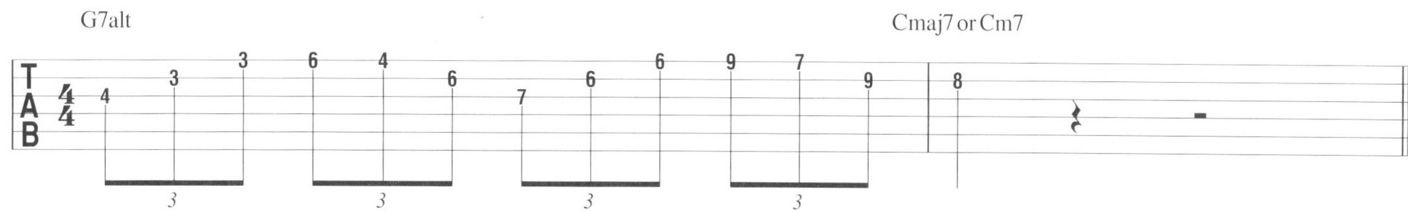


### 997: I-VI-ii-V Turn

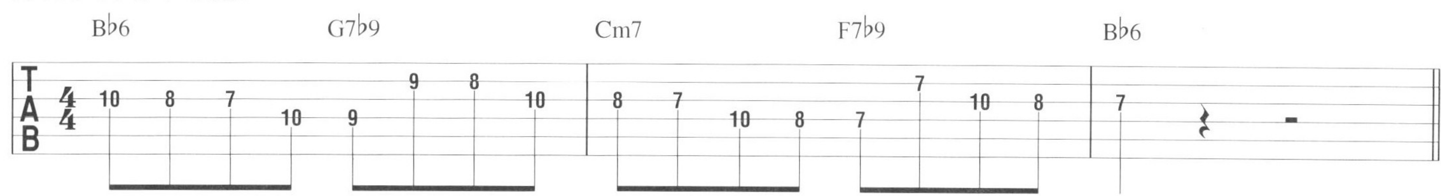


### 998: Follow Your Ear

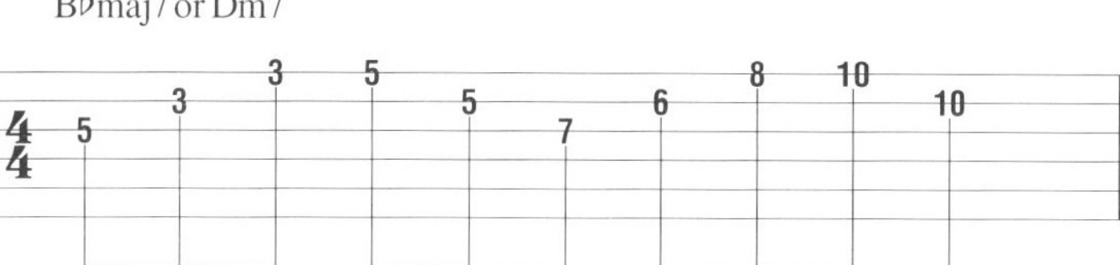


### 999: Octave Displacement

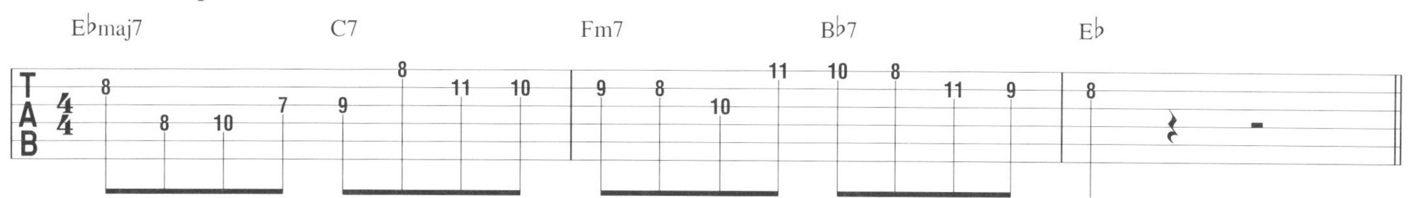


### 1000: Avoid the 3rd

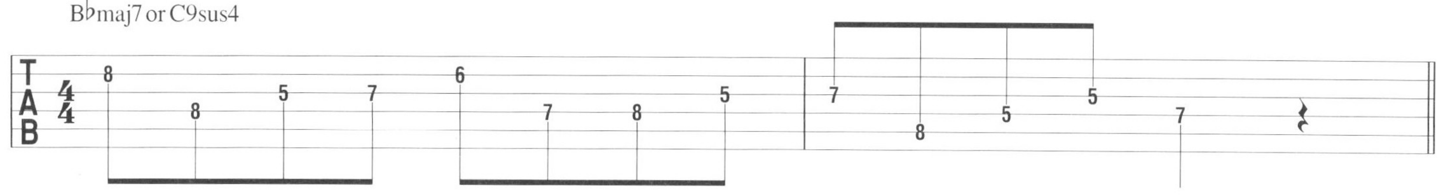

### 987: Nice Curves

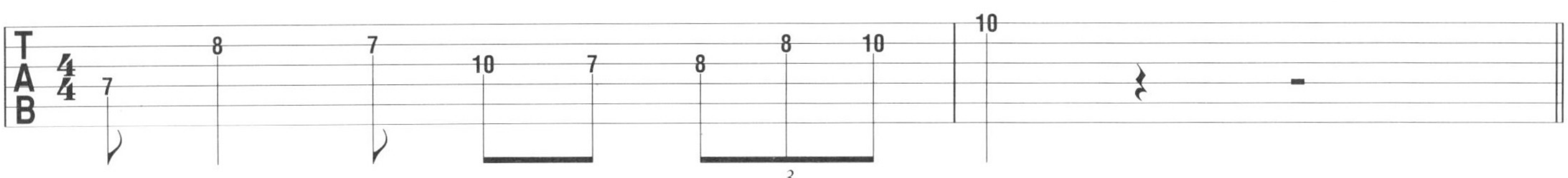


### 988: Whole-Tone Sweeps

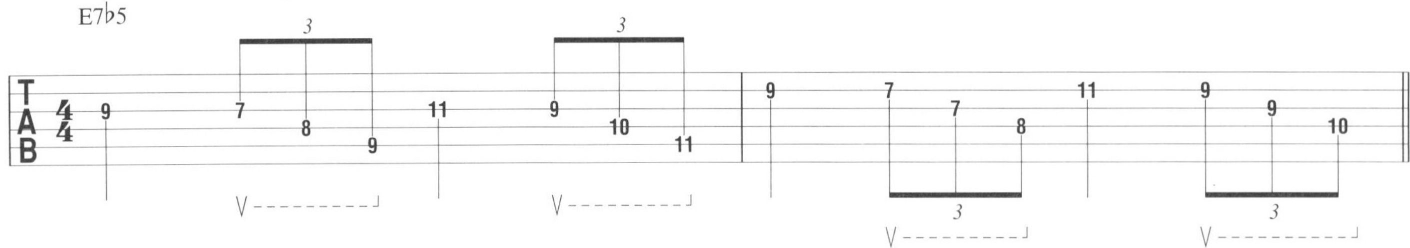


### 989: Rhythm Lab

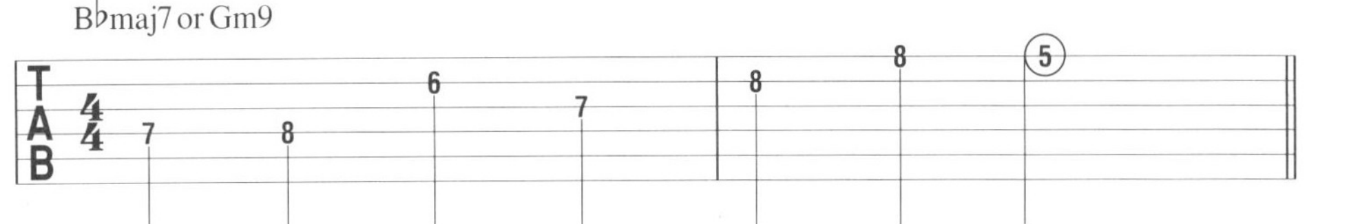


### 990: Spooky Scale

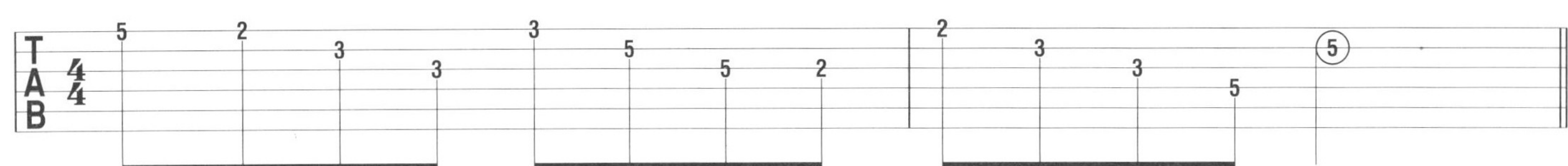

### 991: ii-V Continuity

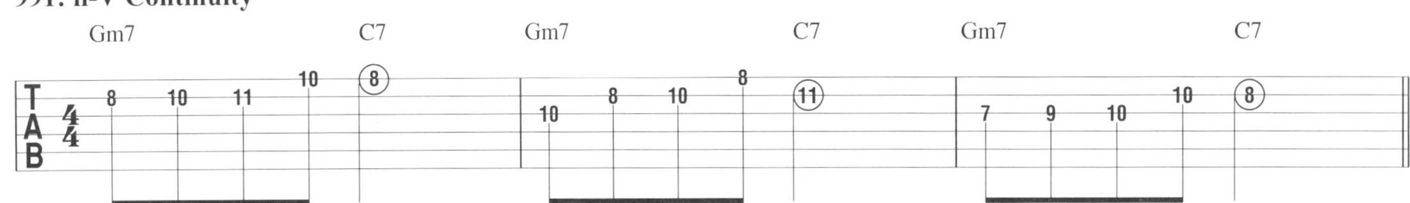


### 992: Dizzy Design

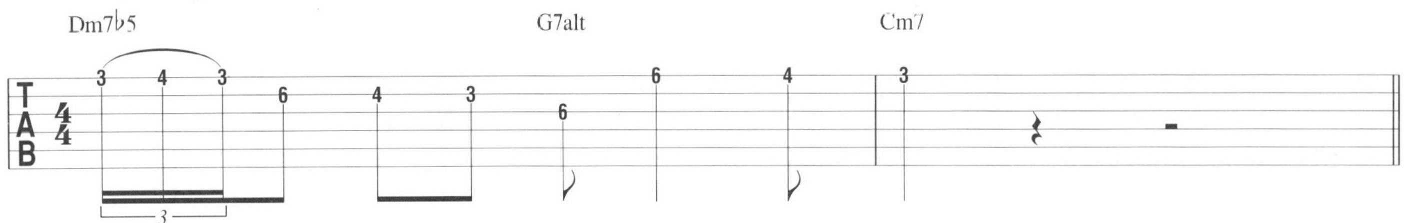


### 993: Bop Tones

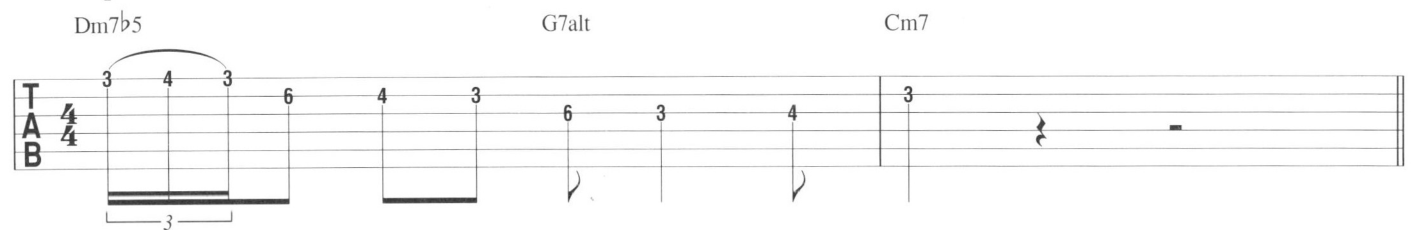